T0257930

Circuits and Systems: Design and Applications

Volume V

Circuits and Systems: Design and Applications

Volume V

Circuits and Systems: Design and Applications Volume V

Edited by **Helena Walker**

New Jersey

Published by Clanrye International,
55 Van Reypen Street,
Jersey City, NJ 07306, USA
www.clanryeinternational.com

Circuits and Systems: Design and Applications
Volume V
Edited by Helena Walker

International Standard Book Number: 978-1-63240-101-4 (Hardback)

Printed in the United States of America.

Contents

Preface

At a very fundamental level, a circuit refers to an overall, complex arrangement of components such as resistors, conductors etc. which are connected in order to ensure a steady flow of current. It is only through circuits that signals or information is conveyed to the destination. Without a proper circuit system, the functional ability of any device becomes more or less redundant. The complexity and design of electronic circuits is ever increasing. Circuits are classified into analog circuits, digital circuits and mixed-signal circuits.

Circuits and systems in this book explain the handling of theory and applications of circuits and systems, signal processing, and system design methodology. The practical implementation of circuits, and application of circuit theoretic techniques to systems and to signal processing are the topics covered under this discipline. From radio astronomy to wireless communications and biomedical applications, the application of circuits and systems can be found across a varying range of subjects.

Circuits and Systems is an interesting discipline and is emerging as a coveted career option for many students. A lot of research, to develop more efficient systems is also being conducted.

I'd like to thank all the contributors for sharing their studies with us and make this book an enlightening read. I would also like to thank them for submitting their work within the set time parameters. Lastly, I wish to thank my family, whose support has been crucial for the completion of this book.

Editor

1

A Modified Eigenvector Method for Blind Deconvolution of MIMO Systems Using the Matrix Pseudo-Inversion Lemma*

Mitsuru Kawamoto[1], Kiyotaka Kohno[2], Yujiro Inouye[3], Koichi Kurumatani[1]
[1]*Information Technology Research Institute, National Institute of Advanced Science and Technology*, Tsukuba, *Japan*
[2]*Department of Electronic Control Engineering, Yonago National College of Technology, Yonago-city, Japan*
[3]*Department of Electronic and Control Systems Engineering, Shimane University, Matsue, Japan*

Abstract

Recently we have developed an eigenvector method (EVM) which can achieve the blind deconvolution (BD) for MIMO systems. One of attractive features of the proposed algorithm is that the BD can be achieved by calculating the eigenvectors of a matrix relevant to it. However, the performance accuracy of the EVM depends highly on computational results of the eigenvectors. In this paper, by modifying the EVM, we propose an algorithm which can achieve the BD without calculating the eigenvectors. Then the pseudo-inverse which is needed to carry out the BD is calculated by our proposed matrix pseudo-inversion lemma. Moreover, using a combination of the conventional EVM and the modified EVM, we will show its performances comparing with each EVM. Simulation results will be presented for showing the effectiveness of the proposed methods.

Keywords: Blind Signal Processing, Blind Deconvolution, Eigenvector Methods, Super-Exponential Mthods, MIMO Systems, Matrix Pseudo-Inversion Lemma

1. Introduction

In this paper, we deal with a blind deconvolution (BD) problem for a multiple-input and multiple-output (MIMO) infinite-impulse response (IIR) channels. A large number of methods for solving the BD problem have been proposed until now (see [1], and reference therein). In order to solve the BD problem, this paper focuses on the eigenvector method (EVM).

The first proposal of the EVM was done by Jelonnek *et al.* [2]. They have proposed the EVM for solving blind equalization (BE) problems of single-input single-output (SISO) channels and single-input multiple-output (SIMO) channels. The most attractive feature of the EVM is that its algorithm can be derived from a closed-form solution using reference signals. Then, a generalized eigenvector problem can be formulated and the eigenvector calculation is carried out in order to solve the BE problem. Owing to the property, differently from the algorithms derived from steepest descent methods, the EVM does not need many iterations to achieve the BE, but works so as to solve the BE problem with one iteration.

Recently, we extended the EVM to the case of MIMO-IIR channels [3,4]. Then we proved that the proposed EVM can work so as to recover all source signals from their mixtures with one iteration. However, in the EVM, its performance accuracy depends highly on computational results of the eigenvectors.

In this paper, we modify the EVM and then an algorithm for solving the BD is proposed, in which the proposed algorithm can be carried out without calculating the eigenvectors. Namely, the proposed algorithm can achieve the BD with as less computational complexity as possible, compared with the conventional EVMs. Moreover, a combination of the conventional EVM and the modified EVM is proposed. The combined EVM has such properties that the BD can be achieved with as less computational complexity as possible and with good accuracy compared with each EVM.

The present paper uses the following notation: Let Z denote the set of all integers. Let C denote the set of all complex numbers. Let $\boldsymbol{C}^n$ denote the set of all n-column vectors with complex components. Let $\boldsymbol{C}^{m\times n}$ denote the set of all $m\times n$ matrices with complex components. The super-

*A preliminary version of this paper was presented at the 2010 IEEE International Symposium on Circuits and Systems (ISCAS2010).

scripts T, $*$, and H denote, respectively, the transpose, the complex conjugate, and the complex conjugate transpose (Hermitian) of a matrix. The symbol† denotes a pseudo-inverse of a matrix. The symbols block-diag $\{\cdots\}$ and diag $\{\cdots\}$ denote respectively a block diagonal and a diagonal matrices with the block diagonal and the diagonal elements $\{\cdots\}$. The symbol cum$\{x_1, x_2, x_3, x_4\}$ denotes the fourth-order cumulant of x_i's. Let $i = \underline{1, n}$ stand for $I = 1, 2, \cdots, n$.

2. Problem Formulation and Assumptions

We consider a MIMO system with n inputs and m outputs as described by

$$y(t) = \sum_{k=-\infty}^{\infty} H^{(k)} s(t-k) + n(t), \ t \in Z, \qquad (1)$$

where $\boldsymbol{s}(t)$ is an n-column vector of input (or source) signals, $\boldsymbol{y}(t)$ is an m-column vector of system outputs, $\boldsymbol{n}(t)$ is an m-column vector of Gaussian noises, and $\{\boldsymbol{H}^{(k)}\}$ is an $m \times n$ impulse response matrix sequence.

The transfer function of the system is defined by $\boldsymbol{H}(z) = \sum_{k=-\infty}^{\infty} H^{(k)} z^k$, $z \in C$.

To recover the source signals, we process the output signals by an $n \times m$ deconvolver (or equalizer) $\boldsymbol{W}(z)$ described by

$$\begin{aligned} v(t) &= \sum_{k=-\infty}^{\infty} W^{(k)} y(t-k) \\ &= \sum_{k=-\infty}^{\infty} G^{(k)} s(t-k) + \sum_{k=-\infty}^{\infty} W^{(k)} n(t-k), \end{aligned} \qquad (2)$$

where $\{\boldsymbol{G}^{(k)}\}$ is the impulse response matrix sequence of $\boldsymbol{G}(z) := \boldsymbol{W}(z)\boldsymbol{H}(z)$, which is defined by $\boldsymbol{G}(z) = \sum_{k=-\infty}^{\infty} G^{(k)} z^k$, $z \in C$. The cascade connection of the unknown system and the deconvolver is illustrated in **Figure 1**.

Here, we put the following assumptions on the system, the source signals, the deconvolver, and the noises.

A1) The transfer function $\boldsymbol{H}(z)$ is stable and has full column rank on the unit circle $|z| = 1$, where the assumption **A1)** implies that the unknown system has less inputs than outputs, *i.e.*, $n \le m$, and there exists a left stable inverse of the unknown system. Please do not revise any of the current designations.

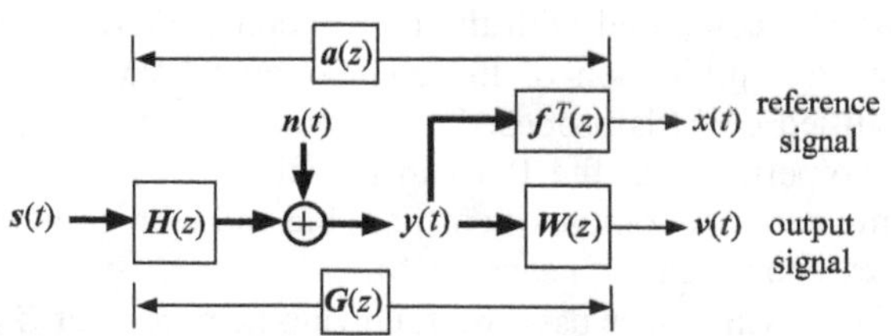

Figure 1. The composite system of the unknown system $H(z)$ and the deconvolver $W(z)$, and the reference system $f(z)$ with m inputs and single output $x(t)$. It is the case of single reference.

A2) The input sequence $\{\boldsymbol{s}(t)\}$ is a complex, zero-mean and non-Gaussian random vector process with element processes $\{s_i(t)\}$, $i = \underline{1,n}$ being mutually independent. Each element process $\{s_i(t)\}$ is an i.i.d. process with a variance $\sigma_{s_i}^2 \neq 0$ and a nonzero fourth-order cumulant $\gamma_i \neq 0$ defined as

$$\gamma_i = \mathrm{cum}\{s_i(t), s_i(t), s_i^*(t), s_i^*(t)\} \neq 0. \qquad (3)$$

A3) The deconvolver $\boldsymbol{W}(z)$ s an FIR system, that is, $\boldsymbol{W}(z) = \sum_{k=L_1}^{L_2} \boldsymbol{W}^{(k)} z^k$, where the length $L := L_2 - L_1 + 1$ is taken to be sufficiently large so that the truncation effect can be ignored.

A4) The noise sequence $\{\boldsymbol{n}(t)\}$ is a zero-mean, Gaussian vector stationary process whose component processes $\{n_j(t)\}$, $j = \underline{1,m}$ have nonzero variances $\sigma_{n_j}^2 \neq 0$, $j = \underline{1,m}$.

A5) The two vector sequences $\{\boldsymbol{n}(t)\}$ and $\{\boldsymbol{s}(t)\}$ are mutually statistically independent.

Under **A3)**, the impulse response $\{\boldsymbol{G}^{(k)}\}$ of the cascade system is given by

$$\boldsymbol{G}^{(k)} := \sum_{\tau=L_1}^{L_2} \boldsymbol{W}^{(\tau)} \boldsymbol{H}^{(k-\tau)}, \ k \in Z \qquad (4)$$

In a vector form, (4) can be written as

$$\tilde{g}_i = \tilde{H}\tilde{w}_i, \quad i = \underline{1,n} \qquad (5)$$

where $\tilde{g}_i$ is the column vector consisting of the i-th output impulse response of the cascade system defined by $\tilde{g}_i := \left[g_{i1}^T, g_{i2}^T, \cdots, g_{in}^T\right]^T$, $\boldsymbol{g}_{ij}$ is expressed as

$$g_{ij} := \left[\cdots, g_{ij}(-1), g_{ij}(0), g_{ij}(1), \cdots\right]^T, \ j = \underline{1, n} \qquad (6)$$

where $g_{ij}(k)$ is the (i, j)-th element of matrix $\boldsymbol{G}^{(k)}$, and $\tilde{w}_i$ is the mL-column vector consisting of the tap coefficients (corresponding to the i-th output) of the deconvolver defined by $\tilde{\boldsymbol{w}}_i := [w_{i1}^T, w_{i2}^T, \cdots, w_{in}^T]^T \in \boldsymbol{C}^{mL}$, w_{ij} is defined by

$$w_{ij} := \left[w_{ij}(L_1), w_{ij}(L_1+1), \cdots, w_{ij}(L_2)\right]^T \in C^L, j = \underline{1,m}, \qquad (7)$$

where $w_{ij}(k)$ is the (i,j)-th element of matrix $\boldsymbol{W}^{(k)}$, and $\tilde{H}$ is the $n \times m$ block matrix whose (i,j)-th block element $\boldsymbol{H}_{ij}$ is the matrix (of L columns and possibly infinite number of rows) with the (l,r)-th element $[\boldsymbol{H}_{ij}]_{lr}$ defined by $[\boldsymbol{H}_{ij}]_{lr} := h_{ji}(l - r)$, $l = 0, \pm1, \pm2, \cdots$, $r = \underline{L_1, L_2}$, where $h_{ij}(k)$ is the (i,j)-th element of the matrix $\boldsymbol{H}^{(k)}$.

In the MIMO deconvolution problem, we want to adjust $\tilde{\boldsymbol{w}}_i$'s ($i = \underline{1,n}$) so that

$$[\tilde{g}_1, \cdots, \tilde{g}_n] = \tilde{H}[\tilde{w}_1, \cdots, \tilde{w}_n] = [\tilde{\delta}_1, \cdots, \tilde{\delta}_n]P, \qquad (8)$$

where $\boldsymbol{P}$ is an $n \times n$ permutation matrix, and $\tilde{\delta}_i$ is the

n-block column vector defined by $\tilde{\delta}_i = [\delta_{i1}^T, \delta_{i2}^T, \cdots, \delta_{in}^T]^T, i = \underline{1,n}$, $\delta_{ij} := \hat{\delta}_i$ for $i = j$, otherwise. $(\cdots,0,0,0,\cdots)^T$ Here, $\hat{\delta}_i$ is the column vector (of infinite elements) whose r-th element $\hat{\delta}_i(\tau)$ is given by $\hat{\delta}_i(\tau) = d_i\delta(r - k_i)$, where $\delta(t)$ is the Kronecker delta function, d_i is a complex number standing for a scale change and a phase shift, and k_i is an integer standing for a time shift.

3. The Conventional Eigenvector Algorithms

Jelonnek *et al.* [2] have shown in the single-input case that from the following problem, that is, Maximize $D_{v_i x} = \text{cum}\{v_i(t), v_i^*(t), x(t), x^*(t)\}$

under $$\sigma_{v_i}^2 = \sigma_{s\rho_i}^2, \tag{9}$$

a closed-form solution expressed as a generalized eigenvector problem can be led by the Lagrangian method, where $\sigma_{v_i}^2$ and $\sigma_{s\rho_i}^2$ denote the variances of the output $v_i(t)$ and a source signal $s_{\rho_i}(t)$, respectively, ρ_i is one of integers $\{1,2\cdots,n\}$ such that the set $\{\rho_1, \rho_2, \cdots, \rho_n\}$ is a permutation of the set $\{1,2,\cdots,n\}$, $v_i(t)$ is the i-th element of $\boldsymbol{v}(t)$ in (2), and the reference signal $x(t)$ is given by $f^T(z)y(t)$ using an appropriate filter $\boldsymbol{f}(z)$ (see **Figure 1**). The filter $\boldsymbol{f}(z)$ is called a *reference system*. Let $\boldsymbol{a}(z) := H^T(z)f(z) = [a_1(z), a_2(z), \cdots, a_n(z)]^T$, then $x(t) = f^T(z)H(z)s(t) = a^T(z)s(t)$. The element $a_i(z)$ of the filter $\boldsymbol{a}(z)$ is defined as $a_i(z) = \sum_{k=-\infty}^{\infty} a_i(k)z^k$ and the reference system $\boldsymbol{f}(z)$ is an m-column vector whose elements are $f_j(z) = \sum_{k=L_1}^{L_2} f_j(k)z^k$, $j = \underline{1,m}$, where differently from the $w_{ij}(k)$, the parameter $f_j(k)$ is any fixed value.

In our case, $D_{v_i x}$ and $\sigma_{v_i}^2$ can be expressed in terms of the vector $\tilde{\boldsymbol{w}}_i$ as, respectively, $D_{v_i x} = \tilde{\boldsymbol{w}}_i^H \tilde{\boldsymbol{B}} \tilde{\boldsymbol{w}}_i$ and $\sigma_{v_i}^2 = \tilde{\boldsymbol{w}}_i^H \tilde{\boldsymbol{R}} \tilde{\boldsymbol{w}}_i$ where $\tilde{\boldsymbol{B}}$ is the $m \times m$ block matrix whose (i,j)-th block element $\boldsymbol{B}_{ij}$ is the matrix with the (l,r)-th element calculated by cum $\{y_j(tL_1 r+1), y_i^*(tL_1 l+1), x^*(t), x(t)\}$ $(l,r = \underline{1,L})$ and $\tilde{R} = E[\tilde{y}^*(t)\tilde{y}^T(t)]$ is the covariance matrix of m-block column vector $\tilde{y}(t)$ defined by

$$\tilde{y}(t) := [y_1^T(t), y_2^T(t), \ldots, y_m^T(t)]^T \in C^{mL} \tag{10}$$

where

$$y_j(t) := [y_j(t-L_1), y_j(t-L_1-1), \cdots, y_j(t-L_2)]^T \in C^L,$$

$j=\underline{1,m}$. It follows from (10) that $\tilde{y}(t)$ is expressed as $\tilde{y}(t) = \boldsymbol{D}_c(z)\boldsymbol{y}(t)$, where $\boldsymbol{D}_c(z)$ is an $mL \times m$ converter (consisting of m identical delay chains each of which has L delay elements when $L_1 = 1$) defined by $\boldsymbol{D}_c(z) :=$ block-diag $\{d_c(z), \cdots, d_c(z)\}$ with m diagonal block elements all being the same L-column vector $\boldsymbol{d}_c(z)$ defined by $\boldsymbol{d}_c(z) = [z^{L_1}, \cdots, z^{L_2}]^T$. Therefore, by the similar way to as in [2], the maximization of $|D_{v_i x}|$ under $\sigma_{v_i}^2 = \sigma_{s\rho_i}^2$ leads to the following generalized eigenvector problem;

$$\tilde{\boldsymbol{B}}\tilde{\boldsymbol{w}}_i = \lambda_i \tilde{\boldsymbol{R}}\tilde{\boldsymbol{w}}_i. \tag{11}$$

Moreover, Jelonnek *et al.* have shown in [2] that the eigenvector corresponding to the maximum magnitude eigenvalue of $\tilde{\boldsymbol{R}}^\dagger \tilde{\boldsymbol{B}}$ becomes the solution of the blind equalization problem, which is referred to as an *eigenvector algorithm* (EVA). It has been also shown in [3] that the BD for MIMO-IIR systems can be achieved with the eigenvectors of $\tilde{\boldsymbol{R}}^\dagger \tilde{\boldsymbol{B}}$, using only one reference signal. Note that since Jelonnek *et al.* have dealt with SISO-IIR systems or SIMO-IIR systems, the constructions of $\tilde{B}$, $\tilde{w}_i$, and $\tilde{R}$ in (11) are different from those proposed in [2].

Castella *et al.* [5] have shown that from (9), a BD can be iteratively achieved by using $x_i(t) = \tilde{\boldsymbol{w}}_i\tilde{y}(t)$ $(i = \underline{1,n})$ as reference signals (see **Figure 2**), where the number of reference signals corresponds to the number of source signals and $\tilde{\boldsymbol{w}}_i$ is a vector obtained by $\tilde{\boldsymbol{R}}^\dagger \tilde{\boldsymbol{B}}_i$ divided by λ_i in the previous iteration, where $\tilde{B}_i$ represents $\tilde{B}$ in (11) calculated by $x_i(t) = \tilde{\boldsymbol{w}}_i\tilde{y}(t)$. Namely, they considered the following equation;

$$\tilde{\boldsymbol{R}}^\dagger \tilde{\boldsymbol{B}}_i \tilde{\boldsymbol{w}}_i = \lambda_i \tilde{\boldsymbol{w}}_i. \tag{12}$$

Then a deflation method was used to recover all source signals. However, the EVM proposed by Castella *et al.* requires the calculation of the eigenvectors of the matrix $\tilde{\boldsymbol{R}}^\dagger \tilde{\boldsymbol{B}}_i$ to achieve the BD.

4. The Proposed Algorithm

Here, the Equation (12) can be interpreted as follows. Suppose that the value $\tilde{\boldsymbol{w}}_i$ in the left-hand side of (12) is a vector obtained by $\tilde{\boldsymbol{R}}^\dagger \tilde{\boldsymbol{B}}_i$ divided by λ_i in the previous iteration. Also, let $\tilde{\boldsymbol{d}}_i$ denote $\tilde{\boldsymbol{B}}_i\tilde{\boldsymbol{w}}_i$. Then (12) can be expressed as

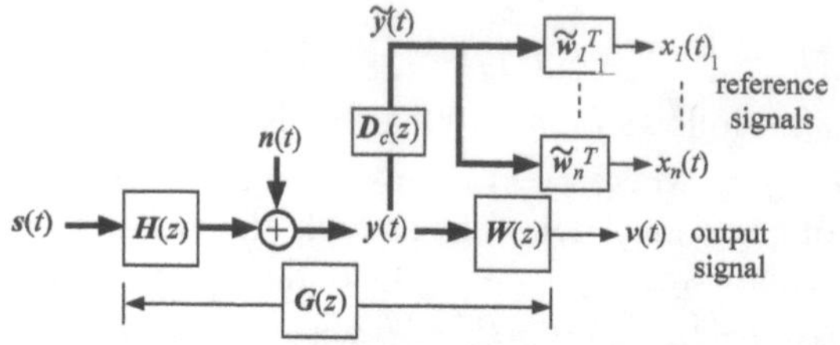

Figure 2. The composite system of the unknown system $H(z)$ and the deconvolver $W(z)$, and the reference system with m inputs and n outputs, where $D_c(z)$ is an $mL\times m$ converter. It is the case of multiple reference system.

$$\tilde{w}_i = \frac{1}{\lambda_i}\tilde{R}^{\dagger}\tilde{d}_i,\ i=\underline{1,n}, \tag{13}$$

where on the details of $\tilde{d}_i = \tilde{B}_i\tilde{w}_i$, see (30) in Appendix. Differently from the EVM in [5], (13) means that $\tilde{w}_i$ is modified iteratively by the value of the right-hand side of (13) without calculating the eigenvectors of $\tilde{R}^{\dagger}\tilde{B}_i$ where $\tilde{w}_i$ in both $x_i(t)$ and $\tilde{d}_i$ is the value of the left-hand side of (13) in the previous iteration. Moreover, the EVMs in [2,6] must select the appropriate parameter for the reference system $f(z)$, but our proposed algorithm does not need such a troublesome process. The scalar λ_i is fixed to be 1, but $\tilde{w}_i$ obtained by (13) should be normalized at each iteration, that is

$$\tilde{w}_i := \frac{\tilde{w}_i}{\sqrt{\tilde{w}_i^H\tilde{R}\tilde{w}_i}},\quad i=1,n. \tag{14}$$

It can be seen that the iterative algorithm (13) is nothing but an iterative procedure of the super-exponential method (SEM) [7-9] (see Appendix), where the first proposal of the SEM was done by Shalvi and Weinstein [9]. Therefore, our proposed algorithm for achieving the BD is that the vector $\tilde{w}_i$ is modified by using the value $\tilde{R}^{\dagger}\tilde{d}_i$ in (13), and then the modified vector, that is, $\tilde{w}_i$ in the left-hand side of (13) is normalized by (14).

Here, the calculation of $\tilde{R}^{\dagger}$ is implemented by using the following algorithm based on the matrix pseudo-inversion lemma proposed in [10]. The reason is that in the case that the pseudo-inverse is calculated using data block, the convergence speed is increased and the computational complexity is reduced, compared with the conventional pseudo-inverse algorithms, for example, the built-in function "pinv" in MATLAB [11]. Therefore, in order to provide a recursive formula based on block data for time-updating of pseudo-inverse, the block index "k" is defined, and then $\tilde{R}$ and $\tilde{R}^{\dagger}$ are described as $\tilde{R}(\mathrm{k})$ and $P(\mathrm{k})$, respectively, where the k-th block of data is defined as

$$t = \mathrm{k}l + i,\ i = \underline{1,l-1},\ \mathrm{k}\in Z \tag{15}$$

the parameters l and t denote the block length and the original discrete (or sample) time, respectively. The matrix $\tilde{R}(k)$ is obtained by

$$\tilde{R}(\mathrm{k}) = (1-\alpha_{\mathrm{k}})\tilde{R}(\mathrm{k}-1) + \alpha_{\mathrm{k}}Y^{*}(\mathrm{k})Y^{T}(\mathrm{k}), \tag{16}$$

where

$$Y(\mathrm{k}) = \left[\tilde{y}\{(\mathrm{k}-1)l\}, \tilde{y}\{(\mathrm{k}-1)l+1\}, \cdots, \tilde{y}\{(\mathrm{k}-1)l+l-1\}\right] \in C^{mL\times l} \tag{17}$$

and α_{k} is a positive number close to, but greater than zero, which accounts for some exponential weighting factor or forgetting factor [12]. Moreover, the following parameters are defined;

$$Y(k) = \sqrt{\alpha_k}\tilde{Y}^{*}(k), \tag{18}$$

$$Y_1(k) = \tilde{R}(k-1)P(k-1)Y(k), \tag{19}$$

$$Y_2(k) = \{I - \tilde{R}(k-1)P(k-1)\}Y(k). \tag{20}$$

Then the pseudo-inverse $P(\mathrm{k})$ can be explicitly expressed, as follows:

$$P(k) = P_B^{\dagger}(k) - P_B^{\dagger}(\mathrm{k})\left[Y_1(\mathrm{k}), Y_2(\mathrm{k})\right]P_D^{-1}(\mathrm{k})\left[Y_1(\mathrm{k}), Y_2(\mathrm{k})\right]^H P_B^{\dagger}(\mathrm{k}) \tag{21}$$

where $P_B^{\dagger}(k)$ and $P_D^{-1}(k)$ are respectively defined by

$$P_B^{\dagger}(\mathrm{k}) := \frac{\left[P(\mathrm{k}-1) - P(\mathrm{k}-1)Y_1\mathrm{k}P_A^{-1}Y_1^H(\mathrm{k})P(\mathrm{k}-1)\right]}{1-\alpha_{\mathrm{k}}} + \left(Y_2^H(\mathrm{k})\right)^{\dagger}Y_2^{\dagger}(\mathrm{k}), \tag{22}$$

and

$$P_D^{-1}(\mathrm{k}) := \begin{bmatrix} -\Delta^{-1}(\mathrm{k})P_2(\mathrm{k}) & \Delta^{-1}(\mathrm{k}) \\ I + E_1(\mathrm{k})\Delta^{-1}(\mathrm{k})E_2(\mathrm{k}) & -E_1(\mathrm{k})\Delta^{-1}(\mathrm{k}) \end{bmatrix} \tag{23}$$

with

$$\Delta(\mathrm{k}) := I - E_2(\mathrm{k})E_1(\mathrm{k}), \tag{24}$$

where

$$E_1(\mathrm{k}) = B_1^H(\mathrm{k})P_B^{\dagger}(\mathrm{k})B_1(\mathrm{k}), \tag{25}$$

$$E_2(\mathrm{k}) = B_2^H(\mathrm{k})P_B^{\dagger}(\mathrm{k})B_2(\mathrm{k}),$$

We treat $P(\mathrm{k})$ as $\tilde{R}^{\dagger}$, and $\tilde{w}_i$ is iteratively modified using (13) and (14), where λ_i in (13) is assumed to be fixed to 1 and $\tilde{d}_i := \tilde{B}_i\tilde{w}_i$ in (13) is estimated by using $Y(\mathrm{k})$.

Thus, the proposed iterative algorithm for solving the BD problem is summarized, as follows:

1) Choose appropriate initial values of $\tilde{w}_i(0)$, $P(0)$, $\tilde{R}(0)$, $\tilde{d}_i(0)$, $i=\underline{1,n}$ and set $\mathrm{k} = 1$.

2) Estimate $\tilde{R}(k-1)$, $\tilde{\mathrm{d}}_i(\mathrm{k}-1)$, by their moving averages, and $P(k-1)$ by (21).

3) Calculate the $\tilde{w}_i(k)$, from $P(k-1)\tilde{w}_i(k)$, and then $\tilde{w}_i(\mathrm{k})$ is normalized by $\sqrt{\tilde{w}_i^H(\mathrm{k})\tilde{R}(\mathrm{k}-1)\tilde{w}_i(\mathrm{k})}$.

4) Put k = k + 1 and stock the $\tilde{w}_i$ obtained in (13).

If k = k' (where k' denotes an appropriate iteration number), stop the iterations, otherwise go to **2**).

5. Simulation Results

To demonstrate the proposed algorithm, we considered a MIMO system $\boldsymbol{H}(z)$ with two inputs (n = 2) and three outputs (m = 3), and assumed that the system $\boldsymbol{H}(z)$ is FIR and the length of channel is three, that is $\boldsymbol{H}^{(k)}$'s in (1) were set to be

$$\boldsymbol{H}(z) = \sum_{k=0}^{2} \boldsymbol{H}^{(k)} z^k = \begin{bmatrix} 1+0.15z+0.1z^2 & 0.65+0.25z+0.15z^2 \\ 0.5-0.1z+0.2z^2 & 1+0.25z+0.1z^2 \\ 0.6+0.1z+0.4z^2 & 0.1+0.2z+0.1z^2 \end{bmatrix}$$

The source signals $s_1(t)$ and $s_2(t)$ were a sub-Gaussian signal which takes one of two values, −1 and 1 with equal probability 1/2. The parameters L_1 and L_2 in $\boldsymbol{W}(z)$ were set to be 0 and 9, respectively. As a measure of performances, we used the *multichannel intersymbol interference* ($\mathrm{M_{ISI}}$) [8], which was the average of 50 Monte Carlo runs. In each Monte Carlo run, using 300 data samples, $\tilde{w}_i$ is modified by (13) and (14), and the total number of modification times is 10. About the block length l, the following two cases were considered: l = 1 and l = 2. For obtaining the pseudo-inverse of the correlation matrix, the initial values of $\tilde{R}$ $\tilde{d}_i$, and $\boldsymbol{P}$ were estimated using 30 data samples. The value of α_{k} was chosen as $\alpha_{\mathrm{k}} = \frac{1}{\mathrm{k}\, l}$ for each k.

Figure 3 shows the results obtained by the conventional EVM (ConEVM), the modified EVM (ModEVM), and their combined EVM (ComEVM) in the case of l = 1. As a ConEVM, we selected the EVM proposed by Castella *et al.*. Then, the pseudo-inverse of $\tilde{R}$ in (12) was calculated by the built-in function "pinv" in MATLAB and our proposed matrix pseudo-inversion lemma, denoted by "mpinvl". In the ComEVM, the ConEVM was carried out at the first modification and from the second modification the ModEVM was carried out, where the pseudo-inverse $\tilde{R}$ in (12) was calculated by "mpinvl". From the figure, the ConEVM with mpinvl provides a better performance compared with the other EVMs, except for the ComEVM. However, the average of the execution time of the ConEVM with mpinvl is longer than the one of the ModEVM with mpinvl (see **Table 1**).

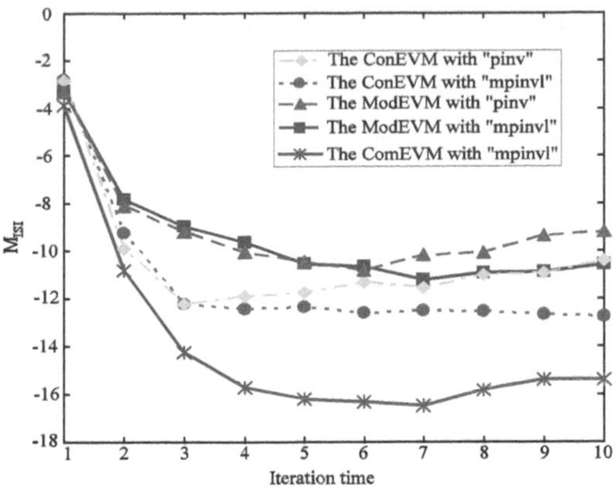

Figure 3. The performances of the proposed algorithm and the conventional methods (l = 1).

On the other hand, the ComEVM with mpinvl is carried out with a little bit longer execution time than the ModEVM with mpinvl but the performance of the ComEVM with mpinvl is better than the other EVMs. From these results, we recommend to use the ComEVM with mpinvl to achieve the BD in the case of l = 1.

Figure 4 shows the results obtained by the EVMs in the case of l = 2. From **Figure 4**, one can see that the ModEVMs with mpinvl provides better performances than the other EVMs. Therefore we recommend to use the ModEVM with mpinvl to achieve the BD in the case of l = 2.

Table 1 shows the average of the execution times for the proposed method and the conventional EVM, using a personal computer (Windows machine) with 3.33 GHz processor and 3 GB main memories. From the **Table 1**, one can see that the execution time of the ModEVM with mpinvl is the fastest compared with other EVMs. The reasons are that the ModEVM is carried out without calculating the eigenvectors of $\tilde{\boldsymbol{R}}^{\dagger}\tilde{\boldsymbol{B}}_i$ in (12) and the mpinvl has a property written in [13].

6. Conclusions

In this paper, by modifying the EVM, we have proposed an algorithm which can achieve the BD without calculating eigenvectors. Moreover, a combination of the modified EVM and the conventional EVM has been proposed. It can be seen that the combined EVM provides a better performance than the other EVMs in the case of l = 1, and the ModEVA with mpinvl provides a better performance than the other EVMs in the case of l = 2, but the average of execution time of the combined EVM is a little bit longer than the modified EVM. Although there exists such a trade-off, we conclude that our proposed EVM is more useful for solving the BD problem, because we consider that the performance accuracy is most important for achieving the BD.

Table 1. Comparison of the averages of the execution times.

Methods	*times* [*sec*] ($l = 1$)	*times* [*sec*] ($l = 2$)
The ModEVM with "pinv"	0.1429	0.1205
The ModEVM with "mpinvl"	0.1353	0.1168
The ModEVM with "mpinvl"	0.1492	0.1218
The ConEVM with "mpinvl"	0.1380	0.1179
The ComEVM with "mpinv"	0.1362	0.1175

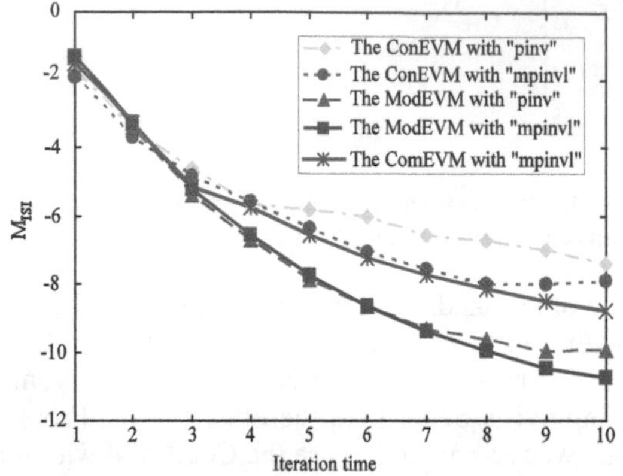

Figure 4. The performances of the proposed algorithm and the conventional methods ($l = 2$).

7. Acknowledgements

This work was supported by the Grant-in-Aids for the Scientific Research by the Ministry of Education, Culture, Sports, Science and Technology of Japan, No.21500 088 and No.22500079.

8. References

[1] Special Issue on Blind System Identification and Esti-Mation, *Proceedings of the IEEE*, Vol. 86, No. 10, 1998, pp. 1907-2089.

[2] B. Jelonnek and K. D. Kammeyer, "A Closed-form Solution to Blind Equalization," *Signal Processing*, Vol. 36, No. 3, 1994, pp. 251-259.

[3] M. Kawamoto, K. Kohno, Y. Inouye and K. Kurumatani, "A Modified Eigenvector Method for Blind Deconvolution of MIMO Systems Using the Matrix Pseudo-Inversion Lemma," *International Symposium on Circuits and Systems* 2010, Paris, 30 May-2 June 2010, pp. 2514-2517.

[4] M. Kawamoto, K. Kohno and Y. Inouye, "Eigenvector Algorithms for Blind Deconvolution of MIMO-IIR Systems," *International Symposium on Circuits and Systems* 2007, New Orleans, 25-28 May 2007, pp. 3490-3493.

[5] B. Jelonnek, D. Boss and K. D. Kammeyer, "Generalized Eigenvector Algorithm for Blind Equalization," *Signal Processing*, Vol. 61, No. 3, 1997, pp. 237-264.

[6] M. Kawamoto, Y. Inouye and K. Kohno, "Recently Developed Approaches for Solving Blind Deconvolution of MIMO-IIR Systems: Super-Exponential and Eigenvector Methods," *International Symposium on Circuits and Systems* 2008, Seattle, 18-21 May 2008, pp. 121-124.

[7] M. Castella, *et al.*, "Quadratic Higher-Order Criteria for Iterative Blind Separation of a MIMO Convolutive Mixture of Sources," *IEEE Transactions. Signal Processing*, Vol. 55, No. 1, 2007, pp. 218-232.

[8] Y. Inouye and K. Tanebe, "Super-Exponential Algorithms for Multichannel Blind Deconvolution," *IEEE Transaction on Signal Processing*, Vol. 48, No. 3, 2000. pp. 881-888.

[9] K. Kohno, Y. Inouye and M. Kawamoto, "Super Exponential Methods Incorporated with Higher-Order Correlations for Deflationary Blind Equalization of MIMO Linear Systems,"*5th International Conference on Independent Component Analysis and Blind Signal Separation*, Granada, 22-24 September 2004, pp. 685-693.

[10] O. Shalvi and E. Weinstein, "Super-Exponential Methods for Blind Deconvolution," *The IEEE Transactions on Information Theory*, Vol. 39, No. 2, 1993, pp. 504-519.

[11] K. Kohno, Y. Inouye and M. Kawamoto, "A Matrix Pseudo-Inversion Lemma for Positive Semidefinite Hermitian Matrices and Its Application to Adaptive Blind Deconvolution of MIMO Systems," *IEEE Transactions Circuits and Systems-I*, Vol. 55, No. 1, 2008, pp. 424-435.

[12] S. Haykin, "Adaptive Filter Theory," 3rd Edition, PrenticeHall, New Jersey, 1995.

[13] K. Kohno, M. Kawamoto and Y. Inouye, "A Matrix Pseudo-Inversion Lemma and Its Application to Block-Based Adaptive Blind Deconvolution of MIMO Systems," *IEEE Transactions Circuits and Systems-I*, Vol. 57, No. 7, 2010, pp. 1449-1462.

Appendix

The relationship between (13) and the SEM

The matrices $\widetilde{\boldsymbol{R}}$ and $\widetilde{\boldsymbol{B}}_i$ can be expressed as

$$\widetilde{\boldsymbol{R}} = \widetilde{\boldsymbol{H}}^H \widetilde{\boldsymbol{\Sigma}} \widetilde{\boldsymbol{H}}, \quad \widetilde{\boldsymbol{B}}_i = \widetilde{\boldsymbol{H}}^H \widetilde{\boldsymbol{\Lambda}}_i \widetilde{\boldsymbol{H}} \tag{28}$$

where $\widetilde{\boldsymbol{\Sigma}}$ is a block-diagonal matrix which is denoted as $\tilde{\Sigma} := \text{block-diag}\{\Sigma_1, \cdots, \Sigma_n,\}$ $\Sigma := \text{diag}\{\cdots, \sigma_{s_i}^2, \sigma_{s_i}^2, \cdots\}$, $i = \underline{1,n}$, $\widetilde{\boldsymbol{\Lambda}}_i$ is a block-diagonal matrix which is represented as $\widetilde{\boldsymbol{\Lambda}}_i := \text{block-diag}\{\Lambda_{i1}, \cdots, \Lambda_{in}\}$,

$$\Lambda_{ij} := \text{diag}\left\{\cdots, |g_{ij}(-1)|^2 \gamma_j, |g_{ij}(0)|^2 \gamma_j, \cdots\right\}, \tag{29}$$

$j = \underline{1,n}$. Then, from (5) and (28), $\widetilde{\boldsymbol{d}}_i = \widetilde{\boldsymbol{B}}_i \widetilde{\boldsymbol{w}}_i$ can be expressed as

$$\widetilde{\boldsymbol{d}}_i = \widetilde{\boldsymbol{B}}_i \widetilde{\boldsymbol{w}}_i = \widetilde{\boldsymbol{H}}^H \widetilde{\boldsymbol{\Lambda}}_i \widetilde{\boldsymbol{g}}_i. \tag{30}$$

It can be seen from (29) that the elements of $\widetilde{\boldsymbol{\Lambda}}_i \widetilde{\boldsymbol{g}}_i$ are $|g_{ij}(k)|^2 g_{ij}(k)\gamma_j$, $k = \underline{-\infty,\infty}$. Here, we define the following equation:

$$f_{ij}(k) = \frac{\gamma_j}{\sigma_{s_j}^2} |g_{ij}(k)|^2 g_{ij}(k). \tag{31}$$

This can be used for the SEM with respect to $g_{ij}(k)$, using the 4th order cumulant. [7] Substituting (31) into (30), we obtain the following equation:

$$\widetilde{\boldsymbol{d}}_i = \widetilde{\boldsymbol{H}}^H \widetilde{\boldsymbol{\Sigma}} \widetilde{\boldsymbol{f}}_i, \tag{32}$$

where

$\tilde{f}_i = \left[f_{i1}^T, f_{i2}^T, \cdots, f_{in}^T\right]^T = \left[\cdots, f_{ij}(1), f_{ij}(0), f_{ij}(1), \cdots\right]^T$.

Moreover, substituting (28) and (32) into (13), then (13) can be expressed as

$$\tilde{w}_i = \left(\tilde{H}^H \tilde{\Sigma} \tilde{H}\right)^{\dagger} \tilde{H}^H \tilde{\Sigma} \tilde{f}_i, \tag{33}$$

where λ_i is assumed to be 1. (33) is the first step of the SEM with respect to $\widetilde{\boldsymbol{w}}_i$ [8]. In the SEM, the second step, that is, the normalization step is implemented using (14). Therefore, (13) and (14) are nothing but the iterative algorithm of the SEM. This completes the proof.

A Novel Multifunction CFOA-Based Inverse Filter

Hung-Yu Wang[1], Sheng-Hsiung Chang[2], Tzu-Yi Yang[1], Po-Yang Tsai[1]
[1]*Department of Electronic Engineering, National Kaohsiung University of Applied Sciences, Kaohsiung, Taiwan, China*
[2]*Department of Optoelectronic Engineering, Far East University, Hsin-Shih, Taiwan, China*

Abstract

We present a novel multifunction inverse biquad configuration based on current feedback operational amplifiers (CFOAs) and grounded passive elements. The proposed scheme can be used to realize inverse lowpass, inverse bandpass and inverse highpass filter functions. The relevant coefficients of the inverse filters are orthogonal adjustable by independent passive elements. All the passive elements in the proposed scheme are grounded to benefit easier electronic tunability. With the high input impedance and low output impedance properties, the scheme is input and output cascadable for voltage operation. The feasibility of the proposed scheme is demonstrated by HSPICE simulations.

Keywords: Multifunction, Inverse Filter, CFOA

1. Introduction

In communication, control and instrumentation systems, there are numerous situations in which an electrical signal is altered through a linear or nonlinear transformation by a processing or a transmission system. So it is necessary to recover the input signal from the available distorted output signal resulted from the signal progress. This can often be done by using a system that has an inverse transfer characteristic of the original system [1]. For digital signal processing, several methods for obtaining digital inverse filters have been established [2]. Nevertheless, for analog signal processing, only a few works are known for realizing continuous-time analog inverse filters [1,3-6].

In [1], a general approach is presented for obtaining the inverse transfer function for linear dynamic systems and the inverse transfer characteristic for non-linear resistive circuits. In [3], a procedure for deriving current-mode, four-terminal floating nullor (FTFN)-based inverse filter from the voltage-mode filter is given. It uses the method in [1] and dual transformation [7] during the procedure. Due to the use of dual transformation, this approach can only be applied to planar circuit. By the use of adjoint transformation, another easier procedure for deriving current-mode FTFN-based inverse filter from the voltage-mode filter is presented and it is applicable to nonplanar circuits [4]. All the proposed approaches in [1,3,4] are useful for obtaining single-input single-output inverse filters. Additional various inverse current-mode and voltage-mode filters are presented in [5] and [6], respectively. However, each circuit proposed in [5,6] has one inverse filter function. In this paper, we present a novel inverse filter scheme based on CFOAs and grounded passive elements. By slight modification of the passive elements of the proposed scheme, various inverse filter functions can be realized. The presented scheme possesses high input impedance and low output impedance which enables the convenience of connecting with the other stage in cascade. The workability of the proposed scheme is verified by HSPICE simulations. The simulated results confirm the theoretical prediction.

2. The Proposed Circuit

The current-feedback operational amplifier, such as AD844 from Analog Devices Inc. [8], has gained the acceptance of researchers as a building block in circuit design. The advantages of CFOAs are their constant bandwidths, independent closed-loop gains and high slew-rate capabilities [9]. The CFOA can be described using the following matrix-relations:

$$\begin{bmatrix} V_x \\ I_y \\ I_z \\ V_w \end{bmatrix} = \begin{bmatrix} 0 & 1 & 0 & 0 \\ 0 & 0 & 0 & 0 \\ 1 & 0 & 0 & 0 \\ 0 & 0 & 1 & 0 \end{bmatrix} \begin{bmatrix} I_x \\ V_y \\ V_z \\ I_w \end{bmatrix}. \quad (1)$$

Considering the proposed scheme in **Figure 1**, three CFOAs are used to construct the circuit functions. The transfer functions can be expressed as:

$$\frac{V_{o1}}{V_{in}} = \frac{V_{o3}}{V_{in}} = \frac{y_1 y_3 + y_2 y_4}{y_0 y_4} \tag{2}$$

$$\frac{V_{o2}}{V_{in}} = \frac{y_1}{y_4} \tag{3}$$

If the admittances are $y_0 = G_0$, $y_1 = sC_1$, $y_2 = sC_2+G_2$, $y_3 = sC_3$ and $y_4 = G_4$, the functions of inverse lowpass filter and inverse integrator can be realized at V_{o1} and V_{o2}, respectively. They are given by

$$\frac{V_{o1}}{V_{in}} = \frac{V_{o3}}{V_{in}} = \frac{s^2 C_1 C_3 + sC_2 G_4 + G_2 G_4}{G_0 G_4} \tag{4}$$

$$\frac{V_{o2}}{V_{in}} = \frac{sC_1}{G_4} \tag{5}$$

From Equation (4), it is clear that the coefficients of the s^2, s^1 and s^0 terms in the numerator and the term in denominator are tunable by the values of C_1, C_2, G_2 and G_0 respectively. So the system parameters, such as the corner angular frequency ω_o and quality factor Q of the inverse filter are tunable by independent passive elements.

In Equation (2), if the admittances are $y_0 = sC_0$, $y_1 = sC_1$, $y_2 = sC_2+G_2$, $y_3 = sC_3$ and $y_4 = G_4$, the functions of inverse bandpass filter and inverse integrator can be realized at V_{o1} and V_{o2}, respectively. They can be given by

$$\frac{V_{o2}}{V_{in}} = \frac{sC_1}{G_4} \tag{6}$$

$$\frac{V_{o1}}{V_{in}} = \frac{V_{o3}}{V_{in}} = \frac{s^2 C_1 C_3 + sC_2 G_4 + G_2 G_4}{sC_0 G_4} \tag{7}$$

Similarly, if the admittances are $y_0 = sC_0$, $y_1 = G_1$, $y_2 = sC_2+G_2$, $y_3 = G_3$ and $y_4 = sC_4$, the functions of inverse highpass filter and inverse differentiator can be realized at V_{o1} and V_{o2}, respectively. They can be expressed by

$$\frac{V_{o1}}{V_{in}} = \frac{V_{o3}}{V_{in}} = \frac{s^2 C_2 C_4 + sC_4 G_2 + G_1 G_3}{s^2 C_0 C_4} \tag{8}$$

$$\frac{V_{o2}}{V_{in}} = \frac{G_1}{sC_4} \tag{9}$$

The output of V_{o3} has the same function as V_{o1}, it provides the additional output which makes the filter application more flexible.

From (2) and (3), after the restricting ourselves only to the using of six passive elements, we can derive all the filter functions as shown in **Table 1**. It can be found that the coefficients of all terms in the numerator and denominator of the transfer functions are adjustable by independent passive elements. Furthermore, for the presented scheme in **Figure 1**, it can be observed that all the employed passive elements are grounded. The use of grounded passive elements conduces to easier electronic tunability and integrated-circuit implementation [10]. A number of realizations of tunable grounded passive elements can be found in the literature [10-13]. The passive sensitivities of corner angular frequency are equal to 0.5 for the inverse filter realizations in **Table 1**, so they can be classified as insensitive. In addition, the proposed configuration in **Figure 1** possesses the characteristics of input and output cascadability due to its high input impedance and low output impedance. So it is convenient to connecting other stages at both input and output terminals for signal processing. It must be noted that the proposed inverse lowpass and inverse bandpass filters in [6] are included in the filter realizations of **Table 1**. The presented scheme in **Figure 1** provides more flexible functions and different realization with identical configuration.

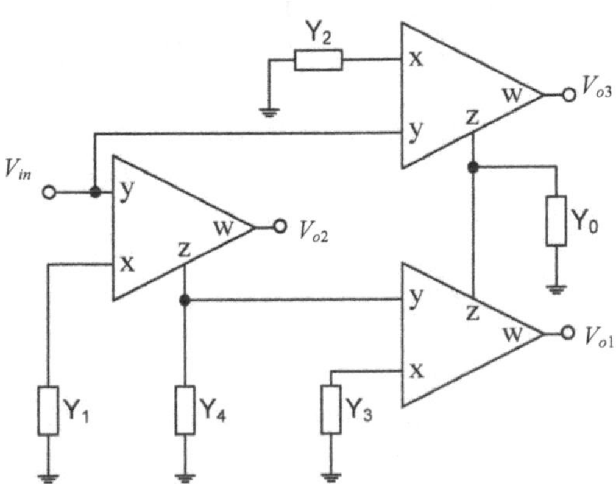

Figure 1. The proposed inverse filter scheme.

3. Simulation Results

To verify the potentialities of the proposed scheme, circuit simulations of the presented multi-function inverse filters have been carried out. The commercial current feedback amplifiers AD844 macromodel with ± 12 V voltage supply is used to realize the CFOA in **Figure 1** [12]. Using an AD844 IC to realize the CFOA, its equivalent model can be shown in **Figure 2**. It is important to understand that the low input impedance at x ter-

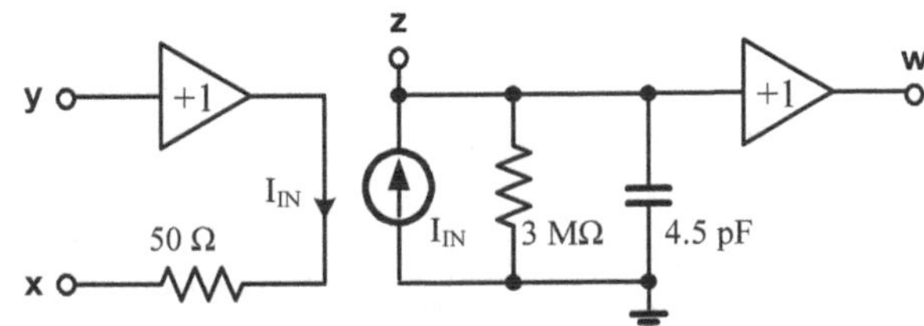

Figure 2. The realization of CFOA with an AD844 IC.

Table 1. All the inverse filter functions using six passive elements.

Case	Function at V_{o1}	Function at V_{o2}	y_0	y_1	y_2	y_3	y_4
1	Inverse lowpass	Differential	G_0	sC_1	sC_2+G_2	sC_3	G_4
2	Inverse lowpass	Inverse lowpass	G_0	sC_1+G_1	G_2	sC_3	G_4
3	Inverse lowpass	Differential	G_0	sC_1	G_2	sC_3+G_3	G_4
4	Inverse bandpass	Differential	sC_0	sC_1	sC_2+G_2	sC_3	G_4
5	Inverse bandpass	Inverse lowpass	sC_0	sC_1+G_1	G_2	sC_3	G_4
6	Inverse bandpass	Differential	sC_0	sC_1	G_2	sC_3+G_3	G_4
7	Inverse bandpass	Integration	G_0	G_1	sC_2+G_2	G_3	sC_4
8	Inverse bandpass	Integration	G_0	G_1	sC_2	sC_3+G_3	sC_4
9	Inverse bandpass	Inverse highpass	G_0	sC_1+G_1	sC_2	G_3	sC_4
10	Inverse highpass	Integration	sC_0	G_1	sC_2	sC_3+G_3	sC_4
11	Inverse highpass	Inverse highpass	sC_0	sC_1+G_1	sC_2	G_3	sC_4
12	Inverse highpass	Integration	sC_0	G_1	sC_2+G_2	G_3	sC_4

minl is locally generated and does not depend on feedback. This is very different from the "virtual ground" of a conventional operational amplifier used in the current summing mode which is essentially an open circuit until the loop settles [8]. In the simulation, the values of all resistors and all capacitors are 40 kΩ and 1 nF, respectively.

It is found that the workability of all the inverse biquids in **Table 1** is in good agreement with our theoretical prediction. The typical frequency responses of inverse lowpass (the case 1 of **Table 1**), inverse bandpass (the case 4 of **Table 1**) and inverse highpass (the case 12 of **Table 1**) are shown in **Figure 3**. The deviation to theoretical response is due to the parasitic impedance of nonideal CFOA [14].

4. Conclusions

We have proposed a novel scheme for the realization of an input and output cascadable voltage-mode multifunction inverse filter. It consists of CFOAs and grounded-passive elements. Many various inverse filter functions are realized by slight modification of the passive elements of the proposed scheme. It offers more convenient

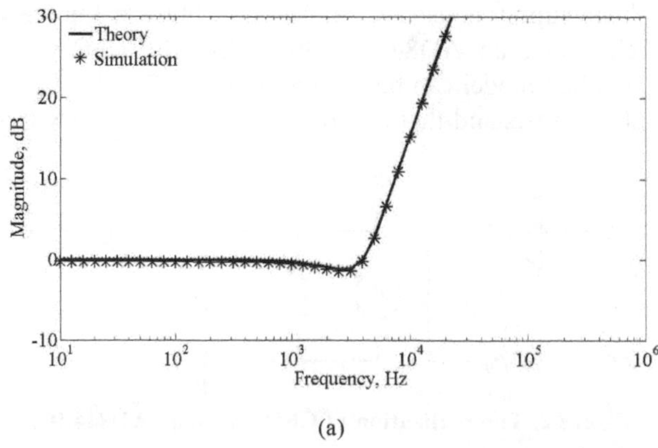

(a)

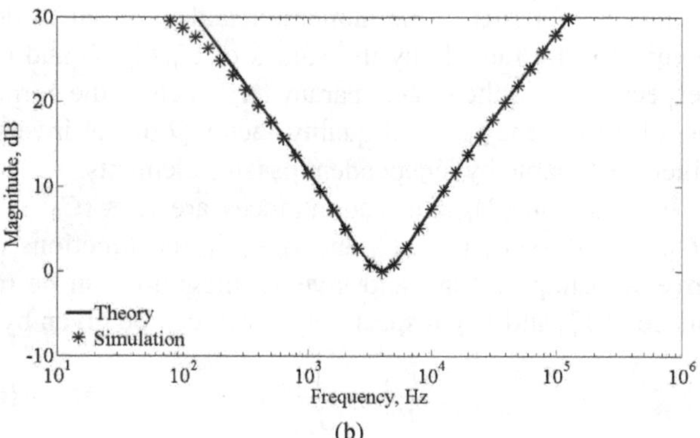

(b)

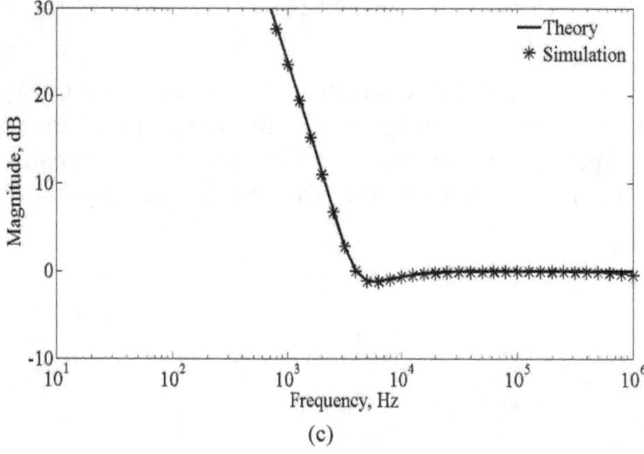

(c)

Figure 3. Typical frequency responses of inverse filters: (a) inverse lowpass; (b) inverse bandpass; (c) inverse highpass.

realizations for inverse filter functions. The feasibility of the proposed circuit is verified by simulation results.

5. References

[1] A. Leuciuc, "Using Nullors for Realisation of Inverse Transfer Functions and Characteristics," *Electronics Letters*, Vol. 33, No. 11, 1997, pp. 949-951.

[2] R. Kuc, "Introduction to Digital Signal Processing," McGraw-Hill, New York, 1988.

[3] B. Chipipop and W. Surakampontorn, "Realisation of Current-Mode FTFN-Based Inverse Filter," *Electronics Letters*, Vol. 35, No. 9, 1999, pp. 690-692.

[4] H. Y. Wang and C. T. Lee, "Using Nullors for Realisation of Current-Mode FTFN-Based Inverse Filters," *Electronics Letters*, Vol. 35, No. 22, 1999, pp. 1889-1890.

[5] M. T. Abuelma'atti, "Identification of Cascadable Current-Mode Filters and Inverse-Filters Using Single FTFN," *Frequenz*, Vol. 54, No. 11, 2000, pp. 284-289.

[6] S. S. Gupta, D. R. Bhaskar, R. Senani and A. K. Singh, "Inverse Active Filters Employing CFOAs," *Electrical Engineering*, Vol. 91, No. 1, 2009, pp. 23-26.

[7] G. H. Wang, Y. Fukui, K. Kubota and K. Watanabe, "Voltage-Mode to Current-Mode Conversion by an Extended Dual Transformation," *IEEE Proceedings International Symposium on Circuits and Systems*, Singapore, 11-14 June 1991, pp. 1833-1836.

[8] Analog Devices, 60 MHz 2000 V/μs Monolithic Op Amp AD844 Data sheet, Revision E, 2003. http://www.analog.com/static/imported-files/data_sheets/AD844.pdf

[9] A. Fabre, "Insensitive Voltage-Mode and Current-Mode Filters from Commercially Available Transimpedance Opamps," *Circuits, Devices and Systems, IEE Proceedings G*, Vol. 140, No. 5, 1993, pp. 319-321.

[10] B. Nauta, "Analog CMOS Filters for Very High Frequencies," Kluwer Academic Publishers, Norwell, 1993.

[11] I. A. Khan and M. T. Ahmed, "OTA-Based Integrable Voltage/Current-Controlled Ideal C-Multiplier," *Electronics Letters*, Vol. 22, No. 7, 1986, pp. 365-366.

[12] K. Vavelidis and Y. Tsividis, "Design Considerations for a Highly Linear Electronically Tunable Resistor," *ISCA* '93, 1993 *IEEE International Symposium on Circuits and Systems*, Vol. 2, Chicago, 3-6 May 1993, pp. 1180-1183.

[13] A. Worapishet and P. Khumsat, "Sub-Threshold R-MOSFET Tunable Resistor Technique," *Electronics Letters*, Vol. 43, No. 7, 2007, pp. 390-392.

[14] J. A. Svoboda, L. McGory and S. Webb, "Applications of a Commercially Available Current Conveyor," *International Journal of Electronics*, Vol. 70, No. 1, 1991, pp 159-164

3

Phase and Quadrature Pulsed Bias LC-CMOS VCO

Stefano Perticaroli[1], Fabrizio Palma[1], Adriano Carbone[2]
[1]*Department of Information Engineering, Electronics and Telecommunications, Sapienza Università di Roma, Rome, Italy*
[2]*Rhea System S. A., Louvain-La-Neuve, Belgium*

Abstract

Pulsed bias is an attempt to improve the performance of oscillators in integrated circuits as a result of architectural innovation. Given the relatively low value of resonator quality factor achievable on-chip, for a specified bias voltage level, pulsed bias may result in a lower power consumption and in an improvement of the spectral purity of the oscillation. The main drawback of this approach is the need to introduce a certain time delay in order to properly position pulses with respect to oscillation waveform. Delay accumulation requires further energy dissipation and introduce additional jitter. In this paper we present a new architecture capable to avoid unnecessary delay, based on the idea to apply the pulsed bias approach to a quadrature oscillator. A first circuit-level implementation of this concept is presented with simulation results.

Keywords: Phase And Quadrature VCO, Pulsed Bias Oscillator, Floquet Eigenvectors Noise Decomposition

1. Introduction

All the recent theories of phase noise point out the intrinsic time-varying nature of its generation[1-4]. Ocillators in fact are nonlinear systems with a periodically time-variant steady state. For this reason, internal noise sources, whose variances depend on the operating point, must be described as cyclostationary processes. Furthemore, periodicity implies that also the conversion process of noise sources into phase and orbital deviation is described by a linear periodically time-variant (LPTV) system. Floquet eigenvectors decomposition is widely acknowledged as a correct approach for the analytical treatment of noise sources in such LPTV systems [3].

Following the Floquet decomposition it can be stated that determination of power density spectrum (PDS) of oscillator depends on mean values of noise sources variances multiplied by the square of noise sources projections onto the system's Floquet eigenvectors. In particular, projections onto the "first eigenvector", *i. e.* the vector tangent to the space state orbit, are indicated as the main contributors to the PDS close to the fundamental [5].

In order to obtain a higher spectral purity, the mentioned mean values should be minimized. This result may be achieved if noise sources are allowed to enter the system only when their projections onto eigenvectors are possibly around a minimum. Since noise in integrated circuits is due mainly to active devices, we may search for architectures that switch on bias currents, and thus add noise, only in certain time intervals during the oscillation period. These time intervals should be chosen to obtain a minimum of the projection onto eigenvectors. We notice that, in a single VCO this implies the need for a circuitry which produces a delay between a threshold crossing and the switching of devices: Additional noise is then introduced as jitter in accumulation of delay time. Uncertainty related to this jitter affects the time instant when the large current needed to sustain oscillations is provided. For this reason, jitter can be not negligible and may overwhelm any improvement obtained through pulsed biasing.

In this paper we present a new architecture based on the idea to apply the pulsed bias approach to a quadrature oscillator including two resonators. In particular we propose to adopt a threshold at zero differential voltage of one resonator and apply the consequent pulse, with no delay, at the second one, taking advantage of the natural phase relationship between the zero and the maximum in quadrature signals.

Quadrature VCOs are fundamental components in many RF transceiver systems. Especially when low-IF or direct conversion architecture is required, the generation of two periodic signal in quadrature of phase is a critical issue. One of the main problems with quadrature oscillators, obtained closing in a loop two identical resonators, is the frequency shift between the actual oscillating frequency f_{osc} and their nominal resonance frequency f_0. In fact, at resonance frequency resonators do not introduce large phase shifts and energy refill process may produce sensible changes in the nominal period of oscillation. A pulsed current architecture, with pulses placed close to the maximum of the oscillation voltage, may result in the reduction of this phenomenon. Benefits of this architecture can be compared with results of other techniques recently proposed for the shaping/filtering of bias currents in single VCO [6,7] or with several quadrature oscillators architectures [8], however we remark our approach is based directly on system's Floquet eigenvectors.

In this paper we propose a first implementation of a pulsed bias phase and quadrature LC-CMOS oscillator, with the aim to pursue an architectural improvement in oscillator phase noise.

The architecture will be also evaluated with respect to other important aspects in actual implementations of phase-quadrature oscillators as common mode oscillation amplitude, third harmonic distortion and quadrature error.

2. Implementation of the Proposed Oscillator

The implementation of the idea illustrated in introduction may vary. One of the simplest implementation has been object of a patent [9] and will be reported here.

Two LC lossy tanks resonators are the core of the phase and quadrature (hereafter *I&Q*) oscillator. Outputs are taken as differential voltage mode of tanks terminals. Every tank is connected between V_{dd} bias and ground through logic gates implementing a function that we call *pulse shaper*. The circuit is reported in **Figure 1**. The *pulse shaper* function is obtained by mean of a stack of three transistor of the same type, *i. e.* NMOS or PMOS. We define the stack to have one output as the drain node connected to the tank and three inputs as the nodes of the transistors gates that build the stack.

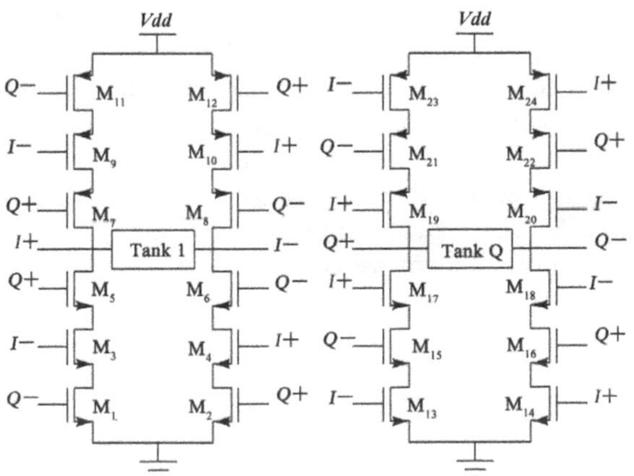

Figure 1. Schematic of the proposed *I&Q* pulsed bias LC-CMOS oscillator.

Every oscillator has four stacks and every tank terminal has a pair of stack connected, a NMOS and a PMOS.

To explain the operation mode of the stack, we consider, as an example, NMOS transistors M_{14}, M_{16} and M_{18} .

Let us assume that a periodic steady state condition in quadrature of phase is reached. Hence, for reasonable quality factor of the resonators, the voltage signals at nodes $I+$, $I-$ and $Q+$, $Q-$ are nearly sinusoidal. These signals are sketched in **Figure 2(a)**.

As shown in **Figure 2(b)**, the stack implements an AND-like boolean function f_{ps} among the three inputs $\underline{X}(t) = I+, I-, Q+$ as described by

$$f_{ps}\left(\underline{X}(t), V_{thn}\right) = \prod_{X=I+,I-,Q+} \frac{1+\operatorname{sgn}\left(X(t)-V_{thn}\right)}{2} \quad (1)$$

in which we define value "1" as the high/on state. In fact, NMOS are assumed to have channel formed once voltages of their gates nodes are greater than the threshold voltage V_{thn}. In this condition, the stack provides a path to ground only during "small" time intervals. These time intervals occur once per period and are located around the zero-crossing of the differential voltage across tank *I* when, at the same time, the signal $Q+$ is high. With these input signals, the *pulse shaper*, designed as a series of three MOS devices, provides a current to the node $Q-$ that

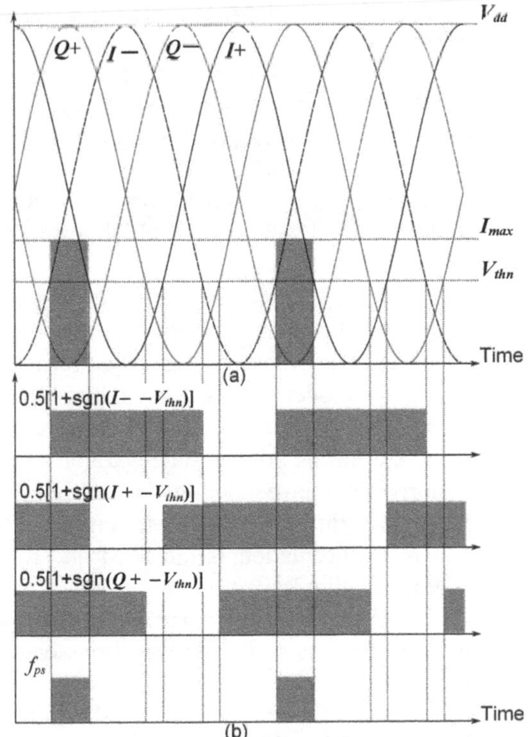

Figure 2. Sketch of single ended voltages at tanks terminals and of current pulses (a), logic states implementing the *pulse shaper* function (b).

is a train of pulses at frequency f_{osc} located exactly around the minimum of the $Q-$ voltage.

The amplitude of pulses depends on the width of MOS devices and on tanks impedance at resonance. In the following discussion we approximate pulses using a rectangular shape. The approximation is valid if pulse duration is reasonably small compared to the oscillation period, so that voltage $Q-$ does not vary considerably around its minimum.

Analogous description may be developed for a PMOS stack. It has to be noticed that as long as $V_{thn} < V_{cm}$ and $(V_{dd} - V_{thp}) > V_{cm}$ (where V_{cm} is the half-sum of tank terminals voltages), a NMOS stack is "active" during the same time intervals when the PMOS stack connected to the other terminal of the same tank is also active, giving rise to pulses of current I_{pI} and I_{pQ} respectively. In conclusion, the stack formed by M_{14}, M_{16} and M_{18} and the stack formed by M_{19}, M_{21} and M_{23} create a path from V_{dd} to ground through the tank Q once time per period. This path alternates with the one formed by M_{13}, M_{15} and M_{17} and by M_{20}, M_{22} and M_{24}.

As overall result, the proposed circuit topology shown in **Figure 1** is able to generate trains of current pulses injected in each tank synchronously with their peak of differential voltages, thus accomplishing a positive feedback capable to sustain oscillations despite losses in the tanks.

3. Phase Noise Evaluation Based on Floquet Eigenvectors

In order to obtain an interpretation of the architecture response to noise perturbation we present here a description of the orbital deviation based on the Floquet eigenvectors. Eigenvectors are obtained from the simplified circuital model reported in **Figure 3** which accounts for the differential modes only.

The model presents four state variables, corresponding to the capacitors voltages and the inductors currents of two tanks. This assumption can be seen as a rather drastic simplification for a model of a real oscillator, nevertheless, if the stacks do not introduce parasitics comparable to those in tanks, the additional state variables can be neglected. Moreover, the assumption is justified by the fact that once a large differential oscillation is established, any common mode oscillation is inhibited and remains within negligible amplitudes.

In our treatment we derive the noise response by direct considering contributions of noise projections onto Floquet eigenvectors [5].

We recall that the "first eigenvector", $\underline{u}_1(t)$, is tangent to the space state orbit and has unitary eigenvalue. In a stable configuration other eigenvectors have corresponding eigenvalues lower than 1.

The main contribution to the overall power density spectrum at frequencies close to the fundamental is due to noise projections on first eigenvector. On the contrary contributions arising from other eigenvectors become relevant only at high frequency offsets $\omega > \gamma_{J=2,3,4}$ (where $\gamma_{J=2,3,4}$ are the poles pulsations related to Floquet multipliers of eigenvectors) due to their low-pass shape with respect to the fundamental.

We assume noise perturbations to be independent realizations of white process with zero time average. Since we are dealing with a parallel RLC tanks, noise is introduced as parallel current sources. Such noisy currents cause a variation of the capacitors voltages, hence we have two normalized noise perturbations through a constant matrix B_w (4x2)

$$B_w = \begin{bmatrix} 0 & 0 & 1 & 0 \\ 1 & 0 & 0 & 0 \end{bmatrix}^T . \qquad (2)$$

The matrix maps perturbations at nodes $[V_I \;\; V_Q]^T$ on the vector of state variables defined as $\underline{S}(t) = [V_{C\_I} \;\; I_{L\_I} \;\; V_{C\_Q} \; I_{L\_Q}]^T$.

A dedicated MATLAB simulator has been developed to compute Floquet eigenvalues and eigenvectors as well as the projections of the components of matrix B_w onto the eigenvectors. Simulator implements a shooting algorithm on the differential equations of the nonlinear model reported in **Figure 3**. Shooting is reached by the use of Interface matrices correction [10] in the calculation of the Monodromy matrix in every iterative step. Interface matrices are essential to reach the convergence, since they allow to properly take into account state variables variations on non-derivable points. Computed eigenvalues are reported in **Table 1** in the case we set resonators parameters ($Q_I = Q_Q = 18$, $L_I = L_Q = 912$ pH, $C_I = C_Q = 1.05$ pF) to be comparable with simulation of implementation with real device models presented in section 4. The working frequency predicted by shooting is $f_{osc} = 5.1275$ GHz.

We want to remark that two very close eigenvalues are found, *i. e.* λ_2 and λ_3. This result suggests to perform the circuital simulation with great care on such system in order to avoid convergence difficulties.

In **Figure 4(a)** the shooting waveforms voltages are reported whereas **Figure 4(b)** shows the projections of matrix $\underline{B}_w$ components onto eigenvector $\underline{u}_1(t)$. For the sake of our treatment we choose to not express physical

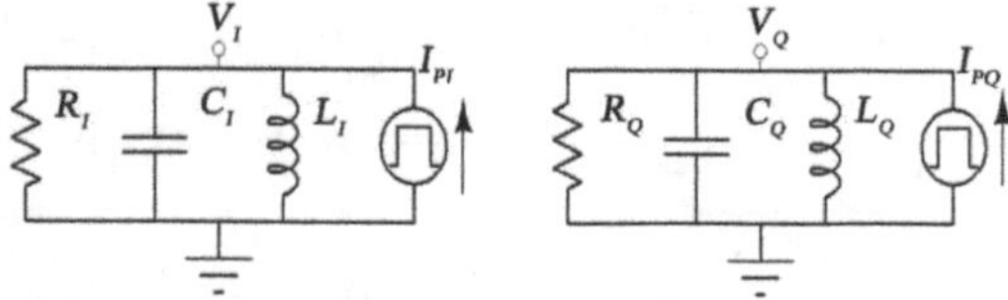

Figure 3. Simplified differential mode model of the *I&Q* pulsed bias oscillator.

Table 1. Floquet eigenvalues of *I&Q* oscillator.

λ_1	λ_2	λ_3	λ_4
1.0039	0.8422	0.8396	0.6991

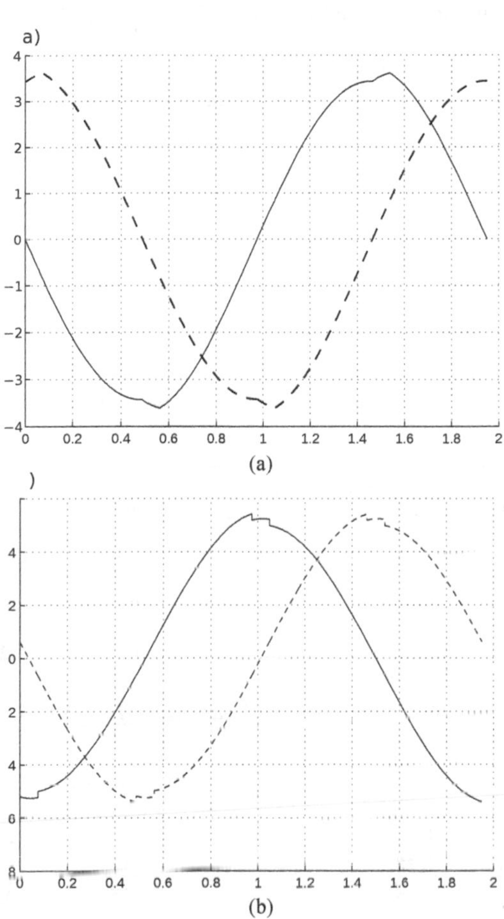

Figure 4. (a) Shooting voltage waveforms of V_I (continue trace) and V_Q (dashed trace) and (b) simulated projections of $[1\ 0\ 0\ 0]^T$ (continue trace) and $[0\ 0\ 1\ 0]^T$ (dashed trace) noise vectors onto first Floquet eigenvector.

dimensions of projections since they could appear meaningless. Eigenvectors, in fact, give a representation in a transformed space, then projections on eigenvectors need to be reconverted into the original space before they can be expressed as voltages or currents.

We notice that the projections are around the zero crossing in correspondence of the current pulse on their relative voltage waveforms ($[1\ 0\ 0\ 0]^T$ for V_I and $[0\ 0\ 1\ 0]^T$ for V_Q), ensuring minimization of the noise distribution close to the fundamental. Additional relevant behaviour can be found in the limited increase of the maximum value of the projection. This maximum could greatly increase in case the other eigenvectors become non orthogonal to the first eigenvector, and enhance the effect of a noise present all along the orbit, e.g. the noise due to parasitic resistance of the tanks.

In conclusion, the model indicates that the architecture appears to be suitable in reduction of both the effect of noise due to bias current and to parasitic resistance. In addition, since the architecture does not require change to position of the pulse, a delay is not required. This further reduces the unavoidable jitter noise introduced by stacks of transistors.

4. Simulation Results

Very accurate circuit simulations, including all the second order effects that were previously discarded, have been performed using the SpectreRF simulator within CADENCE IC5.1.41 environment. Devices models are taken from ST 0.13µm technology library.

In the following, results obtained for two different configurations at *layout versus schematic* (LVS) level are reported. Both configurations reflect schematics in **Figure 1** but the first configuration consists of fixed tanks whereas varactors are introduced in the second one to build a VCO. We choose to set the working frequency in the 4-5 GHz range.

We define as W_{int} the width of the stack transistor which is connected to the tank, whereas W_{mid} is related to the median transistor and finally W_{ext} is related to the transistor connected to the voltage supply. Transistors widths of both NMOS and PMOS stacks are chosen as follows: $W_{int} = 85$ µm, $W_{mid} = 0.5\ W_{int}$ and $W_{ext} = 0.3\ W_{int}$ with a total number of 8 fingers.

In the first configuration the tank is constituted by an octagonal spiral inductor *ind_sym_la* of 912 pH bundled in the RF ST design kit and a capacitor of 1pF to form a parallel resonator. Inductor has 500 µm external diameter and exhibits a quality factor Q peak of approximately 18 around 4.5 GHz. A differential amplitude of oscillation of 3.08 V at f_{osc} = 4.77 GHz has been obtained from a biasing of 1.8 V. The total power consumption is about P_{diss}= 6.5 mW. Noise level at 3 MHz offset from the fundamental is $L\{3\ MHz\} = -147$ dB_C. In order to compare these results with literature ones, relative to oscillators working at different frequencies, with different biasing voltages and tank quality factors, the following Figure of Merit (*FoM*) is used:

$$FoM = -L\{\Delta f\} + 20\log_{10}\left(\frac{f_{osc}}{\Delta f}\right) + 10\log_{10}\left(\frac{1\,\text{mW}}{P_{diss}}\right) \quad (3)$$

The resulting FoM for this configuration is equal to 202. Other results of interest are summarized in **Table 2**.

As stated in introduction, the proposed approach can be compared with other bias current shaping techniques also if, at the knowledge of the authors, they have been used in single oscillators rather than in *I&Q* ones. Both techniques found in [6,7] are based on the suppression of

Table 2. Main characteristics of proposed oscillator.

Frequency	4.77 GHz
Differential mode amplitude	3.08 V
Phase Noise @ 3 MHz offset	−147 dBc
Power consumption @ 1.8 V supply	6.53 mW
FoM as in (3)	202
Quadrature phase error	0.03°
Common mode amplitude @ $2f_{osc}$	37 mV
HD_3	−40.4 dB

devices noise injected at $2f_{osc}$. Since architectures of [6,7] require a tail current source, noise around second harmonic is down-converted to the fundamental, thus increasing phase noise. In [6] an *LC* filter is considered whereas in [7] a phase displacement of pulsed current at $2f_{osc}$ is used to reduce the down-conversion phenomenon. In the proposed architecture instead there is no need of a tail current source and pulsed biasing currents flow at fundamental frequency. Results of comparison are reported in **Table 3**.

For the second configuration a parallel branch is added to the tanks. The branch is constituted of two varactors in series and the control voltage V_{CTRL} is the common node in the series. The total area occupied by varactors is 20 m^2.

In **Figure 5** transient waveforms are reported from postlayout simulation in case f_{osc} = 4.63 GHz for V_{ctrl} = 1.5 V. Periodic steady state occurs in about *10ns* without any startup circuitry. A 600 mV difference in amplitude between the two differential voltage modes *I* and *Q* is observed, however quadrature of signals is maintained. A close-up of pulsed currents bias is also reported. It has to be noticed that these current waveforms result both from displacement of parasitics as well as form conduction in devices, since a single component cannot be isolated. Moreover, when the peak of a pulse is expected, devices of stack are pushed into triode region by the tank terminal voltage, giving rise to deformation of the pulse itself.

The obtained tuning range with the above mentioned varactors dimensions is about 300 MHz around 4.55 GHz, *i. e.* 7% relative tenability, and allows the comparison of the proposed architecture with recent literature works as shown in **Table 4** Comparison is based on largely adopted *PTFN* defined as

$$PTFN = -L\{\Delta f\} + 20\log_{10}\left(\frac{f_{max} - f_{min}}{\Delta f}\right) + 10\log_{10}\left(\frac{K_B T}{P_{diss}}\right) \quad (4)$$

Table 3. Comparison with phase noise reduction techniques.

Ref.	$L\{\Delta f\}$@3 MHz [dBc]	Frequency [GHz]	Power consumption [mW]	FOM
[6]	−153	1.2	9.25	195
[7]	−135	1.77	2.25	186
This work	−147	4.77	6.53	202

Table 4. Comparison with literature *I&Q* VCO.

Ref.	Technology [μm]	Tuning range [GHz]	Power consumption [mW]	PTFN
[11]	0.25	1.73−1.99	20	−2.44
[12]	0.18	5.4−6.6	18	−1.84
[13]	0.25	4.07−4.72	15	−3.17
This work	0.13	4.3−4.64	14	−4.36

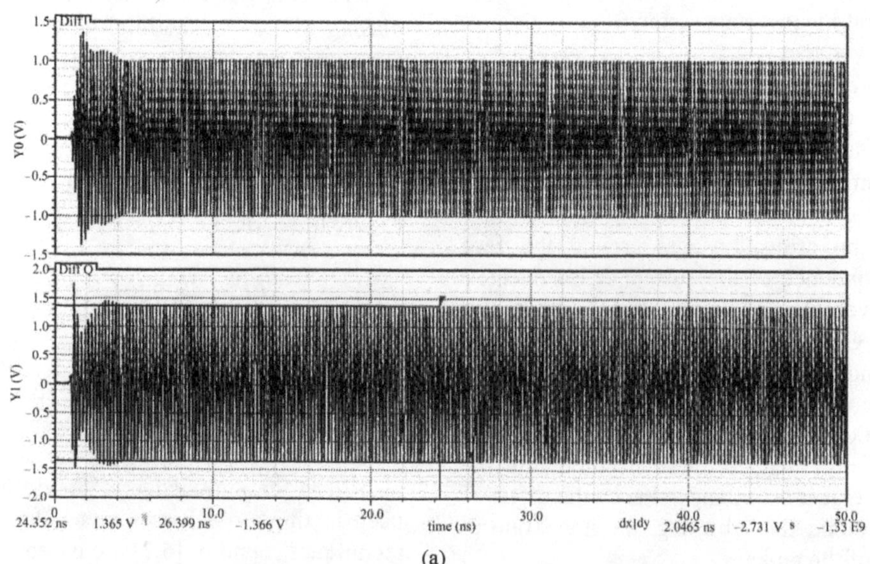

(a)

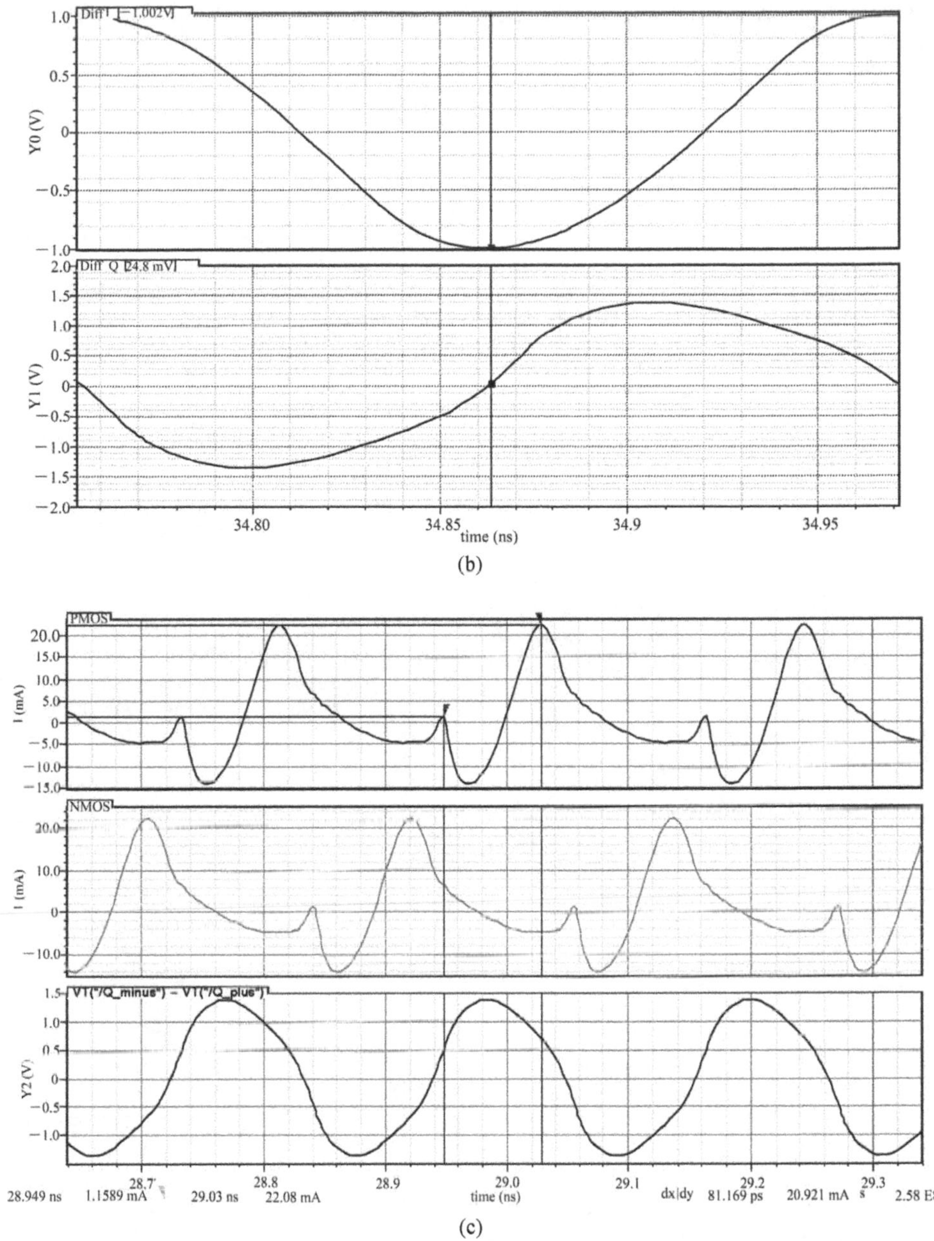

(c)

Figure 5. (a) Transient of tanks differential voltages at startup, (b) signals in quadrature of phase at PSS and (c) close-up of pulsed currents bias of two PMOS and NMOS stacks with respect to differential voltage of tank *Q*.

where $f_{max} - f_{min}$ is VCO tuning range, f is offset from fundamental, K_B is the Boltzmann constant and T is the absolute temperature.

5. Concluding Remarks

In this paper the pulsed bias phase and quadrature oscillator has been introduced as an architectural solution for phase noise reduction. The discussion of noise response of the proposed architecture has been based on the evaluation of noise projections onto the first Floquet eigenvector of the system. Simulations of the pulsed bias I&Q oscillator and VCO implemented in ST 0.13 µm technology appear to validate noise analysis. Result of this work in comparison with other phase noise reduction techniques as well as with recent measurements of prototypes is promising and encourages a real implementation of the described *I&Q* pulsed bias architecture.

6. References

[1] F. X. Kaertner, "Analysis of White and f^{α} Noise in Oscillators," *Inernational Journal of Circuit Theory and Applications*, Vol. 18, No. 5, 1990, pp. 485-519.

[2] A. Hajimiri and T. H. Lee, "A General Theory of Phase Noise in Electrical Oscillators," *IEEE Journal Solid-State Circuits*, Vol. 33, No. 2, 1998, pp. 179-194.

[3] A. Demir, "Floquet Theory and Non-linear Perturbation Analysis Foroscillators with Differential-Algebraic Equations," *International Journal of Circuit and Theory Applications*, Vol. 28, No. 2, 2000, pp. 163-185.

[4] A. Carbone, A. Brambilla and F. Palma, "Using Floquet Eigenvectors in the Design of Electronic Oscillators," *Emerging Technologies: Circuits and Systems for* 4 G *Mobile Wireless Communications*, No. 6, 23-24 June 2005, pp. 100-103.

[5] A. Carbone and F. Palma, "Considering Orbital Deviations on the Evaluation of Power Density Spectrum of Oscill-Ators," *IEEE Transactions on Circuits and Systems-II: Express Briefs*, Vol. 53, No. 6, 2006, pp. 438-442.

[6] E. Hegazi, H. Sjoland and A. Abidi, "A Filtering Technique to Lower LC Oscillator Phase Noise," *IEEE Journal of Solid State Circuits*, Vol. 36, No. 12, 2001, pp. 1921-1930.

[7] B. Soltanian and P. Kinget, "Tail Current Shaping to Improve Phase Noise in LC Voltage Controlled Oscillators," *IEEE Journal of Solid State Circuits*, Vol. 41, No. 8, 2006, pp. 1792-1802.

[8] L. B. Oliveira *et al.*, "Analysis and Design of Quadrature Oscillators," Springer, Berlin, 2008.

[9] United States Patent No. US 2008/0218280 A1.

[10] A. Carbone and F. Palma, "Discontinuity Correction in Piece-Wise-Linear Models of Oscillators for Phase Noise Characterization," *International Journal of Circuit Theory and Applications*, Vol. 35, No. 1, 2007, pp. 93-104.

[11] M. Tiebout, "A Differentially Tuned Quadrature CMOS," *Proceedings of the 26th European Solid-State Circuits Conference*, Montreux, 18-22 September 2006.

[12] J. H. Chang, *et al.*, "A New 6 GHz Fully Integrated Low Power Low Phase Noise LC Quadrature VCO," *Proceedings of* 2003 *Radio Frequency Integrated Circuits Symposium Philadelphia*, Philadelphia, 8-10 June 2003, pp. 295-298.

[13] F. Yang *et al.*, "A 4.8 GHz CMOS LC Balanced Oscillator with Symmetry Noise Filtering Technique," *International Conference on Solid-State Integrated Circuits Technology*, Vol. 2, No. 7, 2004, pp. 1315-1320.

Remotely Controlled Automated Horse Jump

Ibrahim Al-Bahadly, Joel White
School of Engineering and Advanced Technology Massey University, Palmerston North, New Zealand

Abstract

With the application of automation, a horse jump can be controlled with the push of a button, or even a remote control. This enables the rider to adjust the jump to suit their needs while still on their horse. The objective of this work is to design and build a wireless remote motor controller which will be applied to a prototype horse jump. The user will be able to control the forward and reverse direction of the motor by pushing a button or switch via RF remote control. A horse jump prototype consisting of a single jump stand will be constructed.

Keywords: Automation, Horse Jump, Dc Motor, RF Remote Control

1. Introduction

Horse jumping is one of the most exciting of all equine sports and one of the few to enjoy the prestige of being an Olympic event. For many riders, the tedious routine of setting up jumps and constantly adjusting their height seems like an un-avoidable task. With the application of automation, a horse jump can be controlled with the push of a button, or even a remote control. This enables the rider to adjust the jump to suit their needs while still on their horse.

The objective of this work is to design and build a wireless remote motor controller which will be applied to a prototype horse jump. The user will be able to control the forward and reverse direction of the motor by pushing a button or switch via RF remote control.

Potential benefits are:

- Inexpensive
- Simple and efficient to use
- Easy control
- More effective horse training

The block diagram in **Figure 1** represents the approach used to implement the automation.

1.1. Power supply

The power supply is two 12 V lead acid batteries in series. It supplies the power to the converter circuit and the DC Motor.

1.2. User Inputs

The input is two buttons that will allow a user to execute the following operations: Up and down control of the motor. The input signal is sent to the controller through the wireless RF interface.

1.3. Wireless Interface

The interface receives an RF signal from the user input and sends it to the controller. The RF module sends the encoded signal from a transmitter to a receiver. The received signal is decoded to the appropriate logic signal which is then fed into the control circuit.

1.4. Controller

The controller will receive a direction command from the user inputs. The appropriate output signal is fed into the H-Bridge circuit in order to allow the motor drive in the desired direction.

1.5. H-Bridge

The H-Bridge circuit enables the motor to travel in both directions. The H-Bridge circuit receives signals from the control circuit for the user defined action.

1.6. Motor

A 24 V permanent magnet dc motor is used. It operates at a continuous load at about 100 W.

2. Background

2.1. H-Bridge Drive

The H-bridge drive circuit is shown in **Figure 2**.

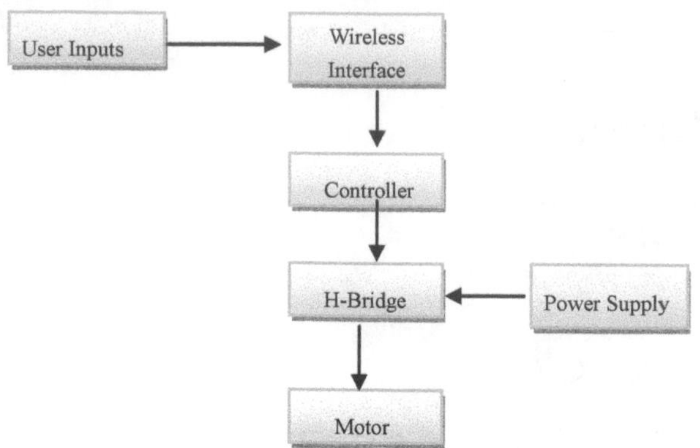

Figure 1. Block diagram for the overall proposed automated system.

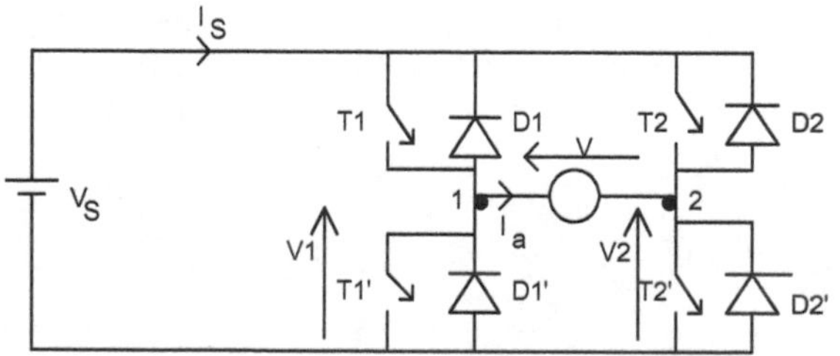

Figure 2. H-bridge circuit.

The H-Bridge arrangement [1] is used to reverse the polarity of the motor, but can also be used to "brake" the motor, or to let the motor "free run" to a stop, as the motor is effectively disconnected from the circuit. **Table 1** summarises the operation.

2.2. Logic Gates

A logic gate performs a logical operation on one or more logic inputs and produces a single logic output. This is the simplest yet effective way of processing logical operations. Initially the use of an 8051 microcontroller [2] was prospected but it was deemed over excessive as the same result could be attained through Boolean algebra [3]. From simplified Boolean algebra a circuit can be developed using inverters AND gates OR gates etc. As it is cheaper and simpler to produce the same logic gates using combinations of one type of gate, a circuit consisting of the above gates is converted into a NAND gate equivalent circuit. **Figure 3** shows the NAND equivalent of logical operations.

Table 1. The operations of the dc motor.

T1	T2	T1'	T2'	Result
1	0	0	1	Motor moves right
0	1	1	0	Motor moves left
0	0	0	0	Motor free runs
0	1	0	1	Motor brakes
1	0	1	0	Motor brakes

2.3. The Horse in Motion

In order to design a good horse jump the mechanics of a horse jumping needed to be considered. When the horse is approaching an obstacle it needs to see, appraise and accept the jump. Therefore the jump needs to be simple and clearly outlined. As it is seen in **Figure 4**, during takeoff and landing the horses forelimbs have potential to strike the top of the jump, therefore a collapsible jump pole is needed that will fall when hit with a horizontal force.

Key jumping factors in horse training are:

- The horse should be able to learn from its mistakes
- The horse should be confident

When the rider has to stop and alter the jump, the horse drops its momentum, with jump height alterations being made while riding, the horses momentum is not lost resulting in much more effective horse training.

2.4. Horse Jump Design

Horse jumps are made up of three main parts: Stands, Cups and Poles [4].

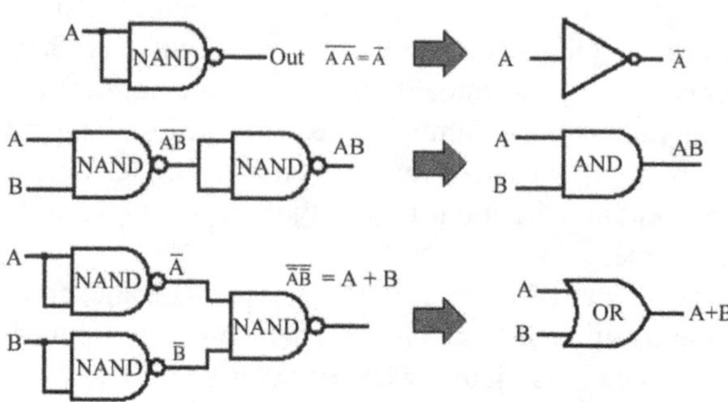

Figure 3. The NAND equivalent logical operations.

Figure 4. The horse in motions.

The stands are available in many different types of materials such as wood, aluminium and plastic. **Figure 5** shows an example of a stand. The main design requirements in a stand are:

- Can be easily transported by hand
- Will not fall over in the weather
- Have no sharp edges
- Can withstand the weight of the poles

The cups main purpose is to mount onto the stands and provide support for the poles. They are mostly made from various metals and plastics. **Figure 6** shows the cups. Their design requirements are:

- Can lock into place at desired height
- Can hold poles stable but will release when knocked
- Will fail at 135 kg of pressure (if a horse was to fall onto the poles)

3. Design and Development

3.1. Standards and Safety

The RF link must be compliant with the Federal Communications Commission (FCC) [5] rules under Section 47, Chapter 1, Part 15, entitled "Radio Frequency Devices". This section lays out the rules and regulations involved with operating a radio controlled device without a license. The device must not cause harmful interference and it must accept any interference that may cause undesired operation. Part 15, 23 specifies that "home-built" devices need only be compliant with FCC regulations to the best of the builder's extent, but does not have to comply otherwise.

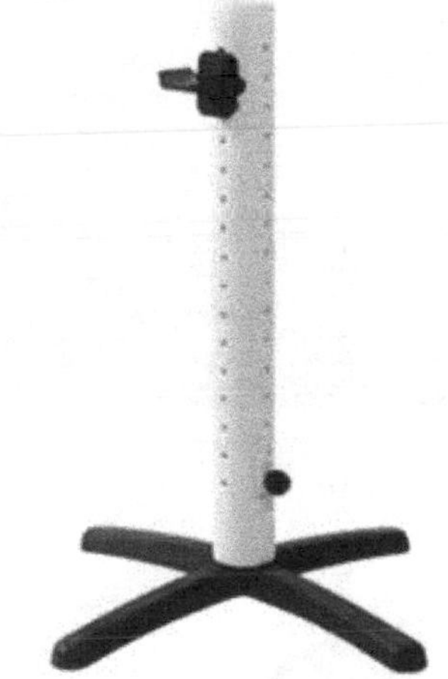

Figure 5. Example of a stand.

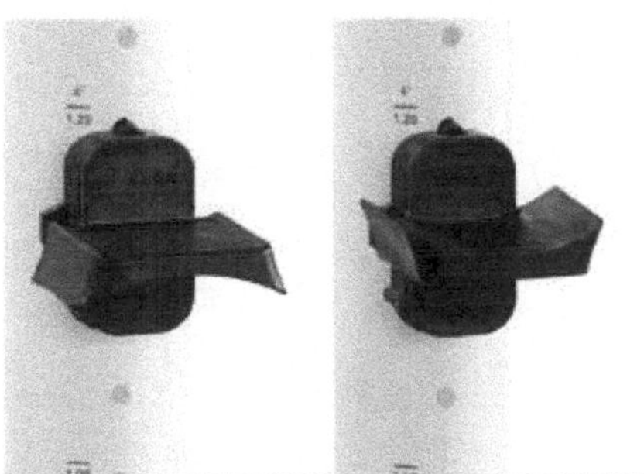

Figure 6. The cups.

The horse jump must ideally have no sharp edges incase the rider or horse shall collide with the stand or any other component. The poles must also collapse when a reasonable pressure is applied to prevent further injury to the horse.

3.2. The Proposed Horse Jump

3.2.1. Design

The key design constraints considered were:

- Height (a variable jump pole from 50 cm to 1 m)
- Lightweight (able to place in yard by one person)
- Durable (can tolerate outdoors, curious horses and shock loads from jump poles being knocked around or undesirable collisions)
- Can withstand the weight of the poles
- Poles are held stable but release when knocked
- Stand will comfortably hold load from pole of 100 N (10 Kg)

Additional design parameters were:

- Simple and affordable due to a low prototype budget
- Locking mechanism to hold jump pole in place
- Ease of manufacture

With these parameters in mind 3 key concepts were developed.

<u>Concept design 1</u>

Figure 7 shows the first design concept.

This design seems very ideal as both sides will remain horizontal. It was decided to disregard this concept due the larger number of mechanical components and potential elasticity in load-bearing components. Also with such a large frame, moving it around will be difficult. Also due to its sturdiness, if the horse or rider were to collide with the sides of the frame, injuries could be caused.

<u>Concept design 2</u>

The second concept design proposed is shown in **Figure 8**. This concept proposed a large belt to rotate around the stand, Poles could then be attached to the rotating belt where desired. The major challenge with this design is that a motor brake needed to be incorporated into the design which results very inefficient operation. Also the large belt seemed hazardous and after consulting experienced horse jumpers, more noticeable moving objects will be likely to spook their horse resulting in ineffective jumping.

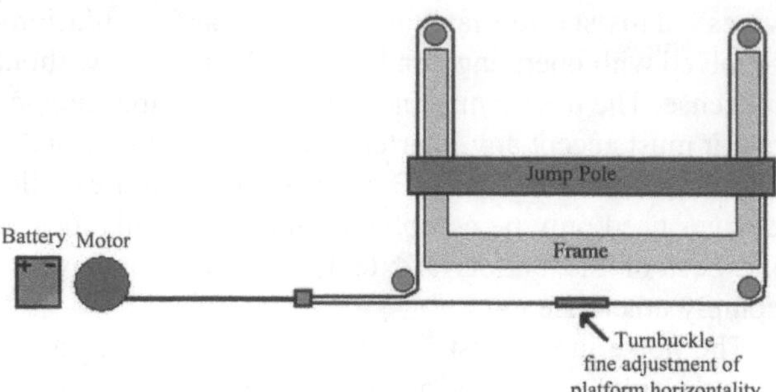

Figure 7. Design concept 1.

Figure 8. Design concept 2.

Concept design 3

Figure 9 shows concept design 3.

The third and final design is ideal. It conforms to all constraints and parameters proposed initially. The major advantage is that the screw style lift prevents the need for a motor brake.

3.2.2. Implementation

The next step of the design process was to simulate major points of fatigue while ensuring the prototype can be easily constructed with readily available materials. To do this a stress test using CosmosWork™ [6] was conducted. Detail in [6] indicates major points of stress are experienced at the nut where the cup is connected to the vertical shaft. An extra block was inserted to improve axial stress on the threaded rod as shown in **Figure 10**.

With the added block, the factor of safety was im-

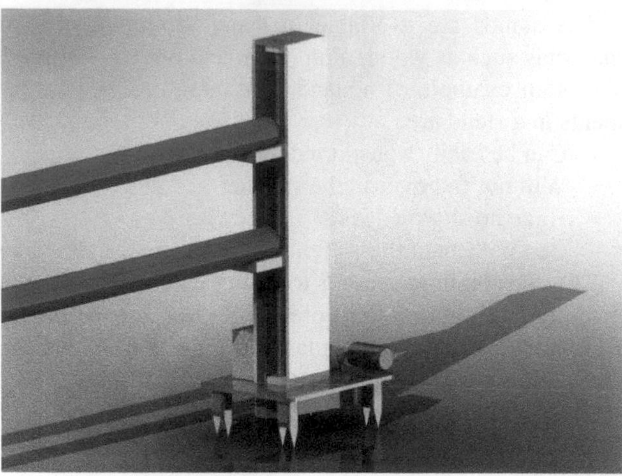

Figure 9. Concept design 3.

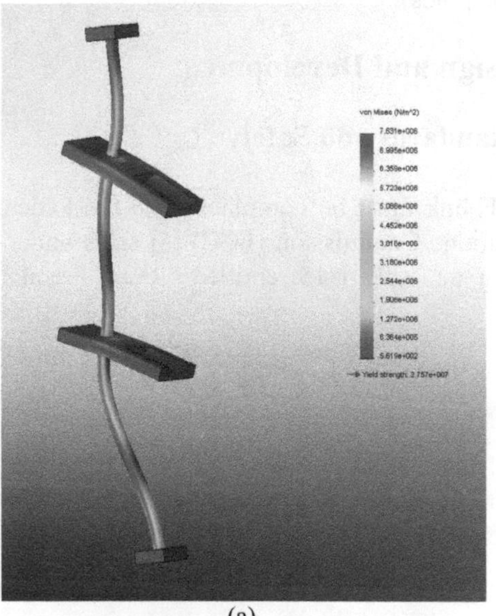

(a)

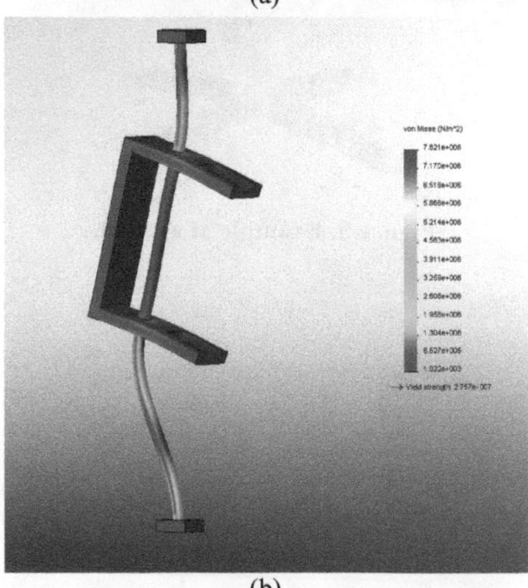

(b)

Figure 10. Stress test results for (a) without extra block and (b) with added block to improve axial stress.

proved from 3.2 to 4.5. Both of these results are acceptable but because the threaded rod used is not purpose built, the threads are susceptible to fraying. Therefore the highest attainable factor of safety was sought after.

With a finalized design, workshop staff proceeded to construct the jump. Small additional changes, such as a one piece aluminum casing, were made to improve ease of manufacture.

3.3. Motor Selection

The desired lifting speed of 1 cm/sec was aimed for. To achieve this, appropriate gearing and motor power needed to be considered [see **Figure 11**].

By using a gear ratio of 1:5, incline angle of 0.1 degrees and RPM of 300. The Torque needed at the motor was 0.2 Nm.

From these results the desired power needed from the motor was calculated as <u>40 W</u>.

A cost effective PMDC gear motor [7] was selected and then tested in the lab for its characteristics.

It produced easily 100 W at 24 VDC drawing 1.6 A at no load. With a simulated load it was noticed that there was almost no change in RPM (due to the gearing) and the motor was drawing 2.6 A. From these results the design constraints for the motor control module were set to be able to satisfy 4 A load at 24 VDC.

3.4. RF Link

3.4.1. Analysis

According to a survey conducted to pony club attendants, the desired control of the horse jump was Up and Down control via portable remote control. Infra Red [8] was not ideal due to the rider would be uncomfortably pointing the remote constantly, Other means such as WiFi [9] and Bluetooth [10] were over excessive therefore RF control was ideal.

Figure 11. Gearing arrangement for the motor.

3.4.2. Design

The RF link consists of three modules; Transmitter, Receiver and Logic Control.

<u>**Transmitter**</u>

The Transmitter design constraints were:

- Transmit at least 2 channels of data
- Powered by replaceable batteries
- Small enough to meet expected aesthetics of a remote control

Figure 12 shows the schematic of the transmitter which was developed in Altium Designer™ [11].

The transmitter module was purchased from JayCar Electronics [12]. When a button is pressed the encoder is activated, producing serial data to be sent to the transmitter module for transmission. A specific 8 bit data address can be set to minimize any interference caused by any surrounding RF devices. This circuit is capable of transmitting another 2 channels of data. These channels can be used for upgrading the horse jump, such as remotely activating a pickup sequence when a pole is knocked off.

<u>**Receiver**</u>

The Receiver design constraints were:

- Receive at least 2 channels of data
- Powered by 5 V Regulated supply
- Produce logical outputs to be processed by the Logic Control module

The schematic for the receiver which was developed in Altium Designer™ is shown in **Figure 13**.

The receiver module was purchased from JayCar Electronics. When a data signal is received that correspond to the Data Address, The decoder then demodulates the signal and produces a Logic output to be processed by the Logic control module.

<u>**Logic Control**</u>

The Logic Control design constraints were:

- Process logic signals from receiver
- Process logic signals from limit switches (two switches at each maximums of travel)
- Powered by 5 V Regulated supply
- Produce Desired outputs for Motor Control module

A NAND gate equivalent schematic was formed in Altium Designer™ as shown in **Figure 14.**

3.4.3. Implementation

The transmitter and receiver were tested running on bench supply. Data was successfully transmitted between modules. **Figure 15** shows a 12 bit serial data being transmitted and received.

The outputs of the receiver were measured using an oscilloscope to ensure data can be processed by the Logic Control module.

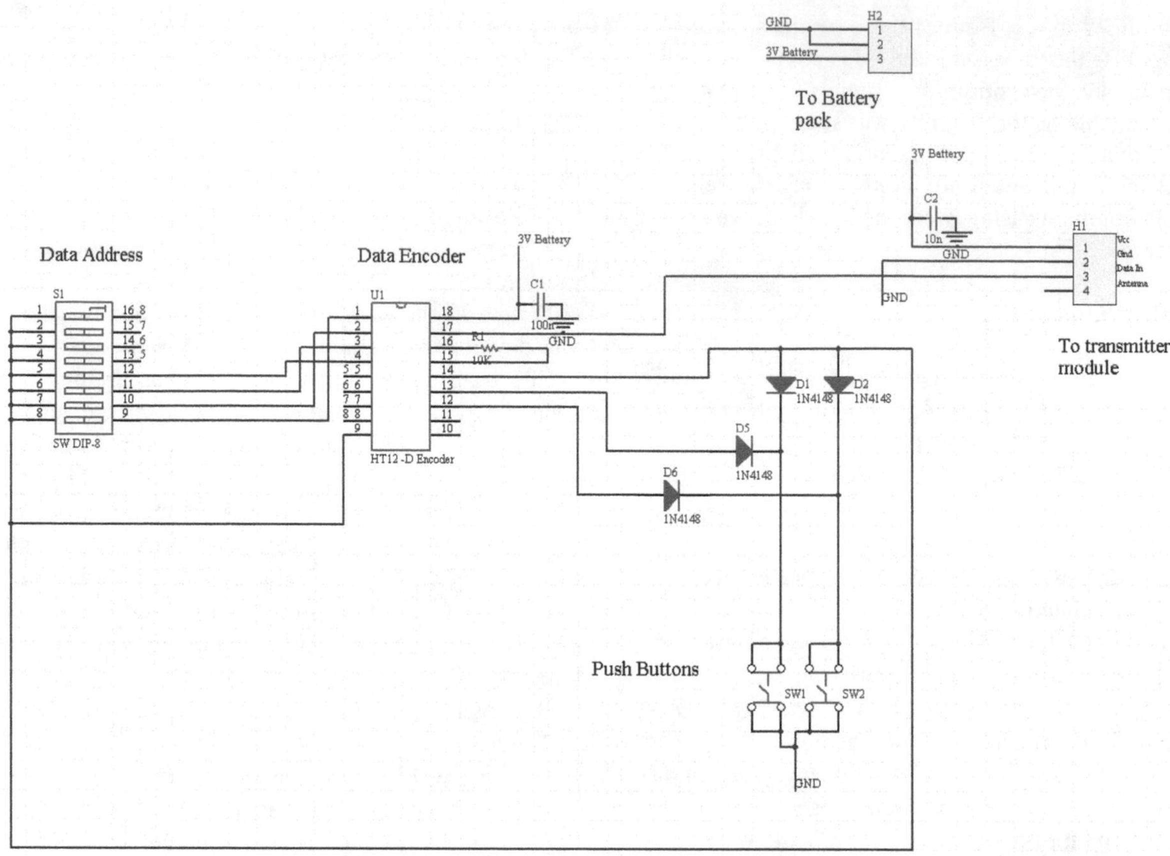

Figure 12. Schematic of the transmitter.

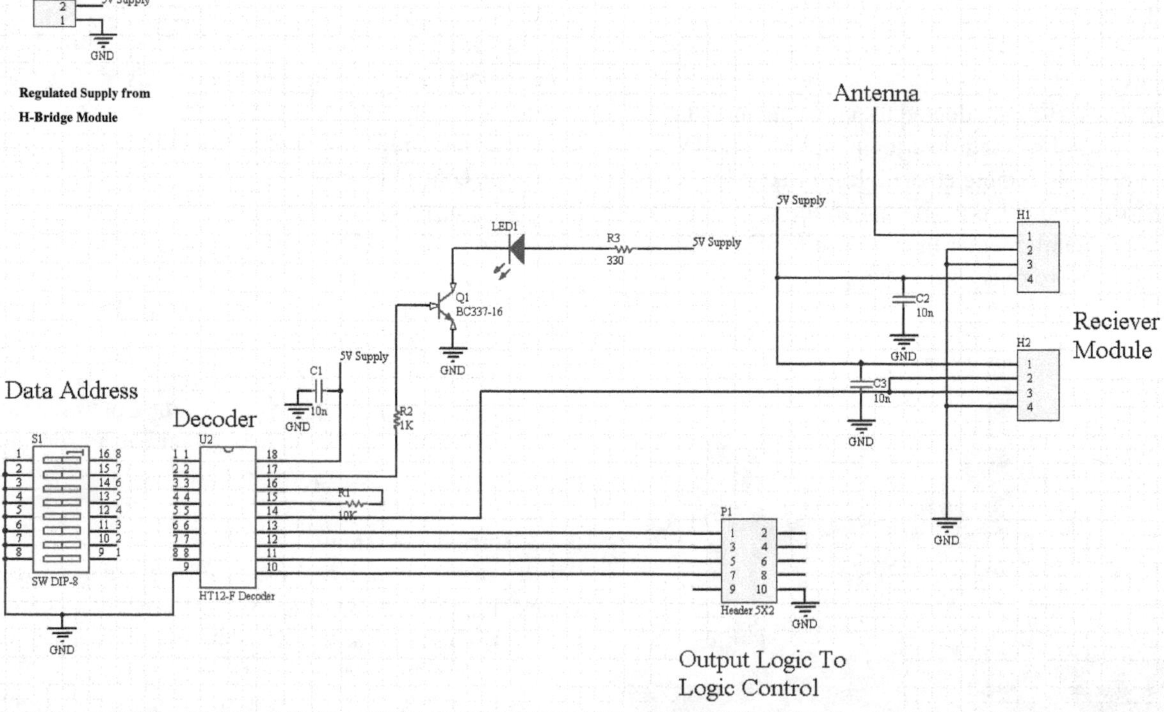

Figure 13. Schematic for the receiver.

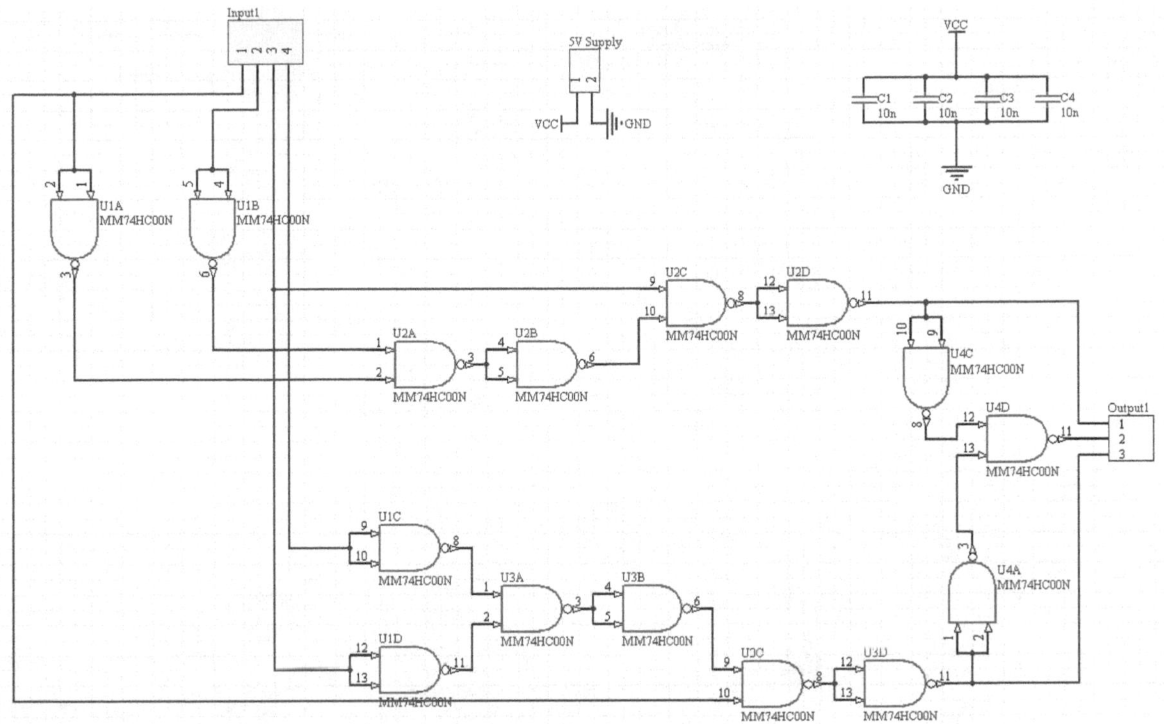

Figure 14. NAND gate equivalent schematic.

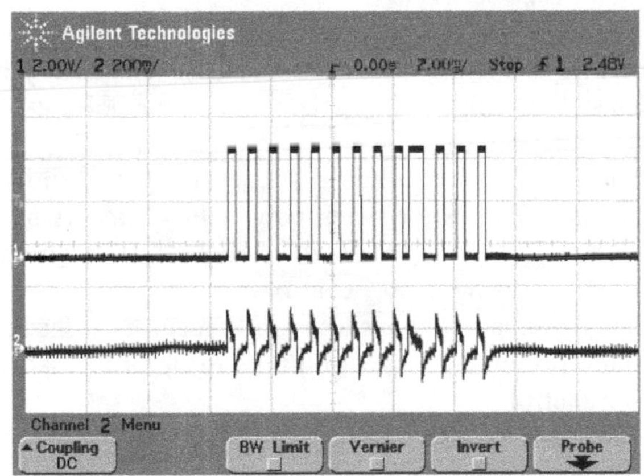

Figure 15. 12 bit serial data transmitted and received.

3.5. DC Motor Control

3.5.1. Analysis

The Motor Control design constraints were:

- Process logic signals from Logic Control
- Produces 5 V Regulated supply to power other modules and itself
- Have forward and reverse motor control
- Produce 24 V at 4 A for motor

3.5.2. Design

The schematic in **Figure 16** was developed in Altium Designer™ and assessed for reliability.

The L298 Dual H-Bridge driver was used in parallel as each H-Bridge was capable of 50 V at 2 A, therefore connected in parallel created potential motor supply of 50 V at 4 A continuously. The 5 V regulator is capable of regulating an input supply voltage of 36 V but has a recommended input voltage of around 9 V, Therefore an input voltage of 24 V is acceptable. Because of the large voltage difference a heat sink needed to be added to the voltage regulator. Also the L298 needed a large heat sink due to the High amperage passing through.

3.5.3. Implementation

The motor Control circuit was then tested in the advanced electronics lab, a 24 V bench supply powered the module while 5 V logic also created from the bench supply was used to survey motor response. The L298 and 5 V regulator didn't show any major signs of overheating. All modules were then tested together before integrating them with the prototype as shown in **Figure 17**.

4. Conclusions

The finalized horse jump prototype was capable of lifting two jump poles at a steady rate of 1 cm/sec over a height range of about 40 cm to 1.2 M. The prototype is only a single jump stand and further development is needed to

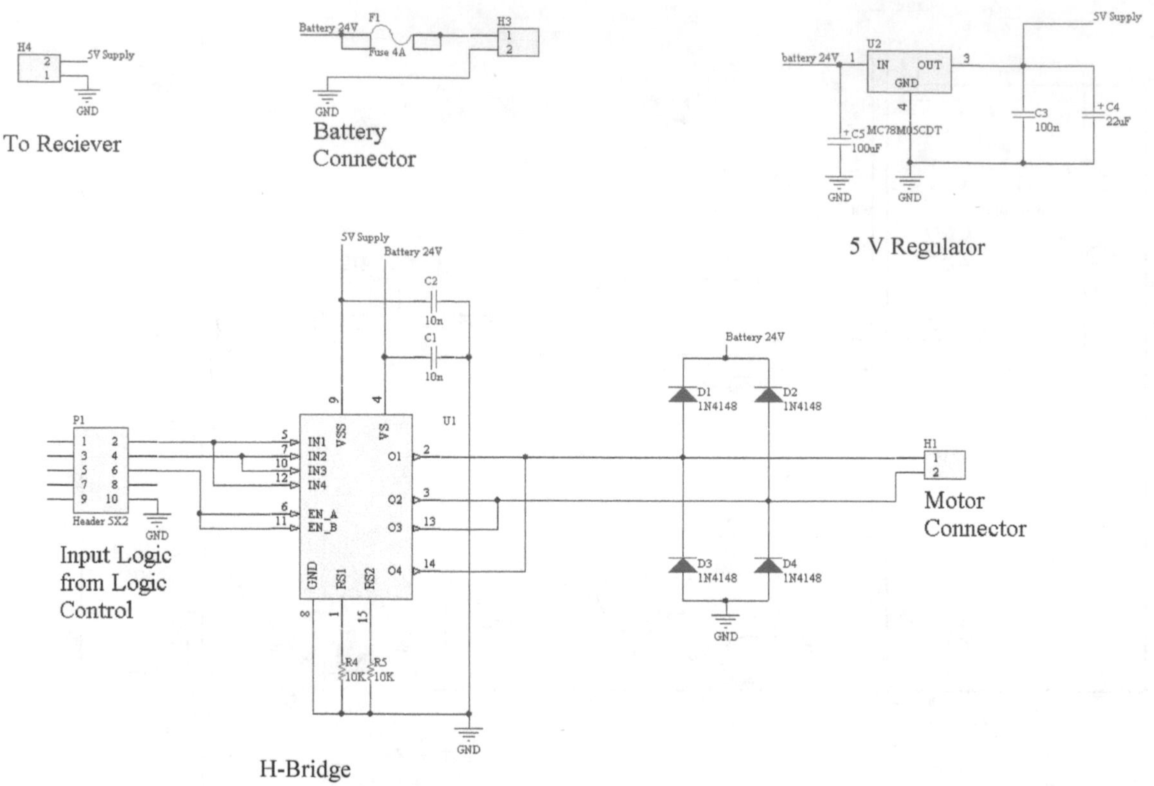

Figure 16. Schematic for the DC motor control circuit.

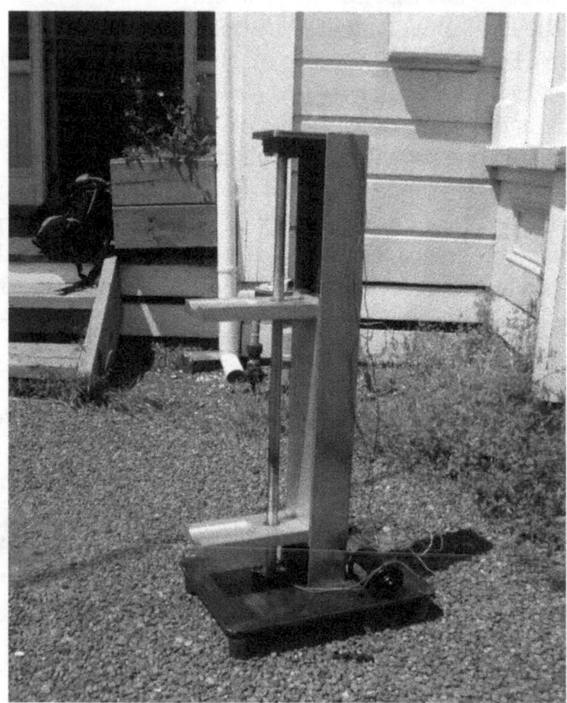

Figure 17. Prototype.

incorporate two jump stands. The prototype is very mechanically sound and is capable of several repetitive height adjustments. The cups can hold standard jump poles stable, with a solid horizontal tap, the poles can be clearly knocked off.

The Transmitter module successfully transmits 2 channels of data while being powered by 2xAAA batteries, the dimensions are small enough to fit in an aesthetically pleasing remote control case.

The Receiver module successfully receives 2 channels of data, producing logical outputs to be processed for motor control.

The H-Bridge circuit successfully controls the direction of the motor when given the correct logical operations. Overheating of the circuit was prevented well.

The motor drives the prototype well, operating within its design specifications. The maximum current of 4 A that the H-Bridge can supply is very unlikely to be reached.

Further development of a pickup sequence needs to be considered for the horse jump to be fully automated. A process where a motor "reels" in the fallen pole can be implemented in the future.

5. References

[1] J. J. Michael, "Power Electronics: Principles and Applications," Delmar Thomson Learning, USA, 2002.

[2] J. W. Stewart and J. J. Mistovich, "The 8051 Microcontroller: Hardware, Software and Interfacing," 2nd Edition, Prentice Hall, New Jersey, 1998.

[3] W. J. Eldon, "Boolean Algebra and Its Applications," Dover Publications, USA, 2010.

[4] M. Summers, "Building Showjumping Courses: A Guide for Beginners," The Pony Club, 2006.

[5] 2010. http://www.fcc.gov/

[6] 2010. http://www.solidworks.com/

[7] R. Krishnan, "Permanent Magnet Synchronous and Brushless Dc Motor Drives," CRC Press, Boca Raton, 2009.

[8] G. K. Shen, "Remote Control Using Inferared with Message Recording," Master's Thesis, Universiti Teknologi Malaysia, 2008.

[9] J. Ross, "The Book of Wi-Fi: Install, Configure and Use 802.11 b Wireless Networking," No Starch Press, USA, 2003.

[10] D. D. M. Bakker and D. M. Gilster, "Bluetooth: End to End," John Wiley & Sons, Inc., New York, 2002.

[11] 2010. http://www.altium.com/products/altium-designer/

[12] 2010. http://www.jaycar.co.nz/

Voltage-Mode Lowpass, Bandpass and Notch Filters Using Three Plus-Type CCIIs

Jiun-Wei Horng, Zhao-Ren Wang, Chih-Cheng Liu
Department of Electronic Engineering, Chung Yuan Christian University, Chung-Li, Taiwan, China

Abstract

A single input and three outputs voltage-mode biquadratic filter using three plus-type second-generation current conveyors (CCII), two grounded capacitors and five resistors is presented. The proposed circuit offers the following features: realization of three filter functions, which are, lowpass, bandpass and notch filters, simultaneously, the use of only grounded capacitors. PSPICE simulation results are also included.

Keywords: Active Filter, Current Conveyor, Voltage-Mode, Biquad

1. Introduction

There is a growing interest in designing active filters using current conveyors. This is attributed to their high signal bandwidths, greater linearity and larger dynamic range [1,2]. The second-generation current conveyor (CCII) proves to be a versatile building block that can be used to implement a variety of high performance circuits, which are simple to construct. The current-feedback amplifier (CFA) exhibits the potentiality of extended operating bandwidth and relatively large value of slew rate compared to the conventional voltage-feedback amplifier. Note that a CFA is equivalent to a plus-type CCII with a voltage follower [3]. On the other hand, the use of only plus-type CCII in filters design has received considerable attention because of its simplicity [4-6].

The circuits consist of more filter functions mean more applications they can be used. Therefore, many cicuits with one input terminal and multiple output terminals were presented [7-11]. In 1994, Soliman [7] presented two CCII-based circuits that equivalent to the Kerwin-Huelsman-Newcomb biquad (KHN biquad) [8]. Both of these circuits use five CCIIs (three plus-type, two minus-type), six (or seven) resistors and two grounded capacitors to realize lowpass, bandpass and highpass transfer functions simultaneously as in the KHN circuit. In 1995, Senani and Singh [9] provided another approach to realize KHN biquad using CCIIs. The circuit uses five CCIIs (two plus-type, three minus-type), six grounded resistors and two grounded capacitors to obtain the lowpass, bandpass and highpass filter functions. In 1996, Soliman [10] presented several circuits that can realize lowpass, bandpass and highpass filters simultaneously using CFAs. In 1997, Horng *et al.* [11] proposed a lowpass, bandpass and highpass filter uses four plus-type CCIIs and seven passive components. Recently, several KHN biquads using various active elements were proposed in [12-15]. However, the notch filter cannot be obtained without additional circuitry from these circuit configurations [7-15]. In 1994, [16] Chang proposed a lowpass, bandpass and notch filter using three CFAs, three resistors and two grounded capacitors.

In this paper, we proposed a voltage-mode biquadratic filter with single input and three outputs using three plus-type CCIIs, two grounded capacitors and five resistors. Lowpass, bandpass and notch filters can be obtained simultaneously from the same circuit configuration. With respect to the previous CFA based lowpass, bandpass and notch biquadratic filter circuit in [16], the proposed circuit employs simpler active components (plus-type CCIIs).

2. Circuit Description

Using standard notation, the port relations of an ideal plus-type CCII can be characterized by

$$\begin{bmatrix} i_y \\ v_x \\ i_z \end{bmatrix} = \begin{bmatrix} 0 & 0 & 0 \\ 1 & 0 & 0 \\ 0 & 1 & 0 \end{bmatrix} \begin{bmatrix} v_y \\ i_x \\ v_z \end{bmatrix} \qquad (1)$$

The proposed configuration is shown in **Figure 1**. Assuming $R_3 = R_4 = R_5 = R$, The transfer functions can be expressed as

$$\frac{V_{out1}}{V_{in}} = \frac{\dfrac{G_1G^2}{C_1C_2(G_1+G-G_2)}}{s^2 + s\dfrac{G^2}{C_1(G_1+G-G_2)} + \dfrac{G^2}{C_1C_2}} \tag{2}$$

$$\frac{V_{out2}}{V_{in}} = \frac{-s\dfrac{G_1G}{C_1(G_1+G-G_2)}}{s^2 + s\dfrac{G^2}{C_1(G_1+G-G_2)} + \dfrac{G^2}{C_1C_2}} \tag{3}$$

$$\frac{V_{out3}}{V_{in}} = \frac{s^2\dfrac{G_1}{G_1+G-G_2} + \dfrac{G_1G^2}{C_1C_2(G_1+G-G_2)}}{s^2 + s\dfrac{G^2}{C_1(G_1+G-G_2)} + \dfrac{G^2}{C_1C_2}} \tag{4}$$

From (2)-(4) it can be seen that a lowpass response is obtained from V_{out1}, a bandpass response is obtained from V_{out2} and a notch response is obtained from V_{out3}. The proposed circuit uses three plus-type CCIIs, two grounded capacitors and five resistors. The design of using only grounded capacitors is attractive, because grounded capacitor can be implemented on a smaller area than the floating counterpart and it can absorb equivalent shunt capacitive parasitics [17-19]. In all cases the resonance angular frequency ω_o and the quality factor Q are given by

$$\omega_o = G\sqrt{\frac{1}{C_1C_2}} \tag{5}$$

and

$$Q = \frac{G_1+G-G_2}{G}\sqrt{\frac{C_1}{C_2}} \tag{6}$$

The resonance angular frequency can be controlled by G. The quality factor can be orthogonally controlled by G_1 or G_2.

3. Sensitivity Analysis

Taking into account the non-idealities of the plus-type

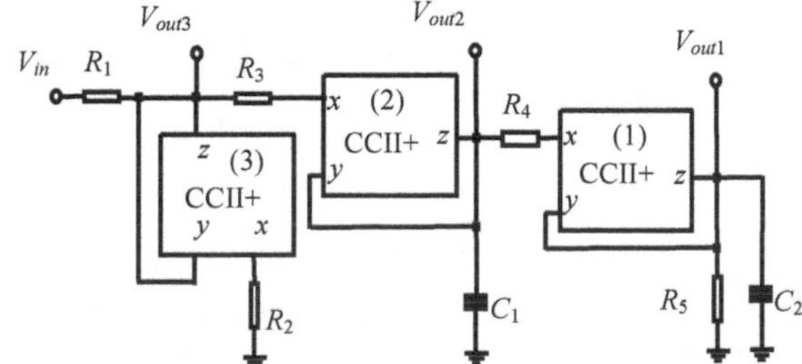

Figure 1. The proposed voltage-mode biquadratic filter.

CCII, the characteristics of the non-ideal CCII can be given by $i_y = 0$, $i_z = \alpha(s)\, i_x$ and $v_x = \beta(s)\, v_y$, where $\alpha(s)$ and $\beta(s)$ represent the frequency transfers of the internal current and voltage followers of the plus-type CCII, respectively. They can be approximated by the following first order lowpass functions [20].

$$\alpha(s) = \frac{\alpha_o}{1+s/\omega_\alpha} \tag{7}$$

$$\beta(s) = \frac{\beta_o}{1+s/\omega_\beta} \tag{8}$$

where $\alpha_o = 0.9914$, $\omega_\alpha = 3.8\times10^9$ rad/s, $\beta_o = 0.9999$, $\omega_\beta = 6.48\times10^9$ rad/s. Assuming the circuits are working at frequencies much lower than the corner frequencies of $\alpha(s)$ and $\beta(s)$, namely, $\alpha(s) = \alpha = 1-\varepsilon_1$ and ε_1 ($|\varepsilon_1| \ll 1$) denotes the current tracking error and $\beta(s) = \beta = 1-\varepsilon_2$ and ε_2 ($|\varepsilon_2| \ll 1$) denotes the voltage tracking error of the plus-type CCII. The denominator of the non-ideal output voltage function for **Figure 1** is

$$D(s) \cong s^2 + s\frac{G^2\alpha_2\beta_2}{C_1(G_1+G-G_2\alpha_3\beta_3)} + \frac{G^2\alpha_1\beta_1}{C_1C_2} \tag{9}$$

The resonance angular frequency ω_o and quality factor Q are obtained by

$$\omega_o = G\sqrt{\frac{\alpha_1\beta_1}{C_1C_2}} \tag{10}$$

and

$$Q = \frac{G_1+G-G_2\alpha_3\beta_3}{G\alpha_2\beta_2}\sqrt{\frac{C_1\alpha_1\beta_1}{C_2}} \tag{11}$$

Because of the tolerances in component values and the non-idealities of the plus-type CCIIs, the response of the actual assembled filter will deviate from the ideal response. As a means for predicting such deviations, the filter designer employs the concept of sensitivity. The sensitivity function is defined as:

$$S_x^y = \frac{\partial y}{\partial x}\frac{x}{y} \tag{12}$$

The active and passive sensitivities of ω_o and Q of the proposed filter are:

$$S_G^{\omega_o} \cong 1,\quad -S_{C_1,C_2}^{\omega_o} \cong S_{\alpha_1,\beta_1}^{\omega_o} \cong \frac{1}{2},\quad S_G^Q \cong \frac{-G_1+G_2}{G+G_1\text{-}G_2},$$

$$S_{G_1}^Q \cong \frac{G_1}{G+G_1-G_2},\quad S_{G_2}^Q \cong \frac{-G_2}{G+G_1-G_2},$$

$$S_{C_1}^Q \cong -S_{C_2}^Q \cong S_{\alpha_1,\beta_1}^Q \cong \frac{1}{2},\quad S_{\alpha_3,\beta_3}^Q \cong \frac{-G_2}{G+G_1-G_2}.$$

These values have been calculated by assuming that α_1, α_2, α_3, β_1, β_2 and β_3 are near unity.

4. Simulation Results

The proposed circuit was simulated using PSPICE. The plus-type CCII was implemented using one AD844. The supply voltages are chosen as $\pm$ 12 V. The following setting were selected to obtain the lowpass, bandpass and notch filters: $R_1 = R_2 = R_3 = R_4 = R_5 = 1$ kΩ, $C_1 = C_2 = 1$ nF with $Q = 1$ and $f_o = 159.15$ KHz. **Figures 2 (a), (b)** and **(c)** represent the simulated frequency responses for the lowpass (V_{out1}), bandpass (V_{out2}) and notch (V_{out3}) filters of **Figure 1**, respectively. The simulation results are coherent with the theoretical analyses. The CCII has parasitic resistor from the z terminal to the ground (R_z [21]). When the z terminal load of the CCII is a capacitor (C), it in troduces a pole produced by R_z and C at low frequency. This explains why **Figure 2(b)** has non-ideal phase responses at low frequencies. This effect can be minimized by using larger loading capacitor or operating the filter in high frequencies.

5. Conclusions

In this paper, a new single input and three outputs voltage-mode biquadratic filter is presented. The proposed circuit uses three plus-type CCIIs, two grounded capacitors and five resistors. The new circuit offers several advantages, such as the realization of lowpass, bandpass, and notch filter functions, simultaneously, in the same circuit configuration; the use of only three plus-type CC -IIs; orthogonally controllable of resonance angular frequency and quality factor and the use of only grounded capacitors.

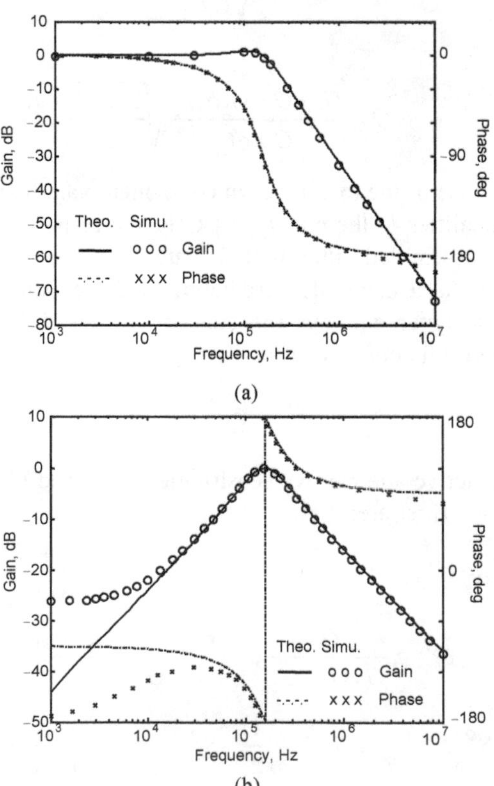

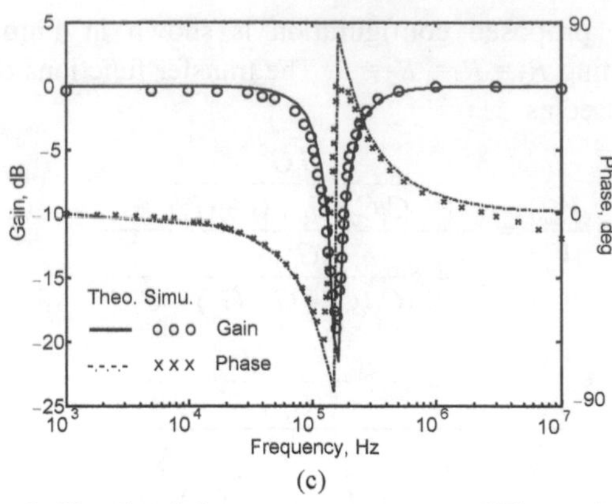

Figure 2. Simulated frequency responses of Figure 1 design with $C_1 = C_2 = 1$ nF and $R_1 = R_2 = R_3 = R_4 = R_5 = 1$ kΩ. (a) lowpass filter (V_{out1}); (b) bandpass filter (V_{out2}), (c) notch filter (V_{out3}).

6. References

[1] C. Toumazou, F. J. Lidgey and D. G. Haigh, "Analogue IC Design: The Current-mode Approach," Peter Peregrinus Ltd., London, 1990.

[2] G. W. Roberts and A. S. Sedra, "All Current-Mode Frequency Selective Circuits," *Electronics Letters*, Vol. 25, No. 12, 1989, pp. 759-761.

[3] J. A. Svoboda, L. McGory and S. Webb, "Applications of a Commercially Available Current Conveyor," *International Journal of Electronics*, Vol. 70, No. 1, 1991, pp. 159-164.

[4] M. Higashimura and Y. Fukui, "Universal Filter Using Plus-Type CCIIs," *Electronics Letters*, Vol. 32, No. 9, 1996, pp. 810-811.

[5] T. Tsukutani, Y. Sumi and N. Yabuki, "Versatile Current-Mode Biquadratic Circuit Using Only Plus Type CCCIIs and Grounded Capacitors," *International Journal of Electronics*, Vol. 94, No. 12, 2007, pp. 1147-1156.

[6] J. W. Horng, "Voltage/Current-Mode Universal Biquadratic Filter Using Single CCII+," *Indian Journal of Pure & Applied Physics*, Vol. 48, No. 10, 2010, pp. 749-756.

[7] A. M. Soliman, "Kerwin-Huelsman-Newcomb Circuit using Current Conveyors," *Electronics Letters*, Vol. 30, No. 24, 1994, pp. 2019-2020.

[8] W. Kerwin, L. Huelsman and R. Newcomb, "State Variable Synthesis for Insensitive Integrated Circuit Transfer Functions," *IEEE Journal of Solid State Circuits*, Vol. 2, No. 3, 1967, pp. 87-92.

[9] R. Senani and V. K. Singh, "KHN-Equivalent Biquad Using Current Conveyors," *Electronics Letters*, Vol. 31, No. 8, 1995, pp. 626-628.

[10] A. M. Soliman, "Applications of the Current Feedback Amplifiers," *Analog Integrated Circuits and Signal Processing*, Vol. 11, 1996, pp. 265-302.

[11] J. W. Horng, J. R. Lay, C. W. Chang and M. H. Lee, "High Input Impedance Voltage-Mode Multifunction Filters Using Plus-Type CCIIs," *Electronics Letters*, Vol. 33, No. 6, 1997, pp. 472-473.

[12] E. Altuntas and A. Toker, "Realization of Voltage and Current Mode KHN Biquads Using CCCIIs," *AEU International Journal of Electronics and Communications*, Vol. 56, No. 1, 2002, pp. 45-49.

[13] A. M. Soliman, "Kerwin Huelsman Newcomb Filter Using Inverting CCII," *Journal of Active and Passive Electronic Devices*, Vol. 3, 2008, pp. 273-279.

[14] S. Minaei and M. A. Ibrahim, "A Mixed-Mode KHN-Biquad Using DVCC and Grounded Passive Elements Suitable for Direct Cascading," *International Journal of Circuit Theory and Applications*, Vol. 37, 2009, pp. 793-810.

[15] J. Koton, N. Herencsar and K. Vrba, "Single-Input Three-Output Variable Q and ω_0 Filters Using Universal Voltage Conveyors," *International Journal of Electronics*, Vol. 97, No. 5, 2010, pp. 531-538.

[16] C. M. Chang, C. S. Hwang and S. H. Tu, "Voltage-Mode Notch, Lowpass and Bandpass Filter Using Current-Feed-Back Amplifiers," *Electronics Letters*, Vol. 30, No. 24, 1994, pp. 2022-2023.

[17] M. Bhushan and R. W. Newcomb, "Grounding of Capacitors in Integrated Circuits," *Electronic Letters*, Vol. 3, No. 4, 1967, pp. 148-149.

[18] E. Yuce and S. Minaei, "ICCII-Based Universal Current-Mode Analog Filter Employing Only Grounded Passive Components," *Analog Integrated Circuits and Signal Processing*, Vol. 58, 2009, pp. 161-169.

[19] C. M. Chang, A. M. Soliman and M. N. S. Swamy, "Analytical Synthesis of Low-Sensitivities High-Order Voltage-Mode DDCC and FDCCII-Grounded R and C All-Pass Filter Structures," *IEEE Transactions on Circuits and Systems I: Regular Papers*, Vol. 54, No. 7, 2007, pp. 1430-1443.

[20] A. Fabre, O. Saaid and H. Barthelemy, "On the Frequency Limitations of the Circuits Based on Second Generation Current Conveyors," *Analog Integrated Circuits and Signal Processing*, Vol. 7, 1995, pp. 113-129.

[21] J. W. Horng, "High-Order Current-Mode and Transimpedance-Mode Universal Filters with Multiple-Inputs and Two-Outputs Using MOCCIIs," *Radioengineering*, Vol. 18, No. 4, 2009, pp. 537-543.

6

Switchable PLL Frequency Synthesizer and Hot Carrier Effects*

Yang Liu, Ashok Srivastava, Yao Xu
Department of Electrical and Computer Engineering Louisiana State University, Baton Rouge, U.S.A

Abstract

In this paper, a new strategy of switchable CMOS phase-locked loop frequency synthesizer is proposed to increase its tuning range. The switchable PLL which integrates two phase-locked loops with different tuning frequencies are designed and fabricated in 0.5 μm n-well CMOS process. Cadence/Spectre simulations show that the frequency range of the switchable phased-locked loop is between 320 MHz to 1.15 GHz. The experimental results show that the RMS jitter of the phase-locked loop changes from 26 ps to 123 ps as output frequency varies. For 700 MHz carrier frequency, the phase noise of the phase-locked loop reaches as low as −81 dBc/Hz at 10 kHz offset frequency and −104 dBc/Hz at 1 MHz offset frequency. A device degradation model due to hot carrier effects has been used to analyze the jitter and phase noise performance in an open loop voltage-controlled oscillator. The oscillation frequency of the voltage-controlled oscillator decreases by approximately 100 to 200 MHz versus the bias voltage and the RMS jitter increases by 40 ps under different phase-locked loop output frequencies after 4 hours of stress time.

Keywords: CMOS Phase-Locked Loop, Voltage-Controlled Oscillator, Hot Carrier Effects, Jitter, Phase Noise

1. Introduction

Phase-locked loops (PLLs) have been widely used in high speed data communication systems. The design, underlying principle of operation and applications are described in numerous publications and text books [1-8]. Present day frequency synthesizers need a broad tuning range for the PLL which sometimes limit the operation of the communication systems. In this paper, we propose a switchable PLL, which combines two relatively narrow bandwidth PLLs into a single chip and uses a frequency detector to decide which PLL to choose according to the reference frequency. As a result, the switchable PLL can work over a wide tuning range and at a high frequency. It also achieves a short locking time without sacrificing the jitter and phase noise performance.

In submicron CMOS devices, the performance of integrated circuits is influenced by the hot carrier effect due to increased lateral channel electric field which results in circuit degradation. Thus, jitter and phase noise may also be affected. Xiao and Yuan [9] have studied hot carrier effects on the performance of voltage-controlled oscillator (VCO). More detailed studies on hot carrier effects in CMOS VCO which is one of the modules of the PLL have been conducted by Zhang and Srivastava [10,11]. In this work, hot carrier effect has been considered and its effect on phase noise and jitter of the CMOS phase-locked loop integrated circuit has been studied.

2. Switchable PLL Design

The design of a switchable PLL is shown in **Figure 1**. Two PLL frequency synthesizers are integrated in a single chip design, one is working in high frequency range and the other is working in low frequency range. Both PLLs include phase-frequency detector (PFD), charge pump (CP), second order loop filter, current starved VCO and 1-by-8 divider. The input range is from 40 MHz to 144 MHz and output range is from 320 MHz to 1.15 GHz. The charge pump and second order low pass loop filter are used to make the system stable and minimize the high frequency noise. The phase frequency detector is designed by using NOR gates and D-flip flops.

*Part of the work is reported in Proc. GLSVLSI, pp. 481-486, 2009.

The current starved single-ended voltage control ring oscillator is shown in **Figure 1**. The MOSFETs M1 and M4 operate as an inverter. MOSFETs M7 and M8 operate as a current source, which control the current flowing into the inverter. The oscillation is obtained by charging and discharging the capacitance in each stage of the VCO. To investigate hot carrier effects, VCO circuits in both PLLs are using two modes of operations. The two operation modes are the stress mode and the oscillation mode. V_{mode} control signal realizes the switches of the two operation modes. In both modes, V_{DD} is 5 V. When V_{mode} = 0 V, VCO is working in oscillating mode and is like a normal one. When V_{mode} = 5 V, the transistors connected to V_{mode} are on and act as switches. Thus, a 5 V voltage appears at the drains of transistors M1-M6 as a V_{stress} and hot carriers are injected into their drains. The VCO is not oscillating in stress mode at this stage. After a certain period of stress time, the measurements of jitter, phase noise and oscillation frequency can be obtained and compared by switching between oscillating and stress modes.

The divider-by-2 cell circuit is built in C^2MOS, which is implemented with only 9 transistors as shown in **Figure 2** [12]. Three inverting buffers are used to drive the divider after VCO. There are three cells of divider-by-2 which are connected in series to make 1-by-8 divider work. It can work up to a maximal frequency of 1.5 GHz clock signal.

As shown in **Figure 3**, the switch includes a local oscillator, frequency detector (FD) and a two input multiplexer (MUX). The same kind of VCO as used in PLL design is working as a local oscillator but the difference is that local VCO doesn't have stress mode and the oscillation frequency is locked at 80 MHz. The FD compares the signal from the local VCO with the input reference signal. When the input frequency is higher than 80 MHz, the output of the FD is high which means the

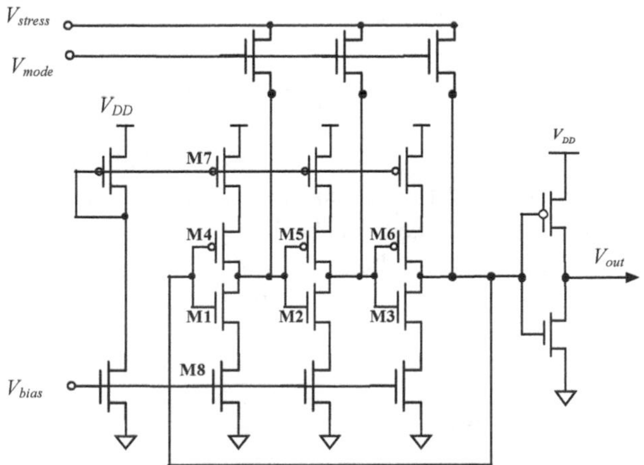

Figure 1. Single-ended CMOS VCO.

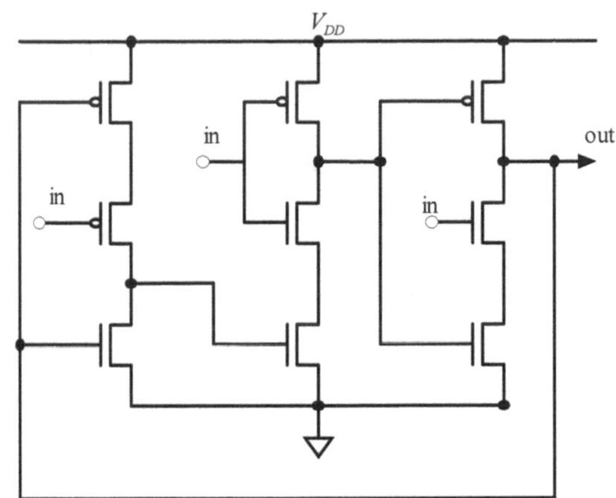

Figure 2. A divide by 2 cell circuit. Note: All three inputs (in) are connected and act as a single input.

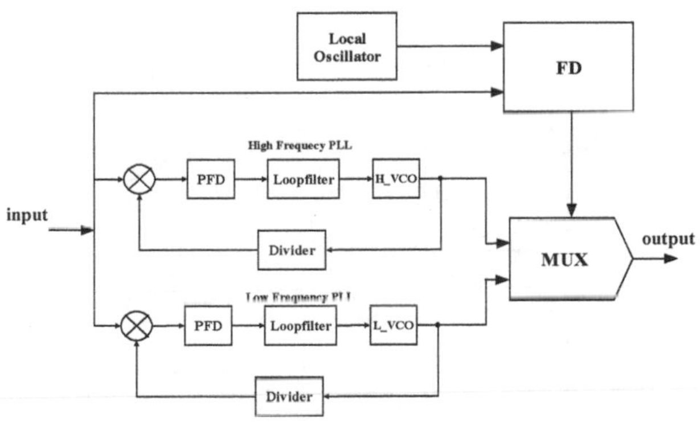

Figure 3. Single-ended CMOS VCO.

high frequency PLL (H_PLL) output signal will go out via the MUX. On the other hand, when the input signal frequency is lower than 80 MHz, the output of the fre-quency detector is low and the low frequency PLL (L_PLL) output signal will go out via the MUX.

The FD circuit schematic is shown in **Figure 4**. The structure of the detector is same with the PFD in each PLL. The RC circuit transfers the output ac signals of PFD to relatively high and low dc voltage signals and comparator compares these two signals to give high or low voltage, which drives the MUX.

Figure 5 shows the loop filter circuit with PFD and charge pump. **Figure 6** shows the schematic of a phase-frequency detector. "Clk" in PFD is from the divider and in FD it is from the "input" in **Figure 3**. **Figure 7** shows the D-flip-flop circuit used in PLL design. The D-flip-flop is a controllable flip-flop that is built with inverters and transmission gates.

3. Hot Carrier Effects (HCE)

As device size shrinks to sub-micron, MOSFETs experience high electric fields with large drain to source

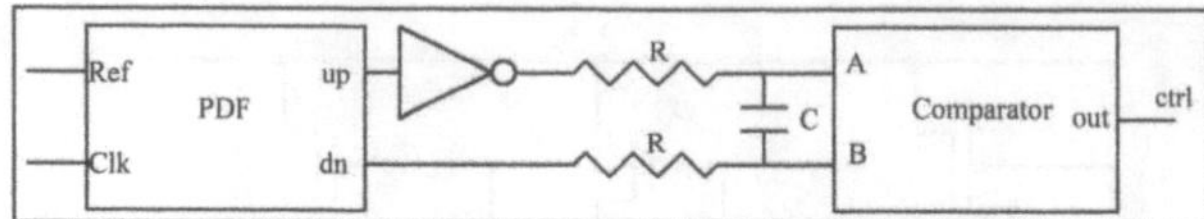

Figure 4. Frequency detector architecture.

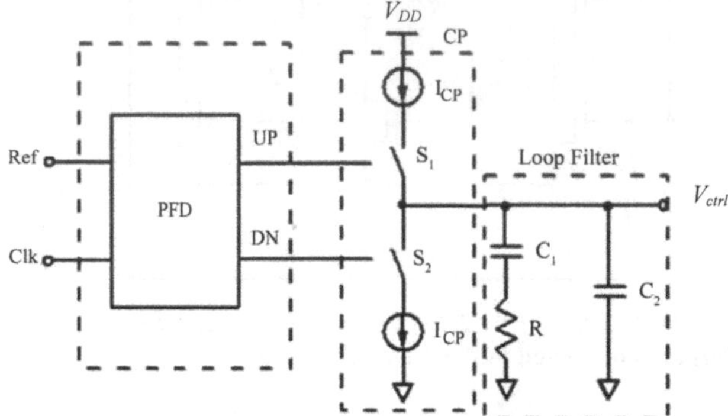

Figure 5. A loop filter with PFD and charge pump.

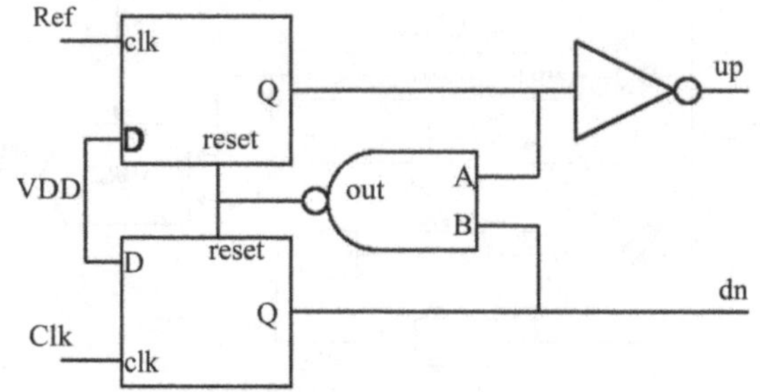

Figure 6. Schematic of a phase-frequency detector (PFD).

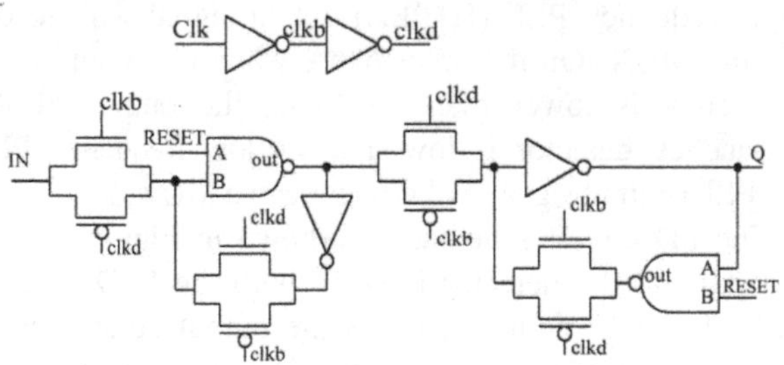

Figure 7. D-flip-flop.

voltage. While the velocity saturation occurs in high electric field, the kinetic energy of the carriers continues to increase. These carriers are known as hot carriers. Hot carriers can cause interface traps and oxide trapped charges. The small geometry devices can be especially influenced and it should be taken into account when dealing with high frequency applications [13]. Hu *et al.* [14] developed a physical model of HCE. When hot electrons gain the energy over 3.7 eV, the interface traps are generated. The interface traps reduce the mobile carrier mobility and density of carriers in the MOSFET which effectively results in increase of the MOSFET threshold voltage.

Here the hot carrier effects are investigated under a few hours of stress on MOSFETs. The stress is from external bias voltages on the gate and drain. A few hours of stress generates the degradation of device para- meters.

The parameters of the MOSFETs determine the features of PLL circuit and the stress of hot carrier injection affects the device parameters including the increase of threshold voltage V_t and the decrease of electron and hole mobilities, μ_0.

Zhang and Srivastava [11] have described an experimental model for the degradation of MOS trans- istors due to hot carrier injection. The threshold voltage shift (ΔV_t) from its original value is presented as follows:

$$\Delta V_t = At^m \tag{1}$$

In Equation (1), A is the degradation constant, which is strongly affected by the gate to source stress voltage (V_{GS}) and drain to source stress voltage (V_{DS}). The power, m mainly depends on V_{GS} and less on V_{DS}.

The n-MOSFET and p-MOSFET have the same channel length in ring oscillator of **Figure 1**. The oscillation frequency is given by,

$$f_0 = \frac{1}{2nt_D} = \frac{I_D}{nC_L V_{DD}} \tag{2}$$

where V_{DD} is the supply voltage t_D is the delay time of a single inverter and n is the stage number of the ring oscillator. C_L is the load capacitor and I_D is the drain current of M1, M2 and M3 given by Equation(3). V_{DD} is 5 V and n is 3 in this circuit.

$$I_D = \frac{1}{2}\mu_o C_{OX}\frac{W}{L}(V_{BIAS} - V_t)^2 \tag{3}$$

In Equation (3), μ_o is the electron mobility, C_{OX} is gate oxide capacitance per unit area, W/L is the channel width to length ratio of n-MOSFET, which decides the frequency of VCO output. V_{BIAS} is the bias voltage and V_t is the threshold voltage. Thus, the gain of VCO output frequency is given by,

$$K_V = \frac{\partial f_0}{\partial V_{BIAS}} = \frac{\mu_o C_{OX}}{n}\frac{W}{L}\frac{V_{BIAS} - V_t}{C_L V_{DD}} \tag{4}$$

From Equation (4), it is shown that the drain currents of n-MOSFETs M1, M2 and M3 affect the frequency and the frequency gain of the VCO. It means that the device parameters of those n-MOSFETs have impacted the VCO performance by hot carrier injection. The hot carrier effects can be modeled by modifying n-MOSFETs parameters, μ_0 and V_t.

3.1. VCO Jitter

The jitter proportionality constant κ is given by [12],

$$\kappa \approx \sqrt{\frac{8}{3\eta}} \cdot \sqrt{\frac{kT}{P} \cdot \frac{V_{DD}}{V_{char}}} \quad (5)$$

where T is the temperature in Kelvin and k is the Boltzmann constant. η is the proportionality constant relating the delay of the VCO which is 0.75 for sub-micron MOSFETs. V_{char} is the characteristic voltage of the device, $V_{char} = \Delta V/\gamma$. γ is the noise ratio between the saturation and linear regions, and is $4/3$ for a short channel device. ΔV is the overdrive voltage on the gate given by,

$$\Delta V = V_{DD}/2 - V_t - \Delta V \quad (6)$$

P is the power dissipation given by,

$$P = nV_{DD}I_{DD} \quad (7)$$

The variability of VCO jitter accumulates as a function of ΔT, interval time between the reference clock and the observed clock. ΔT is equal to 6.7 ns due to difference in delay between the signal input of oscilloscope and the trigger input. We use the threshold crossing time, $\sigma_{\Delta T}$ to quantitatively denote the deviation of the jitter as follows,

$$\sigma_{\Delta T} = \kappa\sqrt{\Delta T} \quad (8)$$

3.2. VCO Phase Noise

Jitter and phase noise are different ways to express the same phenomenon. The method described in subsection 3.1 can be used to model VCO phase noise. For CMOS single-ended VCO, the expression of phase noise is given by [15,16],

$$L\{\Delta f\} \approx \frac{8kT \cdot V_{DD}}{3\eta \cdot P \cdot V_{char}} \cdot \frac{f_0^2}{\Delta f^2} \quad (9)$$

4. Analysis

Figure 8 shows the output of the switchable PLL at different frequencies where 320 MHz waveform is the low frequency PLL (L_PLL) output and 1.12 GHz waveform is the high frequency PLL (H_PLL) output.

Figure 9 shows the variation of PLL output frequency versus control voltage, with and without hot carrier effects. Both the oscillation frequency and frequency range of the PLLs decrease. For the worst case, the over-lapping frequency range, which is 250 MHz without hot carrier effects, decreased to 200 MHz.

The function of RC in the frequency detector is to translate the FD output pulses into dc voltages, which are shown in **Figure 10**. If the input frequency is less than the reference frequency, which is output of the local oscillator defined as 80 MHz, the output is at low level; while if the input frequency is higher than the reference frequency, the output is at high level. But if the input frequency is closer to the reference frequency it will take more time to obtain the dc output. **Figure 11** shows this phenomenon.

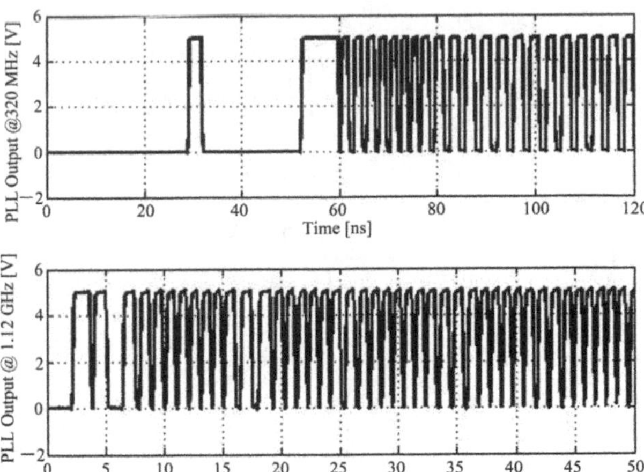

Figure 8. Switchable PLL outputs at different frequencies.

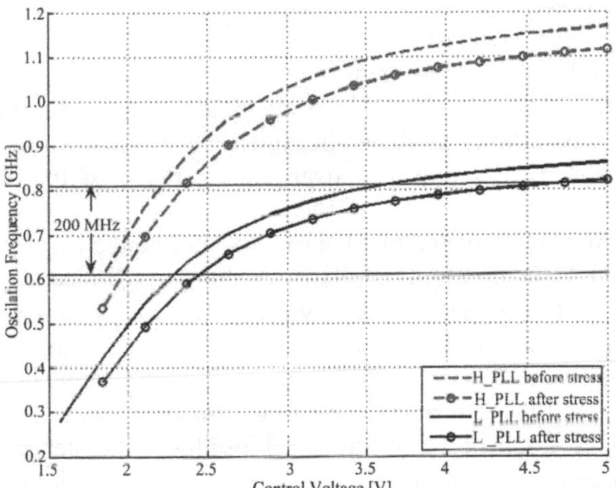

Figure 9. Hot carrier effects on frequency synthesizer.

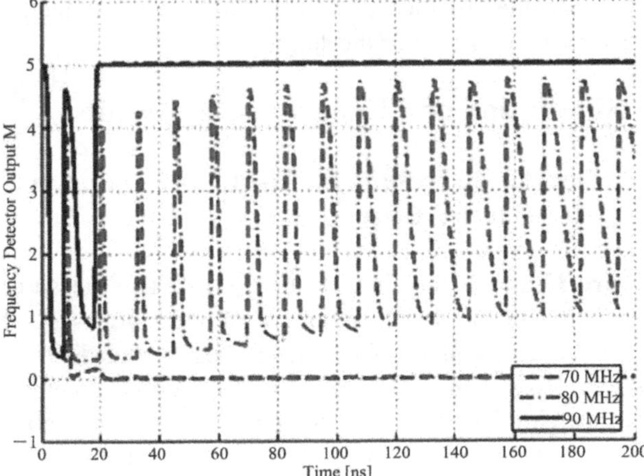

Figure 10. Frequency detector output.

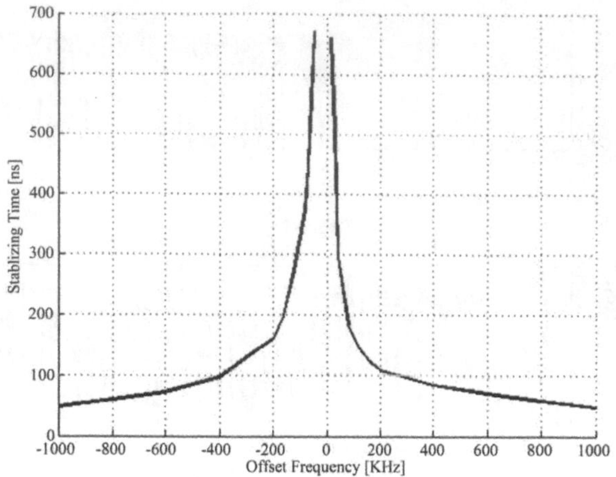

Figure 11. Frequency detector stabilizing time versus frequency.

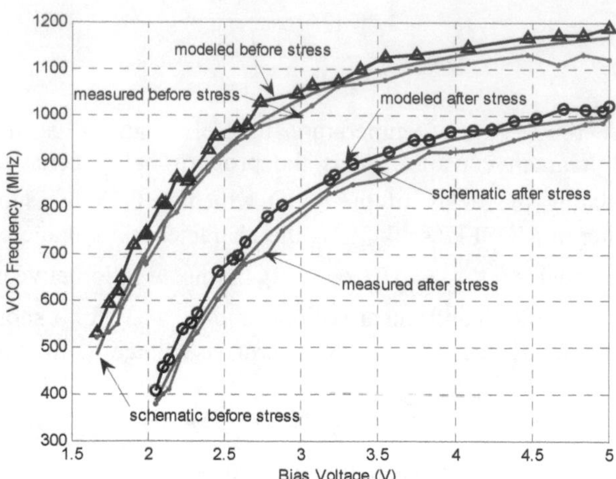

Figure 12. The degradation of VCO frequency due to hot carrier effects.

When the input frequency equals the reference frequency, the output will be oscillating and the stable time will be infinity as shown in **Figure 11**. To deal with this problem, the frequency over-lapping range of the two PLLs is expanded.

It can be noticed that the over-lapping range is at least 200 MHz in **Figure 9**. Thus, if the input frequency is close to reference frequency (80 MHz) the control voltage of the local oscillator can be adjusted to change the reference frequency higher or lower. The large overlapping range guarantees that the difference between the input frequency and the local oscillator frequency is large enough so that the stabilizing time is smaller than 200 ns, which is the stabilizing time of the high frequency PLL. As a result, the stabilizing time of the switchable PLL is decided by the PLLs, while the operation range is much larger than that of the single PLL.

5. Simulation and Experimental Results

5.1. Simulation Results for H-PLL VCO due to Hot Carrier Effects

Figure 12 shows the simulation, modeled and measured results of the oscillation frequency of open loop VCO in H_PLL before and after hot carrier stress versus different bias voltages. The modeled results are in good agreement with the simulation and measured results. The simulation results are performed by Cadence/Spectre. It is shown that at a 4 V bias, the frequency is around 1150 MHz before stress and it is about 950 MHz after stress. This is the effect on VCO output frequency due to hot carrier injection in MOSFETs.

Figure 12 includes experimental data on tuning range of VCO whose operation frequency is slightly lower than the simulation one. Phase noise and jitter measured under hot carrier stress for both VCO and PLL are reported in subsection 5.2. Threshold voltage increases by approximate 120 mV and the electron mobility decreases by about 80 $cm^2/Vsec$ [9] after 4 hours of stress on MOSFETs.

Figure 13 shows the decrease of H_PLL VCO frequency gain at 2.5 V bias voltage versus stress time, which agrees with the Equation (4). After 4 hours of hot carrier injection, the VCO gain decreases by about 33%, from 460 MHz to 310 MHz.

Figure 14 shows the simulation result for the variation of the jitter proportionality parameter, κ changing with the oscillation frequency before and after 4 hours of stress. κ increases by about 10%, which means the value of the jitter of 3-stage single-ended VCO increases by about $0.2\sqrt{\Delta T}ns$ due to hot carrier effects from Equation (5). ΔT is the time difference between rising edge of trigger clock and the observed clock. Thus, the jitter $\sigma_{\Delta T}$ mainly depends on κ, which varies with different tuning frequencies.

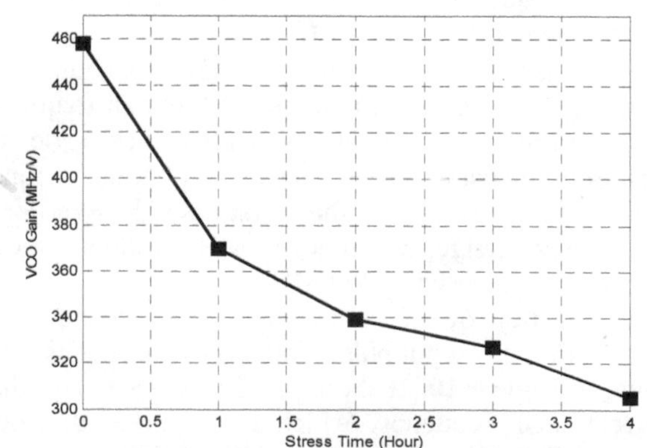

Figure 13. VCO gain versus stress time.

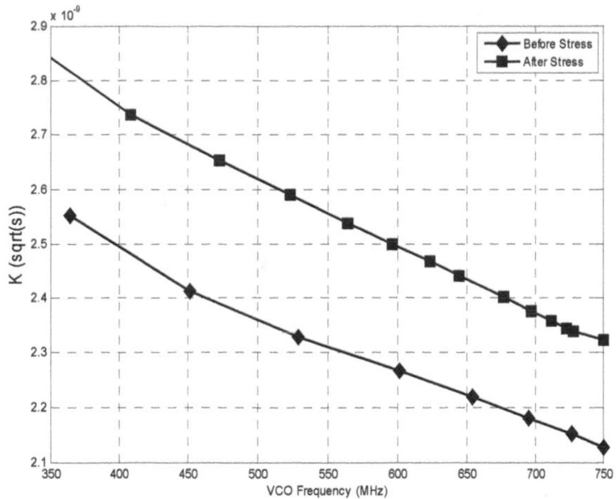

Figure 14. The dependence of K and VCO frequency due to hot carrier effects.

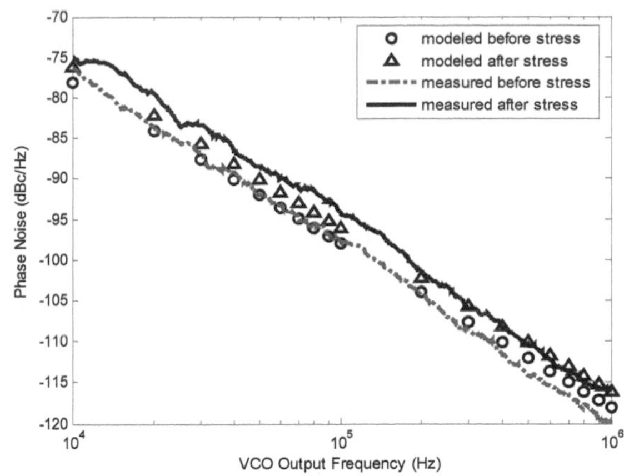

Figure 15. Degradation on phase noise performance under 1 GHz oscillation frequency.

5.2. Experimental Results

Figure 15 shows the experimental and modeled phase noises of the open loop VCO at 1 GHz oscillation frequency before and after hot carrier stress. The experimental results which are from open loop VCO circuit in the chip are in good agreement with the modeled phase noises which are calculated from Equation (9).

Figure 16 shows the experimental results of device degradation on RMS jitter performance under different PLL output frequencies due to hot carrier effects. A 40 ps increase is observed after 4 hours of stress.

The experimental results for PLL output frequencies with and without hot carrier effects are listed in **Table 1**, measured using Tektronix 11801A Digital Sampling Oscilloscope and Agilent ESA-E4404B Spectrum Analyzer.

Figure 17 shows a photograph of the switchable PLL jitter performance measured by a digital sampling oscilloscope.

Figure 18 shows the experimental results of PLL output phase noise at 700 MHz carrier frequency by using Agilent ESA-E4404B Spectrum Analyzer, before and after stress. The offset frequency is from 10 kHz to 1 MHz. In **Figure 18**, the PLL phase noise before stress is −81 dBc/Hz at 10 kHz offset frequency and is around −104 dBc/Hz at 1 MHz offset frequency. The PLL phase noise increases by about 1-2 dB relative to carrier power per Hertz after four hours of hot carriers stress.

The switchable PLL described in the present work was fabricated in 0.5 μm n-well CMOS process. **Figures 19** and **20** show the cadence/virtuoso layout and the microphotograph of the fabricated switchable PLL chip. **Figure 21** shows the RF test board with mounted PLL chip which is specially designed for this experiment. The chip output is connected to Agilent ESA-E4404B Spectrum Analyzer with built-in phase noise module. The RF module is powered by VDD = 5 V and VSS = 0 V.

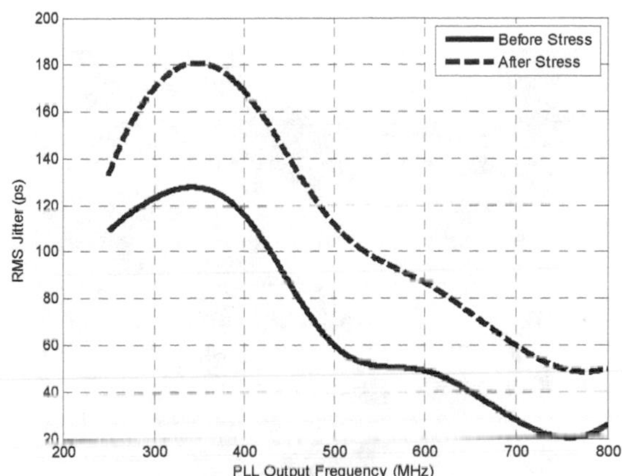

Figure 16. Experimental results of PLL jitter.

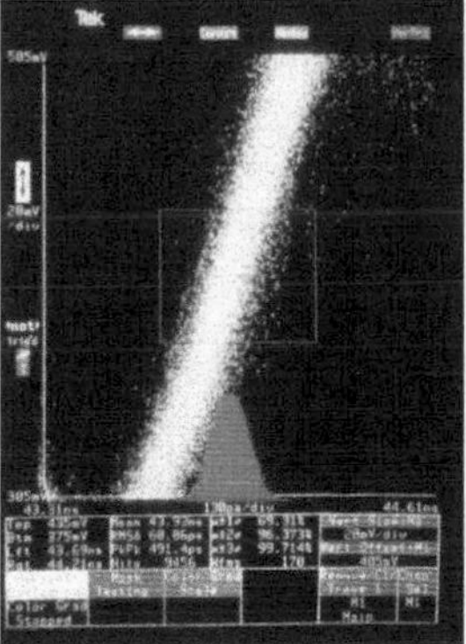

Figure 17. A photograph of PLL jitter.

6. Conclusions

A new design is proposed to expand PLL tuning range without sacrificing its speed and jitter and phase noise

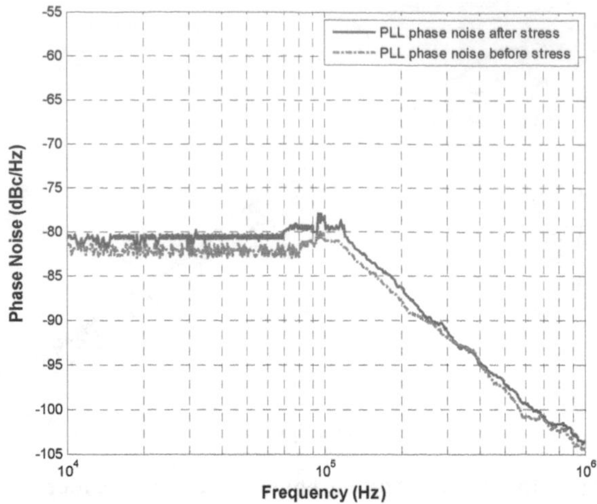

Figure 18. Experimental results of PLL phase noise at 700 MHz carrier frequency.

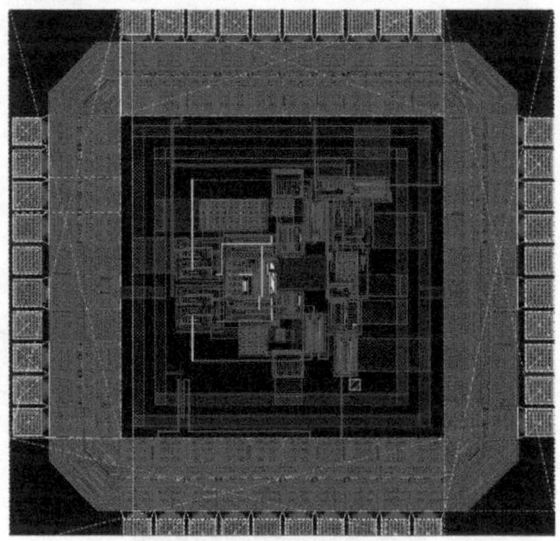

Figure 19. Layout of switchable PLL frequency synthesizer.

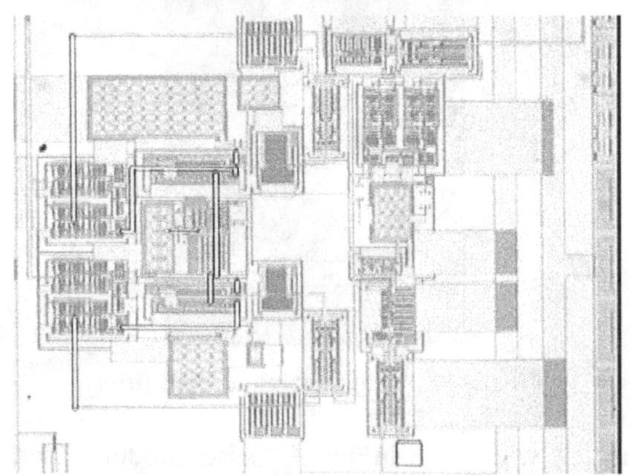

Figure 20. Microphotograph of fabricated switchable PLL.

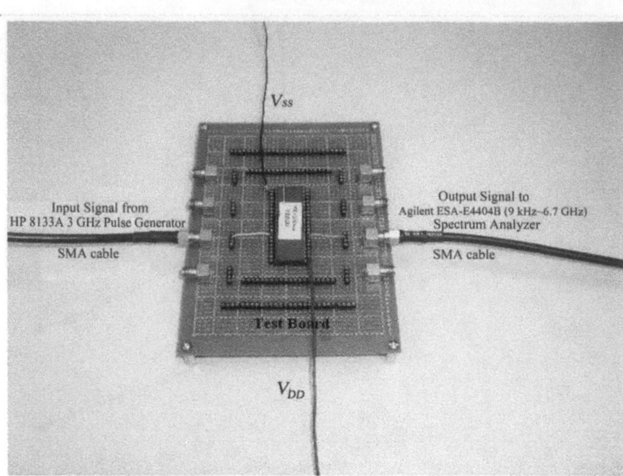

Figure 21. Photograph of RF test board with mounted PLL chip.

performances. The two CMOS PLLs are integrated on a single chip. Cadence/Spectre has been used for post-layout simulations for jitter, phase noise and switchable frequency range. The chip is experimentally tested for jitter, phase noise and switchable frequency range with and without hot carrier effects. A model is presented to address the hot carrier effects on the VCO jitter and phase noise performance. The modeled results are in good agreement with both the simulation and experimental results. It is demonstrated that the jitter can be predicted by the jitter proportionality parameter, κ. The measured jitter and phase noise ranges of the PLL are around 26 to 123 ps and around −69 to −126 dBc/Hz under the entire PLL tuning frequency, 200 MHz–700 MHz.

7. References

[1] G. C. Hsieh and J. C. Hung, "Phase-Locked Loop Techniques-A Survey," *IEEE Transactions Industrial Electronics*, Vol. 42, No. 6, 1996, pp. 609-615.

[2] F. M. Gardner, "Phaselock Techniques," Wiley Interscience, Hoboken, 2005.

[3] S. L. J. Gierkink, D. Li and R. C. Frye, "A 3.5-GHz PLL for Fast Low-IF/Zero-IF LO Switching in an 802.11 Transceiver," *IEEE Journal of Solid-State Circuits*, Vol. 40, No. 9, 2005, pp. 1909-1921.

[4] R. E. Best, "Phase-Locked Loops-Design, Simulation, and Applications," 6th Edition, McGraw-Hill, New York, 2007.

[5] W. Rhee, K. A. Jenkins, J. Liobe and H. Ainspan, "Experimental Analysis of Substrate Noise Effect on PLL Performance," *IEEE Transactions on Circuits and Systems-II*, Vol. 55, No. 7, 2008, pp. 638-642.

[6] C. Jeong, D. Choi and C. Yoo, "A Fast Automatic Frequency Calibration (AFC) Scheme for Phase-Locked Loop (PLL) Frequency Synthesizer," *Proceedings of Radio Frequency Integrated Circuits Symposium*, San-Diego, 7-9 January 2009, pp. 583-586.

FIC.2009.5135609

[7] C. Hsu and Y. Lai, "Low-Cost CP-PLL DFT Structure Implementation for Digital Testing Application," *IEEE Transactions on Instrumentation and Measurement*, Vol. 58, No. 6, 2009, pp. 1897-1906.

[8] Y. Guo and Z. Xie, "Design of PLL Frequency Synthesizer in Frequency Hopping Communication System," *Proceeding of International Conference on Communications and Mobile Computing*, Shenzhen, 12-14 April 2010, pp. 138-141.

[9] E. Xiao and J. S. Yuan, "Hot Carrier and Soft Breakdown Effects on VCO Performance," *IEEE Transactions on Microwave Theory and Techniques*, Vol. 50, No. 11, 2002, pp. 2453-2458.

[10] C. Zhang and A. Srivastava, "Hot Carrier Effects on Jitter and Phase Noise in CMOS Voltage-Controlled Oscillators," *Proceedings of SPIE-Noise in Devices and Circuits III*, Austin, 23-26 May 2005, pp. 52-62.

[11] C. Zhang and A. Srivastava, "Hot Carrier Effects on Jitter Performance in CMOS Voltage Controlled Oscillators," *Fluctuation and Noise Letters*, Vol. 6, No. 3, 2006, pp. 329-334.

[12] S. Pellerano, S. Laventin, C. Samori and A, Lacaita, "A 13.5-mW 5-GHz Frequency Synthesizer with Dynamic-logic Frequency Divider," *IEEE Journal of Solid-State Circuits*, Vol. 39, No. 2, 2004, pp. 378-383.

[13] E. Takeda, C. Y. Yang and A. Miura-Hamada, "Hot-Carrier Effects in MOS Devices," Academic Press, San Diego, 1995.

[14] C. Hu and S. Tam, *et al.*, "Hot-Electron Induced MOSFET Degradation-Model, Monitor, Improvement," *IEEE Transactions on Electron Devices*, Vol. ED-32, 1985, pp. 375-385.

[15] A. Hajimiri, S. Limotyrakis and T. H. Lee, "Jitter and Phase Noise in Ring Oscillators," *IEEE Journal of Solid-State Circuits*, Vol. 34, No. 6, 1999, pp. 790-804.

[16] A. Hajimiri and T. H. Lee, "A General Theory of Phase Noise in Electrical Oscillators," *IEEE Journal of Solid-State Circuits*, Vol. 33, No. 2, 1998, pp. 179-194.

Investigation of the Mechanism of Tangent Bifurcation in Current Mode Controlled Boost Converter

Ling-ling Xie[1], Ren-xi Gong[1], Kuang Wang[2], Hao-ze Zhuo[1]
[1]*College of Electrical Engineering, Guangxi University, Nanning, China*
[2]*Airline Mechanical Company Ltd., Shenzhen, China*

Abstract

Tangent bifurcation is a special bifurcation in nonlinear dynamic systems. The investigation of the mechanism of the tangent bifurcation in current mode controlled boost converters operating in continuous conduction mode (CCM) is performed. The one-dimensional discrete iterative map of the boost converter is derived. Based on the tangent bifurcation theorem, the conditions of producing the tangent bifurcation in CCM boost converters are deduced mathematically. The mechanism of the tangent bifurcation in CCM boost is exposed from the viewpoint of nonlinear dynamic systems. The tangent bifurcation in the boost converter is verified by numerical simulations such as discrete iterative maps, bifurcation map and Lyapunov exponent. The simulation results are in agreement with the theoretical analysis, thus validating the correctness of the theory.

Keywords: Tangent Bifurcation, Discrete Iterative Map, Boost Converter, Continuous Current Mode (CCM)

1. Introduction

In recent years, ones are quite interested in chaos exhibited in the field of power electronics. They are becoming the hot spots of the study in the field. DC-DC converters are a kind of strong nonlinear system. They exhibit various bifurcation and chaos behavior under some operating conditions, such as period-doubling bifurcation [1-5], Hopf bifurcation [6-8], border collision bifurcation [9-11], tangent bifurcation [12,13] and chaos behavior [14-20]. Bifurcation is a complex structure in nonlinear system. The chaos is characteristic of non-repeat, uncertainty and is extreme sensitive to initial conditions. These nonlinear phenomena make the nonlinear dynamic characteristics of DC-DC converter more complex. Deep investigation of these nonlinear phenomena is of great benefit to understanding the nonlinear behavior and practical design.

Up to now, most published papers are mainly about the period-doubling bifurcation in DC-DC converters. The tangent bifurcation, which is a special bifurcation, has been less investigated. The most studies of tangent bifurcation mainly focus on the numerical simulation modeling. The main approaches used for simulation include bifurcation diagram, Lyapunov exponent. The two methods are characteristics of simpleness and intuition, but the main shortcoming of that is large computing quantity, time consuming and blindness. The essential mechanism causing tangent bifurcation was not analyzed in these simulation methods. However, no rigorous attempts have been made to analyze formally the essential mechanism leading to the tangent bifurcation in DC-DC converters.

Boost converters are a kind of important converters with wide applications. Current mode control, being one of the most commonly used control schemes in DC-DC converters, has received much attention to power electronics engineers. Although the work in [12] gives no theoretical insights into the underlying cause of tangent bifurcation in such system, it does prompt the important question of what mechanism may give rise to tangent bifurcation behavior. This paper attempts to answer to this question in the light of the theories of nonlinear dynamic systems. The investigation of the mechanism of the tangent bifurcation in current mode controlled boost converters operating in continuous conduction mode (CCM) is deeply studied. In fact, there are strict stability criteria and the conditions leading to the tangent bifurcation in mathematics based on the theories of nonlinear dynamic systems [13,14]. Based on the tangent bifurcation theorem, the conditions leading to the tangent bifurcation in the discrete iterative model of the boost converter are demonstrated mathematically. Discrete iterative maps, bifurcation diagram, Lyapunov exponent are done to analyze the mechanism and evolution of leading to the tangent bifurcation. The simulation results are in agreement with the theoretical analysis, thus validating the correctness of the theory. The methods proposed in the paper can also be suitable to analysis of the tangent bifurcation and chaos of other kinds of converter circuits.

2. Discrete Iterative Map of a Boost Converter

In **Figure 1**, the circuit model of a boost converter is shown, which consists of a switch S, a diode D, a capacitor C, an inductor L and the load resistor R connected in parallel with the capacitor. The assumptions are made as follows:

1) The boost converter operates in continuous conduction mode.

2) All the components in the boost converter circuit are ideal, no parasitic effects are considered.

Hence, there are two circuit states depending on whether S is closed or open. Assume that the circuit is at the switch state 1 when the switch S is off and diode D is on, and at the switch state 2 when S is on and D is off. The two switch states toggle periodically.

The boost converter is controlled under the current mode. Switch S is controlled by a feedback path that consists of a flip-flop and a comparator. The comparator compares the inductor current i_L with a reference current I_{ref}. The switch is triggered to ON when the clock pulse is received and is triggered to OFF when the inductor current reaches the reference current I_{ref}. Specifically, switch S is turned on at the beginning of each cycle, *i.e.* at $t=nT$, where n is an integer, T is the switching period. The inductor current i_L increases linearly while switch S is on. As i_L approaches to the value of I_{ref}, switch S is turned off, and remains off until the next cycle begins.

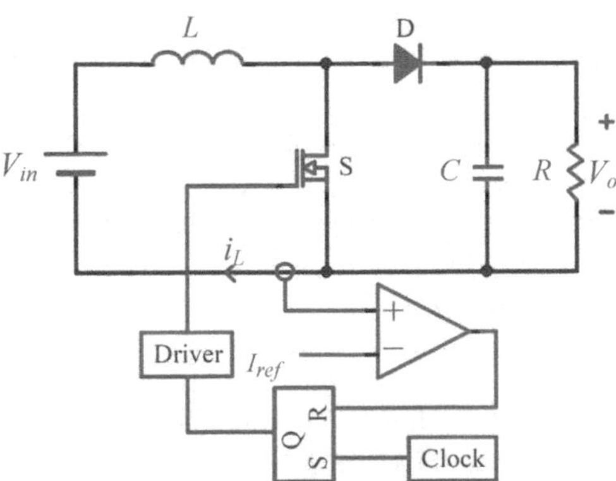

Figure 1. Circuit configuration of current-mode boost converter.

When the switch S closed, diode D is reverse biased. **Figure 2** shows the inductor current waveform. The circuit parameters of the boost converter are listed in **Table 1**.

Let x denote the state vector of the circuit, *i.e.*,

$$x = \begin{bmatrix} v_c \\ i_L \end{bmatrix} \tag{1}$$

where v_C is the voltage across the capacitor and i_L is the current through the inductor.

The state equation for the circuit in any switch state can be written in the form of

$$\dot{x} = A_i x + B_i V_{in} \tag{2}$$

where A_i and B_i are the system matrices in switch state i, and V_{in} is the input voltage. In switch state 1, we have

$$A_1 = \begin{bmatrix} \frac{1}{RC} & 0 \\ 0 & 0 \end{bmatrix}, \quad B_1 = \begin{bmatrix} 0 \\ \frac{1}{L} \end{bmatrix}$$

And in switch state 2, we have

$$A_2 = \begin{bmatrix} \frac{-1}{RC} & \frac{1}{C} \\ \frac{-1}{L} & 0 \end{bmatrix}, \quad B_2 = \begin{bmatrix} 0 \\ \frac{1}{L} \end{bmatrix}$$

The switch S is turned off when the inductor current i_L reaches reference current I_{ref}. The closed-state time t_n can be obtained from (2) by integration, therefore the closed-state time t_n is calculated by the Equation (3).

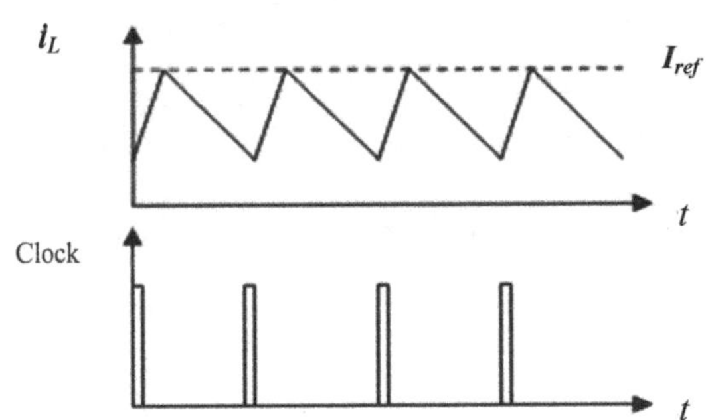

Figure 2. Inductor current waveform.

Table 1. Circuit parameters.

Circuit Components	Values
Switching period T	100 μs
Input Voltage V_{in}	10 V
Load Resistor R	20 Ω
Inductor L	1 mH
Capacitor C	12 μF
Reference Current I_{ref}	0.5~5.5 A

$$t_n = \frac{L}{V_{in}}(I_{ref} - i_n) \tag{3}$$

Subscript n denotes the value at the beginning of the nth cycle, *i.e.*, $i_n = i(nT)$, $v_n = v(nT)$.

The capacitor voltage corresponding to instant t_n is calculated by the following equation

$$v_C(t_n) = v_n e^{-\frac{t_n}{RC}} \tag{4}$$

The discrete iterative model of the boost converter can be derived as follows from the two cases, *i.e.*, $t_n \geq T$ and $t_n < T$.

Case 1. $t_n \geq T$. It means that the converter is in switch state 1 during a switching period T. The instantaneous value of i_n and v_n at next clock instant, i_{n+1} and v_{n+1}, can be calculated with i_n and v_n as initial values.

$$i_{n+1} = i_n + \frac{V_{in}}{L}T \tag{5}$$

$$v_{n+1} = v_n e^{-\frac{T}{RC}} \tag{6}$$

Case 2. $t_n < T$. It means that the converter is switched from switch state 1 to switch state 2 during a switching period T. The instantaneous value of i_n and v_n at next clock instant, i_{n+1} and v_{n+1}, can be calculated with I_{ref} and $v_n e^{-\frac{t_n}{RC}}$ as initial values.

The solution depends on the parameters of circuit values of R、L and C. From **Table 1**, we have $1 - \frac{4R^2C}{L} < 0$. In this case, the solutions of the characteristic equation corresponding to the switch state 2 are a pair of complex conjugate roots. It leads to a damped oscillatory process. Hence, the discrete iterative maps of the boost converter can be derived

$$i_{n+1} = e^{-kt_{n1}}\left[A_1 \sin\beta t_{n1} + A_2 \cos\beta t_{n1}\right] + \frac{V_{in}}{R} \tag{7}$$

$$v_{n+1} = V_{in} - Le^{-kt_{n1}}\left[B_1 \sin\beta t_{n1} + B_2 \cos\beta t_{n1}\right] \tag{8}$$

where,

$$k = \frac{1}{2RC},\ t_{n1} = T\left[1 - \frac{t_n}{T}\right],\ \beta = \frac{1}{2RC}\sqrt{\frac{4R^2C}{L} - 1},$$

$$A_2 = I_{ref} - \frac{V_{in}}{R},\ A_1 = \frac{V_{in} - v_n e^{-2kt_n} + kLA_2}{L\beta},$$

$$B_1 = \frac{kv_n e^{-2kt_n} - kV_{in} - A_2/C}{\beta},\quad B_2 = V_{in} - v_n e^{-2kt_n}$$

From (5-8), the discrete time values of x at $t=nT$ for all n can be obtained. The bifurcation diagram of the boost converter with reference current I_{ref} as parameter is shown in **Figure 3**, the horizontal direction is the reference current I_{ref} which is between 0.5 A and 5 A, the vertical direction is the state variable i_L which ranges from 0.5 A and 5 A. The bifurcations, subharmonics and chaotic behavior are indicated in the diagram. As shown in **Figure 3**, the boost converter goes through period-1, period-2 and eventually exhibits chaos. The period-1 solution is stable until I_{ref}= 1.7059 A whereupon a period doubling bifurcation takes place. The converter eventually goes to chaos when I_{ref} = 2.7 A. It can be interestingly observed that a small periodic window, which also exhibits period doubling cascade, is embedded in the chaos region. In the periodic widow, the converter experiences period-3 to period-6 and so on just above I_{ref} = 4.791 A. The phenomenon that system transits from chaos to period-3 is known as tangent bifurcation.

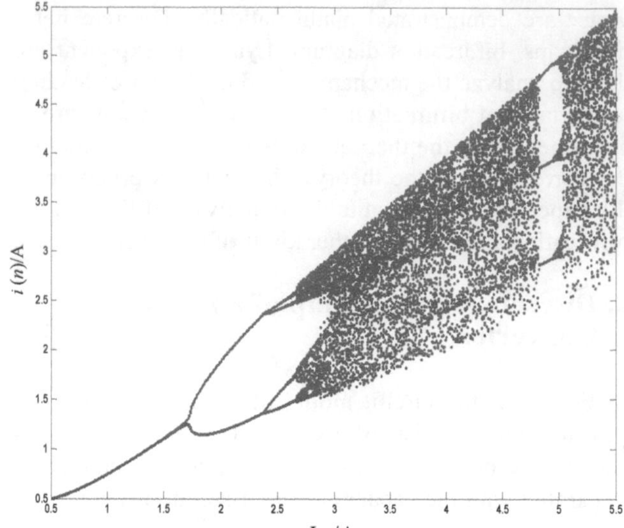

Figure 3. Bifurcation diagram of the boost converter with I_{ref} as parameter.

In **Figure 4**, the larger of the Lyapunov exponents is plotted as a function of the parameter I_{ref} over the same range as in **Figure 3**. It is well known that the presence of chaos is signaled by positive Lyapunov exponent. A negative Lyapunov exponent is characteristic of dissipative (non-conservative) systems, which exhibit point stability. A Lyapunov exponent of zero is characteristic of a cycle-stable system. In this case, the orbits maintain their separation. The tangent bifurcation will be happened when the Lyapunov exponent is changed from the started positive value to zero then to negative value. At $I_{ref} = 1.7059\,\text{A}$, where the fixed point changes from attracting to repelling and an attracting periodic orbit is born, the Lyapunov exponent is 0. Just above $I_{ref} = 2.7\,\text{A}$, the Lyapunov exponent is positive, which means that the system is chaotic. This is the same range in which the bifurcation diagram given in **Figure 3** showed a whole interval. For larger values of I_{ref}, above 4.791 A, there is another short parameter interval in which there is an attracting period-3 orbit and the Lyapunov exponent is negative. Therefore, the tangent bifurcation will be happened.

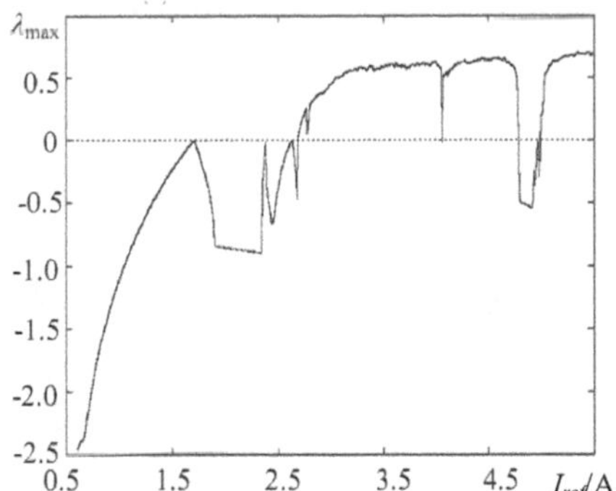

Figure 4. Larger Lyapunov exponent diagram.

3. The Conditions Leading to Tangent Bifurcation

3.1. A Theorem of Tangent Bifurcation

The theorem of tangent bifurcation is briefly reviewed in this section.

Consider the discrete-time nonlinear system

$$x = f(x, \mu) \tag{9}$$

where x is the system variable and μ is a parameter.

A point x^* is called a fixed point or a stationary point if $x^* = f(x^*, \mu^*)$.

It is convenient to have a notation for these functions. We write $f^0(x) = x$ for the 0th iterate that is the identity, $f^1(x)$ for $f(x)$, and $f^2(x)$ for the composition of f with f, that is $f^2(x) = f(f(x))$. Continuing by induction, we obtain $f^{(n)}(\mu, x) = f(f^{n-1}(x))$, is the composition of f with itself n times. Using this notation, for the initial condition x_0, $x_1 = f(x_0)$, $x_2 = f^2(x_0)$, and $x_n = f^n(x_0)$.

Theorem 1 [13,14] (Tangent Bifurcation). Assume that f is a C^2 function from R^2 to R. We write $f(x, \mu) = f_\mu(x)$. Assume that there is a bifurcation value μ^* that has a fixed point x^* with derivative equal to one

1). $f(x^*, \mu^*) = x^*$

2). $f'_{\mu^*}(x^*) = 1$

3). The second derivative $f''_{\mu^*}(x^*) \neq 0$, so the graph of f_{μ^*} lies on one side of the diagonal for x near x^*.

4). The graph of f_μ is moving up or down as the parameter μ varies, or more specifically,

$$\frac{\partial f}{\partial \mu}(x^*, \mu^*) \neq 0$$

The tangent bifurcation takes place in the nonlinear system at the fixed point (x^*, μ^*),

3.2. Derivation of One-Dimensional Discrete Iterative Map

The research of tangent bifurcation should be start from one-dimensional discrete iterative map [12,13]. With one state vector be fixed, reduction of dimension can be done in the boost converter so that the boost converter is transformed into one-dimensional dynamic system. In this study, the capacitor voltage is taken as the state variable needing to be fixed, and the inductor current is chosen as the state variable. The capacitor voltage v_c is assumed to be a constant V_{CO}, then, the inductor current increases and decreases linearly during any period. The following one-dimensional discrete iterative map can be derived by substituting of $v_c = V_{CO}$ into (5-8),

Case 3. $t_n \geq T$.

$$i_{n+1} = f(i_n) = i_n + \frac{V_{in}}{L}T \tag{10}$$

Case 4. $t_n < T$.

$$\begin{aligned} i_{n+1} &= f(i_n) \\ &= e^{-kt_{n1}}\left[A_3 \sin\beta t_{n1} + A_2 \cos\beta t_{n1}\right] + \frac{V_{in}}{R} \end{aligned} \tag{11}$$

where $A_3 = \dfrac{V_{in} - V_{co}e^{-2kt_n} + kLA_2}{L\beta}$

From (10) and (11), $f^2(i_n)$ is obtained

Case 5. $t'_{n2} \geq T$.

$$i_{n+2} = f(i_{n+1}) = f^2(i_n) = i_n + 2\cdot\frac{V_{in}}{L}T \tag{12}$$

Case 6. $t'_{n2} < T$.

$$\begin{aligned} i_{n+2} &= f(i_{n+1}) = f^{(2)}(i_n) \\ &= e^{-kt_{n2}}\left[A_4 \sin\beta t_{n2} + A_2 \cos\beta t_{n2}\right] + \frac{V_{in}}{R} \end{aligned} \tag{13}$$

where, $t_{n2} = T\left[1 - \dfrac{t'_{n2}}{T}\right]$, $t'_{n2} = \dfrac{L}{V_{in}}\left(I_{ref} - i_{n+1}\right)$,

$$A_4 = \frac{V_{in} - V_{co}e^{-2kt'_{n2}} + kLA_2}{L\beta}$$

Similarly, $f^3(i_n)$ is obtained

Case 7. $t'_{n3} \geq T$.

$$i_{n+3} = f(i_{n+2}) = f^3(i_n) = i_n + 3\cdot\frac{V_{in}}{L}T \tag{14}$$

Case 8. $t'_{n3} < T$.

$$\begin{aligned} i_{n+3} &= f(i_{n+2}) = f^{(3)}(i_n) \\ &= e^{-kt_{n3}}\left[A_5 \sin\beta t_{n3} + A_2 \cos\beta t_{n3}\right] + \frac{V_{in}}{R} \end{aligned} \tag{15}$$

where, $t_{n3} = T\left[1 - \dfrac{t'_{n3}}{T}\right]$, $t'_{n3} = \dfrac{L}{V_{in}}\left(\pi I_{ref} - i_{n+2}\right)$,

$$A_5 = \frac{V_{in} - V_{co}e^{-2kt'_{n3}} + kLA_2}{L\beta}$$

The graph of $f(i_n)$ and the diagonal is shown in **Figure 5**, and the graph of $f^3(i_n)$ and the diagonal is shown in **Figure 6**, in which the parameters are same as those in [12], that is, $V_{CO} = 17.2\text{ V}, I_{ref} = 4.7915\text{ A}$, $i_n \in [2\text{ A}, 5\text{ A}]$.

Compared with [12], the discrete iterative map of $f(i_n)$ is different at the interval of [4.75, 5], and that of $f^3(i_n)$ is different at the interval of [4.85, 5]. But the difference has no effect on the analysis of the equilibrium point. These results testify the validity and practicality of the proposed discrete iterative map method of $f(i_n)$ and $f^3(i_n)$.

3.3. The Conditions Leading to Tangent Bifurcation

Definition 1. The graph of a function f is the set of points $\{(x, f(x))\}$. The diagonal, denoted by $\triangle$, is the graph of the identity function that takes x to x: $\triangle = \{(x, x)\}$

Obviously, a point p is fixed for a function f if and only if $(p, f(p))$ is on the diagonal $\triangle$.

In theorem 1, a fixed point is requested according to condition (a). The condition (b) indicates that the iterative map function lose the stability in the instability boundary, in other words, the tangent bifurcation will happen in the instability boundary. Form **Figure 6**, it can be seen that there are four fixed points, *i.e.*, $f^{(3)}(2.82, 4.7515) = 2.82$, $f^{(3)}(3.82, 4.7515) = 3.82$, $f^{(3)}(4.25, 4.7515) = 4.25, f^{(3)}(4.79, 4.7515) = 4.79$, thus satisfying the condition (a) of theorem 1.

Three fixed points $(i^{*1}_n = 2.82, i^{*2}_n = 3.82, i^{*4}_n = 4.79)$ are tangent to the diagonal that the slopes of them are +1,

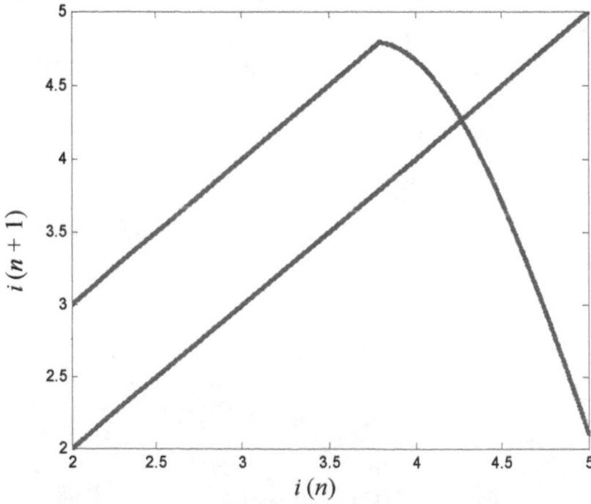

Figure 5. Graph of $f(i_n)$.

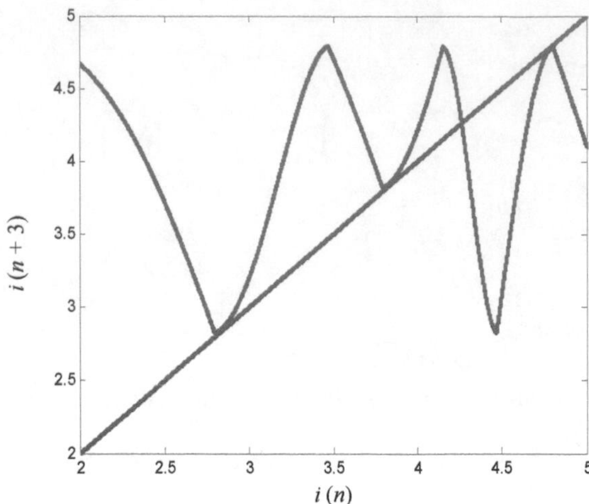

Figure 6. Graph of $f^3(i_n)$.

and the slope of the fixed point $(i^{*3}_n = 4.25)$ is –2. It means that

$$\frac{\partial}{\partial i_n} f^{(3)}(i_n, I_{ref},)\Big|_{i_n=2.82, I_{ref}=4.7915} = +1$$

$$\frac{\partial}{\partial i_n} f^{(3)}(i_n, I_{ref},)\Big|_{i_n=3.82, I_{ref}=4.7915} = +1$$

$$\frac{\partial}{\partial i_n} f^{(3)}(i_n, I_{ref},)\Big|_{i_n=4.79, I_{ref}=4.7915} = +1$$

It satisfies the condition (b) of theorem 1.

From (14) and (15), $\partial f^{(3)}(i_n)/\partial I_{ref}$ can be worked out,

Case 7. $t'_{n3} \geq T$.

$$\partial f^{(3)}(i_n)/\partial I_{ref} = 0 \tag{16}$$

Case 8. $t'_{n3} < T$.

$$\frac{\partial}{\partial i_{ref}} f^{(3)}(i_n, I_{ref}) = \frac{de^{-ktn_3}}{dI_{ref}}(A_5 \sin\beta t_{n3} + A_2 \cos\beta t_{n3}) + e^{-ktn_3} \left(\frac{dA_5}{dI_{ref}}\sin\beta t_{n3} + A_5\frac{d\sin\beta t_{n3}}{dI_{ref}} + \frac{dA_2}{dI_{ref}}\cos\beta t_{n3} + A_2\frac{d\cos\beta t_{n3}}{dI_{ref}}\right) \tag{17}$$

Substituting of circuit parameters and the values of V_{CO}, I_{ref} into (16) and (17), gives

$$\frac{\partial}{\partial I_{ref}} f^{(3)}(i_n, I_{ref})\Big|_{i_n=2.82, I_{ref}=4.7915} = -0.1952 \neq 0$$

$$\frac{\partial}{\partial I_{ref}} f^{(3)}(i_n, I_{ref})\Big|_{i_n=3.82, I_{ref}=4.7915} = -0.1952 \neq 0$$

$$\frac{\partial}{\partial i_{ref}} f^{(3)}\left(i_{ref}, x\right)\Big|_{i_{ref}=4.7915, i_n=4.79} = 0.1639 \neq 0$$

There is no question that it satisfies condition (c) of theorem 1.

The secondary partial derivative $\frac{\partial^2}{\partial^2 i_n} f^{(3)}\left(i_n, I_{ref}\right)$ can be also obtained according to (14) and (15), which is as follows

Case 7. $t'_{n3} \geq T$.

$$\frac{\partial^2}{\partial^2 i_n} f^{(3)}\left(i_n, I_{ref}\right) = 0 \quad (18)$$

Case 8. $t'_{n3} < T$.

$$\frac{\partial^2}{\partial^2 i_n} f^{(3)}\left(i_n, I_{ref},\right) = \frac{\partial^2 e^{-kt_{n3}}}{\partial^2 i_n}\left(A_5 \sin \beta t_{n3} + A_2 \cos \beta t_{n3}\right)$$
$$+e^{-kt_{n3}} \frac{\partial^2}{\partial^2 i_n}\left(A_5 \sin \beta t_{n3} + A_2 \cos \beta t_{n3}\right) \quad (19)$$

Similarly, substituting of the parameters values into (18) and (19), gives

$$\frac{\partial^2}{\partial^2 i_n} f^{(3)}\left(i_n, I_{ref}\right)\Big|_{i_n=2.82, I_{ref}=4.7915} = 14.4706 \neq 0$$

$$\frac{\partial^2}{\partial^2 i_n} f^{(3)}\left(i_n, I_{ref}\right)\Big|_{i_n=3.82, I_{ref}=4.7915} = 14.4706 \neq 0$$

$$\frac{\partial^2}{\partial^2 i_n} f^{(3)}\left(i_n, I_{ref}\right)\Big|_{i_n=4.79, I_{ref}=4.7915} = -47.7344 \neq 0$$

Without question, it satisfies condition (d) of theorem 1.

In summary, the current mode controlled boost converter operating in CCM satisfies the hypothesis of theorem 1. Therefore, the discrete iterative map of $f^3(i_n)$ undergoes the tangent bifurcation at the fixed point, and the tangent bifurcation behavior occurs in this system.

4. Conclusions

The mechanism of tangent bifurcation in the current mode controlled boost converter operating in CCM is explored in this paper. Based on the discrete iterative map of the boost converter, by taking the capacitor voltage as a constant, and choosing the inductor current as the state variable, the one-dimensional discrete iterative maps of $f(i_n)$ and $f^{(3)}(i_n)$ have been derived. It is demonstrated in mechanism that the tangent bifurcation will happen inevitably in the boost converter according to the tangent bifurcation theorem. The computer simulations, such as discrete iterative maps, bifurcation diagram with reference current I_{ref} as parameter, Lyapunov exponent are used to verify the phenomenon. It has been shown that tangent bifurcation does exist for this system. The method presented in the paper provides the theoretical basics for analyzing the tangent bifurcation and chaos. It has generality and can be also used to analyze the tangent bifurcation of other kinds of DC-DC converters.

5. References

[1] F. Angulo, G. Olivar and M. di Bernardo, "Two-Parameter Discontinuity-Induced Bifurcation Curves in a ZAD-Strategy-Controlled DC–DC Buck Converter," *IEEE Transactions on Circuits and Systems I: Regular Papers*, Vol. 55, No. 8, 2008, pp. 2393-2401.

[2] X. Q. Wu, S.-C. Wong, C. K. Tse and J. Lu, "Bifurcation Behavior of SPICE Simulation of Switching Converters: A Systematic Analysis of ErroneousResults," *IEEE Transactions on Power Electronics*, Vol. 22, No. 5, 2007, pp. 1743-1752.

[3] A. El Aroudi and R. Lewa, "Quasi-Periodic Route to Chaos in a PWM Voltage-Controlled DC-DC Boost Converter," *IEEE Transactions on Circuits and Systems I: Fundamental Theory and Applications*, Vol. 48, No. 8, 2001, pp. 967-978.

[4] Ch. Bi, J. M. Wang, Z. W. Lan, K. L. Jia and T. Hu, "Investigation of Bifurcation and Chaos in Forward Converter," *Proceedings International Conference on Mechatronics and Automation*, Harbin, 5-8 August 2007, pp. 663-668.

[5] X.-M. Wang, B. Zhang and D.-Y. Qiu, "Mechanism of Period-Doubling Bifurcation in DCM DC-DC Converter," *Acta Physica Sinice*, Vol. 57, No. 6, 2008, pp. 2728-2736.

[6] A. Kavitha and G. Uma, " Experimental Verification of Hopf Bifurcation in DC-DC Luo Converter," *IEEE Transactions on Power Electronics*, Vol. 23, No. 6, 2008, pp. 2878-2883.

[7] M. B. D'Amico, J. L. Moiola and E. E. Paolini, "Hopf Bifurcation for Maps: A Frequency-Domain Approach," *IEEE Transactions on Circuits and Systems I: Fundamental Theory and Applications*, Vol. 49, No. 3, 2002, pp. 281-288.

[8] M. Debbat, A. El Aroud, R. Giral and L. Martinez-Salamero, "Hopf Bifurcation in PWM Controlled Asymmetrical Interleaved Dual Boost DC-DC Converter," *Proceedings IEEE International Conference on Industrial Technology*, Vol. 2, Maribor, 10-12 December 2003, pp. 860-865.

[9] Z. T. Zhusubaliyev, E. A. Soukhoterin and E. Mosekilde, "Quasi-Periodicity and Border-Collision Bifurcations in a DC-DC Converter with Pulsewidth Modulation," *IEEE Transactions on Circuits and Systems I: Fundamental Theory and Applications*, Vol. 50, No. 8, 2003, pp. 1047-1057.

[10] M. Yue, C. K. Tse, T. Kousaka and H. Kawakami, "Connecting Border Collision with Saddle-Node in Switched Dynamical Systems," *IEEE Transactions on Circuits and Systems II: Express Briefs*, Vol. 52, No. 9, 2005, pp. 581-585.

[11] H. Khammari and M. Benrejeb, "Tangent Bifurcation in Doubling Period Process of a Resonant Circuit's Responses," *Proceedings IEEE International Conference on Industrial Technology*, Vol. 3, Hammamet, 8-10 December 2004, pp. 1281-1286.

[12] Y. F. Zhou and J. N. Chen, "Tangent Bifurcation and Intermittent Chaos in Current-Mode Controlled Boost Converter," *Proceedings of the Chinese Society for Electrical Engineering*, Vol.25, No.1, 2005, pp. 23-26.

[13] B. L. Hao, "Starting with Parabolas, an Introduction to Chaotic Dynamics," Shanghai Scientific and Technological Education Publishing House, Shanghai, 1993.

[14] R. C. Robinson, "An Introduction to Dynamical Systems: Continuous and Discrete," Pearson Prentice Hall, New Jersey, 2004.

[15] C. K. Tse, "Flip Bifimcation and Chaos in the Three-State Boost Switching Regulars," *IEEE Transactions on Circuits Systems I: Fundamental Theory and Applications*, Vol. 41, No. 1, 1994, pp. 16-23.

[16] C. K. Tse and M. di Bernardo, "Complex Behavior in Switching Power Converters," *Proceedings of the IEEE*, Vol. 90, No. 5, 2002, pp. 768-781.

[17] B. Basak and S. Parui, "Exploration of Bifurcation and Chaos in Buck Converter Supplied from a Rectifier," *IEEE Transactions on Power Electronics*, Vol. 25, No. 6, 2010, pp. 1556-1564.

[18] F.-H. Hsieh, K.-M. Lin and J.-H. Su, "Chaos Phenomenon in UC3842 Current-Programmed Flyback Converters," *Proceedings IEEE Conference on Industrial Electronics and Applications*, Xi'an, 25-27 May 2009, pp. 166-171.

[19] J. H. Chen, K. T. Chau and C. C. Chan, "Analysis of Chaos in Current-Mode-Controlled DC Drive Systems," *IEEE Transactions on Industrial Electronics*, Vol. 47, No. 1, 2000, pp. 67-76.

[20] K. W. E. Cheng, M. J. Liu and Y. L. Ho, "Experimental Confirmation of Frequency Correlation for Bifurcation in Current-Mode Controlled Buck-Boost Converters," *IEEE Power Electronics Letters*, Vol. 1, No. 4, 2003, pp. 101-103.

8

Single MO-CCCCTA-Based Electronically Tunable Current/Trans-Impedance-Mode Biquad Universal Filter

Sajai Vir Singh[1], Sudhanshu Maheshwari[2], Durg Singh Chauhan[3]
[1]*Department of Electronics and Communications, Jaypee University of Information Technology, Waknaghat, India*
[2]*Department of Electronics Engineering, Zakir Hussain College of Engineering and Technology, Aligarh Muslim University, Aligarh, India*
[3]*Department of Electrical Engineering, Institute of Technology, Banaras Hindu University, Varanasi, India*

Abstract

This paper presents an electronically tunable current/trans-impedance-mode biquad universal filter employing only single multi-output current controlled current conveyor trans-conductance amplifier (MO-CCCCTA) and two grounded capacitors. The proposed filter realizes all the standard filter functions *i.e.* low pass (LP), band pass (BP) and high pass (HP), notch and all pass (AP) filters in the current form at high impedance output through appropriate selection of the input signals, without any matching conditions. Simultaneously, it can also realize all the standard filter functions in trans-impedance form from the same circuit topology. The circuit does not require inverting-type input current signal(s) and double input current signal(s) to realize all the responses in the design. The validity of proposed filter is verified through PSPICE simulations.

Keywords: Universal, Current-Mode, Trans-Impedance-Mode, Biquad Filter

1. Introduction

Analog electronic filters are important blocks, widely employed in continuous time signal processing. They are present in just about every piece of electronic equipment that are obvious types of equipments, such as radios, televisions and stereo systems. Test equipments such as spectrum analyzers and signal generators also need filters even where signals are connected into digital form, using digital to analog converters; analog filters are usually needed to prevent aliasing. Universal biquadratic filters belong to most popular analog filters, providing all standard filter functions (LP, BP, HP, Notch and AP), without modifying the circuit topology. Several filter realizations either in current-mode, where the input and the output variables are current, or in voltage-mode, where the input and output variables are voltage, have been reported using different active elements [1-22]. These filter circuits are classified as single input multiple output (SIMO) [1-10], multiple input single output (MISO) [11-19] and multiple input multiple output (MIMO) [20-22]. However, there are a number of applications in analog signal processing where it may be desirable to have active filters with input variable as current and output variable as voltage that is trans-impedance filters. Such filters can be used as an interface circuit connecting a current-mode circuit to a voltage-mode circuit and find direct applications with some sensors, the receiver base band (BB) blocks of modern radio systems and D/A converters which provide a current as output signal, avoiding a current to voltage conversion [23,24]. There are a small number of filter topologies operating in trans-impedance-mode reported in the literature [25-27]. These filter topologies reported in [24-26] cannot realize all the standard filter functions (LP, BP, HP, Notch and AP). As far as the topic of this paper is concerned, the filter circuits operated in either current-mode or trans-impedance-mode or in both modes simultaneously, using a single active element, are of interest. Single active element based current-mode filters with multi-input are reported in [18-20]. The circuits in references [18,19] use three inputs and one output and realize all the standard filter functions at high impedance output terminal. The filter circuit of [18] employs single CCCII, two grounded capacitors and one floating resistor and suffers from the following disadvantages: 1) requirement of passive component matching conditions, 2) requirement of inverting-type input current signal, 3) use of floating resistor which is not suitable for IC fabrications while other filter circuit of [19] uses single CCCCTA, two grounded capacitors and suffers from the following two disadvantages: requirement of double input current signal to obtain an all-pass response and use of one capacitor at port X which limits the use of filter in high frequency range since it effectively appears in series with X terminal resistance [28]. Lastly, a three inputs and two outputs current-mode single DO-CCCDTA based filter circuit [20] also realizes all the standard filter functions at high impedance outputs but it still require double input current signal to obtain an all-pass response. Up until now, no previous paper has reported a filter based on single active element which can realize all the standard responses in current as well as trans-impedance form, together, without any matching conditions, from the same topology. In this paper a single MO-CCCCTA-based electronically tunable current/trans-impedance-mode biquad universal filter is proposed. It also uses two grounded capacitors. The proposed filter realizes all the standard filter functions *i.e.* LP, BP, HP, notch and AP filters in the current form at high impedance output through appropriate selection of the input signals, without any matching conditions. Simultaneously, it can also realize all the standard filter functions in trans-impedance form from the same circuit topology. The proposed circuit does not require inverting-type input current signal(s) and double input current signal(s) to realize all the responses in the design. The proposed circuit does not use capacitor at port X so this circuit is suitable in high frequency range. The circuit possesses low active and passive sensitivity. Moreover, the pole frequency (ω_o) can be independently tuned without disturbing the parameter ω_o/Q through adjusting the bias current of MO-CCCCTA. The performance of proposed circuit is illustrated by PSPICE simulation using 0.35 μ CMOS parameters.

2. Proposed Circuit

CCCCTA is relatively new proposed current mode active building block [19] which is the modified version of CCTA. This device can be operated in both current and voltage modes, providing flexibility. In addition, it can offer several advantages such as high slew rate, high speed, wider bandwidth and simpler implementation. Moreover, in the CCCCTA one can control the parasitic resistance at X (R_X) port by input bias current. The MO-CCCCTA properties can be described in the following matrix equation

$$\begin{bmatrix} I_Y \\ V_X \\ I_{-Za,-Zc} \\ I_{Zb} \\ I_{-Ob} \\ I_{-Oc} \end{bmatrix} = \begin{bmatrix} 0 & 0 & 0 & 0 & 0 & 0 \\ R_x & 1 & 0 & 0 & 0 & 0 \\ -1 & 0 & 0 & 0 & 0 & 0 \\ 1 & 0 & 0 & 0 & 0 & 0 \\ 0 & 0 & -g_{mb} & 0 & 0 & 0 \\ 0 & 0 & 0 & -g_{mc} & 0 & 0 \end{bmatrix} \begin{bmatrix} I_X \\ V_Y \\ V_{Zb} \\ V_{-Zc} \\ V_{-Ob} \\ V_{-Oc} \end{bmatrix} \quad (1)$$

where R_X is the parasitic resistance at X terminal. g_{mb} and g_{mc} are trans-conductance of CCCCTA. The schematic symbol of MO-CCCCTA is illustrated in **Figure 1**. CMOS implementation of MO-CCCCTA is shown in **Figure 2**. For a CMOS CCCCTA [29], the R_X, g_{mb} and g_{mc} can be expressed to be

$$R_X = \frac{1}{\sqrt{8\beta_n I_B}}, \quad g_{mb} = \sqrt{\beta_n I_{Sb}} \text{ and } g_{mc} = \sqrt{\beta_n I_{Sc}} \quad (2)$$

where

$$\beta_n = \mu_n C_{OX} \frac{W}{L} \quad (3)$$

where μ_n, C_{OX} and W/L are the electron mobility, gate oxide capacitance per unit area and transistor aspect ratio, respectively. I_B, I_{Sb} and I_{Sc} are the biasing currents of MO-CCCCTA.

The proposed biquad filter circuit as shown in **Figure 3** uses only single MO-CCCCTA and two grounded capacitors. By routine analysis of the circuit in **Figure 3**, the output current I_O and output voltage V_O can be obtained as

$$I_O = \frac{I_1 s^2 C_1 C_2 - I_2 s C_2 g_{mc} + I_3 g_{mb} g_{mc}}{s^2 C_1 C_2 + s C_2 g_{mc} + g_{mb} g_{mc}} \quad (4)$$

$$V_O = \frac{R_x \left(I_1 s^2 C_1 C_2 - I_2 s C_2 g_{mc} + I_3 g_{mb} g_{mc} \right)}{s^2 C_1 C_2 + s C_2 g_{mc} + g_{mb} g_{mc}} \quad (5)$$

From Equations (4) and (5), various filter responses in current form as well as in trans-impedance form can be

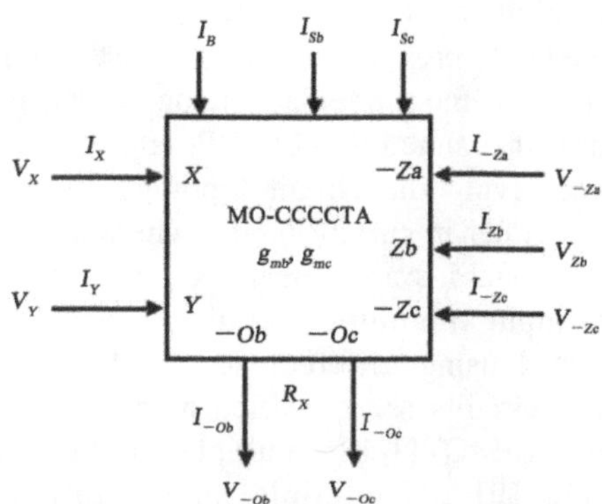

Figure 1. MO-CCCCTA symbol.

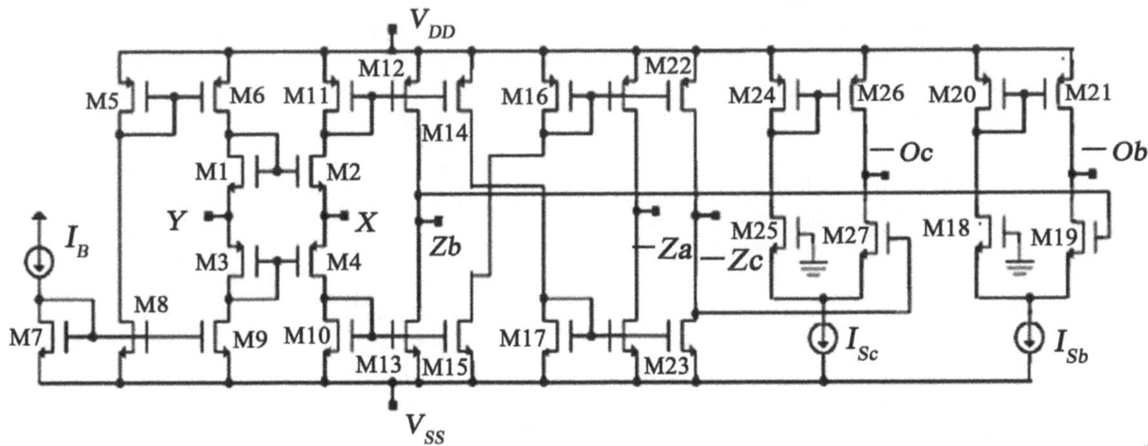

Figure 2. CMOS implementation of MO-CCCCTA.

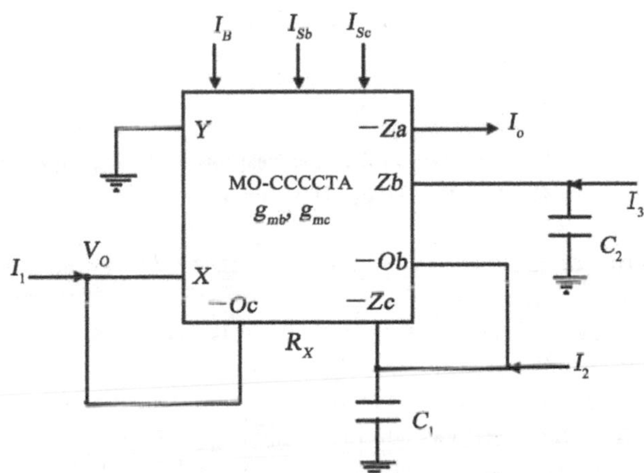

Figure 3. proposed current/trans-impedance-mode universal filter.

obtained through appropriate selection of input currents.

1) High pass response in current form as well as in trans-impedance form, with $I_1 = I_{in}, \ I_2 = I_3 = 0$.

2) Low pass response in current form as well as in trans-impedance form, with $I_1 = I_2 = 0, \ I_3 = I_{in}$.

3) Inverted band pass response in current form as well as in trans-impedance form, with $I_1 = I_3 = 0, \ I_2 = I_{in}$.

4) Notch response in current form as well as in trans-impedance form, with $I_1 = I_3 = I_{in}, \ I_2 = 0$.

5) All pass response in current form as well as in trans-impedance form, with $I_1 = I_2 = I_3 = I_{in}$.

Thus, the circuit is capable of realizing all the standard filter responses in current as well as in trans-impedance-mode from the same configuration, without any matching constraints. Moreover, there is no requirement of inverting-type input current signal(s) and double input current signal(s) to realize all the responses in the design.

The filter parameters pole frequency (ω_o), the quality factor (Q) and bandwidth (BW) ω_o/Q can be expressed as

$$\omega_o = \left(\frac{g_{mc}g_{mb}}{C_1C_2}\right)^{\frac{1}{2}} = \left(\frac{1}{C_1C_2}\beta_n\right)^{\frac{1}{2}}\left(I_{Sc}I_{Sb}\right)^{\frac{1}{4}},$$

$$Q = \left(\frac{C_1g_{mb}}{C_2g_{mc}}\right)^{\frac{1}{2}} = \left(\frac{C_1}{C_2}\right)^{\frac{1}{2}}\left(\frac{I_{Sb}}{I_{Sc}}\right)^{\frac{1}{4}} \quad (6)$$

and

$$BW = \frac{\omega_O}{Q} = \frac{g_{mc}}{C_1} = \frac{1}{C_1}\left(\beta_n I_{Sc}\right)^{\frac{1}{2}} \quad (7)$$

From (6) by maintaining the ratio I_{Sb} and I_{Sc} to be constant, it can be remarked that the pole frequency can be adjusted by I_{Sb} and I_{Sc} without affecting the quality factor. In addition, pole frequency can be controlled by I_{Sb} without affecting bandwidth (BW) of the system. To see the effects of non idealities, the defining equations of the MO-CCCCTA can be rewritten as the following.

$$V_X = \beta V_Y + I_X R_X, \ I_{-Za} = -\alpha_a I_X, \ I_{Zb} = \alpha_b I_X \quad (8)$$

$$I_{-Zc} = -\alpha_c I_X, \ I_{-Ob} = -\gamma_b g_{mb} V_{Zb}, \ I_{-Oc} = -\gamma_c g_{mc} V_{-Zc} \quad (9)$$

where β, α_a, α_b, α_c, γ_b and γ_c are transferred error values deviated from one. In the case of non-ideal and re-analyzing the proposed filter in **Figure 3**, it yields the current output and voltage output as

$$I_O = \frac{\alpha_a(I_1s^2C_1C_2 - I_2s\gamma_cC_2g_{mc} + I_3\gamma_b\gamma_cg_{mb}g_{mc})}{s^2C_1C_2 + s\gamma_c\alpha_cC_2g_{mc} + \gamma_b\gamma_c\alpha_bg_{mb}g_{mc}} \quad (10)$$

$$V_O = \frac{\alpha_aR_X\left(I_1s^2C_1C_2 - I_2s\gamma_cC_2g_{mc} + I_3\gamma_b\gamma_cg_{mb}g_{mc}\right)}{s^2C_1C_2 + s\gamma_c\alpha_cC_2g_{mc} + \gamma_b\gamma_c\alpha_bg_{mb}g_{mc}} \quad (11)$$

In this case, the ω_o and Q are changed to

$$\omega_o = \left(\frac{\gamma_b\gamma_c\alpha_bg_{mb}g_{mc}}{C_1C_2}\right)^{\frac{1}{2}}, \ Q = \frac{1}{\alpha_c}\left(\frac{\gamma_b\alpha_bC_1g_{mb}}{\gamma_cC_2g_{mc}}\right)^{\frac{1}{2}} \quad (12)$$

The all active and passive sensitivities can be found as

$$S^{\omega_o}_{C_1,C_2} = -\frac{1}{2},\ S^{\omega_o}_{\gamma_b,\gamma_c,\alpha_b,g_{mb},g_{mc}} = \frac{1}{2},\ S^{\omega_o}_{\alpha_a,\alpha_c,\beta,R_X} = 0 \quad (13)$$

$$S^{Q}_{C_2,g_{mc},\gamma_c} = -\frac{1}{2},\ S^{Q}_{C_1,\alpha_b,\gamma_b,g_{mb}} = \frac{1}{2},\ S^{Q}_{\alpha_c} = -1\ \ S^{Q}_{\alpha_a,\beta,R_X} = 0 \quad (14)$$

From the above results, it can be observed that all the active and passive sensitivities are equal or less than 1 in magnitude.

3. Simulation Results

The PSPICE simulations are carried out to demonstrate the feasibility of the proposed circuit using CMOS implementation as shown in **Figure 2.** The simulations use a 0.35 μm MOSFET [30] from TSMC. The dimensions of PMOS are determined as $W = 3$ μm and $L = 2$ μm. In NMOS transistors, the dimensions are $W = 3$ μm and $L = 4$ μm. The circuit is designed for $Q = 1$ and $f_o = \omega_o/2\pi = 1.57$ MHz. The active and passive components are chosen as $I_B = 7.5$ μA, $I_{Sb} = I_{Sc} = 30.65$ μA and $C_1 = C_2 = 7.5$ pF. **Figure 4** Shows the simulated gain and phase responses of the HP, LP, BP, Notch and AP in the current form, of the proposed circuit in **Figure 3**. The supply voltages are $V_{DD} = -V_{SS} = 2.5$ V. The simulated pole frequency is obtained as 1.35 MHz. It is noted that simulation results agree quite well with theoretical ones as expected, whereas the difference between them arises from non-idealities such as non ideal gain and parasitic elements. The power dissipations of the proposed circuit for the design values is found as 0.629 mW that is a low value.

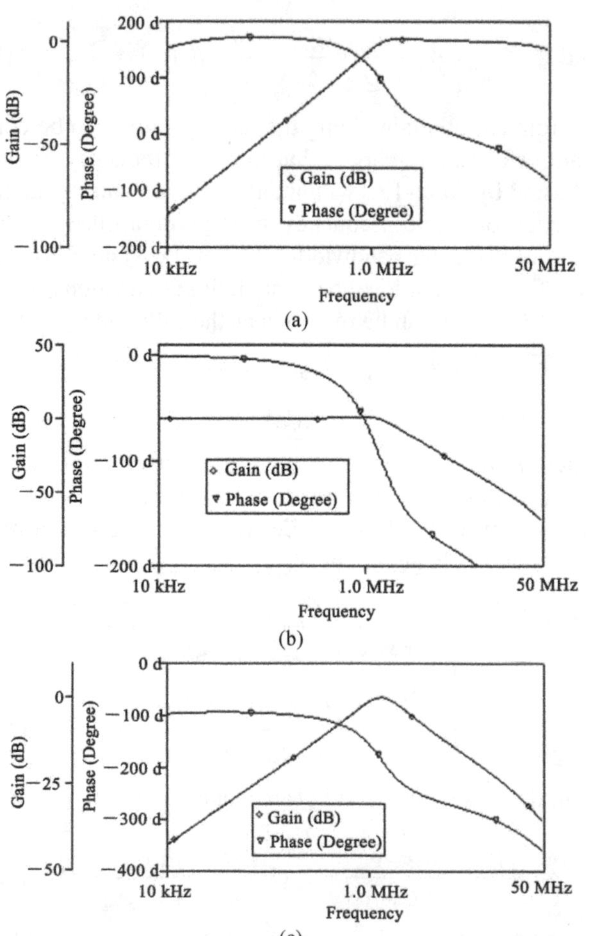

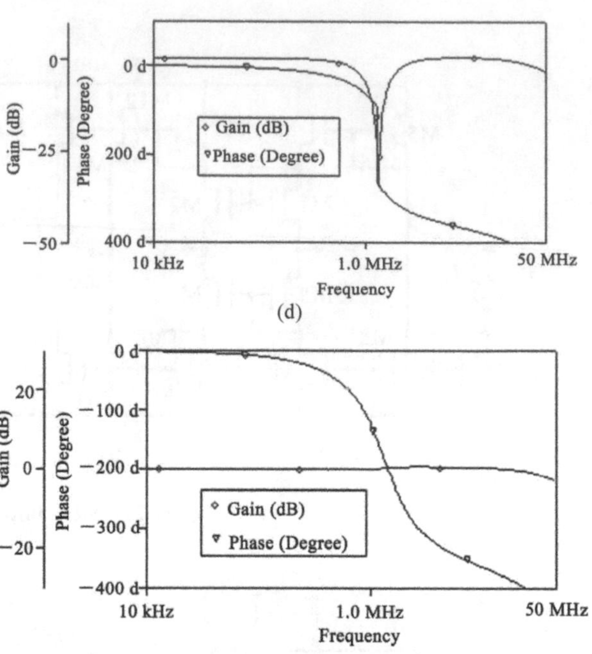

Figure 4. Current gain and Phase responses of the proposed filter (a) HP, (b) LP, (c) BP, (d) Notch and (e) AP.

Next, the frequency tuning aspect of the circuit is verified for a constant Q (= 1) value for the BP response in current-mode. The bias currents I_{Sb} and I_{Sc} are varied simultaneously, by keeping its ratio to be constant. The pole frequency variation, for $Q = 1$, is shown in **Figure 5**. The frequency is found to vary as 650 kHz, 990 kHz, 1.34 MHz and 1.8 MHz for four values of $I_{Sb} = I_{Sc} = 6$ μA, 15 μA, 30 μA and 60 μA, respectively. Further simulations are carried out to verify the total harmonic distortion (THD). The circuit is simulated for THD analysis at BP output in current-mode, by applying sinusoidal input current of varying amplitude and constant frequency. The THD values for the input current signal having amplitude less than 40 μA, at frequency 1.35 MHz remain in acceptable limits *i.e.* 4%. The time domain response of band-pass output in current form is shown in **Figure 6**. It is observed that 40 μA peak to peak input current sinusoidal signal levels are possible without significant distortions. Thus both THD analysis and time domain response of BP output in current-mode confirm the practical utility of the proposed circuit.

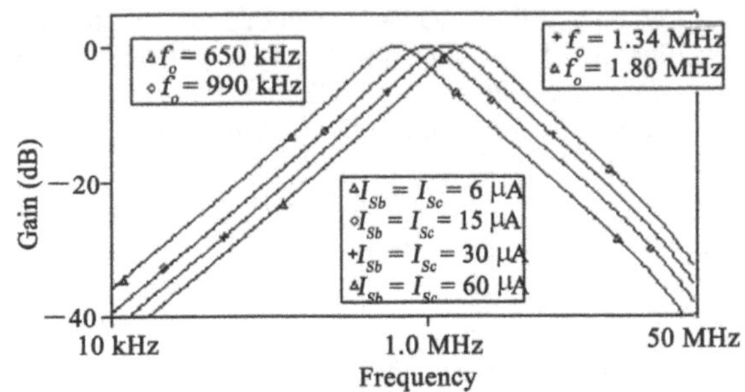

Figure 5. Band pass responses in current-mode for different values of $I_{Sb} = I_{Sc}$ of the proposed filter.

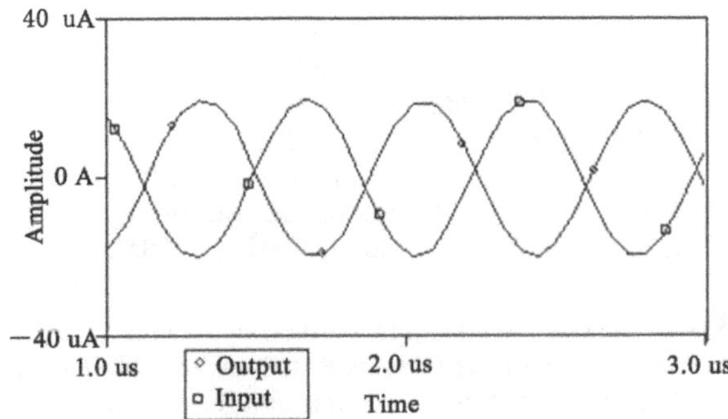

Figure 6. The sinusoidal input having frequency of 1.35 MHz and corresponding band pass output waveforms in current-mode of the proposed filter.

4. Conclusions

This paper presents an electronically tunable current/trans-impedance-mode biquad universal filter using single MO-CCCCTA. The proposed filter offers the following advantages: 1) realization of LP, HP, BP, Notch and AP responses in current form as well as in trans-impedance form without changing the circuit topology; 2) both the capacitors being permanently grounded; 3) low sensitivity figures, low THD and low power consumptions; 4) independent current control of ω_o without disturbing ω_o/Q; 5) no requirement of components matching conditions to get all filter responses; 6) no requirements of inverting-type input current signal(s) and double input current signal(s) to realize the response(s) in the design; 7) single active element.

5. References

[1] S. Minaei and S. Türköz, "New Current-Mode Current-Controlled Universal Filter with Single Input and Three Outputs," *International Journal of Electronics*, Vol. 88, No. 3, 2001, pp. 333-337.

[2] T. Katoh, T. Tsukutani, Y. Sumi and Y. Fukui, "Electronically Tunable Current-Mode Universal Filter Employing CCCIIs and Grounded Capacitors," *International Symposium on Intelligent Signal Processing and Communications*, 2006, pp. 107-110.

[3] S. Minaei and S. Türköz, "Current-Mode Electronically Tunable Universal Filter Using Only Plus-Type Current Controlled Conveyors and Grounded Capacitors," *Electronics and Telecommunication Research Institute Journal*, Vol. 26, No. 4, 2004, pp. 292-296.

[4] I. A. Khan and M. H. Zaidi, "Multifunction Translinear-C Current Mode Filter," *International Journal of Electronics*, Vol. 87, No. 6, 2000, pp. 1047-1051.

[5] M. Soliman, "Current Mode Universal Filters Using Current Conveyors," *Circuits Systems and Signal Processing*, Vol. 27, No. 3, 2008, pp. 405-427.

[6] T. Tsukutani, Y. Sumi, S. Iwanari and Y. Fukui, "Novel Current-Mode Biquad Using MO-CCCIIs and Grounded Capacitors," *Proceedings of* 2005 *International Symposium on Intelligent Signal Processing and Communication Systems*, 13-16 December 2005, pp. 433-436.

[7] D. R. Bhaskar, A. K. Singh, A. K. Sharma and R. Senani, "New OTA-C Universal Current-Mode/Trans-Admittance Biquads," *Institute of Electronics, Information and Communication Engineering Electronics Express*, Vol. 2, No. 1, 2005, pp. 8-13.

[8] J. Wu and E. I. El-Masry, "Universal Voltage and Current-Mode OTAs Based Biquads," *International Journal of Electronics*, Vol. 85, No. 5, 1998, pp. 553-560.

[9] C. M. Chang and M. J. Lee, "Voltage-Mode Multifunction Filter with Single Input and Three Outputs Using Two Compound Current Conveyors," *IEEE Transactions on Circuits and Systems- I: Fundamental Theory and Applications*, Vol. 46, No. 11, 1999, pp. 1364-1365.

[10] S. Maheshwari, "Analogue Signal Processing Applications Using a New Circuit Topology," *IET Circuits, Devices and Systems*, Vol. 3, No. 3, 2009, pp. 106-115.

[11] T. Praveen, M. T. Ahmed and I. A. Khan, "A Canonical Voltage-Mode Universal CCCII-C Filter," *Journal of Active and Passive Devices*, Vol. 4, No. 1-2, 2009, pp. 7-12.

[12] S. Maheshwari, "High Performance Voltage-Mode Multifunction Filter with Minimum Component Count," *WSEAS Transactions on Electronics*, Vol. 5, No. 6, 2008, pp. 244-249.

[13] M. T. Abuelma'atti and N. A. Tassaduq, "A Novel Three Inputs and One Output Universal Current-Mode Filter Using Plus-Type CCIIs," *Microelectronics Journal*, Vol. 30, No. 3, 1999, pp. 287-292.

[14] R. Senani, "New Universal Current Mode Biquad Employing All Grounded Passive Components but Only Two DOCCs," *Journal of Active and Passive Devices*, Vol. 1, No. 3-4, 2006, pp. 281-288.

[15] M. T. Abuelma'atti and M. L. Al-qahtani, "Universal

Current-Contolled Current-Mode Filter with Three Inputs and One Output Using Current Controlled Conveyor," *Active Passive Electronics Components*, Vol. 21, No. 1, 1998, pp. 33-41.

[16] W. Tangsriart and W. Surakampontorm, "Electronically Tunable Current-Mode Universal Filter Employing Only Plus-Type Current-Controlled Conveyors and Grounded Capacitors," *Circuits Systems and Signal Processing*, Vol. 25, No. 6, 2006, pp. 701-713.

[17] W. Tangsrirat and W. Surakampontorm, "Low-Component Current-Mode Universal Filter Using Current-Controlled Conveyors and Grounded Capacitors," *Journal of Active and Passive Devices*, Vol. 4, No. 3, 2009, pp. 259-264.

[18] C. M. Chang, "Universal Active Current Filter Using Single Second-Generation Current Controlled Conveyor," *International Journal of Circuits, Systems and Signal Processing*, Vol. 1, No. 1, 2007, pp. 194-198.

[19] M. Siripruchyanun and W. Jaikla, "Current Controlled Current Conveyor Transconductance Amplifier (CCCCTA): A Building Block for Analog Signal Processing," *Electrical Engineering*, Vol. 90, No. 6, 2008, pp. 443-453.

[20] M. Siripruchyanun and W. Jaikla, "Electronically Controllable Current-Mode Universal Biquad Filter Using Single DO-CCCDTA," *Circuits System Signal Processing*, Vol. 27, No. 1, 2008, pp. 113-122.

[21] W. Tangsriart, "Current-Tunable Current-Mode Multifunction Filter Based on Dual-Output Current-Controlled Conveyors," *International Journal of Electronics and Communications*, Vol. 61, No. 8, 2007, pp. 528-533.

[22] T. Tsukutani, Y. Sumi and N. Yabuki, "Versatile Current Mode Biquadratic Circuit Using Only Plus Type CCCIIs and Grounded Capacitors," *International Journal of Electronics*, Vol. 94, No. 12, 2007, pp.1147-1156.

[23] Y. Wang and R. Raut, "A Design of Transresistance Amplifier for High Gain-Bandwidth Applications," *Proceedings of the* 2003 10*th IEEE International Conference on Electronics, Circuits and Systems*, 14-17 December 2003, pp. 185-188.

[24] A. Carlosena and E. Cabral, "Novel Transimpedance Filter Topology for Instrumentation," *IEEE Transactions on Instrumentation and Measurement*, Vol. 46, No. 4, 1997, pp. 862-867.

[25] M. Soliman, "Mixed-Mode Biquad Circuits," *Microelectronics Journal*, Vol. 27, No. 6, 1996, pp. 591-594.

[26] J. Ramirez-Angulo, M. Robinson and E. Sanchez-Sinencio, "Current-Mode Continuous-Time Filters: Two Design Approaches," *IEEE Transactions on Circuits and Systems-II: Analog and Digital Signal Processing*, Vol. 39, No. 6, 1992, pp. 337-341.

[27] S. Minaei, G. Topcu and O. Cicekoglu, "Low Input Impedance Trans-Impedance Type Multifunction Filter Using Only Active Elements," *International Journal of Electronics*, Vol. 92, No. 7, 2005, pp. 385-392.

[28] A. Fabre, O. Saiid and H. Barthelemy, "On the Frequency Limitations of the Circuits Based on Second Generation Current Conveyors," *Analog Integrated Circuits and Signal Processing*, Vol. 7, No. 2, 1995, pp. 113-129.

[29] M. Siripruchyanun, P. Silapan and W. Jaikla, "Realization of CMOS Current Controlled Current Conveyor Transconductance Amplifier and Its Application," *Journal of Active and Passive Devices*, Vol. 4, No. 1-2, 2009, pp. 35-53.

[30] E. Yuce, S. Tokar, A. Kizilkaya and O. Cicekoglu, "CCII-Based PID Controllers Employing Grounded Passive Componensts," *International Journal of Electronics and Communications*, Vol. 60, No. 5, 2006, pp. 399-403.

9

Voltage/Current-Mode Multifunction Filters Using One Current Feedback Amplifier and Grounded Capacitors

Jiun-Wei Horng, Chun-Li Hou, Wei-Shyang Huang, Dun-Yih Yang
Department of Electronic Engineering,Chung Yuan Christian University,Chung-Li, Taiwan, China

Abstract

One configuration for realizing voltage-mode multifunction filters and another configuration for realizing current-mode multifunction filters using current feedback amplifiers (CFAs) are presented. The proposed voltage-mode circuit exhibit simultaneously lowpass and bandpass filters. The proposed current-mode circuit exhibit simultaneously lowpass, bandpass and highpass filters. The proposed circuits offer the following features: No requirements for component matching conditions; low active and passive sensitivities; employing only grounded capacitors and the ability to obtain multifunction filters from the same circuit configuration.

Keywords: Current Feedback Amplifier, Active Filter, Voltage-Mode, Current-Mode

1. Introduction

The current feedback amplifier (CFA) can provide not only constant bandwidth independent of closed-loop gain but also high slew-rate capability. Thus, it is beneficial to use a current feedback amplifier as a basic building block to realize analogue signal processing circuits [1-12].

In 1992 [7], Fabre proposed a voltage-mode bandpass and highpass filters circuit by using two CFAs, one grounded capacitor, one floating capacitor and three resistors. In 1993 [8], Fabre proposed another voltage-mode or current-mode biquads. The voltage-mode biquad exhibits simultaneously bandpass and highpass filters by using one CFA, one grounded capacitor, one floating capacitor and two resistors. The current-mode biquad exhibits simultaneously bandpass and highpass filters by using one CFA, two grounded capacitors and two resistors. Several single-CFA voltage-mode biquads were proposed in [9-11]. However, only one filter function (lowpass, bandpass or highpass) can be obtained in each realization, which implies the need to change the circuit topology to obtain other types of filter functions. Moreover, these single-CFA voltage-mode biquads employ floating capacitors. In 1995 [12], Liu proposed four voltage-mode biquads with high input impedance for realization lowpass, bandpass or highpass filters by using two CFAs, two (or three) capacitors and three (or two) resistors. However, only one filter function can be obtained in each realization. Moreover, two topologies of Liu's circuits used floating capacitors. In 1996 [10], Soliman proposed many voltage-mode biquadratic filter circuits. The four two-CFA biquads in [10] realize lowpass and bandpass filters simultaneously and using only grounded capacitors.

In this paper, a new configuration is proposed to realize voltage-mode lowpass and bandpass filters simultaneously by using one CFA, two grounded capacitors and three resistors. One more filtering signal can be obtained with respect to the previous single-CFA biquads in [9-11] and two-CFA biquads in [12]. With respect to the voltage-mode biquads in [7-8], the proposed circuit uses only grounded capacitors. The use of grounded capacitors makes the proposed circuit attractive for integrated circuit implementation [13]. With respect to the voltage-mode two-CFA lowpass and bandpass biquads in [10], the proposed circuit uses one less active components.

One new configuration is proposed to realize current-mode lowpass, bandpass and highpass filters simultaneously. One more filtering signal can be obtained with respect to the previous current-mode biquad in [8]. Critical component matching conditions are not required in the design of all proposed circuits.

2. Voltage-Mode Circuit

Using standard notation, the port relations of a CFA can

be characterized by
$v_x = v_y$, $v_o = v_z$, $i_z = i_x$ and $i_y = 0$. The proposed voltage-mode circuit is shown in **Figure 1**. The output transfer functions of **Figure 1** can be expressed as

$$\frac{V_{lp}}{V_{in}} = \frac{-G_1G_3}{s^2C_1C_2 + sC_2(G_1+G_2+G_3)+G_2G_3} \quad (1)$$

$$\frac{V_{bp}}{V_{in}} = \frac{sC_2G_1}{s^2C_1C_2 + sC_2(G_1+G_2+G_3)+G_2G_3} \quad (2)$$

Thus, the circuit realizes an inverting lowpass signal at V_{lp} and a non-inverting bandpass signal at V_{bp}, simultaneously. The circuit employs two grounded capacitors, three resistors and only one CFA. Critical component matching conditions are not required. Because the output impedance of the CFA (terminal v_o) is very small, the output terminal of V_{lp} can be directly connected to the next stage. The various parameter values of **Figure 1** are given by:

$$\omega_o = \sqrt{\frac{G_2G_3}{C_1C_2}}, \quad \frac{\omega_o}{Q} = \frac{G_1+G_2+G_3}{C_1} \quad \text{and}$$

$$Q = \frac{1}{G_1+G_2+G_3}\sqrt{\frac{C_1G_2G_3}{C_2}} \quad (3)$$

The gain constants are

$$H_{o(lp)} = -\frac{G_1}{G_2} \quad \text{and} \quad H_{o(bp)} = \frac{G_1}{G_1+G_2+G_3} \quad (4)$$

One possible design equations for the specified ω_o and Q can be obtained by

$$\begin{cases} C_1 = 9C_2Q^2 \\ G_1 = G_2 = G_3 = 3C_2\omega_oQ \end{cases} \quad (5)$$

Under the design Equation (5), the gain constants of **Figure 1** become

$$H_{o(lp)} = -1 \quad \text{and} \quad H_{o(bp)} = \frac{1}{3} \quad (6)$$

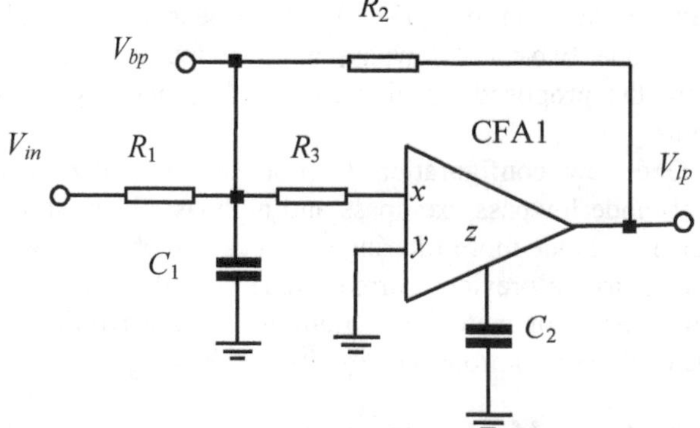

Figure 1. The proposed voltage-mode lowpass and bandpass filter.

All capacitors are grounded in **Figure 1**. The use of grounded capacitors is particularly attractive for integrated circuit implementation [13]. Moreover, the capacitor C_2 in **Figure 1** is connected to the z terminals of the CFA, this design offers another feature of a direct incorporation of the parasitic compensation capacitance (C_p) as a part of the main capacitance [14]. Note that, while cascade the bandpass signal of **Figure 1**, other buffering device is needed because the output impedance of V_{bp} in **Figure 1** is not small.

Taking into account the tracking errors of CFA, namely $v_x = \beta(s)v_y$, $v_o = \gamma(s)v_z$ and $i_z = \alpha(s)i_x$, where $\alpha(s)$ and $\beta(s)$ represent the frequency transfers of the internal current and voltage followers of the CFA, respectively, and $\gamma(s)$ represents the frequency transfer of the output voltage follower of the CFA. They can be approximated by the first order lowpass functions [8]. Assuming the circuits are working at frequencies much less than the corner frequencies of $\alpha(s)$, $\beta(s)$ and $\gamma(s)$, that is, $\beta = 1-\varepsilon_1$ and $\varepsilon_1(|\varepsilon_1| << 1)$ is the input voltage tracking error, $\gamma = 1-\varepsilon_2$ and $\varepsilon_2(|\varepsilon_2| << 1)$ is the output voltage tracking error, $\alpha = 1-\varepsilon_3$ and $\varepsilon_3(|\varepsilon_3| << 1)$ is the current tracking error of a CFA. The resonance angular frequency ω_o, bandwidth ω_o/Q and quality factor Q of **Figure 1** become

$$\omega_o = \sqrt{\frac{G_2G_3\alpha_1\gamma_1}{C_1C_2}}, \quad \frac{\omega_o}{Q} = \frac{G_1+G_2+G_3}{C_1} \quad \text{and}$$

$$Q = \frac{1}{G_1+G_2+G_3}\sqrt{\frac{C_1G_2G_3\alpha_1\gamma_1}{C_2}} \quad (7)$$

The active and passive sensitivities of this filter are

$$S^{\omega_o}_{G_2,G_3,\alpha_1,\gamma_1} = -S^{\omega_o}_{C_1,C_2} = \frac{1}{2}, \quad S^{Q}_{C_1,\alpha_1,\gamma_1} = -S^{Q}_{C_2} = \frac{1}{2},$$

$$S^{Q}_{G_1} = -\frac{G_1}{G_1+G_2+G_3}, \quad S^{Q}_{G_2} = \frac{1}{2} - \frac{G_2}{G_1+G_2+G_3},$$

$$S^{Q}_{G_3} = \frac{1}{2} - \frac{G_3}{G_1+G_2+G_3}.$$

All the active and passive sensitivities are no larger than 1.

3. Current-Mode Circuit

The proposed current-mode circuit is shown in **Figure 2**. The output transfer functions of **Figure 2** can be expressed as

$$\frac{I_{lp}}{I_{in}} = \frac{-G_3G_4}{s^2C_1C_2 + sC_2(G_1+G_2+G_3)+G_2G_3} \quad (8)$$

$$\frac{I_{bp1}}{I_{in}} = \frac{sC_2G_1}{s^2C_1C_2 + sC_2(G_1+G_2+G_3)+G_2G_3} \quad (9)$$

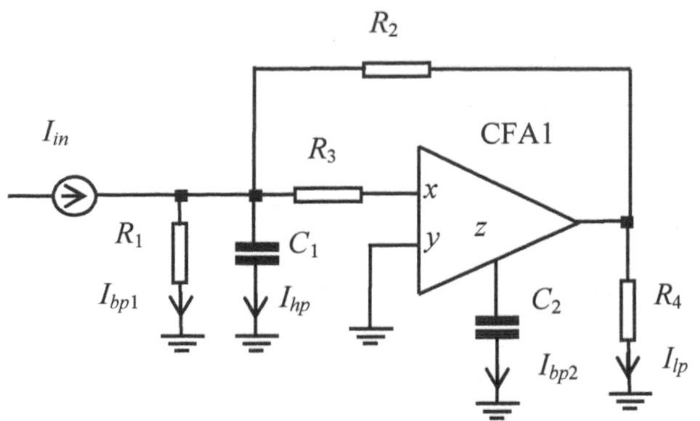

Figure 2. The first proposed current-mode filter.

$$\frac{I_{bp2}}{I_{in}} = \frac{-sC_2G_3}{s^2C_1C_2 + sC_2(G_1 + G_2 + G_3) + G_2G_3} \quad (10)$$

$$\frac{I_{hp}}{I_{in}} = \frac{s^2C_1C_2}{s^2C_1C_2 + sC_2(G_1 + G_2 + G_3) + G_2G_3} \quad (11)$$

Thus, the circuit realizes an inverting lowpass signal at I_{lp}, a non-inverting bandpass signal at I_{bp1}, an inverting bandpass signal at I_{bp2} and a non-inverting highpass signal at I_{hp}, simultaneously. The resonance angular frequency, ω_o, bandwidth, ω_o/Q, and quality factor, Q, have the same values as in Equation (3). The gains of **Figure 2** are

$$H_{o(lp)} = -\frac{G_4}{G_2},\ H_{o(bp1)} = \frac{G_1}{G_1 + G_2 + G_3},$$
$$H_{o(bp2)} = -\frac{G_3}{G_1 + G_2 + G_3} \text{ and } H_{o(hp)} = 1 \quad (12)$$

4. Non-ideal Equivalent Circuit of CFA

The non-ideal equivalent circuit model of the CFA is shown in **Figure 3**, where R_x is the x terminal input resistance, $R_y//(1/sC_y)$ represents the y terminal parasitic input impedance, $R_p//(1/sC_p)$ represents the parasitic impedance at the compensation terminal z [8]. The typical data sheet values of the various parasitics for the bipolar CFAs (such as AD844) are: $R_x = 50\,\Omega$, $C_p = 5.5$ pF, $R_p = 3$ MΩ, $R_y = 2$ MΩ and $C_y = 2$ pF. When non-ideal equivalent circuit model of the CFAs are used instead of ideal ones and assuming the circuits are working at frequencies much less than the corner frequencies of $\alpha(s)$, $\beta(s)$ and $\gamma(s)$, namely, $\alpha \cong \beta \cong \gamma \cong 1$, the voltage transfer functions of **Figure 1** become

$$\frac{V_{lp}}{V_{in}} = \frac{-G_1G_3'}{D(s)} \quad (13)$$

$$\frac{V_{bp}}{V_{in}} = \frac{sC_2'G_1 + G_1G_{p1}}{D(s)} \quad (14)$$

where

$$D(s) = s^2C_1C_2' + s\left[C_2'(G_1 + G_2 + G_3') + C_1G_{p1}\right] + G_2G_3' + G_{p1}(G_1 + G_2 + G_3') \quad (15)$$

$$G_3' = 1/(R_3 + \mathrm{R}_{X1});\ C_2' = C_2 + C_{p1} \quad (16)$$

From Equations (13) to (16), undesirable factors are yielded by the effects of CFA's parasitic impedances. It is found that such factors can be made negligible by operating the filters in high frequencies. But, if the filters are used for lower frequencies, the parasitic impedances could not be negligible. So the characteristics will depart from the theoretical values, especially for the bandpass filter signal in **Figure 1**. Note that the influence of the parasitic elements on the frequency response of the current-mode filter in **Figure 2** can be studies by a similar procedure, as above.

5. Experimental Results

Experiments were carried out to demonstrate the feasibility of the proposed circuits. The CFA was imple-

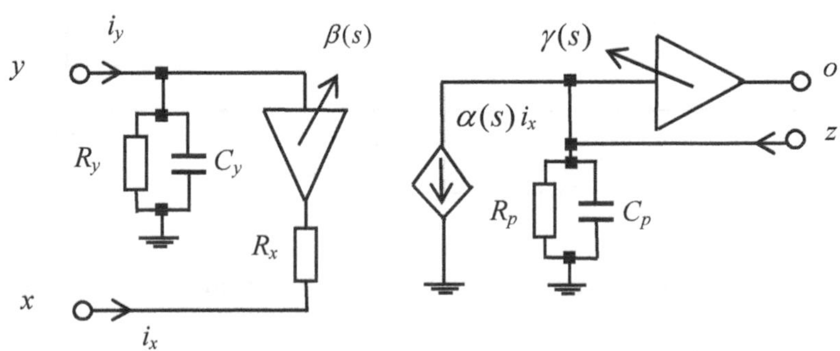

Figure 3. Non-ideal equivalent circuit of the CFA includes the parasitic impedances.

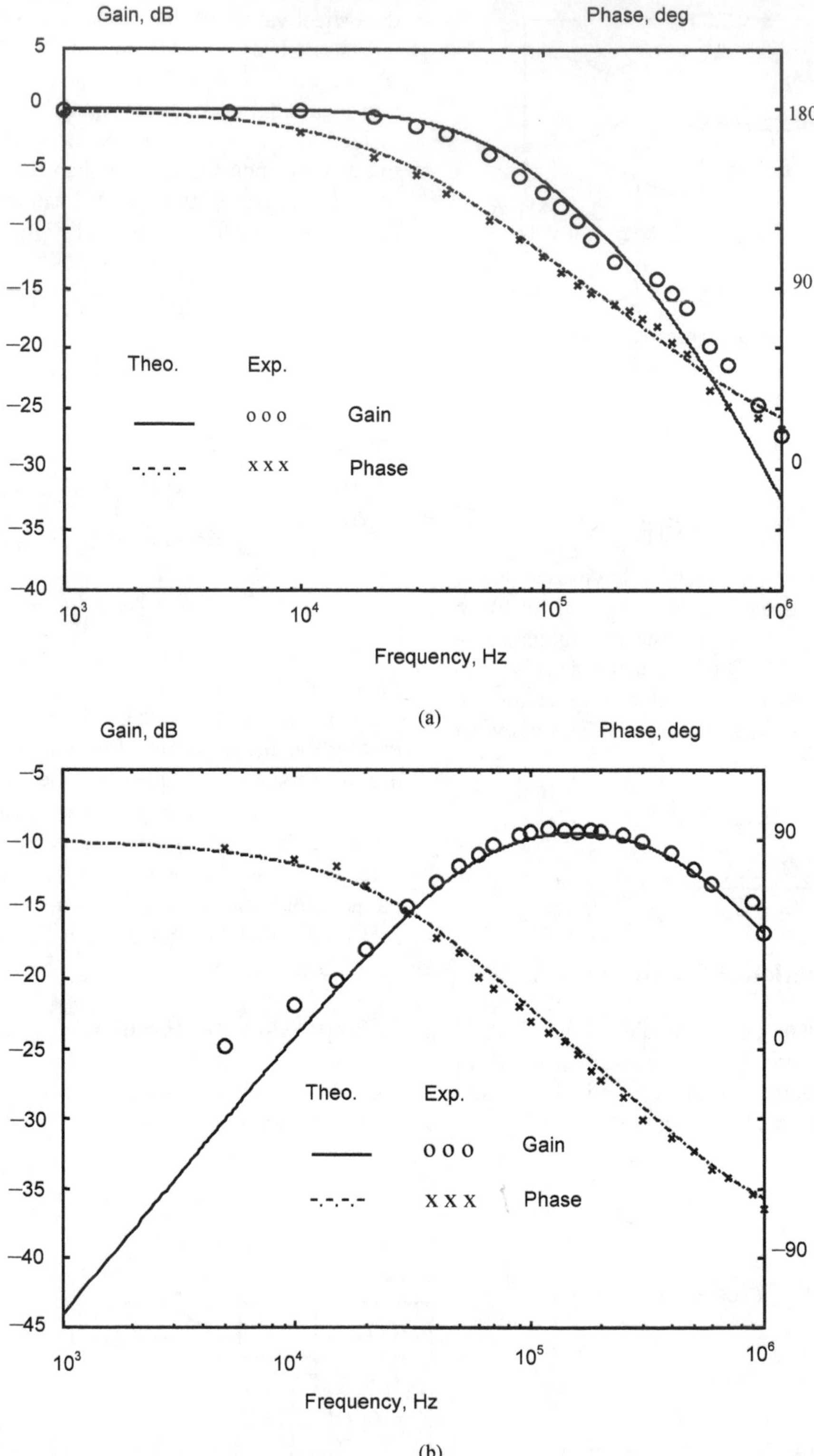

(a)

(b)

Figure 4. Experimental frequency responses of Figure 1 design with $C_1 = C_2 = 100$ pF and $R_1 = R_2 = R_3 = 10$ kΩ. (a) Lowpass filter (V_{lp}), (b) bandpass filter (V_{bp}).

mented using one AD844. **Figure 4 (a)** and **(b)** represent the frequency responses for the lowpass and bandpass filters of **Figure 1**, respectively, designed with $C_1 = C_2 =$ 100 pF and $R_1 = R_2 = R_3 = 10\ \text{k}\Omega$. Experimental results confirm the theoretical analysis.

6. Conclusions

In this paper, a configuration for realizing voltage-mode multifunction filters and a configuration for realizing current-mode multifunction filters using CFAs are presented. The proposed voltage-mode circuit exhibits simultaneously lowpass and bandpass filters by using one CFA, two grounded capacitors and three resistors. The proposed current-mode circuit exhibit simultaneously lowpass, bandpass and highpass filters by using one CFA, two grounded capacitors and four resistors. The proposed circuits have no requirements for component matching conditions. The active and passive sensitivities are low.

7. References

[1] S. S. Gupta, D. R. Bhaskar and R. Senani, "New Voltage Controlled Oscillators Using CFOAs," *International Journal of Electronics and Communications* (*AEU*), Vol. 63, No. 3, 2009, pp. 209-217.

[2] E. Yuce, "Novel Lossless and Lossy Grounded Inductor Simulators Consisting of a Canonical Number of Components," *Analog Integrated Circuits and Signal Processing*, Vol. 59, No. 1, 2009, pp. 77-82.

[3] R. Nandi, T. K. Bandyopadhyay, S. K. Sanyal and S. Das, "Selective Filters and Sinusoidal Oscillators Using CFA Transimpedance Pole," *Circuits, Systems and Signal Processing*, Vol. 28, No. 3, 2009, pp. 349-359.

[4] J. W. Horng, P. Y. Chou and J. Y. Wu, "Voltage/Current-Mode Multifunction Filters Using Current-Feedback Amplifiers and Grounded Capacitors," *Active and Passive Electronic Components*, Vol. 2010, 2010, pp. 1-5.

[5] K. Kumar and K. Pal, "High Input Impedance Voltage Mode Universal Biquad Filter," *Indian Journal of Pure and Applied Physics*, Vol. 48, No. 4, 2010, pp. 292-296.

[6] N. Nikoloudis and C. Psychalinos, "Multiple Input Single Output Universal Biquad Filter with Current Feedback Operational Amplifiers," *Circuits, Systems and Signal Processing*, Vol. 29, No. 6, 2010, pp. 1167-1180.

[7] A. Fabre, "Gyrator Implementation from Commercially Available Transimpedance Operational Amplifiers," *Electronics Letters*, Vol. 28, No. 3, 1992, pp. 263-264.

[8] A. Fabre, "Insensitive Voltage-Mode and Current-Mode Filters from Commercially Available Transimpedance Opamps," *Proceedings of the Institution of Electrical Engineers*, Vol. 140, No. 5, 1993, pp. 319-321.

[9] S. I. Liu and Y. S. Hwang, "Realisation of R-L and C-D Impedances Using a Current-Feedback Amplifier and Its Applications," *Electronics Letters*, Vol. 30, No. 5, 1994, pp. 380-381.

[10] A. M. Soliman, "Applications of the Current Feedback Amplifiers," *Analog Integrated Circuits and Signal Processing*, Vol. 11, No. 3, 1996, pp. 265-302.

[11] A. M. Soliman, "A New Filter Configuration Using Current Feedback Op-Amp," *Microelectronics Journal*, Vol. 29, No. 7, 1998, pp. 409-419.

[12] S. I. Liu, "High Input Impedance Filters with Low Component Spread Using Current-Feedback Amplifiers," *Electronics Letters*, Vol. 31, No. 13, 1995, pp. 1042-1043.

[13] M. Bhushan and R. W. Newcomb, "Grounding of Capacitors in Integrated Circuits," *Electronic Letters*, Vol. 3, No. 4, 1967, pp. 148-149.

[14] R. Senani, "Realization of a Class of Analog Signal Processing/Signal Generation Circuits: Novel Configurations Using Current Feedback Op-Amps," *Frequenz*, Vol. 52, No. 9-10, 1998, pp. 196-206.

Electronically-Controlled Current-Mode Second Order Sinusoidal Oscillators Using MO-OTAs and Grounded Capacitors

Data Ram Bhaskar[1], Kasim Karam Abdalla[1], Raj Senani[2]
[1]*Department of Electronics and Communication Engineering, Faculty of Engineering and Technology, Jamia Millia Islmia, New Delhi, India*
[2]*Division of Electronics and Communication Engineering, Netaji Subhas Institute of Technology, Delhi, India*

Abstract

Five new electronically-controllable second order current-mode sinusoidal oscillators using three multi-output operational transconductance amplifiers (MO-OTAs) and two grounded capacitors (GC) have been presented. Simulation results are included to confirm the theoretical analysis based upon CMOS OTAs implementable in 0.5 μm technology.

Keywords: Oscillators, Analog Electronics, Current Mode Circuits, Operational Transconductance Amplifiers

1. Introduction

Recently, Tsukutani, Sumi and Fukui [1] presented two current-mode OTA-C sinusoidal oscillators each of which employs three MO-OTAs and three grounded capacitors (GC) and provides three explicit current outputs. However, whereas one of the circuits of [1] does not have independent controllability of the condition of oscillation (CO) and the frequency of oscillation (FO) through different transconductances (which is not only a desirable but also an expected property which one likes to see in any OTA-C oscillator), on the other hand, both the circuits employ three GCs and hence, are not canonic.

The main objective of this paper is to present five new current-mode electronically-controllable second order sinusoidal oscillators which use only three MO-OTAs like the circuits of [1] but in contrast to the circuits of [1], the proposed circuits use no more than two GCs and are capable of providing a non-interacting and independent control of both CO and FO and in addition also provide quadrature outputs which find numerous applications (for instance, in communications for quadrature mixers and single-sideband generators and in instrumentation for vector generator or selective voltmeters [2] etc.).

2. The Proposed Circuits

The proposed circuits are shown in **Figure 1**. For an ideal MO-OTA with transconductance g_m, the current output I_o is given by $I_o = g_m (V_+ - V_-)$, where V_+ and V_- are the input voltages at non-inverting input terminal and inverting input terminal respectively. Routine analysis yields, the condition of oscillation (CO) and the frequency of oscillation (FO) for all circuits as summarized in **Table 1**, which also shows the relevant modes of availability of quadrature outputs in all cases. From the expressions of FO given in **Table 1**, it can be easily deduced that magnitude of all active and passive sensitivities of FO, in all the five circuits, would be in the range of 0 to 1/2 and circuits thus, enjoy low sensitivity properties.

3. Simulation Results

To verify the validity of the proposed configurations, circuit simulation of the oscillators has been carried out using the CMOS MO-OTA circuit from [1] (presented here as **Figure 2**). In PSPICE simulation, implementation was based upon a CMOS OTA in 0.5 μm technology. The aspect ratios of the MOSFETs were taken as shown in **Table 2**. The CMOS OTAs were biased with DC power supply voltages $V_{DD} = +2.5$ V, $V_{SS} = -2.5$ V. The generated waveforms, transient and the frequency spectrum for the proposed circuits obtained from simulations are shown in **Figure 3**, **Figure 4** and **Figure 5**,

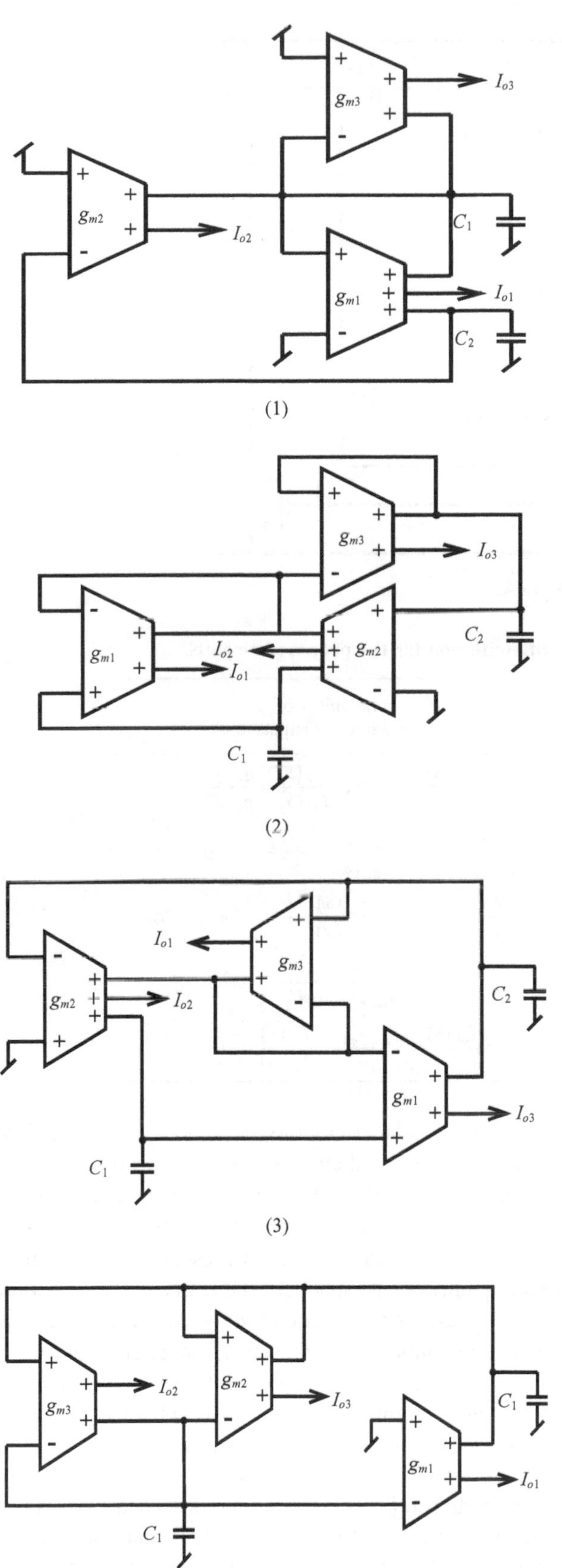

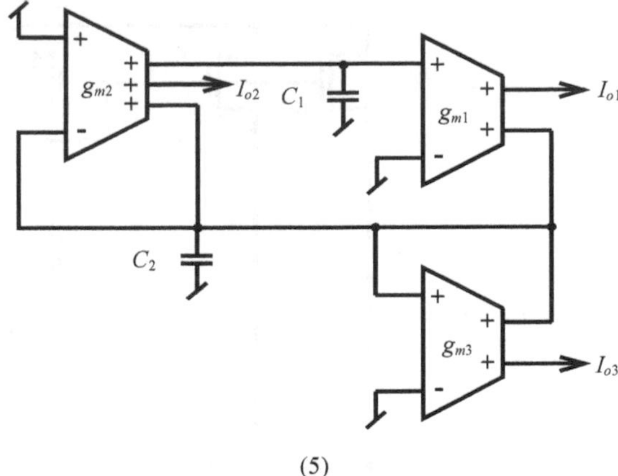

(5)

Figure 1. Proposed configurations.

respectively. The element values used in the simulations along with the theoretical and practical output frequency and total harmonic distortions (THD) for the proposed circuits are summarized in **Table 3**. All the proposed oscillators have been checked for robustness using Monte-Carlo simulations, however, to conserve space, a sample result has been shown in **Figure 6** for the oscillator (5) of **Figure 1**, which confirms that for ±15% variations in the value of g_{m3}, the value of oscillation frequency remains close to its normal value of 1.1996 MHz and hence almost unaffected by change in g_{m3} (which should be the case since g_{m3} does not feature in the expression of FO).

In all cases, a very good correspondence between designed values and those observed from PSPICE simulations has been obtained. The simulation results, thus, confirm the workability of the proposed configurations.

4. Comparison with Other Previously Known OTA-Based Oscillators

It is now useful to compare the proposed new circuits with some of the earlier proposed OTA-based oscillators. Recently, Kamat, Anand Mohan and Prabhu [3] presented a quadrature oscillator employing two MO-OTAs, two single output OTAs and two GCs. The circuit does not have independent controllability of CO and FO. It may also be recalled in this context that much earlier, in reference [4], two minimum-component electronically-tunable sinusoidal oscillators using two OTAs and two GCs had been presented however, these circuits too did not have independent controllability of CO and FO. Furthermore, there is another class of OTA-based RC oscillators known earlier [5-9] which employ one or two OTAs along with a number of resistors and two capacitors. However, when these OTA-RC oscillators from [5-9] can be transformed into OTA-C oscillators, by simulating the resistors with OTAs, the resulting entirely-OTA-based oscillators will

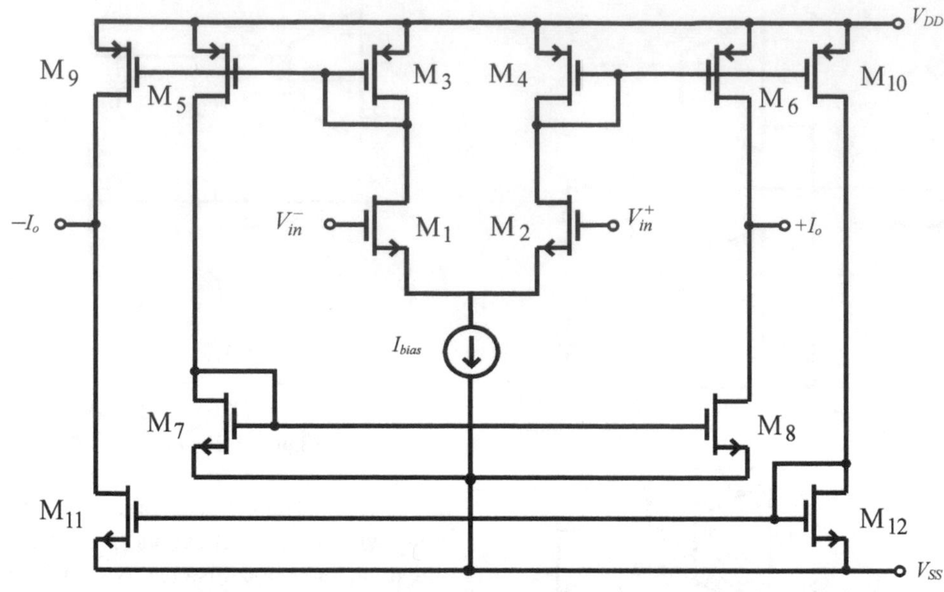

Figure 2. MO-OTA.

Table 1. Condition of oscillation and frequency of oscillation for the proposed circuits.

Circuit No.	Condition of Oscillation (CO)	Frequency of Oscillation (FO)	Availability of Quadrature Outputs
1	$(g_{m3} - g_{m1}) \le 0$	$\frac{1}{2\pi}\sqrt{\frac{g_{m1}g_{m2}}{C_1C_2}}$	$\frac{I_{o2}(s)}{I_{o1}(s)} = \frac{-g_{m2}}{sC_2}$, $\frac{I_{o2}(s)}{I_{o3}(s)} = \frac{g_{m1}g_{m2}}{g_{m3}sC_2}$
2	$(g_{m2} - g_{m1}) \le 0$	$\frac{1}{2\pi}\sqrt{\frac{g_{m2}g_{m3}}{C_1C_2}}$	$\frac{I_{o3}(s)}{I_{o1}(s)} = \frac{g_{m3}}{sC_1}$, $\frac{I_{o3}(s)}{I_{o2}(s)} = \frac{-g_{m3}}{sC_1}$ for $g_{m1} = g_{m2}$
3	$(g_{m1} - g_{m2}) \le 0$	$\frac{1}{2\pi}\sqrt{\frac{g_{m2}g_{m3}}{C_1C_2}}$	$\frac{I_{o3}(s)}{I_{o1}(s)} = \frac{-g_{m3}}{sC_1}$, $\frac{I_{o3}(s)}{I_{o2}(s)} = \frac{g_{m3}}{sC_1}$ for $g_{m1} = g_{m2}$
4	$(C_2 g_{m3} - C_1 g_{m1}) \le 0$	$\frac{1}{2\pi}\sqrt{\frac{g_{m1}g_{m2}}{C_1C_2}}$	$\frac{I_{o1}(s)}{I_{o2}(s)} = \frac{-g_{m1}}{sC_1}$
5	$(g_{m2} - g_{m3}) \le 0$	$\frac{1}{2\pi}\sqrt{\frac{g_{m1}g_{m2}}{C_1C_2}}$	$\frac{I_{o1}(s)}{I_{o3}(s)} = \frac{g_{m2}g_{m1}}{g_{m3}sC_1}$, $\frac{I_{o1}(s)}{I_{o2}(s)} = \frac{-g_{m1}}{sC_1}$

Table 2. Aspect ratios of MOSFETs used in the MO-OTA implementation.

MOSFET	W(μm)	L(μm)
M_1, M_2	20	1.8
M_3, M_4, M_5, M_6, M_9, M_{10}	43	0.5
M_7, M_8, M_{11}, M_{12}	43	1.25

not remain as efficient and practically viable due to the requirement of an excessive number of OTAs.

In comparison, the new circuits are free from above mentioned deficiencies of the circuits presented earlier in [3-9].

5. Concluding Remarks

Five new current-mode electronically controllable OTA-C sinusoidal oscillators have been presented. Like the recently proposed circuits of [1], the proposed circuits also employ only three MO-OTAs and grounded capacitors as preferred for IC fabrication [10] and [11]. However, by contrast to the circuits presented in [1] both of which require three capacitors and hence are non-canonic, the proposed circuits require only two capacitors and hence, are canonic. All the proposed circuits enjoy the feature of independent controllability of oscillation frequency and condition of oscillation, which is not available in one of the circuits presented in [1]. The new circuits are also free from the drawbacks of the circuits presented earlier in [3-9]. Also, all the proposed circuits provide quadrature outputs as an additional feature not available in the circuits of [1]. The active and passivesensitivities of all the circuits are very low. The workability

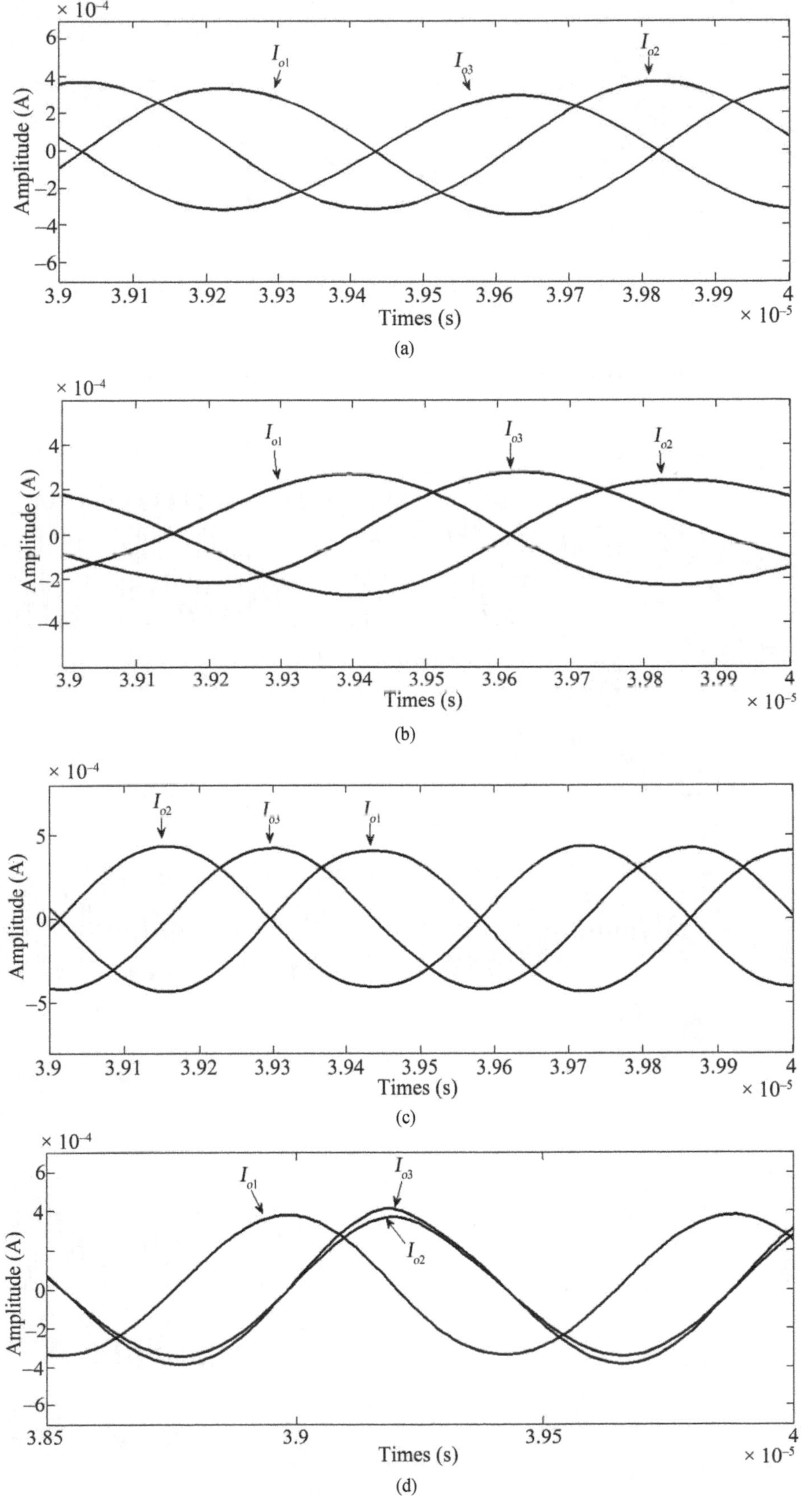
× 10⁻⁴
Amplitude (A)
Times (s)
× 10⁻⁵
I_o1
I_o2
I_o3
(a)
(b)
(c)
(d)

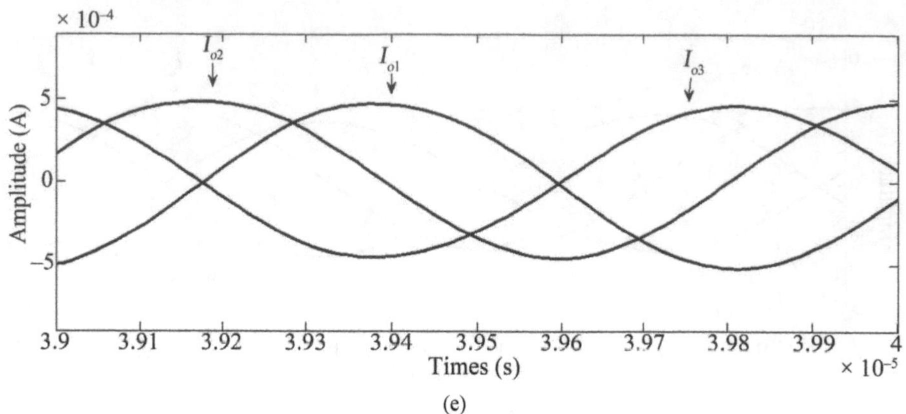

(e)

Figure 3. Output waveforms of (a) circuit 1 (b) circuit 2 (c) circuit 3 (d) circuit 4 (e) circuit 5.

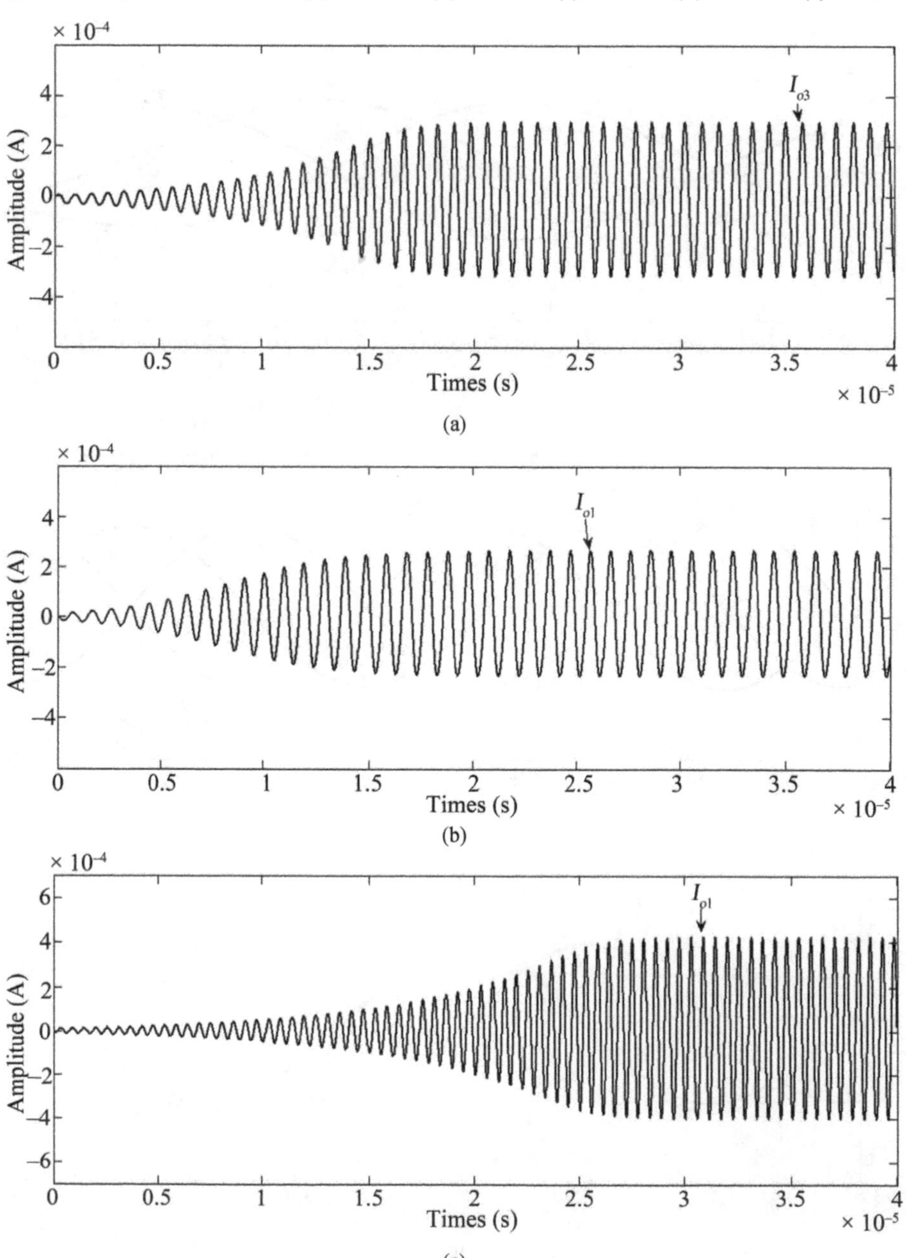

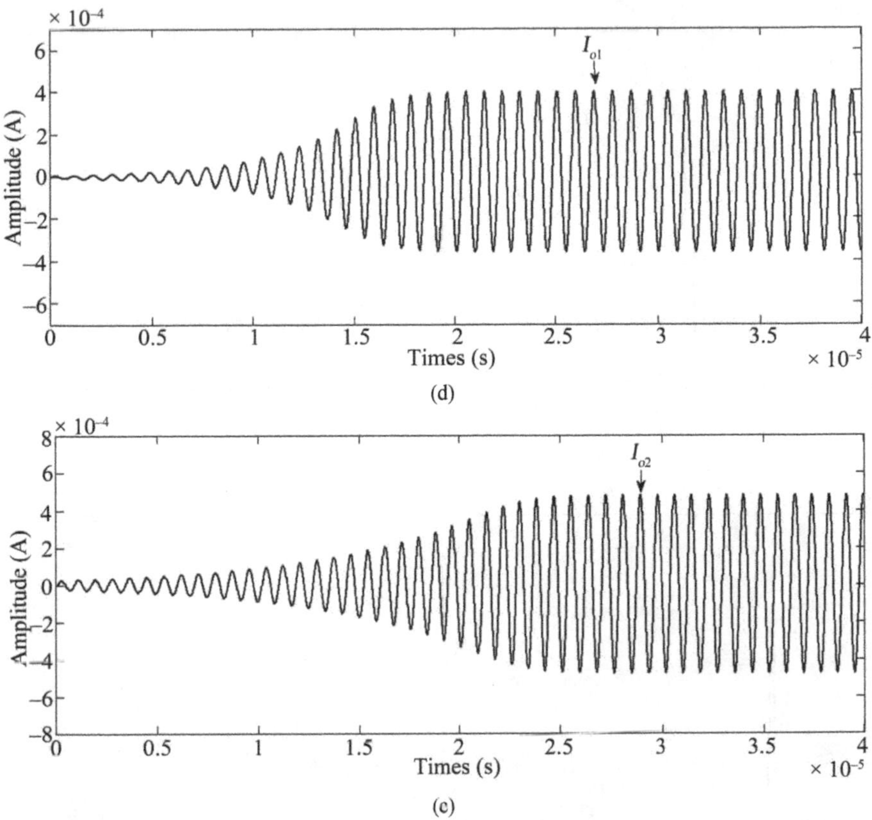

Figure 4. Output transient of (a) circuit 1 (b) circuit 2 (c) circuit 3 (d) circuit 4 (e) circuit 5.

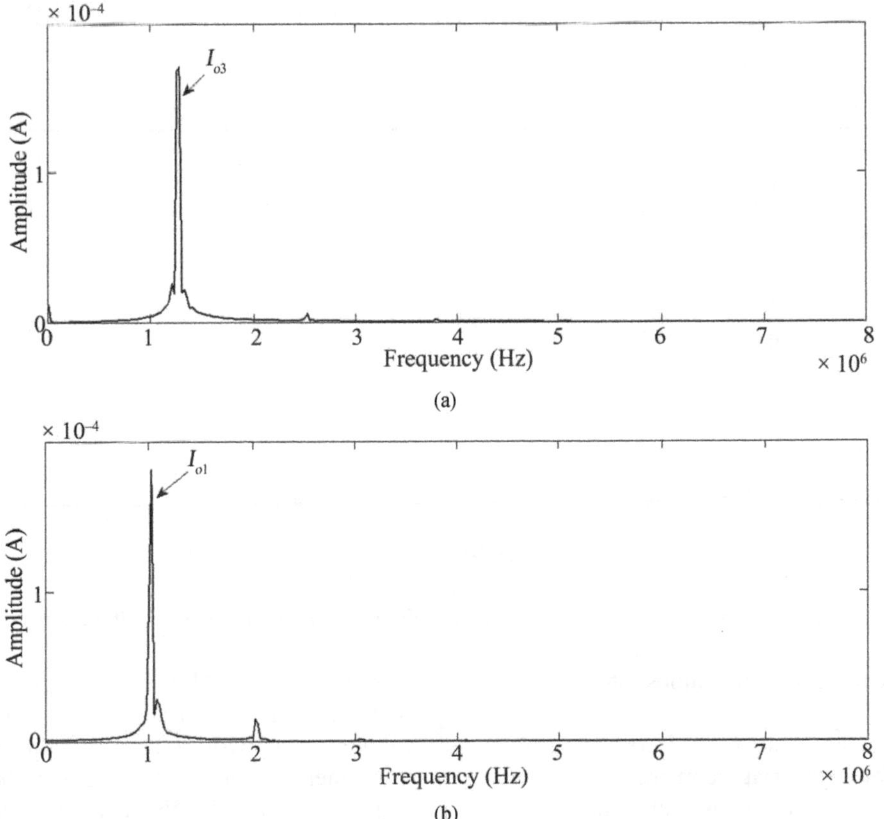

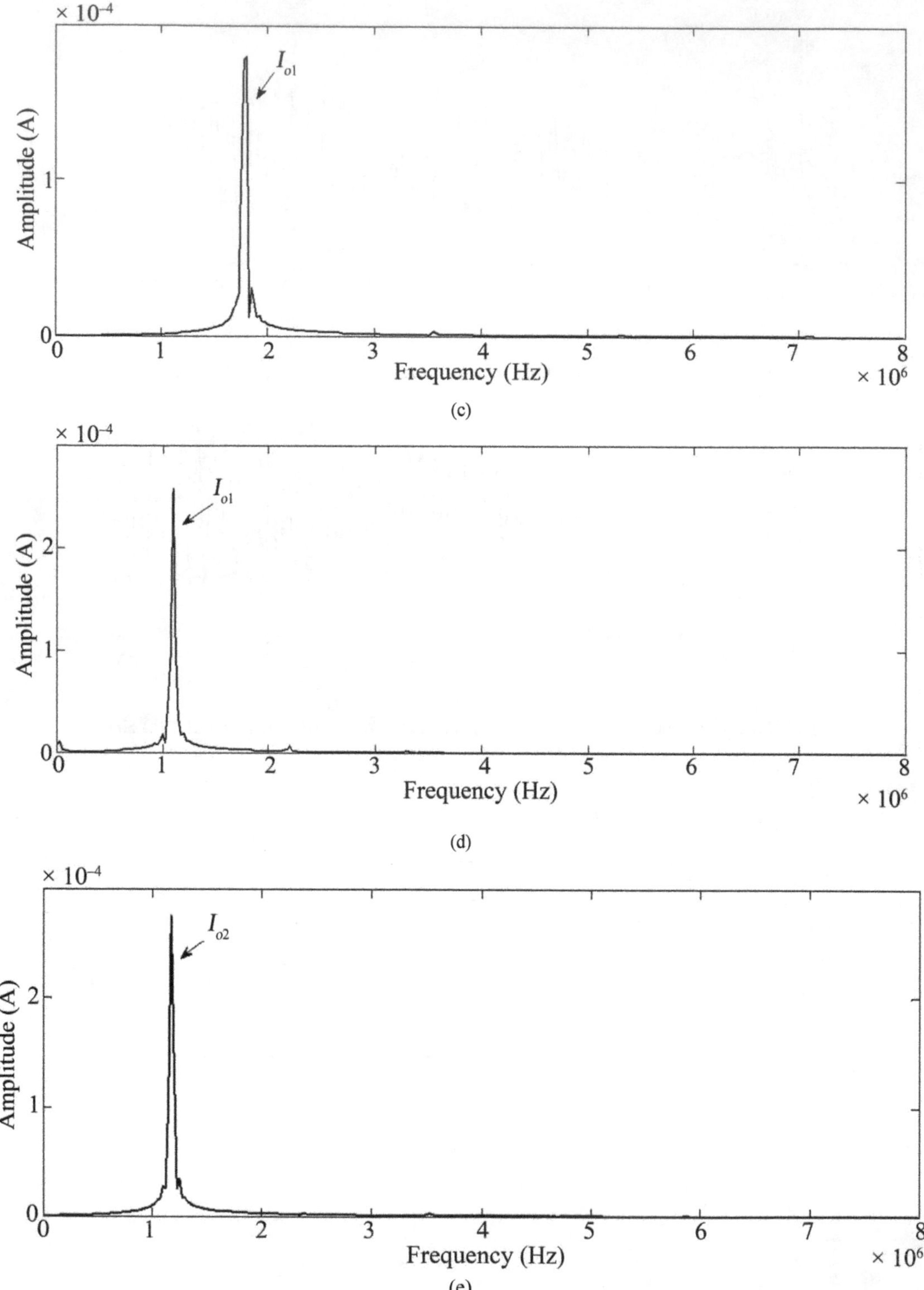

Figure 5. Frequency spectrum of (a) circuit 1 (b) circuit 2 (c) circuit 3 (d) circuit 4 (e) circuit 5.

of the proposed circuits has been demonstrated by SPICE simulation results.

The transconductance of an OTA is temperature dependent this calls for appropriate temperature compensation for which numbers of schemes are known in the literature [12-14]. However, the study of modified versions of the proposed circuits incorporating temperature compensation would require considerable additional work; therefore, it was considered to be outside the scope of present work. Lastly, it may be mentioned that the

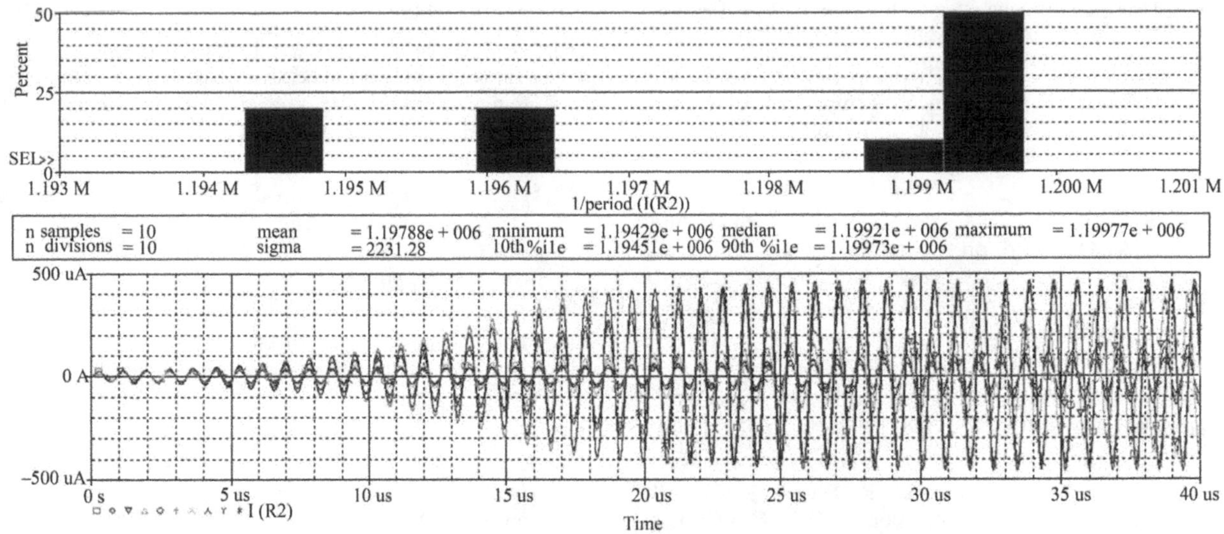

Figure 6. Result of the Monte-Carlo Simulation of oscillator circuit (5) of Figure 1.

Table 3. The values of the capacitors and transconductances for various oscillators.

Circuit No.	g_{m1} (mA/V)	I_{b1} (mA)	g_{m2} (mA/V)	I_{b2} (mA)	g_{m3} (mA/V)	I_{b3} (mA)	C_1 (nF)	C_2 (nF)	$F_{Theoretical}$ (MHz)	$F_{Practical}$ (MHz)	THD
1	0.7954	2.8	0.7954	2.8	0.712	1.47	0.1	0.1	1.265918	1.277	2.6%
2	0.793	2.73	0.715	1.5	0.804	3.4	0.12	0.1	1.101566	1.1803	5.2%
3	0.7523	1.95	0.794	2.75	0.7718	2.26	0.07	0.07	1.732487	1.734	1.6%
4	0.7954	2.8	0.7046	1.4	0.788	2.6	0.11	0.11	1.083157	1.1514	2.3%
5	0.785	2.53	0.715	1.5	0.777	2.36	0.1	0.1	1.192361	1.1996	1%

circuits proposed in this paper are inspired by the ideas contained in [15-19].

6. References

[1] T. Tsukutani, Y. Sumi and Y. Fukui, "Electronically Controlled Current-Mode Oscillators Using MO-OTAs and Grounded Capacitors," *Frequenz*, Vol. 60, No. 11-12, 2006, pp. 220-223.

[2] W. Tangsrirat, " Current Differencing Transconductance Amplifier-Based Current-Mode Four-Phase Quadrature Oscillator," *Indian Journal of Engineering and Material Sciences,* Vol. 14, No. 4, 2007, pp. 289-294.

[3] D. V. Kamat, P. V. A. Mohan and K. G. Prabhu, " Novel First-Order and Second-Order Current-Mode Filters Using Multiple-Output Operational Amplifiers," *Circuits Syst Signal Process*, Vol. 29, No. 3, 2010, pp. 553-576.

[4] M. T. Abuelma'atti, "New Minimum Componet Electronically Tunable OTA-C Sinusoidal Oscillators," *Electronics Letters,* Vol. 25, No. 17,1989, pp. 1114-1115.

[5] M. T. Abuelma'atti and M. H. Khan, "Grounded Capacitor Oscillators Using a Single Operationl Transconductance Amplifier,'' *Active and Passive Electronic Components*, Vol. 19, No. 2, 1996, pp. 91-98.

[6] Y. Tao and J. K. Fidler, "Generation of Second-Order Single-OTA RC Oscillators," *IEE Proceedings of Circuits Devices Systems,* Vol. 145, No. 4, 1998, pp. 271-277.

[7] Y. Tao and J. K. Fidler, "Electronically Tunable Dual-OTA Second-Order Sinusoidal Oscillator/Filters with Non-interacting Controls: A Systematic Synthesis Approach," *IEEE Transactions on Circuits Systems I,* Vol. 47, No. 2, 2000, pp. 117-129.

[8] V. Singh, "Equivalent Forms of Dual-OTA RC Oscillators with Application to Grounded-Capacitor Oscillators," *IEE Proceedings of Circuits Devices Systems,* Vol. 153, No. 2, 2006, pp. 95-99.

[9] V. Singh, "Equivalent Forms of Single-Operational Transconductance Amplifier RC Oscillators with Application to Grounded-Capacitor Oscillators," *IET Circuits Devices Systems*, Vol. 4, No. 2, 2010, pp. 123-130.

[10] B. Bhushan and R. W. Newcomb, "Grounding of Capacitors in Integrated Circuits," *Electronics Letters,* Vol. 3, No. 4, 1967, pp.148-149.

[11] R. Senani, "Realization of a Class of Analog Signal Processing/Signal Generation Circuits: Novel Configura-

tion Using Current-Feedback Op-Amps," *Frequenz*, Vol. 52, No. 9-10, 1998, pp. 196-206.

[12] H. S. Malvar and M. Luettgen, "Temperature Compensation of OTA-Based Filters and Multipliers," *Electronics Letters*, Vol. 23, No. 17, 1987, pp. 890-891.

[13] W.-S. Chung, H.-W. Cha and K.-H. Kim, "Temperature-Stable VCO Based on Operational Transconductance Amplifiers," *Electronics Letters*, Vol. 26, No. 22, 1990, pp. 1900-1901.

[14] C. A. Karybakas, C. Kosmatopoulos and T. Laopoulos, "Improved Temperature Compensation of OTAs," *Electronics Letters*, Vol. 28, No. 8, 1992, pp. 763-764.

[15] R. Senani, M. P. Tripathi, D. R. Bhaskar and A. K. Banerjee, "Systematic Generation of OTA-C Sinusoidal Oscillators," *Electronics Letters*, Vol. 26, No. 18, 1990, pp. 1457-1459.

[16] D. R. Bhaskar, M. P. Tripathi and R. Senani, "A Class of Three-OTA-Two-Capacitor Oscillators with Non-interacting Controls," *International Journal of Electronics*, Vol. 74, No. 3, 1993, pp. 459-463.

[17] D. R. Bhaskar, M. P. Tripathi and R. Senani, "Systematic Derivation of All Possible Canonic OTA-C Sinusoidal Oscillators," *Journal of the Franklin Institute*, Vol. 330, No. 5, 1993, pp. 885-903.

[18] R. Senani, "New Electronically Tunable OTA-C Sinusoidal Oscillator," *Electronics Letters*, Vol. 25, No. 4, 1989, pp. 286-287.

[19] M. T. Abuelma'atti, "Two New Integrable Active-C OTA-Based Voltage (Current) Controlled Oscillators," *International Journal of Electronics*, Vol. 66, No. 1, 1989, pp. 135-138.

A 12-Bit 1-Gsample/s Nyquist Current-Steering DAC in 0.35 μm CMOS for Wireless Transmitter

Peiman Aliparast[1,2], Hossein B. Bahar[2], Ziaadin D. Koozehkanani[2], Jafar Sobhi[2], Gader Karimian[2]

[1]*Young Research Club, Islamic AZAD University of Sofian, Sofian, Iran*

[2]*Faculty of Electrical and Computer Engineering, University of Tabriz, Tabriz, Iran*

Abstract

The present work deals with 12-bit Nyquist current-steering CMOS digital-to-analog converter (DAC) which is an essential part in baseband section of wireless transmitter circuits. Using oversampling ratio (OSR) for the proposed DAC leads to avoid use of an active analog reconstruction filter. The optimum segmentation (75%) has been used to get the best DNL and reduce glitch energy. This segmentation ratio guarantees the monotonicity. Higher performance is achieved using a new 3-D thermometer decoding method which reduces the area, power consumption and the number of control signals of the digital section. Using two digital channels in parallel, helps reach 1-GSample/s frequency. Simulation results show that the spurious-free-dynamic-range (SFDR) in Nyquist rate is better than 64 dB for sampling frequency up to 1-GSample/s. The analog voltage supply is 3.3 V while the digital part of the chip operates with only 2.4 V. Total power consumption in Nyquist rate measurement is 144.9 mW. The chip has been processed in a standard 0.35 μm CMOS technology. Active area of chip is 1.37 mm^2.

Keywords: Wireless Transmitter, 3-D Thermometer Decoding, Current Steering DAC, WLAN, Integrated Circuits, CMOS

1. Introduction

The rapid improvement in the field of wireless communications and the image signal processing area requires the designers to put an increasing amount of design effort in the integration of digital and analog systems on a chip (SoC). High performance DACs find applications in the area of wireless transceivers such as Wireless Local Area Networks (WLAN) and Wireless Metropolitan Area Networks (WMAN), image signal processor such as High Definition Television (HDTV), digital signal synthesizers, and etc. CMOS current mode DACs are the natural candidate for such applications Because of their high speed, low power, and cost effectiveness [1]. Nowadays the WLAN products are increasing in the market. The WLAN infrastructure such as access points connected to the internet exists now everywhere in homes, offices, and public spaces such as WLAN hotspots. New services or applications are being created by connecting various kinds of WLAN products with the WLAN infrastructure. **Figure 1** shows the typical structure of a direct conversion (zero-IF) transmission chain for wireless applications.

Two DACs are needed to convert the *I* and *Q* digital modulated signals coming from the digital signal processor (DSP) into analog waveforms, which are smoothed by the following low-pass reconstruction filters. These baseband signals are then shifted to radio frequency (RF) by two quadrature mixers, and summed up to obtain the final waveform to be transmitted at the antenna, after the amplification provided by the power amplifier (PA) [2]. The baseband sections of such telecom standard transmitters typically consist of cascading of a digital-to-analog con-

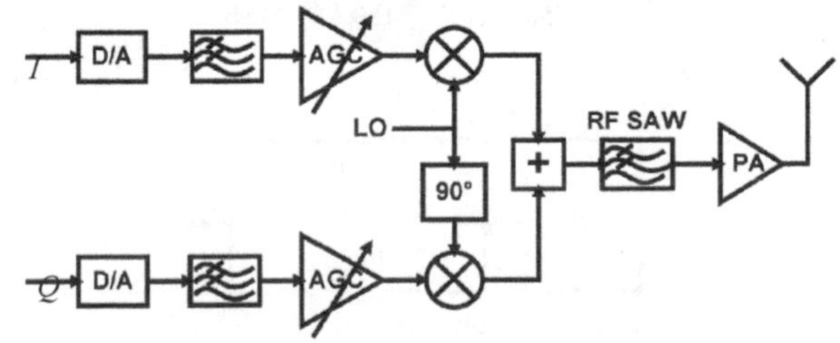

Figure 1. General block diagram of direct conversion for wireless transmitter chain.

verter (DAC), receiving the digital signal processor (DSP) bit-stream, and an analog reconstruction filter, which has to suppress the DAC spectral images. Digital interpolations filter to be situated between the DSP (which typically operates at Nyquist frequency) and the DAC, to enhance the data-rate to the desired value. The design of such a baseband section of wideband wireless communication systems has to optimize the trade-off between two possible approaches: A low DAC conversion frequency, implies a low power interpolation filter, with demand to a high-order, power-hungry analog reconstruction filter, and a high DAC conversion frequency, implies a digital filter with a high interpolation factor, that relaxes the required performance of the analog smoothing filter. This trade-off is presently optimized with a DAC data-rate about 8-10 times the signal bandwidth and a 4-6th order analog reconstruction filter. For instance, in the case of the WLAN IEEE 802.11a standard (whose signal bandwidth is equal to 10 MHz), the DAC data-rate is around 100 MHz as illustrated in **Figure 2** [2-4].

Due to the upcoming higher data rate standards (IEEE 802.16 and 802.11n, for instance), future implementations will involve with several critical issues on this baseband section architecture. As the new standards will present a larger signal bandwidth (25 MHz for the upcoming IEEE 802.16, for instance [5]), the use of traditional transmission (TX) baseband architectures will result in a more and more critical design of the analog filters, since their cut-off frequency has to be increased (with an increasing sensitivity to the lower CMOS gain and to the non-dominant poles) [6]. **Figure 3** shows this work which exploits the DAC oversampling ratio (OSR) to avoid the use of an active analog reconstruction filter [2]. As a matter of fact, the DAC conversion frequency is increased up to 1 GHz.

2. High Speed Conventional Current-Steering DACs

2.1. Binary Weighted Architecture VS. Unary Decoded Architecture

Current-steering DACs are based on an array of matched current sources which are unity decoded or binary weighted [7]. As shown in **Figure 4**, the reference source is simply replicated in each branch of the DAC, and each branch current is switched on or off based on the input code. For the binary version, the reference current is multiplied by a power of two, creating larger currents to represent higher-magnitude digital signals. In the unit-element version, each current branch produces an equal amount of current, and thus 2N current source elements are needed. The performance of the DAC is specified through static parameters: Integral Non-Linearity (INL), Differential Non-Linearity (DNL) and parametric yield; and dynamic parameters: glitch energy, settling time and SFDR [8]. Static performance is mainly dominated by systematic and random errors. Systematic errors caused by process, temperature and electrical slow variation gradients are almost cancelled by proper layout techniques [9]. Random errors are determined solely by mismatch due to fast variation gradients.

Advantages and disadvantages of these structures are

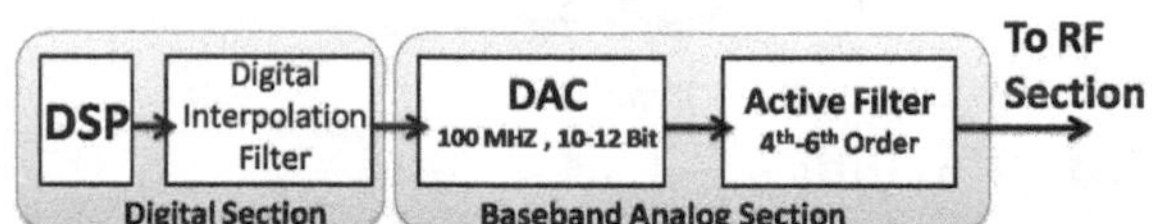

Figure 2. Traditional baseband analog section for wireless transmitters.

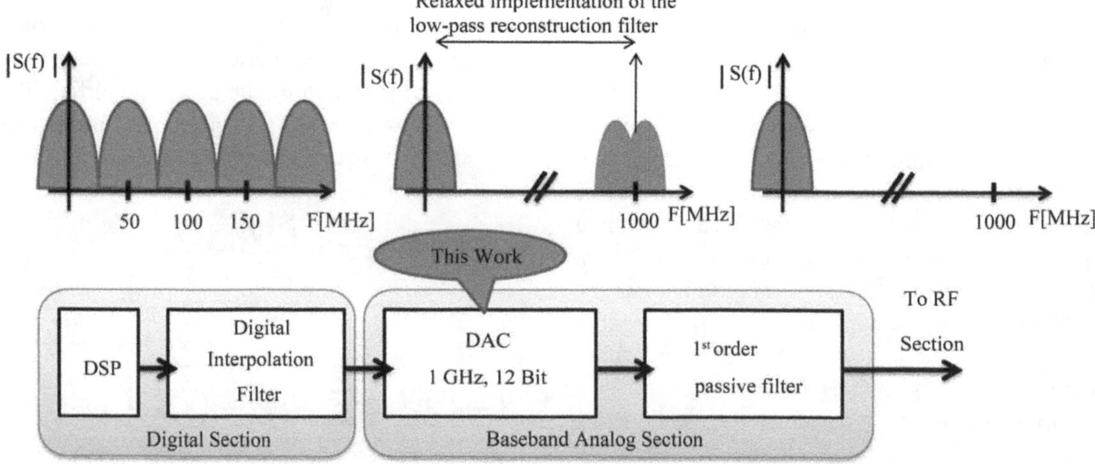

Figure 3. This work which exploits impact of the DAC conversion frequency on the filter implementation.

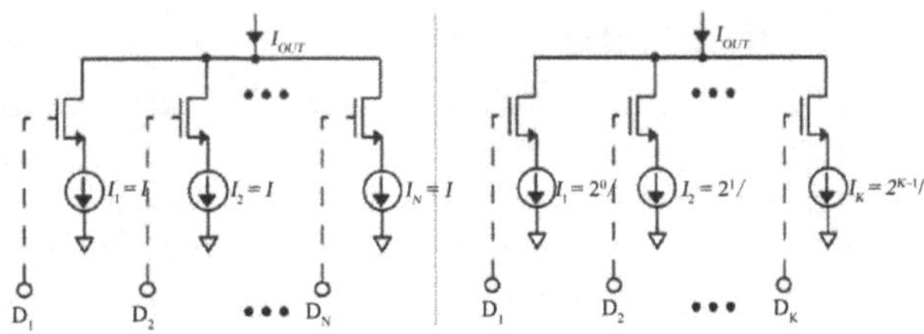

Figure 4. (a) Unit-element current-steering DAC; (b) Binary current-steering DAC.

summarized below:

➢ Thermometer:

✓ Advantages

- Low glitch energy
- Monotonicity
- Small DNL errors

✓ Disadvantages

- Digital decoding with more area and power consumption
- Increased number of control signals

➢ Binary:

✓ Advantages

- Low digital power consumption
- Small number of control signals

✓ Disadvantages

- Monotonicity not guaranteed
- Larger DNL errors
- Large glitch energy

Figure 5 also summarizes aforementioned points graphically.

2.2. Segmented DAC Structure

Usually, to leverage the clear advantages of the thermometer-coded architecture and to obtain a small area simultaneously, a compromise is found by using segmentation [10]. The DAC is divided into two sub-DACs, one for the MSBs and one for the LSBs. Thermometer coding is used in the MSB where the accuracy is needed mostly. Because of the reduced number of bits in this section, the size is considerably smaller than a true thermometer coded design. The LSB section can either be done using the binary-weighted or the thermometer-coded approach. We will refer to a fully binary-weighted design as 0% segmented, whereas a fully thermometer-coded design is referred to as 100% segmented. The design of current-steering DAC starts with an architectural selection to find the optimum segmentation ratio (**m** over **n**) that minimizes the overall digital and analog area [10-12]. The INL is independent of the segmentation ratio and depends only on the mismatch if the output impedance is made large enough [7].

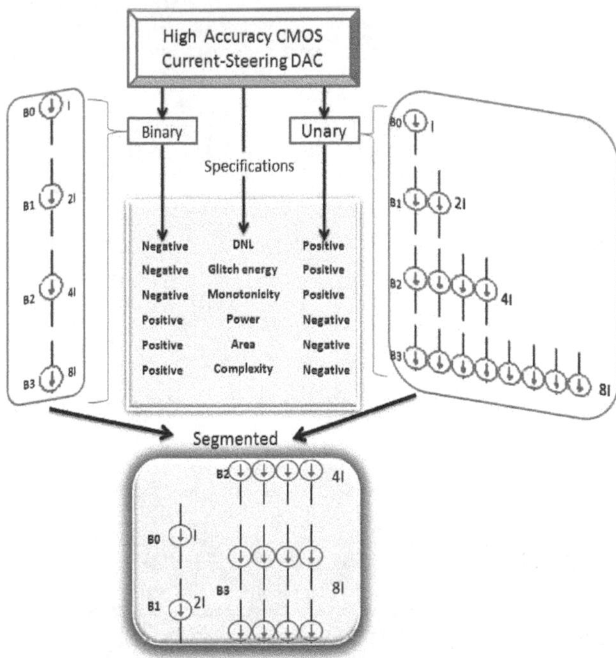

Figure 5. Binary weighted versus Unary-decoded.

The DNL speciation depends on the segmentation ratio but it is always satisfied provided that the INL is below 0.5 LSB for reasonable segmentation ratios. The glitch energy is determined by the number of binary bits b, being the optimum architecture in this sense a totally unary DAC. However, this is unfeasible in practice due to the large area and delay that the thermometer decoder would exhibit. The minimization of the glitch energy is then done in circuit level design and layout of the switch and latch array and current source cell [13].The optimum segmentation is workout 75% in [10,12] so we have used this segmentation to achieve the best performance in high-speed design. Thus we consider 9-bit as thermometer-coded and 3-bit as binary-weighted. **Figure 6** shows a typical block diagram of an **n**-bit segmented current-steering DAC which uses the advantages of both architectures. Input word is segmented between **b** less significant bits that switch a binary weighted array and **m= n – b** most significant bits that control switching of a unary current source array. The **m** input bits are thermometer decoded to switch individually each of the unary sources [14-16]. A dummy decoder is placed in the binary weighted input path to equalize the delay. A latch is placed just before the switch transistors of each current source to minimize any timing error [10].

3. New Thermometer Decoding Architecture

Figure 7 shows a block diagram of a conventional row and column decoded 12-bit current-steering DAC. In this

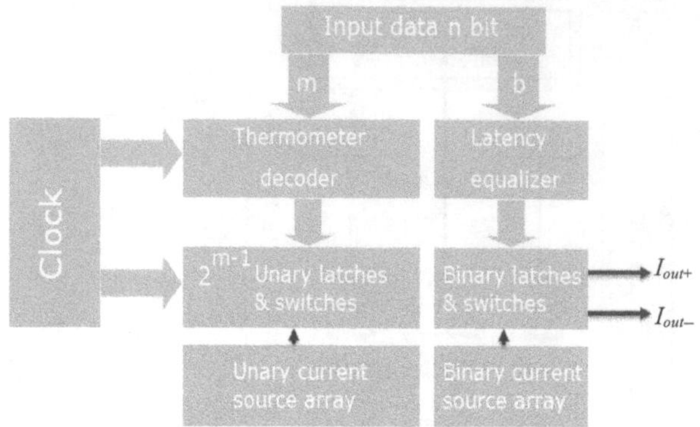

Figure 6. A typical segmented current-steering DAC architecture.

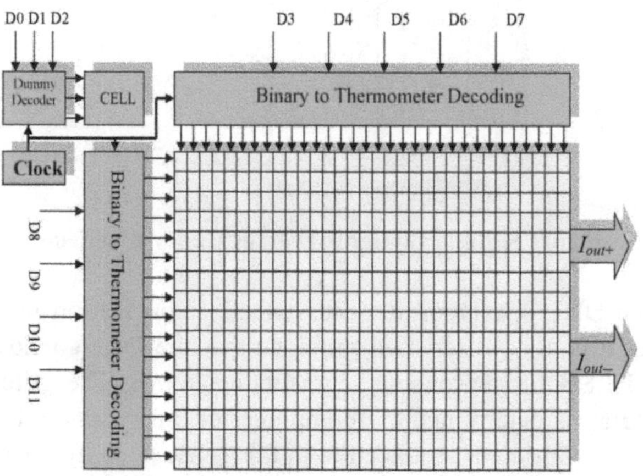

Figure 7. Block diagram of a conventional row and column decoded 12-bit current-steering DAC.

block diagram, the lower significant bits are applied to a dummy decoder [17]. This decoder creates a delay proportional to the Binary-to-Thermometer decoder and causes the signal to arrive at the switches synchronously. The five LSB bits are column decoded and the four MSB bits are row decoded. Column decoder is a 5-input 31-output Binary-to-Thermometer Decoder and row decoder is a 4-input 15-output Binary-to-Thermometer Decoder. Outputs of the decoders control 511 current cells in the main matrix. But if we think about Binary-to-Thermometer Decoder structure we understand that β-bit increase of the input of the decoder cause the area, complexity, number of control signal and power consumption of the decoder increase with 2^{β}. In fact power and area are doubled with only one bit increase in the input of the decoder and we can write:

$$P(4\text{to}15\text{ BTD}) = 2\times P(3\text{to}7\text{BTD}) \quad (1)$$

$$A(4\text{to}15\text{ BTD}) = 2\times A(3\text{to}7\text{BTD}) \quad (2)$$

Thus:

$$P(5\text{to}31\text{BTD}) = 4\times P(3\text{to}7\text{ BTD}) \quad (3)$$

$$A(5\text{to}31\text{ BTD}) = 4\times A(3\text{to}7\text{ BTD}) \quad (4)$$

where BTD is Binary-to-Thermometer Decoder, P is the power consumption of the decoder and A is active area that the decoder uses. Now consider **Figure 8** that shows a 3D decoding architecture. In this block diagram three BTD have been used. Three bits for height, three bits for row and three bits for column and every cell is selected with 3 parameters (R, C and H). In fact we have only used three (3to7 BTD) instead of two (5to31 BTD) and (4to15 BTD) thus power consumption and area of the circuit have been improved two times because:

$$\begin{aligned} &P(4\text{to}15\text{ BTD}) = 2\times P(3\text{to}7\text{ BTD}) \\ +\ &P(5\text{to}31\text{ BTD}) = 4\times P(3\text{to}7\text{BTD}) \\ \hline &P(4\text{to}15\text{ BTD}) + P(5\text{to}31\text{ BTD}) = 6\times P(3\text{to}7\text{BTD}) \end{aligned} \quad (5)$$

And for area we have:

$$\begin{aligned} &A(4\text{to}15\text{ BTD}) = 2\times A(3\text{to}7\text{BTD}) \\ +\ &A(5\text{to}31\text{ BTD}) = 4\times A(3\text{to}7\text{ BTD}) \\ \hline &A(4\text{to}15\text{ BTD}) + A(5\text{to}31\text{ BTD}) = 6\times A(3\text{to}7\text{ BTD}) \end{aligned} \quad (6)$$

In this structure 3 LSB bits are column decoded, 3 middle bits are row decoded and 3 MSB bits are height decoded. On the other hand, we have only used 21 control signals instead of 46 control signals thus the number of control signals has been decreased by 55 percent hence we can achieve the best speed and performance.

4. The Current Cell, Latch and Driver

Static and dynamic performance of current-steering

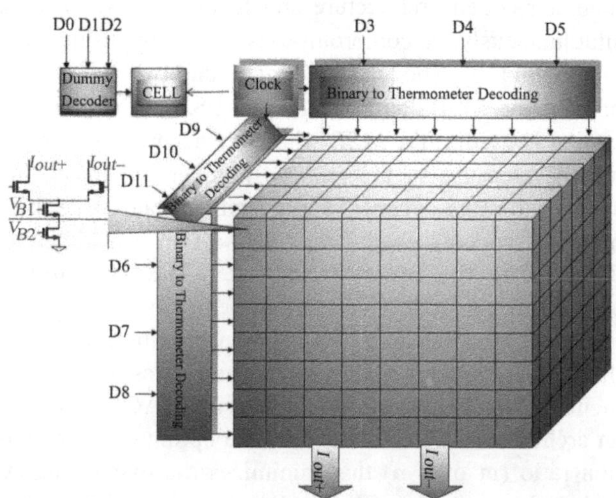

Figure 8. Block diagram of a novel method row and column and height decoded 12-bit 3-D DAC.

DACs is mostly determined by the accuracy of the current sources, finite output impedance, and switching time. **Figure 9** shows a current source transistor M_{CS}, an additional cascode transistor M_{CAS} that increases the output impedance and two complementary switch transistors M_{SW}. This figure shows cascode current source and switch structure for 1LSB while for realizing unary current source cell (8LSB) we used same structure with 8 parallel transistors. In proposed 12-bit DAC three bits are binary weighted so it uses the current source of **Figure 9** and remaining 9 bits are thermometer decoded and need unary current sources. Since two D/A converters processed in the same technology do not necessarily have the same specifications due to technological variations, therefore it is of the utmost importance to know the relationship that exists between the specifications of the circuit and the matching properties of used technology. For a current-steering D/A converter, the INL is mainly determined by the matching behavior of the current sources. A parameter that is well suited for expressing this technology versus DAC specification relation is the INL yield [16]. This INL yield is defined as the ratio of the number of D/A converters with an INL smaller than 1 LSB to the total number of tested D/A converters. As defined by Pelgrom, mismatch "is the process that causes time- independent random variations in physical quantities of identically designed devices" [18]. Pelgrom's paper has become the de facto standard for analysis of transistor matching, and thus his formula for the standard deviation of saturation current for two identically sized devices has been used for the design. This formula is:

$$\frac{\sigma^2(I)}{I^2} = \frac{4\sigma^2(V_T)}{(V_{GS}-V_T)^2} + \frac{\sigma^2(\beta)}{\beta^2} \quad (7)$$

where

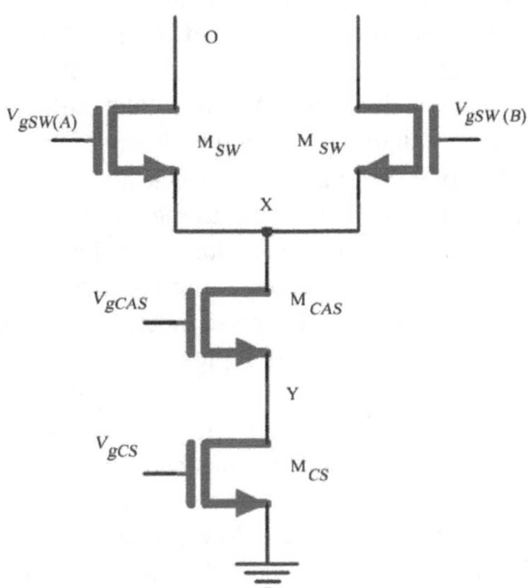

Figure 9. Current source cell topology.

$$\sigma^2(V_T) = \frac{A_{VT}^2}{WL} + S_{VT}^2 D^2 \quad (8)$$

and

$$\frac{\sigma^2(\beta)}{\beta^2} = \frac{A_\beta^2}{WL} + S_\beta^2 D^2 \quad (9)$$

Most of these variables are process-dependent constants. Using these results, an equation for the minimum size device that still provides a reasonable current standard deviation can be determined [13]:

$$\frac{\sigma I^2}{I^2} = \frac{1}{2WL_{cs\,min}}\left(A_\beta^2 + \frac{4A_{VT}^2}{(V_{GS}-V_T)^2}\right) \quad (10)$$

where A_β, A_{VT}, V_{GS} and V_T are process parameters, while I is the current generated by a given source and σI is the relative standard deviation of one current source. The same aspect ratio can be obtained for different areas $W \times L$, except for the M_{CS} transistor, because the usual INL-mismatch specification eliminates one degree of freedom. The relative standard deviation of a unit current source $\sigma I/I$ has to be small enough to fulfil the INL< 0.5 LSB specification given a parametric yield [17]:

$$\frac{\sigma I^2}{I^2} \le \frac{INL_{upper-bound}}{inv\_normal\left(0.5 + \frac{yield}{2}\right).\sqrt{2^{N-1}}} \quad (11)$$

where ***inv_normal*** is the inverse cumulative normal distribution. The M_{CS} transistor size is found by:

$$W^2 = \frac{I}{\mu_n C_{ox}\left(\frac{\sigma I}{I}\right)^2}\left[\frac{A_\beta^2}{\Delta V^2} + \frac{4A_{VT}^2}{\Delta V^4}\right] \quad (12)$$

$$L^2 = \frac{\mu_n C_{ox}}{4I.\left(\frac{\sigma I}{I}\right)^2}\left[A_\beta^2.\Delta V^2 + 4A_{VT}^2\right] \quad (13)$$

where $\mu_n C_{OX}$ is the MOS transistor gain factor and $\Delta V = (V_{GS} - V_T)$. Applying Equations (12) and (13) we arrived in W_{min} = 4 μm and L_{min} = 5 μm for the current source. But in design of cascode current sources, to achieve high speed, we need to choose the size of cascode transistor as small as possible. With different size for W_{CAS} and W_{CS}, we have to use contact in node Y (**Figure 9**) which increases parasitic capacitance and decreases the speed. So in a trade off, we decided to decrease W_{CS} as small as possible and use the same size with W_{CAS}. In other words we have chosen $W_{CAS} = W_{CS}$ = 2 μm, and avoid using contact in node Y. To compensate for reduction in W_{CS} in Equation (14), we increase the values of L_{CS} (L_{CS} = 10 μm) and ΔV while we keep L_{CAS} at its minimum size 0.35 μm. Thus we do not use these Equations (12) and (13) and use only mismatch Equation (10) to reach a minimum sizing of current cell. With this method, the speed of switch is high also INL < 0.5 LSB is satisfied. The small-signal output impedance for the current source topology of **Figure 9** is given by:

$$R_{out} \approx gm_{SW} \cdot gm_{CAS} \cdot r_{dsSW} \cdot r_{dsCAS} \cdot r_{dsCS} \quad (14)$$

The optimum M_{SW} and M_{CAS} gate bias voltages concerning the output impedance are found by differentiating R_{out} with respect to V_{gSW} and V_{gCAS}. For the SW and CAS gate bias voltages that maximize output impedance are found as:

$$V_{gCAS} = V_T + \frac{1}{3}\left(V_{omin} + 2\Delta V_{CS} + 2\Delta V_{CAS} - \Delta V_{SW}\right) \quad (15)$$

$$V_{gSW} = V_T + \frac{1}{3}\left(2V_{omin} + \Delta V_{CS} + \Delta V_{CAS} + \Delta V_{SW}\right) \quad (16)$$

Figure 10 shows the biasing scheme for the cascoded current sources. The PMOS sections of the biasing circuits are labeled as **Global biasing** while the NMOS sections are labeled as **Local biasing**. In the actual implementation, the global biasing is realized using a common-centroid layout to reduce effects of gradients. The local biasing is separated into four quadrants. There is no direct connection between any two quadrants. This will improve both DNL as well as INL performance [10]. A driver circuit with a reduced swing placed between the latch and the switch reduces the clock feed-through to the output node as well [19,20]. **Figure 11(a)** shows a current source, switch, latch and driver cell. A new swing-reduced-device (SRD) circuit is designed (shown in **Figure 11(b)**). The latch circuit complementary output levels and non-symmetrical cross point are designed to minimize glitches [13]. The waveforms of the different nodes are shown in **Figure 11(c)** without SRD circuit and **Figure 11(d)** with SRD circuit. Signals with symmetrical crossing point are fed from the left and SRD makes a non-symmetrical crossing point which reduces the spike at node V_X considerably. In SRD circuit, M_{SRD1} is always on and when M_{SRD2} is off, V_{gSW} approaches 2.4 V (power supply value of digital part). When M_{SRD2} is on with proper sizing of M_{SRD2}, V_{gSW} can be set to desired value because V_{gSW} in this case will be equal to V_{SG} of M_{SRD2} transistors. In this circuit for complete switching of M_{SW} transistors we need 350 mV differential voltage, so V_{SG} of M_{SRD2} is set to 2.05 V. On the other hand for non-symmetric crossing it's enough to choose bigger size for M_{SRD1} than M_{SRD2}. Size of M_{SRD1} and M_{SRD2} has been given in **Table 1**, also SRD output wave forms and its effect in reducing spike in node V_X is shown in **Figure 11(d)**. The capacitive coupling to the analog output is minimized by limiting the amplitude of the control signals just high enough to switch the tail current completely to the desired output branch of the differential

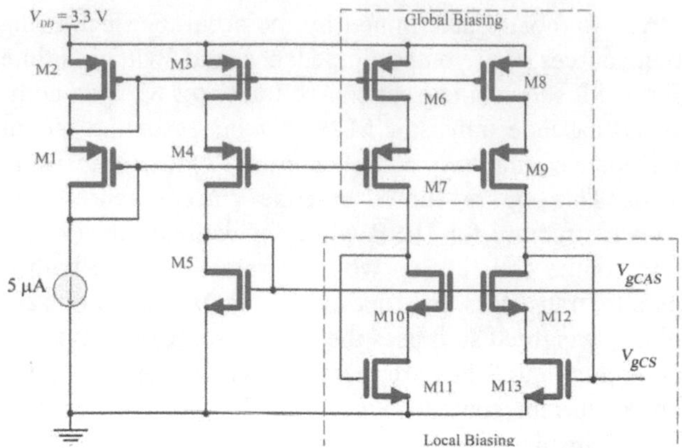

Figure 10. Biasing scheme for current sources.

pair. In addition the switch transistors are kept relatively small in order to avoid large parasitic capacitances.

Table 1. Current source and SRD transistors dimensions and currents.

Transistor	Size	I_D
M_{CS}	W = 2 μm, L = 10 μm	5 μA
M_{CAS}	W = 2 μm, L = 0.35 μm	5 μA
M_{SW}	W = 0.5 μm, L = 0.35 μm	-
M_{SRD1}	W = 1.5 μm, L = 2 μm	-
M_{SRD2}	W = 1 μm, L = 2 μm	-

5. Layout and a Few Techniques to Achieve High Speed

Clock distribution for 1 GHz is very difficult and getting data in this speed is very hard thus we have used 2 channels for digital section. Every channel works at 500MHz and then results of two channels are combined at the input of the switch to get 1 GHz. **Figure 12** shows the structure used for digital section of the DAC. Channel 1 samples input data with clock and channel 2 samples input data with clock-not. A buffer just before switch combines the output of two digital channels. It sends the output of digital channel 1 with clock and the output of digital channel 2 with clock-not to the input of switch. In fact in one period of clock we take 2 samples of the input code and at the output it seems that the circuit works at 1 GHz. On the other hand, we use master-slave operation in all digital circuits and use pipelining scheme, so in overall the digital circuit only senses one gate-delay. For example the structure of one of 3-input 7-output Binary-to-Thermometer Decoder has been shown in **Figure 13**. Layout of all digital section has been done manually to guarantee the best speed, low power and minimum area. **Figure 14** shows the complete layout of the DAC, latches and switches which are grouped in a separated

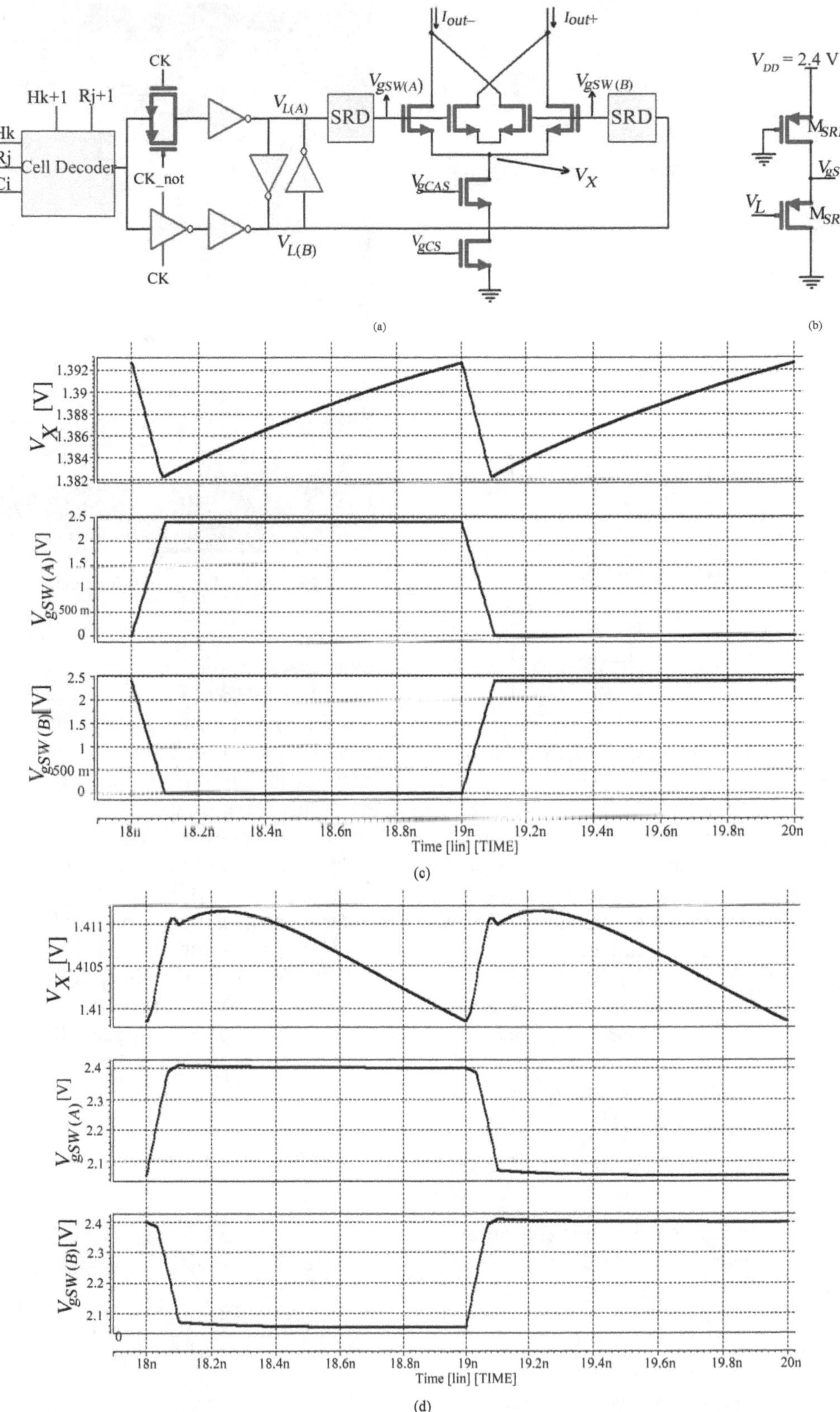

Figure 11. Non-symmetrical crossing point reduces current source drain spike and clock feed-through scheme, (a) current source, switch, latch and driver cell, (b) SRD circuit, (c) drain spike and driver voltages without SRD circuit, and (d) drain spike and driver voltages with SRD circuit.

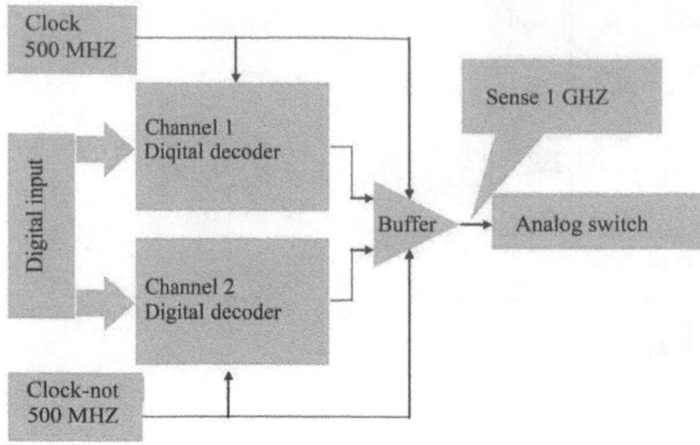

Figure 12. Using two 500 MHz digital channels to achieve 1 Gsample/s.

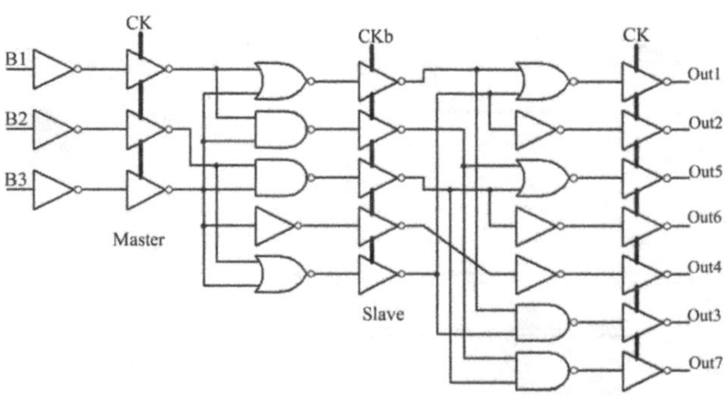

Figure 13. Gate level structure of 3-input 7-output Binary-to-Thermometer Decoder.

array placed between the decoders and the current source arrays to isolate these noisy digital circuits from the sensitive analog circuits that generate the current. A guard ring has been used to separate analog section from digital section. Layout of the decoder circuit has been drawn manually and pipelining used to reach the maximum speed and improvement of the parasitic capacitance and sizing of transistors has been done with simulation. For reduced systematic errors each unary current source is divided into 16 sub-current sources and Q^2 Random Walk distribution scheme is applied [21].

6. Simulation Results

Simulations have been performed on a differential 50-load. The internal node interconnection capacitance has been estimated to be 400 fF, and the output capacitance 1pF. The analog voltage supply is 3.3 V while the digital part of the chip operates at only 2.4 V. Total power consumption in the Nyquist rate measurement is 144.9 mW. SFDR is better than 64 dB in Nyquist rate. **Figure 15** shows differential output spectrum where DAC worked with 1 GSample/s speed and input code near to Nyquist rate (495 MHz) with 1 mV (rms) noise voltage on analog

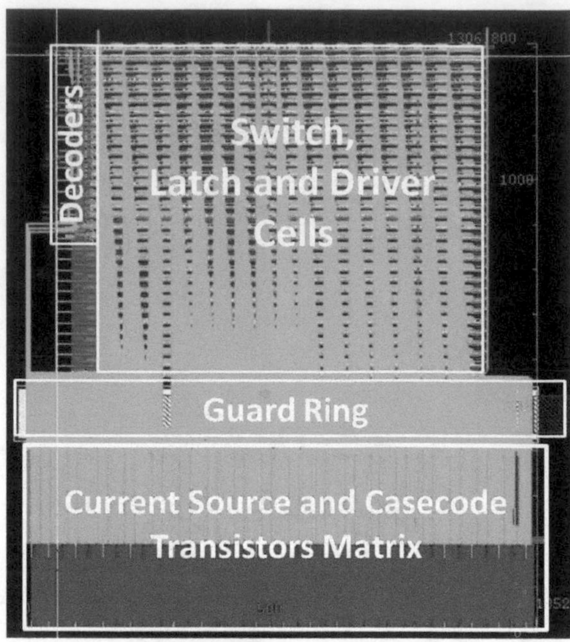

Figure 14. Layout of designed 12-bit DAC.

power supply. Also **Figures 16** and **17** show differential outputs spectrum for 1 GSample/s speed with input signals in 100 MHz and 25 MHz respectively. Measured SFDR for both of them was better than 70 dB. **Figure 18** shows the measured SFDR versus various input frequency for the proposed DAC at a 1 GHz sampling frequency. In **Figure 19**, a dual-tone SFDR measurement is shown. Two sinusoidal signals around 15 MHz with 5-MHz spacing have been applied to the D/A converter at an update rate of 1 GSample/s. The SFDR equals 71 dB. In order to make simulation of glitch energy transition of input digital codes from 011111111111 has been made to 100000000000, such that the glitch energy has been obtained to be 2.3 pV.s. **Figures 20** and **21** show DNL and INL characteristics of designed DAC for in creasing

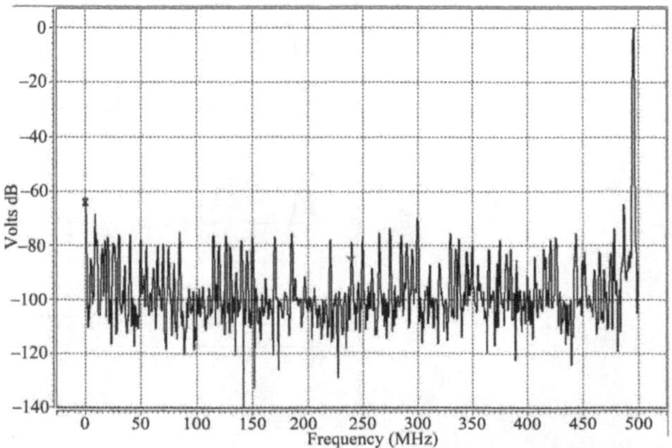

Figure 15. Sinewave spectrum for Fs = 1 GSample/s, Fsig = 495 MHz.

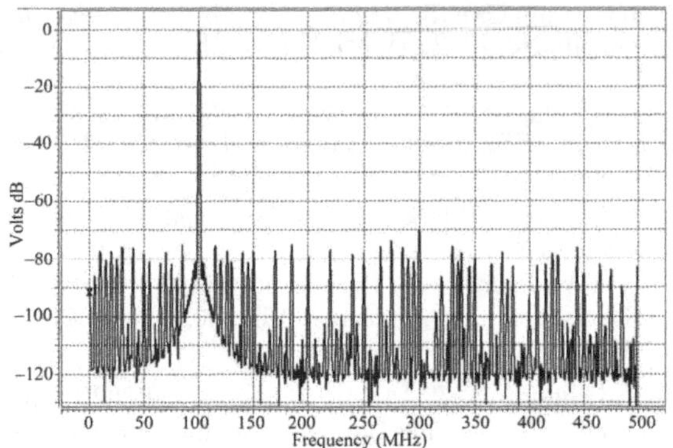

Figure 16. Sinewave spectrum for Fs = 1 GSample/s, Fsig = 100 MHz.

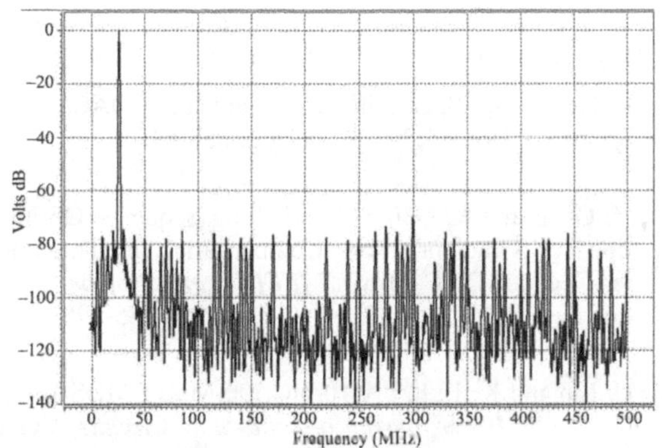

Figure 17. Sinewave spectrum for Fs = 1 GSample/s, Fsig = 25 MHz.

input code from 0 to 4096. The INL and DNL obtained from post layout four corners Monte-Carlo simulations considering process mismatch parameters are better than 0.74 LSB and 0.49 LSB, respectively. **Table 2**

Table 2. Performance summary.

Technology	0.35 μm (1P4M) TSMC Mixed Mode CMOS
Resolution	12-bit
Update rate	Up to 1 GS/s
Max. output swing	$2V_{pp}$ diff.
DNL	Better than 0.49LSB
INL	Better than 0.74LSB
SFDR (495 MHz@1 GS/s)	64 dB
SFDR (100 MHz@1 GS/s)	70 dB
SFDR (25 MHz@1 GS/s)	71 dB
SFDR (1 MHz@1 GS/s)	72 dB
ENOB (25 MHz@1 GS/s)	10.7-bit
ENOB (1 MHz@1 GS/s)	11-bit
Analog Power consumption (at 1 GS/s)	69.3 mW (21 mA from 3.3 V)
Digital Power consumption (at 1 GS/s)	75.6 mW (31.5 mA from 2.4 V)
Total Power consumption (at 1 GS/s)	144.9 mW
Analog/Digital voltage supply	3.3 V/2.4 V
Active area	1306 μm×1052 μm

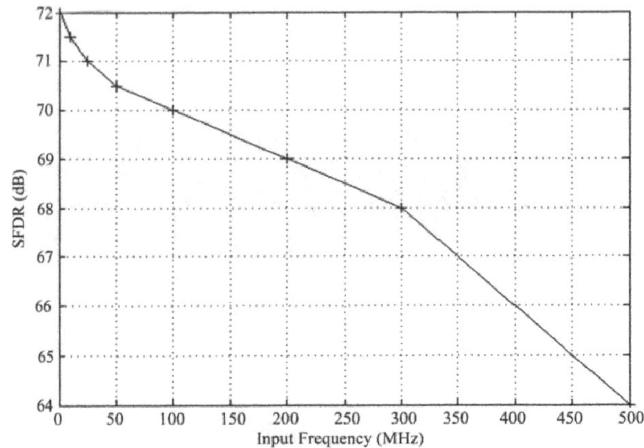

Figure 18. SFDR versus input frequency for the proposed DAC at 1 GHz sampling frequency.

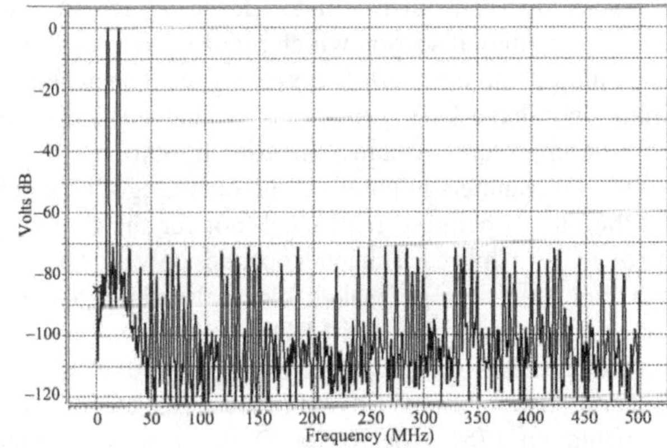

Figure 19. Simulated dual-tone spectrum for Fs = 1 GSample/s, Fsig = 20 MHz and 10MHz.

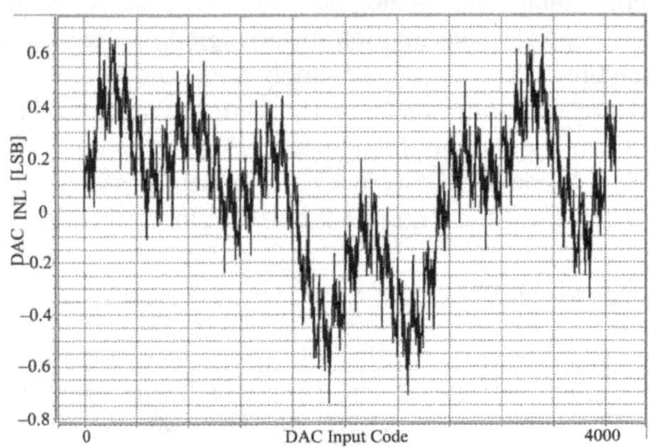

Figure 20. DAC INL characteristic.

summarizes some of important performance parameters of the DAC.

7. Conclusion

In this article a 3.3 V, 12-bit, current-steering, 9 + 3 seg-

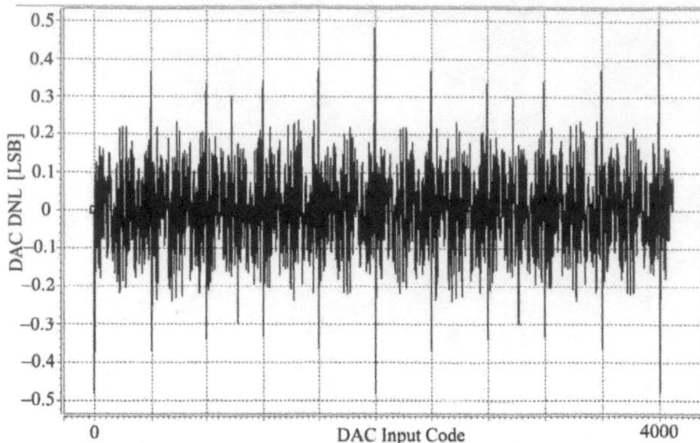

Figure 21. DAC DNL characteristic.

mented architecture digital to analog converter for base-band of wireless transmitter circuits has been presented. A new 3-D thermometer decoding scheme has been used in digital section which reduces the area power consumption and number of control signals considerably. Simulations have been performed to analyze and solve some of important dynamic linearity limitations. Using two digital channels in parallel, one operating with clock and the other operating with clock-not for the sampling rate of 1 GS/s while each channel operates only at 500 MHz. This clocking strategy makes clock distribution much easier. Analog switches and SRD circuits have been optimized not only to get minimum area and maximum speed but also to improve dynamic behavior of the DAC. Segmentation (75%) decreases DNL error and glitch energy considerably and guarantees needed improvement of SFDR. Separate power supplies have been used for digital and analog parts. Digital section operates at lower supply voltage than analog part. This increases speed and reduces power consumption of the digital part and at the same time decreases power supply noise and improve the performance of the analog part. The technology used is a 0.35 µm, single-poly four-metal, 3.3 V, standard TSMC Mixed Mode CMOS process. The active area of the DAC, as shown in **Figure 14**, is 1052 µm × 1306 µm.

8. References

[1] S. M. Ha, T. K. Nam and K. S. Yoon, "An I/Q Channel 12-bit 120 Ms/s CMOS DAC with Three Stage Thermometer Decoders for WLAN," *Proceedings of the IEEE Asia Pacific Conference on Circuits and Systems*, Singapore, 4-7 December 2006, pp. 355-358.

[2] N. Ghittori, *et al.*, "1.2-V Low-Power Multi-Mode Dac+Filter Blocks for Reconfigurable (WLAN/UMTS, WLAN/Bluetooth) Transmitters," *IEEE Journal of Solid-State Circuits,* Vol. 41, No. 9, 2006, pp. 1970-1982.

[3] S. Khorram, *et al.*, "A Fully Integrated SOC for 802.11 b in 0.18 µm CMOS," *IEEE Journal of Solid-State Circuits,* Vol. 40, No. 12, 2005, pp. 2492-2501.

[4] S. Mehta, *et al.*, "An 802.11 g WLAN SOC," *IEEE Journal of Solid-State Circuits,* Vol. 40, No. 12, 2005, pp. 2483-2491.

[5] C. Eklund, R. Marks, K. Stanwood and S. Wang, "IEEE Standard 802.16: A Technical Overview of the Wireless Man Air Interface for Broadband Wireless Access," *IEEE Communications Magazine*, Vol. 40, No. 6, 2002, pp. 98-107.

[6] N. Ghittori, *et al.*, "An IEEE 802.11 and 802.16 WLAN Wireless Transmitter Baseband Architecture with a 1.2-V, 600-Ms/s, 2.4-mW DAC," *Analog Integrated Circuits and Signal Processing*, Vol. 59, No. 3, 2009, pp. 231-242.

[7] B. Razavi, "Principles of Data Conversion Systems," Wiley-IEEE Press, New Jersey, 1995.

[8] P. Hendriks, "Specifying Communication DACs," *IEEE Spectrum,* Vol. 34, No. 7, 1997, pp. 58-69.

[9] Y. Cong and R. Geiger, "Switching Sequence Optimization for Gradient Error Compensation in Thermometer-Decoded DAC Arrays," *IEEE Transaction on Circuits and Systems-II*, Vol. 47, No. 7, 2000, pp. 585-595.

[10] C. Lin.and K. Bult, "A 10-bit, 500-Ms/s CMOS DAC in 0.6 mm^2," *IEEE Journal of Solid-State Circuits,* Vol. 33, No. 12, 1998, pp. 1948-1958.

[11] J. Vandenbussche, *et al.*, "Systematic de Sign of High-Accuracy Current-Steering D/A Converter Macro Cells for Integrated VLSI Systems," *IEEE Transaction on Circuits and Systems II*: *Analog and Digital Signal Processing,* Vol. 48, No. 3, 2001, pp. 300-309.

[12] J. Gonzalez and E. Alarcon, "Clock-Jitter Induced Distortion in High-Speed CMOS Switched-Current Segmented Digital to Analog Converters," *International Symposium on Circuits and Systems* (*ISCAS*'01), Sydney, 6-9 May 2001, pp. 1512-1515.

[13] J. Bastos, M. Steyaert and W. Sansen, "A High Yield 12-Bit 250-Ms/s CMOS D/A Converter," *IEEE Custom Integrated Circuits Conference* (*CICC*), San Diego, 5-8 May 1996, pp. 431-434.

[14] L. Sumanen, M. Waltari and K. Halonen, "A 10-Bit High-Speed Low-Power CMOS D/A Converter in 0.2 mm^2," *IEEE International Conference on Electronics, Circuits and Systems*, Lisboan, 7-10 September 1998, pp. 15-18.

[15] Y. Nakamura, T. Miki, A. Maeda, H. Kondoh and N. Yazwa, "A 10-b 70-Ms/s CMOS D/A Converter," *IEEE Journal of Solid-State Circuits*, Vol. 26, No. 4, 1991, pp. 637-642.

[16] M. Albiol, J. Gonzalez and E. Alarcon, "Mismatch and Dynamic Modeling of Current Sources in Current-Steering CMOS D/A Converters: An Extended Design Procedure," *IEEE Transactions on Circuits and Systems I*: *Regular Papers,* Vol. 51, No. 1, 2004, pp. 159-169.

[17] A. Bosch, M. Borremans, M. Steyaert and W. Sansen, "A 10-Bit 1-Gs/s Nyquist Current Steering CMOS D/A Converter," *IEEE Journal of Solid-State Circuits*, Vol. 36, No. 3, 2001, pp. 315-324.

[18] M. Pelgrom, A. Duinmaijer and A. Welbers, "Matching Properties of MOS Transistors," *IEEE Journal of Solid-State Circuits,* Vol. 24, No. 5, 1989, pp. 1433-1440.

[19] H. Kohno, *et al.*, "A 350-Ms/s 3.3V 8-Bit CMOS D/A Converter Using a Delayed Driving Scheme," *IEEE Custom Integrated Circuits Conference* (*CICC*), Santa Clara, 1-4 May 1995, pp. 211-214.

[20] L. Luh, J. Choma, J. Draper, " A High-Speed Fully Differential Current Switch," *IEEE Transactions on Circuits and Systems-II*: *Analog and Digital Signal Processing*, Vol. 47, No. 4, 2000, pp. 358-363.

[21] G. Van der Plas, *et al.*, "A 14-Bit Intrinsic Accuracy Q^2 Random Walk CMOS DAC," *IEEE Journal of Solid-State Circuits*, Vol. 34, No. 12, 1999, pp. 1708-1718.

Nth Order Voltage Mode Active-C Filter Employing Current Controlled Current Conveyor

Ashish Ranjan, Sajal K. Paul
Department of Electronics Engineering, Indian School of Mines, Dhanbad, India

Abstract

This paper proposes an nth order (where $n = 2,3,\cdots,n$) voltage mode active-C filter using n number of current controlled current conveyors (CCCIIs) and n number of equal valued grounded capacitors. The proposed topology can implement both band pass and low pass responses without alteration of any components. The filters offer the following important features: use of minimum number of current controlled current conveyors (CCCIIs) and passive components, no matching constraint, use of all grounded capacitors and absence of external resistor suitable for integration, cut off frequency can easily be electronically adjusted using AMS 0.35 μm CMOS technology. PSPICE simulation results of third order band pass and low pass responses are provided. The results are found to agree well with the theory.

Keywords: Analog Filters, Active-C Filter, Higher Order Voltage Mode Filter, CCCII

1. Introduction

Nowadays, current conveyors play an important role for the realization of various analog signal processing circuits and systems. They are accepted to have high performance properties such as wide signal bandwidth, high dynamic range, low power consumption and occupy less chip area [1,2]. The basic second generation current conveyor (CCII) does not have in built tuning property, whereas second generation current controlled current conveyor (CCCII) possesses this property because of the adjustability of intrinsic resistance at port X of CCCII by bias current [3-5]. Already a number of analog biquadratic filters have been reported in [6-9] and references cited there in. However, the nth order filter can be flexibly used to realize any higher order filter function and hence serves a wide range of applications. Higher order filters can be obtained by various methods such as cascading of lower order filters or state variable technique or signal flow graph. Already a number of current conveyor (CCII or CCCII) based higher order current mode [10-14] and voltage mode [15-18] filters have been reported. As this paper is concerning higher order voltage mode filters, hence only the study of the features of already reported higher order voltage mode filters [15-18] are made in **Table 1**.

In this work, an attempt is made to propose a new nth order (where, $n = 2,3,\cdots,n$) voltage mode filter. Both low pass and band pass responses can be obtained from the same topology using n CCCIIs and grounded n capacitors. It does not require any resistor. The proposed topology is an active-C filter and hence ideal for IC implementation. The use of CCCIIs in the circuit provides electronic tunability [5] of the filter parameters.

2. Circuit Description

The circuit symbol of the DOCCCII is shown in **Figure 1** The port relationship of a DOCCCII can be defined as

$$I_Y = 0,\ V_X = V_Y + I_X |R_X|,\ I_{Z\pm} = \pm I_X \quad (1)$$

where, the positive and negative signs define a positive and a negative DOCCCII respectively. In this equation R_X, the intrinsic series input resistance of the conveyor at X port is electronically tunable via I_0 of the CMOS based CCCII shown in **Figure 2** and R_X may be defined as [5]

$$R_x = \frac{1}{\sqrt{g_{m2} + g_{m4}}} \quad (2)$$

$$g_{mi} = 2\beta_i I_0 \quad (i = 2,4) \quad (3)$$

$$\beta_i = \frac{\varepsilon_0 \varepsilon_{ins} \mu_i W_i}{t_{ox} L_i} \quad (4)$$

Table 1. Comparative study of the available nth order voltage mode filter.

Ref. No.	Active element used and number of active elements required	Number of capacitors required	Number of resistors required	All passive elements are grounded	In built tunability of filter parameters	Types of filter implemented	Require to change the hardware to change filter type
15	CCII, $3n-2$	$n+1$	$3n-1$	Yes	No	Universal filter	Yes
16	CCII, $n+1$	n	$n+2$	No	No	Low pass	Not Applicable
17	CCII, $n+2$	Minimum	$2n+3$	No	No	Universal filter	Yes
18	CCCII, $n+1$	n	1	Yes	Yes	Low pass	Not Applicable
Proposed	CCCII, n	n	Nil	Yes	Yes	Low pass & Band pass	No

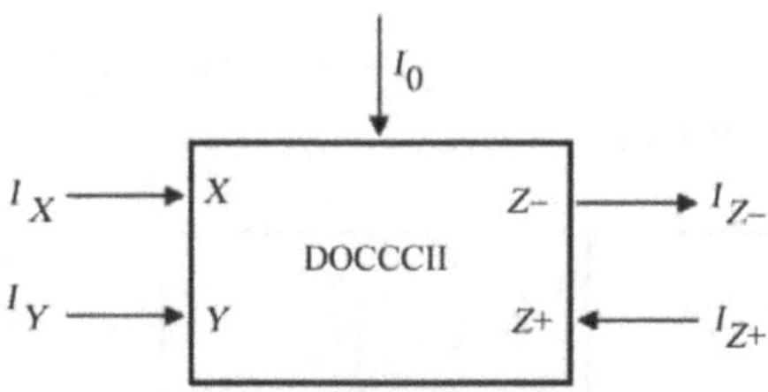

Figure 1. Block diagram of DOCCCII.

where, g_{m2} and g_{m4} are the transconductances of M_2 and M_4 respectively, I_0 is bias current of DOCCCII. The proposed voltage mode nth order filter circuit is shown in **Figure 3**.

The routine analysis of the circuit of **Figure 3** gives the transfer function for an nth order filter as

$$V_{out} = \frac{V_{in1} - sV_{in2}R_xC}{D(S)} \tag{5}$$

where

$$D(S) = a_{nn}\left(R_x^nC^n\right)s^n + \left[\sum_{j=1}^{n-2} a_{n(n-j)}\left(R_xC\right)^{n-j}s^{n-j}\right] + a_{n1}R_xC\,s + a_{n0} \tag{6}$$

$$n = 2,3,\cdots,n \tag{7}$$

$$a_{nn} = 1 \tag{8}$$

$$a_{n(n-j)} = a_{(n-j)(n-j)} + a_{(n-j)(n-j-1)} \quad (j = 1,2,\cdots,n-2) \tag{9}$$

$$a_{n1} = 2 \tag{10}$$

$$a_{n0} = 1 \tag{11}$$

From above equations we can see that specialization in the numerator of (5) results in the following filter responses:

1) Low pass Response

- At V_{out} with $V_{in1} = V_{in}$ and $V_{in2} = 0$

2) Band pass Response

- At V_{out} with $V_{in1} = 0$ and $V_{in2} = V_{in}$

Hence, the proposed circuit gives an inverted nth order band pass filter and nth order low pass filter from the same topology.

As an example, a third order transfer function

$$V_{out} = \frac{V_{in1} - sV_{in2}R_xC}{s^3R_x^3C^3 + 3s^2R_x^2C^2 + 2sR_xC + 1} \tag{12}$$

is realized using (5)–(11) and the corresponding third order circuit obtained from the nth order circuit of **Figure 3** is given in **Figure 4**.

With $V_{in1} = V_{in}$ and, Equation (12) simplifies to

$$V_{out} = \frac{V_{in}}{s^3R_x^3C^3 + 3s^2R_x^2C^2 + 2sR_xC + 1} \tag{13}$$

which is a low pass response.

Similarly, with $V_{in1} = 0$ and, Equation (12) simplifies to

$$V_{out} = \frac{-sV_{in}R_xC}{s^3R_x^3C^3 + 3s^2R_x^2C^2 + 2sR_xC + 1} \tag{14}$$

which is a band pass response.

The forth order filters is obtained by adding section shown in **Figure 5** between 2nd and 3rd CCCII- of **Figure 4**. Similarly, fifth and higher order filters are obtained by adding one section shown in **Figure 5** for each higher order.

Comparision of the available nth order filters [15-18] and the proposed one is given in **Table 1**. It reveals that the proposed circuit uses minimum number of current conveyors and passive components and no resistor. It can realize both band pass and low pass responses in contrast to only low pass response in [16,18] and does not require to change any hardware to change filter type. The uni-

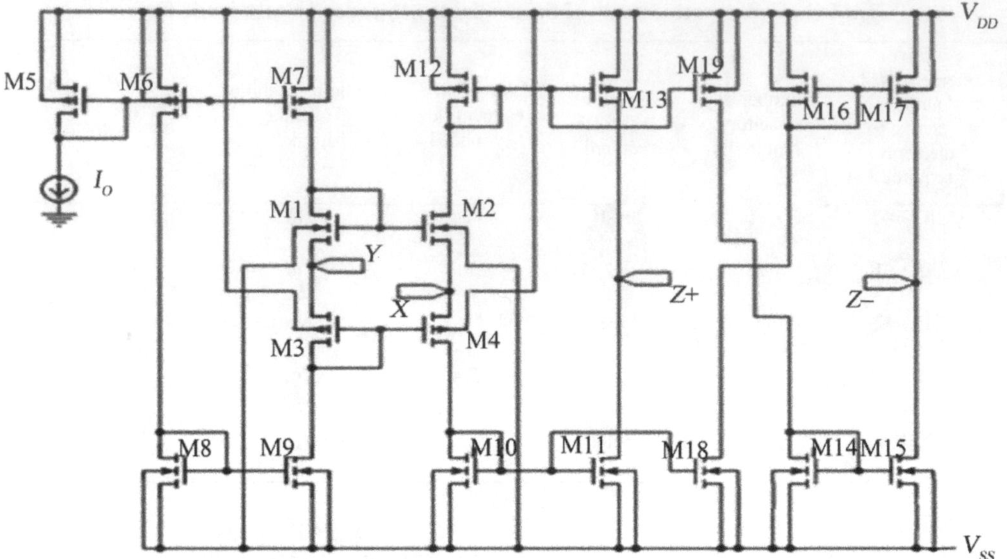

Figure 2. Internal structure of DOCCCII.

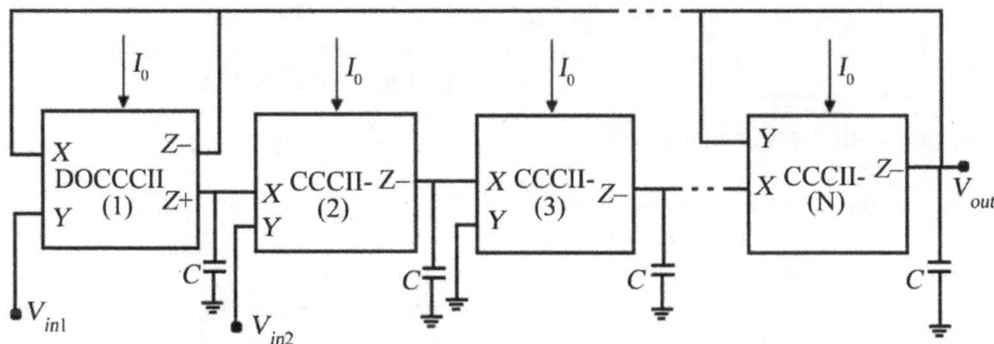

Figure 3. Proposed voltage mode nth order low pass and band pass filters.

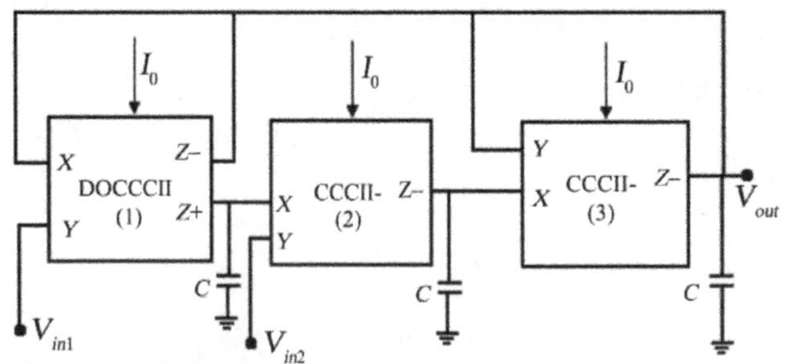

Figure 4. Proposed voltage mode third order low pass and band pass filters.

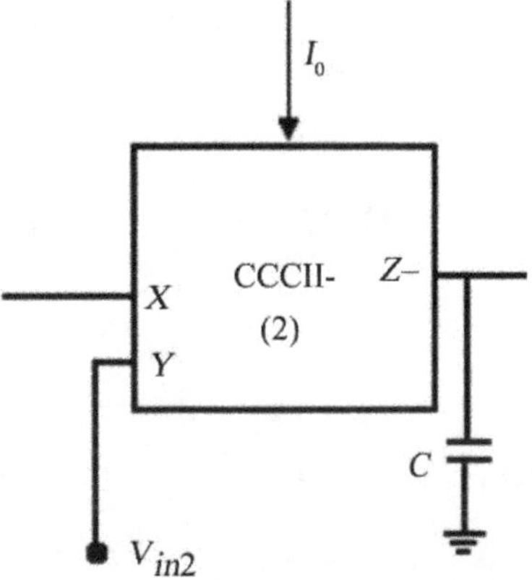

Figure 5. Section to be added for higher order filter.

versal filters realized by structures in [15,17] are attractive, but the changing of the filter type would required the change of hardware of the filter circuits. Hence they are not suitable for monolithic IC implementation.

3. Simulation and Results

To verify the theory, the proposed voltage mode nth order filter circuit is simulated with PSPICE using 0.35 µm AMS CMOS based CCCII circuit given in **Figure 2** [5] with supply voltage of ±2.5 volts and aspect ratio of transistors as given in **Table 2**.

As an example, a third order low pass filter and a band

Table 2. MOS dimensions used in the circuit.

Transistors	W(μm)	L(μm)
M_1, M_2	20	0.35
M_3, M_4	60	0.35
M_5, M_6, M_7	30	2
M_8, M_9	10	2
$M_{10}, M_{11}, M_{14}, M_{15}$	10	1
$M_{12}, M_{13}, M_{16}, M_{17}$	30	1

pass filter are obtained with C = 50 pF and I_0 = 200 μA. Frequency responses of the proposed low pass and band pass filters are shown in **Figure 6** and **Figure** 7 respectively. The response for the low pass filter exhibits a –60 dB/dec slope for frequencies higher than f_0. The response for the band pass filter, as shown in **Figure 7**, exhibits an asymmetrical third order nature with a slope of 20 dB/dec for frequencies lower than f_0 and −40 dB/dec for frequencies higher than f_0. The results show a close matching with the theoretical values. The deviation at higher frequency may be due to parasites of DOCCCII/CCCIIs. The time-domain response of the band pass filter is shown in **Figure 8**. Large signal behavior of the proposed filter is investigated by observing the dependence of the output total harmonic distortion (%THD) upon the level of input signal. The result as illustrated in **Figure 9**, shows that the %THD is well within the reasonable limit of 4% [19] for input peak-to-peak voltage level of 2 V. Responses as shown in **Figures 8** and **9** reveal that the output is of good quality.

4. Conclusions

In this paper a generalized nth order (where $n = 2,3,\cdots,n$) voltage mode active-C filter topology is proposed. Both nth order band pass and low pass responses may be realized using same topology. The topology uses n equal value grounded capacitors, single dual output current controlled current conveyor (DOCCCII) and (n-1) current controlled current conveyors (CCCIIs). The verification of the theory is performed by using AMS 0.35 μm CMOS based DOCCCII/CCCII. Comparison with the reported publications [15-18] reveals that the proposed topology uses minimum number of active analog building blocks and minimum passive components. All of the used capacitors are grounded. It does not use any resistor and there is no requirement of changing any hardware for changing filter type from low pass to band pass or

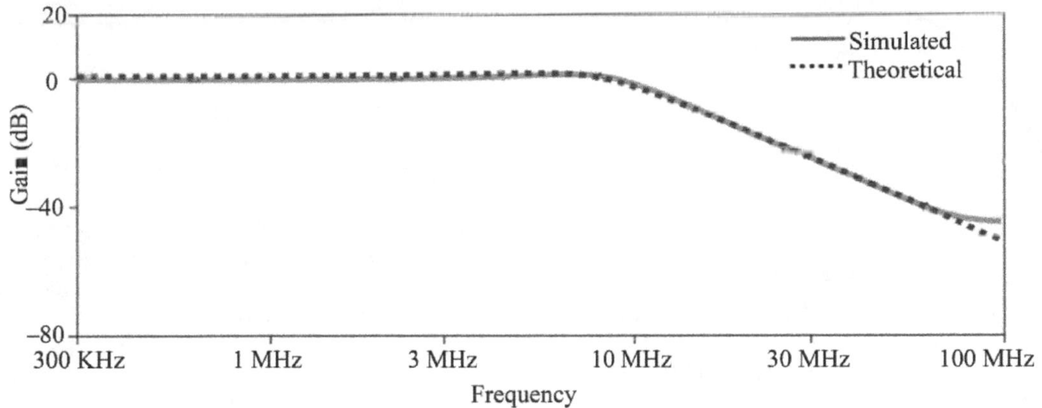

Figure 6. Frequency response of the third order low pass filter.

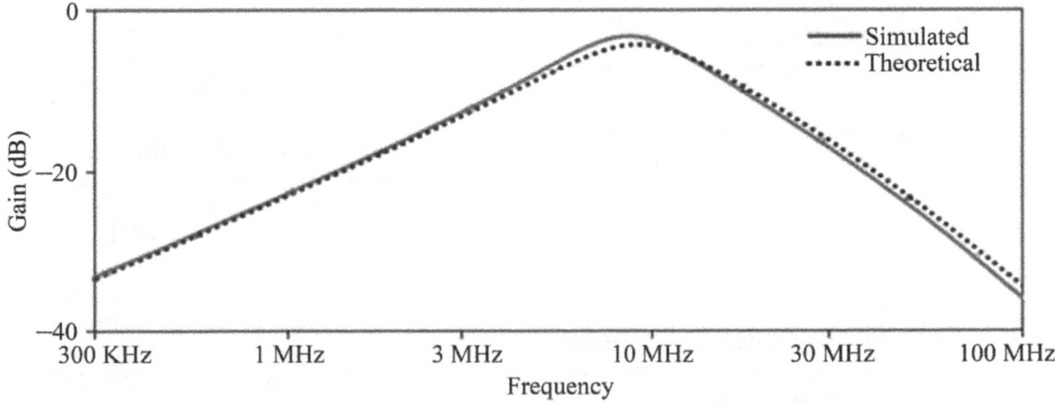

Figure 7. Frequency response of the third order band pass filter.

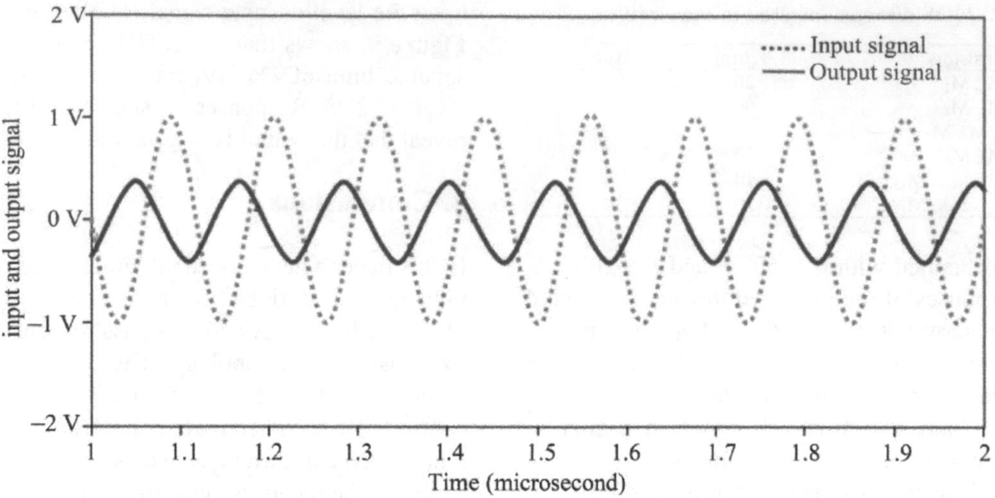

Figure 8. Time response of the band pass filter for input peak-to-peak voltage of 2 V.

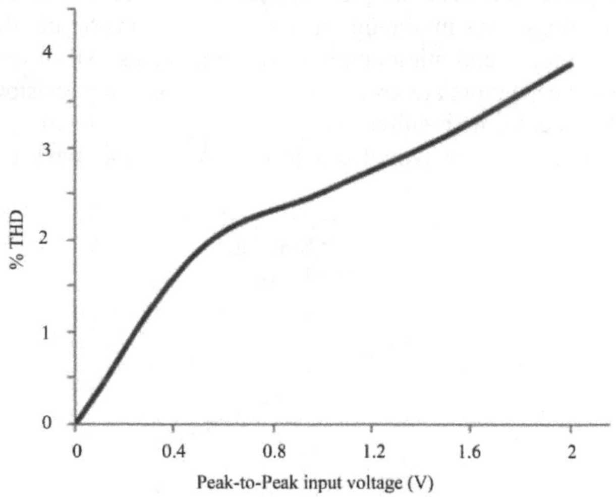

Figure 9. %THD verses input voltage at 10 MHz.

vice-versa, hence suitable for monolithic IC implementation.

5. References

[1] C. Toumazou, F. J. Lidgey and D. G. Haigh, "Analogue IC Design: The Current-Mode Approach," Peter Peregrinus Ltd, London, 1990.

[2] G. Ferri and N. C. Guerrini, "Low-Voltage Low-Power CMOS Current Conveyors," Kluwer Academic Publishers, London, 2003.

[3] A. Fabre, O. Saaid and F. C. Boucheron, "Current Controlled Band Pass Filter Based on Translinear Conveyors," *Electronics Letters*, Vol. 31, No. 20, 1995, pp. 1727-1728.

[4] H. Barthelemy and A. Fabre, "A Second—Generation Current Controlled Conveyor with Negative Intrinsic Resistance," *IEEE Transactions on Circuit Systems-I*, Vol. 49, No. 1, 2002, pp. 63-65.

[5] E. Altuntas and A. Toker, "Realization of Voltage and Current Mode KHN Biquads Using CCCIIs," *International Journal of Electronics and Communication*, Vol. 56, No. 1, 2002, pp. 45-49.

[6] C. M. Chang, "Multifunction Biquadratic Filters Using Current Conveyors," *IEEE Transactions on Circuit Systems-II*, Vol. 44, No. 11, 1997, pp. 956-958.

[7] J. W. Horng, "High-Input Impedance Voltage-Mode Universal Biquardratic Filter Using Three Plus-Type CCIIs," *IEEE Transactions on Circuit Systems-II, Analog and Digital Signal Processing*, Vol. 48, No. 10, 2001, pp. 996-997.

[8] A. K. Singh and R. Senani, "A New Four-Cc-Based Configuration for Realizing a Voltage-Mode Biquad Filters," *Journal of Circuits, Systems and Computers*, Vol. 11, No. 3, 2002, pp. 213-218.

[9] Y. H. Wang and C. T. Lee, "Versatile Insensitive Current-Mode Universal Biquad Implementation Using Current Conveyors," *IEEE Transactions on Circuit Systems-II, Analog and Digital Signal Processing*, Vol. 48, No. 4, 2001, pp. 409-413.

[10] M. Koksal and M. Sagbas, "A Versatile Signal Flow Graph Realization of a General Current Transfer Function," *AEU-International Journal of Electronics and Communication*, Vol. 62, No. 1, 2008, pp. 33-40.

[11] M. Altun, H. Kuntman, S. Minaei and O. K. Sayin, "Realization of Nth-Order Current Transfer Employing ECCIIs and Application Examples," *International Journal of Electronics*, Vol. 96, No. 11, 2004, pp. 1115-1126.

[12] A. A. Hussain, A. N. Tasadduq and A.-E. Osama, "Digitally Programmable High-Order Current-Mode Universal Filteres," *Analog Integrated Circuits and Signal Processing*, Vol. 67, No. 2, 2010, pp. 179-187.

[13] H. Kuntaman, O. Cicekoglu and S. Ozcan, "Realization

of Current-Mode Third Order Butterworth Filters Employing Equal Valued Passive Elements and Unity Gain Buffers," *Analog Integrated Circuits and Signal Processing,* Vol. 30, No. 3, 2002, pp. 253-256.

[14] E. Yuce and S. Minaei, "On the Realization of High-Order Current Mode Filter Employing Current Controlled Conveyors," *Computers and Electrical Engineering,* Vol. 34, No. 3, 2008, pp. 165-172.

[15] E. O. Gunes and F. Anday, "Realization of Nth-Order Voltage Transfer Function Using CCII+," *Electronics Letters,* Vol. 31, No. 13, 1995, pp. 1022-1023.

[16] C. Acar, "Nth-Order Low Pass Voltage Transfer Function Synthesis Using CCII+s: Signal-Flow Graph Approach," *Electronics letters,* Vol. 32, No. 3, 1996, pp.159-160.

[17] C. Acar and S. Ozoguz, "High-Order Voltage Transfer Function Synthesis Using CCII+ Based Unity Gain Current Amplifiers," *Electronics letters,* Vol. 32, No. 22, 1996, pp. 2030-2031.

[18] J. Zaho, J. G. Ziang and J. N. Liu, "Design of Tunable Biquadratic Filters Employing CCCIIs: State Variable Block Diagram Approach," *Analog Integrated Circuits and Signal Processing,* Vol. 62, No. 3, 2010, pp.397-406.

[19] E. S. Erdogan, R. O. Topaloglu, H. Kuntaman and O. Cicekoglu, "New Current Mode Special Function Continuous-Time Active Filters Employing Only OTAs and OPAMPs," *International Journal of Electronics*, Vol. 91, No. 6, 2004, pp. 345-359.

13

A Scalable Model of the Substrate Network in *Deep N-Well* RF MOSFETs with Multiple Fingers

Jun Liu[1,2], Marissa Condon[2]

[1]*Key Laboratory of RF Circuits and Systems, Ministry of Education, Hangzhou Dianzi University, Hangzhou, China*
[2]*School of Electronic Engineering, Dublin City University, Dublin, Ireland*

Abstract

A novel scalable model of substrate components for *deep n-well* (*DNW*) RF MOSFETs with different number of fingers is presented for the first time. The test structure developed in [1] is employed to directly access the characteristics of the substrate to extract the different substrate components. A methodology is developed to directly extract the parameters for the substrate network from the measured data. By using the measured two-port data of a set of nMOSFETs with different number of fingers, with the *DNW* in grounded and float configuration, respectively, the parameters of the scalable substrate model are obtained. The method and the substrate model are further verified and validated by matching the measured and simulated output admittances. Excellent agreement up to 40 GHz for configurations in common-source has been achieved.

Keywords: *Deep N-Well* (*DNW*), RF Mosfets, Substrate Network, Scalable Model

1. Introduction

THE incorporation of a *Deep N-Well* (*DNW*) implantation into a standard CMOS technology has become a popular choice for reducing undesired interference in CMOS mixed-signal/RF SoC designs [2-6]. Substrate network parameters are of the utmost importance in accurately modeling the output admittance of RF MOSFETs. For mixed-signal/RF SoC design, a scalable model of RF MOSFETs is useful. Many papers have reported about scalable models of substrate network components [7-13]. However, there are few detailed works on scalable models with substrate network components in *DNW* RF MOSFETs with different number of fingers. In contrast to the RF MOSFET without *DNW* implantation (as seen from the nMOSFETs in **Figure 1**), the *DNW* actually partitions the substrate of a *DNW* RF MOSFET into three parts [1]: The *DNW* itself, the p-well in the *DNW*, and the original substrate where the *DNW* is formed. The *DNW* layer forms a capacitive coupling path in the substrate, which exists no matter what the electrical configuration is. Furthermore, most previous works [7-19] dealt with substrate parasitic effects in RF MOSFETs by using resistance networks only. The capacitive coupling effect, which is physically in existence, is always neglected. All of these make the previously reported substrate models less physically reasonable to use for accurately extracting the substrate network components of *DNW* RF MOSFETs.

In this paper, a compact, physically based substrate network is proposed targeted specifically at *DNW* RF MOSFET modeling. A novel test structure proposed in [1] is expanded and employed in deriving and extracting the N_f- dependent equations involving substrate components in multi-finger *DNW* RF MOSFETs. The geometric effects such as shallow trench isolation (STI), which have never been considered in previous reported works, are accurately modeled. The results show that the substrate components within the p-well and the capacitances caused by the *DNW* are strongly dependent on N_f, while the parasitic components in the original p-substrate have a slight dependence on N_f in multi-finger devices.

To verify the validity of the derived scalable model of the substrate network components, a macro-model consisting of the BSIM3v3.2 model core with the proposed substrate-network based on the extracted parameters, is simulated in Agilent Advanced Design System (ADS). Excellent agreement between the simulated and measured output admittance for a set of devices with different number of fingers up to 40 GHz validated the accuracy of the methodology proposed for *DNW* RF-MOSFET modeling in this paper.

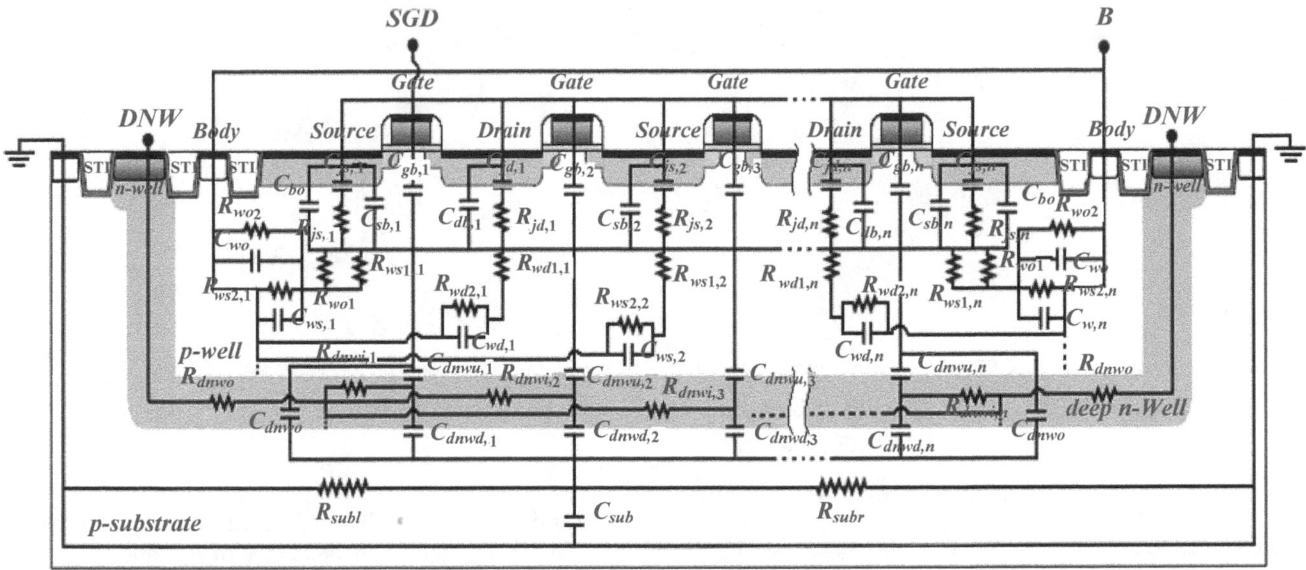

Figure 1. Equivalent circuit for the substrate resistance and capacitance networks of multi-finger (*Nf*) *DNW* RF MOSFET with all the source (*S*), drain (*D*) and gate (*G*) terminals for different fingers connected together. Source, drain, and gate resistances are ignored for their slight contribution to the output impedance.

2. Analysis of the Substrate Network and the Scalable Model Derivation

A multi-finger *DNW* RF MOSFET with the test configuration proposed in [1] is investigated. All of the source (*S*), drain (*D*) and gate (*G*) terminals for different fingers are connected together and used as port one, while the body (*B*) terminal is port two, and the p-substrate is grounded, for two-port measurement. **Figure 1** shows the substrate network when the junction diodes are turned off. In **Figure 1**, $C_{js,i}$, $C_{jd,i}$ are each *S/D* junction region capacitors, $R_{js,i}$, $R_{jd,i}$ are each *S/D* junction resistors. C_{dnwo}, which combined with C_{wo}, C_{bo}, R_{wo1}, R_{wo2} and R_{wo}, is used to capture the difference between the inner and outer *S/D* regions in this work. $C_{dnwu,i}$ and $C_{dnwd,i}$ represent the p-well-to-*DNW* and the *DNW*-to-p-substrate capacitors under each finger region. $C_{ws,i}$ and $C_{wd,i}$ are each finger capacitors from the bottom of the *S/D* regions to *B* within the *Deep N-Well*. $R_{ws1,i}$, $R_{wd1,i}$, $R_{ws2,i}$ and $R_{wd2,i}$ represent the single finger resistors between the bottom of the *S/D* region and *B*. $C_{sb,i}$, $C_{db,i}$ and $C_{gb,i}$ are the *S*-to-*B*, *G*-to-*B* and *D*-to-*B* capacitors of each finger region, R_{subl}, R_{subr} and C_{sub} are the capacitor and the resistor of the p-substrate, $R_{dnw,i}$ represent the resistors of the *DNW* under each finger region. R_{dnwo} represents the n-well ring resistor.

Based on the equivalent circuits identified in **Figure 1**, a simplified substrate network, as shown in **Figure 2**, with the following relationships can be obtained for any number of fingers:

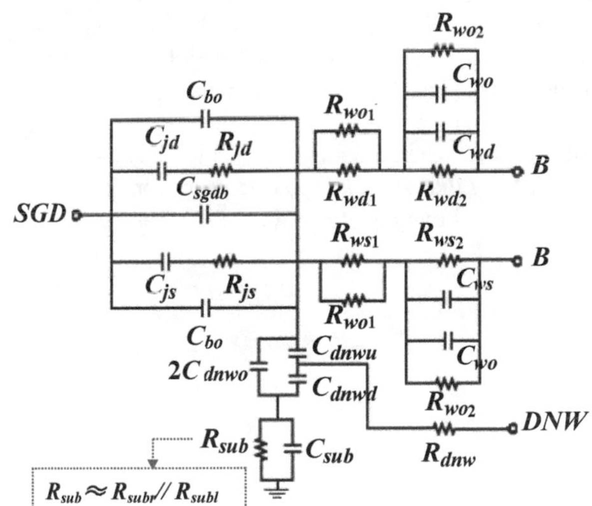

Figure 2. Equivalent circuit of multi-finger *DNW* RF MOSFETs with *S/G/D* terminals connected together.

$$C_{js/jd} = \sum_{i=1}^{N_{s/d}} C_{js/jd,i} \tag{1a}$$

$$R_{js/jd}^{-1} = \sum_{i=1}^{N_{s/d}} R_{js/jd,i}^{-1} \tag{1b}$$

$$C_{sgdb} = \sum_{i=1}^{N_f} \left[C_{sb,i} + C_{gb,i} + C_{db,i} \right] \tag{1c}$$

$$C_{ws/wd} = \sum_{i=1}^{N_{s/d}} C_{ws/wd,i} \tag{1d}$$

$$R_{ws1/wd1}^{-1} = \sum_{i=1}^{N_{s/d}} R_{ws1/wd1,i}^{-1} \quad (1e)$$

$$R_{sub}^{-1} = R_{subl}^{-1} + R_{subr}^{-1} \quad (1f)$$

$$R_{ws2/wd2}^{-1} = \sum_{i=1}^{N_{s/d}} R_{ws2/wd2,i}^{-1} \quad (1g)$$

$$C_{dnwu} = \sum_{i=1}^{N_f} \left[C_{dnwu,i} \right] \quad (1h)$$

$$C_{dnwd} = \sum_{i=1}^{N_f} \left[C_{dnwd,i} \right] \quad (1i)$$

$$R_{dnw} = 2R_{dnwo} + \left[\sum_{i=1}^{N_f} \left[R_{dnw,i}^{-1} \right] \right]^{-1} \quad (1j)$$

where, C_{js}, C_{jd} represent the total *S/D* junction region capacitances, R_{js}, R_{jd} represent the total *S/D* junction resistances, R_{sub} represents the total resistance of the p-substrate, C_{dnw} represents the total capacitance caused by the *DNW*, C_{ws}, C_{wd} are the total capacitances from the bottom of the *S/D* regions to *B* within the *Deep N-Well*, $R_{ws1/wd1}$ and $R_{ws2/wd2}$ are the total resistances between the bottom of the *S/D* regions and *B* within the *Deep N-Well* and N_s and N_d represent the numbers of source and drain diffusion regions, respectively. In the model, when the number fingers is odd, $N_s = N_d = (N_f + 1)/2$. $N_s = N_f/2 + 1$ and $N_d = N_f/2$ when the number of fingers is even.

Assuming that there are no differences in the inner *S/D* regions, the above equations, (1a)-(1h), can be formed as follows:

$$C_{js/jd} = N_{s/d} C_{j,i} \quad (2a)$$

$$R_{js/jd} = R_{j/i} / N_{s/d} \quad (2b)$$

$$C_{sgdb} = N_f \left[2C_{sdb,i} + C_{gb,i} \right] \quad (2c)$$

$$C_{ws/wd} = N_{s/d} C_{w,i} \quad (2d)$$

$$R_{ws1/wd1} = \frac{R_{w1,i}}{N_{s/d}} \quad (2e)$$

$$R_{ws2/wd2} = \frac{R_{w2,i}}{N_{s/d}} \quad (2f)$$

$$C_{dnwu} = N_f C_{dnwu,i} \quad (2g)$$

$$C_{dnwd} = N_f C_{dnwd,i} \quad (2h)$$

$$R_{dnw} = 2R_{dnwo} + \frac{R_{dnwi}}{N_f} \quad (2i)$$

where

$$C_{j,i} = C_{js,i} = C_{jd,i}\ R_{j,i} = R_{js,i} = R_{jd,i}, C_{sdb} = C_{sb,i} = C_{db,i}$$

$$C_{w,i} = C_{ws,i} = C_{wd,i}, R_{w1,i} = R_{ws1,i} = R_{wd1,i}$$

and $R_{w2,i} = R_{ws2,i} = R_{wd2,i}$.

In this paper, the following equations are used to empirically model the N_f- dependence of R_{sub} and C_{sub}:

$$R_{sub} = R_{subl} + N_f R_{subunit} \quad (2j)$$

$$C_{sub} = C_{subl} + N_f C_{subunit} \quad (2k)$$

where R_{subl} and C_{subl} represent the p-substrate resistance and capacitance of a one-finger device, $R_{subunit}$ and $C_{subunit}$ are used to explain the increase in R_{sub} and C_{sub} with the increase in the number of gate fingers.

3. Scalable Model Parameter Extraction

In order to accurately predict the scalability of the substrate elements, a direct parameter extraction methodology is of the utmost importance. In this work, two different test configurations are used. One has the *DNW* floating (as shown in **Figure 3(a)**) and the other has the *DNW* grounded (as shown in **Figure 4(a)**). In each case, all *S/D/G* terminals for different fingers are connected together as port one, the *B* terminal is port two, and the p-substrate grounded. The equivalent circuits shown in **Figure 3(b)** and **Figure 4(b)** can easily be derived from the complete equivalent circuit shown in **Figure 2**, for

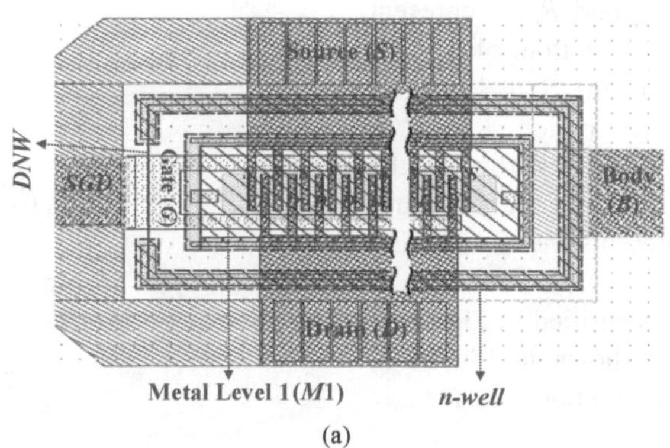

(a)

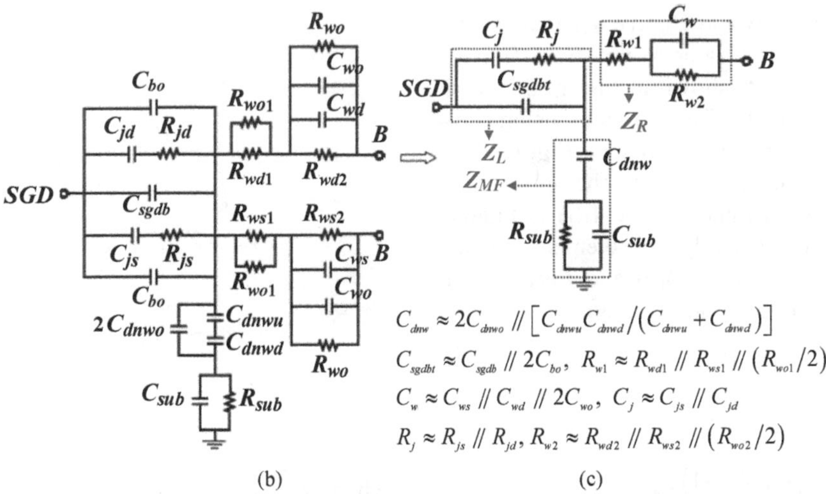

SGD
B
B
SGD
B
Z_L
Z_R
Z_{MF}
$C_{dnw} \approx 2C_{dnwo} // \left[C_{dnwu}C_{dnwd}/(C_{dnwu}+C_{dnwd})\right]$
$C_{sgdbt} \approx C_{sgdb} // 2C_{bo},\ R_{w1} \approx R_{wd1} // R_{ws1} // (R_{wo1}/2)$
$C_w \approx C_{ws} // C_{wd} // 2C_{wo},\ C_j \approx C_{js} // C_{jd}$
$R_j \approx R_{js} // R_{jd},\ R_{w2} \approx R_{wd2} // R_{ws2} // (R_{wo2}/2)$
(b)
(c)

Figure 3. (a) Simplified layout plane figure of *DNW* RF-MOSFETs with *S/G/D* terminals connected together, while the *DNW* is floating. (b) Equivalent circuit model for the device shown in Figure 3(a). R_{dnw} is ignored for its slight influence on two-port measurement. (c) Simplified equivalent circuit for parameter extraction.

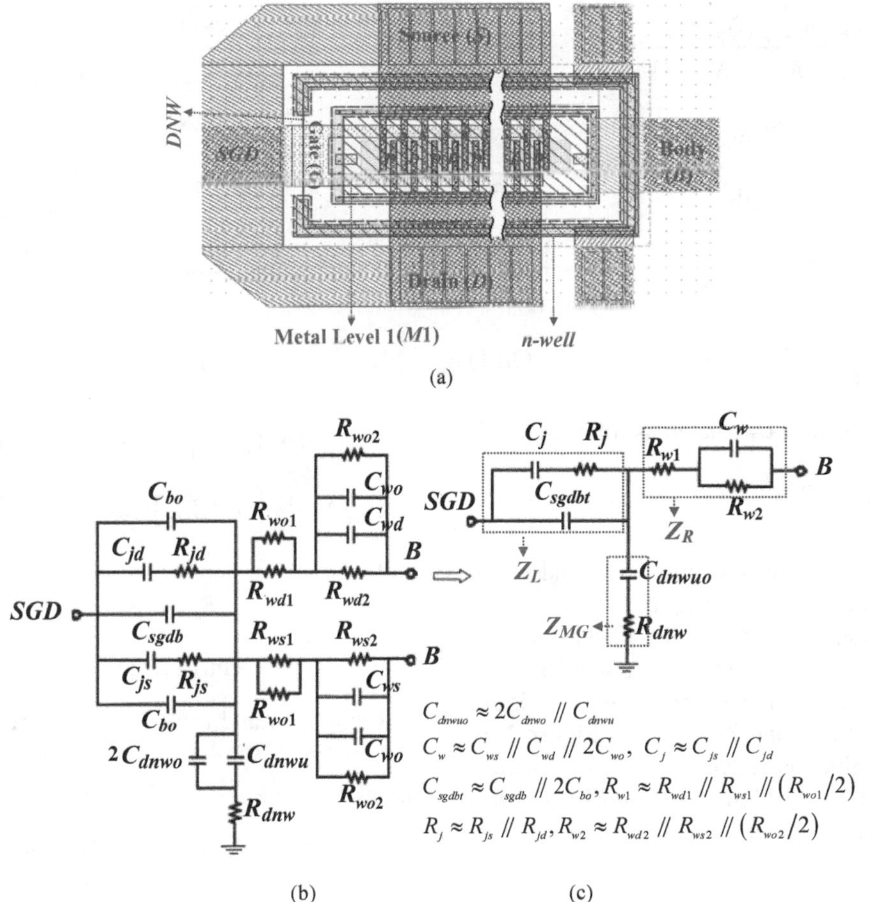

Figure 4. (a) Simplified layout plane figure of *DNW* RF-MOSFETs with *S/G/D* terminals connected together, with the *DNW* grounded. (b) Equivalent circuit model for device shown in Figure 4(a). Since R_{dnw} is much smaller than R_{sub}, the contribution of C_{dnwd}, R_{sub} and C_{sub} to *Z*-parameters becomes so slight that it can be ignored. (c) Simplified equivalent circuit for parameter extraction.

modeling the above two test structures (e.g., with the *DNW* in grounded or float configuration, respectively).

As seen from **Figure 3(b)** and **Figure 4(b)**, since the topologies from *S* to *B* are the same as that from *D* to *B*, both of the equivalent circuits shown in **Figure 3(b)** and **Figure 4(b)** can be reduced to *T*-networks by using simple approaches as shown at the bottom of **Figure 3(c)** and **Figure 4(c)**. Based on (2a)-(2i) and the approaches used to simplify **Figure 3(b)** and **Figure 4(b)** to **Figure 3(c)** and **Figure 4(c)**, respectively, the elements of the two *T*-networks shown in **Figure 3(c)** and **Figure 4(c)** can be calculated with the following equations:

$$C_j = \left(N_f + 1\right) C_{j,i} \tag{3a}$$

$$R_j = R_{j,i} \big/ \left(N_f + 1\right) \tag{3b}$$

$$C_w = 2C_{wo} + \left(N_f + 1\right) C_{w,i} \tag{3c}$$

$$R_{w1} = \frac{0.5R_{wo1} R_{w1,i} \big/ \left(N_f + 1\right)}{0.5R_{wo1} + R_{w1,i} \big/ \left(N_f + 1\right)} \tag{3d}$$

$$R_{w2} = \frac{0.5R_{wo2} R_{w2,i} \big/ \left(N_f + 1\right)}{0.5R_{wo2} + R_{w2,i} \big/ \left(N_f + 1\right)} \tag{3e}$$

$$C_{sgdbt} = 2C_{bo} + N_f \left[2C_{sdb,i} + C_{gb,i}\right] \tag{3f}$$

$$C_{dnwuo} = 2C_{dnwo} + N_f C_{dnwu,i} \tag{3g}$$

$$C_{dnw} = 2C_{dnwo} + N_f C_{dnw,i} \tag{3h}$$

where

$$C_{dnw,i} = \frac{C_{dnwu,i} C_{dnwd,i}}{C_{dnwu,i} + C_{dnwd,i}} \tag{3h.1}$$

Using (3h.1), $C_{dnw,i}$ can be calculated as follows:

$$C_{dnwd,i} = \frac{C_{dnwu,i} C_{dnw,i}}{C_{dnwu,i} - C_{dnw,i}} \tag{3h.2}$$

(2c), (2g)-(2k) and (3a)-(3h) give the N_f-dependent equations of the equivalent circuit in **Figure 2**. This enables the direct identification of the scalability of the substrate components. This will be shown later in this section.

As the Z_L and Z_R of the *T*-network shown in **Figure 4(c)** are the same as the Z_L and Z_R shown in **Figure 3(c)**, with the ground terminal as reference, the *Z*-parameters of the T-networks shown in **Figure 3(c)** and **Figure 4(c)** can be calculated approximately with the following equations:

$$\begin{aligned}\left[Z_L\right]^{-1} &= \left[Z_{dnw\_floating,11} - Z_{dnw\_floating,12}\right]^{-1} \\ &= \left[Z_{dnw\_grounded,11} - Z_{dnw\_grounded,12}\right]^{-1} \\ &= \frac{\omega^2 C_j^2 R_j}{1 + \omega^2 C_j^2 R_j^2} + j\frac{\omega C_j}{1 + \omega^2 C_j^2 R_j^2} + j\omega C_{sgdbt}\end{aligned} \tag{4a}$$

$$\begin{aligned}Z_R &= Z_{dnw\_floating,22} - Z_{dnw\_floating,12} \\ &= Z_{dnw\_grounded,22} - Z_{dnw\_grounded,12} \\ &= R_{w1} + \frac{R_{w2}}{1 + \omega^2 R_{w2}^2 C_w^2} - j\omega \frac{R_{w2}^2 C_w}{1 + \omega^2 R_{w2}^2 C_w^2}\end{aligned} \tag{4b}$$

$$\begin{aligned}Z_{MF} = Z_{dnw\_floating,12} &= \frac{R_{sub}}{1 + \omega^2 R_{sub}^2 C_{sub}^2} \\ &- j\omega \frac{R_{sub}^2 C_{sub}}{1 + \omega^2 R_{sub}^2 C_{sub}^2} - j\frac{1}{\omega C_{dnw}}\end{aligned} \tag{4c}$$

$$Z_{MG} = Z_{dnw\_grounded,12} = R_{dnw} + \frac{1}{j\omega C_{dnwuo}} \tag{4d}$$

where $Z_{dnw\_floating}$ and $Z_{dnw\_grounded}$ are measured *Z*-parameters of *DNW* RF MOSFETs with *S/G/D* terminals connected together, when the *DNW* is floating or grounded, respectively.

Further, the real and imaginary parts of the above *Z*-parameter expressions can be rearranged as follows:

$$\frac{\omega^2}{\mathrm{Re}\left\{\left[Z_L\right]^{-1}\right\}} = \omega^2 R_j + \frac{1}{C_j^2 R_j} \tag{5a}$$

$$C_{sgdbt} = \omega^{-1}\left\{\mathrm{Im}\left\{\left[Z_L\right]^{-1}\right\} - \frac{\omega C_j}{1 + \omega^2 C_j^2 R_j^2}\right\} \tag{5b}$$

$$-\frac{\omega}{\mathrm{Im}\left[Z_R\right]} = \omega^2 C_w + \frac{1}{R_{w2}^2 C_w} \tag{5c}$$

$$R_{w1} = \mathrm{Re}\left[Z_R\right] - \frac{R_{w2}}{1 + \omega^2 R_{w2}^2 C_w^2} \tag{5d}$$

$$\left\{\mathrm{Re}\left[Z_{MF}\right]\right\}^{-1} = R_{sub}^{-1} + \omega^2 R_{sub} C_{sub}^2 \tag{5e}$$

$$C_{dnw} = -\left\{\omega\left[\mathrm{Im}\left[Z_{MF}\right] + \omega R_{sub}^2 C_{sub} / \left(1 + \omega^2 R_{sub}^2 C_{sub}^2\right)\right]\right\}^{-1} \tag{5f}$$

$$R_{dnw} = \mathrm{Re}\left[Z_{MG}\right] \tag{5g}$$

$$\left[-\mathrm{Im}\left(Z_{MG}\right)\right]^{-1} = \omega C_{dnwuo} \tag{5h}$$

Using (5a) and (5c), R_j and C_w can be extracted from the slopes of the linear regression curves of the experimental $\omega^2 \big/ \mathrm{Re}\left\{\left[Z_L\right]^{-1}\right\}$ and $-\omega \big/ \mathrm{Im}\left[Z_R\right]$ versus ω^2, respectively. (5a) and (5c), after subtracting R_j and C_w, give C_j and R_{w2}. Further, (5b) and (5d) give C_{sgdbt} and R_{w1}. Using (5e), R_{sub} and C_{sub} can be determined from the intercept of the linear regression curve of the experimental $1 \big/ Re\left[Z_{MF}\right]$ versus ω^2, and the slope gives C_{sub} after subtracting R_{sub}. After subtracting R_{sub} and C_{sub}, (5f) gives C_{dnw}. Using (5h), C_{dnwuo} can be extracted from the slope of the linear regression curve of the experimental

$\mathrm{Im}(Z_{MG})$ versus ω, while (5g) gives R_{dnw} directly. Thus, all elements of the equivalent circuit of **Figure 3(c)** and/or **Figure 4(c)** are extracted.

For extracting the values of the derived scalable model parameters in (2c), (2g)-(2k) and (3a)-(3h), two different test structures for nine devices with different number of fingers (N_f of each device is 1, 2, 4, 8, 16, 24, 32, 48 and 64, the length (L_f) and width (W_f) for each finger are fixed at 0.18 μm and 2.5 μm), with the *DNW* floating and grounded, respectively, were fabricated using the SMIC 0.18 μm 1P6M RF-CMOS process. *M*1 is used to connect all of the *S/D/G* terminals for different fingers together as port one, while the *B* terminal is port two for two-port RF measurement.

In this work, two-port *S*-parameters were measured and de-embedded (*Open* + *Short*) for parasitics introduced by the GSG PAD using an Agilent E8363B Network Analyzer and a CASCADE Summit probe station. Then, the de-embedded *S*-parameters were transformed to *Z*-parameters for directly extracting all the parameters of the *T*-networks shown in **Figure 3(c)** and **Figure 4(c)** using the parameter extraction methodology developed in this section.

As mentioned in [1], when the junctions become significant, the equivalent circuit in **Figure 2** and its corresponding parameter values are less reasonable. Thus, in this work, the extraction of the substrate network parameters is executed at $V_B = -1$ V and $V_{SGD} = 0$ V. A detailed extraction procedure for a 32-finger *DNW* nMOSFET ($L_f = 0.18$ μm and $W_f = 2.5$ μm for each finger) is given in **Figure 5** to **Figure 8**. Excellent linear regressions validated the feasibility and accuracy of the parameter extraction methodology developed in this section. Similar extraction procedures are finally used for substrate parameter value extraction for the nine fabricated devices with different number of fingers at $V_B = -1$ V and $V_{SGD} = 0$ V. The extracted results are plotted in **Figure 9**.

4. Scalable Model Verification and Validation

Once R_j, C_j, C_w, R_{w1}, R_{w2}, C_{sgdbt}, R_{dnw}, R_{sub}, C_{sub}, C_{dnwuo} and C_{dnw} are extracted, by using (3a)-(3h) and (2i), $R_{j,i}$, $C_{j,i}$, C_{wo}, $C_{w,i}$, R_{wo1}, $R_{w1,i}$, R_{wo2}, $R_{w2,i}$, C_{bo}, ($2C_{sdbi} + C_{gbi}$), R_{dnwo}, R_{dnwi}, R_{subl}, $R_{subunit}$, C_{subl}, $C_{subunit}$, C_{dnwo}, C_{dnwui} and C_{dnwi} can be obtained with a simple optimization procedure from the relationships between the total extracted results and N_f. After determining C_{dnwui} and C_{dnwi}, (3h.2) gives $C_{dnwd,i}$. Thus, (2a)-(2k) and (3a)-(3h) become only $N_{s/d}$– and N_f– dependence equations. **Table 1** gives the extracted scalable model parameter values. **Figure 9** depicts the comparisons between the extracted substrate resistances and capacitances of the nine *DNW* nMOSFETs and the modeled results based on the extracted parameter values shown in **Table 1**. The excellent agreement between the extracted and modeled N_f- dependent substrate network components verifies that the proposed scalable model ((3a-3h)) can accurately describe the scalabilities of the substrate network components of *DNW* MOSFETs.

To verify the validity of the proposed substrate network, the accuracy of the derived scalable model and the developed methodology for parameter extraction, multi-finger *DNW* nMOSFETs, with the *G* terminal defining port one, the *D* terminal defining port two and the *S*, *B* and the p-substrate connected together with ground serving as the common terminal (*i.e.* common-source test configuration) with the *DNW* connected to ground, are also fabricated and tested. A macro-model (as shown in

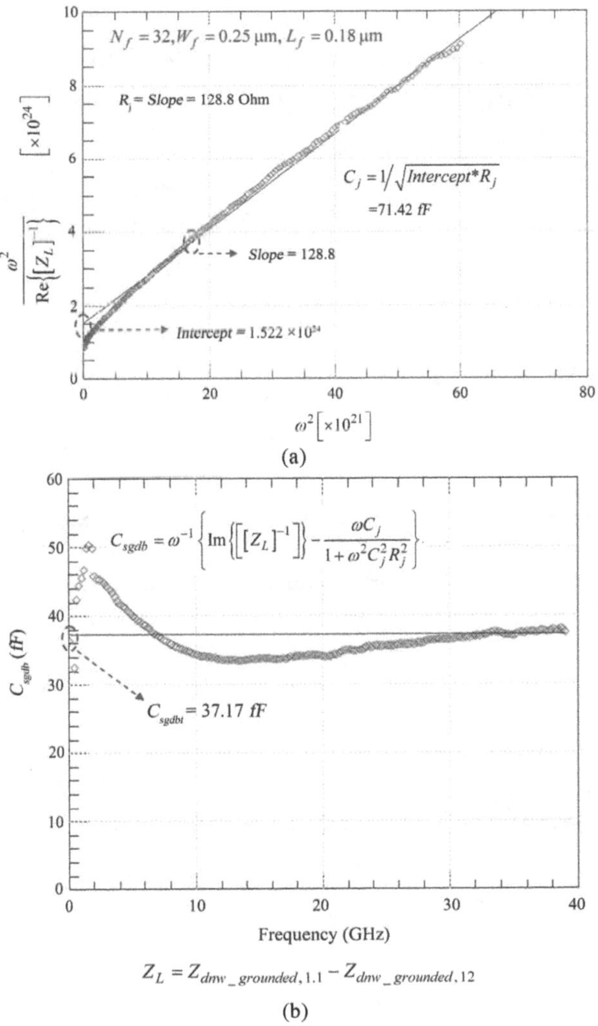

Figure 5. (a) Determine R_j from the slope of the linear regression curve of the experimental $w^2/\mathrm{Re}\{[Z_L]-1\}$ versus ω^2. C_j can be calculated from the intercept. (b) After subtracting R_j and C_j, (5b) gives C_{sgdbt}.

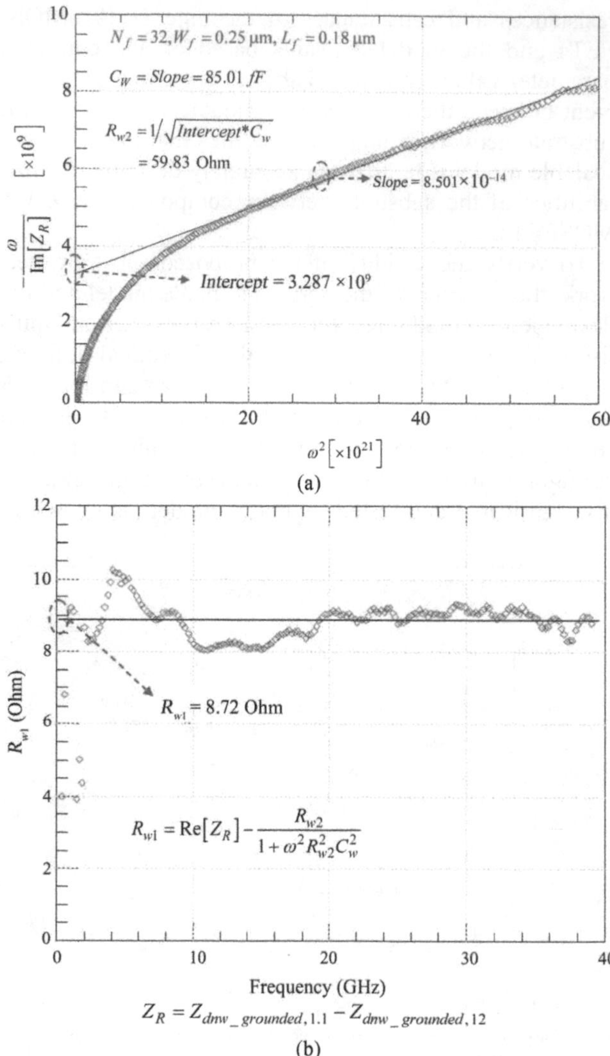

Figure 6. (a) Extract C_w from the slope of the linear regression curve of the experimental $-w/\mathrm{Im}[ZR]$ versus w^2. R_{w2} can be extracted from the intercept. (b) After subtracting R_{w2} and C_w, (5d) gives R_{w1}.

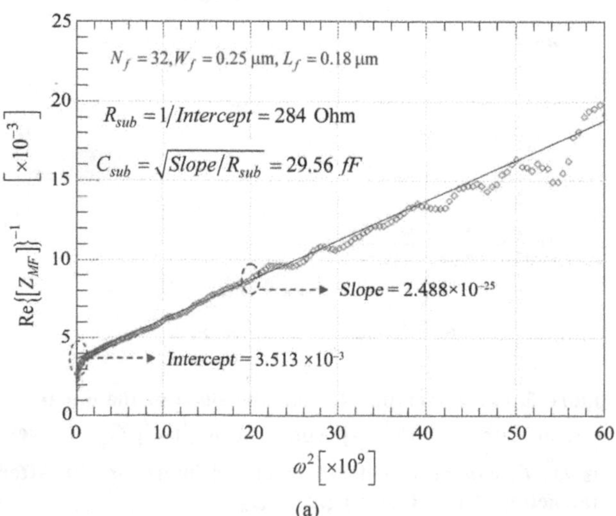

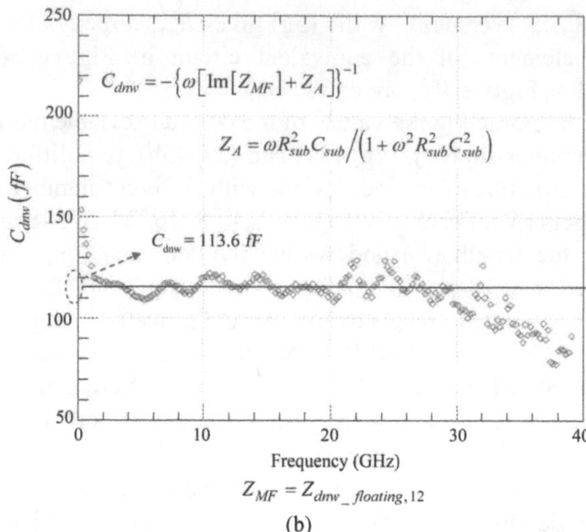

Figure 7. (a) Extract R_{sub} from the intercept of the experimental $\{\mathrm{Re}[Z_{MF}]\}-1$ versus w^2, and the slope gives C_{sub} after subtracting R_{sub}. (b) After subtracting R_{sub} and C_{sub}, (5f) gives C_{dnw}.

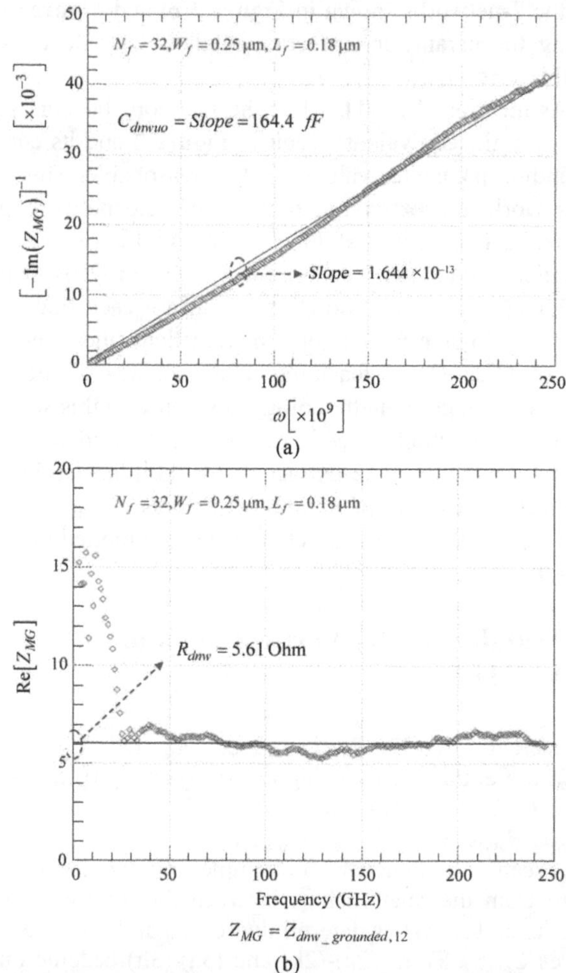

Figure 8. (a) Extract C_{dnwuo} from the slope of the linear regression curve of the experimental $\mathrm{Im}[Z_{MG}]$ versus w. (b) R_{dnw} can be determined from the real part of Z_{MG}.

Figure 10) for common-source connected *DNW* RF MOSFETs modeling was developed. The model consists of the BSIM3v3.2 model core with the proposed new substrate-network and is simulated in Agilent Advanced Design System (ADS) directly.

In **Figure 10**, R_g, R_d, and R_s are *G*, *D* and *S* terminal series resistances, C_{ds} is *D*-to-*S* capacitance. C_{gs}, and C_{gd} represent the *G*-to-*S* and *G*-to-*D* capacitances, respectively. C_{gb}, C_{db} and C_{sb} indicate the *G*-to-*B*, *D*-to-B, *S*-to-*B* capacitances, and the sum of the three components has been extracted in section 4. A conventional method developed in [13] is used to extract the initial values of three terminal series resistances from de-em-

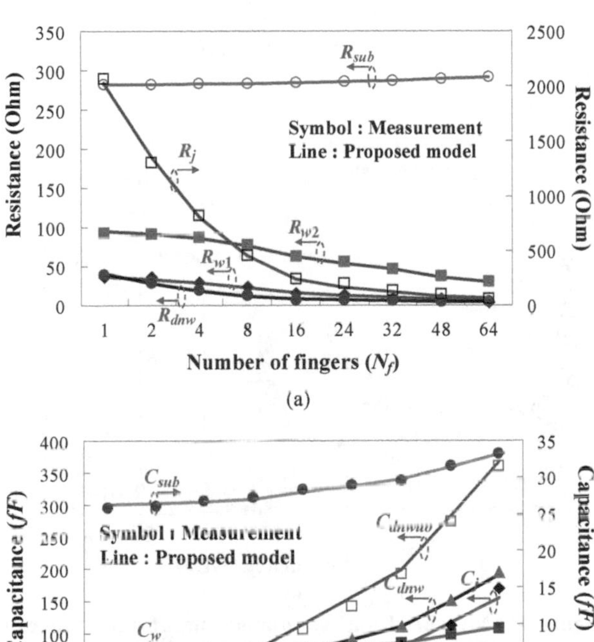

Figure 9. (a) Extracted and modeled substrate resistances and (b) capacitances of *DNW* nMOSFETs with different number of fingers, while the length (L_f) and width (W_f) for each finger are fixed at 0.18 μm and 2.5 μm.

Table 1. Extracted parameter values of the proposed model of the substrate network in *DNW* RF MOSFETs

$R_{j,i}$ (Ω)	$C_{j,i}$ (fF)	C_{wo} (fF)	$C_{w,i}$ (fF)	R_{wo1} (Ω)
4162	2.395	30.64	0.737	87.78
R_{wo2} (Ω)	$R_{w2,i}$ (Ω)	C_{bo} (fF)	$2C_{sdbi}+C_{gbi}$ (fF)	
203.7	2775	5.471	0.91	
R_{dnwi} (Ω)	R_{subI} (Ω)	$R_{subunit}$ (Ω)	C_{subI} (fF)	$C_{subunit}$ (fF)
73.79	282.8	0.137	26.18	0.11
C_{dnwui} (fF)	C_{dnwdi} (fF)	$R_{w1,i}$ (Ω)	R_{dnwo} (Ω)	C_{dnwo} (fF)
5.045	4.771	447.7	3.46	15.2

Table 2. Values of the extracted external capacitors from common source connected devices with different N_f, at zero bias.(L_f = 0.18 μm; W_f = 2.5 μm)

N_f	$C_{gs/d}$ (fF)	C_{gb} (fF)	C_{ds} (fF)
1	0.66	3.4	0.68
2	3.5	4.2	1.02
4	3.9	7.2	3.1
8	8.6	8.5	10.7
16	18.4	10.3	24.1
24	28.3	13.2	41.2
32	36.1	15.5	54.6
48	55.4	16.2	83.4
64	72.2	17.5	110.2

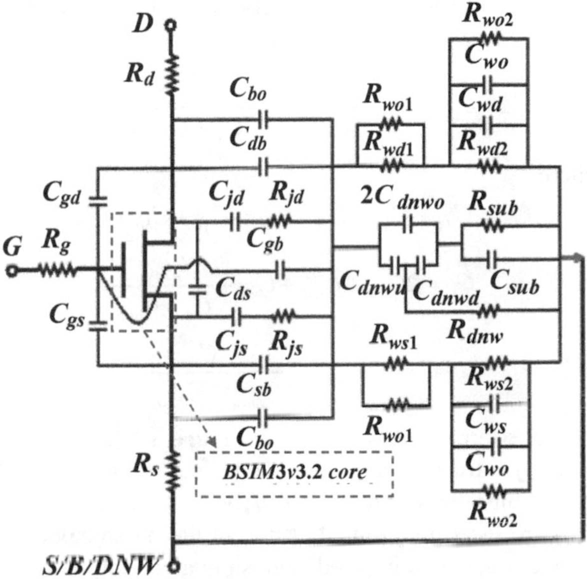

Figure 10. Macro-model for *DNW* RF-MOSFETs modeling when *S/D* junctions are not significant. The test configuration with the *G* terminal defining port one, the *D* terminal defining port two and the *S*, *B* and the p-substrate connected together with ground serving as the common terminal (*i.e.* common-source test configuration), with the *DNW* is tied to ground using M1 (metal level 1), are used in two-port measurement. All the parameters of the BSIM3v3.2, including the terminal resistances R_d, R_g and R_s, are extracted beforehand.

bedded *Y*-parameters. By using the extraction method proposed in [13], the following equations are employed for the remaining components extraction:

$$C_{gd} = \frac{\operatorname{Im}(Y_{12})}{\omega} \tag{6a}$$

$$C_{gs} = C_{gd} \tag{6b}$$

$$C_{gb} = \frac{\operatorname{Im}(Y_{11} + Y_{12})}{\omega} - C_{gd} \tag{6c}$$

According to (1c), the total C_{gb} of an RF MOSFET with the number of fingers is N_f can be calculated as follows:

$$C_{gb} = N_f C_{gb,i} \tag{6d}$$

Thus, $C_{gb,i}$ can be extracted for two or more devices with different number of fingers. Once $C_{gb,i}$ is obtained, (3f) gives $C_{sdb,i}$.

$$C_{sdb,i} = \frac{\left[C_{sgdbt} - 2C_{bo} - N_f C_{gb,i}\right]}{2N_f} \tag{6e}$$

In this work, the extracted values of $C_{gb,i}$ and $C_{sdb,i}$ for multi-finger devices with the length *(L)* and width *(W)* for each finger fixed at 0.18 μm and 2.5 μm, are 0.338 *f*F and 0.285 *f*F, respectively. C_{ds} in **Figure 10** is calculated from de-embedded *Y*-parameters of the common-source connected nMOSFET as follows:

$$C_{ds} = \frac{\operatorname{Im}\left(Y_{22} - Y_{12}\right)}{\omega} - \frac{C_d\left(C_s + C_t\right)}{C_d + C_s + C_t} \tag{6f}$$

where

$$C_d = C_{jd} + C_{bo} + C_{db}, \quad C_s = C_{js} + C_{bo} + C_{sb},$$

$$C_t = 2C_{wo} + C_{wd} + C_{ws} + \frac{C_n C_{sub}}{C_n + C_{sub}}$$

and $$C_n = 2C_{dnwo} + \frac{C_{dnwu} C_{dnwd}}{C_{dnwu} + C_{dnwd}}.$$

The external capacitances in **Figure 10** (*i.e.* C_{gd}, C_{gs} and C_{ds}) extracted from the nine devices with different N_f at zero-bias condition ($V_G = 0$ V; $V_D = 0$ V and $V_{S/B/DNW} = 0$ V) are listed in **Table 2**. After all the parameters have been extracted, measured and simulated output admittances (Y_{22}) at zero-bias for the nine devices with different number of fingers are compared and plotted in **Figure 11**. Excellent agreement is achieved between the measured and simulated results. Due to the oscillation of the measurements at high frequencies, the resistive parasitics of the substrate are hard to be extracted accurately, which is further introducing errors between the measured and simulated results of the real parts of the output admittances of transistors.

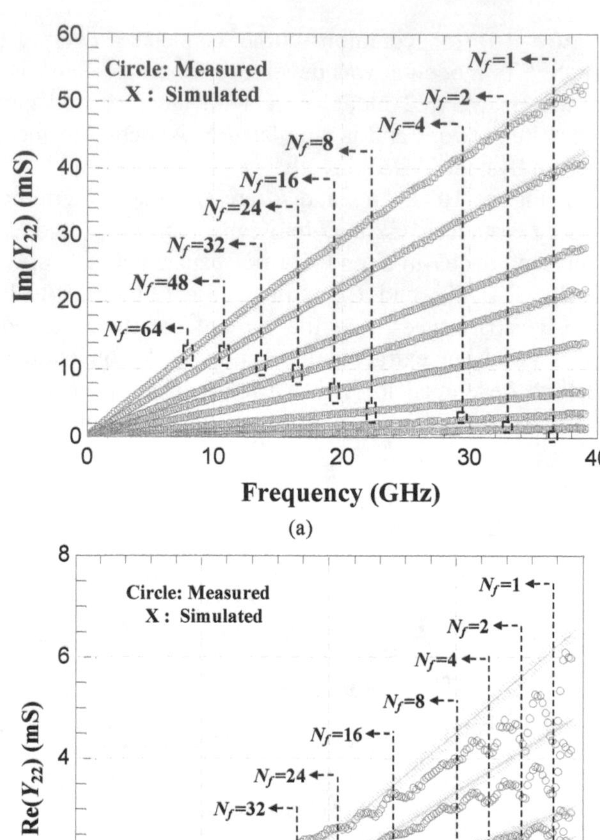

Figure 11. Measured and simulated output admittances of *DNW* nMOSFETs with different number of fingers at zero bias ($V_G = 0$ V, $V_D = 0$ V and $V_{S/B/DNW} = 0$ V). All the devices are connected in common source configuration, while the *DNW* is grounded.

5. Summary

A compact, physically based scalable model for the substrate network of *DNW* RF MOSFETs has been demonstrated. All of the substrate components are directly extracted from two-port measurements. The derived and extracted scalable model is directly used to capture the substrate characteristics of common-source connected devices. The model shows excellent agreement with measured output admittances of devices with different number of fingers at an operation frequency up to 40 GHz. The model and methodology developed in this paper also can be used to accurately extract the substrate network in RF MOSFETs without *DNW* implantation by removing the sub-network for the *DNW*.

6. References

[1] J. Liu, L. L. Sun, L. L. Lou, H. Wang and C. McCorkell, "A Simple Test Structure for Directly Extracting Substrate Network Components in *Deep N-Well* RF CMOS Modeling," *IEEE Electron Device Letters*, Vol. 30, No. 11, 2009, pp. 1200-1202.

[2] J. G. Su, H. M. Hsu, S. C. Wong, C. Y. Chang, T. Y. Huang and J. Y. C. Sun, "Improving the RF Performance of 0.18-um CMOS with *Deep N-Well* Implantation," *IEEE Electron Device Letters*, Vol. 22, No. 10, 2001, pp. 481-483.

[3] K. W. Chew, J. Zhang, K. Shao, W. B. Loh, and S. F. Chu, "Impact of *Deep N-Well* Implantation on Substrate Noise Coupling and RF Transistor Performance for Sys-

tems-on-a-Chip Integration," *Proceeding of the 32nd European Solid-State Device Research Conference*, Bologna, 24-26 September 2002, pp. 251-254.

[4] D. Kosaka, M. Nagata, Y. Hiraoka, I. Imanishi, M. Maeda, Y. Murasaka and A. Iwata, "Isolation Strategy Against Substrate Coupling in CMOS Mixed-Signal/RF Circuits," *Symposium on VLSI Circuits Digest of Technical Papers*, Kyoto, 16-18 June 2005, pp. 276-279.

[5] J. Kang, D. Yu, Y. Yang and B. Kim, "Highly Linear 0.18-m CMOS Power Amplifier with Deep-N-Well Structure," *IEEE Journal of Solid-State Circuits*, Vol. 41, No. 5, 2006, pp. 1073-1080.

[6] S. F. W. M. Hatta and N. Soin, "Performance of the Forward-Biased RF LNA with *Deep N-Well* NMOS Transistor," *Proceeding of International Conference on Semiconductor Electronics*, Johor Bahru, 25-27 November 2008, pp. 465-469.

[7] J. Han and H. Shin, "A Scalable Model for the Substrate Resistance in Multi-Finger RF MOSFETs," *IEEE MTT-S International Microwave Symposium Digest*, Philadelphia, 8-13 June 2003, pp. 2105-2108.

[8] Y. Cheng and M. Matloubian, "Parameter Extraction of Accurate and Scaleable Substrate Resistance Components in RF MOSFETs," *IEEE Electron Device Letters*, Vol. 23, No. 4, 2002, pp. 221-223.

[9] N. Srirattana, D. Heo, H. M. Park, A. Raghavan, P. E. Allen and J. Laskar, "A New Analytical Scalable Substrate Network Model for RF MOSFETs," *IEEE MTT-S Microwave Symposium Digest*, Fort Worth, 6-11 June 2004, pp. 699-702.

[10] I. M. Kang, S. J. Jung, T. H. Choi, H. W. Lee, G. Jo, Y. K. Kim, H. G. Kim and K. M. Choi, "Scalable Model of Substrate Resistance Components in RF MOSFETs with Bar-Type Body Contact Considered Layout Dimensions," *IEEE Electron Device Letters*, Vol. 30, No. 4, 2009, pp. 404-406.

[11] S. P. Voinigescu, M. Tazlauanu, P. C. Ho and M. T. Yang, "Direct Extraction Methodology for Geometry-Scalable RF-CMOS Models," *International Conference on Microelectronic Test Structures*, Awaji, 22-25 March 2004, pp. 235-240.

[12] S. P. Kao, C. Y. Lee, C. Y. Wang, J. D.-S. Deng, C. C. Chang and C. H. Kao, "An Analytical Extraction Method for Scalable Substrate Resistance Model in RF MOSFETs," 2007 *International Semiconductor Device Research Symposium*, College Park, 12-14 December 2007, pp. 1-2.

[13] B. Parvais, S. Hu, M. Dehan, A. Mercha and S. Decoutere, "An Analytical Extraction Method for Scalable Substrate Resistance Model in RF MOSFETs," *Custom Integrated Circuits Conference*, San Jose, 16-19 September 2007, pp. 503-506.

[14] Y. Cheng, M. J. Deen and C. H. Chen, "MOSFET Modeling for RF IC Design," *IEEE Transactions on Electron Devices*, Vol. 52, No. 7, 2005, pp. 1286-1303.

[15] M. M. Tabrizi, E. Fathi, M. Fathipour and N. Masoumi, "Extracting of Substrate Network Resistances in RF CMOS Transistors," *Topical Meeting on Silicon Monolithic Integrated Circuits in RF Systems*, Atlanta, 8-10 September 2004, pp. 219-222.

[16] J. Han, M. Je and H. Shin, "A Simple and Accurate Method for Extracting Substrate Resistance of RF MOSFETs," *IEEE Electron Device Letters*, Vol. 23, No. 7, 2002, pp. 434-436.

[17] Y. S. Lin, "An Analysis of Small-Signal Source-Body Resistance Effect on RF MOSFET for Low-Cost System-on-Chip (SoC) Applications," *IEEE Transactions on Electron Devices*, Vol. 52, No. 7, 2005, pp. 1442-1451.

[18] S. C. Rustagi, L. Huailin, S. Jinglin and Z. X. Yong, "BSIM3 RF Models for MOS Transistors: A Novel Technique for Substrate Network Extraction," *Proceeding of IEEE International Conference on Microelectronic Test Structures*, Monterey, 17-20 March 2003, pp. 118-123.

[19] U. Mahalingam, S. C. Rustagi and G. S. Samudra, "Direct Extraction of Substrate Network Parameters for RF MOSFET Modeling Using a Simple Test Structure," *IEEE Device Letters*, Vol. 27, No. 2, 2006, pp. 130-132.

14

A New Chaotic Behavior from Lorenz and Rossler Systems and Its Electronic Circuit Implementation

Qais H. Alsafasfeh[1], **Mohammad S. Al-Arni**[2]
[1]*Electrical Engineering Department, Tafila Technical University, Tafila, Jordan*
[2]*Electrical Engineering Department, Tafila Technical University, Tafila, Jordan*

Abstract

This paper presents a new three-dimensional continuous autonomous chaotic system with ten terms and three quadratic nonlinearities. The new system contains five variational parameters and exhibits Lorenz and Rossler like attractors in numerical simulations. The basic dynamical properties of the new system are analyzed by means of equilibrium points, eigenvalue structures. Some of the basic dynamic behavior of the system is explored further investigation in the Lyapunov Exponent. The new system examined in Matlab-Simulink and Orcad-PSpice. An electronic circuit realization of the proposed system is presented using analog electronic elements such as capacitors, resistors, operational amplifiers and multipliers.

Keywords: Chaos, Lorenz System, Rossler System, Lyapunov Exponent, Bifurcation

1. Introduction

The science of nonlinear dynamics and chaos theory has sparked many researchers to develop mathematical models that simulate vector fields of nonlinear chaotic physical systems. Nonlinear phenomena arise in all fields of engineering, physics, chemistry, biology, economics, and sociology. Examples of nonlinear chaotic systems include planetary climate prediction models, neural network models, data compression, turbulence, nonlinear dynamical economics, information processing, preventing the collapse of power systems, high-performance circuits and devices, and liquid mixing with low power consumption [1-3].

The Lorenz system of differential equations arose from the work of meteorologist/mathematician Edward N. Lorenz, who was studying thermal variations in an air cell underneath a thunderhead.

The Lorenz equations are a fairly simple model in which to study chaos [3].

$$\left.\begin{aligned}\dot{x} &= \sigma(y-x)\\ \dot{y} &= rx-y-xz\\ \dot{z} &= xy-\beta\ z\end{aligned}\right\} \tag{1}$$

The arbitrary parameters σ, r and $\beta > 0$ and for this example are $\sigma = 10$, $r = 28$ and $\beta = 8/3$. The Rossler system has only one quadratic nonlinearity xz numerical integration shows that this system has a strange attractor for $a = b = 0.2$, $c = 5.7$ [2].

$$\left.\begin{aligned}\dot{x} &= -y-z\\ \dot{y} &= x+ay\\ \dot{z} &= b+z(x-c)\end{aligned}\right\} \tag{2}$$

This paper propose a new chaotic system based on adding two chaotic system (Lorenz and Rosslere) and it compares the results with the chaotic system and an electronic circuit realization of the proposed system is presented using analog electronic elements, The remainder of the paper is organized as follows: Section 2 discusses the proposal of a new chaotic system and its analysis, section 3 present deal with circuit realization of the new attractor and section 4 discusses and examines a new scheme [4].

2. A New Chaotic System and Its Analysis

Most researchers developed a new chaotic system depending on one chaotic system like Lorenz or Rossler systems the proposed scheme in this paper based on merging two chaotic systems Lorenz chaotic system and Rossler chaotic system. Therefore will be added two chaotic systems in (1) and (2), a new system is shown in (3).

$$\left.\begin{aligned}\dot{x} &= \sigma(y-x)-y-z\\ \dot{y} &= rx-y-xz+x+ay\\ \dot{z} &= xy-\beta z+b+z(x-c)\end{aligned}\right\} \tag{3}$$

We note after adding the two chaotic systems, it is noticed (1) and (2) that the control parameter increased from three (δ, r, β) to six (δ, r, β, b, a, c) but to check the new system is suitable for achieving the chaotic requirements, by plot phase plane for a new system we note a new system loss chaotic behavior shown in **Figure 1**.

Therefore we try to manipulate the above equation to achieve a chaotic behavior, so we will add cuomo Circuit shown in (4) (linear transformation of Lorenz equations with a new scale) [2,5] to Rossler equations after changing z instead x in last equation of Rossler system, the final system is shown below in (5) and (6).

$$\left.\begin{aligned} \dot{u} &= \sigma(v-u) \\ \dot{v} &= ru - v - 20uw \\ \dot{w} &= 5uv - \beta w \end{aligned}\right\} \qquad (4)$$

$$\left.\begin{aligned} \dot{x} &= \sigma(y-x) - y - z \\ \dot{y} &= rx - y - 20xz + x + ay \\ \dot{z} &= 5xy - \beta z + b + x(z-c) \end{aligned}\right\} \qquad (5)$$

$$\left.\begin{aligned} \dot{x} &= (\delta-1)y - \delta x - z \\ \dot{y} &= (r+1)x - (1-a)y - 20xz \\ \dot{z} &= 5xy - \beta z + b + xz - cx \end{aligned}\right\} \qquad (6)$$

To check that the new system has a chaotic behavior or not, no definition of the term chaos has been universally accepted yet but most researchers agree on the three ingredients used in following definition "Chaos is aperiodic long term behavior in a deterministic system that exhibits dependence on initial condition" [1-4,6]. Even though the definition of chaos has not been agreed upon by mathematicians, two properties that are generally agreed to characterize it are sensitivity to initial conditions and the presence of period-doubling cycles leading to chaos.

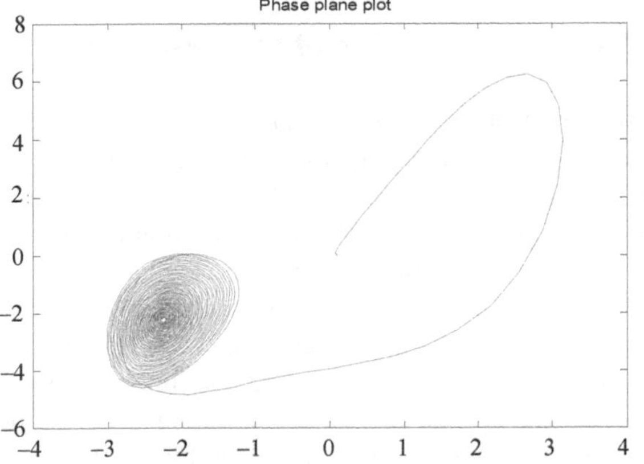

Figure 1. Phase plane at adding Lorenz with Rossler systems.

The new system has six terms, two quadratic nonlinearities (xz, xy) and six real constant parameters (δ, r, a, b, β and c). The state variables of the system are x, y, and z. The new system equations have one equilibrium point. This point which satisfies this requirement is found by setting x, y, $z = 0$, in (5), and solving for x, y and z:

$$\left.\begin{aligned} 0 &= \sigma(y-x) - y - z \\ 0 &= rx - y - 20xz + x + ay \\ 0 &= 5xy - \beta z + b + x(z-c) \end{aligned}\right\} \qquad (7)$$

The fixed point just we have one point (0,0,0), The Jacobian of the system is:

$$\boldsymbol{J} = \begin{bmatrix} -\delta & (\delta-1) & -1 \\ (r+1-20z) & (a-1) & -20x \\ 5y+z-c & 5x & -\beta+x \end{bmatrix}$$

For the case when the fixed point is $(x^*, y^*, z^*) = (0,0,0)$, the Jacobian becomes

$$\boldsymbol{J} = \begin{bmatrix} -\delta & (\delta-1) & -1 \\ (r+1) & (a-1) & 0 \\ -c & 0 & -b \end{bmatrix}$$

The eigenvalues are found by solving the characteristic equation, $|\boldsymbol{J} - \lambda \boldsymbol{I}| = 0$, for which is yielding eigenvalues $\lambda_1 = 18.4561$, $\lambda_2 = -30.6770$ and $\lambda_3 = -8.279$ the equilibrium points are unstable and this implies chaos. Thus, the system orbits around the unstable equilibrium point. Using a Matlab-Simulink model as shown in **Figure 2**. The xy, xz, and yz phase portraits of the new system achieved are shown in **Figure 3**, **Figure 4**, and **Figure 5**, also the time series for the new chaotic system is shown in **Figure 6.**

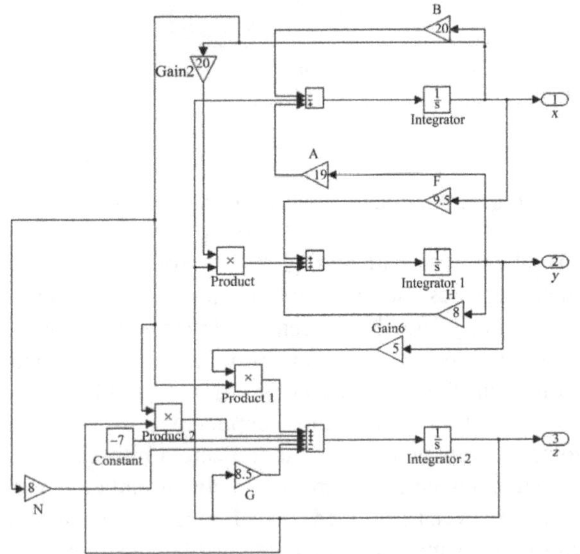

Figure 2. The Matlab-Simulink model of the new system.

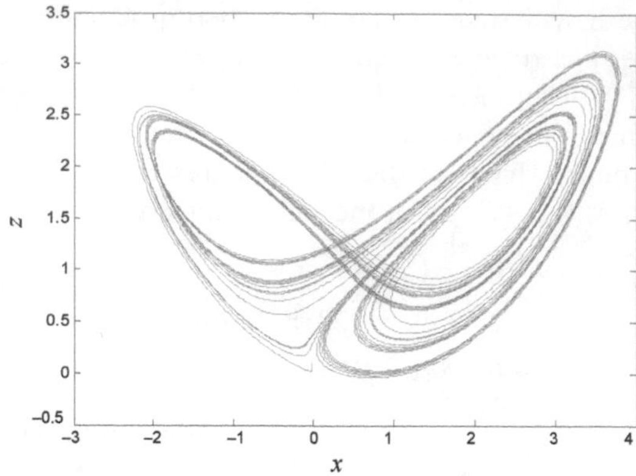

Figure 3. *xz* phase portrait of the new system.

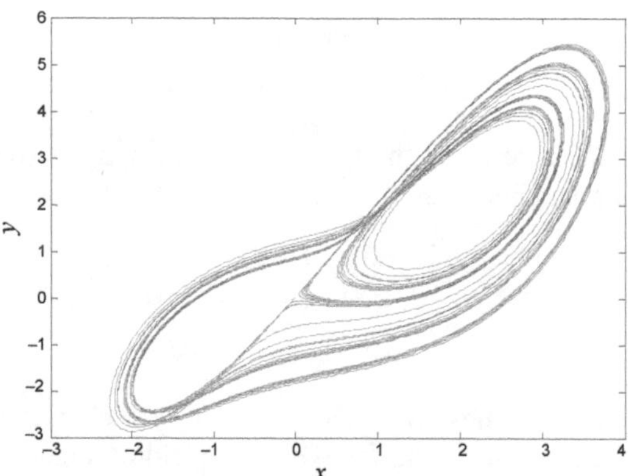

Figure 4. *xy* phase portrait of the new system.

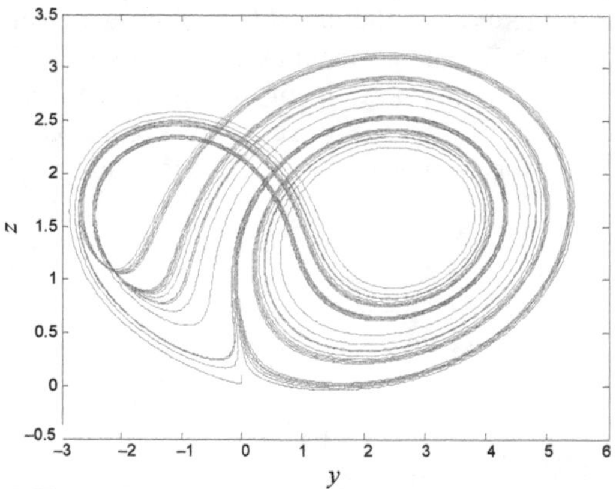

Figure 5. *yz* phase portrait of the new system.

Another important test is the Lyapunov exponents, which measures the exponential rates of divergence and convergence of nearby trajectories in state space, and the Lyapunov exponent spectrum provides additional useful information about the system as shown in **Figure 7**. A positive and zero Lyapunov exponent indicates chaos, two zero Lyapunov exponents indicate a bifurcation, and a zero and a negative Lyapunov exponent indicates periodicity, however as noticed from Lyapunov exponent the sum of the Lyapunov exponents must be negative. A positive Lyapunov exponent reflects a "direction" of stret-

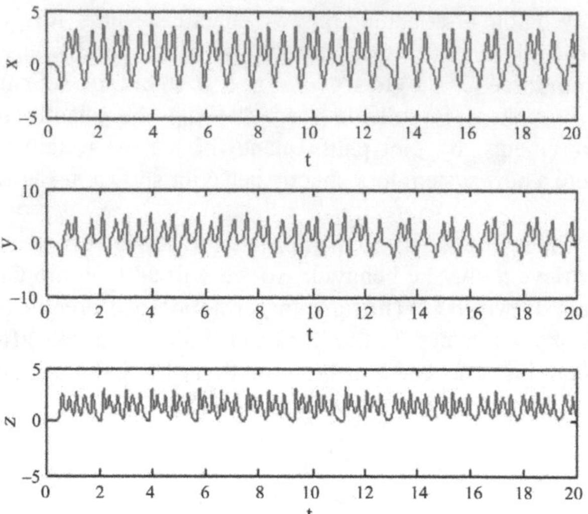

Figure 6. The time series for new chaotic system.

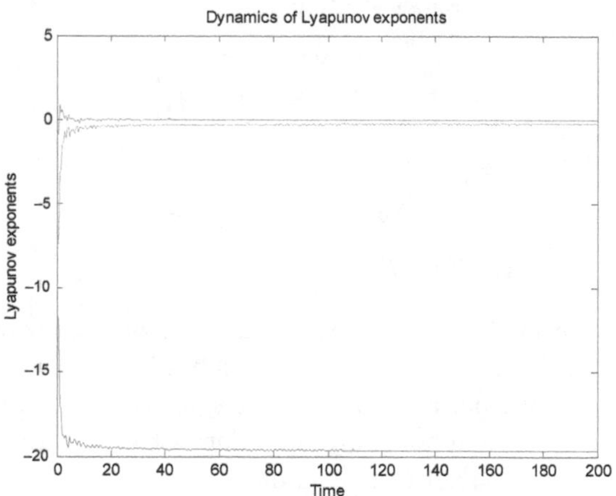

Figure 7. Dynamics Lyapunov exponent of the new system.

ching and folding and therefore determines chaos in the system, 3D continuous dissipative $(\lambda_1,\lambda_2,\lambda_3)$,(+,0,–)—A strange attractor; (0,0,–)—A two-torus; (0,–,–)—A limit cycle; (–,–,–)—A fixed point [7-11].

3. Circuit Realization of the New Attractor

A simple electronic circuit is designed, so that it can be used to study chaotic phenomena. The circuit employs simple electronic elements, such as resistors, and operational amplifiers, the operational amplifiers and associated circuitry perform the operations of addition, subtraction, and integration. Analog multipliers implement the nonlinear terms in the circuit equations, and is easy to construct [12]. Circuit schematic for implementing the new chaotic system in (6). By applying standard node analysis techniques to the circuit of **Figure 8**, a set of state equations that govern the dynamical behavior of the circuit can be obtained. This set of equations is given by

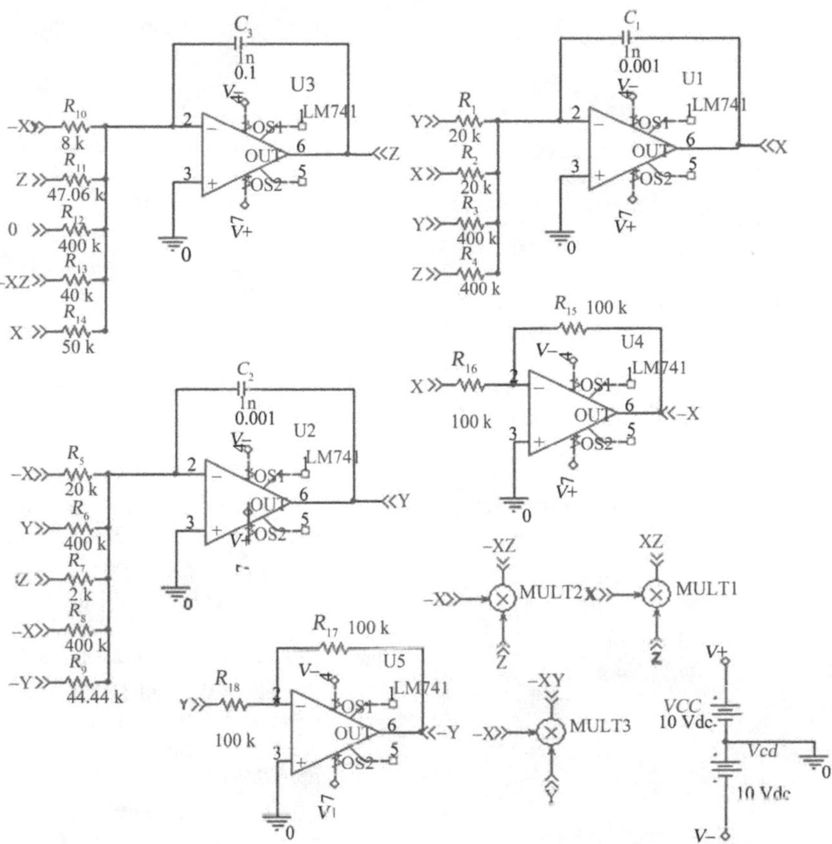

Figure 8. The electronic circuit schematic of the new chaotic system.

(8):

$$
\left.
\begin{aligned}
\dot{x} &= \left(\frac{1}{R_1C_1}-\frac{1}{R_3C_1}\right)y-\frac{1}{R_1C_1}x-\frac{1}{R_4C_1}z \\
\dot{y} &= \left(\frac{1}{R_5C_2}-\frac{1}{R_8C_2}\right)x-\left(\frac{1}{R_6C_2}-\frac{1}{R_9C_2}\right)y-\frac{1}{R_7C_2}xz \\
\dot{z} &= \frac{1}{R_{10}C_3}xy-\frac{1}{R_{11}C_3}z+\frac{1}{R_{12}C_3}d+\frac{1}{R_{13}C_3}xz-\frac{1}{R_{14}C_3}x)
\end{aligned}
\right\}
\tag{8}
$$

For the chosen component value is equivalent to after rescaling time by a factor of 1500. An electronic circuit of the new chaotic system is implemented with parameters of ($\delta = 20$, $r = 20, a = 9$, $\beta = 8.5$, $b = 0$ and $c = 8$) and initial conditions x0 = 0.0010, y0 = 0.001, z0 = 0.1 LM741 opamps, and the analog multipliers are used with $R_1 = R_2 = R_5 = 20$ K, $R_3 = R_4 = R_6 = R_8 = R_{12} = 400$ K, $R_9 =$ 44.44 K, $R_{10} = 8$ K, $R_{11} = 47.06$, $R_7 = 2$ K, $R_{13} = 40$ K and $R_{14} = 50$ K and $C_1 = C_2 = C_3 = 1$ nF. The output voltage is the products of the inputs multiplied by 10 V. PSpice simulations of the new chaotic system are also attained in **Figure 9**, **Figure 10**, and **Figure 11** for *xy, xz,* and *yz* attractors, respectively. In this simulation, the parameters (δ, r, a, β, b and c) are set at a value of 20,20,9,8.5,0 and 8.

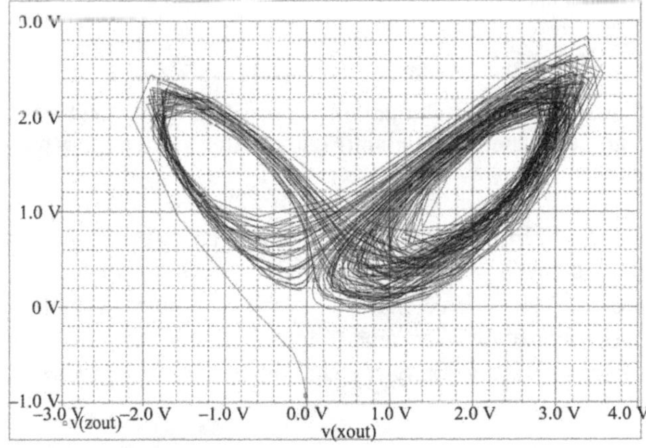

Figure 9. PSpice simulation result of the new chaotic system's electronic oscillator (Figure 3) for *xz* strange attractor.

4. Conclusions

In this paper, we have displayed a three-dimensional continuous autonomous chaotic system modified from the Lorenz system and Rössler system, which the first equation has not non-linear cross-product term but the second equation has one non-linear cross-product term

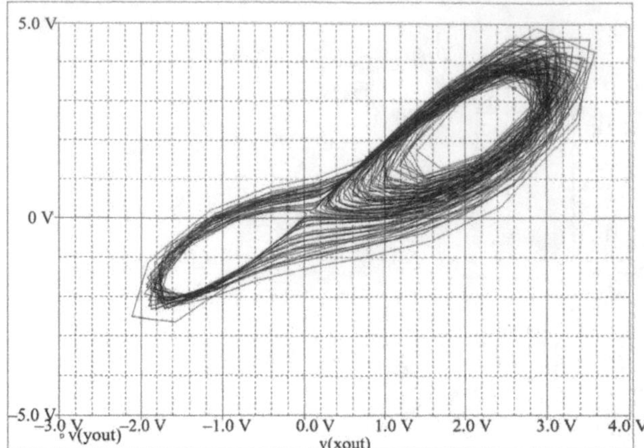

Figure 10. PSpice simulation result of the new chaotic system's electronic oscillator (Figure 4) for *xy* strange attractor.

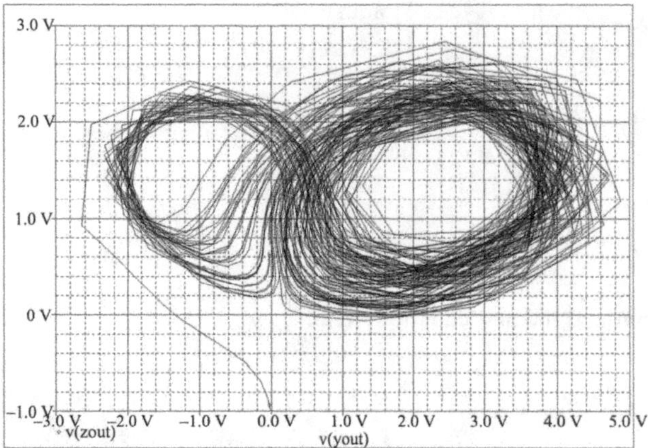

Figure 11. PSpice simulation result of the new chaotic system's electronic oscillator (Figure 5) for *yz* strange attractor.

and the third one has two non-linear cross-product term. Part of the basic dynamic behavior of the system is explored further investigation in the Lyapunov Exponent and bifurcation diagrams. Moreover, this was the new system also physically realized using analogue electronic circuits.

5. References

[1] G. Chen and X. Dong, "From Chaos to Order: Methodologies, Perspectives and Applications," World Scientific Publishing, Singapore, 1998.

[2] K. M. Cuomo, A. V. Oppenheim and S. H. Strogatz, "Synchronization of Lorenz-Based Chaotic Circuits with Applicationsto Communications," *IEEE Transactions on Circuits and Systems-II: Analog and Digital Signal Processing*, Vol. 40, No. 10, 1993, pp. 626-633.

[3] E. N. Lorenz, "Deterministic Nonperiodic Flow," *Journal of Atmospheric Sciences*, Vol. 20, No. 2, 1963, pp. 130-141.

[4] O. E. Rossler, "An Equation for Continuous Chaos," *Physics Letters A*, Vol. 57, No. 5, 1976, pp. 397-398.

[5] W. Yu, J. Cao, K. Wong and J. Lu, "New Communication Schemes Based on Adaptive Synchronization," *Chaos*, Vol. 17, No. 3, 2007, pp. 33-114.

[6] J. H. LÜ, G. Chen, D. Cheng and S. Celikovsky, "Bridge the Gap between the Lorenz System and the Chen System," *International Journal of Bifurcation and Chaos*, Vol. 12, No. 12, 2002, pp. 2917-2926.

[7] S. Celikovsky and G. Chen, "On a Generalized Lorenz Canonical Form of Chaotic Systems," *International Journal of Bifurcation and Chaos*, Vol. 12, No. 8, 2002, pp. 1789-1812.

[8] J. LÜ, G. Chen and S. Zhang, "Dynamical Analysis of a New Chaotic Attractor," *International Journal of Bifurcation and Chaos*, Vol. 12, No. 5, 2002, pp. 1001-1015.

[9] S. Nakagawa and T. Saito, "An RC OTA Hysteresis Chaos Generator," *IEEE Transactions on Circuits Systems Part I: Fundamental Theory and Applications*, Vol. 43, No. 12, 1996, pp. 1019-1021.

[10] J. LÜ and G. Chen, "Generating Multiscroll Chaotic Attractors: Theories, Methods and Applications," *International Journal of Bifurcation and Chaos*, Vol. 16, No. 4, 2006, pp. 775-858.

[11] M. E. Yalcin, J. A. K. Suykens, J. Vandewalle and S. Ozoguz, "Families of Scroll Grid Attractors," *International Journal of Bifurcation and Chaos,* Vol. 12, No. 1, 2002, pp. 23-41.

[12] K. M. Cuomo and A. V. Oppenheim, "Circuit Implementation of Synchronized Chaos with Applications to Communications," *Physical Review Letters*, Vol. 71, No. 65, 1993, pp. 65-68.

15

High Frequency Oscillator Design Using a Single 45 nm CMOS Current Controlled Current Conveyor (CCCII+) with Minimum Passive Components

Mohd Yusuf Yasin, Bal Gopal
Department of Electronics and Communication Engineering, Integral University, Lucknow, India

Abstract

In the field of analog VLSI design, current conveyors have reasonably established their identity as an important circuit design element. In the literature published during the past few years, numerous application have been reported which are based on a variety of current conveyors. In this paper, an oscillator circuit has been proposed. This oscillator is designed using a single positive type second generation current controlled current conveyor (CCCII+). A CCCII has parasitic input resistance on it's current input node. This resistance could be exploited to reduce circuit complexities. Thus in this accord, a novel oscillator circuit is proposed which utilizes the parasitic resistance of the CCCII+ along with a few more passive components.

Keywords: Current Mode (CM) Circuit Applications, Current Conveyor (CC), Current Controlled Current Conveyor (CCC) Applications, CCCII Oscillator Circuit; Single CCCII+ Oscillator Circuit, Low Power Oscillator Circuit

1. Introduction

In the recent past, the analog VLSI has emerged as a promising technology for the future demands of low power and high bandwidth requirements. Current mode (CM) design approach is fast gaining in and establishing a trend setting reputation in the design of the modern day VLSI. It proves to be a viable technique that can help applying various design considerations which are ineffective or hard to apply otherwise. Because of it's superiority over the voltage mode approach, [1], the CM design approach appears to be a fit candidate for the next generation of analog VLSI.

Current mode design approach is one where circuits are operated on current stimuli and also the states of the circuits are represented in terms of currents rather than in terms of voltages. Current mode approach has numerous remarkable features, like, superior bandwidth, higher speed and better operational accuracy. It does not require highly sophisticated designs as demanded by the good performance VM amplifiers. Further, this approach can also manage with comparatively low precision design components. The CM design approach has been successfully applied to a variety of circuit applications. For example, several important CM applications are proposed in [2]. These applications are based on various CM devices like CCII, CCIII, CFA, OFC.

Current conveyor (CC) is an important and versatile current mode active building block, which has been considered superior to operational amplifiers [3], and can offer higher design flexibility than conventional operational amplifiers. It can be elegantly applied to a variety of analog circuit design problems. CC versions of various standard applications are found simpler and more elaborate than their voltage mode counterparts. In a CC, the voltage follower action between the input nodes and the current conveyance between input output nodes are the principal actions [1], and are controllable over a wide range [3]. A CC facilitates the use of both positive and negative feedbacks with equal ease, and can be used to simulate negative resistance. Current controlled current conveyor (CCC) is yet another CM active building block, where considerable parasitic resistance appears at the current input node and is controllable by the controlling (biasing) current. Both of these devices also offer the features of current duplication and current negation without any deterioration in the operation of the principal circuit. A brief review of the well known characteristics of an ideal CCCII+ are given in Equation (1) and **Figure 1** [4,5].

$$\begin{bmatrix} I_Y \\ V_X \\ I_Z \end{bmatrix} = \begin{bmatrix} 0 & 0 & 0 \\ 1 & R_X & 0 \\ 0 & 1 & 0 \end{bmatrix} \begin{bmatrix} V_Y \\ I_X \\ V_Z \end{bmatrix} \quad (1)$$

In a type CCCII+, both I_X and I_Z may flow into or out of the device simultaneously. For the other two possible combinations of these currents, the device is typed as CCCII-. The R_X is input resistance at the node X and depends upon the circuit structure.

In this work, an oscillator is realized using CMOS version of the CCCII+ shown in **Figure 1**. Resistance R_X of the CCCII+ is exploited and is treated like any other passive resistor with the aim of reducing the demand of external passive resistors.

2. Oscillator Circuit Scheme

Several oscillator circuits have been published recently [4,6-10]. These circuits have invariably been proposed on the basis of the multiple use of CC/CCC along with two or more passive components, incorporating both inverting and non inverting outputs, and, in some cases, a few more design building blocks, etc. A number of oscillator topologies are presented in [11]. ICCII is the active device used in all these topologies. However, the minimum passive component count is irredundantly four, along with at least one ICCII.

Here in this work, a novel scheme is proposed as depicted in **Figure 2**. This scheme is quite simple and employs only one single output CCCII+ with a possible minimum passive component count. Here the basic circuit structure is proposed with four passive components, however, the subsequent analysis helps in reducing the external component count to three. The circuit also has the added features like, very low power requirement,

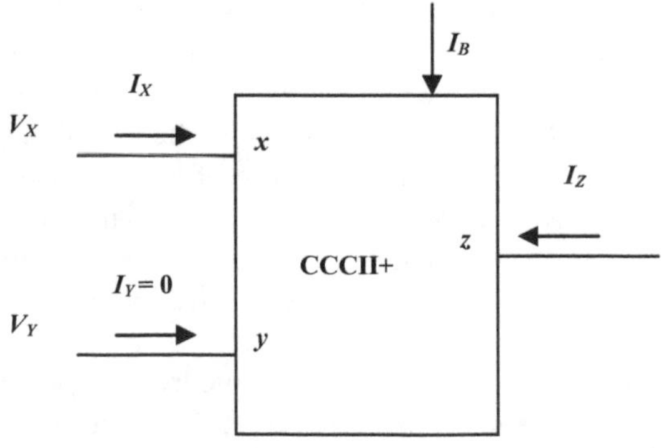

Figure 1. Block Diagram representation of the 2nd generation CCCII+.

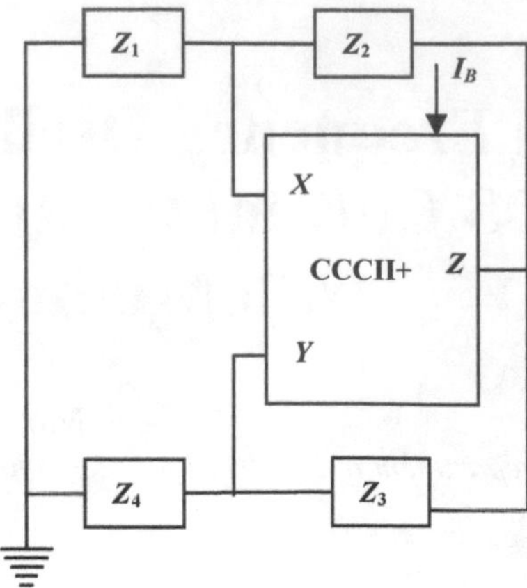

Figure 2. Generalized scheme for the proposed Oscillator. All Z_i's are impedances.

capability of generating high oscillation frequency, low turn-on time [6], and electronically tunable frequency through I_B.

Routine analysis of the scheme of **Figure 2**, gives the following characteristic equation:

$$\begin{aligned} Z_2 Z_4 &= Z_4 R_X + Z_1 Z_2 + 2 Z_1 Z_3 \\ &+ R_X \left(Z_1 + Z_2 + Z_3 \right) \end{aligned} \quad (2)$$

For a real frequency of oscillation, and the gain adjustment, a suitable second order polynomial is required, so that the real and imaginary components yield. This requirement of Equation (2) can be fulfilled for the following specific choice of external components as given in Equation (3). Arrows in Equation (3) indicate the operation of replacing the impedances by the corresponding passive components (for example, impedance Z_1 is replaced by the capacitor C_1).

$$Z_1 \to C_1; Z_2 \to C_2; Z_3 \to R_3; Z_4 \to R_4 \quad (3)$$

The choice of Equation (3) is incorporated in the scheme of **Figure 2** and the following s-domain characteristic polynomial is obtained.

$$\begin{aligned} & s^2 C_1 C_2 R_X \left(R_3 + R_4 \right) + \\ & s \left(C_1 R_X + C_2 R_X + 2 C_2 R_3 - C_1 R_4 \right) + 1 = 0 \end{aligned} \quad (4)$$

Equation (4) gives the necessary gain condition and the frequency of oscillations.

$$C_1 R_X + C_2 R_X + 2 C_2 R_3 = C_1 R_4 \quad (5)$$

$$\omega_O = \frac{1}{\sqrt{C_1 C_2 R_X \left(R_4 + R_3 \right)}} \quad (6)$$

Equations (5) and (6) clearly show the insignificance of R_3. If it is shorted, ($R_3 = 0$), both the Equations (5) and (6) are further simplified.

$$R_4 = 2 R_X \quad (7)$$

$$\omega_O = \frac{1}{\sqrt{2}CR_X} \quad (8)$$

Thus it is possible to realize the oscillator using a single CCCII+, one Resistor and two equal capacitors. The final complete circuit is presented in **Figure 3**.

On the basis of **Figure 3** and the Equations (7) and (8), a few observations are worth noting. Equation (7) depicts ideal condition, and thus Equation (8) remains a valid equation when expressed in terms of R_4. Further, from **Figure 3**, the feedback signal with respect to node Y is $V_2 = \frac{R_X - R_4 - sCR_XR_4}{R_4(1+2sCR_X)}V_3$. For large values of R_4 and ω, $\frac{V_2}{V_3} \rightarrow -\frac{1}{2}$. It clearly indicates that a larger value of R_4 is necessary to build up the required level of the Y node feed back signal and 180° phase shift so that the circuit sustains oscillations. Therefore the oscillation frequency should better be defined using Equation (8) instead of using the suggestion of Equation (7), as it predicts only the ideal condition for oscillations. Simulation results also suggest the independence of the frequency of oscillations of R_4.

Ignoring the body effect, the estimate of resistance R_X of the above circuit, is given by $R_X \approx \frac{1}{g_{m10}+g_{m9}}$. For matched transistors M9 and M10, $R_X \approx \frac{1}{\sqrt{8\beta I_B}}$, β being the device transconductance of M9 [5].

3. Circuit of the CCCII+

For realization of the above oscillator, the class AB CCCII+ circuit adopted is shown in **Figure 4**, and is readily available in literature. It's bipolar version is studied by many authors, [12,13]. It's CMOS version can be found in references [5,10]. In the present work, this circuit is redesigned in 45 nm CMOS and is simulated using the "Predictive Technology Model Beta Version 45 nm MOS Parameters" compatible with HSPICE [14]. The design details of this circuit are presented in **Table 1.**

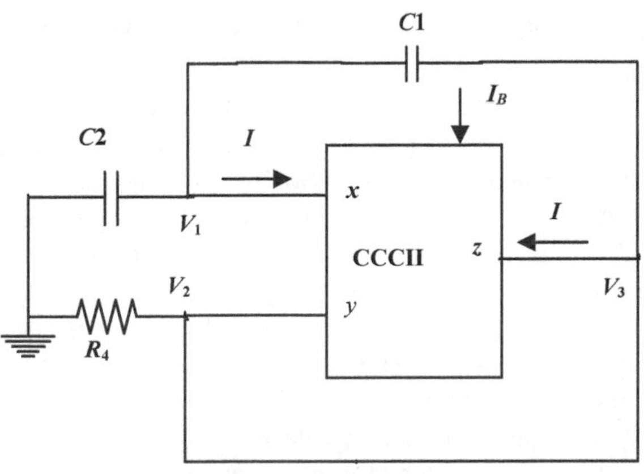

Figure 3. Simplified circuit schematic of the CCCII+ based oscillator.

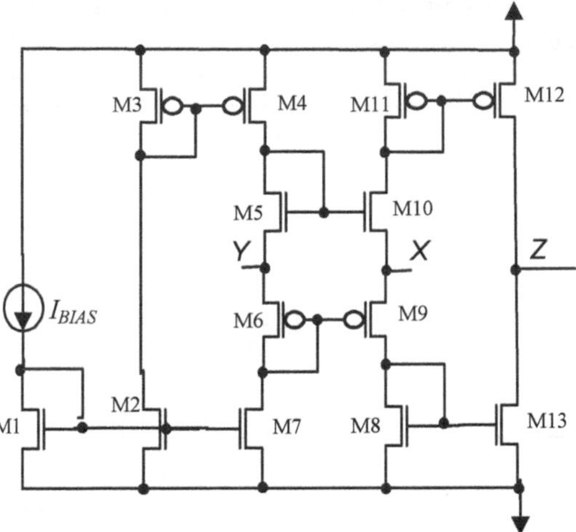

Figure 4. CCCII+ circuit for testing the proposed oscillator. Upward arrow is to V_{DD} and the downward arrow is to V_{SS}.

4. Verification and Results

CCCII+ of **Figure 4** is designed in 45 nm CMOS, and is applied to the realization of the proposed oscillator.

The application is then simulated on HSPICE and the performance of the oscillator (node Z voltage signal) is presented in **Figure 5**. For clarity of the necessary details, **Figure 5** is windowed between 600 ns and 800 ns; and is presented in **Figure 6**. However, the simulation is done for the entire 0.1 ms interval.

Fourier analysis, with respect to the principal frequency (38.48 MHz), is performed on the node Z signal to ascertain the quality of the oscillations. Result of this analysis is presented in **Figure 7**. Peaks in **Figure 7** correspond to the principal frequency of the oscillator and it's harmonic frequencies. Third harmonic component is significant (–27 dB) compared to the second harmonic component (–30 dB). Estimates of the total harmonic distortion (THD) and the DC component of the node Z signal are important quality matrices. Both these parameters are found reasonably very low. The simulation results are summarized in **Table 2.**

It is noteworthy that the sustainable oscillations are established without requiring a trigger signal. Further, the value of resistor R_4 estimated by Equation (6) above, would theoretically establish oscillations. It is observed that higher values of R_4 enhance the voltage buildup

Table 1. Design details of the circuits of Figure 3 & Figure 4.

Design Parameter	Value
R_4	15 kΩ
$C_1 = C_2$	1 pF
Supply Voltage	± 1.0V
I_{BIAS}	3 μA
W/L	0.98 μm/0.2 μm (all NMOS)
W/L	8.3 μm/0.36 μm (all PMOS)
Parameters	45 nm (β version), HSPICE

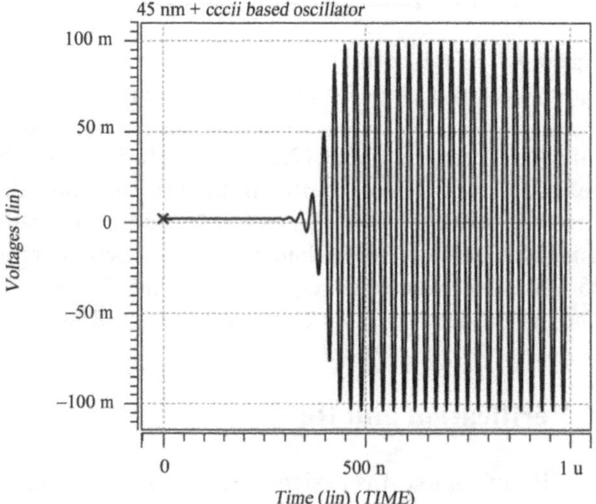

Figure 5. Output of the proposed oscillator (node *Z*). I_B = 3 μA, *C* = 10 pF. Figure shows startup time ≈ 400 ns.

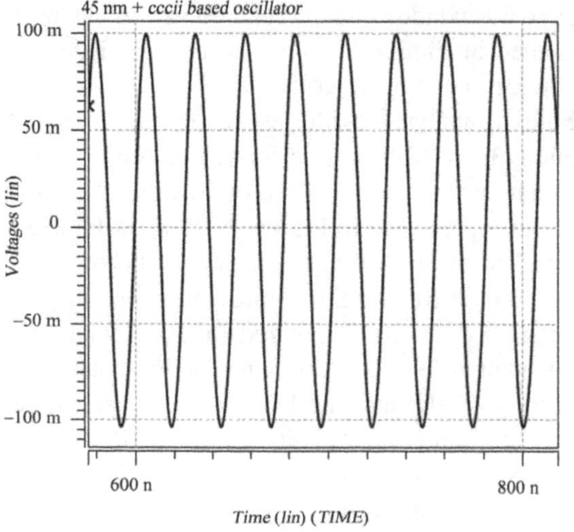

Figure 6. Expanded view of the output signal (node *Z*) in Figure 5.

quicker and hence the oscillations start up earlier. It is also observed that R_4 do not affect the oscillation frequency though Equation (8) can be expressed in terms of R_4. This is merely because of Equation (7).

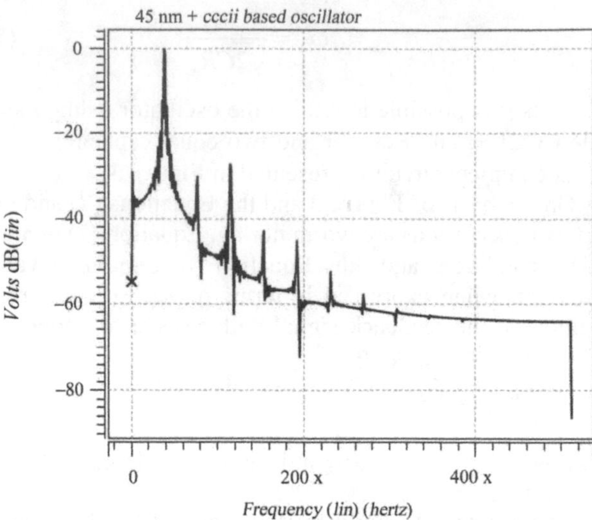

Figure 7. Fourier analysis of the signal at node z of Figure 5. First peak appears at 38.5 MHz. Subsequent peaks occur at harmonic frequencies.

Table 2. Performance results of the proposed oscillator.

Performance Parameters	Detail
Frequency	38.5 MHz
THD	–31.4 dB,(2.7%)
DC Component	–1.8 mV
Peak Average Magnitude	–104 mV to 99.4 mV
Total Power Dissipation(biasing source)	257 μW
Oscillations start-up Time	~400 ns
SNR at output node	–0.75 dB

Authors of reference [4] reported frequency of operation in kHz range for their proposed oscillators with a THD of 0.5% using CC/CCC based upon bipolar technology.

Authors of reference [11] use 1.2 μm CMOS based ICCII using ±2.5 V supply voltages. The total active area for the proposed ICCII was 2096 μm^2. Also the proposed oscillators gradually build up to final peak to peak amplitude of oscillations in about 400 μs. Test results in [11] are presented for 39.78 kHz.

The circuit scheme proposed here in this work is a low voltage, low power scheme, based on CCCII designed in 45 nm CMOS technology, biased at ±1 V and simulation results are summarized in **Table 2**. In addition, the proposed circuit can generate frequencies up to 100 MHz(at I_B= 2.79 μA, C_1= C_2= 0.225 pf), and requires only 19.6 μm^2 active area, which is quite small [11].

Figure 8 shows a logarithmic plot for frequency variation with respect to capacitance. The graph shows a natural trend of as frequency drops with increasing capacitance.

In **Figures 9** a plot for frequency variation with biasing current of the CCCII+ is presented on logarithmic scale. Simulation results show that a variation in the bias current, $\Delta I_B = 2.9$ μA (0.4 μA to 3.3 μA), cause the oscillator frequency to vary as $\Delta f = 25.78$ MHz (15.2 MHz to 40.98 MHz). For the sake of analysis, a figure of merit could be defined as the current to frequency transfer coefficient, K_{fi}, [15]. Thus for $C_1 = C_2 = 1$ pf, $K_{fiN} = 25.78$ MHz /2.9 μA = 8.9 MHz/μA. $K_{f\text{-}I}$ depends on capacitances and the biasing current. It varies directly with the I_B and inversely with the capacitances.

5. Non Idealities of CCCII+ and Their Impact on Circuit Performance

In the above analysis, the CCCII+ is considered ideal. However, a number of non-idealities are present in a practical CCCII+. Considering some of these non-idealities, the device model of the CCCII+ of **Figure 1** can be described as below:

$$I_Z = \pm \alpha I_X \tag{9}$$

$$V_X = I_X R_X + \beta V_Y \tag{10}$$

$$I_Y = I_\delta \tag{11}$$

where α in Equation (9), is the current conveyance coefficient between nodes X and Z; β in Equation (10), is the voltage gain from node Y to node X and is usuall $y < 1$. I_δ in Equation (11) is the input current at node Y. For analytical simplicity in the proposed oscillator scheme, it is assumed that this current is a function of the voltage at node Z. Therefore, $I_\delta = V_Z/R_\delta$, where R_δ is the corresponding resistance at the Y node. Also, as usual, $C_1 = C_2 = C$. Using these assumptions, analysis of circuit in **Figure 3**, gives the following modified characteristic equation:

$$s^2C^2R_4R_X + sC\left(2R_X - 2\alpha\beta R_4 + R_4 + \beta R_4 - \alpha R_4 R_X + 2\frac{R_4}{R_X}\right) + \left(1 + \frac{R_4}{R_\delta}\right) = 0 \tag{12}$$

On solving Equation (12), the results are:

$$\frac{1}{R_4} + \frac{1}{R_\delta} = \frac{\alpha(1+2\beta) - (1+\beta)}{2R_X} = \frac{K}{2R_X} \tag{13}$$

$$\omega^2 = \frac{\frac{1}{R_\delta} + \frac{1}{R_4}}{C^2 R_X} = \frac{K}{2C^2R_X^2} \tag{14}$$

$$\omega = \sqrt{K}\frac{1}{\sqrt{2}CR_X} = \sqrt{K}\omega_O \tag{15}$$

$$\frac{\omega}{\omega_O} = \sqrt{K} < 1 \tag{16}$$

Equation (13) relates R_4, R_X, and R_δ. Equation (15) shows a possible elimination of R_δ. Hence either of R_4 and R_X or both may get modified on account of the voltage and current tracking errors of the CCCII. Here it is assumed that the circuit non-idealities do not cause significant change in the value of R_X. Equation (16) shows that the oscillation frequency ω under non-ideal conditions is lesser than the ideal oscillation frequency ω_o . Further more,

$$K = \alpha(1+2\beta) - (1+\beta) \tag{17}$$

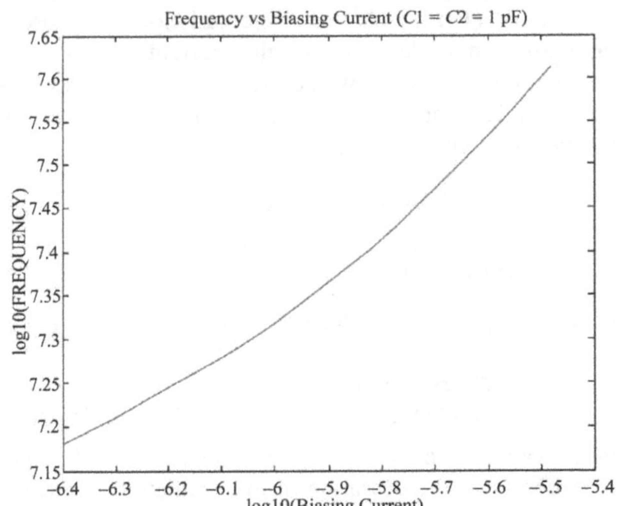

Figure 9. Frequency variation with biasing current. Case 2 : C = 1 pF.

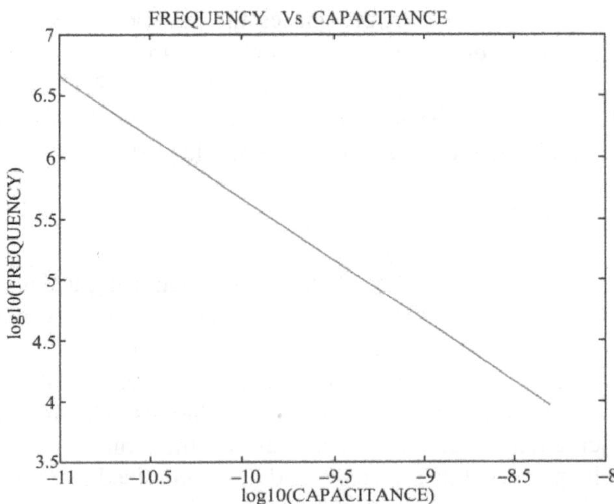

Figure 8. Frequency variation with Capacitor ($C_1 = C_2 = C$).

Equation (17) indicates that the variation in the oscillator frequency depends on the current and voltage tracking errors, and shows no effect of the current existing at node Y of the CCCII+. Percent decrease in the frequency can be described as:

$$\frac{\omega_O - \omega}{\omega_O} = 1 - \sqrt{K} \tag{18}$$

For an ideal situation, $\alpha \to 1$, $\beta \to 1$, $I_\delta = 0$ and $R_\delta \to \infty$; hence Equation (13) reduces to $\frac{1}{R_4} = \frac{1}{2R_X}$, and Equation (14) reduces to Equation (8), and hence from Equations (16) and (18), $\omega = \omega_O$. But for a 5% tracking error in the values of α, and β, e.g. $\alpha = 0.95$, $\beta = 0.95$, using Equation (18), the deviation in the oscillation frequency is observed to be $\frac{\omega_O - \omega}{\omega_O} = 0.1028$, or 10.3%.

6. Time Domain and Stabilty Considerations

The time domain analysis may be significant in giving better insight in the functioning and performance of the oscillator circuit. Assuming the circuit of **Figure 3** relaxed, it can be described by the following system of equations for $v_1(t)$ and $v_3(t)$ voltages of nodes 1 and 3 respectively

$$(CR_X)^2 R_4 \frac{d^2 v_1}{dt^2} + CR_X(2R_X - R_4)\frac{dv_1}{dt} + R_X v_1 = 0 \tag{19}$$

$$(CR_X)^2 R_4 \frac{d^2 v_3(t)}{dt^2} + CR_X(2R_X - R_4)\frac{dv_3(t)}{dt} - R_X v_3(t) = 0 \tag{20}$$

Equation (19) predicts oscillatory behaviour for the option $R_4 = 2R_x$ as has already been indicated above. Using this option, and defining $\omega'_o = \frac{1}{CR_4}$, general solutions of Equations (19) and (20) are as follows

$$v_1(t) = c_1 e^{j\omega_o' t} + c_2 e^{-j\omega_o' t} \tag{21}$$

$$v_3(t) = c_3 e^{\sqrt{2}\omega_o' t} + c_4 e^{-\sqrt{2}\omega_o' t} \tag{22}$$

In the above Equations (21) and (22), the coefficients C_1, C_2, C_3, and C_4, are arbitrary constants. Equation (21) is oscillatory in nature. In Equation (22), one of the terms rises exponentially to saturation while the other term sharply decays out for large ω'_o and hence oscillations attain their amplitude. $\omega_o = \sqrt{2}\,\omega'_o$

Again one can consider the gain limits of the circuit. For this purpose, feedback signal from node Z to node X is through C_1 and C_2 ($C_1 = C_2$), while to node Y is through R_4. Thus the gain function corresponding to the capacitive feedback arm is:

$$\frac{v_1(s)}{v_3(s)} = \frac{sCR_X + 1}{s2CR_X + 1} = \frac{1}{2}\frac{s + \frac{2}{CR_4}}{s + \frac{1}{CR_4}} = \frac{1}{2}\frac{s + 2\omega'_o}{s + \omega'_o} \tag{23}$$

$$\left|\frac{v_1(s)}{v_3(s)}\right| = \frac{1}{2}\frac{\sqrt{\omega^2 + 4\omega'^2_o}}{\sqrt{\omega^2 + \omega'^2_o}} = \frac{1}{2}\frac{\sqrt{\omega_n^2 + 4}}{\sqrt{\omega_n^2 + 1}} \tag{24}$$

Similarly the gain function corresponding to the resistive arm is

$$\frac{v_3(s)}{v_1(s)} = \frac{(sCR_X - 1)R}{sCRR_X + R_X - R} = \frac{s - \frac{2}{CR_4}}{s - \frac{1}{CR_4}} = \frac{s - 2\omega'_o}{s - \omega'_o} \tag{25}$$

$$\left|\frac{v_3(s)}{v_1(s)}\right| = \frac{\sqrt{\omega^2 + 4\omega'^2_o}}{\sqrt{\omega^2 + \omega'^2_o}} = \frac{\sqrt{\omega_n^2 + 4}}{\sqrt{\omega_n^2 + 1}} \tag{26}$$

Equations (24) and (26) are described as a function of normalized frequency, $\omega_n = \omega/\omega'_o$. From Equation (24), the gain limits are: for $\omega_n \to 0$, $\left|\frac{v_1(s)}{v_3(s)}\right| \to 1$ and $\omega_n \to \infty$, $\left|\frac{v_1(s)}{v_3(s)}\right| \to \frac{1}{2}$. Similarly from Equation (26), $\omega_n \to 0$, $\left|\frac{v_3(s)}{v_1(s)}\right| \to 2$ and $\omega_n \to \infty$, $\left|\frac{v_3(s)}{v_1(s)}\right| \to 1$. In both cases, the gain transitions occur between $1 < \omega_n < 2$. However, the phases for Equations (23) and (25), being opposite to one another, start at 0° phase angle, both attain a peak ($\omega_n \approx 1.4$, $\varphi(\omega) \approx \pm 19.47^\circ$ and then gradually die towards zero individually. It is thus concluded that the system is quite stable [16].

7. Conclusions

In this work, a novel oscillator is designed using a single CCCII+, two passive capacitors to control frequency and one passive resistor to sustain the necessary gain. The simulation results of the oscillator verify the circuit capability to generate megahertz oscillations. Quality of oscillations is also reasonable as per the simulation results presented in **Figures 5** and **6**, summarized in **Table 2**. The DC component of the output is observed about –1.8 mV and the total harmonic distortion in the output node Z signal is about 2.7% (–31.4 dB) at 38.5 MHz frequency (see **Table 2**). The peak to peak amplitude of the output voltage is 203 mV. Also, the simulation shows the average power dissipation low, 257 μW when biased through ±1.0 V and a 3 μA source. The oscillator is also investigated for higher frequencies and found capable of generating 100 MHz at I_B = 2.79 μA, $C_1 = C_2$ = 0.225 pf satisfactorily. It is also supported by the **Figures 8** and **9** that smaller capacitance and larger bias current results higher frequency oscillations.

Further more, it is noticeable that a higher value of R_4 is required to set in the oscillations. The reasons may include

1) Requirement of the feedback loop gain to satisfy the criterion of oscillations.

2) Current, and voltage follow up errors at the relative node pairs (Z, X) and (Y, X) respectively. If R_X assumed unchanged, critical value R_4 requires an upward modification on account of $\alpha \neq 1$, $\beta \neq 1$.

In presence of such non-idealities, however, the model of CCCII described in Equation (1) may be modified to accommodate the tracking errors and the voltage node input current.

$$\begin{bmatrix} I_Y \\ V_X \\ I_Z \end{bmatrix} = \begin{bmatrix} 0 & 0 & 0 \\ \beta & R_X & 0 \\ 0 & \pm\alpha & 0 \end{bmatrix} \begin{bmatrix} V_Y \\ I_X \\ V_Z \end{bmatrix} + \begin{bmatrix} 1 \\ 0 \\ 0 \end{bmatrix} [I_\delta] \quad (27)$$

It is also noticeable that it is the deviations (the absolute values of the coefficients α and β) that affect the results much more than the input current or impedance of the node Y as is clearly indicated by Equation (15). It is further noteworthy that the definition of the parasitic resistance in Equation (1) includes both gate transconductance and body transconductance of M9 and M10. Body transconductnace of the MOSFETs, was ignored in the analysis. Inclusion of the body transconductance of the MOSFETs, however, shows a favorable impact on decreasing R_X, and thus improves the oscillator performance.

8. References

[1] S. Sedra, *et al.*, "The Current Conveyor: History, Progress and New Results," *IEE Proceedings (Part G) of Circuits, Devices and Systems*, Vol. 137, No. 2, April 1990, pp. 78-87.

[2] S. S. Rajput, *et al.*, "Advanced Applications of Current Conveyors: A Tutorial," *Journal of Active and Passive Electronic Devices,* Vol. 2, No. 2, 2007, pp. 143-164.

[3] J. Zhao, *et al.*, "Design of Tunable Biquadratic Filters Employing CCCIIs: State Variable Block Diagram Approach," *Analog Integrated Circuits and Signal Processing*, Vol. 62, No. 3, March 2010, pp. 397-406.

[4] N. Pandey, *et al.*, "Sinusoidal Oscillator—A New Configuration Based on Current Conveyor," *Proceedings of XXVII General Assembly of International Union of Radio Science* (*URSI*), Delhi, 23-29 October 2005, pp 23-29.

[5] M. Siripruchyanun, "A Temperature Compensation Technique for CMOS Current Controlled Current Conveyor (CCCII)," *Proceedings of ECTI-CON* 2005, North Bangkok, 12-13 May 2005, pp. 510-513.

[6] S. B. Salem, *et al.*, "A High Performances CMOS CCII and High Frequency Applications," *Analog Integrated Circuits and Signal Processing*, Vol. 49, No. 1, October 2006, pp. 71-78.

[7] J. Horng, *et al.*, "Sinusoidal Oscillators Using Current Conveyors and Grounded Capacitors," *Journal of Active and Passive Electronic Devices*, Vol. 2, No. 2, 2007, pp. 127-136.

[8] W. Kiranon, *et al.*, "Current Controlled Oscillator Based on Translinear Conveyors," *Electronics Letters*, Vol. 32, No. 15, 1996, pp. 1330-1331.

[9] W. Kiranon, *et al.*, "Electronically Tunable Multifunction Translinear—C Filter and Oscillator," *Electronics Letters,* Vol. 33, No. 7, 1997, p. 573.

[10] J. W. Horng, "A Sinusoidal Oscillator Using Current-Controlled Current Conveyor," *International Journal of Electronics*, Vol. 88, No. 6, 2001, pp. 659-664.

[11] A. Toker, *et al.*, "New Oscillator Topologies Using Inverting Second-Generation Current Conveyors," *Turkish Journal of Electriial Engineering & Computer Science*, Vol. 10, No. 1, 2002, pp. 119-130.

[12] E. Yucel, *et al.*, "Universal Resistorless Current-Mode Filters Employing CCCIIs," *International Journal of Circuit Theory and Applicaitons*, Vol. 36, No. 5-6, 2008, pp. 739-755.

[13] T. Parveen1, *et al.*, "A Canonical Voltage Mode Universal CCCII-C Filter," *Journal of Active and Passive Electronic Devices,* Vol. 4, No. 1-2, 2009, pp. 7-12.

[14] Predictive Technology Model, 2006. http://ptm.asu.edu

[15] S. Soclof, "Design and Applications of Analog Integrated Circuits," Prentice Hall of India, Delhi, 2004.

[16] G. Daryanani, "Principles of Active Network Synthesis and Design," John Wiley and Sons, New York, 1976.

16

A Fluctuation-Dissipation Model for Electrical Noise*

Jose-Ignacio Izpura, Javier Malo
Group of Microsystems and Electronic Materials, Universidad Politécnica de Madrid, Madrid, Spain

Abstract

This paper shows that today's modelling of electrical noise as coming from noisy resistances is a non sense one contradicting their nature as systems bearing an electrical noise. We present a new model for electrical noise that including Johnson and Nyquist work also agrees with the Quantum Mechanical description of noisy systems done by Callen and Welton, where electrical energy fluctuates and is dissipated with time. By the two currents the Admittance function links in frequency domain with their common voltage, this new model shows the connection Cause-Effect that exists between Fluctuation and Dissipation of energy in time domain. In spite of its radical departure from today's belief on electrical noise in resistors, this Complex model for electrical noise is obtained from Nyquist result by basic concepts of Circuit Theory and Thermodynamics that also apply to capacitors and inductors.

Keywords: Admittance-Based, Noise Model, Fluctuation, Susceptance, Dissipation, Resistance

1. Introduction

Current understanding of electrical noise in circuits considers shot and Johnson noises as different physical phenomena each with its own physical model, despite their deep connection found by some authors [1]. Considering electric current as carried by discrete electrons independently of one another, as Johnson did in vacuum devices to study their shot noise [2], this connection isn't too surprising. What is a surprise, however, is that today's works in this field tend to consider noise currents as carried by packets of electrons that, to our knowledge, hardly are found in ordinary matter. We mean proposals like [3] contending that electrical charge piling-up in a lonely resistance R generates shot noise, thus transgressing a Quantum-Mechanical result of [4]: the need for a Complex Admittance function to describe a noisy system.

This transgression and that of Special Relativity that a null C shunting the R of a resistor endures [5], led us to review today's modelling of electrical noise in this paper showing why the PSPICE simulator does not give the right noise of junction diodes [6] and what the effects are of today's unawareness about the Susceptance that shunts the Conductance $G = 1/R$ of any resistor we can make. The paper is organized as follows. In Section 2 we review the Partial Interpretation (PI) in use today of Johnson-Nyquist results that leads to a wrong modelling of electrical noise sometimes. Section 3 shows how to pass from this PI to an Advanced Model (AM) for electrical noise that agreeing with the laws of Physics, also allows a right modelling of this noise where the aforesaid PI fails. This passage is done in frequency domain by the familiar noise densities $S_I(f)$ in A^2/Hz and $S_V(f)$ in V^2/Hz. Section 4, however, considers the generation of electrical noise by Fluctuations and Dissipations of electrical energy in time domain, taking place in the Admittance of two-terminal devices like resistors and capacitors, no matter its physical structure. Some relevant conclusions are drawn at the end.

*Work supported by the Spanish CICYT under the MAT2010-18933 project, by the Comunidad Autónoma de Madrid through its IV-PRICIT Program, and by the European Regional Development Fund (FEDER).

2. Reviewing Current Model for Electrical Noise in Resistors

To a first level, the Susceptance shunting the conductance $G = 1/R$ of a resistor of resistance R is due to a capacitance C_d coming from the dielectric properties of the material used to fabricate this device, whose physical structure appears in **Figure 1** and where the space between two parallel plates (ohmic contacts) contains some material of dielectric permittivity ε and conductivity σ. We mean the Susceptance due to $C_d = \tau_d / R$ that each resistor bears in parallel with its R because the non-null dielectric relaxation time $\tau_d = \varepsilon / \sigma$ of its inner material

[7]. Any stray capacitance as $C_{stray} \approx 0.5$ pF, typical of set-ups used in Low Frequency Noise (LFN) measurements [8], would be added to C_d.

For conducting materials as n-doped Silicon or GaAs, τ_d falls below the ps, thus giving very low C_d values: $C_d \approx 10^{-15}$ F for $R = 1$ kΩ and $\tau_d = 1$ ps. This is why C_d and C_{stray} are considered irrelevant at frequencies $f \leq 1$ MHz where LFN is found. This irrelevance that can be accepted numerically in most cases (e.g. when there are other Admittances in parallel), leads to the misconception underlying the aforesaid PI of the pioneering works of Johnson [9] and Nyquist [10]. This error is so deep-rooted in today's research that reviewers of [3] were not ashamed of publishing a piling-up of electrical charge in a resistance devoid of capacitance C, which links electric charge $Q(t)$ and electric voltage $v(t)$. When a current $i(t)$ produces a change of dipolar charge $\partial Q = i\partial t$ as t passes, it builds a voltage ∂v that is linked with the charge variation at each instant by the Capacitance $C = \partial Q/\partial v$. Thus, $C = 0$ between the two terminals of a resistor means that it could show an electrical voltage between them without electric charges acting as its source or, as we wrote in [5], its material having finite σ to offer a finite R with the structure of **Figure 1**, but having a null permittivity $\varepsilon = 0$ to offer $C_d = 0$, would allow an infinite speed for the electromagnetic wave, thus infringing Einstein's Special Relativity. Besides this conflict with Physics, this PI of Nyquist work is hard to apply out of Thermal Equilibrium (TE) because [10] was done for TE. The footnote of Figure 4.11 of [11] summarizes the essence of this PI by this sentence: "Circuits elements and their noise models. Note that capacitors and inductors do not generate noise".

Figure 2 shows the circuits this PI uses to represent electrical noise in a resistor of resistance R, where a Conductance $G = 1/R$ is shunted by a noise generator of density $S_I(f) = 4kT/R$ A^2/Hz (Nyquist noise) for k being the Boltzmann constant. This leads to a noise density $S_V(f) = R^2 \times S_I(f) = 4kTR$ V^2/Hz (Johnson noise). Thus, a resistor is a noisy resistance [3] for this PI that uses the resistance R of a resistor in TE as a generator of flat $S_I(f)$ and $S_V(f)$ noises up to frequencies $f_Q \approx 6.2$ THz at room T, a quantum limit given in [10].

Let's consider under this PI the circuit of **Figure 3** with $C = 0$, where the voltage of a resistor of $R = 100$ kΩ is sampled and feedback as a current by a feedback factor $\beta = 1/R$ A/V. For this $R = 100$ kΩ giving $S_V(f) = 4kTR \approx 1600\ (\text{nV})^2/\text{Hz}$ and $S_I(f) = 0.16\ (\text{pA})^2/\text{Hz}$, the noiseless sampling and feedback of **Figure 3** could be carried out quite well with today's Operational Amplifiers [12] having input noise parameters as: $e_n^2 = 36(\text{nV})^2/\text{Hz}$ and $i_n^2 = 1(\text{fA})^2/\text{Hz}$. Accordingly to the PI in use today this negative feedback adds a noiseless R in parallel with the noisy R or resistor whose Nyquist noise $S_I(f)$ is the input signal of this feedback circuit. Thus, the $S_I(f)$ of the noisy R is the only source of noise in this circuit that, attenuated by the noiseless R, leads to $S_{VFB}(f) = kTR$ V^2/Hz in it. This result agreeing with

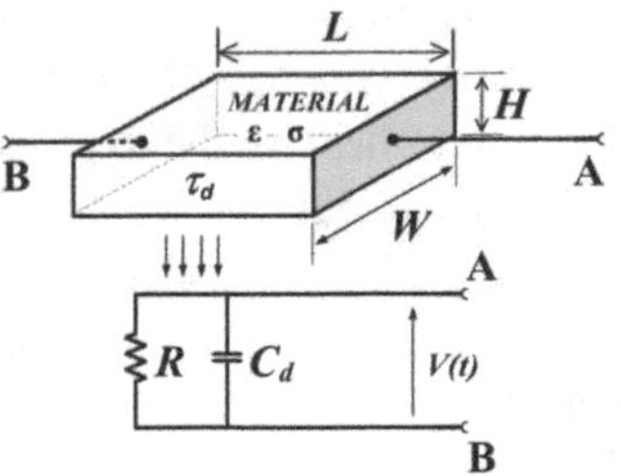

Figure 1. Physical structure of an elemental resistor whose ohmic contacts (shaded area) are the plates that enclose the parallel-plate capacitor of capacitance $C_d = \tau_d/R$ that allows to apply or to measure an electrical voltage between the terminals A and B of its resistance *R*.

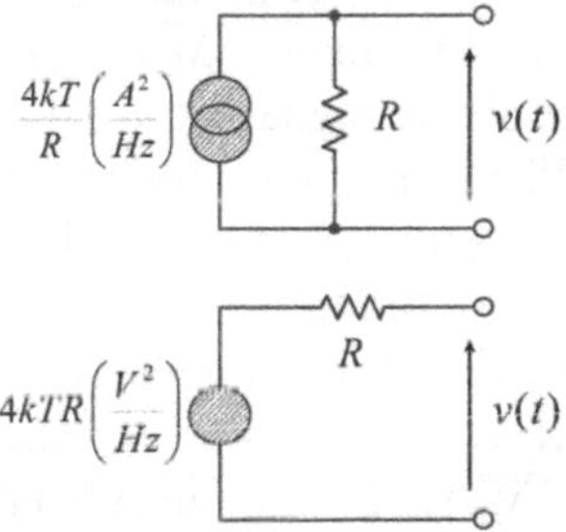

Figure 2. Parallel and series circuits that today's Partial Interpretation (PI) of Johnson and Nyquist results uses to represent the electrical noise of a resistor (see text).

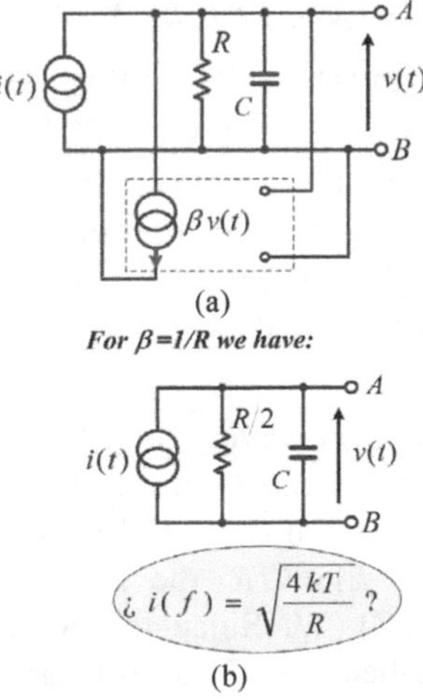

Figure 3. Feedback scheme used to show that today's unawareness about the role of Susceptance in electrical noise, doesn't allow finding the "well known" kT/C noise of the capacitor existing in this circuit.

a "well know" one of this PI, namely: "the available noise power from a resistor of resistance R in TE at some T *is* $N(f) = kT$ W/Hz ", deserves some attention. Because the noisy R and the noiseless R are driven by $S_{VFB}(f) = kTR$ V^2/Hz, they are dissipating $N(f) = S_{VFB}(f)/R = kT$ W/Hz, of course. Since the noisy R is *out of TE* due to its feedback, we find logical this lower dissipation than the $4kT$ W/Hz it dissipated in TE when it was driven by $S_I(f)$. What is less "logical" is the null dissipation R has in the equivalent circuit of **Figure 2** with $S_V(f)$ series connected with R, thus raising doubts about the physical correctness of $S_V(f) = R^2 \times S_I(f)$, whose circuital correctness is well known.

To make some progress, let's consider the noisy R shunted by C = 1 pF in **Figure 3** to represent a pixel of an imaging device becoming charged by m electrons when a short packet of m/η photons is absorbed with quantum efficiency $\eta < 1$. "Short" means that photons are absorbed within a time interval $\Delta t \ll \tau = RC$, where τ is the time constant of this R-C cell. Thus, a photon packet sets a charge of mq C in C (q is the electron charge) and the voltage $\Delta v = mq/C$ V appearing on R will be the aimed Signal on R whose power is: $S = (mq/C)^2/R$ W. Since C will discharge through R, the Signal readout would be done a short time $t_d \ll \tau$ after the photon absorption in order to find the aforesaid power S. Concerning Noise power N, the mean square noise voltage on R is the product of the Johnson noise $S_V(f) = 4kTR$ V^2/Hz by the noise bandwidth $BW_N = (\pi/2) f_C$ of this circuit of cut-off frequency $f_C = 1/(2\pi RC)$ [13]: $N = S_V \times BW_N$. This replaces the integration in f of $S_V(f)$ to allow a fast reasoning using Signal to Noise ratios (S/N). Thus, the noise power in the pixel without feedback is: $N = kT/(RC)$ W and its S/N is: $(S/N)_i = (mq)^2/(kTC)$, the ratio of the square charge signal in C $(mq)^2$ C^2, divided by the square charge noise of C: kTC C^2 [14]. To give some figures, the kT/C noise at room T (e.g. the square root of kT/C) of C = 1 pF is 64 μV$_{rms}$. For a Signal $\Delta v = mq/C$ = 6.4 mV we would have: $S/N|_i = 10^4$ or 40 dB for the pixel without feedback.

With feedback, however, the BW_N doubles due to $R/2$ shunting the same C that this feedback in-phase with the output doesn't vary [15]. From this double BW_N with $S_{VFB}(f) = kTR$ the noise power on R is: $N_{FB} = kT/(2RC)$ W. Since the Signal power on R doesn't change because C doesn't vary, the (S/N) of the pixel with feedback would be doubled, a result well worth patenting provided it was true. Unfortunately, this noise modelling is wrong as we will show in the next Section.

3. An Advanced Model for Electrical Noise in Resistors and Capacitors

Because $C = \partial Q/\partial v$ links charge variations with voltage ones related with electric fields storing energy between terminals, C behaves as the reservoir of electrical energy whose thermal Fluctuations are observed as Johnson noise $v(t)$ in resistors [7]. Using Thermodynamics, C sets the Degree of Freedom to store electrical energy linked with the fluctuating $v(t)$ in a resistor that a lonely resistance doesn't have. Using Quantum Mechanics we will say that eingenstates of electrical energy hardly will be found in a lonely resistance unable to store it by some Susceptance in parallel or by a Reactance in series. Thus, a cogent model for electrical noise in resistors must handle Conductance $G = 1/R$ together with Susceptance, and this also holds for noise modelling of capacitors in TE at some temperature T because they offer a similar Admittance [5].

It is worth noting that these ideas about noise in resistors are present in **Figure 2** if one knows how to read its first circuit or which is the physical meaning of $S_I(f) = 4kTG$ A^2/Hz, a current-like power source proportional to the conductance it is driving. This $S_I(f)$ leads to $S_V(f) = 4kTR$ V^2/Hz, a power density that, being proportional to R while its bandwidth (note that C_d always exists) is proportional to $1/R$, means that the mean square voltage noise has nothing to do with currents in R. Thus, the noise currents that $S_I(f) = 4kT/R$ represents must be currents $i_{nQ}(t)$ orthogonal to noise currents $i_{nP}(t)$ in G that always are in-phase with the voltage noise $v_n(t)$. This means currents $i_{nQ}(t)$ always in quadrature with $v_n(t)$ flowing through a Susceptance shunting $G = 1/R$. The compound device Nyquist used in [10] agrees with this feature of the AM for electrical noise we are going to show. This AM used to explain the $1/f$ excess noise of Solid-State devices [7] and the flicker noise of electron fluxes in vacuum ones [5], never has been described before at this level of detail, especially in time domain.

The Susceptance or ability to store electrical energy our AM uses replacing the Transmission Line of [10], is the circuit element providing a Degree of Freedom to store electrical energy liable to fluctuate thermally in the device. These Fluctuations giving rise to the Johnson noise of resistors, don't take place in R, but in its Susceptance that must be capacitive because the flat $S_V(f) = 4kTR$ V^2/Hz found by Johnson at low f [9] is not possible for an inductive Susceptance with Fluctuations of energy of finite power. To make easier the passage from the PI to our AM let's consider the electrical noise of a two-terminal circuit that can be reduced to a capacitance C at high f. The equipartition value for one

Degree of Freedom applies to C in this case [14] and this gives the mean square voltage noise of C in TE from this equality:

$$\frac{1}{2}kT = \frac{1}{2}C\langle v^2(t)\rangle \Rightarrow \langle v^2(t)\rangle = \frac{kT}{C} \quad (1)$$

thus showing that the mean square voltage of noise has nothing to do with currents in R as we concluded previously from Circuit Theory and why this is so.

Because (1) gives the kT/C noise of capacitive devices that doesn't depend on the R that shunts C [13,14], let us consider the noise of the BAT85 Schottky diode of [6] whose PSPICE model appears in Appendix I. Due to its C_{J0} = 11.1 pF, the kT/C noise of this diode at room T is: $\langle v^2(t)\rangle$ = 3.7 × 10^{-10} V^2 or 19.3 μV$_{rms}$. From its saturation current I_{sat} = 211.7 nA and the ideality factor n = 1.016 of its i-v curve, C_{J0} is shunted in TE by a resistance $r_{d0}=(\partial i/\partial v)^{-1}\big|_{v=0} = nV_T/I_{sat}$ = 124.1 kΩ, where $V_T = kT/q$ is the thermal voltage. Following our AM, the room T noise density of this diode at low f must be: $S_{VAM}(0) = 4kTr_d$ V^2/Hz in TE because this is the value giving $\langle v^2(t)\rangle$ = kT/C_{J0} in C_{J0} to fulfil (1). Therefore, $S_{VAM}(f)$ is this low-pass, Lorentzian spectrum:

$$S_{VAM}(f) = \frac{4kTr_{d0}}{1+(2\pi f r_{d0}C_{J0})^2} = \frac{kT}{C_{J0}}\times\frac{2}{\pi}\times\frac{\frac{1}{f_c}}{1+\left(\frac{f}{f_c}\right)^2} \quad (2)$$

that integrated from $f \to 0$ to $f \to \infty$ gives $\langle v^2(t)\rangle$ = kT/C_{J0} as it must be by Equipartition.

Using PSPICE we have obtained the i-v curve of this diode shown in **Figure 4** with a logarithmic axis to show its exponential character. Besides the simulated i-v we also present (by dots) the i-v solely due to thermoionic current represented by this equation:

$$\begin{aligned} i &= I_{sat}\left(\exp\left(\frac{v}{nV_T}\right)-1\right) \\ &= 211.7\cdot 10^{-9}\left(\exp\left(\frac{v}{1.016\times 25.85\times 10^{-3}}\right)-1\right) \end{aligned} \quad (3)$$

The superposition of the two curves shows that currents through R_1 = 36 MΩ used by PSPICE to get a better fitting in reverse mode (see Appendix I), are negligible. The inset of **Figure 4** shows the i-v curve with linear axis in the region ($v \approx 0$) where a resistance $R^*(v=0)$ = 123.7 kΩ can be found. This R^* is: $R^* = (r_{d0}\times R_1)/(r_{d0}+R_1) \approx r_{d0}$. Curve **a)** of **Figure 5** is the $S_V(f)$ PSPICE gives for this diode in TE (i = 0 in the inset of **Figure 5**), whose flat $S_{VPI}(0)$ = −171.5 dB at low f means 1.13 μV$_{rms}$ noise in this diode whereas our AM states that it will be 19.3 μV$_{rms}$. This $S_{VPI}(0)$ being 24.6 dB *below* $S_{VAM}(0) = 4kTR^*$ = −146.9 dB, is a 292 times lower noise that PSPICE gives because it considers (as the aforesaid PI) that the only source of noise in the diode at v = 0 *is* R_1 = 36 MΩ, whose Nyquist noise $S_I(f) = 4kT/R_1$ drives the parallel circuit of r_{d0}, R_1 and C_{J0}. This gives a low-pass spectrum of amplitude S_{VPI} (0) = $4kT(R^*)^2/R_1$ V^2/Hz at low f that is R_1/R^* times lower than the $S_{VAM}(0) = 4kTR^*$ that our AM states to keep the kT/C_{J0} noise of C_{J0} shunted by R^*. Since $10\log(R_1/R^*) = 24.6$ dB, this explains why today's *PI* of Nyquist result fails to give a well known kT/C noise. Concerning circuit elements, PSPICE consider them perfectly as it is shown by the cut-off frequency f_c = $1/(2\pi R^* C_{J0})$ = 115.6 kHz of curve **a** in **Figure 5**.

Taking advantage of the correctness of the f_c PSPICE gives, we have simulated this diode *out of* TE, under a *forward* current $i = I_{sat}$. The noise spectrum thus obtained is curve **b** of **Figure 5**, whose f_c = 222.4 kHz comes from the low dynamical resistance of the diode under this forward bias: $r_d(i = I_{sat}) = r_{dfw}$ = 62 kΩ, and its similar junction capacitance (slightly higher with the voltage v = 18.2 mV set by this $i = I_{sat}$ biasing the diode). Note that while the diode capacitance varies slightly for such a small voltage, the diode resistance varies as: $\exp(-v/nV_T)$

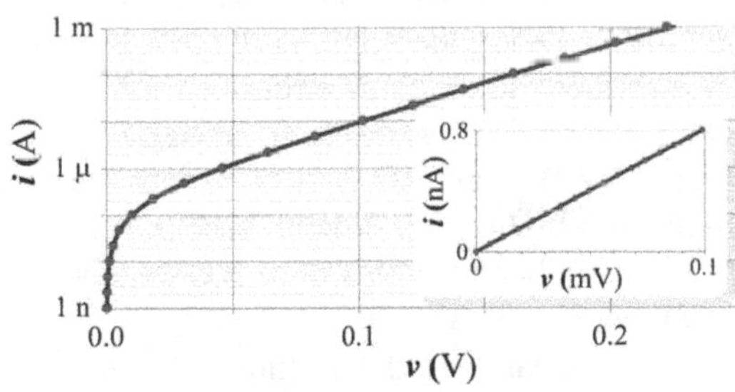

Figure 4. Current-voltage (i-v) characteristics of the BAT85 Schottky diode obtained by PSPICE (line) and its thermoionic values (dots) given by (3) (see text).

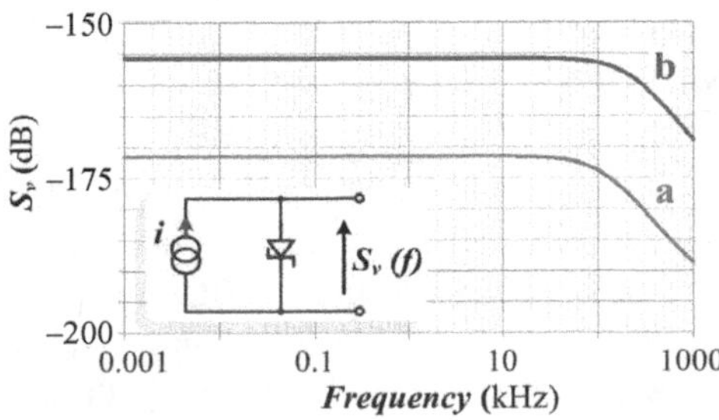

Figure 5. Noise densities $S_V(f)$ obtained by PSPICE for the BAT85 Schottky diode at room T: a) without bias (Thermal Equilibrium, i = 0) and b) under forward bias ($i = I_{sat}$). Curve a) does not give the kT/C noise of its junction capacitance (see text).

[7]. The $S_{VSim}(0) = -155.8$ dB that PSPICE gives at low f for $i = I_{sat}$ is the shot noise of the net current i converted to voltage noise on $r_{dfw} = 62$ kΩ: $10\log(2qI_{sat} \times r_{dfw}^2) = -155.8$ dB. This noise is 7.7 dB below $S_{VAM}(0) = (3/2)4kTr_{dfw} = -148.1$ dB that our AM will give for this case *out of TE* in the next Section. Considering that to deal with shot noise one has to take *all* the independent currents, not its net value [6], and that a net $i = I_{sat}$ is: $i = (+2I_{sat}) + (-I_{sat})$, see (3), we have: $S_I(f) = 2q(I_{sat} + 2I_{sat})$ A^2/Hz that converted to S_V on r_{dfw} gives: $10\log(6qI_{sat} \times r_{dfw}^2) = -151$ dB. This improvement of the PSPICE's prediction appears "converting" shot noise accordingly to a procedure that works fine in TE, where a net $i = 0 = (+I_{sat}) + (-I_{sat})$ leads to: $S_I(f) = 2q(I_{sat} + I_{sat})$ that converted to S_V on R^* gives: $S_V(0) = 10\log[4qI_{sat} \times (R^*)^2]$ (e.g. $S_V(0) = -146.8$ dB) which is similar to $S_{VAM}(0) = 4kTR^* = -146.9$ dB predicted by our AM.

As it is shown in [5,7], this "conversion" by the square of a resistance fails out of TE [5,7] as we will see in the next Section linked with the meaning of Resistance in time domain. A proof favouring our AM that doesn't need this advanced knowledge can be given from a paradox we had in previous Section where a negative feedback seemed to improve the S/N of the pixel of **Figure 3** accordingly to the PI in use today. Following our AM, however, the kT/C noise of C must be kept by taking the low f noise density on R^* as: $S_{VAM}(0) = 4kTR^*$, where R^* is the resistance shunting C no matter its origin. If $R^* = R$ in the pixel without feedback we have: $S_{VAM}(0) = 4kTR$ V^2/Hz and when feedback makes $R^* = R/2$, the noise is: $S_{VAM}(0) = 4kTR/2$ V^2/Hz, always keeping the kT/C noise of C. This keeps the noise power on R: $N_{FB} = kT/(RC)$ W and therefore, this negative feedback doesn't improve the S/N as it is "well known".

When v is negative and few times V_T, an interesting situation appears because the diode current becomes $i \approx -I_{sat}$ that, accordingly to the PI today in use, is a source of "shot" noise $S_I(f) \approx 2q(I_{sat})$ A^2/Hz that converted to voltage noise (V^2/Hz) by $r_d^2(v)$ will track the $\exp(-v/nV_T)$ variation of $r_d(v)$ for $C_{J0}(v) \approx$ constant. This is shown in **Figure 6(a)** by the noise spectra PSPICE gives for the diode biased by three reverse currents i_a, i_b and i_c that set $v_a = -3nV_T$, $v_b = -4nV_T$ and $v_c = -5nV_T$ in the diode respectively. To study the noise of the diode alone, R_1 was removed from the PSPICE model.

Due to the factor $e \approx 2.718\ldots$ dividing $r_d(v)$ as we go from curve a) to curve b) of **Figure 6(a)**, the bandwidth decreases by e whereas their low f value increases by e^2. This gives **Figure 6(a)** looking like the picture representing the Gain × Bandwidth conservation of Operational Amplifiers with resistive feedback. The results of our AM for these cases will be discussed in the next Section.

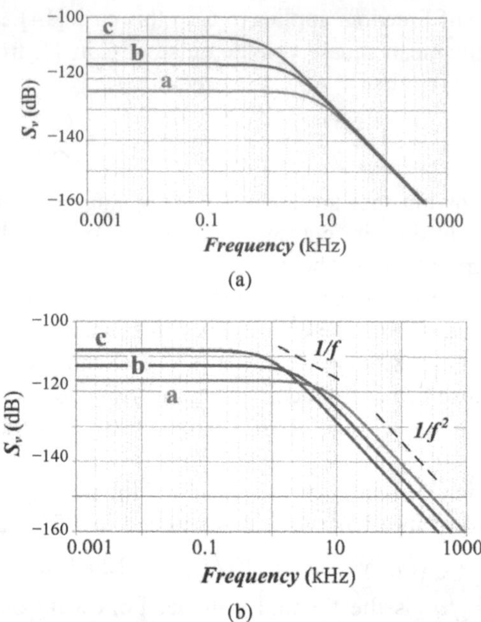

Figure 6. (a) Noise densities $S_V(f)$ obtained by PSPICE for the BAT85 Schottky diode at room T for three reverse currents (see text); (b) Noise densities $S_V(f)$ obtained by our Fluctuation-Dissipation model for electrical noise.

4. Electrical Noise as Fluctuations and Dissipations of Electrical Energy in Time

Because an arbitrary voltage noise $v(t)$ can be built from sinusoidal components (Fourier synthesis) we will use sinusoidal noise voltages $v_n(t)$ and currents $i_n(t)$ except otherwise stated. Being Conductance $G(f)$ the ratio between sinusoidal current and voltage mutually in-phase at frequency f, it doesn't distinguish "ohmic" resistances of resistors from "non-ohmic" ones due to feedback or to junctions for example, because all of them dissipate power by Conduction Currents (CC) in phase with their voltage. To work with a parallel circuit let's use the Admittance function $Y(j\omega) = G(\omega) + jB(\omega)$, whose Real part is Conductance $G(\omega)$ and whose Imaginary part is Susceptance $B(\omega)$, where ω is the angular frequency $\omega = 2\pi f$ and j is the imaginary unit indicating a 90° phase shift (orthogonality or null mean overlap in time for sinusoidal signals).

From the meaning of $Y(j\omega)$, a voltage noise $v_n(t)$ observed between terminals of a noisy device will come from a current in-phase with $v_n(t)$ through $G = 1/R^*$ and from a current in-quadrature through $B(\omega)$. $G = 1/R^*$ means that we will use a Conductance that is independent of f as it uses to happen in the device resistor at low f, because at high f it becomes a capacitor due to τ_d [7]. **Figure 7** shows the circuit our AM uses for the electrical noise of resistors and capacitors in TE. Although it reminds the parallel one of **Figure 2**, it has $C = C_d + C_{stray}$

shunting its R^* that includes ohmic and non-ohmic resistances defining the Conductance $G = 1/R^*$ of the Admittance we will use to handle noise voltage $v(t)$ as the signal linking noise current in its Conductance with noise current in its Susceptance at each f. Being $v_n(t)$ a sinusoidal component of $v(t)$, the noise current through $G = 1/R^*$ is the sinusoidal current in-phase with $v_n(t)$ given by: $i_P(t) = G \times v_n(t)$ (see **Figure 8**).

The noise current $i_Q(t)$ of **Figure 8** is a noise current in-quadrature with $v_n(t)$ given by: $i_Q(t) = jB \times v_n(t)$ that, for this positive B due to C, will be +90° phase-advanced respect to $v_n(t)$. Hence, the time integral of $i_Q(t)$ and $v_n(t)$ have the same Phase, thus suggesting what our AM considers: that the Displacement Current (DC) at each f $i_Q(t)$ is the Cause that, integrated in time by C, produces the Effect $v_n(t)$ that synthesizes Johnson noise in resistors and kT/C noise in capacitors. To study noise coming from Fluctuations in time of electrical energy, let's use the instantaneous power function: $p_i(t) = v_n(t) \times i_n(t)$ where $i_n(t) = i_P(t) + i_Q(t)$ is the whole current in the device. To work in time domain, the noise density $4kT/R^*$ A^2/Hz of **Figure 7** is replaced by the random current $i_{Ny}(t)$ with zero mean shown in **Figure 8**, whose equation on top (Kirchoff's law) we will write as:

$$C\frac{\partial v_n(t)}{\partial t} = -Gv_n(t) + i_{Ny}(t) \tag{4}$$

Equation (4) states that any real $i_{Ny}(t)$ will create both a DC in C and a CC in R^*. To create only a DC, a δ-like $i_{Ny}(t)$ of infinite bandwidth (BW$\rightarrow\infty$) or null duration ($\delta t_c \rightarrow 0$) is needed. For this δ-like $i_{Ny}(t)$ having a weight q in t (charge), the time integral of (4) during $\delta t_c \rightarrow 0$ gives a step $\Delta v_{built} = q/C$ V created instantaneously in C by the δ-like $i_{Ny}(t)$.

For an uncharged C ($v = 0$), a Fluctuation of $q^2/(2C)$ J appears in C, whence it may be seen the need of C to have fluctuations of electrical energy in a resistor. Although pure Fluctuations of energy won't exist in resistors because their $i_{Ny}(t)$ is band-limited [10], there can be fast DC with short δt_c looking like very pure Fluctuations of energy in this circuit. They will include, however, a small, non null Dissipation due to the CC existing during the non null δt_c elapsed, whence it may be seen that an electron leaving one plate with a kinetic energy of $q^2/(2C)$ J exactly is unable to create $\Delta v_{built} = q/C$ V in C because part of its $q^2/(2C)$ energy is dissipated during its transit time δt_c. For $\delta t_c \ll R^*C$ however, this passage of one electron between plates of C is a very energy-conserving event because the term $Gv_n(t)$ "has no time" to dissipate a noticeable energy during this fast DC or thermal jump of an electron of charge q between the ohmic contacts or plates of C. This fast DC would be a pure Fluctuation of energy (e.g. devoid of Dissipation) given the orthogonal character of these two phenomena (see Appendix II).

Let's call Thermal Action (TA) this fast transit of an electron between the ohmic contacts due to thermal activity. For a capacitor made from two metal plates in vacuum, thermoionic emission would produce directly these TA [5], whereas for resistors with conducting material between plates, TA would appear in the way proposed in Appendix III. Once a TA sets a voltage $\Delta v_{built}(t = 0) = q/C$ in C, the response of the circuit to this impulsive driving starts. This response or Reaction is a slower CC driven by $\Delta v_{built}(t)$ itself that decays exponentially with t as the Fluctuation of energy (Cause) is dissipated by the CC or Effect it produces. Thus, this Reaction includes a CC through G together with a simultaneous DC through C to rearrange the dipolar charge $\Delta Q(t) = C \times \Delta v_{built}(t)$ that sustains $\Delta v_{built}(t)$ at each instant of t. Making null $i_{Ny}(t)$ in (4) or in **Figure 8**, the continuity of electrical current states that this exponentially decaying CC in G requires a similar DC in C as C loses the energy fluctuation it received from the previous TA.

Calling this process Device Reaction (DR) electrical noise becomes a random series of Action-Reaction events taking place in an electrical Admittance. This explains and allows an easy simulation of Phase Noise in oscillators based on L-C resonators [16,17] for example. This description in time of the noise densities $S_I(f)$ and $S_V(f)$ considers TA appearing randomly, both in time and sign, at an average rate of λ TA per second to present Conductance G = $1/R$ as a rate of chances to dissipate energy accordingly to (9) in Appendix III, where we have considered these fast DC are carried by electrons independently of one another as Johnson did in 1925 [2].

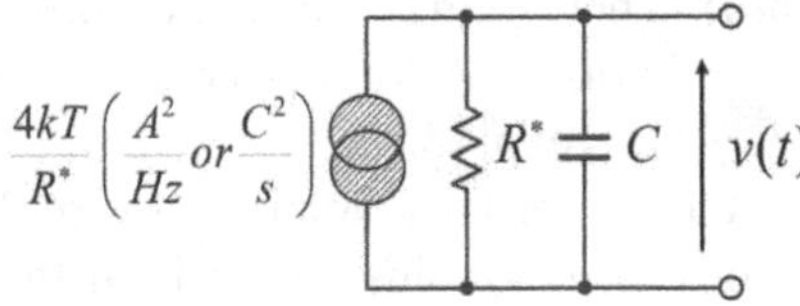

Figure 7. Electrical circuit that represents Johnson noise of resistors or *kT/C* noise of capacitors in Thermal Equilibrium accordingly to our Fluctuation-Dissipation Model for electrical noise.

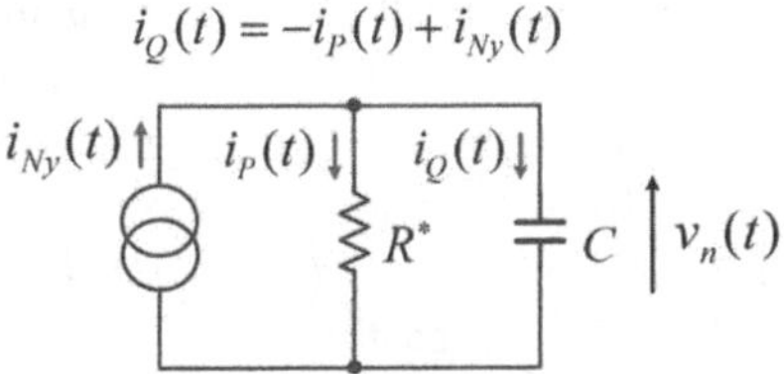

Figure 8. Time-domain counterpart of the Fluctuation-Dissipation Model of Figure 7 used to show the Cause-Effect connection of the Fluctuation-Dissipation pair of events.

This view of G as λ chances per second to dissipate energy suggests the reason why the conversion $A^2/Hz \rightarrow V^2/Hz$ by the square of a resistance fails for very high R^* values, as those found in [7] for the $r_d(v)$ of reverse-biased junctions with tens of V_T. The high noise voltages this conversion gives as $R^* \rightarrow \infty$ would require "packets of electrons" passing together between terminals [5] that, contrarily to [3], we consider unlikely to occur in common devices. This led us to abandon this conversion in [7] replacing it by the AM or Fluctuation-Dissipation Model (FDM) for electrical noise just described, which was used to explain two noises [5,7] that the PI of Nyquist result in use today is unable to explain.

To use this FDM out of TE let's consider the cases of the BAT85 diode whose PSPICE spectra appeared in **Figure 6(a)**. Recalling that for $v = 0$ the diode is in TE with λ TA/s due to its *two* opposed I_{sat}, the rate of *TA* for $i \approx -I_{sat}$, will drop to $\lambda/2$ [5,7]. Since C only has half the charge noise power it had in TE, we don't have to keep $\langle v^2(t) \rangle = kT/C$ in C, but half this value. Particularizing (2) for these cases, we have:

$$S_{VAMOUT}(f) = \frac{2kTr_d(v)}{1+\left(2\pi f r_d(v) C_{J0}(v)\right)^2} = \frac{kT}{C_{J0}(v)} \times \frac{1}{\pi} \times \frac{\frac{1}{f_c(v)}}{1+\left(\frac{f}{f_c(v)}\right)^2} \quad (5)$$

Integrating (5) from $f \rightarrow 0$ to $f \rightarrow \infty$ we obtain: $\langle v^2(t) \rangle = kT/\left[2C_{J0}(v)\right]$. **Figure 6(b)** shows the three noise spectra obtained using (5) with the f_c PSPICE gave in **Figure 6(a)**. They form a ladder of slope $1/f$ whose sum gives a $1/f$ noise spectrum over a band ($f_{LO} - f_{HI}$) such that: $f_{IO}/f_{HI} = \exp\left[(5nV_T - 3nV_T)/V_T\right]$. This means one decade of $1/f$ noise for a voltage span of $2.3V_T$ (e.g. 60 mV at room T), being this the basis of the $1/f$ noise synthesizer that appeared in [5,7] with this FDM for electrical noise based on Admittance.

To end, let's justify the $S_{VAM}(0) = (3/2)\ 4kTr_{dfw} = -148.1$ dB value we proposed in previous Section as the noise for the diode with $i = I_{sat}$, recall curve b) of **Figure 5**. Due to the $-I_{sat}$ and $+2I_{sat}$ existing in this case, we have: $3(\lambda/2)$ TA/s in C or a charge noise power that is 3/2 times higher than the one required to keep the kT/C noise of C by λ TA/s in TE. This means that for $i = I_{sat}$ we don't have to keep $\langle v^2(t) \rangle = kT/C\ V^2$ in C by using $4kTr_{dfw}\ V^2/Hz$ as the low f value of (2). Instead, we have to keep 3/2 times this value, whence it can be seen the reason to write $S_{VAM}(0) = (3/2)\ 4kTr_{dfw} = 6kTr_{dfw}$.

5. Conclusions

The partial interpretation of Nyquist result today in use leads to a 1-Dimensional (1-D) noise model based on Dissipation that is incomplete. A 2-D noise model using a Complex Admittance to handle Fluctuation and Dissipation of electrical energy, not only excels the aforesaid 1-D model, but also studies electrical noise accordingly to its first Quantum Mechanical treatment due to Callen and Welton. In this Complex model, Fluctuations and Dissipations of electrical energy creating electrical noise form a random series of Cause/Effect pairs in time, each linked with an elemental charge noise of one electron.

For this Complex model of electrical noise, $1/f$ "excess noise" in Solid State devices and flicker noise in thermoionic emitters simply are consequences of thermal noise that the 1-D noise model based on Dissipation is unable to explain. This Complex model also shows that the Johnson noise of resistors and the kT/C noise of capacitors, both reflect the same power $4kT/R$ of charge noise in C^2/s or A^2/Hz, appearing thermally between two conductors separated by some finite distance in our physical world. The quantization of electrical noise that results leads to an easy explanation of Phase noise in resonant circuits of electronic oscillators.

6. References

[1] L. Callegaro, "Unified Derivation of Johnson and Shot Noise Expressions," *American Journal of Physics*, Vol. 74, No. 5, 2006, pp. 438-440.

[2] J. B. Johnson, "The Schottky Effect in Low Frequency Circuits," *Physical Review*, Vol. 26, No. 1, 1925, pp. 71-85.

[3] G. Gomila, C. Pennetta, L. Reggiani, M. Sampietro, G. Ferrari and G. Bertuccio, "Shot Noise in Linear Macroscopic Resistors," *Physical Review Letters*, Vol. 92, 2004, Article ID: 226601.

[4] H. B. Callen and T. A. Welton, "Irreversibility and Generalized Noise," *Physical Review*, Vol. 83, No. 1, 1951, pp. 34-40.

[5] J. I. Izpura, "On the Electrical Origin of Flicker Noise in Vacuum Devices," *IEEE Transactions on Instrumentation and Measurement*, Vol. 58, No. 10, 2009, pp. 3592-3601.

[6] J. I. Izpura and J. Malo, "Noise Tunability in Planar Junction Diodes: Theory, Experiment and Additional Support by SPICE," *TAEE*'2006 *Conference*, Madrid, July 2006. http://taee.euitt.upm.es/Congresosv2/2006/papers/2006S1F02.pdf

[7] J. I. Izpura, "1/f Electrical Noise in Planar Resistors: The Joint Effect of a Backgating Noise and an Instrumental Disturbance," *IEEE Transactions on Instrumentation and Measurement*, Vol. 57, No. 3, 2008, pp. 509-517.

[8] M. Sampietro, L. Fasoli and G. Ferrari, "Spectrum Analyzer with Noise Reduction by Cross-Correlation Technique on Two Channels," *Review of Scientific Instrumentation*, Vol. 70, No. 5, 1999, pp. 2520-2525.

[9] J. B. Johnson, "Thermal Agitation of Electricity in Conductors," *Physical Review*, Vol. 32, No. 1, 1928, pp. 97-109.

[10] H. Nyquist, "Thermal Agitation of Electric Charge in Conductor," *Physical Review*, Vol. 32, No. 1, 1928, pp. 110-113.

[11] D. A. Johns and K. Martin, "Analog Integrated Cicuit Design," John Wiley & Sons, New York, 1997.

[12] "Dual Low Noise, Picoampere Bias Current, JFET Input Op Amp," http://www.datasheetcatalog.org/datasheet/lineartechnology/1169fa.pdf

[13] C. D. Motchenbacher and F. C. Fitchen, "Low Noise Electronic Design," John Wiley & Sons, New York, 1973.

[14] D. A. Bell, "Noise and the Solid State," Pentech Press, London, 1985.

[15] J. Malo and J. I. Izpura, "Feedback-Induced Phase Noise in Microcantilever-Based Oscillators," *Sensors and Actuators A: Physical*, Vol. 155, No. 1, 2009, pp. 188-194.

[16] J. Malo and J. I. Izpura, "Feedback-Induced Phase Noise in Resonator-Based Oscillators," *Proceedings of DCIS'09 Conference*, Zaragoza, November 2009, pp. 231-236. http://www.linkpdf.com/ebook-viewer.php?url=http://dcis2009.unizar.es/FILES/CR2/p5.pdf

[17] J. Malo, PhD Thesis, Chapter III (in Spanish). Universidad Politecnica de Madrid, Madrid, pp. 70-145.

Appendix I

SUBCKT BAT85 1 2

* The Resistor R1 does not reflect a physical device. Instead it improves modelling in the reverse mode of operation.

*

R1 1 2 3.6E+07

D1 1 2 BAT85-1

.ENDS

*

.MODEL BAT85-1 D(IS = 2.117E-07, N = 1.016, BV = 36, IBV = 1.196E-06, RS = 2.637, CJO = 1.114E-11, VJ = 0.2013, M = 0.3868, FC = 0, TT = 0, EG = 0.69, XTI = 2)

A similar model can be found in: http://www.nxp.com/models/spicespar/BAT85.html

Appendix II

For a sinusoidal $v_n(t)$ in the circuit of **Figure 8** the current $i_P(t)$ also is sinusoidal whereas $i_Q(t)$ is advanced +90° respect to $v_n(t)$. Thus, the instantaneous power contains Active power $p_{iP}(t) = v_n(t) \times i_P(t)$ always entering R^* and Reactive power $p_{iQ}(t) = v_n(t) \times i_Q(t)$ entering and leaving the Susceptance (e.g. oscillating) at $2f$. Taking $v_n(t) = A \times \sin(\omega t)$ ($\omega = 2\pi f$) as a voltage existing on C and from its related current in C: $i_Q(t) = C \times (\partial v_n(t)/\partial t)$, the instantaneous power $p_{iQ}(t)$ entering C is:

$$\begin{aligned} p_{iQ}(t) &= A\sin(\omega t)\times(A\omega C)\cos(\omega t) \\ &= (A^2\omega C)\times\sin(\omega t)\times\cos(\omega t) \end{aligned} \tag{6}$$

On the other hand, the fluctuating electrical energy stored in C by $v_n(t)$ will be:

$$\begin{aligned} &U_E(t) = \frac{C}{2}\times(A\sin(\omega t))^2 \Rightarrow \\ &\frac{\partial U_E}{\partial t} = (A^2\omega C)\times\sin(\omega t)\times\cos(\omega t) \end{aligned} \tag{7}$$

From (6) and (7) all the power entering C leads to fluctuations of its energy, thus linking Fluctuations of electrical energy with currents in quadrature with $v_n(t)$. Concerning Dissipations of electrical energy, they come from currents in-phase with $v_n(t)$. From the $i_P(t) = v_n(t)/R^*$ that $v_n(t)$ produces in the resistance R^*, the instantaneous power $p_{iP}(t)$ entering R^* is:

$$\begin{aligned} p_{iP}(t) &= A\sin(\omega t)\times\frac{A}{R^*}\sin(\omega t) \\ &= \frac{A^2}{2R^*}(1-\cos(2\omega t)) \end{aligned} \tag{8}$$

Contrarily to (6) whose mean value is null because energy enters and exits C, energy always enters R^* and (8) is the power dissipated in a resistance R^* driven by sinusoidal voltage of amplitude A V: a positive power of mean value $P_{avg} = A^2/(2R^*)$ W. Thus all the instantaneous power entering R^* is dissipated. Hence, Fluctuation of electrical energy in C and Dissipation of electrical energy in R^* are orthogonal processes linked with the Active and Reactive power in the circuit of **Figure 8**.

Appendix III

The idea of electrical noise as due to a random series of Fluctuation-Dissipation events or TA-DR pairs taking place in the Admittance of **Figure 8** leads to consider the evolution of $\Delta v_{built} = q/C$ V created by each TA in C. Being the sign of Δv_{built} positive or negative with equal probability on average, the mean voltage in C will be null ($v = 0$). Taking $\lambda/2$ as the average rate of positive TA, the average rate of TA is λ. For $v = 0$, each TA or Charge fluctuation of one electron in C will set a Fluctuation $\Delta U_{TA} = q^2/(2C)$ J in C. Once this Fluctuation is completed in a short transit time τ_{TA}, its associated voltage $\Delta v_{built} = q/C$ starts to drive a slower DR or the Dissipation by R^* of the ΔU_{TA} stored by the TA. Due to this, the initial Δv_{built} decays with a time constant $\tau = R^*C$ as shown in **Figure 9(a)**. The spectrum of this decay will look like the Lorentzian one of **Figure 9(b)**, which is the Johnson noise $v(t)$ of the circuit of **Figure 7** coming from a random series of pulses like that of **Figure 9(a)**, each following its own TA (Carson's Theorem).

Since the noise power N dissipated in R^* (the kT/C noise of C divided by R^*) has to dissipate the energy fluctuations of λ TAs per second on average, we have:

$$N = \frac{kT}{R^*C} = \lambda \times \frac{q^2}{2C} \Rightarrow R^* = \frac{2kT}{q^2\lambda} \Rightarrow \frac{4kT}{R^*} = 2q(\lambda q) \quad (9)$$

Equation (9) shows that the Resistance R^* of a resistor or capacitor in TE is inversely proportional to the λ opportunities per unit time it has to dissipate energy. It also shows that the noise density $4kT/R^*$ A^2/Hz preserving the kT/C noise of C is the density of shot noise due to the λ TA's per unit time taking place in this device.

Thus, the shot noise $2qI_{TA}$ A^2/Hz of the current $I_{TA} = \lambda q$ associated to the λ TAs per unit time of this device is the source of its electrical noise, no matter if we call it Johnson noise of its resistance R^* or kT/C noise of its capacitance C. This deep connection between "shot" and Johnson noises (also found by other scientists [1]) is the charge noise existing in the capacitance C of a resistor or capacitor in TE due to its λ TA-DR pairs per unit time that are shown in **Figure 10**.

Since each DR has a CC and a DC giving a charge fluctuation of q C each in C and they are uncorrelated in time due to their orthogonal character in f-domain, the mean square charge noise per second (charge noise power) existing in C due to DR is: $2(\lambda q^2) = 4kT/R^*$ C^2/s. This explains the alternative units used in **Figure 7** to reveal neatly the same charge noise underlying Johnson and shot "noises".

It is worth studying what happens if we change the conducting material between plates in **Figure 1** to reduce its R^* to $R^*/10$ while keeping the same ε. Since C does not vary its kT/C noise will remain, but the voltage decays of **Figure 9(a)** will be ten times faster, thus having a ten times broader spectrum (**Figure 9(b)**). Since the voltage $\Delta v_{built} = q/C$ decays ten times faster with t, there must be ten times more TA (10λ) to sustain the same kT/C V^2 in time. This agrees with (9), where 10 times lower R^* at the same T requires a 10 times higher rate of TA or 10 times more charge noise due to TA. Since this happens no matter the material we use, the presence of solid matter between contacts doesn't change the nature of the TA in our FDM: a Charge Noise of one electron.

Although single electrons jumping between plates in vacuum is well know [2], this is not so for electrons doing it between contacts in Solid-State devices due to their possible blockage by the conducting material between them. This is solved, however, by considering that a free electron in a Quantum State (QS) of the Conduction Band (CB) has a wavefunction extending over the whole material between plates. This would allow an electron to jump from a contact to this QS as soon as it is left empty by the electron that, occupying it previously, has been captured by the far contact (Collector). Thus, a QS or energy level of the CB would be a sort of tunnel for the fast transit of each electron between ohmic contacts cladding n-type semiconductor material for example.

Used to electrons transiting between electrodes in vacuum devices that are collected a short transit time τ_T after their emission, the above process looks reversed: an electron of the CB is captured by the Collector a short time τ_T before another electron is emitted from the Emitter contact to the empty QS of the CB. Processes where electrons emitted from a contact to empty QS of the CB are subsequently captured by the other contact acting as a Collector of electrons are equally possible.

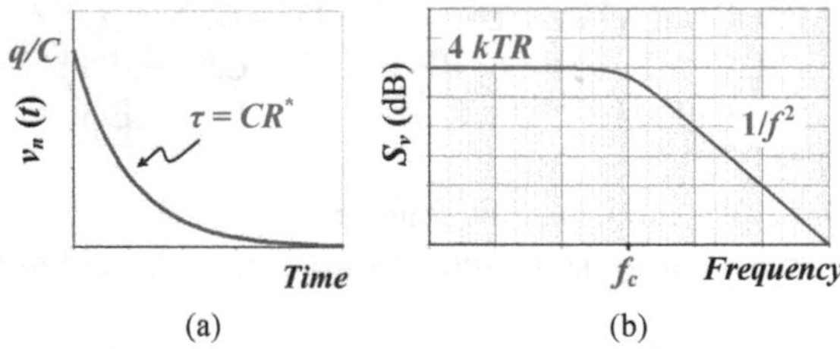

Figure 9. (a) Impulse response of the circuit of Figure 8 driven by current $i_{Ny}(t)$ and taking $v(t)$ as its output signal. (b) Bode plot (modulus) of the Lorentzian spectrum of $v(t)$ mirroring the spectral energy content of the impulse shown in Figure 4.

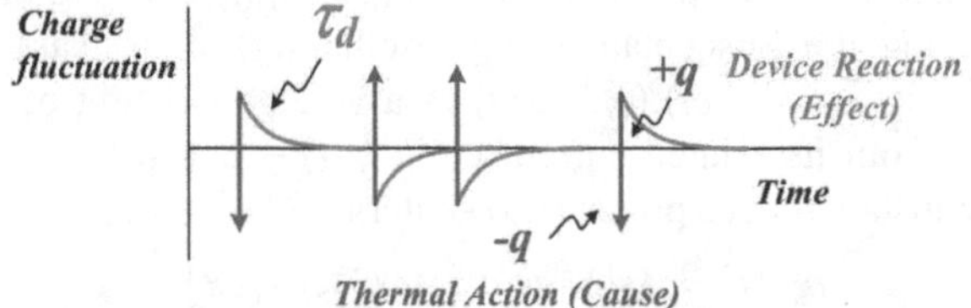

Figure 10. Charge noises in the contacts of a resistor or capacitor due to the (Thermal Action)/(Device Reaction) dynamics described in the text.

17

Analyzing an UWB Bandpass Filter for High Power Applications Using Rectangular Coaxial Cables with Square Inner Conductors

Nasreddine Benahmed[1], Nadia Benabdallah[2], Salima Seghier[3], Fethi Tarik Bendimerad[1], Boumedienne Benyoucef[1]

[1]*University Abou Bekr Belkaid-Tlemcen, Tlemcen, Algeria*

[2]*Preparatory School of Sciences and Technology (EPST-Tlemcen), Tlemcen, Algeria*

[3]*University of Saida, Saida, Algeria*

Abstract

Using the finite element method (FEM) in two dimensions and the CST MICROWAVE STUDIO® (CST MWS) Transient Solver, the electromagnetic (EM) analysis and the design of a novel compact ultra wide-band (UWB) bandpass filter using rectangular coaxial cables with square inner conductors, convenient for high power applications, are presented. The design of the UWB BP filter is based on the use of impedance steps and coupled-line sections. The center frequency around 6.85 GHz was selected, the bandwidth is between 3 - 10 GHz, the insertion-loss amounts to around 0.35 dB and the return loss is found higher than 10 dB in a large frequency range 4 - 9.5 GHz. The simulated results of stopband performances are better than 15 dB for a frequency range up to 11 GHz. For the selected center frequency and on a substrate with a dielectric constant of 2.03, the rectangular coaxial cables BPF with square inner conductors is only 6.7 × 8.9 × 33.4 mm in size.

Keywords: Rectangular Coaxial Cables, Square Inner Conductors, Ultra Wideband Bandpass Filter, Compact Filter, Electromagnetic Parameters, Analysis and Design, FEM Method, CST MWS Transient Solver

1. Introduction

Since the Federal Communications Commission (FCC) released the unlicensed use of ultra-wideband (UWB: 3.1 to 10.6 GHz) wireless systems in February 2002 [1], many researchers have started exploring various UWB components, devices, and systems [2,3]. As one of the key circuit blocks in the whole system, the UWB bandpass filter (BPF) has been studied through the use of the matured filter theory [4] and other techniques [5,6].

On the basis of impedance steps and coupled-line sections as inverter circuits, several works were interested in the design of planar broadband filters with low loss, compact size, high suppression of spurious responses, and improved stopband performances [7,8].

In this work, we propose a novel and a simple compact ultra wideband (UWB) bandpass filter using rectangular coaxial cables with square inner conductors, convenient for high power applications. The filter can be easily designed and fabricated using FeeFEM environment [9], CST MICROWAVE STUDIO® (CST MWS) Transient Solver [10] or other commercial EM software. The design of the UWB filter is based on the use of impedance steps and coupled-line sections. The center frequency around 6.85 GHz was selected, the bandwidth is between 3-10 GHz, the insertion-loss amounts to around 0.35 dB and the return loss is found higher than 10 dB in a large frequency range (4 - 9.5) GHz. The simulated results of stopband performances are better than 15 dB for a frequency range up to 11 GHz. For the selected center frequency and on a substrate with a dielectric constant of 2.03, the rectangular coaxial cable BPF with square inner conductors is only 6.7 × 8.9 × 33.4 mm in size. What follows are the analysis and the design of this compact UWB filter using both FEM method under FeeFEM environment and CST MWS Transient Solver.

2. Rectangular Coaxial Cables

Coupled rectangular coaxial cables can provide signal coupling in a compact form for any characteristic impedance systems. They were used previously in [11] to build a directional coupler. This kind of coupler has excellent performance in terms of high directivity, low VSWR, good isolation, excellent electromagnetic interference (EMI) shielding, high power handling capability, and low cost due to the use of commercial semirigid rectangular coaxial cables and elimination of a mechanical housing.

Figure 1 shows the cross-section of a rectangular coaxial coupled line with square inner conductors. The cable is assumed to be lossless with an inner squared conductor of side ($2a_1$) and an outer rectangular conductor of height ($2a_2$) and width ($2(a_2 + h)$). Dielectric material with dielectric constant (ε_r) fills the inside of the cable. A portion of each cable is cut out and two of these cut cables are joined to form the coupled line. The cut depth is represented by (h) on the cross section as shown in **Figure 1**.

3. Numerical Resolution

The electrical properties of the lossless and homogeneous symmetrical coupler presented in **Figure 1** can be described in terms of its primary parameters [L] and [C], and its secondary parameters k, Z_{0e} and Z_{0o} [12,13].

where: $$[L]=\begin{bmatrix} L_{11} & L_{12} \\ L_{21} & L_{22} \end{bmatrix};\ [C]=\begin{bmatrix} C_{11} & C_{12} \\ C_{21} & C_{22} \end{bmatrix}$$

The inductance matrix [L] contains the self-inductances on the diagonal ($L_{11} = L_{22}$ are the proper inductances) and the mutual inductances ($L_{12} = L_{21}$) between the two coupled lines.

Matrix [C] accounts for the capacitative effects between the two coupled lines, characterizing the electric field energy storage in the coupler. ($C_{11} = C_{22}$) are the proper capacitances and ($C_{12} = C_{21}$) is the coupling capacitance.

$$k=\frac{L_{12}}{L_{11}}=\frac{C_{12}}{C_{11}};$$

is the coupling coefficient and (Z_{0e}, Z_{0o}) are respectively the even- and the odd-modes characteristic impedances of the coupler.

On the other hand, the isolated line of **Figure 2** is described in terms of its inductance and capacitance per unit length (L and C) and in term of its characteristic impedance Z_0.

In reference 14, we successfully realized a numerical tool under FreeFEM environment, used to analyze electromagnetic (EM) parameters for rectangular coaxial couplers with square inner conductors. This numerical tool can be easily adapted to study any other TEM or quasi-TEM structure [15]. Also, we proposed rigorous analytical expressions for the primary parameters (inductance [L] and capacitance [C] matrices) and the impedances (Z_{0e}, Z_{0o}) of the even- and odd-modes for rectangular coaxial couplers with square inner conductors [14]. The analytical expressions are convenient for all coupled rectangular coaxial couplers having square inner conductors with a wide range of cut depths and an outer to inner conductor ratio between 1.4 and 10. We proposed others analytical expressions in order to calculate the EM parameters of squared coaxial lines [16]. All our analytical expressions were deduced from rigorous analyses by the FEM and MoM methods under respectively FreeFEM and LINPAR [17] environments. Using these analytical expressions, an analysis can be readily implemented in modern CAE software tools for the design of microwave and wireless components.

4. UWB Filter Using Rectangular Coaxial Cables

Assuming 50-Ω external feeding lines, **Figures 3(a)** and **3(b)** show respectively the 3D schematic representation and the longitudinal section of the proposed UWB BPF. An isolated rectangular coaxial line with one square inner conductor in the middle and a rectangular coaxial coupled line with square inner conductors at the two ends [18].

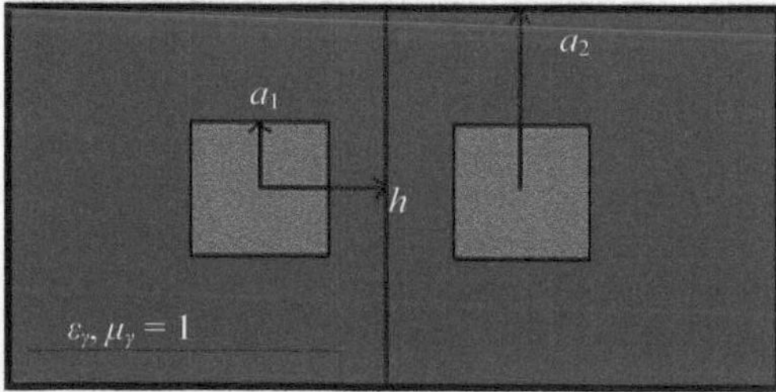

Figure 1. Cross section of the rectangular coaxial coupled line with square inner conductors.

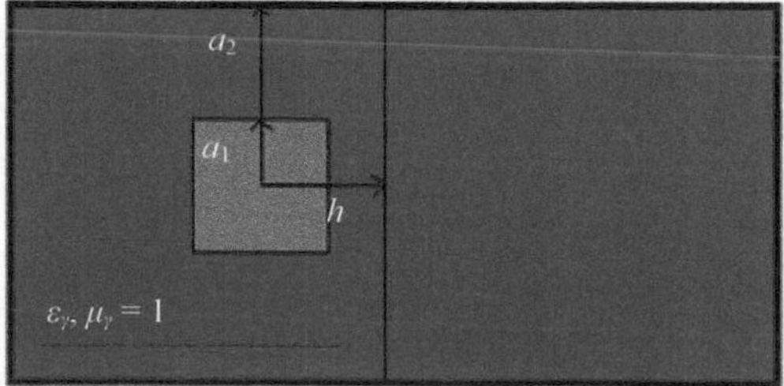

Figure 2. Cross section of the rectangular coaxial line with one square inner conductor.

To achieve the specified UWB bandpass, the three sections of this filter are arranged with the lengths of about one quarter-, one half-, and one quarter-wavelength, *i.e.*, $\lambda/4$, $\lambda/2$ and $\lambda/4$ [18], as marked in **Figure 3(b)**.

5. EM Analyses and Design

As part of the study, we were interested in the design of the 50 Ω-UWB bandpass filter having an inner conductor of side ($2a_1 = 2$ mm), an outer conductor of side ($2a_2 = 6.7$ mm) and a dielectric constant of 2.03, we have varied the cut depth (h) from (a_1) to (a_2) in order to assure for the rectangular coaxial coupler a coupling coefficient less than 5 dB (**Figure 4**).

A coupling coefficient of 2.4 dB was obtained using our previous works based on FEM for a cut depth (h) of 1.1 mm, yielding a characteristic impedance of approximately $\sqrt{Z_{0e} \times Z_{0o}} = 26.24\ \Omega$ and the following primary EM parameters:

$$[L] = \begin{bmatrix} 190.9 & 144.6 \\ 144.6 & 190.9 \end{bmatrix} \left(\frac{nH}{m}\right)$$

$$[C] = \begin{bmatrix} 278.7 & -211.4 \\ -211.4 & 278.7 \end{bmatrix} \left(\frac{pF}{m}\right)$$

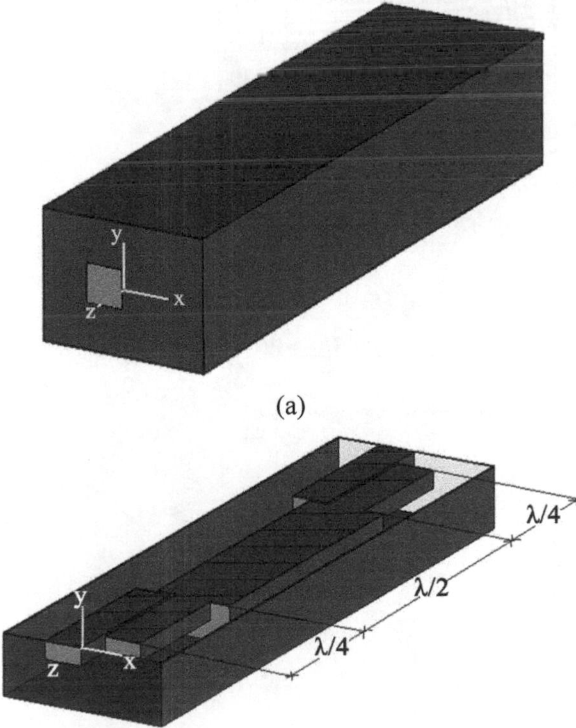

Figure 3. Longitudinal section of the proposed UWB BPF using rectangular coaxial cables with square inner conductors.

For a length of one quarter-wavelength, *i.e.*, $l = \lambda/4$ and in order to verify if the designed coupler has a coupling coefficient less than 5 dB in the frequency range [3.1 - 10.6] GHz, we plotted the resulting coupling coefficient of the rectangular coaxial coupler of **Figure 4** versus frequency as shown in **Figure 5**, using MATPAR software [19]. From this figure, it appears clearly that the coupling coefficient (S_{12}) and the isolation (S_{14}) vary respectively between 4 - 5.5 dB and 11.4 - 11.5 dB in the frequency band [3.1 - 10.6] GHz. In the same frequency band the minimum directivity of the coupler $(|S_{14}| - |S_{12}|)$ is approximately 6 dB.

For the middle line of the UWB BPF represented in **Figure 6**, the outer conductor parameters, the cut depth (h) and the dielectric constant were kept constants (*i.e.* $a_2 = 3.35$ mm, $h = 1.1$ mm and $\varepsilon_r = 2.03$) and the inner conductor side ($2a_1$) was varied as needed in order to get a characteristic impedance (Z_0) of 19 Ω for the middle line. This value of (Z_0) was obtained for ($a_1 = 2.1$ mm), yielding an inductance and a capacitance per unit length respectively of 90.75 nH/m and 248.55 pF/m [14].

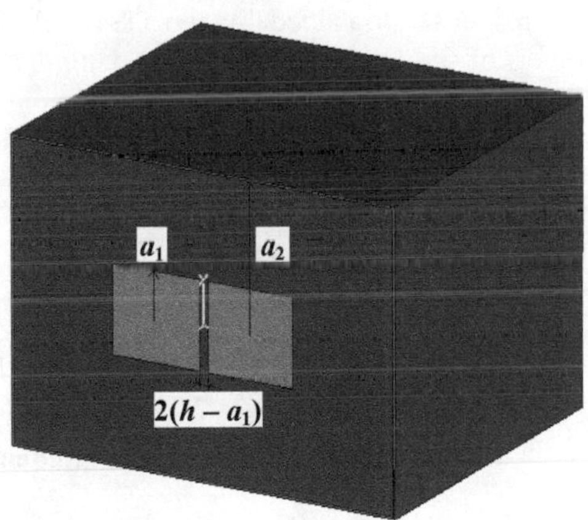

Figure 4. Rectangular coaxial coupler with square inner conductors.

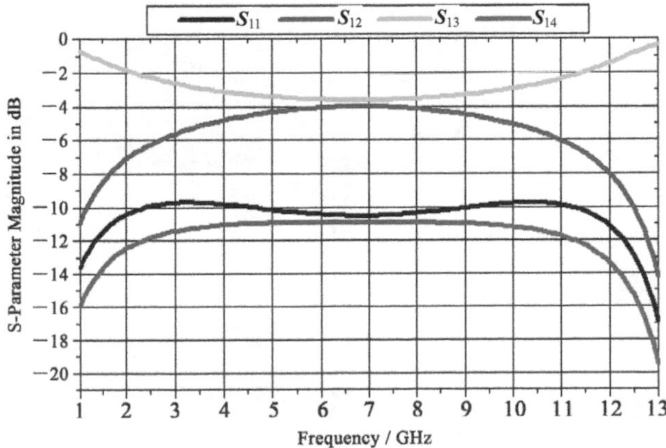

Figure 5. Scattering parameters of the rectangular coaxial coupler presented in Figure 4.

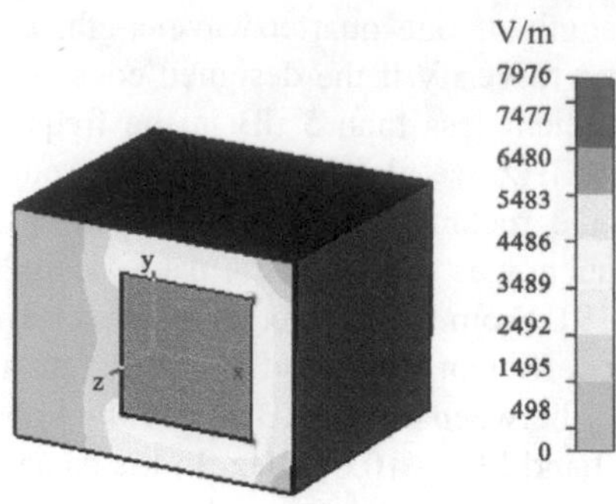

Figure 6. CST simulation of the middle line of the proposed UWB BPF.

We applied the CST MWS Transient Solver in the aim of checking the predicted electrical performance of our proposed and designed UWB BPF using rectangular coaxial cables of **Figure 3**. The designed filter is characterized by the features marked in **Figure 7**.

In the frequency range [1 - 11] GHz, **Figure 8** provides plots of the resulting scattering parameters obtained of the proposed and designed UWB BPF. It can be seen that the simulated responses, obtained by the CST MWS Transient Solver, of the UWB filter using rectangular coaxial cables with square inner conductors, are in very reasonable agreement with those using planar structures. The plotted wideband also accorded the FCC-defined UWB for high power applications.

For the simulated UWB filter using CST, the insertion-loss amounts to around 0.35 dB and the return loss is found higher than 10 dB in a large frequency band (4 - 9.5) GHz. The simulated results of stopband performances are better than 15 dB for a frequency range up to 11 GHz.

For this type of UWB bandpass filter using rectangular coaxial cables with square inner conductors, there are no numerical or experimental results in the scientific literature. In order to check our results obtained by the CST MWS Transient Solver we were obliged, for the same geometrical and physical parameters of our filter, to make simulations using our previous works and estimate the resulting scattering parameters of the designed UWB filter using MATPAR software. The results coefficients (S_{11}) and (S_{12}) as functions of frequency for the proposed UWB BP filter structure are provided in **Figure 9**. The **Figures 8** and **9** show that the responses obtained by the two numerical models (CST and MATPAR) are in a good agreement.

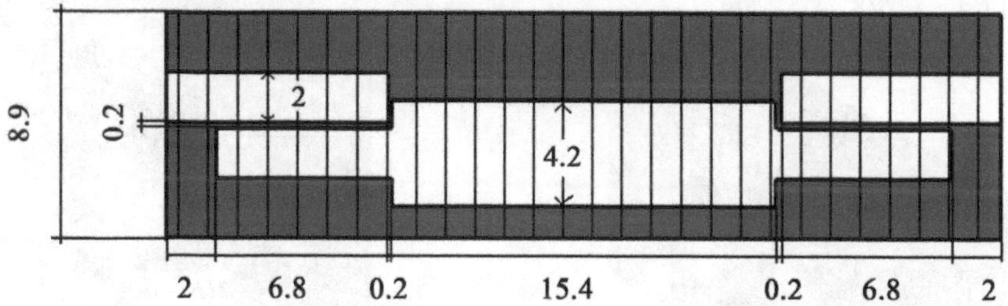

Figure 7. Longitudinal section view of the designed UWB BPF.

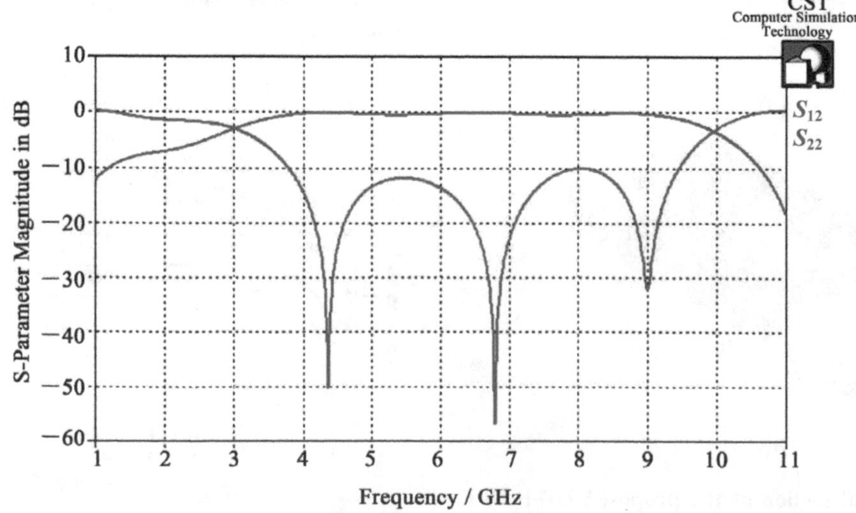

Figure 8. Scattering parameters of the designed 50 Ω-UWB BPF obtained by the CST MWS Transient Solver.

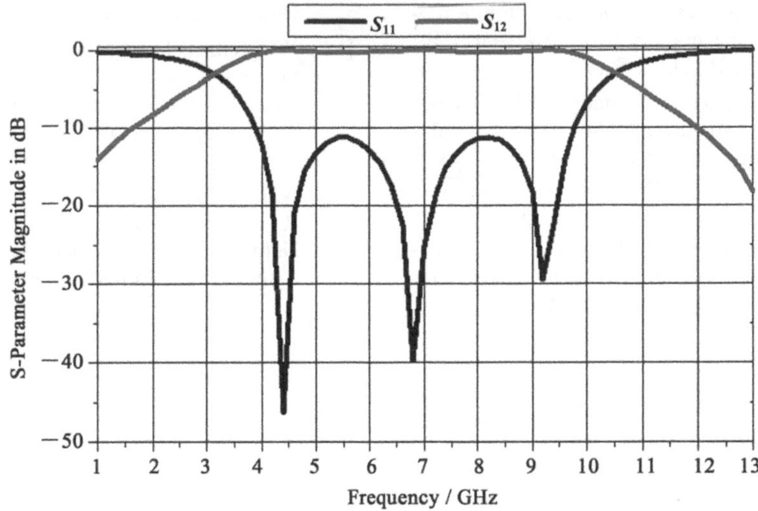

Figure 9. Scattering parameters of the designed 50 Ω UWB BPF obtained by MATPAR software.

6. Conclusions

A novel and a simple compact ultra wideband bandpass filter using rectangular coaxial cables with square inner conductors, convenient for high power applications, is presented, analyzed and designed. The design of the UWB filter is based on the use of impedance steps and coupled-line sections.

The designed rectangular coaxial cable bandpass filter is only 6.7 × 8.9 × 33.4 mm in size and can be easily designed and fabricated using CST MICROWAVE STUDIO® Transient Solver or other commercial EM software. The bandwidth of the designed filter is between 3 - 10 GHz, the insertion-loss amounts to around 0.35 dB and the return loss is higher than 10 dB in a large frequency range. The simulated results of stopband performances are better than 15 dB for a frequency range up to 11 GHz.

7. References

[1] FCC, "Revision of Part 15 of the Commission's Rules Regarding Ultra-Wideband Transmission System," Technical Report ET-Docket 98-153, 14 February 2002.

[2] G. R. Aiello and G. D. Rogerson, "Ultra-Wideband Wireless Systems," *IEEE Microwave Magazine*, Vol. 4, No. 2, 2003, pp. 36-47.

[3] Z. Irahhauten, H. Nikookar, and G. J. M. Janssen, "An Overview of Ultra Wide Band indoor Channel Measurements and Modeling," *IEEE Microwave and Wireless Components Letters*, Vol. 14, No. 8, 2004, pp. 386-388.

[4] G. Matthaei, L. Young and E. M. T. Jones, "Design of Microwave Filters, Impedance-Matching Networks, and Coupling Structures," Artech House, Norwood, 1980.

[5] A. Saito, H. Harada and A. Nishikata, "Development of Bandpass Filter for Ultra Wideband (UWB) Communication Systems," *Proceedings of IEEE Conference on Ultra Wideband Systems and Technologies*, Reston, 16-19 November 2003, pp. 76-80.

[6] L. Zhu, S. Sun and W. Menzel, "Ultra-Wideband (UWB) Bandpass Filters Using Multiple-Mode Resonator," *IEEE Microwave Wireless Components Letters*, Vol. 15, No. 11, 2005, pp. 796-798.

[7] J. Gao, L. Zhu, W. Menzel and F. Bögelsack, "Short- Circuited CPW Multiple-Mode Resonator for Ultra-Wideband (UWB) Bandpass Filter," *IEEE Microwave Wireless Components Letters*, Vol. 16, No. 3, 2006, pp. 104-106.

[8] M. Meeloon, S. Chaimool and P. Akkaraekthalin, "Broadband Bandpass Filters Using Slotted Resonators Fed by Interdigital Coupled Lines for Improved Upper Stopband Performances," *International Journal of Electronics and Communications*, Vol. 63, No. 6, 2009, pp. 454-463.

[9] www.Freefem.org.

[10] www.CST.com.

[11] S. Seghier and N. Benahmed, "Analyse et Conception d'un Coupleur Coaxial Rectangulaire à Conducteurs Internes Circulaires par la Méthode des Eléments Finis," *Afrique Science*, Vol. 2, No. 3, 2006, pp. 300-313.

[12] N. Benahmed and M. Feham, "Rigorous Analytical Expressions for Electromagnetic Parameters of Transmission Lines: Coupled Sliced Coaxial Cable," *Microwave Journal*, Vol. 44, No. 11, 2001, pp. 130-138.

[13] N. Benabdallah, N. Benahmed, S. Seghier and R. Bouhmidi, "Sliced Coaxial Cables form Compact Couplers," *Microwaves and RF*, Vol. 46, No. 7, 2007, pp. 90-94.

[14] N. Benahmed and S. Seghier, "Rigorous Analytical Expressions for the Electromagnetic Parameters of Rectangular Coaxial Couplers with Circular and Square Inner Conductors," *Microwave Journal*, Vol. 49, No. 8, 2006, pp. 164-174.

[15] N. Benahmed, M. Feham and M. Kameche, “Finite Element Analysis of Planar Couplers,” *Applied Microwave & Wireless*, Vol. 12, No. 10, 2000, pp. 28-38.

[16] S. Seghier, N. Benabdallah, N. Benahmed, N. Benmostefa and R. Bouhmidi, “Accurate Closed-Form Formulas for the Electromagnetic Parameters of Squared Coaxial Lines,” *International Journal of Electronics and Communications*, Vol. 62, No. 5, 2008, pp. 395-400.

[17] A. R. Djordjevic, M. B. Bazdar and T. K. Sarkan, “LINPAR for Windows: Matrix Parameters of Multiconductor Transmission Lines, Software and User'S Manual,” Artech House, London, 1999.

[18] W. Menzel, L. Zhu, K. Wu and F. Bogelsack, “On the Design of Novel Compact Broadband Planar Filters,” *IEEE Transactions on Microwave Theory and Techniques*, Vol. 51, No. 2, 2003, pp. 364-370.

[19] A. R. Djordjevic, M. Bazdar, G. Vitosevic, T. Sarkar and R. F. harrington, “Scattering Parameters of Microwave Networks with Multiconductor Transmission Lines,” Artech House, London, 1990.

18

ΔI_{DDQ} Testing of a CMOS Digital-to-Analog Converter Considering Process Variation Effects*

Rajiv Soundararajan[1], Ashok Srivastava[1], Siva Sankar Yellampalli[2]
[1]*Department of Electrical and Computer Engineering, Louisiana State University, Baton Rouge, USA*
[2]*Centre for Advanced Studies (VTU Extension Centre), UTL Technologies Ltd., Bangalore, India*

Abstract

In this paper, we present the implementation of a built-in current sensor (BICS) which takes into account the increased background current of defect-free circuits and the effects of process variation on ΔI_{DDQ} testing of CMOS data converters. A 12-bit digital-to-analog converter (DAC) is designed as the circuit under test (CUT). The BICS uses frequency as the output for fault detection in CUT. A fault is detected if it causes the output frequency to deviate more than ±10% from the reference frequency. The output frequencies of the BICS for various (MOSIS) model parameters are simulated to check for the effect of process variation on the frequency deviation. A set of eight faults simulating manufacturing defects in CMOS data converters are injected using fault-injection transistors and tested successfully.

Keywords: I_{DDQ} Testing, DAC, BICS, Sub-Micron CMOS IC, ΔI_{DDQ} Testing, Process Variation, Background Current

1. Introduction

Quiescent current (I_{DDQ}) testing has become an effective and efficient testing method for detecting physical defects such as gate-oxide shorts, floating gates (open) and bridging faults [1] in circuits. Conventional I_{DDQ} testing is based on the fact that quiescent current in a defect free circuit is less compared to the quiescent current of the circuit with defects. Several available I_{DDQ} test methodologies can be classified into two groups, external (off-chip) and internal (on-chip) I_{DDQ} testing. External I_{DDQ} testing monitors power supply current through the power pins of the integrated circuit package while internal I_{DDQ} testing monitors power supply current through the built-in current sensors (BICS) [2]. On-chip built-in current sensors are advantageous over off-chip current sensors for detecting the defective quiescent current due to better discrimination and higher testing speeds [3].

Currently, in VLSI circuits designed in sub-micron/deep sub-micron CMOS processes, the gap between the defective and defect-free quiescent current is narrowing due to increasing background current [4-6]. Process variation also impacts digital, analog/mixed-signal integrated circuits fabricated in sub-micron/deep sub-micron CMOS technology. Process variation affects the threshold voltage of the circuit and thus the effective leakage current in the circuit. Hence, designing BICS for submicron CMOS process is becoming difficult. However, problems related with I_{DDQ} testing in digital VLSI circuits designed in submicron CMOS processes are well known and have been researched extensively [7]. Many new testing techniques have been proposed and presented in literature to minimize the effect of increased background current and the impact of process variation on the I_{DDQ} measurements to improve defect detectability. Among those, delta I_{DDQ} (ΔI_{DDQ}) testing is particularly attractive because the differential measurement suppresses the impact of the background current. Vazquez and de Gyvez [8,9] have reported a ΔI_{DDQ} BICS which has both on-chip and off-chip components. Most of these new testing techniques to improve the effectiveness of I_{DDQ} testing have been successfully implemented for digital circuits. However testing of analog circuits using I_{DDQ} in submicron CMOS is still a problem due to variation in design parameters from one specific application to other. Hence, in testing of analog circuits the tolerance on the circuit parameters has to be taken into account because it can cause a significant difference between the quiescent

*Part of the work is reported in Proc. IEEE MWSCAS, pp. 284-287, Seattle, 2010.

current of a manufactured circuit and its nominal value. A simple pass/fail test is not a good measure for fault detection. Mixed-signal types of circuits such as data converters are even more difficult to test using I_{DDQ}. We have extensively researched and presented the ΔI_{DDQ} testing for sub-micron CMOS mixed-signal circuits in our previous work [10,11]. In this work, effects of process variation on ΔI_{DDQ} testing for CMOS data converters are studied and presented.

Here we present the design and implementation of a built-in-current sensor for delta I_{DDQ} testing in a 0.5 µm n-well CMOS process for a 12-bit digital-to-analog converter (DAC) to study the effects of process variation. The paper is organized as follows: Section 2 describes the proposed sensor and its circuit implementation, Section 3 describes 12-bit DAC which is being used as the circuit under test (CUT), Section 4 presents the results and discussion and Section 5 gives the conclusion.

2. Built-in Current Sensor for Delta I_{DDQ} Testing

2.1. Proposed Design

The proposed sensor combines the concepts of multi-parameter testing and delta I_{DDQ} testing to detect defective currents and is based on Keating-Meyer approach for I_{DDQ} testing [12] and is a modification of I_{DDQ} measurement (MEAS) block of delta I_{DDQ} BICS by Vazquez and de Gyvez [8,9]. Multi-parameter testing helps in suppressing the high background current while delta I_{DDQ} testing helps in decreasing I_{DDQ} variance. **Figure 1** [8,9] summarizes the sensor's operation; it has two curves corresponding to low and high leakage. After applying an input pattern to the CUT, the on-chip capacitor is allowed to charge and discharge until it reaches the reference voltage V_{REF}.

The expression associated with this discharge is given by [8-11]

$$I_{DDQ} = C\frac{\Delta V}{\Delta t} \quad (1)$$

where $\Delta V = V_{DD} - V_{REF}$ and C is the total circuit capacitance including the discharging capacitor. The time Δt taken by the decaying voltage of the capacitor to reach V_{REF} is measured as frequency by using a comparator and a voltage controlled oscillator (VCO) as shown in **Figure 2**. The comparator gives an output V_{CTRL}, which is used as an input by the VCO to give the output frequency.

In the design, the BICS is on-chip for better testability and higher testing speeds. The proposed sensor also takes into account the process variation after fabrication and self-adjusts for fault detection. This is done by calculating the output frequency of the VCO and subtracting it from the output frequency of the ring oscillator to obtain the final output frequency.

2.2. Circuit Implementation

Figure 2 shows the circuit diagram of the BICS where p-MOSFET in earlier MEAS block [8,9] has been replaced by two transmission gates TG_1 and TG_2 as switches. The two transmission gates are used to isolate CUT from the BICS depending on the mode of operation (normal mode or test mode). In the normal mode of operation, the supply voltage V_{DD1} is given to CUT and the BICS is isolated, so that there will be no performance degradation in the CUT.

In the test mode of operation, the supply voltage is given to V_{DD}. In this mode, initially transmission gate TG_1 between the supply voltage and the CUT is turned on charging the capacitor to V_{DD}, transmission gate TG_2 between the BICS and the CUT is turned off isolating them during this period. A single clock has been used to turn on and off both TG_1 and TG_2 as shown in **Figure 2**. For fault detection TG_1 is turned off and TG_2 is turned on discharging the capacitor C_1 through the CUT. When TG_2 is turned on, the node X of the capacitor C_1 gets connected to the comparator and the voltage at the node X keeps reducing as the capacitor gets discharged through the CUT. The voltage at node X is compared to the reference voltage through the comparator to give a pulse output. The reference voltage to comparator is

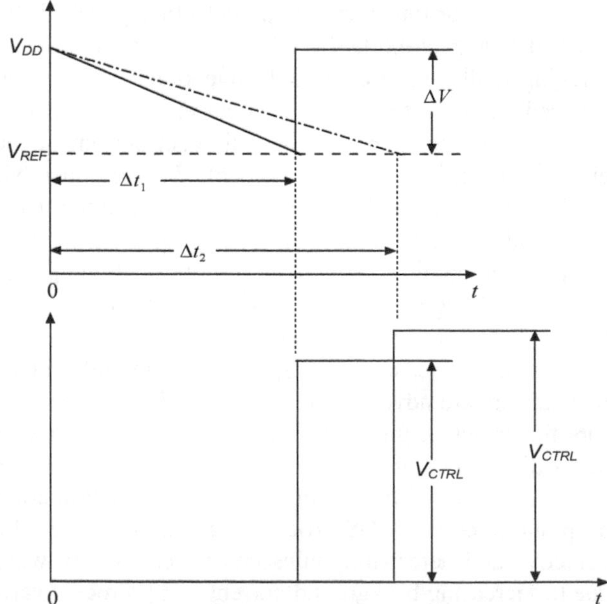

Figure 1. Capacitor discharge transient voltage of the CUT under high and low leakage [8-11]. Solid line: fault free condition, dotted line: faulty condition.

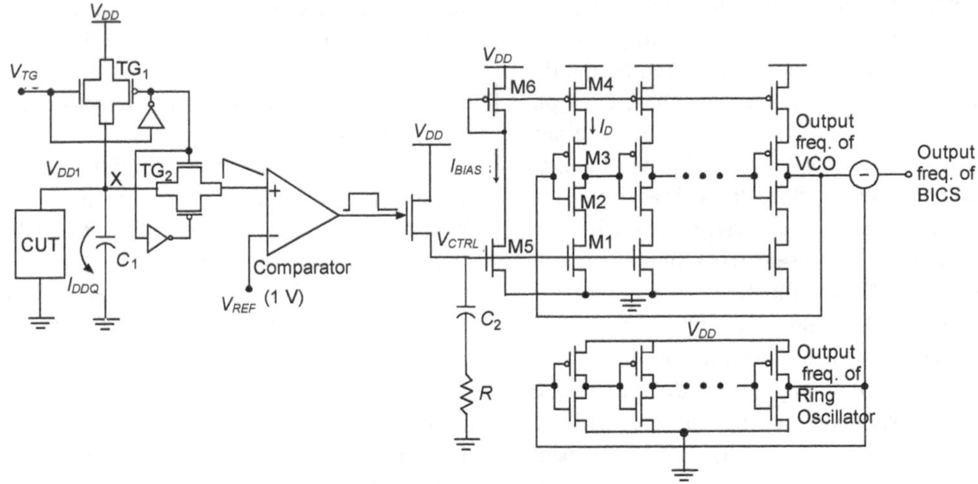

Figure 2. ΔI_{DDQ} built-in current sensor (BICS).

given externally so that the width of the pulse at the output of the comparator can be controlled. The output of the comparator is used as input to the NMOS switch which in turn charges the capacitor C_2 as shown in **Figure 2**.

The voltage across the capacitor C_2, V_{CTRL} depends on the time NMOS switch is on, which in-turn depends on the discharge time of the capacitor C_1. The voltage across the capacitor V_{CTRL} is then given to a VCO. The output of a VCO is a clock signal, whose frequency is dependent on V_{CTRL}. Its operation is similar to that of a ring oscillator. The oscillation frequency of the current starved VCO for n number (an odd number $\geq$ 3) of stages is given by

$$f_O = \frac{1}{n\left(t_r + t_f\right)} \approx \frac{I_D}{n\cdot\left(C_{out} + C_{in}\right)\cdot V_{DD}} \quad (2)$$

where, t_r and t_f are the rise time and the fall time, respectively, and n is the number of stages. V_{DD} is the power supply voltage. I_D is the biasing current. The biasing current can be adjusted by varying the control voltage, which in turn changes the oscillation frequency. The output frequency of the voltage controlled oscillator is subtracted from the frequencies of the ring oscillator to obtain BICS final output frequency as shown in **Figure 2**. This method helps to overcome the process variation in sub-micron CMOS technology.

3. 12-Bit DAC Design (CUT)

The 12-bit DAC design uses a charge scaling architecture and the block diagram is as shown in **Figure 3** [13]. The DAC converts a 12-bit digital input word to a respective analog signal by scaling a voltage reference. The DAC consists of voltage reference, binary switches, scaling network, an operational amplifier and a sample and hold circuit. The multiplexer circuit connected to the other end of each capacitor, selects the voltage which is either V_{REF} or GND to which the capacitor is charged depending upon the control signal "V_S". Initially, the control signal for all multiplexer switches is set to LOW before giving any specified input so that GND is supplied to the capacitor network and reset. Then the capacitor network is supplied with the digital word by switching the particular multiplexer switch for each bit to the desired value of either V_{REF} for "1" or GND for "0". The capacitors whose ends are connected to V_{REF} are charged to +2 V and those, which are connected to GND, are charged to 0 V. Since the capacitor network is connected in parallel, the equivalent voltage is calculated by,

$$V_{OUT} = \left(b_1 2^{-1} + b_2 2^{-2} + b_3 2^{-3} + \cdots + B_N 2^{-N}\right) V_{REF} \quad (3)$$

The capacitor at the end of the network is used as a "terminating capacitor". Depending on the capacitors, which are charged to different voltages based on the input digital word, the effective resultant analog voltage is calculated for the respective digital combination. The analog voltage is passed through the op-amp and the sample-and-hold circuit and appears as an analog voltage. The op-amp and comparator used in DAC is designed for 2.5 V operation.

4. Results and Discussion

Figure 4 shows the chip layout of a 12-bit DAC designed for operation at 2.5 V in 0.5 μm n-well CMOS process with eight defects introduced using fault injection transistors (FITs) as switches [14]. The design integrates an on-chip BICS of **Figure 2** for ΔI_{DDQ} testing of physical defects such as shorts in MOSFETs. The DAC occupies 504 × 501 μm^2 area of the chip. The BICS occupies 20% (670 × 75 μm^2) of the total chip area.

In testing of analog and mixed signal circuits, the dependence of the power supply current on the circuit parameters has to be considered. This can result in a significant difference between the fabricated (manufactured) circuit and its nominal value. So a fault-free circuit can be considered as faulty and vice-versa [10,11,15]. This problem is overcome in the present work by considering a tolerance limit of ±10% on the fault free output frequency value. It thus takes into account the variations due to significant technology and design parameters. The circuit has been designed using the model parameters T69K [16] and the frequency output of the BICS is called the natural frequency (f_N). The BICS has been simulated with various model parameters to check for the effects of process variation on the deviation of the output frequencies from the natural frequency. The results are presented in **Figure 5**.

From **Figure 5**, it can be observed that the deviation of the output frequency of the BICS is less than ±10% for all the model parameters except T5CX [16], T51T [16], T3CU [16] thus falling within the tolerance limit. To check the robustness of the BICS against the process variation, the output frequencies obtained by BICS for the different model parameters have been modified by ± 10 % and their deviation with the natural frequency have also been calculated and shown in **Figure 5**. It can be observed from **Figure 5** that even with the variation of the output frequencies obtained by BICS by either +10% or −10%, the deviation is within ±10% of the natural frequency. Thus, the CUT can be designed using one set of model parameters and the same natural frequency value can be used for fault detection after fabrication using the BICS.

The CUT is then simulated after introducing faults using fault injection transistors one by one. **Table 1** summarizes the output frequency of the BICS along with their deviation from the natural frequency.

Fault-1 simulates a physical short between drain and source of one of the transistors in multiplexer part of the circuit of **Figure 3**, Fault-2 simulates a physical short between drain and source of one of the transistors in multiplexer part of the circuit of **Figure 3**, Fault-3 simulates a physical short between gate and source of one of the transistors of the op-amp part of the circuit of **Figure 3**, Fault-4 simulates a physical short between drain and source of one of the transistors of the op-amp part of the circuit of **Figure 3**. Fault-5 simulates a gate-substrate short in one of the transistors of the op-amp part of the circuit of **Figure 3**. Fault-6 simulates a gate-drain short of one of the transistors of the op-amp part of the circuit of **Figure 3**, Fault-7 simulates a source-substrate short of one of the transistors of the sample-and-hold circuit part of the circuit of **Figure 3** and Fault-8 simulates an inter-gate short between two transistors in the unit gain op-amp of the sample-and-hold circuit part of the circuit of **Figure 3**. From **Table 1** it can be noted that the deviation is greater than ±10% and thus detecting the introduced faults.

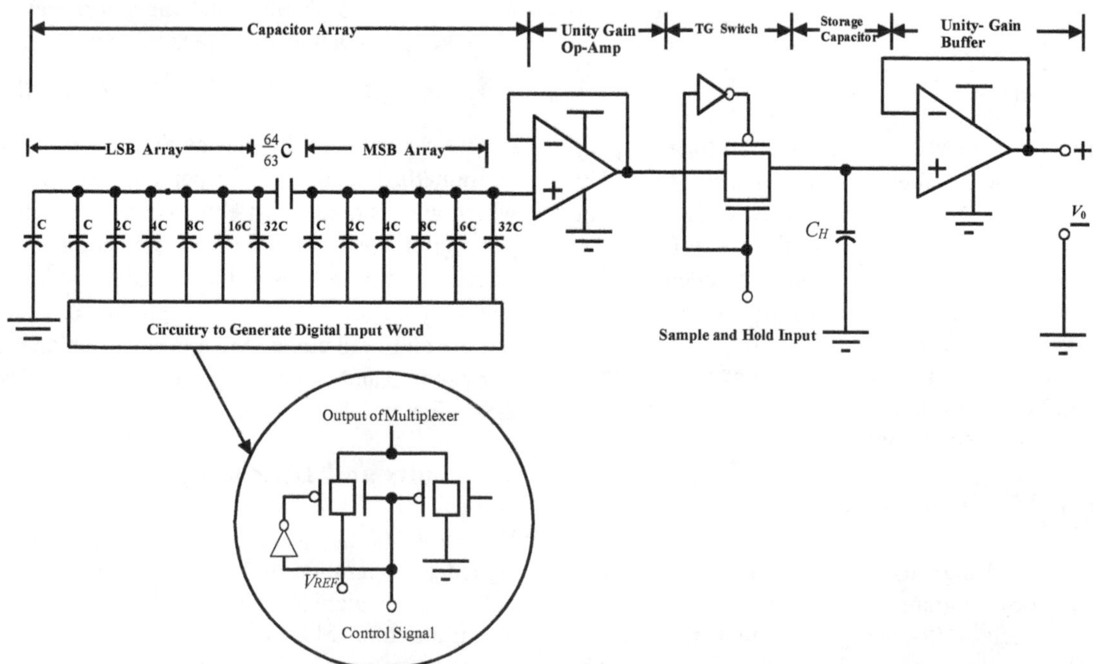

Figure 3. Schematic of a 12-bit charge scaling DAC.

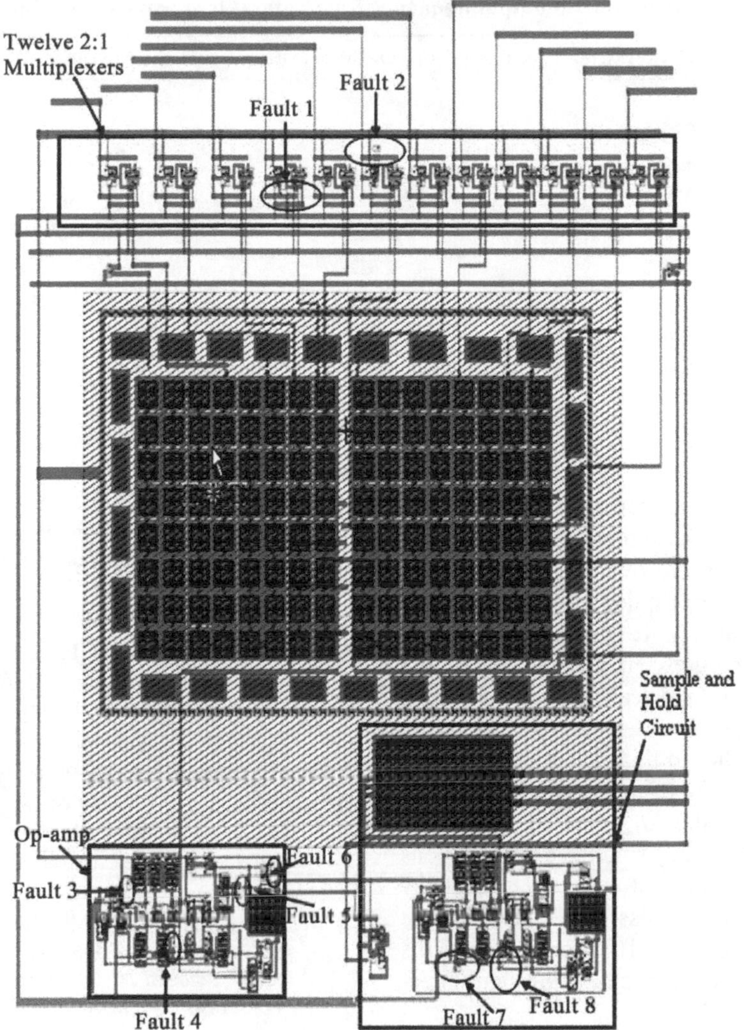

Figure 4. Chip layout of 12-bit DAC and BICS with induced faults.

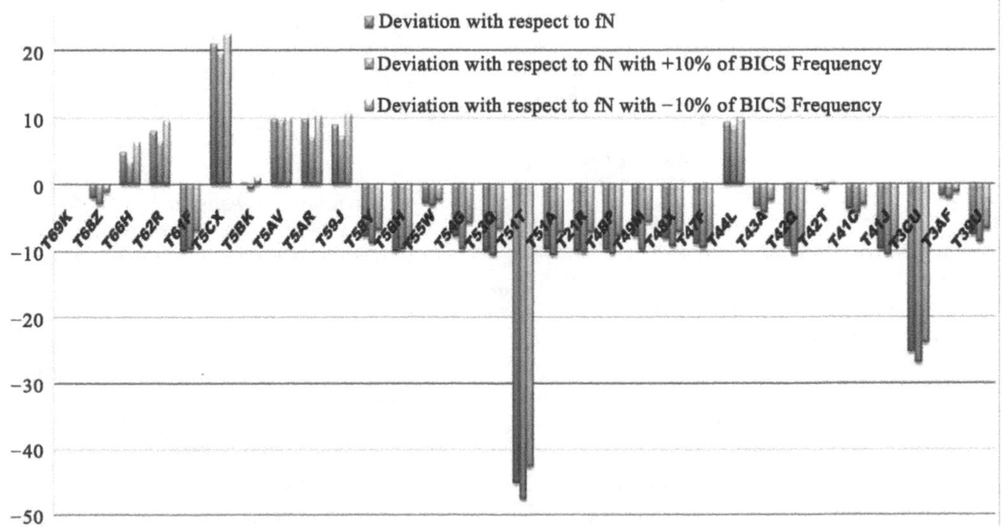

Figure 5. Deviation of BICS output frequency to natural frequency (f_N).

Table 1. Deviation of BICS output frequency from natural frequency with induced faults.

Fault	Output Freq. of VCO (MHz)	Freq. of Ring Oscillator (MHz)	Output Freq. of the BICS (kHz)	Deviation (%)
No Fault	2.632	2.632	0	0
Fault 1	3.226	2.632	594.227	22.58
Fault 2	3.125	2.632	493.421	18.75
Fault 3	2.326	2.632	−305.998	−11.63
Fault 4	2.222	2.632	−409.357	−15.56
Fault 5	2.326	2.632	−305.998	−11.63
Fault 6	2.941	2.632	309.597	11.76
Fault 7	2.326	2.632	−305.998	−11.63
Fault 8	2.222	2.632	−409.357	−15.56

5. Conclusions

We have proposed and implemented a BICS for CMOS data converters fabricated in 0.5 μm n-well CMOS process. The circuits are designed to overcome the problem of increase in absolute value of quiescent current due to increasing background current. It also overcomes the variation in the value of quiescent current due to the change in threshold voltage and leakage current caused by process variation in the circuit. Thus, the increase in quiescent current caused due to defect can be estimated accurately in sub-micron CMOS data converters. The process variation effects on the ΔI_{DDQ} testing of the data converters are considered and simulated for various model parameters. The deviation of the output frequency of the BICS is observed to be less than ±10% for the model parameters and more than ±10% for various faults introduced in the data converter circuit using fault-injection transistors.

6. References

[1] R. Rajsuman, "I_{ddq} Testing for CMOS VLSI," Artech House, London, 1995.

[2] A. Srinivas, "I_{DDQ} Testing of a CMOS 10-Bit Charge Scaling Digital-to-Analog Converter," M.S. Thesis, Louisiana State University, Baton Rouge, 2003.

[3] P. Nigh and W. Maly, "Test Generation for Current Testing," *Design & Test of Computers*, Vol. 7, No. 1, 1990, pp. 26-38.

[4] A. Keshavarzi, K. Roy and C. F. Hawkins, "Intrinsic Leakage in Low Power Deep Submicron CMOS ICs," *IEEE Proceedings of the* 1997 *International Test Conference*, Washington, 1-6 November 1997, pp. 146-155.

[5] B. Kruseman, R. Van Veen and K. Van Kaam, "The Future of Delta-I_{DDQ} Testing," *IEEE Proceedings of the* 2001 *International Test Conference*, Baltimore, 30 October-1 Nobember 2001, pp. 101-110.

[6] R. R. Montanes and J. Figueras, "Estimation of the Defective I_{DDQ} Caused by Shorts in Deep Submicron CMOS ICs," *Proceedings of the Conference on Design Automation and Test in Europe*, Paris, 23-26 February 1998, pp. 490-494.

[7] J. Figueras and A. Ferre, "Possibilities and Limitations of I_{DDQ} Testing in Submicron CMOS," *IEEE Transaction Components, Packaging and Manufacturing Technology—Part B*, Vol. 21, No. 4, November 1998, pp. 352-359.

[8] J. R. Vazquez and J. P. de Gyvez, "Built-in Current Sensor for ΔI_{DDQ} Testing," *IEEE Journal of Solid-State Circuits*, Vol. 39, No. 3, March 2004, pp. 511-518.

[9] J. R. Vazquez and J. P. de Gyvez, "Built-in Current Sensor for ΔI_{DDQ} Testing of Deep Submicron Digital CMOS ICs," *Proceeding of the 22nd IEEE VLSI Test Symposium*, Napa Valley, 25-29 April 2004, pp. 53-58.

[10] S. Yellampalli and A. Srivastava, "ΔI_{DDQ} Based Testing of Submicron CMOS Digital-to-Analog Converter Circuits," *Journal of Active and Passive Electronic Devices*, Vol. 3, No. 3-4, 2008, pp. 341-353.

[11] S. Yellampalli and A. Srivastava, "ΔI_{DDQ} Testing of CMOS Data Converters," *Journal of Active and Passive Electronic Devices*, Vol. 4, No. 1-2, 2009, pp. 63-89.

[12] M. Keating and D. Meyer, "A New Approach to Dynamic I_{DD} Testing," *IEEE Proceedings of the* 1987 *International Test Conference*, Washington DC, 30 August-3 September 1987, pp. 316-321.

[13] R. J. Baker, H. W. Li and D. E. Boyce, "CMOS Circuit Design, Layout and Simulation," IEEE Press, Hoboken, 2003, p. 813.

[14] A. Srivastava, S. Aluri and A. K. Chamakura, "A Simple Built-in Current Sensor for I_{DDQ} Testing of CMOS Data Converters," *Integration, the VLSI Journal*, Vol. 38, No. 4, 2005, pp. 579-596.

[15] G. Gielen, Z. Wang and W. Sansen, "Fault Detection and Input Stimulus Determination for the Testing of Analog Integrated Circuits Based on Power Supply Current Monitoring," *Proceedings of IEEE/ACM International Conference on Computer Aided Design*, Los Alamitos, 6-10 November 1994, pp. 495-498.

[16] The MOSIS Service, 2011. http://www.mosis.com/Technical/Testdata/ami-c5-prm.html

19

Linearized Phase Detector Zero Crossing DPLL Performance Evaluation in Faded Mobile Channels

Qassim Nasir[1], Saleh Al-Araji[2]

[1]*Department of Electrical and Computer Engineering, University of Sharjah, Sharjah, UAE*

[2]*Communication Engineering Department, Khalifa University of Science, Technology and Research, Sharjah, UAE*

Abstract

Zero Crossing Digital Phase Locked Loop with Arc Sine block (AS-ZCDPLL) is used to linearize the phase difference detection, and enhance the loop performance. The loop has faster acquisition, less steady state phase error, and wider locking range compared to the conventional ZCDPLL. This work presents a Zero Crossing Digital Phase Locked Loop with Arc Sine block (ZCDPLL-AS). The performance of the loop is analyzed under mobile faded channel conditions. The mobile channel is assumed to be two path fading channel corrupted by additive white Gaussian noise (AWGM). It is shown that for a constant filter gain, the frequency spread has no effect on the steady state phase error variance when the loop is subjected to a phase step. For a frequency step and under the same conditions, the effect on phase error is minimal.

Keywords: Non-uniform Sampling, Digital Phase Locked Loops, Zero Crossing DPLL, Mobile Faded Channels

1. Introduction

Phase Lock Loops (PLLs) are used in a wider range of communication applications such as carrier recovery synchronization, and demodulation [1]. A PLL is a closed loop system in which the phase output tracks the phase of the input signal. It consists of a phase detector, filter, and voltage controlled oscillator. Digital Phase locked Loops (DPLLs) were introduced to minimize some of the problems associated with the analogue counter part such as sensitivity to DC drift and the need for periodic adjustments [1,2]. Conventional Zero Crossing DPLL (ZCDPLL) is the most widely used due to its simplicity in modeling and implementation [3,4].

In this paper an Arc-Sine ZCDPLL is analyzed under mobile faded channel. The purpose of including the Arc-Sine in the loop is to linearize the phase difference detection. The peak detector guarantees the input amplitude to the Arc-Sine block to remain between −1 and +1. It has been shown that the AS-ZCDPLL loop offers improved performance in the lock range and acquisition with reduced steady state phase error [5]. The proposed ZCDPLL-AS can be characterized by a linear difference equation in module (π/2) sense.

The mobile radio channel is characterized by fast Rayleigh fading and random phase distribution. This considerably degrades the tracking performance and increase the jitter of the loop. In this paper, the performance of ZCDPLL-AS with phase and frequency step inputs in the mobile radio environment is studied. The ZCDPLL-AS, in this work is considered as part of a mobile receiver. The mobile channel is assumed to be a two path fading channel corrupted by additive white Gaussian noise (AWGN). The fading in each path of the channel follows Rayleigh distribution and has power spectral density as given by Jakes [6].

$$S(f) = \frac{\sigma^2}{\pi f_m \sqrt{1 - \left(\frac{f}{f_m}\right)^2}}$$

where $f_m = vfc/c$ is the Doppler frequency that depends on the speed of the vehicle v and carrier frequency fc. The performance of the proposed algorithm will be evaluated for Doppler frequencies of 6 Hz, 100 Hz and 222 Hz, corresponding to a pedestrian (3.5 km/hr) and vehicular channels with speeds of 54 km/hr and 120 km/hr respectively.

The stochastic difference equation describing the ZC-DPLL-AS loop operation is derived in Section 2. Finally, the probability density function (pdf) of the steadystate phase error is derived and calculated numerically in Section 3. Experimental simulation results are presented in Section 4 and finally conclusion are given, in Section 5.

2. ZCDPLL-AS System Operation in Mobile Faded Channels

The ZCDPLL-AS is composed of a sampler as a phase detector, inverse sine block, a digital loop filter, and a Digital Controlled Oscillator (DCO) as shown in **Figure 1** [5]. The input signal to the loop is taken as $x(t) = s_1(t) + n(t)$, where $s_1(t)$ is the noise free input signal to the loop after passing through the mobile channel. If $s(t)$ = $A\sin(\omega_0 t + \theta_i(t))$, $n(t)$ is Additive white Gaussian Noise (AWGN); $\theta_i(t) = \theta_0+\Omega_0 t$, from which the signal dynamics are modeled; θ_0 is the initial phase which we will assume to be zero; Ω_0 is the frequency offset from the nominal value ω_0. Then $s_1(t) = r(t)\sin(\omega_0 t + \theta_i(t) + \varphi_{ch}(t))$, $r(t)$ is Rayleigh faded envelope and $\varphi_{ch}(t)$, is a uniform distribution channel phase.

The input signal is sampled at time instances tk determined by the Digital Controlled Oscillator (DCO). The DCO period control algorithm as given by [7-10] is

$$T_k = T_0 - c_{k-1} = t_k - t_{k-1} \tag{1}$$

where $T_0 = (2\pi/\omega_0)$ is the nominal period, c_{k-1} is the output of the loop digital filter $D(z)$. The sample value of the incoming signal $x(t)$ at t_k is

$$x(t_k) = s_1(t_k) + n(t_k) \tag{2}$$

or

$$x_k = s_k + n_k \tag{3}$$

where $s_k = A\sin(\omega_0 t_k + \theta_i(t_k))$, The sequence x_k is passed through the Arc-Sine block with output $y_k = \sin^{-1}(x_k)$. The output is passed through a digital filter $D(z)$ whose output c_k is used to control the period of the DCO.

The time instances t_k can be rewritten as

$$t_k = \sum_{i=1}^{k} T_i = kT_0 - \sum_{i=0}^{k-1} c_i,\ k = 1,2,3,\cdots \tag{4}$$

Thus

$$x_k = r_k \sin\left[w_0\left(kT_0 - \sum_{i=0}^{k-1} c_i \right) + \theta_k + \phi_{ch,k} \right] + n_k \tag{5}$$

The phase error is defined to be [5]

$$\phi_k = \theta_k + \phi_{ch,k} - w_0 \sum_{i=0}^{k-1} c_i \tag{6}$$

Also

$$\phi_{k+1} = \theta_{k+1} + \phi_{ch,k+1} - w_0 \sum_{i=0}^{k} c_i \tag{7}$$

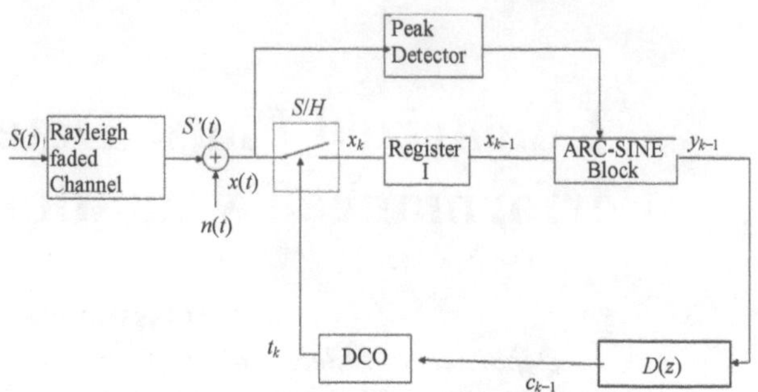

Figure 1. Block diagram of the ZCDPLL-AS.

Taking the difference of (7) and (8) results in

$$\phi_{k+1} - \phi_k = \theta_{k+1} - \theta_k + \phi_{ch,k+1} - \phi_{ch,k} - w_0 c_k \tag{8}$$

The Arc-Sine ($\sin^{-1}$) block has been added to linearize the equation and avoid the nonlinear behaviour of the systems [5]. The output of the Arc-Sine block can be expressed as $y_k = \sin^{-1}(x_k) = \varphi_k$, $-1 \le x_k \le +1$ and $-\pi/2 \le y_k \le +\pi/2$. The z transform of the output of the digital filter is

$$C(z) = D(z)Y(z) \tag{9}$$

where $Y(z)$ is the z transform of $y(t)$. The order of the loop is determined by the type of the digital filter. For first order, the digital filter is simply a gain block $D(z) = G_1$, where G_1 is the block gain. However, for second order loop, $D(z) = G_1 + G_2/(1 - z^{-1})$.

Let us consider a first order AS-ZCDPLL loop, then the digital filter output which controls the DCO is given by

$$c_k = G_1 y_k \tag{10}$$

Then the stochastic difference equation describing the loop behaviour is given by

$$\theta_{k+1} - \theta_k = \phi_{k+1} - \phi_k - \phi_{ch,k+1} + \phi_{ch,k} + w_0 r_k G_1(\phi_k + n_k) \tag{11}$$

For phase step input where $\theta_{k+1} = \theta_k$ for $k \ge 0$, (11) becomes

$$\phi_{k+1} = \phi_k + \phi_{ch,k+1} - \phi_{ch,k} - w_0 r_k G_1(\phi_k + n_k) \tag{12}$$

And for frequency step $\theta_k = (\omega + \omega_0)t_k$ and for $k \ge 0$, (12) becomes

$$\begin{aligned}\phi_{k+1} &= \phi_k + \phi_{ch,k+1} - \phi_{ch,k} \\ &\quad - w r_k G_1(\phi_k + n_k) + (\varpi - \varpi_0)T\end{aligned} \tag{13}$$

In practical mobile communication systems and in the 800 MHz band, an IF frequency of 10.7 MHz is usually used; therefore, the sampling period T is on the order of 0.1 ps. The maximum Doppler frequency shift is on the order of 100 Hz (at vehicle velocity, about 60 mph). In other words, the $\phi_{ch,k+1}$ and $\phi_{ch,k}$ are equal, then (12) and (13) are reduced to

$$\phi_{k+1} = \phi_k - w_0 r_k G_1 \phi_k - w_0 r_k G_1 n_k \quad (14)$$

$$\phi_{k+1} = \phi_k - w r_k G_1 (\phi_k + n_k) + (\varpi - \varpi_0) T \quad (15)$$

For both cases, the probability density function of steady state phase error became a function of two independent random variables $r(k)$ and $n(k)$.

3. Phase Error Probability Density Function (pdf)

3.1. Phase Step without Noise

In steady state $\phi_{k+1} = \phi_k$, (14) can be rewritten as

$$\phi_{k+1} = (1 - \varpi_0 r_k G_1) \phi_k \quad (16)$$

If the expected value of $w_0 G_1 r_k$ is 1, then the expected value of ϕ_k is zero for all values of k. This will lead to rapid convergence of the steady state. Since the probability density function of r_k is Rayleigh then

$$P_{r_k}(r) = \frac{r}{\sigma_s^2} e^{-\frac{r^2}{2\sigma_s^2}}, \quad r \geq 0 \quad (17)$$

which has an average of $\sqrt{\pi/2\sigma_s}$. Therefore, the optimum value of the gain is $G_{opt} = (1/\varpi_0 \sigma_s)\sqrt{2/\pi}$. Let $b = \varpi_0 G_1 \sin(z)$, where $z \neq n\pi$, n is integer. Then the transition pdf can be shown as to be

$$P_{\frac{\phi_{k+1}}{\phi_k}}\left(\frac{u}{z}\right) = \frac{|u-z|}{b^2 \sigma_s^2} e^{-\frac{(u-z)^2}{2b^2\sigma_s^2}}, \quad u > z \quad (18)$$

3.2. Phase Step plus Noise

Let $y = Z \pm \omega_0 G_1 n_k$ be a Gaussian random variable with a mean of z and variance $\varpi_0^2 G_1^2 \sigma_n^2$,where σ_n^2 is the variance of the noise $n(t)$. Then the pdf of y is given by

$$P_y(y) = \frac{1}{\sqrt{2\pi}\varpi_0 G_1 \sigma_n} e^{-\frac{(y-z)^2}{2\varpi_0^2 G_1^2 \sigma_n^2}} \quad (19)$$

So

$$\phi_{k+1} = y + b r_k, \, b = -w_0 G_1 \sin(z) \quad (20)$$

When $z = 0$, ϕ_{k+1} will be zero mean Gaussian. Also when $z = \pm n\pi$, ϕ_{k+1} will be Gaussian with mean of z. The transition pdf can be rewritten as [4]

$$P_{\phi_{k+1}\phi_k}\left(\frac{u}{\pm n\pi}\right) = \frac{1}{\sqrt{2\pi}\varpi_0 G_1 \sigma_n} e^{-\frac{(u \pm n\pi)^2}{2\varpi_0^2 G_1^2 \sigma_n^2}} \quad (21)$$

Given $\phi_k = z$, then

$$\phi_{k+1} = z - \varpi G_1 r_k \sin(z) - \varpi G_1 n_k, + (\varpi - \varpi_0)\frac{2\pi}{\varpi_0} \quad (22)$$

Define a random variable Y as

$$Y = z - \varpi G_1 n_k + (\varpi - \varpi_0)\frac{2\pi}{\varpi_0} \quad (23)$$

Y will be Gaussian with mean $\left(z + 2\pi(\omega/\omega_0 - 1)\right)$ and variance $\omega G_1^2 \sigma_n^2$. Therefore

$$P_Y(y) = \frac{1}{\sqrt{2\varpi} G_1 \sigma_n} e^{-\frac{\left[y - z - 2\pi\left(\frac{\varpi}{\varpi_0} - 1\right)\right]^2}{2\varpi^2 G_1^2 \sigma_n^2}} \quad (24)$$

$$\phi_{k+1} = Y + b' r_k, \; b' = -\varpi G_1 \sin(z) \quad (25)$$

Since ϕ_k is a discrete time continuous variable Markov process, its conditioned on an initial condition error ϕ_0 satisfies Chapman-Kolmogrov equation, then

$$P_{\phi_{k+1}}\left(\frac{\phi}{\phi_0}\right) = P_{\phi_{k+1}\phi_k}\left(\frac{\phi}{z}\right) P_{\phi_k}\left(\frac{z}{\phi}\right) dz \quad (26)$$

Equation (23) is valid whether r_k and r_{k+1} are mutually independent or not. This is solved numerically as was done in [4]. The transition pdf $P(\phi|z)$ is stored in a matrix starting with $P_0(z/\phi_0) = \delta(z - \phi_0)$, $P_{\phi_{k+1}}(\phi/\phi_0)$ is calculated from $P_{\phi_k}(\phi/\phi_0)$ with k = 1,2,⋯, until the values of successive k differ by a prescribed small amount.

4. Simulation Results

The performance of the loop was evaluated in simulation by subjecting it to phase as well as frequency steps. The input signal $s(t)$ = sin(2000_t) is considered as modulation free and the DCO center frequency is 1000 Hz. In the simulation process, the Signal to Noise Ratio is defined as SNRdb = $10\log(1/\sigma_n^2)$, where σ_n^2 represents noise variance. The loop is studied under phase step in the presence of noise. It is noticed from **Figure 2**, and as derived in section (2), that the steady state phase error variance depends on the value of the filter gain, as shown in **Figure 3**. The increase in gain causes the phase error to increase sharply which results in degradation in system's performance. The effect of SNR on the phase error variance is shown in **Figure 4**. This variance is directly proportional to SNR as shown in **Figure 5**. As shown from the figure, the loop performance due to phase jitter improves as SNR increases. The frequency spread has no direct effect on the steady state phase error variance if the filter gain is kept constant, as shown in **Figure 6**. However, if the loop input signal is subjected to a frequency step, then the loop jitter is slightly affected by the step size if the filter gain is kept constant. The Doppler spread will increase the jitter if the spread is increased as shown in **Figure 6**. The loop probability density function of the phase performance when subjected to a frequency step is shown in **Figure 7** for different frequency offsets, while **Figure 8** is for different wireless channel Doppler spreads. It is seen from the figures that the impact of frequency offset and channel speed of variations (Doppler spread) on the system performance is minimal. The loop performance, when a frequency step is applied to the loop, is also affected by the channel SNR as shown in **Figure 9**. The variance of timing error in the loop is increased as the loop gain G_1 is increased and this primary-

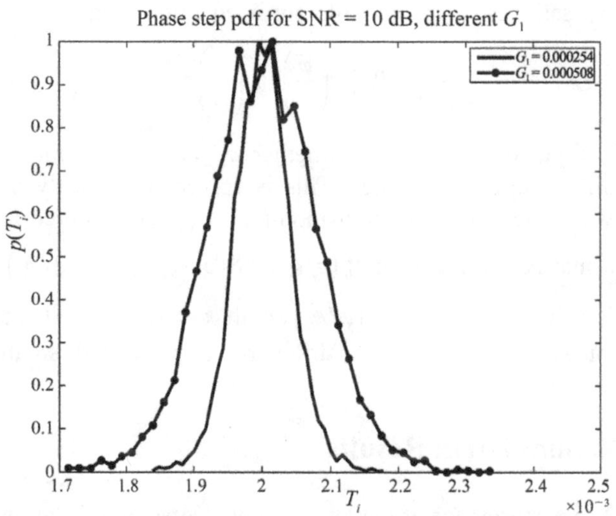

Figure 2. Probability Density Function (pdf) of DCO Period when SNR = 10 dB and when Phase step is applied with different values of filter gain G_1.

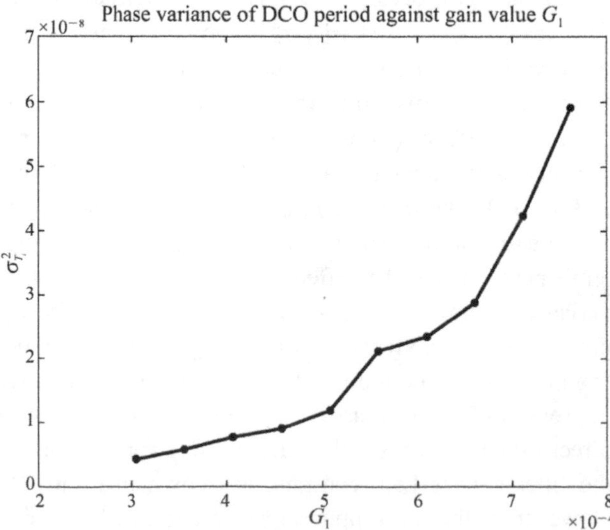

Figure 3. Variance of DCO period against filter gain G_1.

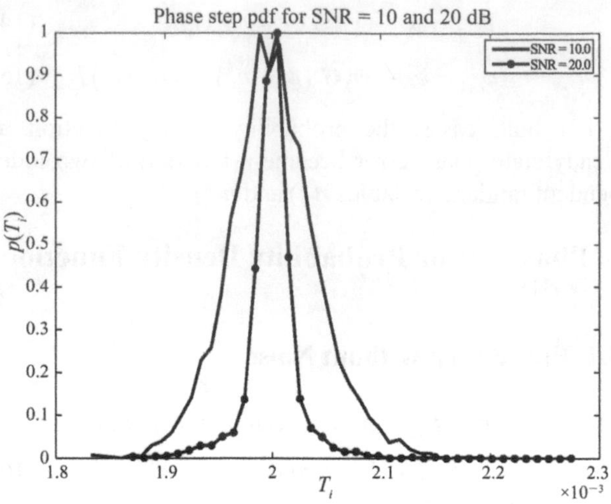

Figure 4. Probability Density Function (pdf) of DCO period for SNR = 10, 20 dB and when phase step is applied.

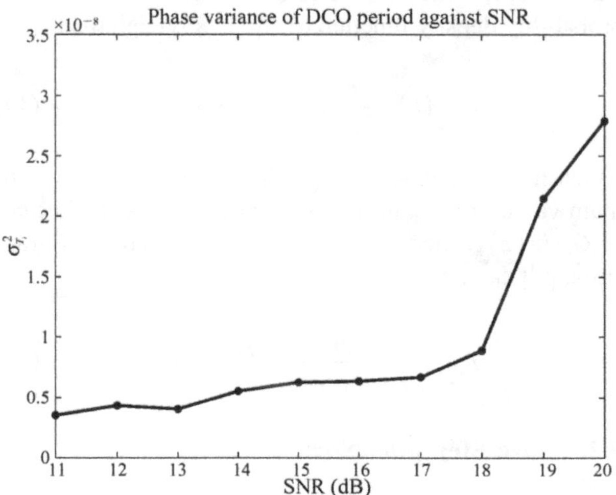

Figure 5. Variance of DCO period versus input signal SNR.

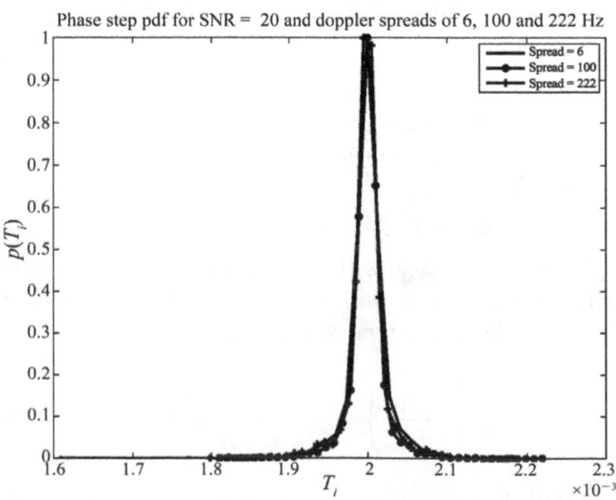

Figure 6. Probability Density Function (pdf) of DCO period for SNR = 20 dB with phase step with different doppler spreads.

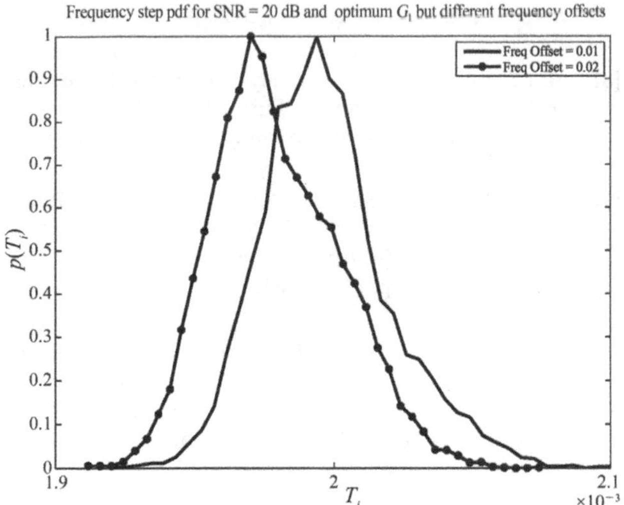

Figure 7. Probability Density Function (pdf) of DCO period for SNR = 20 dB with Frequency step with different frequency spreads.

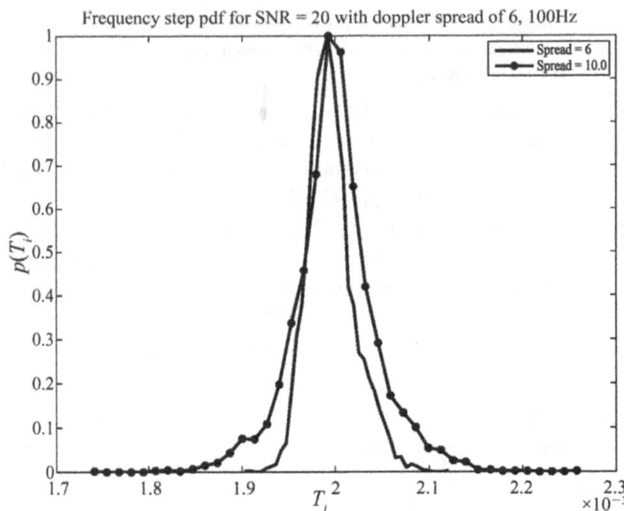

Figure 8. Probability Density Function (pdf) of DCO period for SNR = 20 dB with frequency step with doppler spread of 6 and 100 Hz.

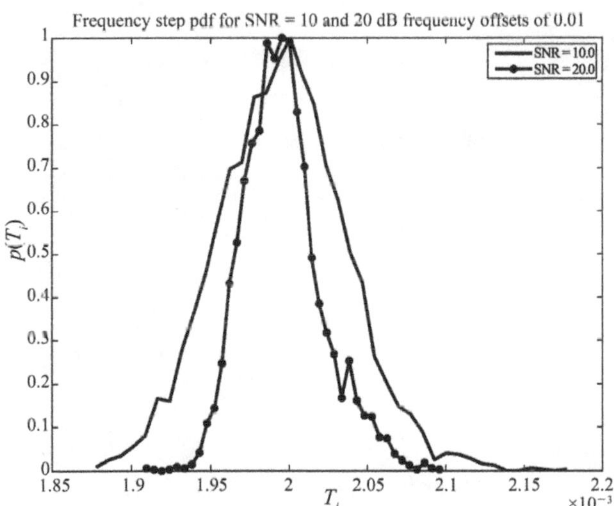

Figure 9. Probability Density Function(pdf) of DCO period for SNR = 10 and 20 dB with frequency step of frequency offset of 0.01.

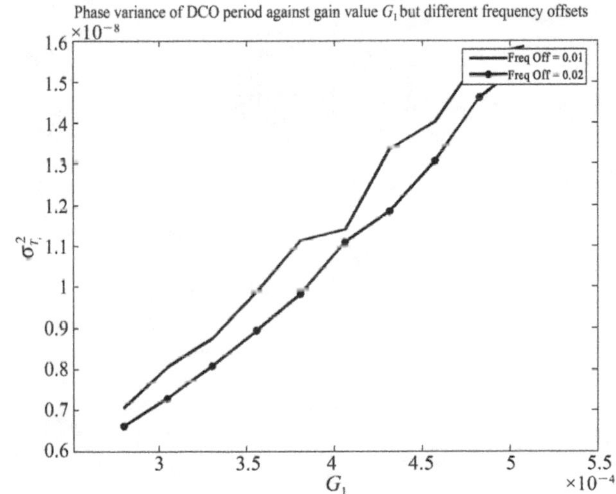

Figure 10. Variance of DCO period versus the loop gain G_1 for different frequency offsets.

ly depends on the value frequency step input as shown in **Figure 10**.

5. Conclusions

The ZCDPLL-AS loop is studied under phase and frequency steps in the presence of noise. It is shown that the frequency spread, under phase step condition, has no direct effect on the steady phase error variance if the filter gain is kept constant. For frequency step, the error is slightly affected under the same conditions. From the results, it has been shown that the variance of the DCO period increases with the Doppler spread. The system was tested with Doppler spreads of 6 Hz, 100 Hz, and 222 Hz. ZCDPLL-AS loop has been tested and has shown to give improved locking and acquisition performance.

6. References

[1] F. M. Gardner, "Phaselock Techniques," 3rd Edition, John Wiley and Sons, Hoboken, 2005.

[2] Q. Nasir and S. R. Al-Araji, "Optimum Perfromance Zero Crossing Digital Phase Locked Loop using Multi-Sampling Technique," *IEEE International Conference on Electronics, Circuits and Systems*, Sharjah, 14-17 December 2003, pp. 719-722.

[3] Q. Nasir, "Digital Phase Locked Loop with Broad Lock

Range Using Chaos Control Technique," *AutoSoft - Intelligent Automation and Soft Computing*, Vol. 12, No. 2, 2006, pp. 183-186.

[4] Q. Nasir, "Extended Lock Range Zero Crossing Digital Phase Locked Loop with Time Delay," *EURASIP Journal on Wireless Communications and Networking*, Vol. 2005, No. 3, 2005, pp. 413-418.

[5] Q. Nasir and S. R. Al-Araji, "Performance Analysis of Zero Crossing DPLL with Linearized Phase detector," *International Journal of Information and Communication Technology*, Vol. 1, No. 3, 2009, pp. 45-51.

[6] W. C. Jakes, "Microwave Mobile Communication," John Wiley and Sons, Hoboken, 1974.

[7] Q. Nasir, "Chaos Controlled ZCDPLL for Carrier Recovery in Noisy Channels," *Wireless Personal Communications*, Vol. 43, No. 4, December 2007, pp. 1577-1582.

[8] H. C. Osborne, "Stability Analysis if an Nth Power Phase-Locked Loop—Part I: First Order DPLL," *IEEE Transactions on Communications*, Vol. 28, No. 8, 1980, pp. 1343-1354.

[9] H. C. Osborne, "Stability Analysis if an Nth Power Phase-Locked Loop—Part II: Second- and Third-Order DPLL's," *IEEE Transactions on Communications*, Vol. 28, No. 8, 1980, pp. 1355-1364.

[10] F. Chao, *et al.*, "A Novel Islanding Detection Method Based on Digital PLL for Grid-Connected Converters," *International Conference on Power System Technology*, Hangzhou, 24-28 October 2010, pp. 1-5.

New Analysis to Measure the Capacitance and Conductance of MOS Structure toward Small Size of VLSI Circuits

Wagah Farman Mohammad
Communications & Electronics Department, Faculty of Engineering, Philadelphia University, Amman, Jordan

Abstract

In this research thin film layers have been prepared at alternate layers of resistive and dielectric deposited on appropriate substrates to form four - terminal R-Y-NR network. If the gate of the MOS structures deposited as a strip of resistor film like NiCr, the MOS structure can be analyzed as R-Y-NR network. A method of analysis has been proposed to measure the shunt capacitance and the shunt conductance of certain MOS samples. Mat lab program has been used to compute shunt capacitance and shunt conductance at different frequencies. The results computed by this method have been compared with the results obtained by LCR meter method and showed perfect coincident with each other.

Keywords: Thin Film R-Y-NR Network, MOS R-Y-NR Network, MOS-VLSI Circuits, MOS Capacitance

1. Introduction

In recent years, there have been rapidly growing interest and activity in thin film integrated circuits as an approach to microelectronics. Electronic circuits have been fabricated on the basis of replacing conventional lumped elements with their thin film equivalents. Essentially the VLSI memory devices are Electronic structures. The Metal-Oxide-Silicon (MOS) structures are an important type of the VLSI memory devises. MOS capacitance is one of the key test structures for VLSI technology characterization. It permits the determination of the electrical characteristics of a given technology such as oxide thickness, substrate doping, the switching speed and the driving capability of VLSI circuits [1].

The MOS capacitor is a Metal-Oxide-Semiconductor structure. **Figure 1** show the MOS capacitor which consists of few layers: semiconductor substrate with a thin oxide layer and a top metal contact also referred to as the gate. A second metal layer forms an ohmic contact to the back of the semiconductor, also referred to as the bulk. The electrical characteristics of MOS structures determine the switching speed of VLSI circuits. The electrical characteristics of MOS structures may be estimated using few simple formulas, such [2]:

The gate capacitance: $C_G = C_{ox}WL$

The channel resistance: $R_C = R_s\ (L/W)$. Where R_s is the sheet resistance, C_{ox} is the oxide capacitance, L is the channel length and W is the channel width. Unfortunately MOS is not simple and computing the channel resistance and gate capacitance is more complicated.

As MOS feature size is getting smaller and smaller, the thickness of layers becomes more and more significant. The correct extraction of parasitic capacitance and resistance in deep submicron VLSI design is getting a major research area. The MOS different modes of operation, namely accumulation, flat band, depletion and inversion [3] are introduced here. The MOS structure has a

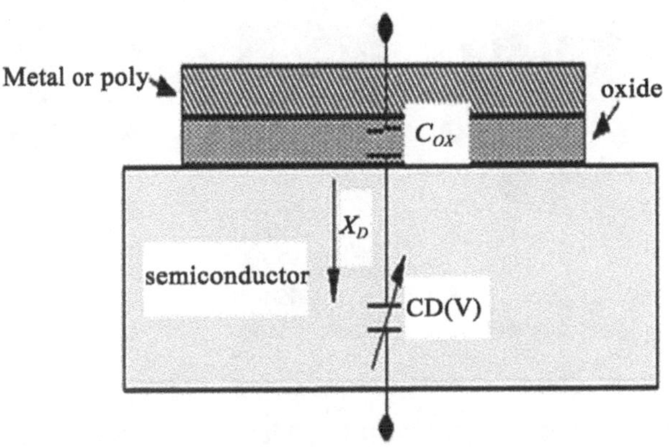

Figure1. Schematic cross section of the MOS.

p-type substrate. The structure will be referred as an n-type MOS capacitor since the inversion layer as discussed below contains electrons.

To understand the different bias modes of an MOS capacitor three different bias voltages were considered. The first one is below the flat band voltage, V_{FB}, a second between the flat band voltage and the threshold voltage V_T, and finally one larger than the threshold voltage.

These bias regimes are called the accumulation, depletion and inversion mode of operation. These three modes as well as the charge distributions associated with each of them are shown in **Figure 2**.

Accumulation occurs typically for negative voltages where the negative charge on the gate attracts holes from the substrate to the oxide-semiconductor interface. Depletion occurs for positive voltages. The positive charge on the gate pushes the mobile holes into the substrate. Therefore, the semiconductor is depleted of mobile carriers at the interface and a negative charge, due to the ionized acceptor ions, is left in the space charge region. The voltage separating the accumulation and depletion regime is referred to as the flat band voltage, V_{FB}. Inversion occurs at voltages beyond the threshold voltage. In inversion, there exists a negatively charged inversion layer at the oxide-semiconductor interface in addition to the depletion-layer. This inversion layer is due to minority carriers, which are attracted to the interface by the positive gate voltage. **Figure 3** represents a typical C(V) behavior for a MOS capacitance test structure, measured at high frequency (1 MHz). The operation ranges are also indicated on this figure: strong inversion, depletion, and accumulation.

The majority of the up-dated work however has been concerned with the investigation of sandwiched three layer rectangular and exponential shaped structures. In

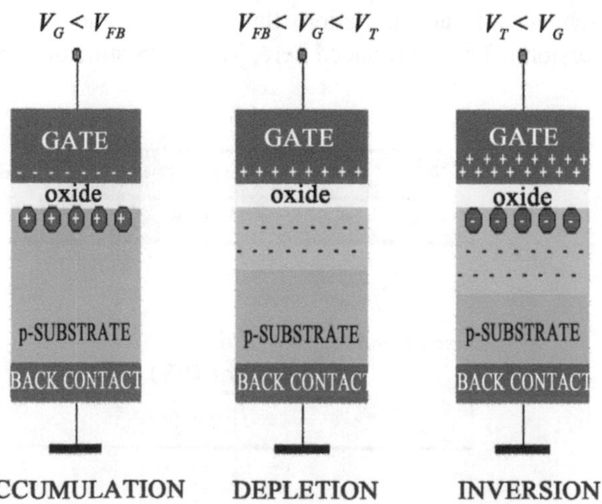

Figure 2. The three bias regimes of MOS structures.

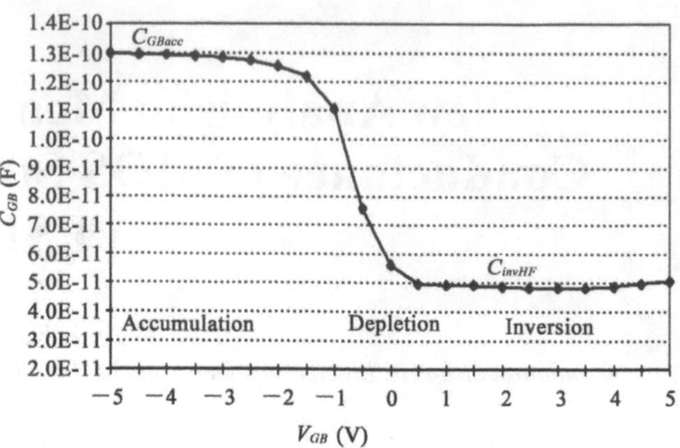

Figure3. C(V) behavior for a MOS capacitance test structure measured at high frequency (1 MHz).

these structures, alternate layers of resistive and dielectric films are deposited on appropriate substrates to form four terminal R-Y-NR networks [4], which is a special type of MOS structure. In this research a new method to measure the capacitance and conductance of MOS structures was derived and discussed. The method of analysis that was used to obtain the steady state ac response and the response to a unit step is rather straightforward. It is shown that the partial differential equation relating voltage, position, and time is of second order homogeneous ordinary linear differential equation [5]. If the MOS gate deposited as a strip of resistor film like NiCr, MOS structure can be analyzed as R-Y-NR network [6].

2. Open Circuit Voltage Transfer Function

The matrix parameter functions (MPFs) of a solvable DP R-Y-NR network are defined with the following symbols [5]:

$$r = \begin{vmatrix} M'_0 & F'_0 \\ M'_L & F'_L \end{vmatrix} \tag{1}$$

$$g = (1+N)R_o \begin{vmatrix} M'_0 & F'_0 \\ M'_L & F'_L \end{vmatrix} \tag{2}$$

$$b = (1+N)R_L \begin{vmatrix} M'_0 & F'_0 \\ M_0 & F_0 \end{vmatrix} \tag{3}$$

$$a = (1+N)R_o \begin{vmatrix} M'_L & F'_L \\ M_L & F_L \end{vmatrix} \tag{4}$$

$$h = (1+N)R_L \begin{vmatrix} M'_0 & F_0 \\ M_L & F_L \end{vmatrix} \tag{5}$$

$$y = (1+N)^2 R_o R_L \begin{vmatrix} M_L & F_L \\ M_0 & F_0 \end{vmatrix} \tag{6}$$

Employing the technique of sub network generation

[7,8], the open circuit voltage transfer function T_{vo} of the exponential distributed parameter two-port three Layer sub networks of **Figure 4** is obtainable in terms of the matrix parameter functions (MPFs). The exponential distributed parameter R-Y-NR structure consists of two resistive layers with per unit length (PUL) series resistance $R = R_o\exp(Kx)$ and $NR = NR_o\exp(Kx)$ for first and second resistive layers respectively. These two resistive layers are separated from each other by an intermediate dielectric layer for which the per unit length (PUL) shunt capacitance is $C = C_o\exp(-Kx)$ and shunt conductance is $G = G_o\exp(-Kx)$ where N is a dimensionless constant representing the ratio of the two resistive layers, R_o is a PUL resistive constant, C_o is a PUL capacitive constant, G_o is a PUL conductive constant and K is a PUL exponential taper constant.

The open circuit voltage transfer function [7] for the Sub network in **Figure 4(a)** is:

$$T_{V_o} = \frac{V_o}{V_i} = \frac{a + Ng}{(1+N)g} \quad (7)$$

And that for the sub network in **Figure 4(b)** is:

$$T_{V_o} = \frac{V_o}{V_i} = \frac{g - a}{(1+N)g} \quad (8)$$

where g and a are (MPFs) for the exponential distributed parameter (DP) R-Y-NR structure. For structure of length L and ac signal, they are identified as [8]:

$$g = \cosh(mL) + \frac{K}{2}\sinh(mL) \quad (9)$$

$$\omega = \text{angular frequency} = 2\pi f$$

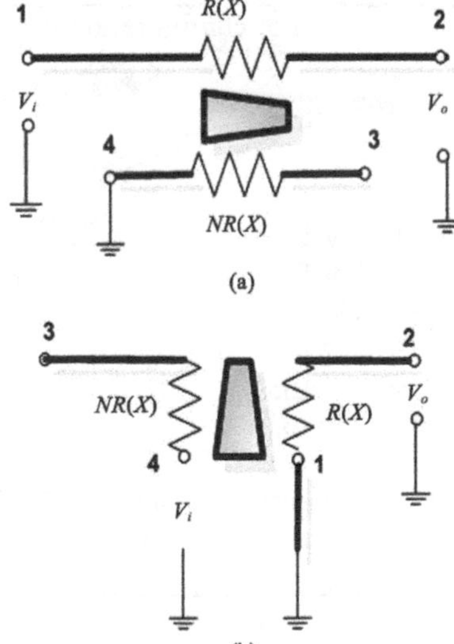

Figure 4. (a) IOFG configuration: 1-input, 2-output, 3-floating and 4-Ground. (b) GOFI configuration: 1-ground, 2-output, 3-floating and 4-input.

For $N = 0$ which means that the second resistive layer is perfect conductive film, Equations (7) and (8) will respectively be abbreviated to:

$$a = m\exp\left(\frac{KL}{2}\right) \quad (10)$$

$$m = \sqrt{(K/2)^2 + (j\omega C_o + G_o)R_o(1+N)}$$

$$\omega = \text{angular frequency} = 2\pi f$$

For $N = 0$ which means that the second resistive layer is perfect conductive film, Equations (7) and (8) will respectively be abbreviated to:

From **Figure 4(a)**:

$$\frac{V_o}{V_i} = \frac{a}{g} \quad (11)$$

From **Figure 4(b)**:

$$\frac{V_o}{V_i} = \frac{g - a}{g} = 1 - \frac{a}{g} \quad (12)$$

Substituting the matrix parameter functions in the Equations (11) and (12) will respectively give:

From **Figure 4(a)**:

$$\frac{V_o}{V_i} = \frac{m\exp\left(\frac{KL}{2}\right)}{m\cosh(mL) + \frac{K}{2}\sinh(mL)} \quad (13)$$

From **Figure 4(b)**:

$$\frac{V_o}{V_i} = 1 - \frac{m\exp\left(\frac{KL}{2}\right)}{m\cosh(mL) + \frac{K}{2}\sinh(mL)} \quad (14)$$

Considering the uniform distributed thin film R-Y-NR network; that means the constant of exponential taper is zero ($K = 0$), and substituting in the Equations (13) and (14) leads respectively to get:

From **Figure 4(a)**:

$$\frac{V_o}{V_i} = \frac{m}{m\cosh(mL)} = \frac{1}{\cosh(mL)} = \text{Sech}(mL) \quad (15)$$

From **Figure 4(b)**:

$$\frac{V_o}{V_i} = 1 - \text{Sech}(mL) \quad (16)$$

where m is a complex angle per unit length and

$$m = \sqrt{j\omega C_o R_o + R_o G_o} \quad (17)$$

Then the complex angle is $mL = m \times L$ and

$$mL = \sqrt{j\omega C_o R_o L^2 + R_o G_o L^2} \quad (18)$$

Let $\frac{V_o}{V_i} = T_{v1}$ and $\frac{V_o}{V_i} = T_{v2}$ for circuit connection in **Figures 4(a)** and **(b)** respectfully.

Then:

$$T_{v1} = \text{Sech}(mL) \tag{19}$$

And:

$$T_{v2} = 1 - \text{Sech}(mL) \tag{20}$$

Subtracting (20) from (19) and manipulating the results lead to:

$$mL = \text{Sech}^{-1}\left(\frac{T_{v1} + 1 - T_{v2}}{2}\right)$$

And hence:

$$(mL)^2 = \left[\text{Sech}^{-1}\left(\frac{T_{v1} + 1 - T_{v2}}{2}\right)\right]^2 \tag{21}$$

From Equation (18):

$$(mL)^2 = j\omega C_o R_o L^2 + R_o G_o L^2 \tag{22}$$

Joining Equations (21) and (22) gives:

$$C = C_o L = \frac{\text{Im}\left[\text{Sech}^{-1}\left(\frac{T_{v1} + 1 - T_{v2}}{2}\right)\right]^2}{\omega R_o L} \tag{23}$$

$$G = G_o L = \frac{\text{Re}\left[\text{Sech}^{-1}\left(\frac{T_{v1} + 1 - T_{v2}}{2}\right)\right]^2}{R_o L} \tag{24}$$

3. Experimental Results

For sake of showing accuracy of the proposed method, shunt capacitance and shunt conductance measurements have been carried out on a certain MOS samples. These samples are accomplished by depositing a strip of NiCr resistor thin film as a gate contact and then depositing two dot aluminum points at the two ends of the strip for measurement purposes.

At the beginning, transfer function of the device has been measured for both configurations shown in **Figure 4**. Response of transfer function magnitude and its phase with respect to frequency have been plotted as shown in **Figures 5** and **6** respectively for positive gate biasing. For negative biasing, transfer function magnitude and phase responses have been plotted as shown in **Figures 7** and **8** respectively. Mat lab program has been used to compute shunt capacitance and shunt conductance for strip gate MOS structure at different frequencies. For a zero bias, shunt capacitance and shunt conductance of the MOS structure at different frequencies have been computed. The computed results and the results obtained using LCR meter method [9] have been plotted, as shown in **Figures 9** and **10**. It is clear that the results obtained from the two methods coincided with each other.

4. Conclusions

In this research the high frequency C-V and G-V device measurements were fulfilled using MOS structure as a

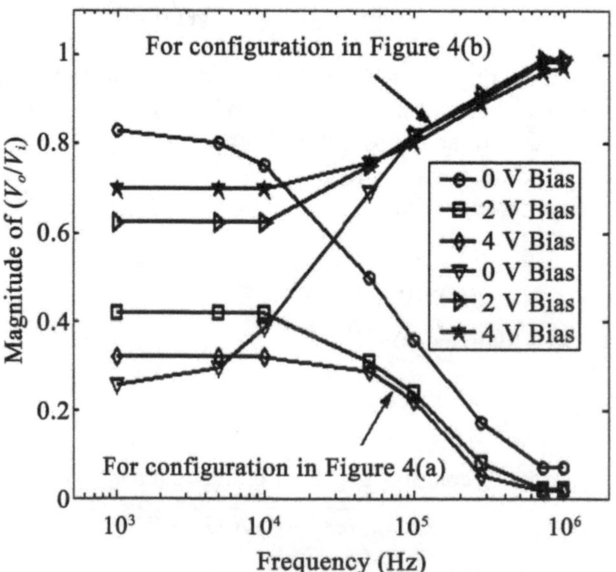

Figure 5. Transfer function magnitude frequency response of a strip gate MOS device for different positive biases.

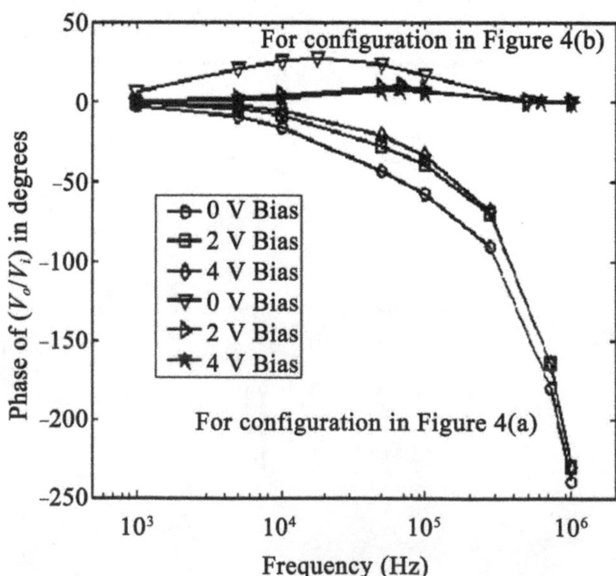

Figure 6. Transfer function phase frequency response of a strip gate MOS device for different positive biases.

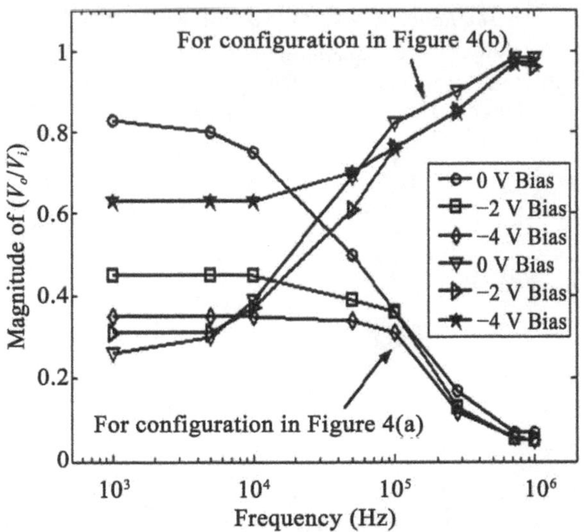

Figure 7. Transfer function magnitude frequency response of a strip gate MOS device for different negative biases.

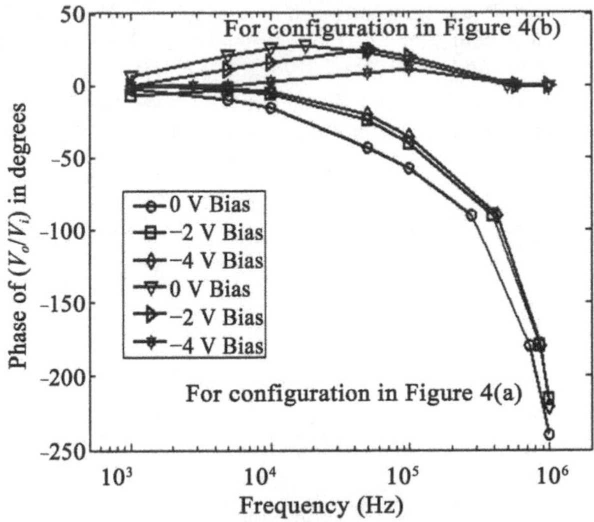

Figure 8. Transfer function phase frequency response of a strip gate MOS device for different negative biases.

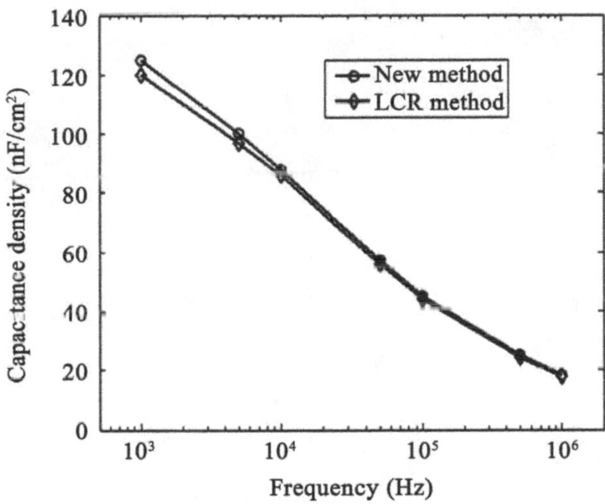

Figure 9. Comparison between capacitance determined by the two methods for zero bias.

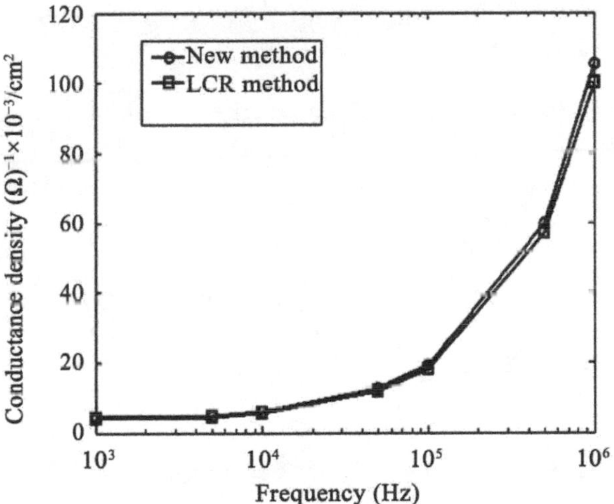

Figure 10. Comparison between leakage conductance dedetermined by the two methods for zero bias.

thin film distributed R-Y-NR structure with four terminal two port network. This conclusion encourage using the proposed method as a tool for C-V and G-V plots at any frequency.

5. References

[1] A. Meinertzhgen, C. Petit, M. Jourdain and F. Mondon, "Anode Hole Injection and Stress Induced Leakage Current Decay in Metal-Oxide-Semiconductor Capacitors," *Solid-State Electronics*, Vol. 44, No. 4, 2000, pp. 623-630.

[2] J. Singh, "Semiconductor Optoelectronics, Physics & Technology," McGraw-Hill, New York, 1995.

[3] W. Monch, "Electronic Properties of Ideal and Interface-Modified Metal-Semiconductor Interface," *Journal of Vacuum Science & Technology B*, Vol. 14, No. 4, 1996, p. 2985.

[4] B. B. Woo and J. M. Bartlemay, "Characteristics and Applications of a Tapered, Thin Film Distributed Parameter Structure," *IEEE International Convention Record*, Vol. 11, No. 2, 1963, pp. 56-75.

[5] K. U. Ahmed, "The Two Port Four Terminal Matrix Parameter Functions of Solvable Distributed Parameter Z--Y-KZ Network," *IEEE Transactions on Circuit Theory*, Vol. 19, No. 5, 1972, pp. 506-508.

[6] P. L. Swart and C. K. Campbell, "Effect of Losses and Parasitic on a Voltage-Controlled Tunable Distributed RC Notch Filter," *IEEE Journal of Solid-State Circuits*, Vol. 8, No. 1, 1973, pp. 35-36.

[7] K. U. Ahmed, "Two Port Sub-networks of Exponential

Distributed Parameter Z-Y-KZ and Y-Z-KY Micro-circuits with Similar Transfer Functions," *Micro Electron Reliable*, Vol. 21, No. 2, 1981, pp. 235-239.

[8] K. U. Ahmed, "A New Band-Reject Filter Configuration of Three-Layer Thin-Film Exponential R-C-KR," *Micro Electron Reliable*, Vol. 21, No. 2, 1981, pp. 241-242.

[9] P. Olivo, T. N. Nguyen and B. Ricco, "High-Field Induced Degradation in Ultra-thin SiO_2 Films," *IEEE Transactions on Electron Devices*, Vol. 35, No. 12, 1988, pp. 2259-2267.

21

A Review of PVT Compensation Circuits for Advanced CMOS Technologies

Andrey Malkov, Dmitry Vasiounin, Oleg Semenov
Freescale Semiconductor, Moscow, Russia

Abstract

The recent high-performance interfaces like DDR2, DDR3, USB and Serial ATA require their output drivers to provide a minimum variation of rise and fall times over Process, Voltage, and Temperature (PVT) and output load variations. As the interface speed grows up, the output drivers have been important component for high quality signal integrity, because the output voltage levels and slew rate are mainly determined by the output drivers. The output driver impedance compliance with the transmission line is a key factor in noise minimization due to the signal reflections. In this paper, the different implementations of PVT compensation circuits are analyzed for cmos45 nm and cmos65 nm technology processes. One of the considered PVT compensation circuits uses the analog compensation approach. This circuit was designed in cmos45 nm technology. Other two PVT compensation circuits use the digital compensation method. These circuits were designed in cmos65 nm technology. Their electrical characteristics are matched with the requirements for I/O drivers with respect to DDR2 and DDR3 standards. DDR2 I/O design was done by the Freescale wireless design team for mobile phones and later was re-used for other high speed interface designs. In conclusion, the advantages and disadvantages of considered PVT control circuits are analyzed.

Keywords: PVT Compensation, PVT Control Circuit, Process Variation, DDR Interface, I/O Driver

1. Introduction

In any manufacturing step during the fabrication process of ICs, there are target specifications and there are manufacturing tolerances around each specification. For example, the gate oxide thickness specification translates to slower devices (higher threshold voltage) for thicker oxides and faster devices for thinner oxides (lower threshold voltage). If such devices were used as a driver element, large variations in driver strengths and slew rates from the pre-driver should be expected. This is turn affects the timing of the outgoing signals.

Providing the higher data processing rate and interface speed are becoming more important to the evolution of multimedia environment. For example, the speed of modern storage interfaces (ATA/ATAPI-6 standard) has rapidly increased up to 100 MB/s [1]. The recent high-performance interfaces like DDR2, DDR3, USB and Serial ATA require their output drivers to provide a minimum variation of rise and fall times over process, voltage, and temperature (PVT) and output load variations. As the interface speed grows up, the output drivers have been important component for high quality signal integrity, because the output voltage levels and slew rate are mainly determined by the output drivers. Any decrease in the skews variation depending on the PVT variations can usually be translated into better timing budgets and signal integrity, resulting in the increase of system I/O speed. To achieve good signal integrity, slew rate also must be kept constant over PVT variations. Large slew rate induces significant switching noise (Ldi/dt noise) and small slew rate decrease the signal timing margin. One method to improve system speed is to provide circuit compensation. The compensation allows the designer to speed up the slower I/O driver and receiver speeds and increase the driver strength for the slow part. At the same time, the fast part is slowed down to match the slow part in speed and drive strength. Various compensation architectures have been previously reported for PVT variation [2-5] and most of them use external resistors to generate a bias current. Generally, the PVT control circuits can be classified on two types with (1) analog and (2) digital compensation methods, as it shown in **Figure 1**. In this paper, the different implementations of PVT compensation circuits are analyzed for cmos45 nm and cmos65 nm technology processes. These new PVT circuits are used for compensation of output resistance variation of high speed DDR I/O drivers implemented in sub-100 nm bulk and SOI technologies. In deep submicron technologies, the PVT control is extremely important due to the higher process variations and process instability. One of the considered PVT compensation circuits uses the analog compensation approach.

This circuit was designed in the cmos45nm SOI technology. The second PVT compensation circuit uses the digital compensation method. This circuit was designed in the cmos65nm bulk technology and its electrical characteristics are matched with the requirements for I/O driver with respect to DDR3 standard. In conclusion, the advantages and disadvantages of considered PVT control circuits are analyzed.

2. Scope of the Problem

One practical method of communication between chips is the transmission lines on a printed circuit boards (PCB). These transmission lines are fast and very economical, which explains their popularity. Generally, these transmission lines are thick metal wires (~1 mil) with a polymer dielectric surrounding it. The driver, the transmission line and termination matching are key factors to clean signaling. Transmission lines that are not well terminated suffer from reflecting. These reflections interfere with signaling as a new data will be affected by the remnants of the previous data that have not settled down. It is very well known that the good impedance matching of I/O driver and transmission line reduces the signal reflection in a transmission line. In this paper, the presented PVT compensation circuits are used for impedance matching of I/O driver and transmission line under the process, voltage and temperature variations.

3. Analog Compensation: General Background

There are different implementations of analog PVT compensation circuits. Some of them are presented in **Figure 2**, where in option (a) transistor stacks reflects the stack up in a pre-driver and option (b) reflects a normal output buffer structure, which directly compensates the output impedance under PVT variations. These schemes are based on equalizing the voltage drop across a resistor and transistor. The compensating device (NMOS or PMOS) is compared to a known external resistor (R3 or R6) and the voltage is fed back to an operational amplifier (OA1 or OA2). The operational amplifier compares this voltage to a known reference voltage. Independing on the chip processing (fast or slow), the correct voltage is generated to make the device drains match the reference voltage. Using this compensation voltage, the I/O buffers can be biased. The strengths of drivers and pre-drivers can be adjusted by rationing the gate widths with respect to the compensated N and P devices. Before the compensating voltage can be used, it has to be distributed on the chip to each buffer. Since the distributed interconnection can couple noise from other digital signal lines and be lengthy, it should be closely shielded. An effective shield is the addition of power interconnects in parallel with the compensation voltage interconnect. For example, the analog voltage delivery scheme using Vss wires to shield and charge share the injected noise. The digital signals should not run in parallel to the analog signals.

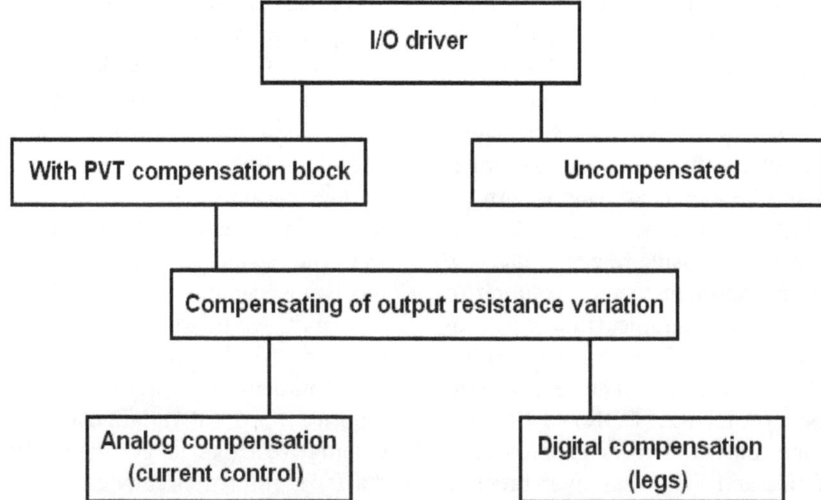

Figure 1. Compensation schemes used for control of output resistance compensation of I/O drivers.

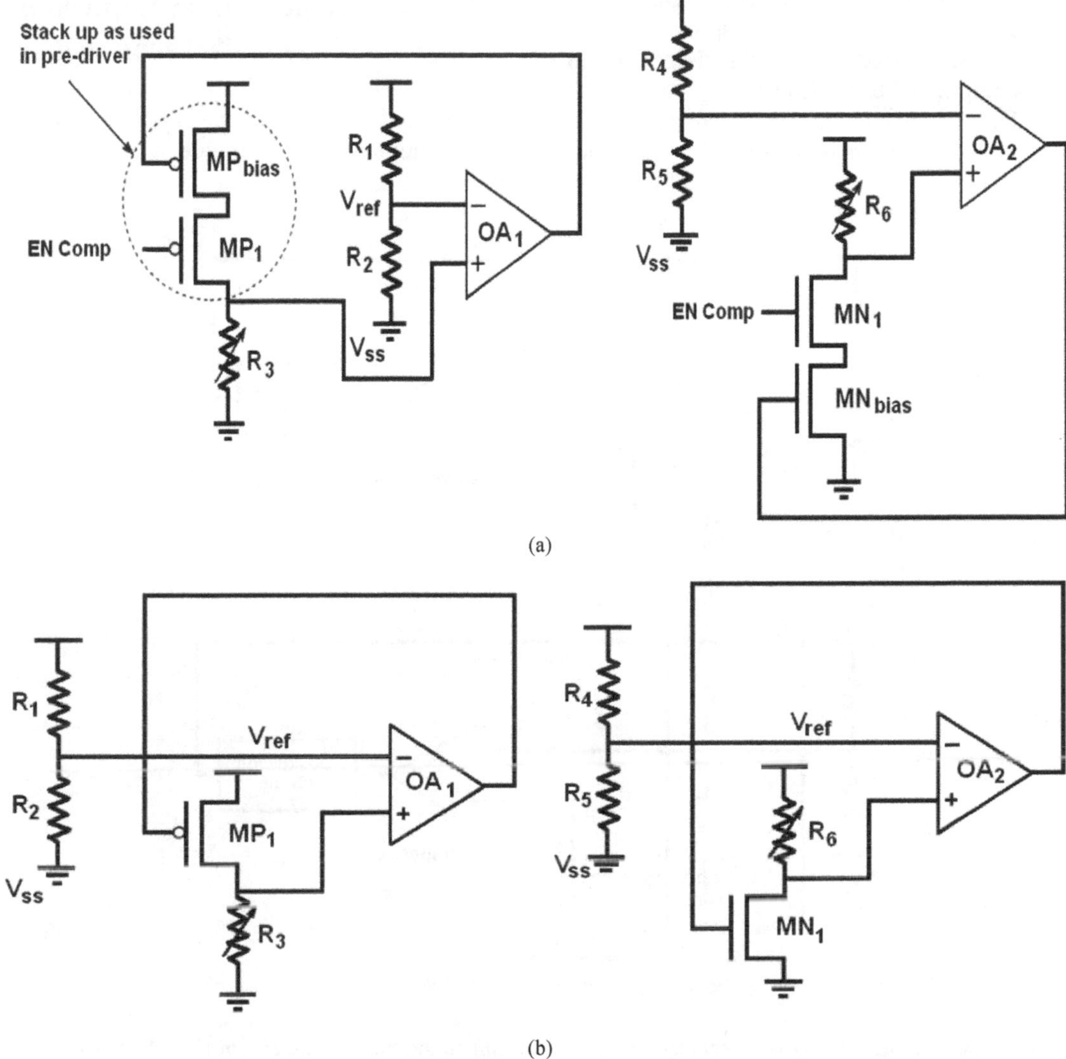

Figure 2. (a) Analog bias generation scheme that can be used to compensate I/O buffers: transistor stack reflects the stack up in a pre-driver (adopted from [6]); (b) Analog bias generation scheme that can be used to compensate I/O buffers: this option is convenient since it reflects a normal output buffer structure (adopted from [6]).

4. Digital Compensation: General Background

The analog techniques are sensitive to noise, as all other analog schemes. This is true in the generation of the compensation voltage and its distribution. An option is to use digital compensation techniques. On of such methods is given in **Figure 3**. Here a circuit similar to the analog case may be used to generate the compensation factor (a series of bits). The calibration transistor is broken into sections. Each leg is then controlled by a control bit. All the "on" legs together represent the driver strength. The control bits are derived from a counter that is fed by a comparator. The comparator senses the voltage division between the resistor and transistor legs and compares it to a reference voltage. A key difference between analog and digital compensation is that in the digital scheme when a leg is turned on it is fully on (Vcc at the gate of an NMOS device), unlike the analog case where all the legs are partially on.

The digital comparator can change states as the feedback loop time permits. The distribution of digital compensated signals is easier because they are all at normal CMOS voltage levels and not at an intermediate analog level, and thus they are less noise sensitive.

One of the implementation of digitally-impedance-controlled output buffer circuit was developed by T. Takahashi *et al.* [5]. This circuit is suitable for chips with a high I/O count due to its stable impedance against various kinds of noise. Impedance of the pull-up NMOS and pull-down NMOS are set to transmission line impedance for obtaining an accurate midpoint level and for avoiding reflection. The schematic of digitally-impedance-controlled output buffer circuit is shown in **Figure 4**. In this circuit, the input buffer judges 0.6 V as a "High", when the output of its output buffer is "Low" and "Low" when the output is "High". This is accomplished by the adjustable voltage divider which is controlled by the core input signal (Din).

5. Digital Compensation: Implementation in CMOS065 nm Bulk Technology

In this section, two practical implementations of digital PVT compensation technique are analyzed for DDR2 and DDR3 I/O circuits.

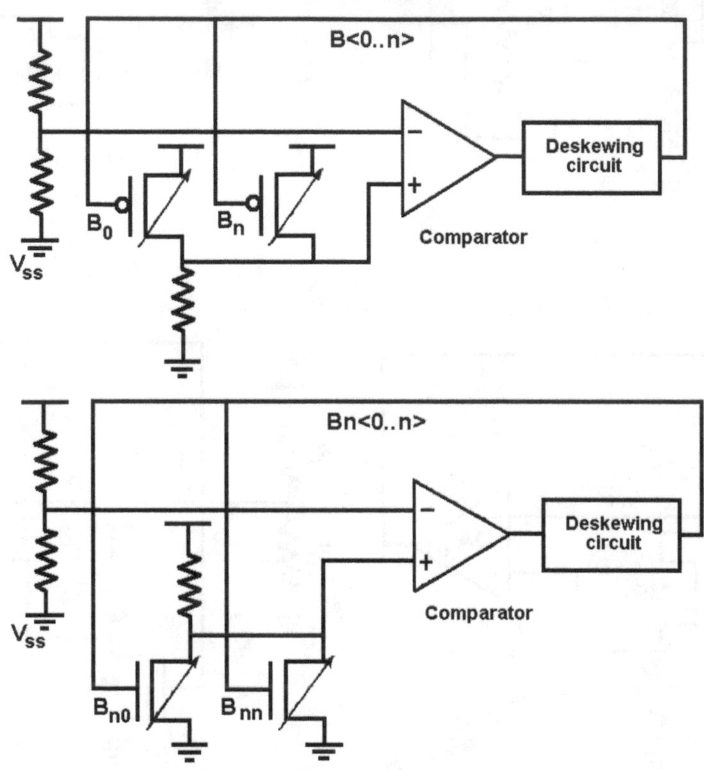

Figure 3. Concept of digital bias generation scheme. It may be similar to analog scheme except that the transistors are not one device but a number of parallel bits capable of being switched on and off independently (adopted from [6]).

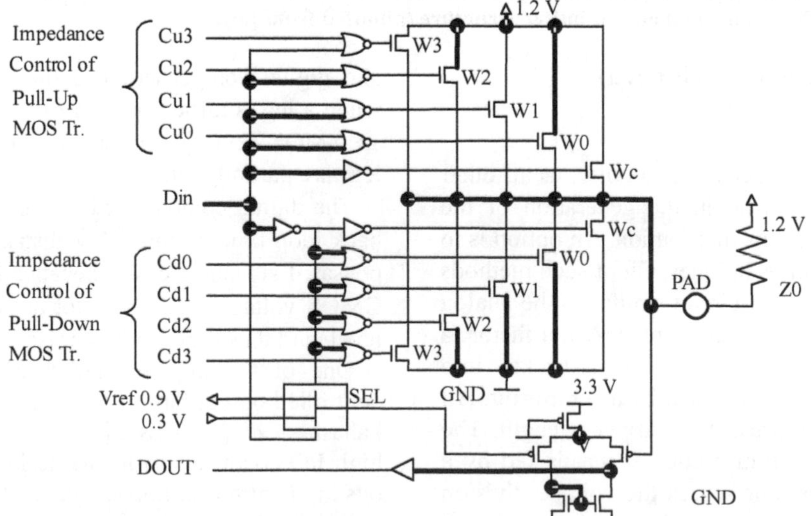

Figure 4. Digitally-impedance-controlled bidirectional I/O circuit [7].

In DDR2 I/O cell, the PVT control circuit consists on PVT sensor block, which is used to track the PVT conditions, and output driver block, which is split on several Legs that are used for the adjustment of output driver impedance according to the detected PVT condition [8]. The schematic of PVT control block is presented in **Figure 5**. The PVT sensor block includes ring oscillator, digital frequency decoder and level shifter. The ring oscillator uses the same OVDD power supply as the DDR drivers in the pad ring. The changing of junction temperature, operating voltage and process variation can be sensed as a changing of oscillation frequency. This oscillation frequency is correlated to the time constant of RC network within of ring oscillator. In the RC network, "R" is determined by the transistor impedance which is a scaled down replica of the output driver. And C represents the metal routing capacitance that has a very low temperature coefficient and has a weak process variation dependency. The ring oscillator output is divided by 256 times prior to the frequency decoder, as shown in **Figure 5**.

Figure 6 shows how the ring oscillator frequency depends on the PVT conditions. "Wcs" corresponds to the lowest frequency, "typ" case corresponds to the medium frequency and "bcs" corresponds to the max frequency. The frequency of ring oscillator is compared to the external reference clock signal (32 KHz CKIL clock). The PVT decoder analysis the difference and generates the 6 bits control signals (s0-s5) to switch ON or OFF the legs in output driver (see **Figure 7**).

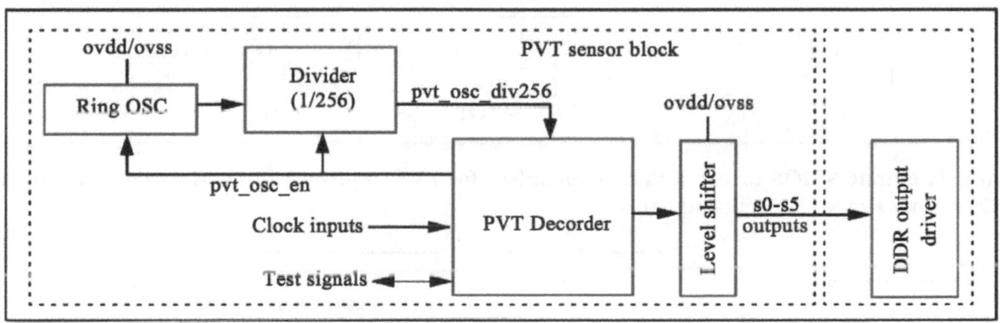

Figure 5. A PVT control circuit used in DDR2 I/O bank [this figure is courtesy of Kiyoshi Kase and Dzung T. Tran from Freescale Semiconductor].

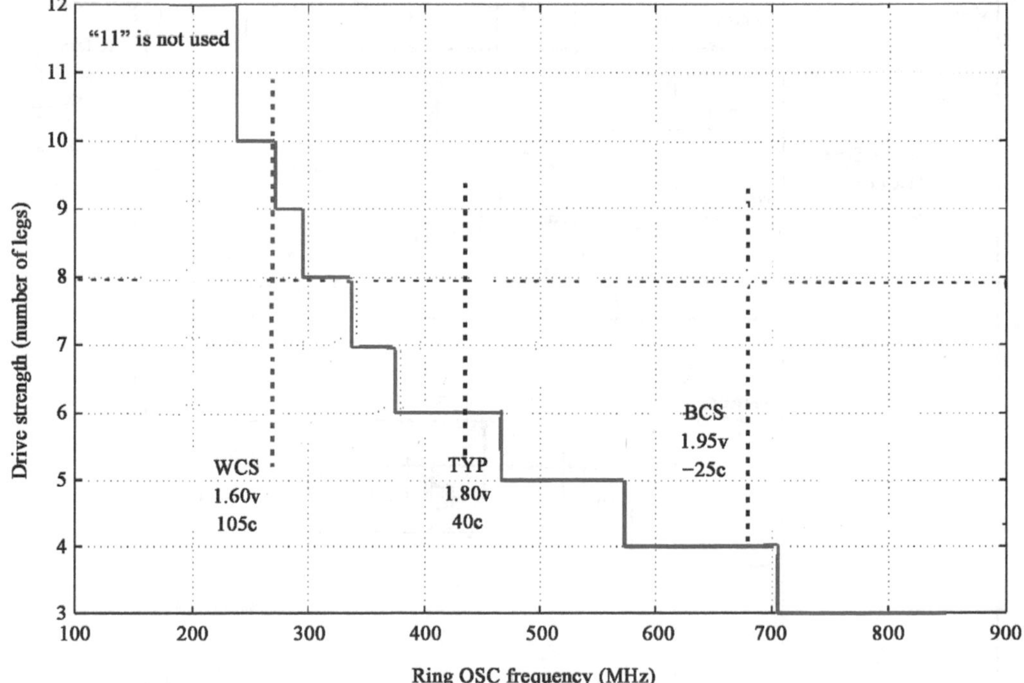

Figure 6. Ring oscillator frequency with respect to the number of output legs that should be connected to keep constant the impedance of output driver [this figure is courtesy of Kiyoshi Kase and Dzung T. Tran from Freescale Semiconductor].

Another digital PVT calibration approach was developed for CMOS065 DDR3 I/O cells set. It uses the external resistor for accurate adjustment of output driver impedance. The schematic of calibration circuit is presented in **Figure 8**. The calibration circuit consists on PMOS and NMOS output drivers that are connected to external resistor, comparator, reference voltage generator, and logical state machine for the generation of calibration signals.

The output NMOS and PMOS drivers have a major transistor, which has a slightly bigger resistance in "bcs" than the external reference resistor, and a number of legs. These are the additional transistors placed in parallel to the major transistor. These legs are used to reduce the total impedance of output driver and match it to the external resistor. In the calibration circuit, the combination of PMOS, NMOS transistors in output drivers and the external reference resistor forms the voltage divider. To monitor the voltage drop on the Xres pin, the comparator is used. It compares the voltage drop on the pin Xres and the reference voltage (OVDD/2) which is generated within of calibration circuit. During the calibration process, the logical state machine activates one by one the additional transistors (Legs) in output PMOS driver using the voh<4:0> signals. As a result, the effective resistance of output PMOS driver is reduced and the voltage drop on the Xres pin is increased. When the voltage drop on the Xres pin is increased to OVDD/2 (the switching

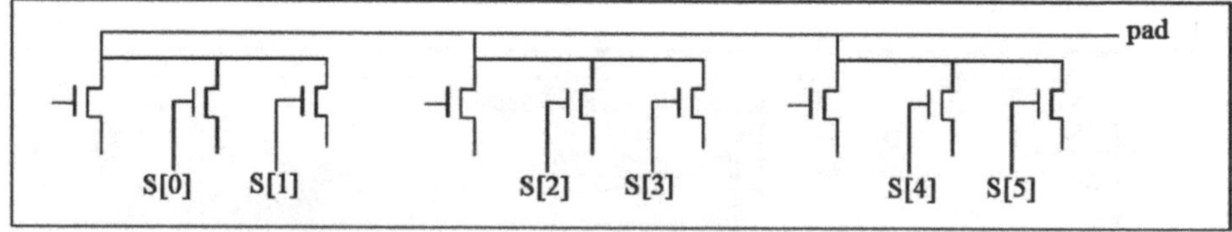

Figure 7. Example of output NMOS driver with additional legs for PVT adjustment [this figure is courtesy of Kiyoshi Kase and Dzung T. Tran from Freescale Semiconductor].

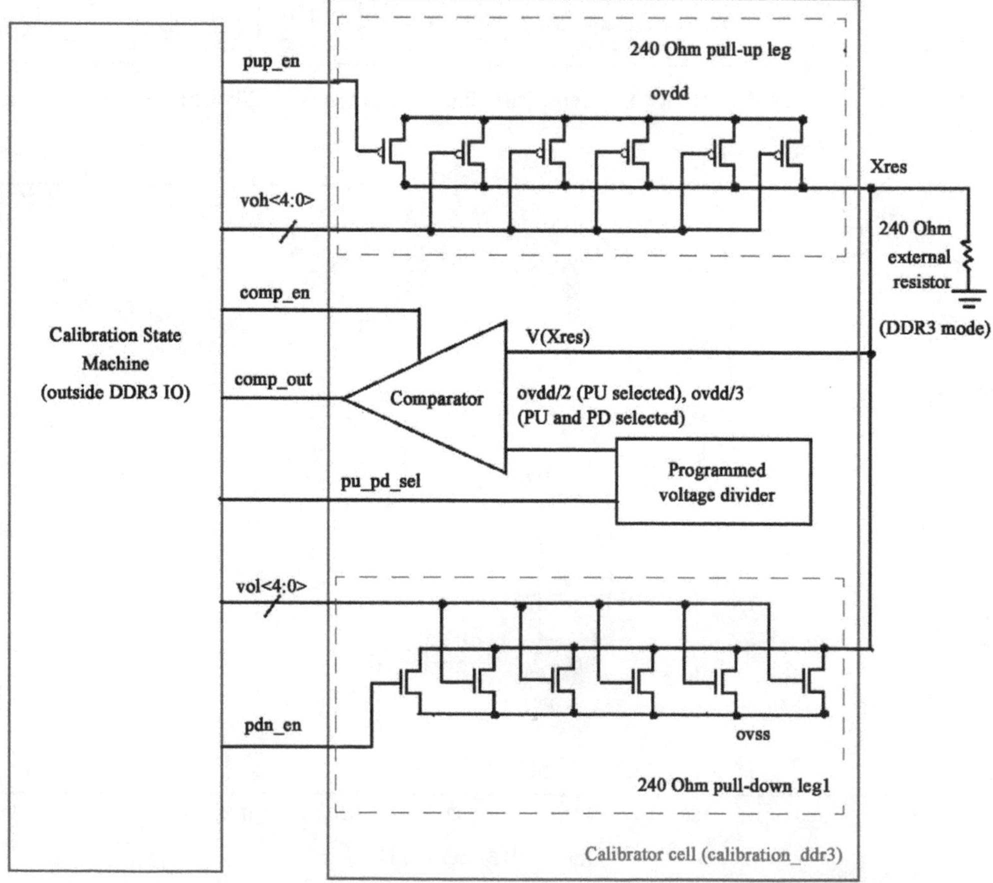

Figure 8. PVT calibration circuit developed for DDR3 I/O banks.

voltage for comparator), the output signal from comparator is changed from 0 to 1. It means that the calibration process of PMOS output driver is completed and the output driver impedance is equaled to the external reference resistor. The calibration codes are stored in the internal register. The next step is the calibration of NMOS output driver. To do this, the previously calibrated PMOS output driver is kept in ON mode and NMOS driver is also switched ON by the vol<4:0> signals. It is necessary because the reference resistor is connected between Xref and VSS. The calibration procedure of NMOS output driver is similar to the calibration process of PMOS output driver, except that the Xref voltage should be compared to OVDD/3 instead of OVDD/2 as it was for PMOS driver. This is because for the NMOS output driver calibration the voltage divider based on PMOS transistor and NMOS transistor with Rext resistor connected in parallel is used.

6. Analog Compensation: Implementation in CMOS045nm SOI Technology

The idea of analog compensation method is based on the control of output driver transconductance. In this method, the output driver of I/O buffer has stacked NMOS and PMOS transistors. One of the stacked transistors is managed by P-pre-driver and N-pre-driver, respectively, as it shown in **Figure 9**, and these transistors are operating in a switch ON/OFF mode. On the gate terminals of second transistors in the stacked transistor pairs are applied the Vbias_n and Vbias_p voltages that keep constant transconductance of stacked transistors under different PVT conditions.

Generally, the analog PVT compensation circuit consists on two major blocks: 1) PVT control block (**Figure 9**) and 2) Reference current block (**Figure 10**). The reference current block has the "OVDD/2" voltage divider, external resistor, operational amplifier and a couple current mirrors. The external resistor is used to specify the reference currents Iref_p and Iref_n that are not dependent on process corners and temperature, and are directly proportional to the OVDD/2 voltage.

The PVT control block consists on two stacked NMOS and PMOS devises and two operational amplifiers. The principle of PVT block operation is the same as the functionality of previously mentioned analog bias generation circuit shown in **Figure 2(a)**. The advantage of analog PVT compensation circuit developed for CMOS045 nm SOI technology is that it requires just one external reference resistor. Most of other implementations of analog PVT compensation circuits given in literature require two external resistors, for example circuit presented in **Figure 2(a)** or circuit developed by Seok-Woo Choi *et al.* [9].

7. Conclusions

In this paper several different implementations of PVT compensation circuits are analyzed for cmos45 nm and cmos65 nm technology processes. One of the considered PVT compensation circuits uses the analog compensation approach. This circuit was designed in cmos045 nm SOI technology. Other two PVT compensation circuits use the digital compensation method. Theses circuits were designed in cmos065 nm technology and their electrical characteristics were matched with the requirements for I/O driver with respect to DDR2 and DDR3 standards.

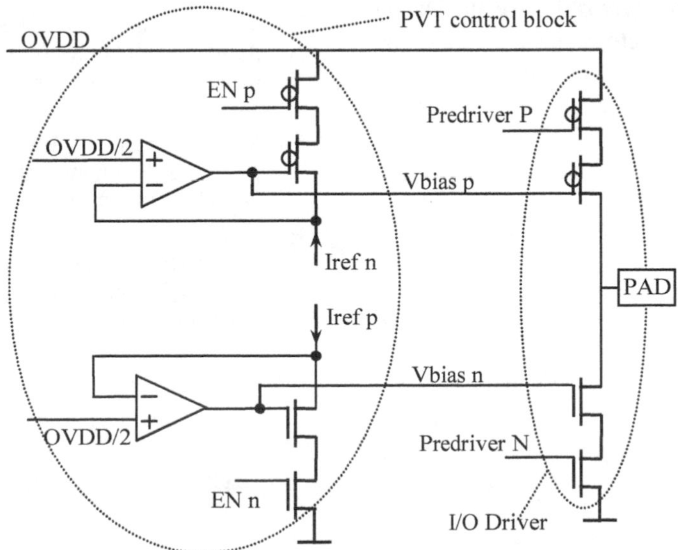

Figure 9. Implementation of PVT control block.

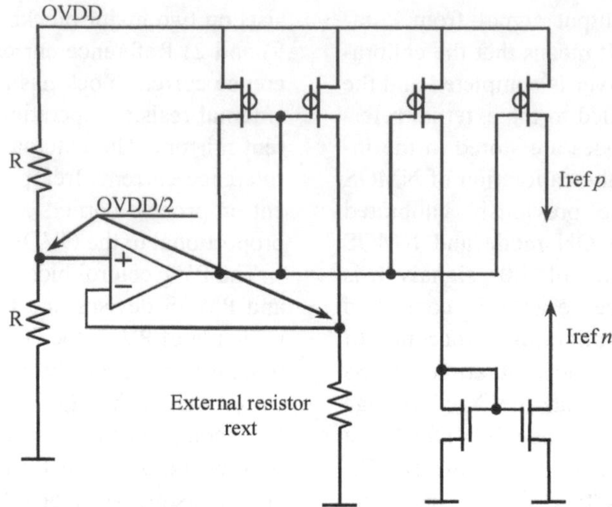

Figure 10. Reference current block.

The advantage of analog-based PVT compensation circuit is that its layout area is typically smaller than the layout area consumed by the digital-based PVT compensation circuit. However, the digital-based PVT compensation circuit is recommended for chips with high I/O count due to its stable impedance against various kinds of noise. Finally, in case of uncompensated I/O drivers, the effect of PVT variations can be reduced by the placement of poly-silicon resistor in series to the transistor of output driver. Typically, poly-silicon resistor has low dependency on PVT variations and it is designed to have significantly higher resistance than the output driver transistor.

8. Acknowledgements

The authors would like to thank Kiyoshi Kase and Dzung T. Tran (Freescale Semiconductor) for providing the figures, reviewing of manuscript and useful comments.

9. References

[1] ATA/ATA-6 Specification, 2001. http://www.t13.org/Documents/UploadedDocuments/project/d1410r3b-ATA-ATAPI-6.pdf

[2] S.-W. Choi and H.-J. Park, "A PVT-Insensitive CMOS Output Driver with Constant Slew Rate," *IEEE Asia-Pacific Conference on Advanced System Integrated Circuits*, Tainan, Taiwan, 4-5 August 2004, pp. 116-119.

[3] H. Chi, D. Stout and J. Chickanosky, "Process, Voltage and Temperature Compensation of off-Chip-Driver Circuits for Sub-0.25-pm CMOS Technology," *10th Annual IEEE International ASIC Conference and Exhibit*, Portland, 7-10 September 1997, pp. 279-282.

[4] H.-S. Jeon, D.-H. You and I.-C. Park, "Fast Frequency Acquisition All-Digital PLL Using PVT Calibration," *IEEE International Symposium on Circuits and Systems*, Seattle, 18-21 May 2008, pp. 2625-2628.

[5] Y. Tsugita, K. Ueno, T. Hirose, T. Asai and Y. Amemiya, "On-Chip PVT Compensation Techniques for Low-Voltage CMOS Digital LSIs," *IEEE International Symposium on Circuits and Systems*, Taipei, Taiwan, 24-27 May 2009, pp. 1565-1568.

[6] S. Dabral and T. Maloney, "Basic ESD and I/O Design," John Wiley & Sons Inc., New York, 1998.

[7] T. Takahashi, M. Uchida and T. Takashi, "A CMOS Gate Array with 600 Mb/s Simultaneous Bidirectional I/O Circuit," *IEEE Journal of Solid-State Circuits*, Vol. 30, No. 12, 1995, pp. 1544-1546.

[8] K. Kase and D. T. Tran, "Performance Variation Compensating Circuit and Method," US Patent No.: US7,508, 246B2, 24 March 2009.

[9] S.-W. Choi and H.-J. Park, "A PVT-Insensitive CMOS Output Driver with Constant Slew Rate," *IEEE Asia-Pacific Conference on Advanced System Integrated Circuits*, Fukuoka, 4-5 August 2004, pp. 116-119.

22

A Thyristor-Only Input ESD Protection Scheme for CMOS RF ICs*

Jin Young Choi, Choongkoo Park
Electronic & Electrical Engineering Department, Hongik University, Chungnam, South Korea

Abstract

We propose an input protection scheme composed of thyristor devices only without using a clamp NMOS device in order to minimize the area consumed by a pad structure in CMOS RF ICs. For this purpose, we suggest low-voltage triggering thyristor protection device structures assuming usage of standard CMOS processes, and attempt an in-depth comparison study with a conventional thyristor protection scheme incorporating a clamp NMOS device. The comparison study mainly focuses on robustness against the HBM ESD in terms of peak voltages applied to gate oxides in an input buffer and lattice heating inside protection devices based on DC and mixed-mode transient analyses utilizing a 2-dimensional device simulator. We constructed an equivalent circuit for the input HBM test environment of the CMOS chip equipped with the input ESD protection devices. And by executing mixed-mode simulations including up to four protection devices and analyzing the results for five different test modes, we attempt a detailed analysis on the problems which can occur in real HBM tests. We figure out strength of the proposed thyristor-only protection scheme, and suggest guidelines relating the design of the protection devices and circuits.

Keywords: ESD Protection, HBM, Thyristor, Mixed-Mode Simulation, RF ICs

1. Introduction

CMOS chips are vulnerable to electrostatic discharge (ESD) due to thin gate oxides used, and therefore protection devices such as NMOS transistors are required at input pads. A large size for the protection devices is needed to reduce discharge current density and thereby to protect them against thermal-related problems. However, using a large size tends to increase parasitic capacitances added to input nodes generating problems such as gain reduction and poor noise characteristics in RF ICs [1].

To reduce the added parasitics, the protection schemes utilizing thyristor or diode protection devices were suggested [2,3] and have been used as fundamental protection schemes in RF ICs. In the protection scheme utilizing thyristor or diode protection devices, it is conventional to include a V_{DD}-V_{SS} clamp NMOS device in the input pad structure to provide discharge paths for all possible human-body model (HBM) test modes [4]. A large size for the clamp NMOS device is essential to prevent thermal device failure. Even though the clamp NMOS device does not add parasitics to the input node since it is not connected to it, adopting a large size makes the design to consume an excessive area for the pad structure. This requirement can be a serious limitation in a chip where a pad size is a critical issue in chip design.

In this paper, we suggest an input protection scheme utilizing low-voltage triggering thyristor devices only without using a clamp NMOS device in input pad structure. This scheme can be implemented into input pad structures of CMOS RF ICs to provide protection against HBM and MM (Machine mode) discharge events. We present a comparative analysis result of the proposed scheme and the conventional thyristor protection scheme incorporating a clamp NMOS device. The characteristics of the latter scheme are already presented in [4].

A 2-dimensional device simulator, together with a circuit simulator, is utilized as a tool for the comparative analysis. The analysis methodology utilizing a device simulator has been widely adopted with credibility [4-6] since it provides valuable information relating the mechanisms leading to device failure, which cannot be obtained by measurements only.

*This work was supported by 2010 Hongik University Research Fund. (*sponsors*)

In Section 2, we suggest low-voltage triggering thyristor protection device structures assuming usage of standard CMOS processes, and introduce device characteristics based on DC device simulations. In Section 3, we briefly explain discharge modes in HBM tests and introduce two input protection scheme utilizing the suggested protection devices. In Section 4, we construct an equivalent circuit model for CMOS chips equipped with the input protection devices to simulate various input HBM test situations, and execute mixed-mode transient simulations. Based on the simulation results, we figure out weak modes in real discharge tests, and present in-depth analysis results relating critical characteristics such as peak voltages developed across gate oxides in input buffers, locations of peak temperature inside protection devices, and so on. In Section 5, based on the simulation results, considerations relating device and circuit design are discussed.

2. Protection Device Structures and DC Characteristics

Figure 1 shows the NMOS protection device structure assumed in this work, which is utilized as a V_{DD}-V_{SS} clamp device. The structure is same with the one suggested in [4]. The p^+ junctions located at the upper left/right corners represent diffusions for substrate ground contacts. A series resistor of 1 MΩ·μm, which is not shown in **Figure 1**, is connected at the bottom substrate node considering distributed resistances leading to substrate contacts located far away.

DC simulations were performed using a 2-dimensional device simulator ATLAS [7]. All necessary physical models including an impact ionization model and lattice-heating models were included in the simulations. The source, the gate, and the substrate were grounded, and the drain bias was varied for simulation.

Figure 2 shows simulated drain current vs. voltage characteristics of the NMOS device in **Figure 1** in a semi-log scale. The underlying physics relating the characteristics in **Figure 2** are fully explained in [4] previously. The device shows an n^+-drain/p-sub junction breakdown when the drain voltage is increased above 9.3 V. A generated hole current by avalanche flows to the substrate terminal to increase the body potential. With a sufficient hole current flowing, a parasitic lateral npn bipolar transistor is triggered. The source, the body, and the drain act as an emitter, a base, and a collector, respectively. As the BJT is being triggered, the required drain-source voltage is reduced to show a snapback, as indicated as "BJT trigger" in **Figure 2**. After the snapback at about 9.4 V, the drain-source voltage drops to about 4.6 V of a bipolar holding voltage.

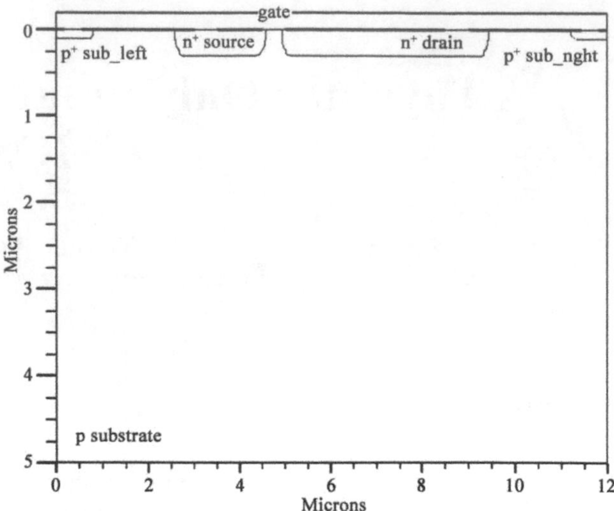

Figure 1. Cross section of the NMOS device.

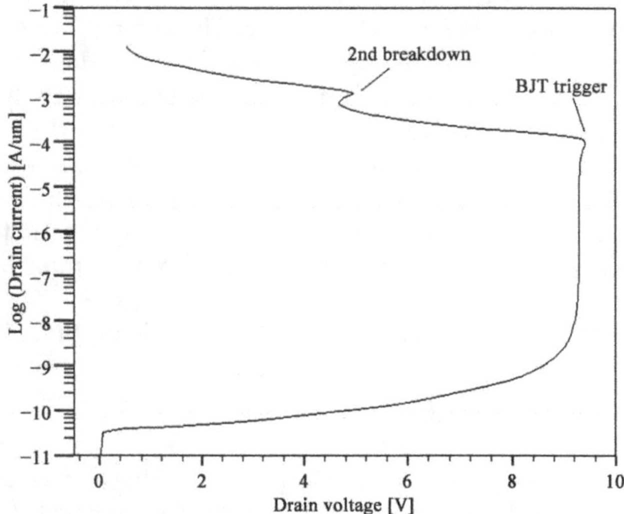

Figure 2. Drain I-V characteristics of the NMOS device.

Figure 3 shows the lvtr_thyristor_down device structure assumed in this work, which is used as a protection device between an input pad and a V_{SS} node. An lvtr_thyristor device is a pnpn-type device suggested to lower the snapback voltage by incorporating an NMOS transistor into it [2]. The drain/gate/source NMOS structure composed of the n^+ well (n^+ region at the right-hand corner of the n well), the gate, and the n^+ cathode is similar to the NMOS structure in **Figure 1**. However, it does not incorporate ESD implant steps, which is implied by the relatively shallow junctions. The structure shown in **Figure 3** is same with the one of the lvtr_thyristor device suggested in [4]. The NMOS gate oxide thickness, the gate length, the effective channel length, and the channel peak doping are same with those in **Figure 1**. A series resistor is also connected at the bottom substrate node as in the NMOS device in **Figure 1**.

The n^+ and p^+ anodes in **Figure 3** are tied together to serve as an anode. The cathode, the gate, and the substrate were grounded, and the anode bias was varied for simulation.

Figure 4 shows the simulated DC anode current vs. voltage characteristics of the lvtr_thyristor_down device in **Figure 3**. The underlying physics relating the characteristics in **Figure 4** are fully explained in [4] previously. The device shows an n^+-drain/p-sub junction breakdown when the anode voltage is increased to above 8.8 V. With a sufficient hole current flowing to the substrate terminal, the p-sub/n^+-cathode junction is forward biased triggering a lateral npn bipolar transistor. The n^+ well, the p substrate, and the cathode act as a collector, a base, and an emitter, respectively. At this situation, a snapback is monitored as shown in **Figure 4**. The collector current from the n^+ anode flows through the n well to decrease the potential of the region under the p^+ anode by an ohmic drop. When the collector current is large enough, the p^+-anode/n-well junction is forward biased to trigger a pnpn (p^+-anode/n-well/p-sub/n^+-cathode) thyristor, which causes another decrease in the anode voltage, as indicated as "pnpn trigger" in **Figure 4**. The resulting holding voltage drops to about 1 V, which is much smaller compared to 4.6 V of the NMOS device in **Figure 2**.

We note here that the device shown in **Figure 3** includes a well conducting thyristor by virtue of the larger n^+–p^+ anode space. This is verified by the fact that the current level for the pnpn trigger is not much higher than that for the bipolar trigger in **Figure 4**. As the anode space decreases, the current level for the pnpn trigger increases [8].

If we want to use the lvtr_thyristor_down device in **Figure 3** as a protection device between a V_{DD} node and a pad in a thyristor-only protection scheme, we should connect the p^+ anode and the n^+ anode to a V_{DD} node, and n^+ cathode to a pad, and the common p substrate to a V_{SS} node. In this case, however, we found that a serious problem occurs in a PD mode (a positive ESD voltage applied to a pad with a V_{DD} pin grounded) since there is no forward diode path from the pad to the V_{DD} node. Without the forward diode path provided, an npn (n^+-cathode/p-sub/n^+-anode) bipolar transistor conducts from the pad to the V_{DD} node to cause a thermal-related problem with a larger holding voltage. **Figure 5** shows the lvtr_thyristor_up device, which is suggested in this work to solve the problem. The device apparently includes a forward diode path from the cathode to the anode.

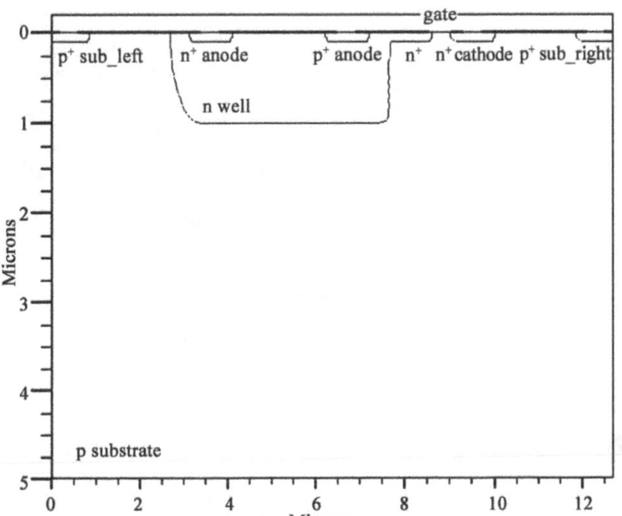

Figure 3. Cross section of the lvtr_thyristor device.

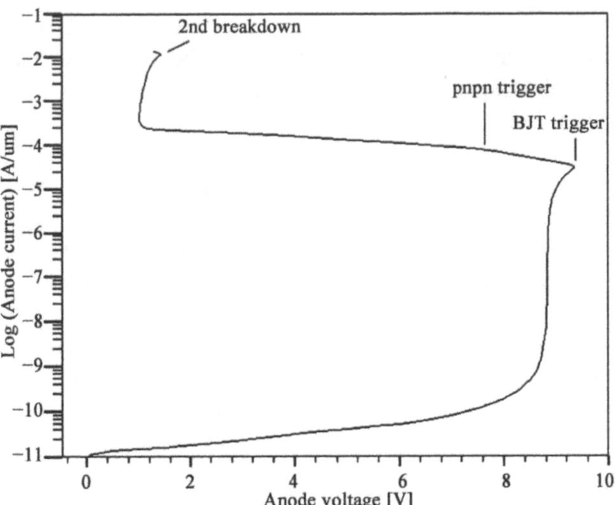

Figure 4. Anode I-V characteristics of the lvtr_thyristor device.

As we can see in **Figure 5**, the device needs addition of a p base region, which is provided in most of standard CMOS processes below 0.35 μm to allow forming simple bipolar transistors. Depth of the p-base region was assumed as 0.5 μm, and the base is assumed to have a channel peak doping of 2.35×10^{17} cm^{-3}, which is similar to that of the NMOS structure in the lvtr_thyristor_down device. Doping profiles of the n well, the n^+ and p^+ junctions are same with those in the the lvtr_thyristor_down device.

The NMOS transistor, which is incorporated in the device to lower the snapback voltage, is located inside the p base. The n^+ well (n^+ region at the left-hand corner of the p base), the gate, and the n^+ cathode play the role of the drain, the gate, and the source, respectively. The NMOS structure in the device is very similar to that in the lvtr_thyristor_down device except a small difference in the acceptor doping profile in the body region. We note that, in deep n-well processes, a p well separated from a p substrate can replace the p base.

The n^+ and p^+ anodes in **Figure 5** are tied together to serve as an anode. The n^+ and p^+ cathodes, the gate, and the substrate were grounded, and the anode bias was varied for simulation.

Figure 6 shows the simulated DC anode current vs. voltage characteristics of the lvtr_thyristor_up device in **Figure 5**. The characteristics and the underlying physics are very similar to those of the lvtr_thyristor_down device except that an npn bipolar transistor is formed by the n^+-well/p-base/n^+-cathode structure and a pnpn thyristor is formed by the p^+-anode/n-well/p-base/n^+-cathode structure. The breakdown voltage in this device corresponds to that of the n^+-well/p-base junction.

Table 1 summarizes the principal DC characteristics of the three protection devices.

3. ESD Protection Schemes

Since parasitics added to an input pad should be minimized, it is desired to connect fewer number of protection devices to an input pad. An effective way to reduce the number is to use a V_{DD}-V_{SS} clamp device since it provides discharge paths without adding parasitics to an input pad. **Figure 7** shows a popular ESD protection scheme utilizing a thyristor device, which minimizes the added parasitics and is chosen for a comparison study with the thyristor-only protection scheme in this work. A CMOS inverter was assumed as an input buffer.

The lvtr_thyristor_down device in **Figure 3** is used for T_1 in **Figure** 7. The NMOS device in **Figure 1** is used for M_2. In M_2, the drain is connected to V_{DD}, and the gate, the source, and the substrate are connected to V_{SS}. In T_1, the p^+ and n^+ anodes are connected to the pad, and the p substrate and the n^+ cathode are connected to V_{SS}. The NMOS gate (G_1) in T_1 is also connected to V_{SS} to maintain an off state in normal operations.

It is important to locate all the protection devices close to the pad to minimize variation of the gate voltage in the input buffer when an ESD voltage is applied to the pad. Even though same discharge paths can be provided with V_{DD}-V_{SS} clamp devices located in other places, there exists an enhanced danger of oxide failure since the voltage applied to the gate oxide of the input buffer may increase due to added high voltage drops in power bus lines with a large discharge current flowing.

Figure 8 shows the thyristor-only protection scheme suggested in this work. The lvtr_thyristor_down device in **Figure 3** is used for T_1, and the lvtr_thyristor_up device in **Figure 5** is used for T_2. Connection of T_1 is same as that in **Figure** 7. In T_2, the p^+ and n^+ anodes are connected to V_{DD}, and the p^+ and n^+ cathodes are connected to the pad. The NMOS gate (G_2) in T_2 is connected to the pad to maintain an off state in normal operations. Although it is not shown in **Figure 8**, the p substrate in T_2 is connected to V_{SS}.

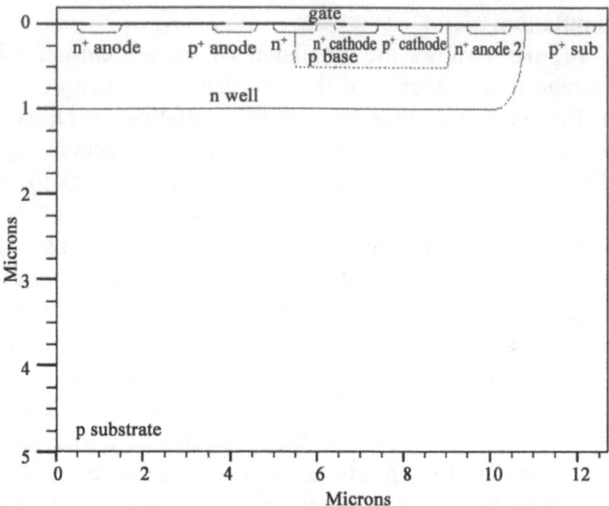

Figure 5. Cross section of the diode device.

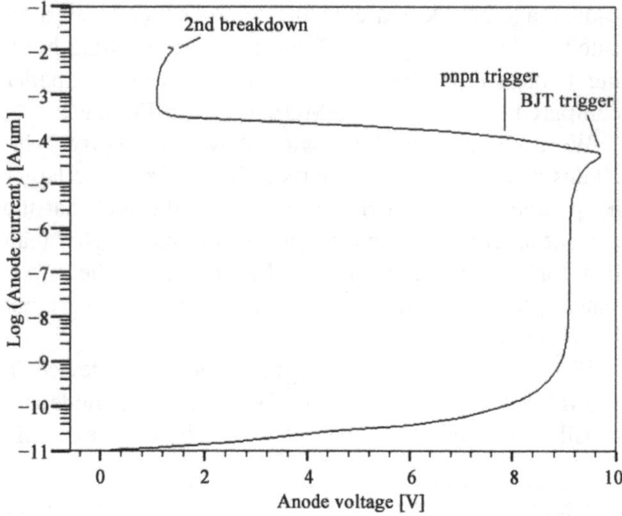

Figure 6. Anode current-voltage characteristics of the lvtr_thyristor_up device.

Table 1. Principal principal DC characteristics of the protection devices.

Protection device	Holding Voltage	Breakdown voltagee	Snapback voltagee
NMOS	4.6 V	9.3 V	9.4 V
lvtr_thyristor_down	1.0 V	8.8 V	9.4 V
lvtr_thyristor_up	1.1 V	9.1 V	9.7 V

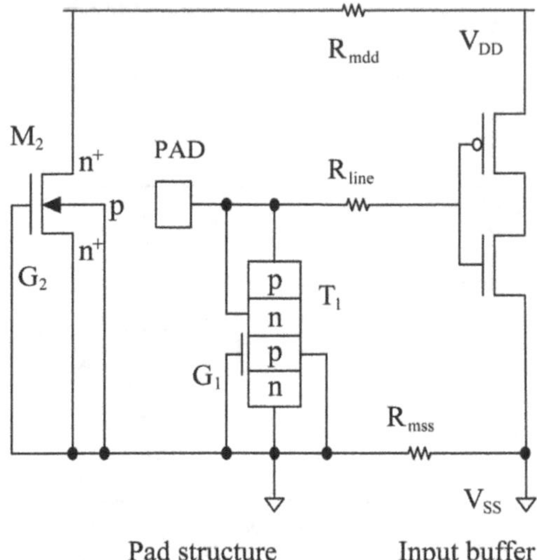

Figure 7. Protection scheme (1) utilizing a thyristor device.

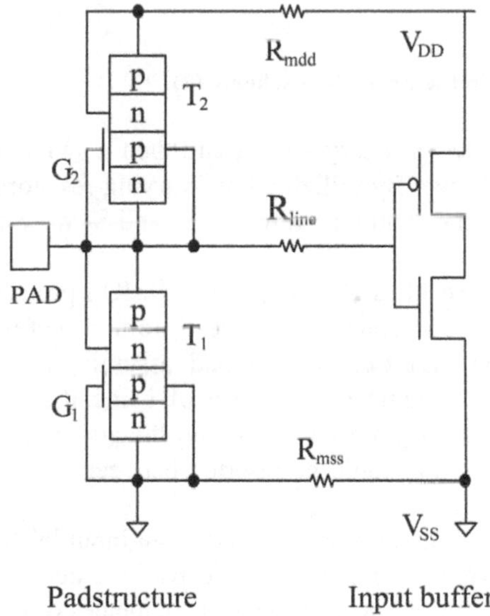

Figure 8. Protection scheme (2) utilizing thyristor devices only.

Input protection schemes utilizing thyristor devices only had been suggested [9,10]; however the trigger voltages of the suggested devices are too high [9] to be used in recent technologies, or the trigger voltages for the two LVTSCR thyristor devices are uneven [10] due to a difference in hole and electron mobilities resulting uneven trigger voltage for different HBM test modes, which is certainly not beneficial, and the PMOS-triggered thyristor structure does not provide a forward diode path from a pad to a V_{DD} node [10] to make the complementary-LVTSCR structure hard to be optimized.

While the amount of added capacitance to an input pad is expected to increase to about twice of that in case of using the protection scheme (1), the area consumed by a pad structure is expected to be reduced a lot by eliminating the clamp NMOS device, and the peak voltages applied to gate oxides of input buffers can be reduced somewhat since the series clamp NMOS device disappears in a discharge path.

Since HBM tests for input pins should include all possible discharge modes, tests are performed for five modes defined as PS, NS, PD, ND, and PTP modes [4].

Main discharge paths for test modes in each protection scheme are shown in **Figures 9** and **10**.

Figure 9 shows main discharge paths for each test mode when using the protection scheme (1). In a PS mode, a pnpn thyristor in T_1 provides a main discharge path, and in an NS mode, a forward-biased pn (p^+-sub/n^+-anode) diode in T_1 provides it. In a PD mode, a pnpn thyristor in T_1 and a forward-biased pn (p^+-sub/n^+-drain) diode in M_2 in series provide a main discharge path, and in an ND mode, a parasitic npn bipolar transistor in M_2 and a forward-biased pn (p^+-sub/n^+-anode) diode in T_1 in series provides it. In a PTP mode, a pnpn thyristor in T_1 and a forward-biased pn (p^+-sub/n^+-anode) diode in T_3, which is located in the other pad, in series provide a main discharge path.

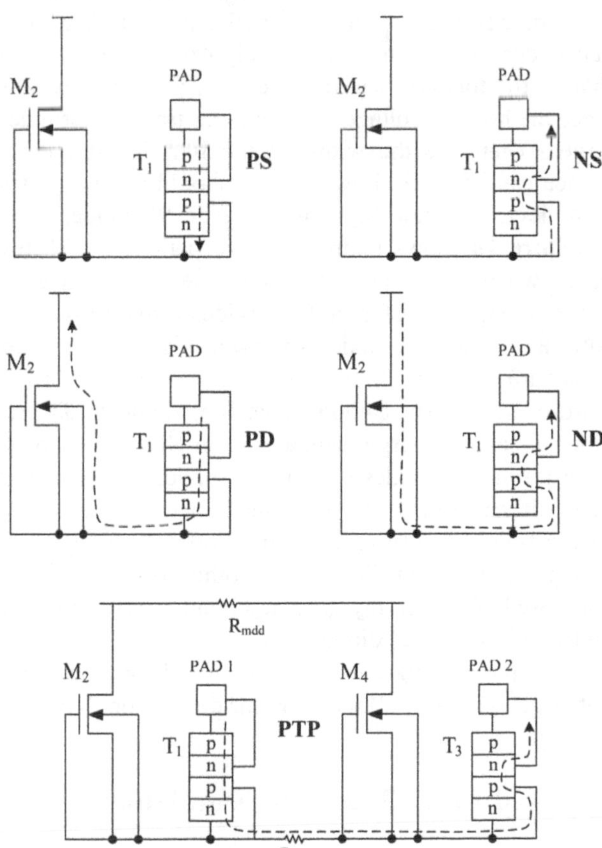

Figure 9. Main discharge paths for each test mode in the protection scheme (1).

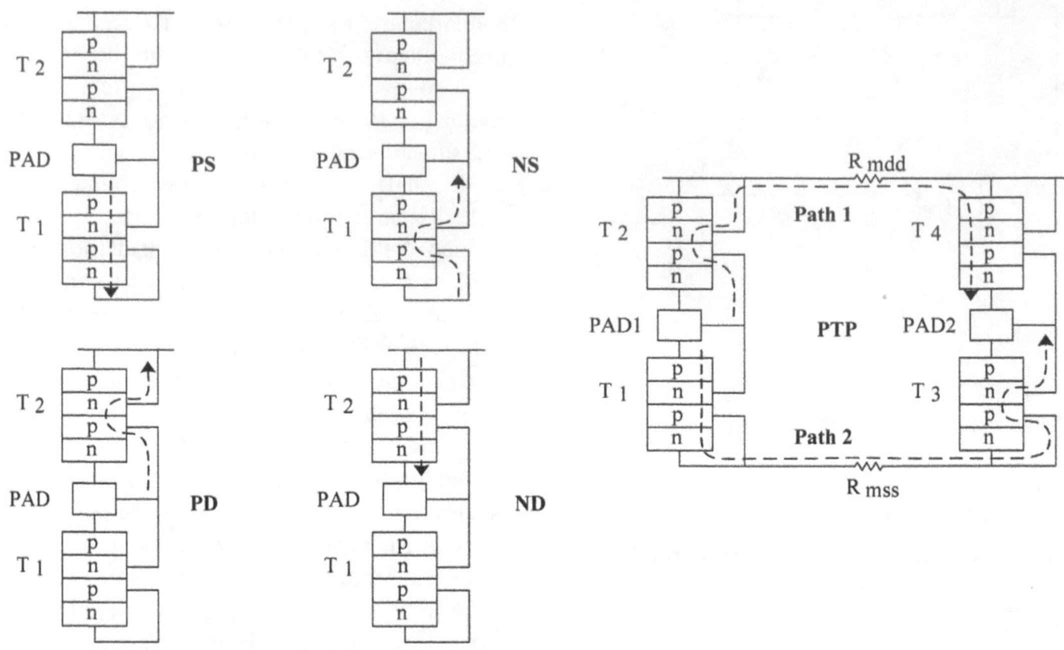

Figure 10. Main discharge paths for each test mode in the protection scheme (2).

Local lattice heating is proportional to a product of current density and electric field intensity, and therefore temperature-related problems in the protection devices can occur in the parasitic npn bipolar transistor rather than in the forward-biased diode or in the pnpn thyristor since the holding voltage of the bipolar transistor is much larger. Therefore the width of the lvtr_thyristor_down device can be small, however, we should assign a sufficient device width to M_2 considering an ND mode.

Figure 10 shows main discharge paths for each test mode when using the protection scheme (2). In a PS mode, a pnpn thyristor in T_1 provides a main discharge path, and in an NS mode, a forward-biased pn (p^+-sub/n^+-anode) diode in T_1 provides it. In a PD mode, a forward-biased pn (p^+-cathode/n^+-anode) diode in T_2 provides a main discharge path, and in an ND mode, a pnpn thyristor in T_2 provides it. In a PTP mode, there exist two main discharge paths. One is a series path composed of a forward-biased pn (p^+-cathode/n^+-anode) diode in T_2 and a pnpn thyristor in T_4, and the other is a series path composed of a pnpn thyristor in T_1 and a forward-biased pn (p^+-sub/n^+-anode) diode in T_3.

Since the holding voltages of the thyristor devices are not large, widths of all the thyristor devices don't need to be large.

4. Mixed-Mode Transient Simulations

Figure 11 shows an equivalent circuit of an input HBM test situation assuming a PS mode, which is fully explained in [4] previously. V_{ESD} is a HBM test voltage, and a switch S_1 charges C_{ESD} and then a switch S_2 initiates discharge. By utilizing time-varying resistors for the switches, the switching times of S_1 and S_2 were set short as 0.15 ns.

In **Figure 11**, a V_{DD}-V_{SS} clamp NMOS protection device M_2 and a protection device T_1 form a representative protection circuit in the input pad, assuming usage of the protection scheme (1). In case of using the protection scheme (2), M_2 is eliminated, and the additional protection device T_2 should be inserted between the V_{DD} node and the pad.

A CMOS inverter is assumed as an input buffer inside a chip, which is modeled by a capacitive network. C_{ngate} and C_{pgate} represent gate-oxide capacitances of an NMOS transistor and a PMOS transistor, respectively. C_{ds} represents an n-well/p-sub junction capacitance. 0.1 pF, 0.1 pF, and 0.01 pF were assumed for C_{ngate}, C_{pgate}, and C_{ds}, respectively.

Using ATLAS, we performed mixed-mode transient simulations utilizing the equivalent circuit in **Figure 11** equipped with two different input protection circuits shown in **Figures 7** and **8**. When a mixed-mode simulation is performed, the active protection devices are solved by device and circuit simulations simultaneously.

For all the mixed-mode transient simulations performed for each test mode, $V_{ESD} = \pm 2000$ V was assumed. To have fair comparison on ESD robustness of the different protection schemes, widths of the protection devices were adjusted to maintain utmost peak lattice temperature inside the protection devices below 500 K in all the mixed-mode simulations, resulting 250 μm, 20 μm, and 20 μm for M_2, T_1, and T_2, respectively.

As an example of the mixed-mode simulation results, **Figure 12** shows variation of the anode current of T_1 as a function of time in a PS mode in case of using the protection circuit (1) in **Figure** 7. The anode current peaks up to 1.37A, and shows decaying characteristics with a time constant of roughly $R_{ESD}C_{ESD}$ = 0.15 μs, which can be expected from the equivalent circuit in **Figure 11**.

Figure 13 shows variations of the voltages developed across C_{ngate} and C_{pgate} in the input buffer from the same simulation result. In **Figure 13**, the pad voltage is not shown since it is almost same with the voltage developed across C_{ngate}.

From the DC simulation result in **Figure 4**, we can estimate transient discharge characteristics of T_1, which lies in the main discharge path in this case. When a positive ESD voltage is applied, the developed voltage across the device will increases at least up to the snapback voltage (9.4 V). As the bipolar transistor and the pnpn thyristor are triggered in order, the developed voltage will drop down to the holding voltage (1 V) and main discharge will proceed. In the later stage of discharge when the discharge current decreases below the holding current for the thyristor action, the developed voltage will increase again at most up to the snapback voltage (9.4 V) and will remain constant around the breakdown voltage (8.8 V) for some duration even though the discharge current decreases. As the discharge current decreases further, the device will go out of the breakdown mode and the developed voltage will decrease towards zero to end the discharge.

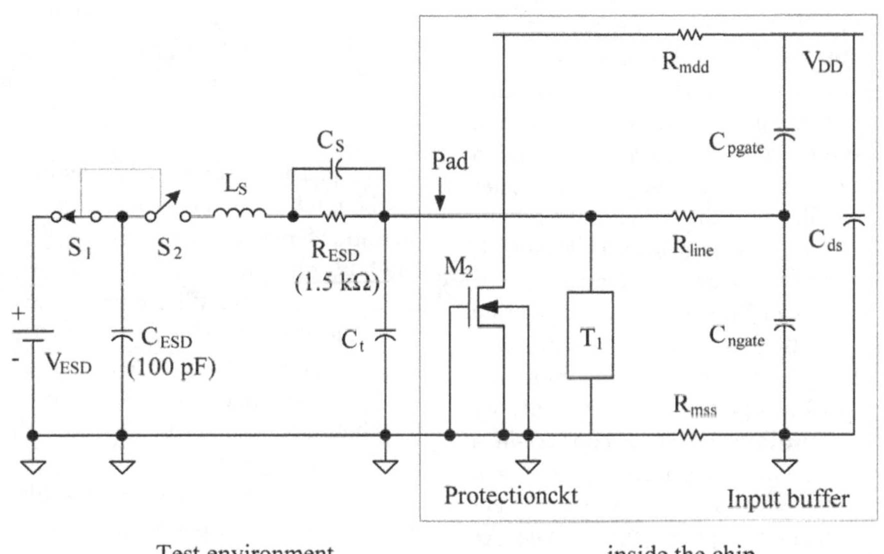

Figure 11. Equivalent circuit of an input-pin HBM test situation.

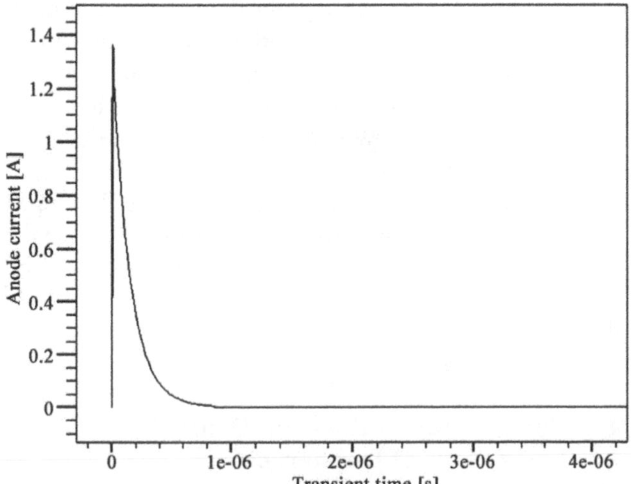

Figure 12. Variation of the anode current of T_1 in a PS mode when using the protection circuit (1).

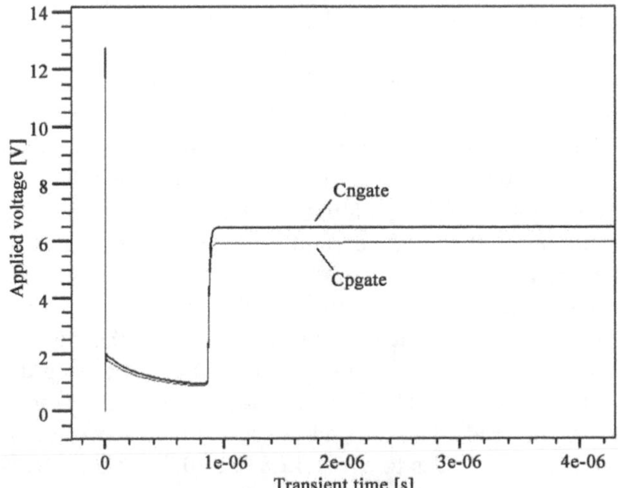

Figure 13. Variations of the voltages developed on C_{ngate} and C_{pgate} in a PS mode when using the protection circuit (1).

With the expectation above in mind, let's examine the results shown in **Figures 12** and **13**. From the results shown in **Figures 12** and **13**, we can see that the parasitic bipolar transistor in T_1 is triggered when the pad voltage in the early stage of discharge increases to about 12.8 V at 0.77 ns after S_2 in **Figure 11** is closed. The trigger voltage is lager than the expected DC value probably due to the time needed for charge redistribution. Main discharge through the pnpn thyristor proceeds as the pad voltage, which is equal to the anode-cathode voltage of T_1, drops to the holding voltage of about 2 V. The pad voltage decreases down to 1 V as the discharge current decreases with time. We can also see that the pad voltage increases again and reaches to 6.5 V at about 0.9 μs, when the anode current is reduced below the holding current for the pnpn thyristor action, and decreases very slowly thereafter. We confirmed from additional simulations that it takes 510 ms for the pad voltage to decrease down to 3 V. We also confirmed that main components of the anode current at 0.9 μs are the leakage current through the n-well/p-sub junction and the weak-inversion MOS current. The developed peak voltage in this later stage of discharge is smaller than the breakdown voltage (8.8 V) of the lvtr_thyristor device shown in **Figure 4**. This seems to be caused by the long duration (0.9 μs) of the main discharge by virtue of the excellent conducting pnpn thyristor. We confirmed that, with the sufficient discharge through the pnpn thyristor, the remaining discharge current level in this stage of discharge is only about 40 nA, which is too low for T_1 to conduct in a breakdown mode. We also confirmed from an additional simulation that, if we decrease the n^+/p^+ anode contact space down to 0.7 μm, the pnpn thyristor turns off earlier at 0.815 μs and the developed peak voltage increases up to 9 V with the remaining discharge current level of about 0.1 mA, which is certainly high enough for the device to conduct in a breakdown mode.

Figure 13 shows that, in overall, a lower voltage by about 1 V is developed on C_{pgate} since the V_{DD} node does not lie in the main discharge path.

Figure 14 shows variations of the voltages developed on C_{ngate} and C_{pgate} in a PS mode in case of using the protection circuit (2) in **Figure 8**. We confirmed that the variation of the anode current of T_1 is similar to that in **Figure 12**.

As we can see from **Figure 14**, the variation of the pad voltage, which is again almost same with the voltage developed on C_{ngate}, is similar to that in case of using the protection circuits (1). The parasitic bipolar transistor in T_1 is triggered when the pad voltage in the early stage of discharge increases to about 12.8 V at 0.77 ns after S_2 is closed. Main discharge through the pnpn thyristor proceeds as the pad voltage drops to the holding voltage of about 2 V.

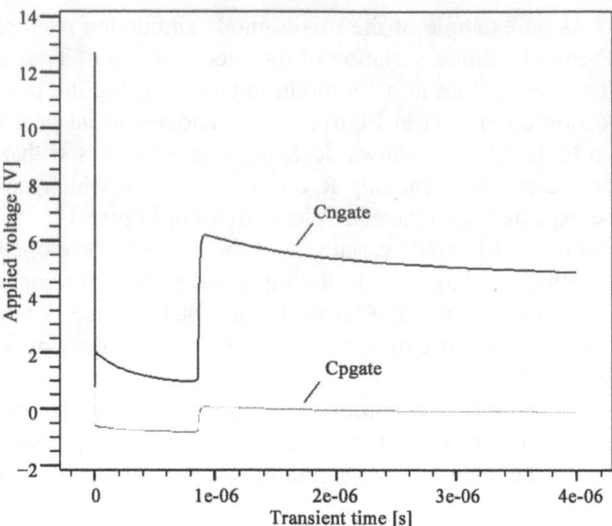

Figure 14. Variations of the voltages developed on C_{ngate} and C_{pgate} in a PS mode when using the protection circuit (2).

The pad voltage increases again and reaches to 6.2 V at about 0.9 μs, and decreases very slowly thereafter. We confirmed that the pad voltage (6.2 V) in this case is slightly lower than that in case of using the protection circuit (1) due to a difference in the current components. We confirmed that, when the pad voltage increases to 6.2 V, a pnp (p^+-cathode/n-well/p^+-sub) bipolar transistor in T_2 is triggered and the pad voltage is limited by the pnp bipolar holding voltage. Since the holding voltage is somewhat large, thermal heating may cause a problem. However, we confirmed that the bipolar current level at this moment is too low to cause thermal heating. The components of the anode current in T_1 in this later stage of discharge also include the leakage current through the n-well/p-sub junction and the weak-inversion MOS current, however the bipolar current through T_2 is a major discharge current for some duration. Due to this current component, the pad voltage in this later stage of discharge decreases faster, compared to the case using the protection circuit (1). We confirmed that it takes 23 ms for the pad voltage to decrease down to 3 V.

In **Figure 14**, we can see that the voltage developed across C_{pgate} remains low all the time. This is because the p^+-cathode/n^+-anode diode is conducting if the V_{DD}-pad voltage becomes larger than the forward diode drop. In the later stage, there is almost no conduction through T_2, and the voltage stays close to zero.

4.1. Voltages across the Gate Oxides in the Early Stage of Discharge

For the two PS modes analyzed above, the trigger time for T_1 is 0.77 ns. Due to this trigger time, the voltage

(12.8 V) larger than the DC snapback voltage is developed across T_1 right after S_2 is closed, resulting the high voltage developed on C_{ngate} in the early stage of discharge in **Figures 13** and **14**.

Depending on test modes, larger peak voltages across the gate oxides in the input buffer appear at C_{ngate} or C_{pgate}. If we define the test modes, which produce larger peak voltages in the mixed-mode transient simulations performed for 5 test modes, as weak modes, the results can be summarized as shown in **Table 2**.

In **Table 2**, 13.3 V on C_{pgate} in the PD mode in case of using the protection scheme (1) corresponds to a sum of the voltages applied on the pnpn structure in T_1 and the forward diode in M_2, which can be easily expected from **Figures 7** and **9**. The voltage applied on the pnpn structure peaks up to 12 V in this case. 13.5 V on C_{pgate} in the ND mode in case of using the protection scheme (1) corresponds to a sum of the voltages applied on the npn structure in M_2 and the forward diode in T_1. The voltage applied on the npn structure peaks up to 10.8 V. 12.3 V on C_{pgate} in the ND mode in case of using the protection scheme (2) corresponds to the voltage applied on the pnpn structure in T_2, which can be easily expected from **Figures 8** and **10**.

The peak voltages in **Table 2** can be regarded as excessive; however, durations of the peak voltages applied are very short. We confirmed that, for example, the durations for which the voltages exceed 10 V are at most 0.2 ns. Therefore it may be inferred that the gate oxides in the input buffer won't be damaged in the early stage of discharge [11].

Notice that the peak voltages can be suppressed by reducing the bipolar trigger voltage of the NMOS transistor in the NMOS protection device or the thyristor protection devices. To make the bipolar trigger voltage of the NMOS transistor even lower than the off-state DC breakdown voltage, the gate-coupled NMOS (gcNMOS) structure [12] can be adopted.

It is possible to obtain a similar result by simply inserting a series resistor between the gate (G_2) and V_{SS} nodes of M_2 in **Figure 7** since the gate-drain overlap capacitance (C_{gd}) already exists in the NMOS structure [4]. For the lvtr_thyristor_down device, the same technique can be applied since it includes the same NMOS structure in it [4]. For the lvtr_thyristor_up device, the same technique can be also applied. A series resistor inserted between the gate (G_2) and the input node in **Figure 8** will do the role.

We performed addition simulations to confirm that the early peaking can be suppressed by adding the series resistor to the gate node. The results are summarized in **Table 3**. For the 250 μm M_2, a 10 kΩ resistor was inserted between the gate and V_{SS} nodes. For the 20 μm T_1, a 125 kΩ resistor was inserted between the gate and V_{SS} nodes. For the 20 μm T_2, a 125 kΩ resistor was inserted between the gate and the input pad nodes. It is certain that the early peaking can be suppressed if needed.

4.2. Voltages across the Gate Oxides in the Later Stage of Discharge

Depending on test modes, larger peak voltages across the gate oxides also appears at C_{ngate} or C_{pgate} in the later stage of discharge. If we define the test modes, which produce larger peak voltages, as weak modes, the results can be summarized as shown in **Table 4**. We confirmed that use of the gate-coupling techniques does not affect the peak voltages in the later stage of discharge at all.

Table 2. Peak voltages developed across the gate oxides in the early stage of discharge.

Protection scheme	Weak mode	Peak voltage [V]		Time [ns]
		C_{ngate}	C_{pgate}	
(1)	PS	12.8		0.77
	PD		13.3	0.66
	ND		13.5	0.82
(2)	PS	12.8		0.77
	ND		12.3	0.80

Table 3. Peak voltages developed across the gate oxides in the early stage of discharge when adopting the gate-coupling technique.

Protection scheme	Weak mode	Peak voltage [V]		Time [ns]
		C_{ngate}	C_{pgate}	
(1)	PS	8.7		0.65
	PD		9.7	0.57
	ND		10.4	0.79
(2)	PS	8.7		0.65
	ND		8.8	0.69

Table 4. Peak voltage developed across the gate oxides in the later stage of discharge.

Protection scheme	Weak mode	Peak voltage [V]		Time [μs]
		C_{ngate}	C_{pgate}	
(1)	PD	7.6		0.92
	ND		10.7	0.50
(2)	PS	6.2		0.92
	ND		8.8	0.89
	PTP	7.4	7.9	0.89

From **Table 4**, we can see that, in case of using the protection scheme (1), the ND mode is the weakest one. 10.7V developed on C_{pgate} corresponds to a sum of the breakdown voltage of M_2 (9.6 V) and the forward diode drop in T_1 (1.1 V) right after the main discharge through M_2 and T_1 is finished, which can be easily expected from **Figures 9** and 7. Differently from the results of the thyristor devices in **Figures 13** and **14**, the peak voltage developed across M_2 in this case is about same with the DC breakdown voltage (9.3 V). This is because the bipolar transistor in M_2 is not as excellent conducting as the pnpn thyristor, and the main discharge through the bipolar transistor ends earlier (at 0.5 μs) compared to that through the pnpn thyristor as shown in **Table 4**.

In case of using the protection scheme (2), the ND mode is also the weakest one. 8.8 V developed on C_{pgate} corresponds to the voltage developed across T_2, which is somewhat smaller than the DC breakdown voltage (9.1 V) of T_2. In a PTP mode, 7.4 V and 7.9 V are developed on C_{ngate} and C_{pgate}, respectively, which correspond to the voltages developed across T_1 and T_4 in **Figure 10**.

We note that high voltages in the later stage of discharge can damage gate oxides in input buffers since they last for long time. When judging from the peak voltages developed across the gate oxides in the later stage of discharge in **Table 4**, the weakest modes in case of using the protection scheme (1) is an ND mode, and the PMOS gate oxide is more vulnerable to HBM ESD damages if the gate-oxide thicknesses of the NMOS and the PMOS are same. In case of using the protection scheme (2), the weakest mode is also an ND mode and the PMOS gate oxide is also more vulnerable.

When judging from the peak voltages developed, the advantage of the protection scheme (2) over the protection scheme (1) is expected to stand out more as the gate oxide thickness shrinks with advanced process technology used.

4.3. Location of Peak Temperature and Weak Modes

In case of using the protection scheme (1), the utmost peak temperature in a PS mode appears at T_1, and **Figure 15** shows the variation of peak temperature inside T_1. Peak temperature increases up to 473 K at about 0.9 ns just before the pnpn thryristor trigger, but decreases down to 330 K as soon as the pnpn thryristor is triggered since the holding voltage decreases. It peaks again up to 421 K at about 45 ns with increasing discharge current, and decreases slowly with the discharge current decreasing. By examining 2-dimensional temperature distributions, we confirmed that peak temperature at 0.9 ns appears at the n^+ well junction, where the electric field intensity is highest, and that at 45 ns appears at the n^+ cathode junction, where the current density is highest.

If we define the test modes, which produce larger temperature increase inside any protection device, as weak modes, the results can be summarized as shown in **Table 5**.

In case of using the protection scheme (1) incorporating the 250 μm NMOS device and 20 μm lvtr_thyristor_down device, the weakest mode is the ND mode, and peak temperature appears in M_2, which conducts as an npn bipolar transistor. Peak temperature inside M_2 appears at the gate-side n^+ drain junction. This is the reason for assigning a large spacing between the gate and the drain contact in **Figure 1** to avoid drain contact melting. The second weakest mode is the PS mode, and the 1st peak temperature appears in T_1, which happens just before the pnpn thyristor is triggered. At this point, peak temperature inside T_1 appears at the n^+ well junction

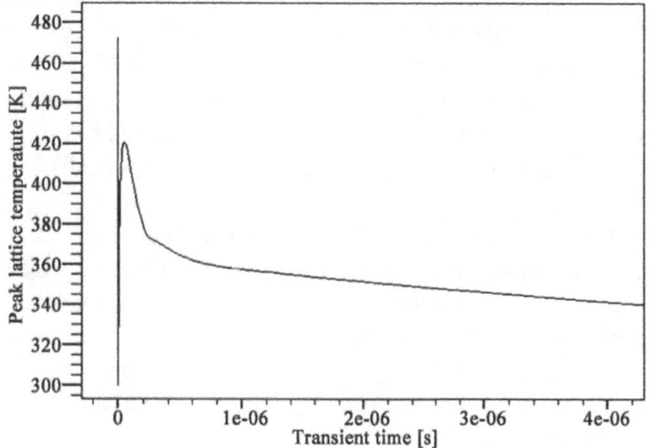

Figure 15. Peak temperature variation inside T_1 in a PS mode when using the protection scheme (1).

Table 5. Peak temperature locations and times.

Protection scheme	Weak mode	Peak temp.[°K]	Peak temperature: Location	Peak temperature: Time [ns]
(1)	PS	473	n^+ well junction in T_1	0.9
		421	n^+ cathode junction in T_1	45
	ND	495	gate-side drain junction in M_2	33
(2)	PS	471	n^+ well junction in T_1	0.8
		421	n^+ cathode junction in T_1	52
	ND	471	n^+ well junction in T_2	0.9
		473	n^+ cathode junction in T_2	44

at the right-hand corner of the n well. However, a problem with contact melting will not occur in this junction since there is no contact on it. The 2nd peak temperature in T_1 appears at the n^+ cathode junction when it conducts as a pnpn thyristor. Junction engineering such as increasing the junction area or adopting ESD ion implantation may be required to restrain temperature increase. However, it will not add parasitics to the input pad since the junction is not connected to it.

In case of using the protection scheme (2) incorporating the 20 μm lvtr_thyristor devices, the weakest mode is the ND mode, and the 1st peak temperature appears in T_2, which happens just before the pnpn thyristor is triggered. Peak temperature inside T_2 appears at the n^+ well junction at the left-hand corner of the p base. However, a problem with contact melting will not occur in this junction since there is no contact on it. The 2nd peak temperature in T_2 appears at the n^+ cathode junction when it conducts as a pnpn thyristor. Junction engineering such as increasing the junction area or adopting ESD ion implantation may be required to restrain temperature increase. This will not add parasitics to the input pad as long as the p-base region is not widened since the n^+ cathode is located inside the p base. As shown in **Table 5**, lattice heating characteristics in a PS mode are very similar to those in case of using the protection scheme (1).

We confirmed from additional simulations incorporating the gate-coupling technique that all the temperature peaking prior to 1ns in **Table 5** are suppressed below 380 K by virtue of the reduced bipolar trigger voltages. This can be easily expected from the results shown in **Table 3**.

From the result shown in **Table 5**, we can see that the 20 μm lvtr_thyristor devices are superior to the 250 μm NMOS device in ESD robustness in terms of thermal heating. Therefore we can save a lot of area consumed by a pad structure by eliminating the large clamp NMOS device.

5. Discussions

5.1. Considerations in Designing the Lvtr_Thyristor_Down Device

By performing additional simulations, we figured out that a serious problem could occur if the p-type substrate contacts are not located close to the lvtr_thyristor_down device as shown in **Figure 3**. When the p^+-sub/n^+-anode forward diodes in T_1 and T_3 in **Figure 10** turn on in the early stage of discharge in the NS and PTP modes, respectively, the parasitic npn (n^+-cath-ode/p-sub/n^+-anode) bipolar transistor inside this small-sized device can be triggered to increase temperature around the n^+ cathode junction a lot, where electric field intensity is high. Therefore it is very important to locate the p^+-sub contacts close as shown in **Figure 3**.

5.2. Considerations in Designing the Lvtr_Thyristor_Up Device

By performing additional simulations, we also figured out that a similar problem could occur if the n^+ anode2 contact at the right-hand side of the p base is not located in the lvtr_thyristor_up device as shown in **Figure 5**. When the p^+-cathode/n^+-anode forward diode in T_2 in **Figure 10** gets on in the early stage of discharge in PD and PTP modes, a parasitic npn (n^+-cathode/p-base/n^+-anode) bipolar transistor inside this small-sized device can be triggered to increase temperature around the n^+ cathode junction a lot. This can be completely solved by providing an additional p^+-cathode/n^+-anode2 forward diode path with the n^+ anode2 contact as shown in **Figure 5**.

We also figured out that there is an important consideration to take care in connecting the gate node (G_2) in T_2 in **Figure 8**. Even though G_2 can be connected to the V_{SS} node without increasing an off-state leakage in normal operations, this may cause a problem by making the pnpn thyristor in T_1 never triggered in the PTP mode shown in **Figure 10**. This is because the voltage developed between the pad (connected to the n^+/p^+ cathodes of T_2) and the V_{SS} node is restrained below 9 V, which is much smaller than the pnpn trigger voltage of 12.8 V, as a result of capacitive coupling between G_2 (connected to the V_{SS} node) and the n^+/p^+ cathodes of T_2. As a result, the discharge current flows mainly through the upper discharge path (Path 1) consisting of T_2 and T_4 in **Figure 10**. At the same time, the pnp (p^+-cathode/n-well/p^+-sub) bipolar transistor in T_2 is triggered to provide another discharge path by way of the forward biased pn (p^+-cathode/n^+-anode) diode in T_3. This causes a thermal heating problem by increasing lattice temperature near the p^+ sub junction at the right-hand corner of T_2 a lot. This pnp (p^+-cathode/n-well/p^+-sub) bipolar transistor is easily triggered since the p^+-cathode/n-well diode is already forward biased due to the conduction through Path 1 in **Figure 10**. This problem is completely solved by making the pnpn thyristor in T_1 easy to be triggered by connecting G_2 to the input pad as shown in **Figure 8**.

5.3. Providing Discharge Paths for VDD-VSS HBM Discharge

We have to check that a chip adopting the thyristor-only protection scheme can provide safe discharge paths when V_{DD}-V_{SS} HBM tests are performed. We note that large clamp devices such as the NMOS device shown in **Figure 1** should be located between V_{DD} and VSS buses in V_{DD} and V_{SS} pad structures and also anywhere a space is available to provide discharge paths for V_{DD}-V_{SS} ESD events and also to reduce a V_{DD} bounce during normal operation by increasing the capacitance between the two buses. We note that the bipolar trigger voltage of the clamp NMOS device without the gate-coupling technique was confirmed as less than 11 V relating the result shown in **Table 3**.

Using a single lvtr_thyristor protection device formed by assuming the lvtr_thyristor_down device in **Figure 3** (T_1) and the lvtr_thyristor_up device in **Figure 5** (T_2) located side by side on a same substrate, we confirmed by a mixed-mode simulation that the V_{DD}-V_{SS} peak voltage of the protection scheme (2) in a V_{DD}-V_{SS} HBM test is 17.6 V. The V_{DD}-V_{SS} voltage decreases down to 4 V (2 V each across T_1 and T_2) with both of the pnpn thyristors in T_1 and T_2 being triggered. Therefore, in a V_{DD}-V_{SS} HBM ESD test, it is certain that the clamp NMOS devices will provide discharge paths before the pnpn path through T_1 and T_2 in any of input pad structures is triggered.

Also when a surge voltage appears between V_{DD} and V_{SS} buses, the clamp NMOS device will constrain the rail voltage below 11 V to suppress the possibility of latch-up through T_1 and T_2. Also the latchup cannot persist since the conduction through T_1 and T_2 in series can be maintained only if the V_{DD}-V_{SS} voltage is higher than 4 V, which is higher than the normal supply voltage in recent technologies.

6. Summary

We proposed an input protection scheme composed of thyristor devices only to minimize the size of an input pad structure. For this purpose, we suggested the low-voltage triggering thyristor protection device structures assuming usage of standard CMOS processes, and attempted an in-depth comparison study with a conventional thyristor protection scheme incorporating a clamp NMOS device based on DC and mixed-mode transient analyses utilizing a 2-dimensional device simulator.

We analyzed in detail the problems which can occur in real HBM tests to provide useful findings regarding the proposed protection scheme as follows.

1) We figured out weak modes in terms of peak voltages developed across gate oxides in input buffers.

2) We figured out weak modes in terms of temperature increase inside the protection devices, and also figured out locations of peak temperature inside the protection devices.

3) We suggested design guidelines for each protection device to minimize temperature increase inside it and to minimize voltages developed across gate oxides in input buffers.

4) We showed how we can incorporate the gate coupling technique into the suggested protection devices.

5) We showed that the suggested thyristor-only protection scheme can be made free from CMOS latch-up.

7. References

[1] P. Leroux and M. Steyaert, "High-Performance 5.2 GHz LNA with on-Chip Inductor to Provide ESD Protection," *Electronics Letters*, Vol. 37, No. 7, 2001, pp. 467-469.

[2] A. Chatterjee and T. Polgreen, "A Low-Voltage Triggering SCR for on-Chip ESD Protection at Output and Input Pads," *IEEE Electron Devices Letters*, Vol. 12, No. 1, 1991, pp. 21-22.

[3] E. R. Worley, R. Gupta, B. Jones, R. Kjar, C. Nguyen and M. Tennyson, "Sub-micron Chip ESD Protection Schemes Which Avoid Avalanching Junctions," *Electrical Overstress/Electrostatic Discharge Symposium Proceedings*, Phoenix, 12 September 1995, pp. 13-20.

[4] J. Y. Choi, "A Comparison Study of Input ESD Protection Schemes Utilizing NMOS, Thyristor, and Diode Devices," *Communications and Network*, Vol. 2, No. 1, 2010, pp. 11-25.

[5] H. Feng, G. Chen, R. Zhan, Q. Wu, X. Guan, H. Xie and A. Z. H. Wang, "A Mixed-Mode ESD Protection Circuit Simulation-Design Methodology," *IEEE Journal of Solid-State Circuits*, Vol. 38, No. 6, June 2003, pp. 995-1006.

[6] B. Fankhauser and B. Deutschmann, "Using Device Simulations to Optimize ESD Protection Circuits," *International Symposium on Electromagnetic Compatibility*, Santa Clara, 9-13 August 2004, pp. 963-968.

[7] Silvaco International, "ATLAS II Framework," Version 5.10.2.R, Silvaco International, Austin, 2005.

[8] J.-Y. Choi, W. S. Yang, D. Kim and Y. Kim, "Thyristor Input-Protection Device Suitable for CMOS RF ICs," *Analog Integrated Circuits and Signal Processing*, Vol. 43, No. 1, April 2005, pp. 5-14.

[9] H. Feng, K. Gong and A. Wang, "A Comparison Study of ESD Protection for RFIC's: Performance vs. Parasitic," 2000 *IEEE Radio Frequency Integrated Circuits Symposium*, Boston, 11-13 June 2000, pp. 143-146.

[10] M.-D. Ker, C.-Y. Wu and H.-H. Chang, "Complementary-LVTSCR ESD Protection Circuit for Submicron CMOS VLSI/ULSI," *IEEE Transactions on Electron Devices*, Vol. 43, No. 4, 1996, pp. 588-598.

[11] Z. H. Liu, E. Rosenbaum, P. K. Ko, C. Hu, Y. C. Cheng, C. G. Sodini, B. J. Gross and T. P. Ma, "A Comparative Study of the Effect of Dynamic Stressing on High-Field

Endurance and Stability of Reoxidized-Nitrided, Fluorinated and Conventional Oxides," *International Electron Devices Meeting*, Washington, 8-11 February1991, pp. 723-726.

[12] G. Chen, H. Fang and A. Wang, "A Systematic Study of ESD Protection Structures for RF ICs," 2003 *IEEE Radio Frequency Integrated Circuits Symposium*, Philadelphia, 8-10 June 2003, Vol. 46, pp. 347-350.

Adaptability of Conservative Staircase Scheme for Live Videos

Sudeep Kanav, Satish Chand
Division of Computer Engineering, Netaji Subhas Institute of Technology, New Delhi, India

Abstract

Existing broadcasting schemes provide services for the stored videos. The basic approach in these schemes is to divide the video into segments and organize them over the channels for proper transmission. Some schemes use segments as a basic unit, whereas the others require segments to be further divided into subsegments. In a scheme, the number of segments/subsegments depends upon the bandwidth allocated to the video by the video server. For constructing segments, the video length should be known. If it is unknown, then the segments cannot be constructed and hence the scheme cannot be applied to provide the video services. This is an important issue especially in live broadcasting applications wherein the ending time of the video is unknown, for example, cricket match. In this paper, we propose a mechanism for the conservative staircase scheme so that it can support live video broadcasting.

Keywords: Conservative Staircase Scheme, Staircase Scheme, Live Video Channel, Channel Transition

1. Introduction

Video broadcasting has been an active research area for last few years and several broadcasting schemes have been developed. The technologies available earlier for these applications could not support high data rate and hence the video services could not gain popularity in spite of their vast applications. Besides the high data rate, their storage requirement is also quite high unless some compression technique is applied. In fact, even after applying a good compression technique the data size is considerably large. In recent years, the communication and computational technologies (including the storage technologies) have been developed significantly. But new applications such as Video-on-Demand (VOD) put a limitation on data rate and the storage devices. So, these resources need to utilize efficiently. Several good schemes have been developed to provide the video services. In almost all the schemes, the video data is transmitted in terms of segments and/or subsegments and the size of a segment and/or subsegment is determined based on the bandwidth allocated to the video. For applying a broadcasting scheme, the video size should be known. In case of live videos, the size of the video object is not known in the beginning and thus the schemes cannot be employed to provide the live video services.

There are generally two main approaches for providing video services. In the first approach, the bandwidth is allocated to the individual users and in the second one the bandwidth is allocated to the individual video objects. In the first case, the immediate video services are provided to user requests and the number of users is the main constraint. In the second case, the video services are independent of the number of users, but all users may not get immediate services. The first approach is called user-centered or true video-on-demand and the second one is called data-centered or near video-on-demand. In both the approaches, the video server is one of the very important entities, which allocates bandwidth to videos. The bandwidth is a scarce resource and must be used efficiently. For allocating bandwidth to the video objects, many researchers have discussed several schemes [1-6] and all these schemes are meant for the stored videos. To the best of authors' knowledge, there does not appear any work that discusses the live video transmission. The possible reason might be the unknown video size in advance as all schemes require constructing the segments/subsegments from the video. To develop a broadcasting scheme to support live video broadcasting is the motivation to carry out this work. In this paper, we propose a technique that makes the conservative staircase scheme to provide live video broadcasting.

The system design consists of a live system that broadcasts the live video using its live video channel. Besides the live system, it contains a video server that stores video data from the live system into its buffer and then broadcasts that data. Storing video data from the live system by the video server is done in terms of pre-specified fixed size durations. We call such durations as time slots and the data downloaded in a time slot is referred to as a segment. The segment size (in time units) determines the user's waiting time. The live system just broadcasts the live video; it does not store. The video server while broadcasting the stored video data from its buffer downloads new data from the live system into its buffer in terms of segments. The new stored segments are broadcast by the video server along with the old segments. This process continues till the live video transmission is there. When the live video broadcasting is over, the video size becomes known and the scheme can function similar to a scheme meant for the video of known size. If the live broadcast continues and all video channels of the video server have been exhausted, then the newly downloaded segments cannot be broadcast. Therefore, we need to make some video channel free for broadcasting the new segments. This can be done if the data occupied by a channel is moved to other channels. While carrying out this activity, all users must get reliable services. To transfer data from one channel to another without interrupting user services is called channel transition. So, we need to apply channel transition mechanism to make the last channel free by transferring its data to other video channels. Thus, the newly downloaded segments can be broadcast using this free channel. This is the concept used in this paper.

The rest of the paper is organized as follows. Section 2 reviews the related work. Section 3 discusses architecture of the scheme for live video transmission. Section 4 presents the results and discussion. Finally, in Section 5 the paper is concluded.

2. Related Work

Several broadcasting schemes have been discussed in literature. Some of the important schemes are harmonic scheme [7], cautious harmonic scheme [8], skyscraper scheme [9], and conservative staircase scheme [10]. The harmonic and cautious harmonic schemes perform better than the skyscraper and conservative staircase schemes, but their implementation is more complex. These schemes use non-uniformly allocated bandwidth logical channels. The skyscraper and conservative staircase schemes use uniformly allocated bandwidth logical channels, called video channels, which are individually divided into uniform subchannels. A subchannel transmits a segment in terms its subsegments. In this paper, we will refer the conservative staircase scheme as the conservative scheme.

In almost all the schemes, the first one or two channels are generally kept undivided and other channels may be divided into subchannels. All these channels are generally video channels. A logical channel with bandwidth equal to the consumption rate of the video is called the *video channel*. The video is divided into equal-sized segments; each segment may further be individually divided into uniform subsegments. The conservative scheme has been developed to overcome the limitation of the staircase scheme [11]. The problem with the staircase scheme is that this scheme does not always provide the video data to all users in time. The staircase scheme has been developed to overcome the excessive buffer requirement of the Fast Broadcasting scheme [12] without increasing the user's waiting time. The proposed scheme is based upon the conservative staircase scheme [10]. So, we briefly review this scheme. In the conservative scheme, the video is uniformly divided into segments and the bandwidth allocated to the video into uniform channels. The video display time is divided into equal time durations, called time slots. The segment size (in time units) is equal to the time slot length. More precisely, a time slot is the duration in which a segment can be viewed exactly at the consumption rate. Let the number of segments of a video of length D be K ($K \geq 3$), denoting them as $S_1, S_2, \cdots, S_K$, and the video channels allocated to it be N. The number of video segments and the number of video channels are related by $K = 3 * 2^{N-2}$. The first segment S_1 is transmitted over the first video channel. The next two segments are transmitted over the second video channel. The segments from $(1 + 3*2^{m-3})^{\text{th}}$ to $(3*2^{m-2})^{\text{th}}$ are transmitted over mth video channel C_m ($m > 2$). For transmitting data over the mth channel, this channel is divided into $3*2^{m-3}$ number of subchannels and the corresponding segments are divided into subsegments. The subsegment $S_{i,j}$ ($3*2^{m-3} < i \leq 3*2^{m-2}$, $m > 2$) is transmitted over the jth subchannel of the mth channel in $(p*3*2^{m-3} + (i + j - 1) \bmod 3*2^{m-3})^{\text{th}}$ time slot, $p = 0,1,2,\cdots$. **Figure 1** shows transmission of the video segments and subsegments over three video channels in the conservative scheme.

The conservative scheme overcomes the limitation of the staircase scheme. In the staircase scheme, all users may not get video data on time. However, the conservative scheme requires more bandwidth as compared to the staircase scheme. Since the conservative scheme is complete in itself, *i.e.*, it provides video data to all users on time, we consider it to support live videos and this is the main contents of this paper. In [13], the live broadcasting mechanism has been discussed for the Fast broadcasting scheme, but the Fast broadcasting scheme requires quite

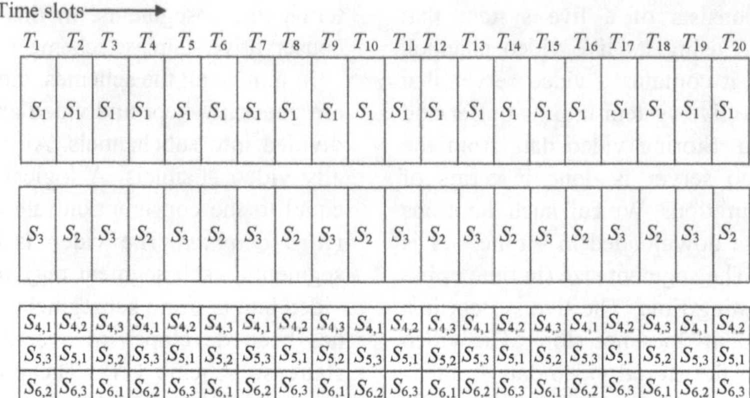

Figure 1. Transmission of segments/subsegments in conservative scheme.

large amount of storage. That is why we consider the conservative staircase scheme for live broadcasting. In next section, we discuss the proposed scheme.

3. Adaptability of Conservative Scheme for Live Videos

The conservative scheme needs the video size in the beginning to partition it into equal-sized segments and subsegments. Generally, in a live video we do not know the video size; so this scheme cannot be applied in its existing form. We modify its basic architecture. We do not divide the segments or video channels any further. For the modified conservative scheme, we discuss a mechanism so that this scheme can support live video broadcasting. We assume that the bandwidth allocated to the video is finite. This assumption is not illogical because for abundant bandwidth there is hardly any issue to discuss.

In the proposed architecture, we have a *live* system that broadcasts the live video using its video channel, called the *live channel*. This live system is active while there is a live video and provides video services only once using its live video channel. There is one more system that stores the video data from the live system into its buffer. This system, called video server, broadcasts the stored video data. The live system broadcasts the video data at the consumption rate. The user requests received till the live system begins to broadcast the video data get all data from the live system directly. These requests require no buffer storage. The live video display is divided into fixed time durations, called *time slots*. The video server stores the video data from the live channel. The data downloaded and stored in a time slot constitutes a video segment. The segment size (in time units) determines the user's waiting time. After storing new segment in its buffer, the video server broadcasts that segment over its video channels and concurrently downloads new segments from the live system into its buffer. A request received after the live system has started the live video gets the missing initial data from the video server and the future data from the live channel. We now discuss the data transmission method used by the video server.

a) Data Transmission Method

All video segments S_i ($i = 1,2,\cdots,K$) are of uniform size (in time units) and they are constructed as discussed above. The video server broadcasts the segments as follows:

1) The first channel C_1 broadcasts the first segment S_1, repeatedly.

2) The second channel C_2 transmits next two segments S_2 and S_3, alternately and repeatedly.

3) The *i*th channel C_i ($i > 2$) broadcasts $3*2^{i-3}$ number of segments from $(3*2^{i-3} + 1)$ to $(3*2^{i-2})$, sequentially and periodically.

Let the video server allocate N video channels C_1, $C_2,\cdots,C_N$ to the desired video. After downloading the first segment S_1, the video server broadcasts this segment over its first video channel C_1, repeatedly, and concurrently downloads the second segment S_2 into its buffer from the live system. After the video server stores the segment S_2 into buffer from the live system, it broadcasts S_2 from the next time slot along with S_1 according to the data transmission Method. When the video server broadcasts S_1 and S_2, it stores third segment S_3 from the live system into its buffer and then broadcasts S_3 along with S_1 and S_2. A user request is allowed to get video data from the live system or the video server at the starting point of a time slot, not in between; thus, a user may have to wait for at most one time slot. If a user request is received when the live system broadcasts S_1, it would get the data from the live system at the start of the second time slot, but by that time this request must has missed S_1. The segment S_1 has already been stored by the video server in its buffer in the first time slot and in the next time slot, *i.e.*, second time slot, it is broadcast by the video server as per the data transmission method. Thus, the request can get S_1 from the video server and its storage requirement is equal to a segment size. The video server downloads future data from the live channel into its buffer and broadcasts the already stored video data from its buffer, if there is a free video channel available. If the live video broadcasting is not over and all video channels of the video server have been exhausted, then there is need to make a video channel free to broadcast the newly stored video segments. The possible solution to handle this problem is to make the last video channel free by transferring its data to other video channels. The important issue while transferring the data from one video channel to other is that the requests which are currently viewing and those which would view in future should get continuous delivery of the video data. For transferring data from the last video channel to other video channels, we need to increase the segments' size. The data transferring approach without disturbing user services is called channel transition mechanism. The channel transition can be an intermediate in which the total size of the video is still unknown, or it can be the final channel transition when the video size is known, *i.e.*, the live video transmission is over.

b) Intermediate Channel Transition

The important point in a channel transition is that the users who have been viewing since prior to the channel transition and those who would view after the channel transition should get continuous delivery of the video data. Here we discuss a channel transition when all video channels allocated to the video by the video server have been exhausted and the live video is still going on. After carrying out the channel transition, the size of a (new) segment becomes double of that of an old segment. Denote old segments before the ith channel transition by S_k^{i-1}, S_{k+1}^{i-1}, ⋯. and new segments after transition by S_k^i, S_{k+1}^i, ⋯ Then, $S_k^i = S_{2k-1}^{i-1} + S_{2k}^{i-1}$, ⋯. After the channel transition, the waiting time for a user request would be equal to two segments. Therefore, it is necessary to delay the channel transition as much as possible, while maintaining continuous delivery of the video data to users. Continuous delivery can be ensured if the channel transition takes place when the second segment S_2 has been transmitted over the second channel C_2. If the channel transition is made after the third segment S_3 has been transmitted over C_2, then the requests that start receiving the video data from the time slot just before the channel transition will not get the data in time because half of the new second segment S_2^1 (which is the old segment S_3^0, S_3^0 is the original third segment S_3) has already been transmitted over C_2 just before the channel transition and S_2^1 will be transmitted over C_2 just after the channel transition. It means that the old users who received the segment S_3 would be expecting S_4. But since the new second segment S_2^1 is transmitted just after the channel transition and its first half, *i.e.*, S_3 will be received again, not S_4. Thus, all users will not get the required data in time. We considered the second channel as an example, but similar problems occur with other channels, too. Non-delivery of the video data can be overcome if the channel transition is made when the second segment S_2 has been transmitted over the second channel C_2. We now illustrate the channel transition with an example.

Illustration

Assume that the video server allocates five video channels to the video. The number of segments that can be transmitted over these five channels is $3*2^{N-2} = 3*2^{5-2} = 24$. Let the live video start at time t_0. The video server is always tuned to the live channel to store the video data into its buffer from the live system. Let the size of a time slot, which is also equal to a segment size (in time units), be 1.0 minute. The video server first downloads video data from the live system for 1.0 minute into its buffer, denoting it as S_1, and then broadcasts this data as per the data transmission method. The requests which have arrived by the time t_0 get video data from the live system. The requests which would arrive after the live video has been started (say, at time t_0 + 0.5) would get video data from the live system at the start of the next time slot, *i.e.*, at time (t_0 + 1.0). Call time durations from t_0 to (t_0 + 1.0), (t_0 + 1.0) to (t_0 + 2.0),⋯, (t_0 + i) to (t_0 + (i + 1)), as 0th time slot T_0, 1st time slot T_1, 2nd time slot T_2, ⋯, *i*th time slot T_i, ⋯, respectively. Denote the data broadcast by the live system in these time slots by S_{0L}, S_{1L}, S_{2L}, ⋯,S_{iL}, ⋯. We denote the video data available in buffer of the video server for broadcasting in the time slots T_0, T_1, T_2, ⋯, T_i, ⋯, respectively, by segments S_0, S_1, S_2, ⋯,S_i, ⋯. It may be seen that $S_0 = 0$, $S_1 = S_{0L}$, $S_2 = S_{1L}$, ⋯. The segment S_0 is zero because no data is available in buffer of the video server for broadcasting in the time slot T_0. *The segment stored into buffer in current time slot will be available for broadcasting in next time slot, not in the current time slot.* The video server stores S_1 into its buffer in time slot T_0 from the live system and this will be available for broadcasting in time slot T_1. It is to note that the request, R_0, arrived at any time in 0th time slot T_0 will not get S_1 from the live system because R_0 would be allowed to receive data from the live system from the time t_0 + 1.0 onward and by that time the live system would have already broadcast S_1. However, the video server has stored S_1 into its buffer in 0th time slot T_0 and broadcasts it from 1st time slot as per the data transmission method. The request R_0 can get S_1 from the video server and the future data from the live system. It is noteworthy to mention that the live system and the video server broadcast the video data, so any number of requests received in any time slot will require same amount of resources as a single request. Therefore, without loss of generality we can represent all the requests received in a time slot by a single request. The requests received in the ith time slot are denoted by R_i. Consider request R_2 that arrives in 2nd time slot T_2. This request will be allowed to join the live channel at time $t_0 + 2.0$ for receiving the future data. So, R_2 does not get S_1 and S_2 because their transmission has already been over by the live system. However, the video server has stored S_1 and S_2 in its buffer in the time slots T_0 and T_1, respectively, from the live system and broadcasts S_1 from time slot T_1 onward and S_2 from time slot T_2 onward. Thus, R_2 can get S_1 and S_2 from the video server. Using similar argument, it is not difficult to show that a request received in any time slot would get the required data in time. This process will continue till all time slots of all video channels have been occupied and the live broadcasting is still there. When all video channels have been exhausted, we need to perform the channel transition to make the last channel free for broadcasting the new segments. It means that the segments occupied by the 5th channel C_5 (*i.e.*, S_{13}, S_{14}, ···, S_{24}) need be broadcast using the first four channels. In the modified conservative scheme, it can easily be done by just making the segment size double because the video channel C_k ($k > 2$) can occupy maximum number of segments that is equal to the sum of all segments occupied by all lower indexed video channels C_{k-1}, C_{k-2}, ···, C_1. Denote new segments and new time slots by S_0^1, S_1^1, S_2^1, ···, S_i^1, ···, and T_0^1, T_1^1, T_2^1, ···, T_i^1, ···, respectively. The size of a new segment (or time slot) is double of that of an old segment (or time slot). Here T_0^1 denotes the time slot just prior to the channel transition and S_0^1 denotes the data downloaded in buffer in time slot T_0^1. The segment S_0^1 contains data of segments that have been stored in the buffer in the time slot just before the channel transition. **Figure 2** shows the first channel transition at thick line of the time point for using five video channels. In **Figures 2-5**, the gray-colored channels represent the live channels and the others are video channels allocated to the video by the video sever. The optimal time point at which the channel transition should be made is ($t_0 + 24$), *i.e.*, at the end of the time slot T_{24} because by that time all time slots of all the video channels of the video server must have been occupied. After carrying out the channel transition, the first new segment S_1^1 comprises S_1 and S_2. The second and third new segments (S_2^1 and S_3^1) comprise S_3 & S_4 and S_5 & S_6 segments, respectively. The transmission of new segments over the video channels takes place exactly in the same way as the old segments according to the data transmission method. The important characteristics of the conservative staircase scheme is that for freeing the last video channel all segments are made double and the channel transition can be delayed optimally. The ith new segment and the ith new time slot can be written in terms of old segments and old time slots, respectively, as

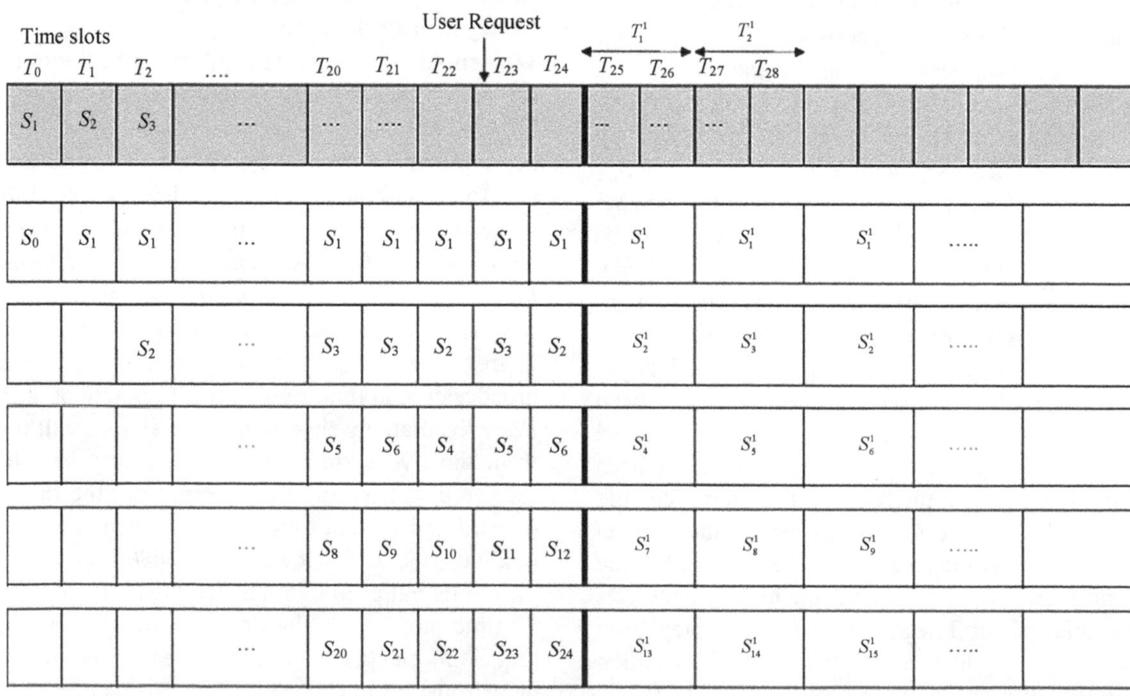

Figure 2. First channel transition.

$$S_i^1 = S_{2i-1}S_{2i}$$

and

$$T_i^1 = T_{24+2i-1} + T_{24+2i};$$

For $i = 1,2,\cdots$, we have

$$S_1^1 = S_1S_2, \quad S_2^1 = S_3S_4, \quad S_3^1 = S_5S_6,\cdots,$$

$$T_1^1 = T_{25} + T_{26},\ T_2^1 = T_{27} + T_{28},\ T_3^1 = T_{29} + T_{30},\cdots,$$

Consider request R_{23} received at any time in 23rd time slot T_{23} (refer to **Figure 2**). This request gets S_1 from the channel C_1, S_2 from the 2nd channel C_2, S_6 from the 3rd channel C_3, S_{12} from the 4th channel C_4, in the time slot T_{24}, and the segments S_{24} onward from the live system. The request R_{23} would require S_{24} for viewing in the T_{47} time slot in terms of new segments. The remaining data (*i.e.*, segments S_1 to S_{23}) is provided by the video server (refer to **Figure 2**). The segment S_3, first part of the segment S_2^1 is provided by the video server just after the channel transition followed by S_4 as it is the second half of S_2^1. The request received after the channel transition gets video data uninterruptedly in terms of new segments. In fact, we can show that for any request received after or before the channel transition will always get the required data in time. This process continues till all new time slots of all video channels have been occupied. Since the size of a current segment is twice of that of an old one, the next time channel transition will take place when there are 24 new segments or 48 old segments. So far the video has been played for 24 minutes. Next time the channel transition will take place when the video must have been played for 48 segments, *i.e.*, 48 minutes. This process will continue for the duration of the live video transmission. **Figure 3** shows the second channel transition. The user's waiting time after the second transition will be 4 minutes as the segment size is four times that of the original one.

*c) **Final Channel Transition***

We now discuss the final channel transition, which is performed only after the live video has been over. To carry out the final channel transition, the number of segments on the last video channel must be less than its capacity. If the number of segments transmitted by the last channel is equal to its capacity, we do nothing and this is the best scenario. Here the "capacity" means the maximum number of segments that can be transmitted by that channel. The final channel transition is necessary for utilizing bandwidth efficiently. Here our objective is that the video segments should occupy all time slots on all video channels. We may assume that the video data always comprises integral segments. If the last segment is not a complete, then this is made a complete segment by adding dummy data. The channel C_1 transmits the segment S_1^{L-1} and the channel C_2 transmits the segments S_2^{L-1} & S_3^{L-1} in normal course of time. After the final channel transition, the segment size decreases as the

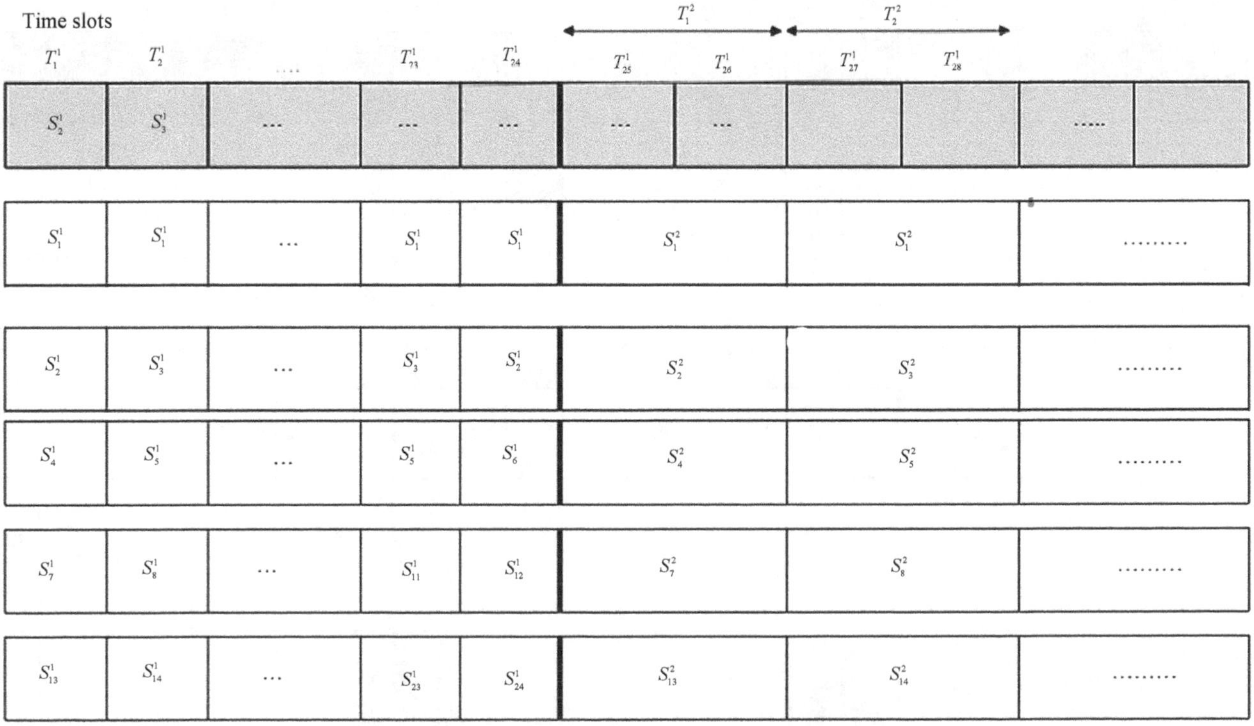

Time slots					T_1^2		T_2^2			
T_1^1	T_2^1	....	T_{23}^1	T_{24}^1	T_{25}^1	T_{26}^1	T_{27}^1	T_{28}^1		
S_2^1	S_3^1	...	...	...	...	...			.....	
S_1^1	S_1^1	...	S_1^1	S_1^1	S_1^2		S_1^2		....	
S_2^1	S_3^1	...	S_3^1	S_2^1	S_2^2		S_3^2		....	
S_4^1	S_5^1	...	S_5^1	S_6^1	S_4^2		S_5^2		....	
S_7^1	S_8^1	...	S_{11}^1	S_{12}^1	S_7^2		S_8^2		....	
S_{13}^1	S_{14}^1	...	S_{23}^1	S_{24}^1	S_{13}^2		S_{14}^2		....	

Figure 3. Second channel transition.

number of segments increases. In other words, some last portion of the segment S_1^{L-1} is added to the beginning of S_2^{L-1} and some last portion S_2^{L-1} is added to the beginning of S_3^{L-1}, and so on. In this way, we increase the number of segments. By doing so, these new segments will occupy all time slots of all video channels. Here an important question is "*will all users get video data in time*?" If not, how to make the segments' allocation over the video channels so that all users can get continuous delivery of the video data. We illustrate this with an example. Let the video be allocated five video channels by the video server. The last channel, fifth one, can occupy 12 segments (from 13th to 24th). The live video can be over at any time, *i.e.*, after 12th or 13th, ··· or 24th segment. If the live video is over after the 24th segment, we do nothing. Assume that the live video is over in the T_i^{L-1} $(12 < i < 24)$ time slot in which the *i*th segment S_i^{L-1} has been downloaded. We would need to carry out the last channel transition after T_i^{L-1} time slot. By delaying one time slot, we get one time slot free on the last video channel and that time slot is used to broadcast the segment S_2^{L-1} or S_3^{L-1} just before the final channel transition depending upon whether the last video segment broadcast by the live channel was even or odd. This is shown as gray-colored time slot on the last channel in **Figure 4**.

Consider request R_{12} that begins downloading video data into its buffer from the live system from the time slot T_{13}^{L-1} onward. It can download, if required, the segments S_4^{L-1}, S_7^{L-1}, S_{13}^{L-1} in T_{13}^{L-1} time slot and the segments S_2^{L-1}, S_5^{L-1}, S_8^{L-1}, S_3^{L-1} in time slot T_{14}^{L-1} from the 2nd, 3rd, 4th, and 5th video channels, respectively. The segment S_1^{L-1} can be viewed while downloading from the first video channel and does not require any storage. The request R_{12} has all initial segments except the segment S_6^{L-1}. This segment would be required for viewing after the segment S_5^{L-1}. After the channel transition, the segment S_6^{L-1} is distributed among the segments S_{10}^L, S_{11}^L, & S_{12}^L. These segments can be downloaded in time while the segments S_2^{L-1}, S_3^{L-1}, S_4^{L-1} are viewed. Consider another request R_{13} that begins downloading the video data into its buffer from the video server from the time slot T_{14}^{L-1} onward and can store, if required, the segments S_2^{L-1}, S_5^{L-1}, S_8^{L-1}, S_3^{L-1} into its buffer. The segment S_4^{L-1} will be required for viewing after the segment S_3^{L-1}. But, this segment is neither in buffer nor available for downloading and after the channel transition will be distributed among the segments S_6^L, S_7^L, and S_8^L. These segments can be downloaded in time while the segments S_2^{L-1} and S_3^{L-1} are viewed because the data required for two old time slots (before the channel transition) would be sufficient for viewing in more

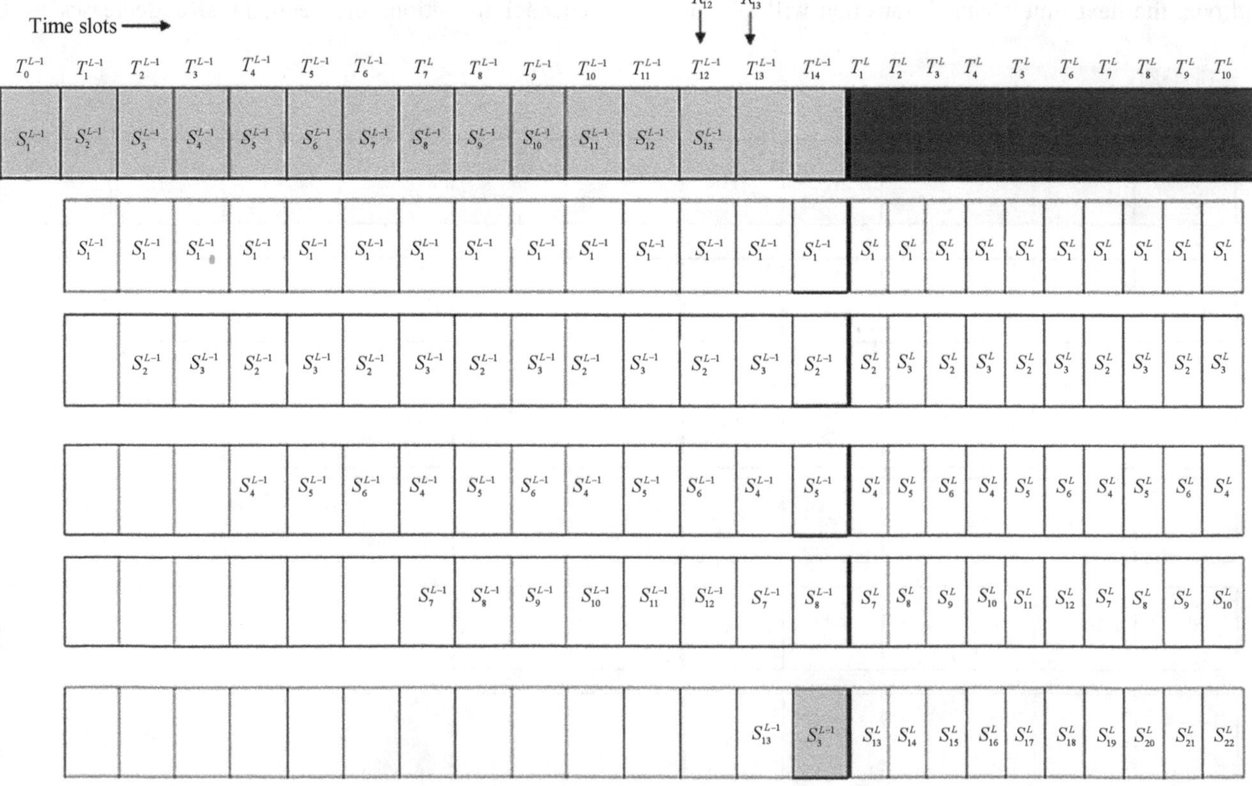

Figure 4. Final channel transition.

than three new time slots (after the channel transition). If any problem related to the data availability is there, it will be for the S_4^{L-1} segment. The request which may have problem of data availability is one that starts receiving video data from the time slot just before the channel transition. For other requests whether received before or after the channel transition, there is no problem of data availability. **Figure 4** shows the final channel transition when the live video is over just after the live system has broadcast the segment S_{13}^{L-1} in T_{13}^{L-1} time slot. Consider another case when the live video is over after the segment S_{14}^{L-1} has been broadcast by the live system. We need to perform channel transition after the time slot T_{15}^{L-1} (it is not shown in figure because of size). The request R_{14} can download, if required, the segments S_3^{L-1}, S_6^{L-1}, S_9^{L-1}, S_2^{L-1} in time T_{15}^{L-1} time slot before the channel transition. It however does not have the segment S_4^{L-1}, which is a part of the segments S_6^L and S_7^L. These segments can be downloaded into buffer in time while the segments S_2^{L-1} and S_3^{L-1} are viewed because the duration of these two segments (*i.e.*, S_2^{L-1} & S_3^{L-1}) is more than that of the three new segments (after the channel transition). So, the segments S_6^L and S_7^L can be downloaded in time. Consider another request, say R_{21}, which receives video data from the video server from the time slot T_{22}^{L-1} onward. In T_{22}^{L-1} time slot, the segments S_2^{L-1}, S_5^{L-1}, S_8^{L-1}, S_3^{L-1} can be downloaded, if required, but the segment S_4^{L-1} is not in buffer and after the channel transition this segment gets distributed among the segments S_4^L and S_5^L. These segments can be downloaded in time when the segments S_2^{L-1} & S_3^{L-1} are viewed. Now the only point to resolve is "*what segments after the channel transition are into which the segment S_4^{L-1} is distributed.*" The smallest and largest indices of new segments (after the channel transition), denoted by I_S and I_L, which contain the data of segment S_4^{L-1} are given by

$I_S = n$ such that $\min_n \left\lfloor \frac{n*p}{K} \right\rfloor \geq 3$ and $I_L = n$ such that $\min_n \left\lfloor \frac{n*p}{K} \right\rfloor \geq 4$

where p is the index of the last segment broadcast by the live system and K is the number of video segments.

For example, consider that the last segment broadcast by the live system is S_{16}^{L-1}. The request R_{16} receives video data from the video server in T_{17}^{L-1} time slot onward, the segment S_4^{L-1} would be distributed among the segments S_5^L and S_6^L. This can easily be verified as follows:

$$S_1^L = \frac{16}{24}S_1^{L-1};\quad S_2^L = \frac{8}{24}\left(S_1^{L-1} + S_2^{L-1}\right);\quad S_3^L = \frac{16}{24}S_2^{L-1};$$

$$S_4^L = \frac{16}{24}S_2^{L-1};\quad S_5^L = \frac{8}{24}\left(S_3^{L-1} + S_4^{L-1}\right);\quad S_6^L = \frac{16}{24}S_4^{L-1}.$$

4. Results and Discussion

The conservative scheme provides video data to users in time, whereas the staircase scheme does not. That is the reason we have considered the conservative scheme for live video broadcasting. Another important characteristics of this scheme is that the number of segments occupied by a video channel C_i is the sum of all the segments transmitted by all video channels having indices 1, 2, ⋯, $i - 1$. Because of this the channel transition can be done at optimal time point, *i.e.*, the transition can be delayed till all time slots of all video channels have been occupied. The buffer storage requirement depends upon the arrival time of the request, but in no case it can be more than 50% of the video length. Consider **Figure 5** in which the gray-colored channel is the live channel and the dark black line in each channel is the channel transition point.

Using similar discussions, we can find out the buffer requirement for any request. **Table 1** shows the buffer requirements for different requests (referring to **Figure 5**) for allocating five video channels to the video.

In **Table 2**, for R_{12} and R_{13} requests, there are two different storage requirements. If the live video is over after the 24th segment, then it is 11S and 11S, respectively; otherwise 12S and 13S. The waiting time in this scheme is pre-decided for the initial users and remains same till the channel transition time. After every channel transition except the last one the waiting time becomes double. When the live transmission is over, the final channel transition is carried out and then the user's waiting time is stabilized. We can find out how many and what the initial time slots are in a new time slot after the live video is over. The size of a time slot after the channel transition except the last one becomes double. If T_i and T_i^1 are the ith time slots before and after the first channel transition, then we have the following relation:

$$T_i^1 = T_{24+2i-1} + T_{24+2i}$$

In general, we have

$$T_i^k = T_{24+2i-1}^{k-1} + T_{24+2i}^{k-1}, \quad \text{for} \quad k = 1, 2, \cdots, L-1, \qquad (1)$$

where T_i^0 denotes the very first ith time slot, *i.e.*, $T_i^0 = T_i$ and L specifies the final channel transition.

It is to note that till the final but one channel transition the time slots become double of the previous ones. We can find the size of a time slot after any channel transition in terms of the original time slots. For example, consider fourth channel transition (assuming it is not the last channel transition). Then, from (1), we have

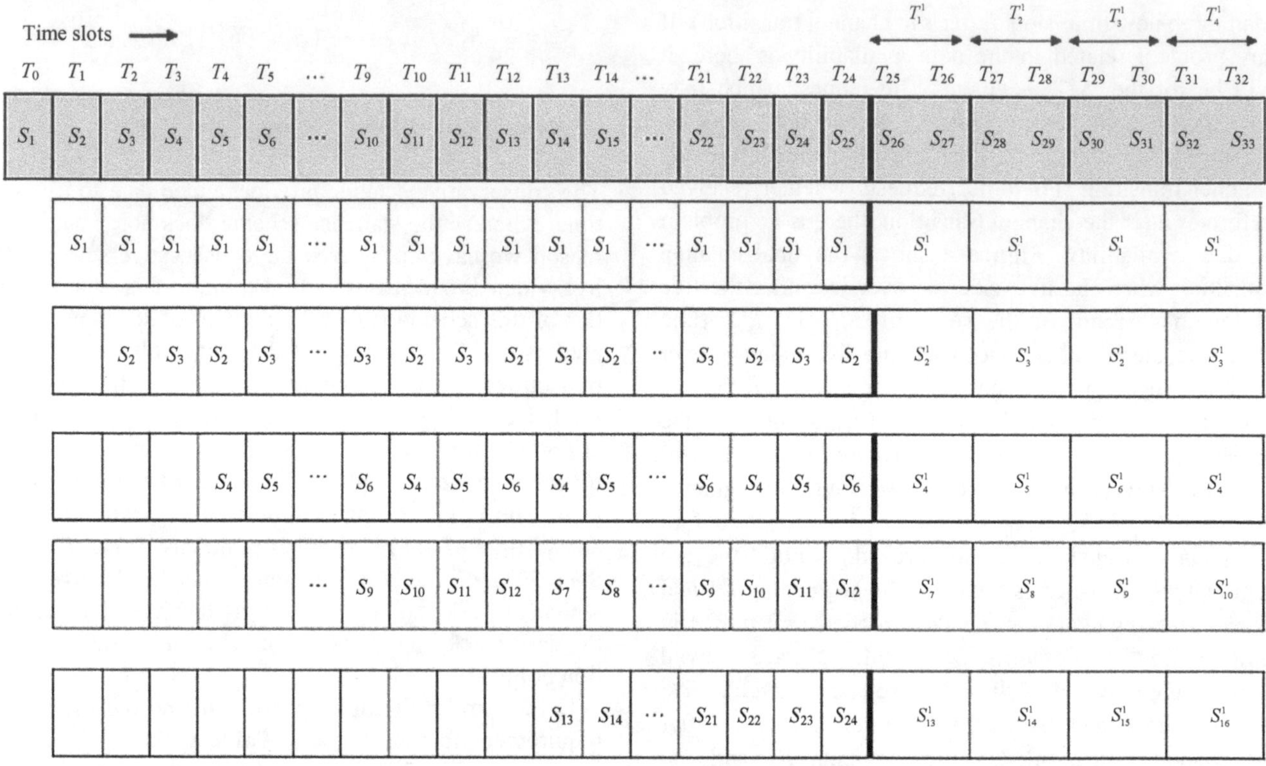

Figure 5. Availability of segments over different channels before and after the channel transition.

Table 1. Segments (seg.) stored from the live system and video server (VS) for R_{10}.

Time slot	*Seg. available for storing from VS*	*Seg. stored from VS*	*Seg. stored from live system*	*Seg. required for viewing*	*Total seg. required*
T_{11}	$S_2 + S_6 + S_{10}$	S_2	S_{12}	S_1	$+1 + 1 = 2$
T_{12}	$S_3 + S_4 + S_{11}$	$S_3 + S_4$	S_{13}	S_2	$+2 - 1 + 1 = 2$
T_{13}	S_5	S_5	S_{14}	S_3	$+1 - 1 + 1 = 1$
T_{14}	S_6	S_6	S_{15}	S_4	$+1 - 1 + 1 = 1$
T_{15}	S_7	S_7	S_{16}	S_5	$+1 - 1 + 1 = 1$
T_{16}	S_8	S_8	S_{17}	S_6	$+1 - 1 + 1 = 1$
T_{17}	S_9	S_9	S_{18}	S_7	$+1 - 1 + 1 = 1$
T_{18}	S_{10}	S_{10}	S_{19}	S_8	$+1 - 1 + 1 = 1$
T_{19}	S_{11}	S_{11}	S_{20}	S_9	$+1 - 1 + 1 = 1$
T_{20}			S_{21}	S_{10}	$-1 + 1 = 0$
T_{21}			S_{22}	S_{11}	$-1 + 1 = 0$
Buffer Storage required for request R_{10} = 11S					

In last column "+" and "–" sign indicate that segment is stored in buffer and read from buffer., e.g., $+1 - 1 + 1 = 1$ means 1 segment are stored from the video server, 1 segment is read from buffer, and 1 segment is stored from the live channel into buffer. Thus, net requirement is 1 segment. S_1 is viewed while downloading.

Table 2. Buffer requirement for different requests allocating five video channels.

Request	*Buffer Requirement*	*Request*	*Buffer Requirement*
R_0	S	R_7	8S
R_1	2S	R_8	9S
R_2	3S	R_9	10S
R_3	4S	R_{10}	11S
R_4	5S	R_{11}	12S
R_5	6S	R_{12}	11S or 12S
R_6	7S	R_{13}	11S or 13S

$$T_i^4 = T_{24+2i-1}^3 + T_{24+2i}^3 \quad (2)$$

We can take $i = 1$ because after any channel transition all time slots are of same durations. Thus, we have from (2),

$$T_1^4 = T_{25}^3 + T_{26}^3$$

We now need T_{25}^3 and T_{26}^3, which are given by

$$T_{25}^3 = T_{24+49}^2 + T_{24+50}^2 = T_{73}^2 + T_{74}^2;$$
$$T_{26}^3 = T_{24+51}^2 + T_{24+52}^2 = T_{75}^2 + T_{76}^2.$$

Again T_{73}^2, T_{74}^2, T_{75}^2, and T_{76}^2 are needed and they are given by

$$T_{73}^2 = T_{24+145}^1 + T_{24+146}^1 = T_{169}^1 + T_{170}^1$$
$$T_{74}^2 = T_{24+147}^1 + T_{24+148}^1 = T_{171}^1 + T_{172}^1$$
$$T_{75}^2 = T_{24+149}^1 + T_{24+150}^1 = T_{173}^1 + T_{174}^1$$
$$T_{76}^2 = T_{24+151}^1 + T_{24+152}^1 = T_{175}^1 + T_{176}^1$$

We need T_{169}^1, T_{170}^1, T_{171}^1, T_{172}^1, T_{173}^1, T_{174}^1, T_{175}^1, and T_{176}^1, and they are given by

$$T_{169}^1 = T_{24+337}^0 + T_{24+338}^0 = T_{361}^0 + T_{362}^0$$
$$T_{170}^1 = T_{24+339}^0 + T_{24+340}^0 = T_{363}^0 + T_{364}^0$$
$$T_{171}^1 = T_{24+341}^0 + T_{24+342}^0 = T_{365}^0 + T_{366}^0$$
$$T_{172}^1 = T_{24+343}^0 + T_{24+344}^0 = T_{367}^0 + T_{368}^0$$
$$T_{173}^1 = T_{24+345}^0 + T_{24+346}^0 = T_{369}^0 + T_{370}^0$$
$$T_{174}^1 = T_{24+347}^0 + T_{24+348}^0 = T_{371}^0 + T_{372}^0$$
$$T_{175}^1 = T_{24+349}^0 + T_{24+350}^0 = T_{373}^0 + T_{374}^0$$
$$T_{176}^1 = T_{24+351}^0 + T_{24+352}^0 = T_{375}^0 + T_{376}^0$$

Here $T_i^0 s$ denote original time slots. So, we have

$$T_1^4 = T_{361} + T_{362} + \cdots + T_{376}$$

The time slot after the final channel transition (*i.e.*, Lth) is α times of a time slot of that of $(L-1)$th channel transition, where $0.5 \le \alpha \le 1$. The value of $\alpha = 0.5$ means that the live video was over at the time when all time slots of all video channels had been occupied by the segments. In that case the last channel transition was not required. This situation is exactly same for $\alpha = 1$. If $\alpha = 1$, then the live video transmission is over just after all time slots of all the channels have been occupied. In this case, the user's waiting time is unchanged. It means that after the final but one channel transition, the number of segments is such that all time slots of the last channel have been occupied and we need not do anything. Here we have discussed for values of $\alpha = 0.5$ and 1. The exact value of α for other cases will depend on when the live video is over. Since we do not know in advance when the live video will be over, the exact value of α cannot be determined in advance. When the live video is over, the entire video data is distributed on all channels as per the scheme's basic architecture.

In other broadcasting schemes including the conservative staircase scheme the user waiting time is decided by the bandwidth allocated to the video, *i.e.*, the size of a video segment, whereas in the proposed scheme it varies after every channel transition. The initial waiting time is decided by the service provider. As we know that the segment size becomes double of the previous size after every channel transition except the last channel transition, so is the user's waiting time. As far as performance of the proposed scheme is concerned, there does not seem to appear alternative work in literature to make a meaningful comparison and hence the comparison is not possible.

5. Conclusions

In this paper, we have proposed a technique for supporting the live video in the conservative scheme. The important characteristics of the conservative scheme is that the number of segments transmitted by a video channel is equal to the sum of all segments transmitted by all lower-indexed channels. This characteristic has been exploited to develop a mechanism for the live video. Providing live video services has wide applications, such as cricket match, interactive education session, etc.

6. References

[1] Y.-C. Tseng, M.-H. Yang and C.-H. Chang, "A Recursive Frequency-Splitting Scheme for Broadcasting Hot Videos in VOD Service," *IEEE Transactions on Communications*, Vol. 50, No. 8, 2002, pp. 1348-1355.

[2] W. F. Poona, K.-T. Lo and J. Feng, "First Segment Partition for Video-on-Demand Broadcasting Protocols," *Computer Communications*, Vol. 26, No. 14, 2003, pp. 1698-1708.

[3] S. Vishwanathan and T. Imielinski, "Metropolitan Area Video on Demand Service Using Pyramid Broadcasting," *Multimedia Systems*, Vol. 4, No. 4, 1996, pp. 197-208.

[4] L. Gao, J. Kurose and D. Towsley, "Efficient Schemes for Broadcasting Popular Videos," *Multimedia Systems*, Vol. 8, No. 4, 2002, pp. 284-294.

[5] Ch.-L. Chan, S.-Y. Huang, T.-C. Su and J.-S. Wang, "Buffer-Assisted on-Demand Multicast for VOD Applications," *Multimedia Systems*, Vol. 12, No. 2, 2006, pp. 89-100.

[6] S. Ramesh, I. Rhee and K. Guo, "Multicast with Cache (Mcache): An Adaptive Zero-Delay Video-on-Demand Service," *IEEE Proceedings of 2th Annual Joint Confer-*

ence of the Computer and Communications Societies, Vol. 1, Anchorage, 22-26 April 2001, pp. 85-94.

[7] L. S. Juhn and L.-M. Tseng, "Harmonic Broadcasting Scheme for Video-on-Demand Service," *IEEE Transactions on Consumer Electronics*, Vol. 43, No. 3, 1997, pp. 268-271.

[8] J.-F. Paris, S. W. Carter and D. D. E. Long, "Efficient Broadcasting Protocols for Video on Demand," *Proceedings of 6th International Symposium on Modeling, Analysis and Simulation of Computer and Telecommunication Systems*, Montreal, 19-24 July 1998, pp. 127-132.

[9] K. A. Hua and S. Sheu, "Skyscraper Broadcasting: A New Broadcasting Scheme for Metropolitan Video on Demand Systems," *ACM SIGCOMM Computer Communication Review*, Vol. 27, No. 4, 1997, pp. 89-100.

[10] Z. Q. Gu and S. Y. Yu, "Conservative Staircase Data Broadcasting Protocol for Video on Demand," *IEEE Transactions on Consumer Electronics*, Vol. 49, No. 4, 2003, pp. 1073-1077.

[11] L. S. Juhn and L. M. Tseng, "Fast Data Broadcasting and Receiving for Popular Video Service," *IEEE Transactions on Broadcasting*, Vol. 44, No. 1, 1998, pp. 100-105.

[12] L. S. Juhn and L. M. Tseng, "Staircase Data Broadcasting and Receiving Scheme for Hot Video Service," *IEEE Transactions on Consumer Electronics*, Vol. 43, No. 4, 1997, pp. 1110-1117.

[13] S. Chand, "Live Video Services Using Fast Broadcasting Scheme," *Journal of Communications and Network*, Vol. 2, No. 1, 2010, pp. 79-85.

24

An Ultra Low-Voltage and Low-Power OTA Using Bulk-Input Technique and Its Application in Active-RC Filters

Arash Ahmadpour
Department of Electronic Engineering, Lahijan Branch, Islamic Azad University, Lahijan, Iran

Abstract

This paper presents the design of a two-stage bulk-input pseudo-differential operational transconductance amplifier (OTA) and its application in active-RC filters. The OTA was designed in 90 nm CMOS process and operates at a single supply voltage of 0.5 V. Using a two-path bulk-driven OTA by the combination of two different amplifiers the DC gain and speed of the OTA is increased. Rail-to-rail input is made possible using the transistor's bulk terminal as in input. Also a Miller-Feed-forward (MFF) compensation is utilized which is improved the gain bandwidth (GBW) and phase margin of the OTA. In addition, a new merged cross-coupled self-cascode pair is used that can provide higher gain. Also, a novel cost-effective bulk-input common-mode feedback (CMFB) circuit has been designed. Simplicity and ability of using this new merged CMFB circuit is superior compared with state-of-the-art CMFBs. The OTA has a 70.2 dB DC gain, a 2.5 MHz GBW and a 70.8° phase margin for a 20 PF capacitive load whereas consumes only 25 μw. Finally, an 8th order Butterworth active Biquadrate RC filter has been designed and this OTA was checked by a typical switched-capacitor (SC) integrator with a 1 MHz clock-frequency.

Keywords: Operational Transconductance Amplifier (OTA), Common-Mode Feedback (CMFB), Bulk-Input, Switched-Capacitor (SC) Integrator, Miller-Feed-Forward (MFF)

1. Introduction

There are growing strong demands for low-voltage supply and low-power consumption circuits and systems. This is especially true for very high integration level and very large scale integrated (VLSI) mixed-signal chips and system-on-a-chip. In mixed-signal systems, the analog circuits are combined with digital circuits in order to get the best performance with low-voltage supply and low-power consumption. This combination should be in an optimal way and the optimization process is application dependent. Also modern portable applications such as medical devices and remote wireless sensors require extending the battery life as well. This trend has forced designers to develop new approaches more amenable to low-voltage and low-power integrated circuits and it poses lots of challenges for all involved such as processes, devices, circuits, and system architectures [1]. Operational transconductance amplifiers (OTAs) are the key active building blocks of continuous-time filters. They can be generally classified into single ended, fully differential and pseudo-differential OTAs. Fully differential OTAs are preferred because they provide larger signal swing, better distortion performance, better CM noise and supply noise rejection. The main drawback of using fully differential OTAs is that a common-mode feedback (CMFB) circuit must be added. The principle of the CM control circuit can be easily applied to the design of differential structures, and it is well suited for low-voltage pseudo-differential architectures. This extra circuit is used to establish the common-mode output voltage and suppress the common mode signal components [2]. The speed of the common-mode path should be comparable to that of the differential path; otherwise the common-mode noise may be significantly amplified such that the output signal becomes distorted. Also, the CMFB circuit is often a source of noise injection and increases the load capacitance that needs to be driven. Regardless of the limitations described above, fully differential OTAs work very well and can substantially improve the system's quality, especially in very unfriendly environments such as mixed-mode applications. However, at lower supply voltages, pseudo differential OTAs could be used to avoid the voltage drop across the tail current source used in the fully differential structures. Taking the tail current source achieves a larger signal swing, but it also results in larger CM gain. So it requires to carefully controlling the CM response for pseudo differential OTAs. The reduced supply voltage will cause many problems when designing analog circuits due to the reduction in available signal swing. This problem is magnified due to the fact that the threshold voltage (V_T) of the transistors has been reduced at a slower rate than the supply voltage. In other words, the threshold-voltage with decreasing the Power supply never reduces linearly. If standard analog design techniques continue to be used, the dynamic range and SNR of the circuits will degrade. The gain of devices such as amplifiers will also decrease because cascode transistors can no longer be used since they limit the output swing. The design of rail-to-rail input circuits is also made more difficult due to the large V_T which must be overcome. One solution for designing low-voltage analog circuits is to operate the transistors in the weak inversion region. The drawbacks to this technique include a limited input signal swing, an increase in the mismatch between transistors, a low slew-rate due to the low bias current levels, and large transistor sizes [3-6]. In order to avoid these drawbacks a bulk-input technique can be used, which allows for operation in the moderate inversion region at supply voltages equal to the V_T of the technology. The voltage applied to the bulk actually reduces the threshold voltage of the transistor, which increases the inversion level. One drawback of the bulk input technique is that the input transistor must sit in an n-well or p-well, so that its bulk is separate from the bulk of the rest of the transistors. This is not a problem in advanced technologies, which make use of triple well structures. In triple-well processes both the NMOS and PMOS can have isolated bulk terminals [5]. This paper presents the design of a novel two-stage bulk-input pseudo differential OTA, which operates at a supply voltage of 0.5 V. The circuit was designed using the 90 nm process in digital CMOS technology. Design procedure for this new merged OTA structure such as main OTA, CMFB and bias circuits are introduced in Section 2. In Section 3, SC integrator and active RC filter design are described. Section 4 presents simulation results. Finally, conclusions and acknowledge are given in Section 5 and 6, respectively.

2. Bulk-Input OTA Circuit Design

2.1. Main Amplifier

A basic body-input stage, capable of operating with very low supply voltage is depicted in **Figure 1**. This structure is a two-path OTA built by the combination of the two different amplifiers. In this circuit a PMOS body-driven OTA is implemented due to the action of M_{1+}, M_{1-}, M_{4+} and M_{4-}, and also a current-mirror bulk-input OTA is composed by transistors M_{2+}, M_{2-}, M_{3-} and M_{3+}. The OTA input consists of two bulk-input split differential pairs; some of the ac current generated by the input transistors is injected to the output transistors, providing a fast path for the current. The other part of the current is delivered to the current mirrors of M_{3+} and M_{3-}. These are the main transistors which the main portion of the currents by the factor n transfer to output transistors of M_{4+} and M_{4-}. If we suppose M_{4+} and M_{4-} have equal effective voltage to M_{1+} and M_{1-}, their transconductances are very much greater than bulk- transconductance of M_{1+} and M_{1-} ($g_{m4} >> g_{mb1}$). It is possible to utilize common-source amplifier which is parallel and in same phase with M_1 when the input signal is implied to the gate of M_4 via feed-forward (FF) compensate capacitor C_{ff} (not shown in **Figure 1**). Moreover, the transistor of the active load current source operates like a common source amplifier. This structure increases the gain and speed of the OTA. M_{3+} and M_{3-} with diode connections utilize for M_{4+} and M_{4-} biasing and use in M_{2+} and M_{2-} as a differential loads.

To further improve the differential gain PMOS devices (M_{5+}, M_{6+} and M_{5-}, M_{6-}) are added. The body-inputs of them are a new merged cross-coupled self-cascode pairs that adds a negative resistance to the output in the form of g'_{mb6} and boosts the differential DC gain. The g'_{mb6} is the g_{mb} of the self-cascode configuration of M_5, M_6. Also, the gate inputs biased at 100 mV, which biases them in moderate inversion. Moreover, these transistors are a self-cascode active load for transistors M_{4+} and M_{4-} which are common source amplifiers.

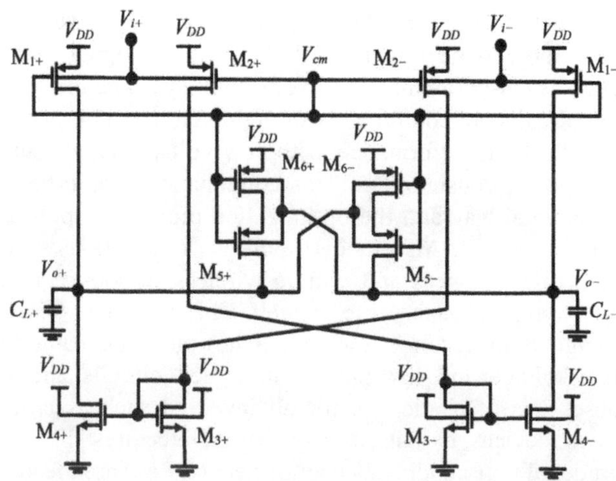

Figure 1. One stage of proposed bulk-input differential pair.

2.2. Bulk-Mode Common-Mode Feedback Circuit

The Fully differential OTAs require a common-mode feedback circuit. A CMFB circuit should behave linearly and only response to common-mode voltage. Lacking these features causes increase the THD of the circuit. Nowadays, designing a CMFB circuit which is able to operate under an ultra low-voltage supply is very difficult, mainly because of the difficulty of detecting of CM voltage. In Reference [5] a CMFB circuit which operated at 0.5 V by using two resistors to sense the output CM levels was designed. But this structure increases the die area and reduces the gain due to longer loads the OTA. To overcome some of these problems, a CMFB circuit has been reported [6]. This structure uses of four PMOS and two NMOS transistors. The NMOS devices is a bulk-input current mirror, which compares the current of the PMOS devices and then difference of these current is fed to the gate of the input transistors for controlling of the output CM voltages. This paper is given a novel continuous-time CMFB circuit that is able to operate with an ultra low-voltage supply. **Figure 2** shows the proposed CMFB circuit for each stage.

In this circuit, a combination of two complementary NMOS and PMOS transistors is used in a bulk-driven configuration. The output voltage of the CMFB circuit can be found using the KCL at the output node (V_{cm}). The difference between currents of PMOS and NMOS transistors is fed to the gate of the input transistors of OTA. The bulks of the PMOS devices M_{cp+} (M_{cp-}) connected to the NMOS devices M_{cn+} (M_{cn-}) and are utilized to maintain the output common voltage at the required level (250 mV), while maximizing the output swing of the OTA. In other words, the inputs to the CMFB circuit are the outputs of the OTA, V_{o+} and V_{o-}. The CMFB circuit amplifies the difference between the average of V_{o+} and V_{o-} and the desired common level V_{cm} (250 mV), and sends a feedback signal V_{cm} to set the bias voltage at the gates of input transistors of the OTA. This structure is able to operate with an ultra low supply voltage (as low as 0.3 V supply voltage).

In addition, this configuration with minimizing of the area cost and power consumption is a very cost-effective CMFB which is much more applicable regarding modern ultra low-voltage and low-power mixed-signal SoCs. Simplicity and ability of using this new merged CMFB circuit to set the output CM voltage of OTA is superior compared with state-of-the-art CMFB.

To obtain adequate gain, identical gain blocks can be cascaded so that a two-stage OTA is obtained. **Figure 3** show the proposed OTA structure in first and second stages without bias and CMFB circuits. In order to improve the phase margin and speed of amplifier, we were used Feed-forward compensation. Finally, the OTA was stabilized by adding Miller compensation capacitors Cc with series resistors Rc for right half-plane zero cancelation. The OTA was designed and classified into two kinds of compensations, such as only Miller compensation and Miller-Feed-forward (MFF) compensation. The comparison of two these methods of compensations are given in **Table 1**. As can be seen, the MFF compensation method increases the phase margin and enhances the open-loop GBW about two times as much.

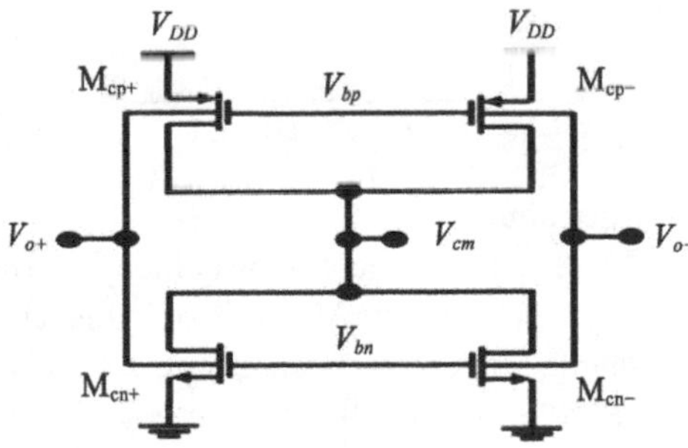

Figure 2. Ultra low-voltage bulk-mode CMFB circuit.

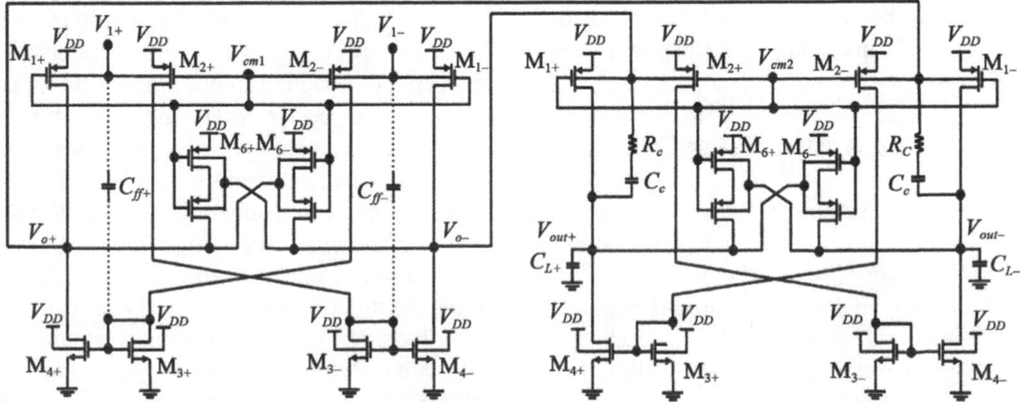

Figure 3. Two-stage bulk-input pseudo-differential OTA without bias and CMFB circuits.

Table 1. Comparison of two compensation methods.

Resistors and Capacitors	Miller-comp.	MFF-comp.
R_c	60 k	68 k
C_c	3 pf	1 pf
C_{ff}	-	3 pf
Open-loop GBW	962 KHz	2.5 MHz
Phase-Margin	65°	70.8°

2.3. Reference Current Generator and Bias Circuit

A low-sensitivity reference current generator and bias circuit are illustrated in **Figure 4**. Because the gate and source of M_{B3} and M_{B4} are common for both transistors, and the aspect ratios are equal, $I_{D\,MB3} = I_{D\,MB4}$. Also, note that $V_{GS\,MB2} = V_{GS\,MB1} + R_B \cdot I_{D\,MB1}$. Thus,

$$\sqrt{\frac{2I_{DM_{B3}}}{\mu_n \cdot C_{ox} \cdot (W/L)_{M_{B2}}}} = \sqrt{\frac{2I_{DM_{B3}}}{\mu_n \cdot C_{ox} \cdot K \cdot (W/L)_{M_{B2}}}} + R_B \cdot I_{DM_{B3}} \quad (1)$$

In the above mentioned equation, K is the ratio between the aspect ratios of M_{B1} and M_{B2}. Rearranging this expression,

$$I_{DM_{B3}} = \frac{1}{R_B^2} \frac{2}{\mu_n \cdot C_{ox} . K \cdot (W/L)_{M_{B2}}} \left(1 - \frac{1}{K}\right) \quad (2)$$

In the target circuit, $k = 1.13$ and $R_B = 1$ k, thus $I_{D\,MB3} = 1.25$ uA. As expected, the circuit is independent of the supply voltage. Transistor M_{B5} mirrors this current to generate a stable 2 uA reference current, which is used in the bias of PMOS devices. In order to ensure that the all transistors operate in the saturation region, fixed bias voltages are applied either to the gate of the PMOS and NMOS transistors in the main OTA and CMFB circuits. The gate voltage all of the NMOS and PMOS transistors biased in about $V_{bn} = 350$ mV and $V_{bp} = 100$ mV, respectively.

3. SC Integrator and Active Filter Circuit

In order to show that the designed OTA will be useful in practical analog circuits, this structure was checked by a typical switched-capacitor (SC) integrator [7,8] with suitable input frequency 1 KHz and sampling frequency 1 MHz. **Figure 5** is shown schematic of this structure. In switched-capacitor integrator design, we utilized two clock-frequencies which have no overlap and used Bootstrapped switches in Reference [9].

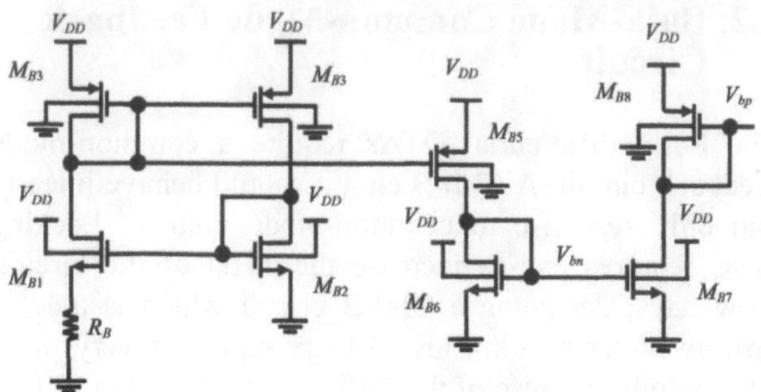

Figure 4. Reference current generator and bias circuit.

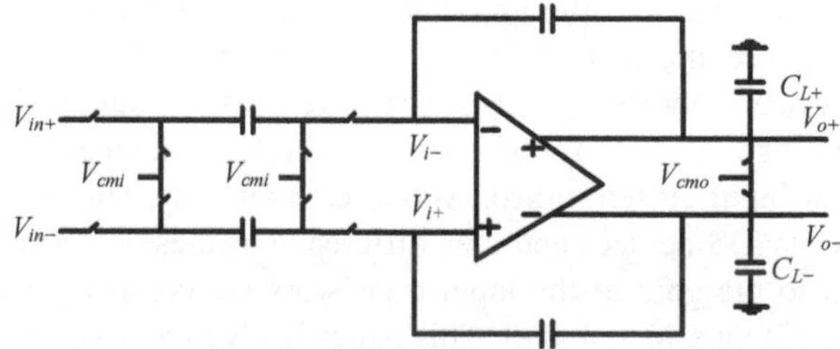

Figure 5. Fully differential switched-capacitor integrato.

Simulation result of this structure is depicted in **Figure 11**.

Filters are systems that can be used to manipulate the frequency spectrum of signals and they are essential in many different applications. The low-pass continuous-time filter is used to limit signal and noise bandwidth and provide anti-aliasing prior sampling. The analog-to- digital converter (ADC) digitizes the filtered output to take the advantages of the Digital Signal Processing (DSP) unit. The equalizer provides the equalization and the equalized signal goes to the decoder. The gain/timing control module is used to adjust the gain of the VGA. Although we are living in a digital age, many digital systems interfacing with the real analog world might use continuous-time filters. There are mainly two types of filters: digital filters and analog filters. While the data samples are discrete for digital filters, analog filters process continuous signals. Analog filters can be further divided into passive filters and active filters. While passive filters comprise passive components only such as resistors, capacitors, and inductors, active filters use active devices such as operational amplifiers and/or operational transconductance amplifiers (OTAs). Active filters can also be classified into Active-RC, Switched-Ca- pacitor (sampled-data filters), OTA-C/Gm-C, and LC filters. Passive filters do not employ amplifiers and usually they are off-chip filters and are not suitable for integrated circuits. But active-RC and SC filters are suitable for low to medium frequency applications.

This OTA was tested in an 8th order active Biquadrate RC filter for maximize the attainable swing. The filter was built by connecting four 2nd orders Thomas BiQuad stage to implement the Butterworth function, shown in **Figure 6**. The equations of the Two-Thomas biquad filter as follow:

$$\omega_o^2 = \frac{1}{R_{s2} \cdot R_{f2} \cdot C_{f1} \cdot C_{f2}}, Q = \frac{R_{f1}}{\sqrt{R_{s2} \cdot R_{f2}}} \sqrt{\frac{C_{f1}}{C_{f2}}}, A_o = \frac{R_{f2}}{R_{s1}} \quad (3)$$

where A_o is the gain of integrator and ω_o and Q are the cut-off frequency and quality factor of integrator, respectively. Assume $R_{s2} = R_{f2}$, $C_{f1} = C_{f2}$, Equation (3) can be written as:

$$\omega_o = \frac{1}{R_{f2} \cdot C_{f1}}, Q = \frac{R_{f1}}{R_{f2}}, A_o = \frac{R_{f2}}{R_{s1}} \quad (4)$$

In the above mentioned equation, Q and A_o are determined by the ratio of resistors and both Q and ω_o can be tuned independently [10]. This 8th order Butterworth filter consists of four cascaded Thomas biquads; and the cut-off frequency is about 400 KHz. The filter was simulated with components values given in **Table 2**. Also, a plot of the frequency response for input CM voltage from rail-to-rail of this filter is shown in **Figure 12**.

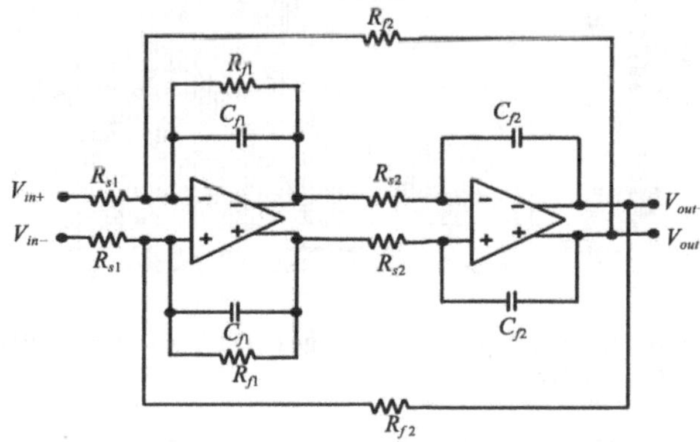

Figure 6. 2nd order Thomas Biquad filter stage.

Table 2. Filter component values.

Components	Stage (1)	Stage (2)	Stage (3)	Stage (4)
R_{s1}	56 k	39 k	47 k	56 k
R_{s2}	56 k	39 k	47 k	56 k
R_{f1}	30 k	87 k	87 k	30 k
R_{f2}	56 k	39 k	47 k	56 k
C_{f1}	10 pf	10 pf	10 pf	12 pf
C_{f2}	10 pf	8 pf	5.4 pf	10 pf

4. Simulation Results

To test op-amp's performance, various configurations were implemented to simulate application condition. Based on the analysis procedure described in the previous sections, an ultra low-voltage OTA at a single 0.5 V supply voltage was designed. The OTA has been designed in 90 nm CMOS process, and then simulated by Hspice. Then this structure was checked by a typical SC integrator with a 1 MHz clock frequency. Also a 8th order active RC-filter with a 400 KHz cut-off frequency was designed. The simulation results are shown in **Figures 7** to **12**. Furthermore, **Table 3** summarizes the simulated performance of this OTA and comparisons of characteristics of proposed OTA with state-of-the-art OTAs. The open-loop frequency response of the OTA for the common-mode input V_{cm} varying from rail-to-rail by a step 0.01 V was tested. The amplitudes and the phases of the proposed OTA were almost independent of the applied V_{cm}. **Figure 5** shows the frequency response of the OTA for V_{cm} = 0.25 V. The result showed a 70.2 dB DC gain, a 2.5 MHz bandwidth and a of 70.8° phase margin. For the closed-loop simulation, the OTA was configured in unity-gain with 1 pf capacitors.

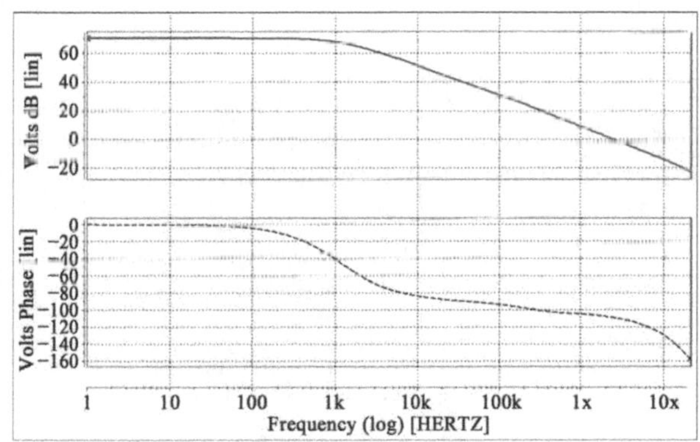

Figure 7. Open-loop frequency response of OTA for V_{cm} = 0.25 V.

Table 3. Comparison of characteristics of proposed OTA with state-of-the-art OTAs.

Parameters	This work	Ref. [5]	Ref. [6]
Technology	90 nm	0.18 μm	0.18 μm
Supply Voltage	0.5 V	0.5 V	0.5 V
Open-loop DC Gain	70.2 dB	62 dB	65 dB
Open-loop GBW	2.5 MHz	10 MHz	550 KHz
Closed-loop GBW	645 KHz	-	475 KHz
Phase-Margin	70.8°	60°	50°
Input ref. noise@1 KHz	139 nV/Hz$^{1/2}$	-	432 nV/Hz$^{1/2}$
FOM	100	133.3	19.6
THD@ 500 mV	0.119%	1%	0.13%
Load Capacitors	20 pf	20 pf	20 pf
Power Consumption	25 μw	110 μw	28 μw

The closed-loop frequency response of the OTA is shown in **Figure 8** for rail-to-rail input common-mod ranges by a step of 50 mV. It is obvious that the frequency responses of OTA have no peak and result a bandwidth of 645 KHz. This shows that the OTA function correctly for rail-to-rail input common-mode voltage values without any considerable decrease in gain.

The main optimization steps were done in transient tests because it is most important behavior. Two inputs were applied to see both small and large signal behavior of OTA in transient mode, when in closed-loop test; the OTA is configured in unity-gain with 1 pf capacitors. For an input common-mode voltage of 250 mV, when 0.1 V step was applied to inputs of OTA, the output voltage was settled to its final value in less than 735 ns (@ 0.01%). Identically, for large signal mode with a 0.3 V step and input common-mode voltage of 250 mV, output voltage was settled in less than 1500 ns for rising and less than 1170 ns for falling (@ 0.02%).

In this case, positive and negative slew-rates are 0.67 V/µs and 0.8 V/µs, respectively. **Figure 9** show transient response of OTA for 0.1 V and 0.3 V inputs, when input common-mode voltage varying from rail-to-rail by a step 50 mV. It is obvious that response has no ring or overshoot because of suitable bandwidth and phase margin.

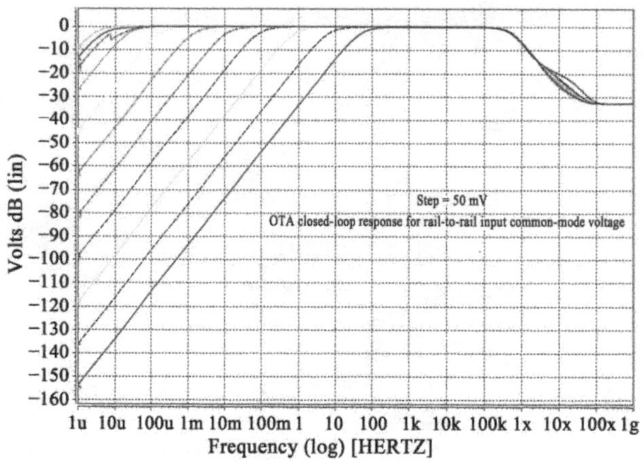

Figure 8. OTA closed-loop response for rail-to-rail common mode input value (Step = 50 mV).

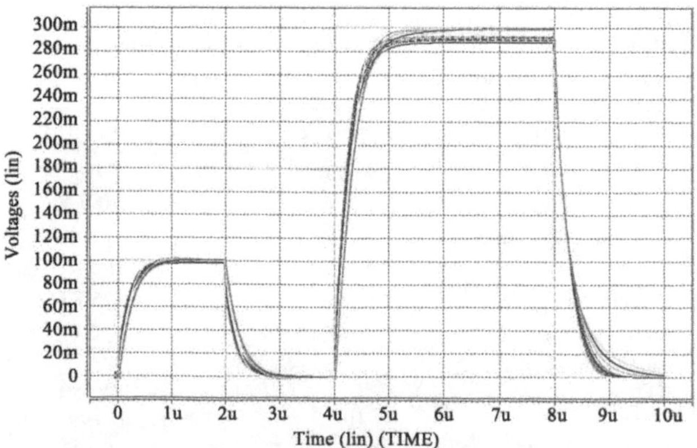

Figure 9. Settling simulated results of OTA for rail-to-rail input common-mode voltage (Step = 50 mV).

The obtained total harmonic distortion of OTA with a 200 mV amplitude and 10 KHz input frequency sampled at 100 KHz is shown in **Figure 10**. The third harmonic is

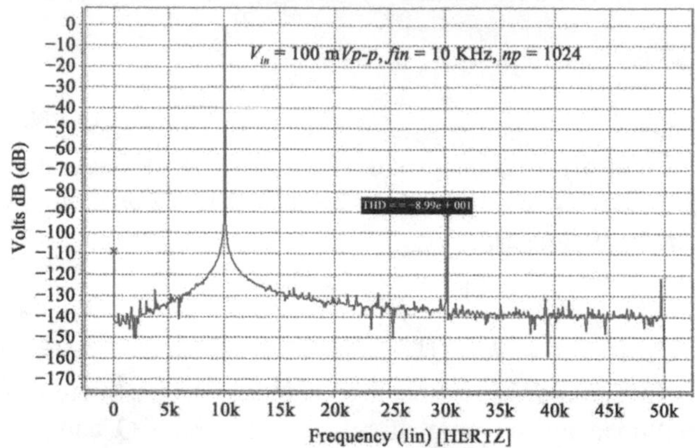

Figure 10. Total harmonic distortion of OTA with f_{in} = 10 KHz and V_{in} = 200 *mVp–p*.

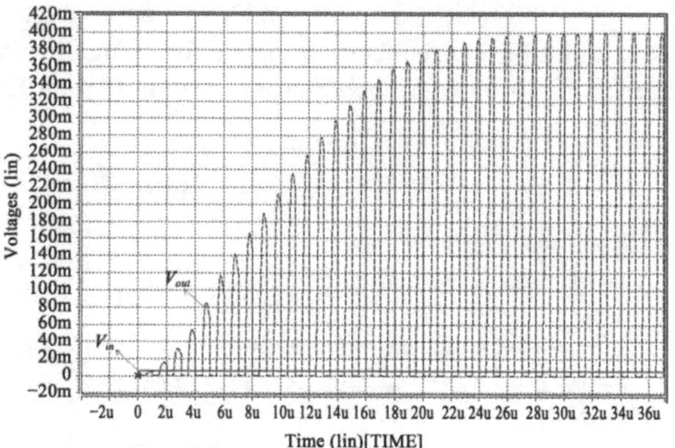

Figure 11. Integrated output voltage of OTA with f_s = 1 MHz and f_{in} = 1 KHz.

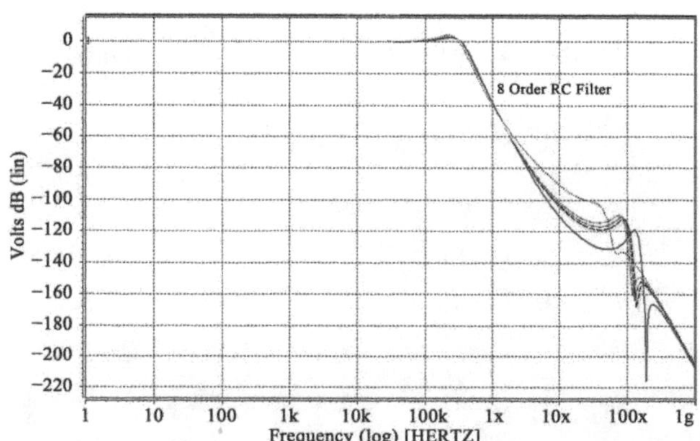

Figure 12. Filter frequency response of OTA v. s input CM voltage from rail-to-rail.

about 90 dB below the fundamental. Also, for 400 mV amplitude, the third harmonic is about −74.4 dB. As can be seen, the extra harmonics except main harmonic has been eliminated in this design.

5. Conclusions

In this paper a novel two-stage configuration of the ultra low-voltage and low-power bulk-input CMOS OTA in 90 nm CMOS process which is able to operate with a single supply voltage as low as 0.5 V has been presented. A new merged cross-coupled self-cascode pair was used and higher DC gain was achieved. In addition, a MFF compensation was utilized which has been improved the GBW and phase margin of the OTA. Also, a new bulk-mode CMFB circuit which no longer loads OTA has been discussed. A large linear signal swing has been achieved due to the well controlled CM behavior. Finally this structure was checked by a typical SC integrator and was tested in an 8th order active Biquadrate RC filter. Correct functionality for this configuration is verified from −30°C to 70°C. In addition, this structure can be used for modern ultra low-voltage and low-power mixed- signal SoCs.

6. Acknowledgements

The work described in this paper is financially supported by a grant from the Research department of the Islamic Azad University-Lahijan Branch. Also, the corresponding author wishes to thank Reviewers for their useful comments and suggestions.

7. References

[1] E. Sanchez-Sinencio and A. G. Andreou, "Low-Voltage and Low Power Integrated Circuits and Systems," *Low-Voltage Mixed-Signal Circuits*, IEEE Press, New York, 1998.

[2] A. N. Mohieldin, "High Performance Continuous-Time Filters for Information Transfer Systems," Ph.D. Dissertation, Department of Electrical Engineering, Texas A & M University, College Station, 2003.

[3] S. Yan and Sanchez-Sinencio, "Low-Voltage Analog Circuit Design Techniques: A Tutorial," *IEICE Transactions on Analog Integrated Circuits and Systems*, Vol. E00-A, No. 2, 2000, pp. 179-196.

[4] S. S. Rajput and S. S. Jamuar, "Low-Voltage Analog Circuit Design Techniques," *IEEE Circuit and System Magazine*, Vol. 2, No. 1, 2002, pp. 24-42.

[5] S. Chatterjee, Y. Tsvidis and P. Kinget, "0.5 V Analog Circuit Techniques and Their Application to OTA and Filter Design," *IEEE Journal of Solid State Circuits*, Vol. 40, No. 12, 2005, pp. 2373-2387.

[6] M. Trakimas and S. Sonkusale, "A 0.5 V Bulk-Input OTA with Improved Common-Mode Feedback for Low--Frequency Filtering Applications," *Analog Integrated Circuits and Signal Processing*, Springer Press, New York, 2009, pp. 83-89.

[7] A. Ahmadpour and R. Fouladi, "A Modified High-Performance Structure of Low-Voltage CMOS Op-Amp," *Proceeding of the* 2008 *IEEE International Conference on Electron Devices and Solid-State Circuits*, Hong Kong, 8-10 December 2008, pp. 1-5.

[8] A. Ahmadpour, "An Ultra Low-Voltage and High-Speed Amplifier for Switched-Capacitor Applications," *6th International Conference on Electrical Engineering/Electronics, Computer, Telecommunications and Information Technology*, Vol. 1, Pattaya, 6-9 May 2009, pp. 552-555.

[9] M. Dessouky and A. Kaiser, "Very Low-Voltage Digital-Audio Modulator with 88-dB Dynamic Range Using Local Switch Bootstrapping," *IEEE Journal of Solid-State Circuits*, Vol. 36, No. 3, March 2001, pp. 349-355.

[10] R. Schaumann and M. E. Van Valkenburg, "Design of Analog Filters," Oxford University Press, Oxford, 2001.

25

Voltage Controlled Ring Oscillator Design with Novel 3 Transistors XNOR/XOR Gates

Manoj Kumar[1], Sandeep Kumar Arya[1], Sujata Pandey[2]
[1]*Department of Electronics & Communication Engineering Guru Jambheshwar, University of Science & Technology, Hisar, India*
[2]*Department of Electronics & Communication Engineering, Amity University, Noida, India*

Abstract

In present work, improved designs for voltage controlled ring oscillators (VCO) using three transistors XNOR/XOR gates have been presented. Supply voltage has been varied from [1.8 - 1.2] V in proposed designs. In first method, the VCO design using three XNOR delay cells shows frequency variation of [1.900 - 0.964] GHz with [279.429 - 16.515] μW power consumption variation. VCO designed with five XNOR delay cells shows frequency variation of [1.152 - 0.575] GHz with varying power consumption of [465.715 - 27.526] μW. In the second method VCO having three XOR stages shows frequency variation [1.9176 - 1.029] GHz with power consumption variation from [296.393 - 19.051] μW. A five stage XOR based VCO design shows frequency variation [1.049 - 0.565] GHz with power consumption variation from [493.989 - 31.753] μW. Simulations have been performed by using SPICE based on TSMC 0.18μm CMOS technology. Power consumption and output frequency range of proposed VCOs have been compared with earlier reported circuits and proposed circuit's shows improved performance.

Keywords: CMOS, Delay Cell, Low Power, VCO, XOR and XNOR Gates

1. Introduction

The Phase locked loops (PLL) are widely used circuit component in data transmission systems and have extensive applications in data modulation, demodulation and mobile communication. Voltage control oscillators (VCO) are the critical and necessary building blocks of these PLL systems. Two widely used VCOs types are LC tank based and CMOS ring circuits. Combination of inductor and capacitor consumes large layout area in LC tank based oscillators [1-3]. CMOS ring based oscillators have advantages due to ease of controlling the output frequency and no requirement for on chip inductors [4,5]. CMOS based ring oscillators are easier to integrate and also gives wide tuning range. Due to flexibility of on chip integration, CMOS based ring oscillators have become essential building blocks in various battery operated mobile communication systems. Rising requirement of portable devices like cellular phones, notebooks, personal communication devices have aggressively enhanced attention for power saving in these devices. Power consumption in very large scale integration (VLSI) systems includes dynamic, static power and leakage power consumption. Dynamic power consumption results from switching of load capacitance between two different voltages and dependent on frequency of operation. Static power is contributed by direct path short circuits currents between supply (V_{dd}) and ground (V_{ss}) and it is dependent on leakage currents components [6,7]. VCOs being the major components in PLL system and is responsible for most of the power consumption. Some draw back of ring based oscillators includes large power consumption, phase noise and the limit of highest achievable frequency. In modern VCOs design power consumption and output frequency range are significant performance metrics [8-13]. A ring oscillator consist of delay stages, with output of last stage fed back to input of first stage. A VCO block diagram with single ended *N*-delay stages is shown in **Figure 1**.

The ring must provide a phase shift of 2π and unity voltage gain for oscillation occurrence. Each delay cell also gives a phase shift of π/N, where N is number of delay stages. The remaining π phase shift is provided by dc inversion using the inverter delay cells. For single ended oscillator design the odd numbers of delay stage are required for dc inversion. Frequency of oscillation with N-single ended delay stages is given by $f_o = 1/(2Nt_d)$, where N is the number of delay stages and t_d is delay of each stage [9,14]. Delay stages are the basic building blocks in any VCO design and improved design of these delay cells will improve the overall performances of VCO. Various types of delay cells have been reported for VCO design including multiple-feed- back loops, dual-delay paths and single ended delays. These delay cells have been implemented by various approaches like simple inverter stage, latches, cross coupled cells etc. [15-18].

In present work modified VCOs circuits with three transistor XNOR/XOR delay cells have been presented with reduced the power consumption and wide output frequency range. The paper is organized as follows: In Section 2 three & five stages XNOR/XOR based ring VCOs have been presented. In Section 3 results for the three proposed VCOs have been obtained and comparisons with earlier reported structures have been made. Finally, in Section 4 conclusions have been drawn.

2. System Description

The frequency of single ended ring VCO is dependent on the delay provided by the each delay cell. In the proposed designs new delay cells based on three transistor XNOR/XOR gates have been used. Inverter operation has been implemented by XNOR/XOR gates. Direct path between V_{dd} and ground has been eliminated in proposed delay cells, due to which leakage power is reduced and the designs are power efficient. The circuits have been designed in 0.18 μm CMOS technology with supply voltage of 1.8 V. Supply voltage/control voltage has been varied from 1.8 to 1.2 V for obtaining the output frequency at different supply voltages.

First proposed delay cell is shown in **Figure 2**. XNOR delay stage is made up of two NMOS transistors and one PMOS transistor. Out of two input terminal of XNOR gate, one is connected to ground and signal is applied to other terminal. This circuits works as inverter without having direct path between V_{dd} and ground with saving in power consumption. A small capacitance of 0.01 pf at output of each delay cell has been included. The gate

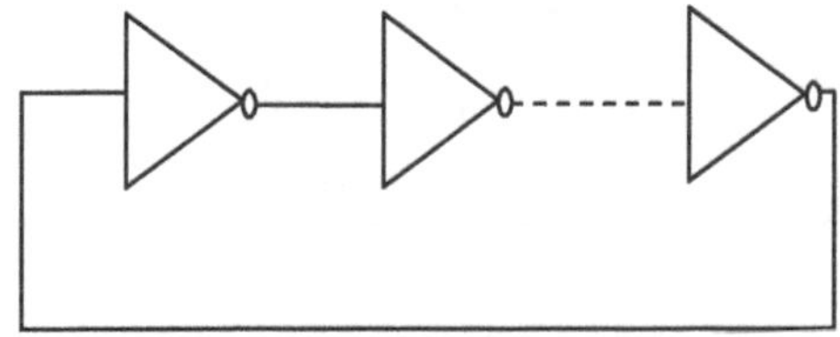

Figure 1. Block diagram of single ended VCO.

lengths of all three transistors have been taken as 0.18 μm. Widths (W_n) of NMOS transistors (N1 & N2) have been taken 2.5 μm and 0.5 μm respectively. Width (W_p) for transistor P1 has been taken as 1.0 μm. Output frequency is controlled by varying the supply voltage of XNOR delay stage. Three and five stages ring VCOs have been designed using proposed XNOR delay cell as shown in **Figures 3(a)** and **(b)**.

Figure 4 shows proposed XOR delay cell, which consist of two PMOS transistors (P1 & P2) and one NMOS transistor (N1). One input terminal of XOR gate is connected to control voltage (V_c) and signal is applied to other terminal so that circuit works as an inverter. The gate length of all three transistors has been taken as 0.18 μm in XNOR delay cell. Width (W_n) of NMOS transistor N1 has been taken 0.25 μm. Width (W_p) for P1 & P2 transistors has been taken as 2.0 μm. Output frequency is controlled by varying the control voltage (V_c) of second input terminal of XOR delay stage. Three and five stages ring VCOs have been designed using proposed XOR delay cell as shown in **Figures 5(a)** and **(b)**.

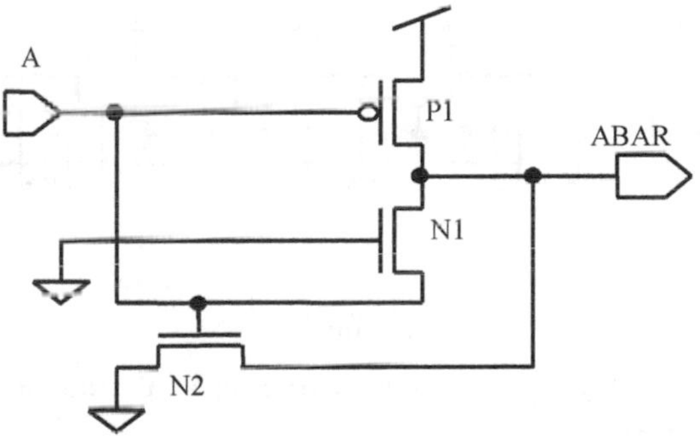

Figure 2. Proposed delay cell based on XNOR gate.

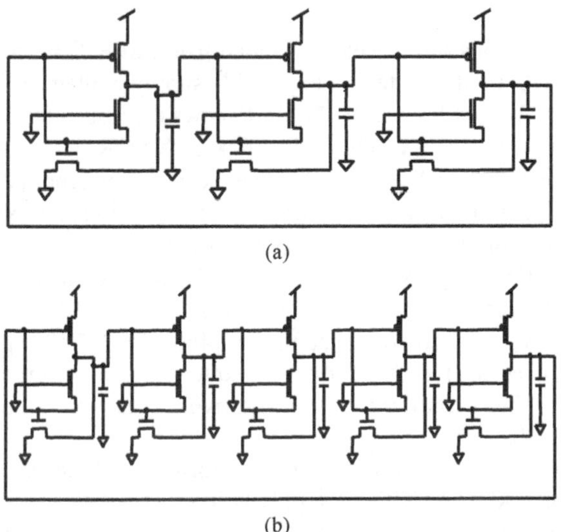

Figure 3. (a) 3 stages, (b) 5 stages ring VCO based on XNOR gate delay cell.

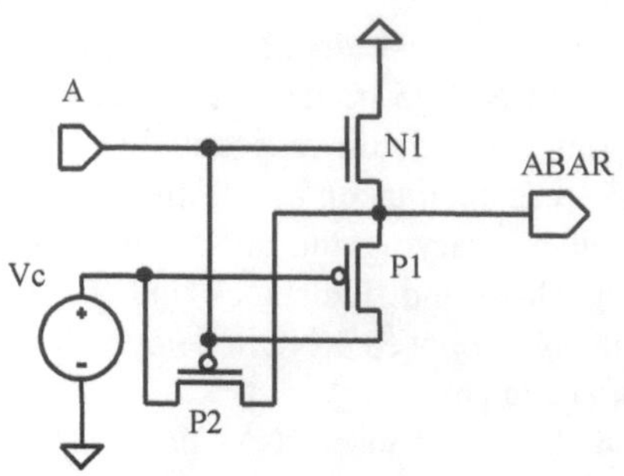

Figure 4. Proposed delay cell based on XOR gate.

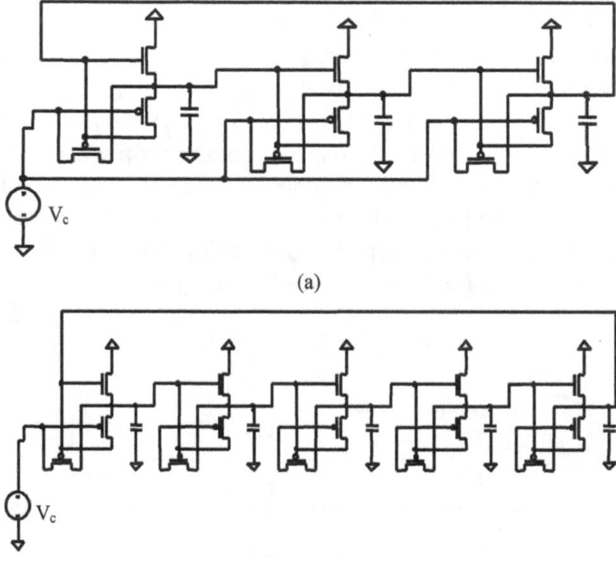

Figure 5. (a) 3 stages, (b) 5 stages ring VCO with on XOR gate delay cell.

3. Results and Discussions

Simulations have been performed using SPICE based on TSMC 0.18 μm technology with supply voltage variations from [1.8 - 1.2] V. **Table 1** shows the results for three and five stages VCOs designed with XNOR delay cells. Supply /control voltage (V_c) has been varied from [1.8 - 1.2] V. Output frequency of three stage VCO shows variation from [1.900 - 0.964] GHz with power consumption variation of [279.429 - 16.515] μW. In five stages ring VCO frequency shows variation from [1.152 - 0.575] GHz with varying power consumption [465.715 - 27.526] μW. **Figures 6(a)** and **(b)** shows frequency and power consumption variation for three and five stages XNOR based ring VCOs.

Figure 7 shows output waveform for three & five stages XNOR VCOs at supply voltage of 1.8 V.

Table 2 shows results for three and five stages ring VCOs designed with XOR delay cells. Control voltage at the second input terminal of delay cells has been varied from [1.8 - 1.2] V. In three stage VCO, output frequency shows variation [1.917 - 1.029] GHz with varying power consumption of [296.393 - 19.051] μW. For five stage XOR VCO frequency varies from [1.049 - 0.565] GHz with varying power consumption of [493.989 - 31.753] μW. **Figures 8(a)** and **(b)** shows frequency and power consumption variation for three and five stages XOR based ring VCOs. **Figure 9** shows output waveform for three & five stages XOR based VCO at supply voltage of 1.8 V.

Table 1. Results for XNOR delay based VCO.

Control voltage (V)	Three stages XNOR VCO		Five stages XNOR VCO	
	Output frequency (GHz)	Power consumption (μW)	Output frequency (GHz)	Power consumption (μW)
1.8	1.900	279.429	1.152	465.715
1.7	1.773	210.349	1.071	350.582
1.6	1.632	151.432	0.978	252.388
1.5	1.469	102.570	0.884	170.950
1.4	1.312	63.786	0.789	106.311
1.3	1.144	35.179	0.686	58.632
1.2	0.964	16.515	0.575	27.526

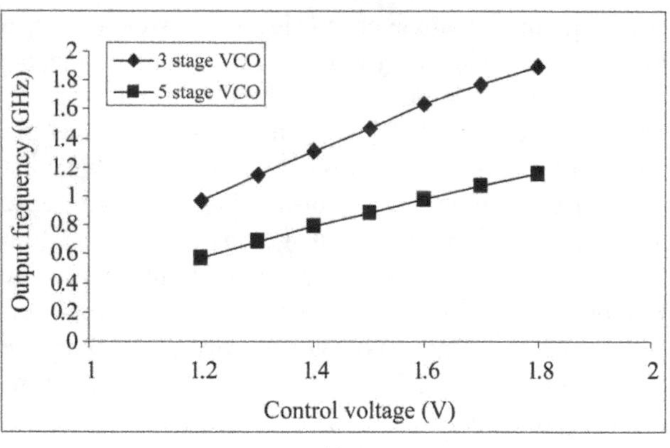

(a)

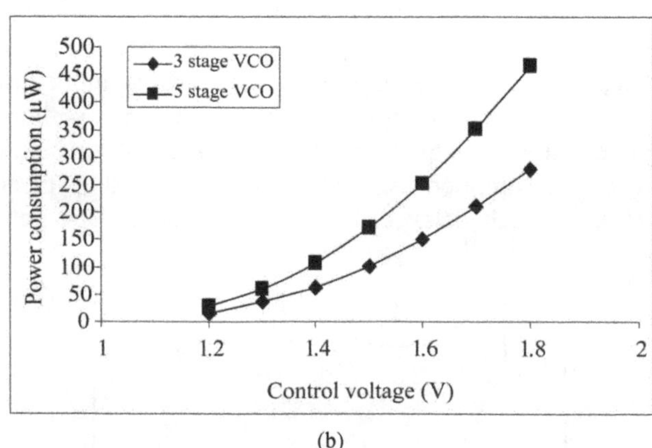

(b)

Figure 6. (a) Frequency, (b) power consumption variations of 3 and 5 stages XNOR based VCO.

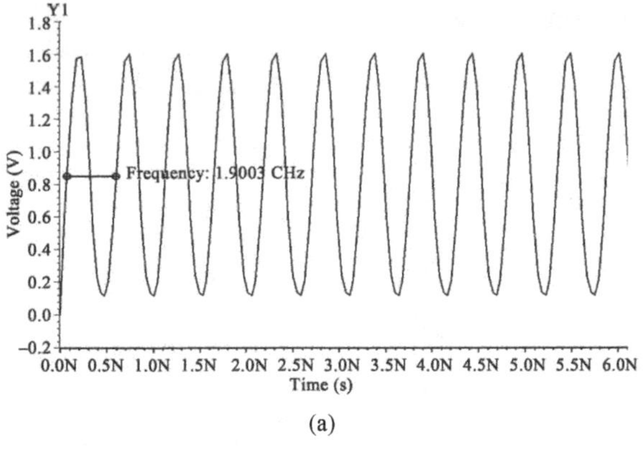

(a)

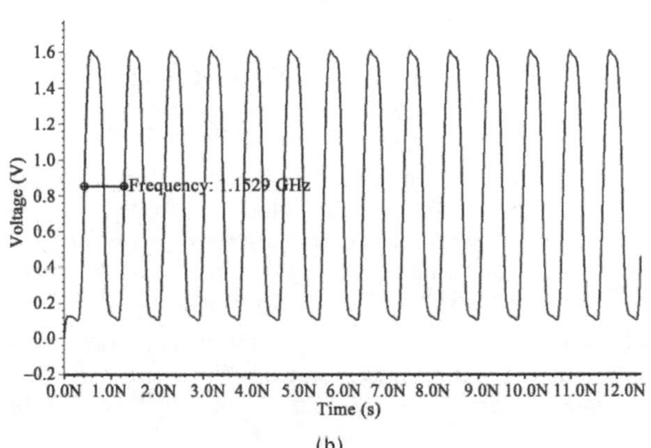

(b)

Figure 7. Wave forms at 1.8 V for (a) 3 stages XNOR VCO, (b) 5 stages XNOR VCO.

Table 2. Results for XOR delay based VCO.

Control Voltage (Vc) (V)	Three stages XOR VCO		Five stages XOR VCO	
	Output frequency (GHz)	Power Consumption (μW)	Output frequency (GHz)	Power Consumption (μW)
1.8	1.917	296.393	1.049	493.989
1.7	1.794	225.614	0.981	376.023
1.6	1.660	164.559	0.908	274.266
1.5	1.507	113.140	0.827	188.568
1.4	1.363	71.500	0.747	119.167
1.3	1.202	40.054	0.656	66.757
1.2	1.029	19.051	0.565	31.753

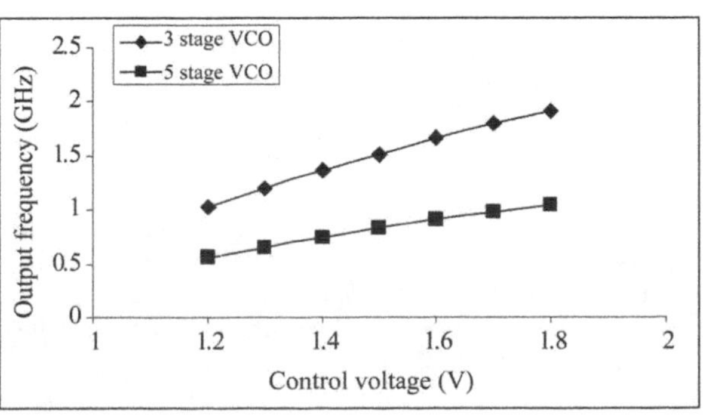

(a)

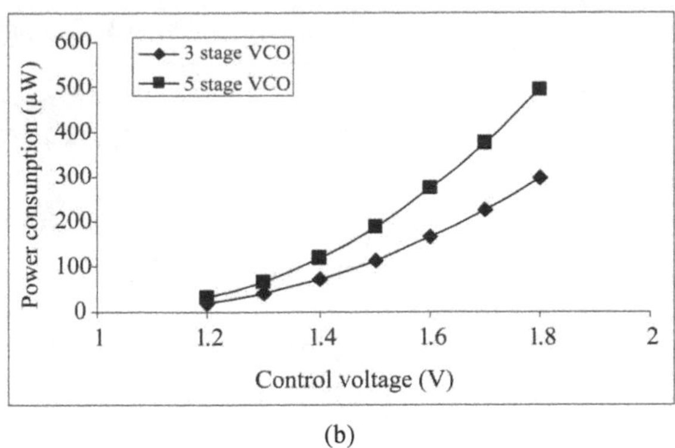

(b)

Figure 8. (a) Frequency, (b) power consumption variations of 3 and 5 stages XOR VCOs.

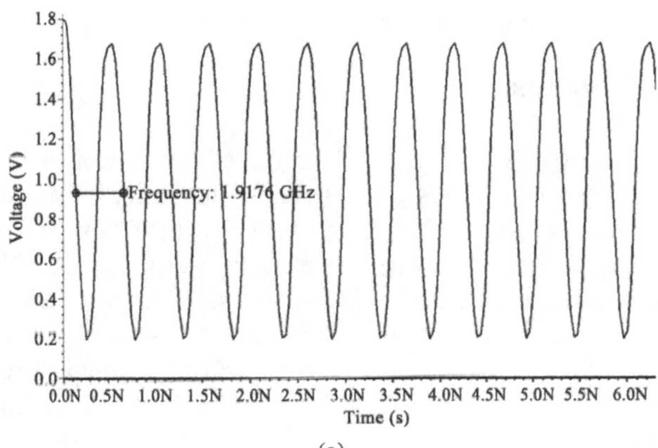

(a)

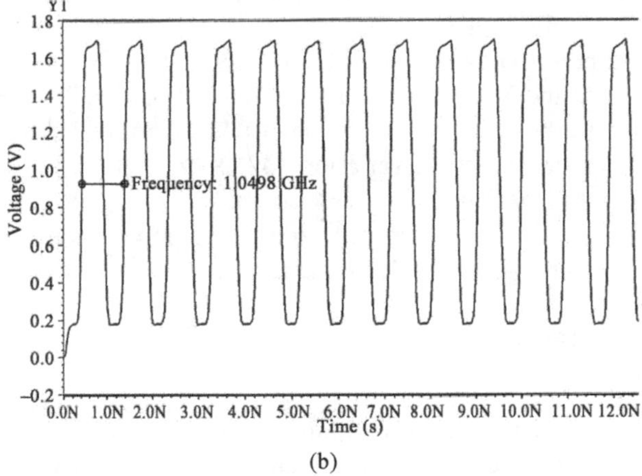

(b)

Figure 9. Wave forms at 1.8 V for (a) 3 stages, (b) 5 stages XOR VCO.

In reported circuits, power consumption is increasing with increase in number of delay stages whereas output frequency is showing downward trend. Number of stages may be decreased or increased depending upon the application, requirement for frequency range and power consumption. A comparison with earlier reported circuits in terms of power consumption and output frequency range is given in **Table 3**. Proposed circuits' shows better

Table 3. Comparison of VCO performance.

VCO designs	Operating frequency (GHz)	Vdd (V)	Technology (μm)	Power consumption
[1]	2.17 - 2.73	0.9	0.18	2.7 mW
[5]	0.39 - 1.41	1.8	0.18	12.5 mW
[10]	0.12 - 1.3	0.5	0.18	0.085 mW
[13]	1.57 - 3.57	1.8	0.090	16.8 mW
[16]	0.65 - 1.6	1.8	0.18	39 mW
Present work [3 stages XNOR]	1.900 - 0.964	1.8	0.18	[279.429 - 16.515] μW
Present work [5 stages XNOR]	1.152 - 0.575	1.8	0.18	[465.715 - 27.526] μW
Present work [3 stages XOR]	1.917 - 1.029	1.8	0.18	[296.393 - 19.051] μW
Present work [5 stages XOR]	1.049 - 0.565	1.8	0.18	[493.989 - 31.753] μW

performance in terms of power consumption and output frequency range than compared circuits.

4. Conclusions

In reported work improved power efficient designs for three and five stages CMOS ring VCOs have been presented. In first methodology design with XNOR delay stages have been presented. Three stages VCO with XNOR shows frequency variation [1.900 - 0.964] GHz with deviation in power consumption from [279.429 - 16.515] μW. Five stages XNOR delay based VCO gives output frequency range [1.152 - 0.575] GHz with power consumption variation [465.715 - 27.526] μW. In the second methodology VCO designed with three stages XOR based delay cell shows frequency variation [1.917 - 1.029] GHz with power consumption variation [296.393 - 19.051] μW. Finally the VCO designed with five stages XOR delay cells shows frequency variation [1.049 - 0.565] GHz with power consumption variation [493.989 - 31.753] μW. Proposed designs have been compared with previously reported design and present approach shows significant power saving with wide tuning range.

5. References

[1] S. Y. Lee and J. Y. Hsieh, "Analysis and Implementation of a 0.9 V Voltage-Controlled Oscillator with Low Phase Noise and Low Power Dissipation," *IEEE Transactions on Circuits and Systems II*, Vol. 55, No. 7, July 2008, pp. 624-627.

[2] J. Craninckx and M. S. J. Steyaert, "A 1.8-GHz CMOS Low-Phase-Noise Voltage-Controlled Oscillator with Prescaler," *IEEE Journal of Solid-state Circuits*, Vol. 30, No. 12, December 1995, pp. 1474-1482.

[3] B. Catli and M. M. Haskell, "A 0.5 V 3.6/5.2 GHz CMOS Multi-Band VCO for Ultra Low-Voltage Wireless Applications," *IEEE International Symposium on Circuits and Systems*, Seattle, 18-21 May 2008, pp. 996-999.

[4] T. Cao, D. T. Wisland, T. S. Lande and F. Moradi, "Low--Voltage, Low-Power, and Wide-Tuning Range VCO for Frequency ΔΣ Modulator," *IEEE Conference on NORCHIP*, Tallinn, 16-17 November 2008, pp.79-84.

[5] L. S. Paula, S. Banpi, E. Fabris and A. A. Susin, "A Wide Band CMOS Differential Voltage-Controlled Ring Oscillators," *Proceeding of 21st Symposium on Integrated Circuits and System Design*, Gramado, 1-4 September 2008, pp. 85-89.

[6] A. P. Chandrakasan, S. Sheng and R. W. Brodersen, "Low--Power CMOS Digital Design," *IEEE Journal of Solid-State Circuits*, Vol. 27, No. 4, April 1992, pp. 473-484.

[7] K. Roy and S. C. Prasad, "Low Power CMOS Circuit Design," Wiely Pvt. Ltd., New Delhi, 2002.

[8] H.-R. Kim, *et al.*, "A Very Low-Power Quadrature VCO with Back-Gate Coupling," *IEEE Journal of Solid-State Circuits*, Vol. 39, No. 6, June 2004, pp. 952-955.

[9] M. J. Deen, *et al.*, "Performance Characteristics of an Ultra-Low Power VCO," *Proceedings of the 2003 International Symposium on Circuits and Systems*, Hamilton, 25-28 May 2003, pp. 697-700.

[10] T. W. Li, B. Ye and J. G. Jiang, "0.5 V 1.3 GHz Voltage Controlled Ring Oscillator," *IEEE International Conference on ASIC*, Changsha, 20-23 October 2009, pp. 1181-1184.

[11] S. K. Enam and A. A. Abidi, "A 300 MHz CMOS Voltage Controlled Ring Oscillator," *IEEE Journal of Solid State Circuits*, Vol. 25, No. 1, 1990, pp. 312-315.

[12] B. Fahs, W. Y. Ali-Ahmad and P. Gamand, "A Two Stage Ring Oscillator in 0.13 um CMOS for UMB Impulse Radio," *IEEE Transaction on Microwave Technology*, Vol. 57, No. 5, May 2009, pp. 1074-1082.

[13] J. K. Panigrahi and D. P. Acharya, "Performance Analysis and Design of Wideband CMOS Voltage Controlled Ring Oscillator," *IEEE International Conference on Industrial and Information Systems*, Mangalore, 29 July-1 August 2010, pp. 234-238.

[14] A. Hajimiri, S. Limotyrakis and T. H. Lee, "Jitter and Phase Noise in Ring Oscillators," *IEEE Journal of Sol-*

id-State Circuits, Vol. 34, No. 6, June 1999, pp. 790-804.

[15] H. Q. Liu, W. L. Goh and L. Siek, "A 0.18-μm 10-GHz CMOS Ring Oscillator for Optical Transceivers," *IEEE International Symposium on Circuits and Systems*, Kobe, 23-26 May 2005, pp. 1525-1528.

[16] S. L. Amakawa, *et al.*, "Low-Phase-NoiseWide-Frequency-Range Ring-VCO-Based Scalable PLL with Sub Harmonic Injection Locking in 0.18 μM CMOS," *IEEE International Microwave Symposium Digest*, Anaheim, 23-28 May 2010, pp. 1178-1181.

[17] C. H. Park and B. Kim, "A Low-Noise, 900-Mhz VCO in 0.6-μm CMOS," *IEEE Journal of Solid-State Circuits*, Vol. 34, No. 5, May 1999, pp. 586-591.

[18] Y. A. Eken and J. P. Uyemura, "A 5.9-GHz Voltage Controlled Ring Oscillator in 0.18-um CMOS," *IEEE Journal of Solid State Circuits*, Vol. 39, No. 1, January 2004, pp. 230-233.

26

A Comparative Study of Analytical Solutions to the Coupled Van-der-Pol's Non-linear Circuits Using the He's Method (HPEM) and (BPES)

Hüseyin Koçak[1], Ahmet Yıldırım[1], Dahong Zhang[2], Karem Boubaker[3], Syed Tauseef Mohyud-Din[4]

[1]*Department of Mathematics, Ege University, Bornova–İzmir, Turkey*
[2]*Department of Physics, South China University, Guangzhou, China*
[3]*École Supérieure des Sciences et Techniques de Tunis, University of Tunis, Tunis, Tunisia*
[4]*Department of Basic Sciences, HITEC University, Taxila Cantt, Pakistan*

Abstract

In this paper, the He's parameter-expanding method (*HPEM*) and the 4q-Boubaker Polynomials Expansion Scheme (*BPES*) are used in order to obtain analytical solutions to the non-linear modified Van der Pol's oscillating circuit equation. The resolution protocols are applied to the ordinary Van der Pol equation, which annexed to conjoint delayed feedback and delay-related damping terms. The results are plotted, and compared with exact solutions proposed elsewhere, in order to evaluate accuracy.

Keywords: Van-der-Pol's Oscillating Circuit, Delayed Feedback, Damping, BPES, HPEM, Exact Solutions, Electrical Triode-Valve Circuit

1. Introduction

Originally, the Van der Pol's equation was associated, in the 1920s, with an electrical triode-valve circuit (**Figure 1**). In the last decades' literature, it was the subject of several investigations due to the panoply of dynamical oddness as relaxation oscillations, elementary bifurcations, quasiperiodicity, and chaos. Its application has already reached nerve pulse propagation and electric potential evolution across neural membranes.

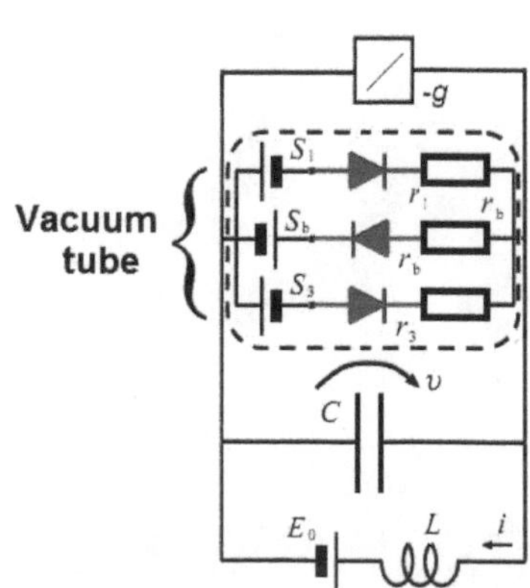

Figure 1. Van der Pol oscillator synoptic scheme.

The actual study tries to give a theoretical supply to the recent attempts to yield analytical solutions to this equation, like the studies of D. D. Ganji *et al.* [1,2] and A. Rajabi *et al.* [3] in the heat transfer domain, the investigations of L. Cveticanin [4] and J. H. He [5-7] on non-linear mechanics, fluid dynamics and oscillating systems modelling (**Figure 2**).

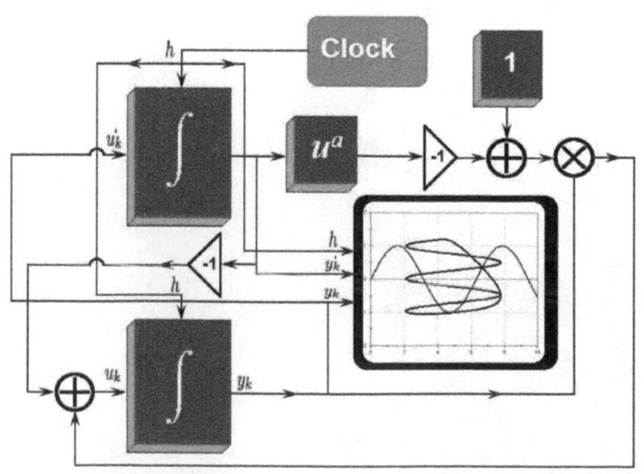

Figure 2. A prototype of Van der Pol oscillating systems modelling (The two integrators are Trapezoidal-type $\{y_k = h/2(u_k + u_{k-1}) + y_{k-1}\}$ **).**

Among the different formulations, the well-known standard boundary value-free Van der Pol oscillator problem (BVFP) is given by F. M. Atay [8] by the following system (1):

$$\begin{cases} x''(t)+x(t)=\varepsilon\times f\left(x(t),x'(t),x(t-\tau)\right) \\ f\left(x(t),x'(t),x(t-\tau)\right)=\left(1-x(t)^2\right)x'(t)+k\times x(t-\tau) \end{cases} \quad (1)$$

where τ is a positive parameter representing the delay, $\varepsilon > 0$ and k is the feedback gain.

A simpler formulation is that of W. Jiang *et al.* [9]:

$$\begin{cases} \dot{x}(t)=y(t) \\ \dot{y}(t)=-x(t)+kf\left(x(t-\tau)\right)-\varepsilon\times\left(x(t)^2-1\right)y(t) \end{cases} \quad (2)$$

In this study, an attempt to give analytical solution to the nonlinear second-order Van der Pol equation annexed to conjoint delayed feedback and delay-related damping terms as presented by A. Kimiaeifar *et al.* [10]:

$$\begin{cases} \dot{x}(t)=y(t) \\ \dot{y}(t)=-x(t)-\varepsilon\times\left(1-x(t)^2\right)y(t)+k\times x(t-\tau) \\ x(0)=x_0=H\neq 0 \\ x'(0)=x'_0=0 \end{cases} \quad (3)$$

2. Analytical Solutions Derivation

2.1. The Enhanced He's Parameter-Expanding Method (HPEM) Solution

The resolution protocol based on the enhanced He's parameter-expanding method (HPEM) is founded on the infinite serial expansions:

$$\begin{cases} x(t)=\sum_{n=0}^{+\infty}\varepsilon^n x_n(t) \\ x(t-\tau)=\sum_{n=0}^{+\infty}\varepsilon^n x_n(t-\tau) \end{cases} \quad (4a)$$

Substituting these expansions in the main equation Equation (3) and processing with the standard perturbation method, it has been demonstrated [10] that a solution of the kind:

$$x_0(t)=H\cos(\omega\times t+\phi) \quad (4b)$$

where H, ω and ϕ are constant, gives:

$$\begin{aligned} &\ddot{x}_1(t)+H\omega\sin(\omega\times t+\phi)+\omega^2 x_1(t)+v_1 H\cos(\omega\times t+\phi) \\ &-H^3\omega\cos^2(\omega\times t+\phi)\sin(\omega\times t+\phi) \\ &-kH\cos(\omega\times t+\phi)\cos(\omega\times\tau+\phi) \\ &-kH\sin(\omega\times t+\phi)\sin(\omega\times\tau+\phi)=0 \end{aligned} \quad (4c)$$

with, as a final solution (Equation (4d)):

$$x(t)=H\cos\left(\pm\frac{\sqrt{2k\varepsilon\left(\sqrt{6k\varepsilon\tau^4+3k^2\varepsilon^2\tau^4-36k\varepsilon\tau^2+36}+3k\varepsilon\tau^2-6\right)}}{k\varepsilon\tau^2}t+\phi\right) \quad (4d)$$

2.2. The Boubaker Polynomials Expansion Scheme (BPES)-Related Solution

The resolution protocol is based on the Boubaker polynomials expansion scheme (BPES) [11-23]. The first step of this scheme starts by applying the expressions:

$$x(t)=\frac{1}{2N_0}\sum_{k=1}^{N_0}\lambda_k\times B_{4k}(t\times r_k) \quad (4e)$$

where B_{4k} are the 4k-order Boubaker polynomials, is the normalized time ($t\in[0,1]$), r_k are B_{4k} minimal positive roots, N_0 is a prefixed integer, and $\lambda_k|_{k=1..N_0}$ are unknown pondering real coefficients.

Consequently, it comes that:

$$y(t)=\dot{x}(t)=\frac{1}{2N_0}\sum_{k=1}^{N_0}\lambda_k r_k\times\frac{\mathrm{d}B_{4k}(t\times r_k)}{\mathrm{d}t} \quad (5)$$

The main advantage of these formulations (Equations (4) and (5)) is the fact of verifying the boundary conditions in Equation (3), at the earliest stage of resolution protocol. In fact, due to the properties of the Boubaker polynomials [12-18], and since $r_k|_{k=1..N_0}$ r_k are the roots of $B_{4k}|_{k=1..N_0}$, the following conditions stand :

$$\begin{cases} x(t)|_{t=0}=-\frac{1}{N_0}\sum_{k=1}^{N_0}\lambda_k=A=x_0\neq 0 \\ \left.\frac{\mathrm{d}x(t)}{\mathrm{d}t}\right|_{t=0}=\frac{1}{2N_0}\sum_{k=1}^{N_0}\lambda_k r_k\times\left.\frac{\mathrm{d}B_{4k}(t\times r_k)}{\mathrm{d}t}\right|_{t=0}=0 \end{cases} \quad (6)$$

By introducing expressions (4) and (6) in the system (3), and by majoring and integrating along the interval $[0,1]$, $x(t)$ is confined, through the coefficients $\lambda_k|_{k=1..N_0}$, to be a weak solution of the system:

$$\begin{cases} \sum_{k=1}^{N_0}r_k^2\lambda_k M_k+\varepsilon\sum_{k=1}^{N_0}r_k\lambda_k P_k-\sum_{k=1}^{N_0}\lambda_k\left(Q_k-k\times R_k(\tau)\right)=0 \\ M_k=\int_0^1\frac{\mathrm{d}^2B_{4k}(t\times r_k)}{\mathrm{d}t^2}\mathrm{d}t \\ P_k=\int_0^1\frac{\mathrm{d}B_{4k}(t\times r_k)}{\mathrm{d}t}\mathrm{d}t \\ Q_k=\int_0^1 B_{4k}(t\times r_k)\mathrm{d}t \\ R_k(\tau)=\int_0^1 B_{4k}\left((t-\tau)\times r_k\right)\mathrm{d}t \\ \sum_{k=1}^{N_0}\lambda_k=-N_0x_0=-N_0H \end{cases} \quad (7)$$

The set of solutions $\hat{\lambda}_k\Big|_{k=1,\cdots,N_0}$ is the one which minimizes, for given values of ε and k the Minimum Square function $\Psi_{MS}(\varepsilon,k)$:

$$\Psi_{MS}(\varepsilon,k) = \left(\sum_{k=1}^{N_0} r_k^2\hat{\lambda}_k M_k + \varepsilon\sum_{k=1}^{N_0} r_k\hat{\lambda}_k P_k - \sum_{k=1}^{N_0}\hat{\lambda}_k\left(Q_k - k\times R_k(\tau)\right)\right)^2 \quad (8)$$

under the intrinsic condition:

$$\sum_{k=1}^{N_0}\hat{\lambda}_k = -N_0 H \quad (9)$$

The condition expressed by Equation (9) ensures a non-zero solution to the system (8). The convergence of the algorithm is tested relatively to increasing values of N_0.

The correspondent solutions are represented in **Figure 3** for the data gathered in **Table 1**, along with the exact solutions given by F. M. Atay [8] and A. Kimiaeifar *et al.* [10]. It is noted that F. M. Atay [8] demonstrated that the presence of delay can change the amplitude of limit cycle oscillations, or suppress them altogether through derivative-like effects, while A. Kimiaeifar *et al.* [10] yielded a highly accurate solution to the same classical Van der Pol equation with delayed feedback and a modified equation where a delayed term provides the damping. The features of the proposed solutions [8-10] (namely behavior at starting phase, first derivatives at limit time, etc.) are concordant with the actually proposed results.

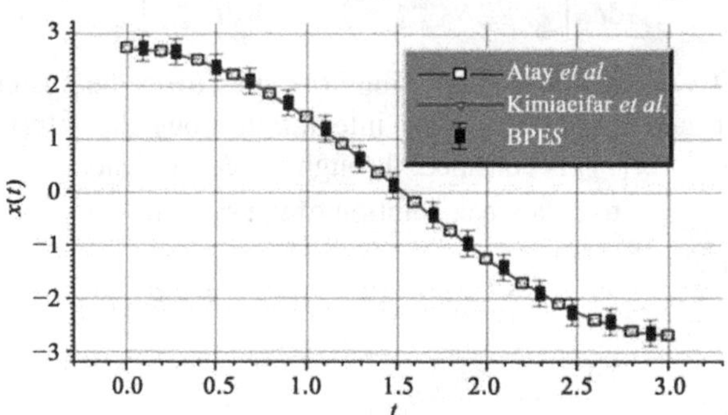

Figure 3. Analytical solutions plots.

Table 1. Solution parameters values.

Parameter	Value
ε	0.1
k	−1.0
τ	1.0
x_0	2.75
$\dot{x}_0$	0.0
N_0	31
ϕ	0.0

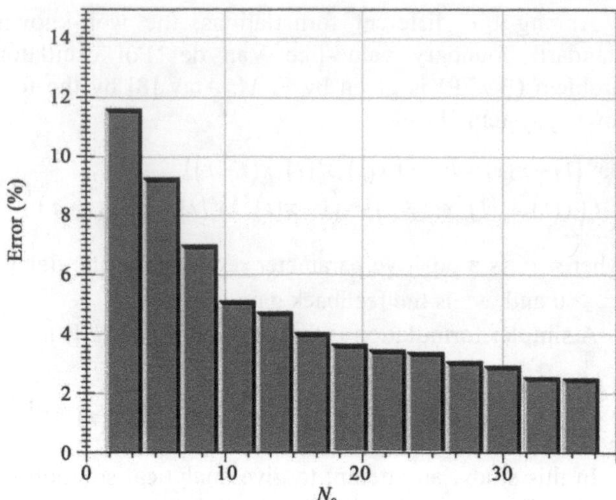

Figure 4. Mean absolute error versus N_0.

3. Results and Discussions

The results show a good agreement between the proposed analytical solutions (**Figure 3**) and those of the recent studies published elsewhere. The mean absolute error (for $N_0 > 30$) was less than 3.33% (**Figure 4**). The convergence of the *BPES*-related protocol has been recorded for the values of N_0 superior to 30.

4. Conclusions

In this paper, we have used the enhanced He's parameter-expanding Method (HPEM) along with the Boubaker Polynomials Expansion Scheme (BPES) in order to obtain the Van der Pol's characteristic periodical solutions.

The obtained solutions were in acceptable agreement with those obtained from values of similarly performed methods. The typical periodical aspect of the oscillations, already yielded [2,10,24-27] by the enhanced He's parameter-expanding method (HPEM) could be reproduced using a simple and convergent polynomial approximation. This method was based on an original protocol which reduces the stochastic nonlinear system into an equivalent deterministic nonlinear system. This simple and controllable reduction is carried out through the verification of the initial conditions, in the solution basic expression, prime to launching the resolution process.

The results show that the methods are very promising ones and might find wide applications, particularly when exact solutions expressions are difficult to establish [28-34].

5. References

[1] D. D. Ganji and A. Rajabi, "Assessment of Homotopy Perturbation and Perturbation Methods in Heat Transfer Radiation Equations," *International Communications in*

Heat and Mass Transfer, Vol. 33, No. 3, 2006, pp. 391-400.

[2] D. D. Ganji and A. Sadighi, "Application of He's Homotopy-Perturbation Method to Nonlinear Coupled Systems of Reaction-Diffusion Equations," *International Journal of Nonlinear Sciences and Numerical Simulation*, Vol. 7, No. 4, 2006, pp. 411-418.

[3] A. Rajabi, D. D. Ganji and H. Taherian, "Application of Homotopy Perturbation Method in Nonlinear Heat Conduction and Convection Equations," *Physics Letters A*, Vol. 360, No. 4-5, 2007, pp. 570-573.

[4] L. Cveticanin, "Homotopy-Perturbation Method for Pure Nonlinear Differential Equation," *Chaos, Solitons & Fractals*, Vol. 30, No. 5, 2006, pp. 1221-1230.

[5] J. H. He, "Homotopy Perturbation Method for Bifurcation of Nonlinear Problems," *International Journal of Nonlinear Sciences and Numerical Simulation*, Vol. 6, No. 2, 2005, pp. 207-208.

[6] J. H. He, "Homotopy Perturbation Method For Solving Boundary Value Problems," *Physics Letters A*, Vol. 350, No. 1-2, 2006, pp. 87-88.

[7] J. H. He, "Limit Cycle and Bifurcation of Nonlinear Problems," *Chaos, Solitons & Fractals*, Vol. 26, No. 3, 2005, pp. 827-833.

[8] F. M. Atay, "Van der Pol's Oscillator under Delayed Feedback," *Journal of Sound and Vibration*, Vol. 218, No. 2, 1998, pp. 333-339.

[9] W. Jiang and J. Wei, "Bifurcation Analysis in Van der Pol's Oscillator with Delayed Feedback," *Journal of Computational and Applied Mathematics*, Vol. 213, No. 2, 2008, pp. 604-615.

[10] A. Kimiaeifar, A. R. Saidi, A. R. Sohouli and D. D. Ganji, "Analysis of Modified Vander Pol's Oscillator Using He's Parameter-Expanding Methods," *Current Applied Physics*, Vol. 10, No. 1, 2010, pp. 279-283.

[11] J. Ghanouchi, H. Labiadh and K. Boubaker, "An Attempt to Solve the Heat Transfert Equation in a Model of Pyrolysis Spray Using 4q-Order m-Boubaker Polynomials," *International Journal of Heat & Technology*, Vol. 26, No. 1, 2008, pp. 49-53.

[12] O. B. Awojoyogbe and K. Boubaker, "A Solution to Bloch NMR Flow Equations for the Analysis of Homodynamic Functions of Blood Flow System Using m-Boubaker Polynomials," *Current Applied Physics*, Vol. 9, No. 3, 2009, pp. 278-288.

[13] H. Labiadh and K. Boubaker, "A Sturm-Liouville Shaped Characteristic Differential Equation As a Guide to Establish a Quasi-Polynomial Expression to the Boubaker Polynomials," *Differential Equations and Control Processes*, Vol. 2, No. 2, 2007, pp. 117-133.

[14] S. Slama, J. Bessrour, M. Bouhafs and K. B. Ben Mahmoud, "Numerical Heat Transfer, Part A: Application," *An International Journal of Computation and Methodology*, Vol. 48, No. 6, 2005, pp. 401-404.

[15] S. Slama, M. Bouhafs and K. B. Ben Mahmoud, "A Boubaker Polynomials Solution to Heat Equation for Monitoring A3 Point Evolution During Resistance Spot Welding," *International Journal of Heat and Technology*, Vol. 26, No. 2, 2008, pp. 141-146.

[16] H. Rahmanov, "Triangle Read by Rows: Row n Gives Coefficients of Boubaker Polynomial B_*n*(*x*), Calculated for X = 2cos(*t*), Centered by Adding –2cos(*nt*), Then Divided by 4, in Order of Decreasing Exponents," OEIS (Encyclopedia of Integer Sequences), A160242.

[17] H. Rahmanov, "Triangle Read by Rows: Row n Gives Values of the 4q-28Boubaker Polynomials B_4q(X) (Named after Boubaker Boubaker (1897-1966)), Calculated for X = 1 (or –1)," OEIS (Encyclopedia of Integer Sequences), A162180.

[18] S. Tabatabaei, T. Zhao, O. Awojoyogbe and F. Moses, "Cut-Off Cooling Velocity Profiling Inside a Keyhole Model Using the Boubaker Polynomials Expansion Scheme," *Heat and Mass Transfer*, Vol. 45, No. 10, 2009, pp. 1247-1255.

[19] S. Fridjine and M. Amlouk, "A New Parameter: An ABACUS for Optimizig Functional Materials Using the Boubaker Polynomials Expansion Scheme," *Modern Physics Letters B*, Vol. 23, No. 17, 2009, pp. 2179-2182.

[20] A. Belhadj, J. Bessrour, M. Bouhafs and L. Barrallier, "Experimental and Theoretical Cooling Velocity Profile Inside Laser Welded Metals Using Keyhole Approximation and Boubaker Polynomials Expansion," *Journal of Thermal Analysis and Calorimetry*, Vol. 97, No. 3, 2009, pp. 911-920.

[21] A. Belhadj, O. Onyango and N. Rozibaeva, "Boubaker Polynomials Expansion Scheme-Related Heat Transfer Investigation Inside Keyhole Model," *Journal of Thermophysics Heat Transfer*, Vol. 23, No. 6, 2009, pp. 639-642.

[22] A. Chaouachi, K. Boubaker, M. Amlouk and H. Bouzouita, "Enhancement of Pyrolysis Spray Disposal Performance Using Thermal Time-Response to Precursor Uniform Deposition," *The European Physical Journal - Applied Physics*, Vol. 37, No. 1, 2007, pp. 105-109.

[23] D. H. Zhang and F. W. Li, "A Boubaker Polynomials Expansion Scheme BPES-Related Analytical Solution to Williams-Brinkmann Stagnation Point Flow Equation at a Blunt Body," *Journal of Engineering Physics and Thermophysics*, Vol. 84, No. 3, 2009, pp. 618-623.

[24] Z. L. Tao, "Frequency–Amplitude Relationship of Nonlinear Oscillators by He's Parameter-Expanding Method," *Chaos, Solitons & Fractals*, Vol. 41, No. 2, 2009, pp. 642-645.

[25] L. Xu, "He's Parameter-Expanding Methods for Strongly Nonlinear Oscillators," *Journal of Computational and Applied Mathematics*, Vol. 207, No. 1, 2007, pp. 148-154.

[26] D. D. Ganji, M. Rafei, A. Sadighi and Z. Z. Ganji, "A Comparative Comparison of He's Method with Perturba-

tion and Numerical Methods for Nonlinear Vibrations Equations," *International Journal of Nonlinear Dynamics in Engineering and Sciences*, Vol. 1, No. 1, 2009, pp. 1-20.

[27] J. H. He, "Determination of Limit Cycles for Strongly Nonlinear Oscillators," *Physical Review Letters*, Vol. 90, No. 17, 2003, pp. 1-11.

[28] Z. M. Odibat and S. Momani, "Application of Variational Iteration Method to Nonlinear Differential Equations of Fractional Order," *International Journal of Nonlinear Sciences and Numerical Simulation*, Vol. 7, No. 1, 2006, pp. 27-34.

[29] E. Yusufoglu, "Variational Iteration Method for Construction of Some Compact and Non Compact Structures of Klein-Gordon Equations," *International Journal of Nonlinear Sciences and Numerical Simulation*, Vol. 8, No. 2, 2007, pp. 152-158.

[30] M. D'Acunto, "Self-Excited Systems: Analytical Determination of Limit Cycles," *Chaos, Solitons & Fractals*, Vol. 30, No. 3, 2006, pp. 719-724.

[31] J. K. Hale, "Averaging Methods for Differential Equations with Retarded Arguments and a Small Parameter," *Journal of Differential Equations*, Vol. 2, No. 1, 1966, pp. 57-73.

[32] A. Golbabai and D. Ahmadian, "Homotopy Pade Method for Solving Linear and Nonlinear Integral Equations," *International Journal of Nonlinear Dynamics in Engineering and Sciences*, Vol. 1, No. 1, 2009, pp. 59-66.

[33] J. H. He, "Some Asymptotic Methods for Strongly Nonlinear Equations," *International Journal of Modern Physics B*, Vol. 20, No. 10, 2006, pp. 1141-1199.

[34] J. H. He, "Book Keeping Parameter in Perturbation Methods," *International Journal of Nonlinear Sciences and Numerical Simulation*, Vol. 2, No. 3, 2001, pp. 257-264.

27

Chip Design of a Low-Voltage Wideband Continuous-Time Sigma-Delta Modulator with DWA Technology for WiMAX Applications

Jhin-Fang Huang, Yan-Cheng Lai, Wen-Cheng Lai, Ron-Yi Liu
Department of Electronic Engineering, National Taiwan University of Science and Technology, Chinese Taipei

Abstract

This paper presents the design and experimental results of a continuous-time (CT) sigma-delta (ΣΔ) modulator with data-weighted average (DWA) technology for WiMAX applications. The proposed modulator comprises a third-order active RC loop filter, internal quantizer operating at 160 MHz and three DAC circuits. A multi-bit quantizer is used to increase resolution and multi-bit non-return-to-zero (NRZ) DACs are adopted to reduce clock jitter sensitivity. The NRZ DAC circuits with quantizer excess loop delay compensation are set to be half the sampling period of the quantizer for increasing modulator stability. A dynamic element matching (DEM) technique is applied to multi-bit ΣΔ modulators to improve the nonlinearity of the internal DAC. This approach translates the harmonic distortion components of a nonideal DAC in the feedback loop of a ΣΔ modulator to high-frequency components. Capacitor tuning is utilized to overcome loop coefficient shifts due to process variations. The DWA technique is used for reducing DAC noise due to component mismatches. The prototype is implemented in TSMC 0.18 um CMOS process. Experimental results show that the ΣΔ modulator achieves 54-dB dynamic range, 51-dB SNR, and 48-dB SNDR over a 10-MHz signal bandwidth with an oversampling ratio (OSR) of 8, while dissipating 19.8 mW from a 1.2-V supply. Including pads, the chip area is 1.156 mm^2.

Keywords: ADC, Analog-to-Digital Conversion, Sigma-Delta Modulator, ΣΔ, DWA

1. Introduction

Sigma-delta modulation techniques have been extended in moderate and high accuracy analog/mixed-signal IC applications, such as analog-to-digital data converters (ADCs), digital-to-analog data converters (DACs), frequency synthesizers, and power amplifiers [1]. Moreover, ΣΔ modulators are widely used in receivers because of their ability to provide high-resolution with relatively low precision components and low power consumption [2,3]. Oversampling ΣΔ ADCs trade digital signal processing complexity for relaxed requirements on the analog components compared to Nyquist-rate ADCs [4]. Due to the over-sampling characteristics, ΣΔ modulators are limited on the application of voice band or lower frequency signals. As the ICs process is improved, recently it makes many researches transfer to wider bandwidth applications gradually, such as GSM, WCDMA, Bluetooth, WiFi, and WiMAX [5]. With the progress of wireless communication, ADCs need higher OSR in order to achieve higher speed and resolution in the system. When OSR is programmable, increasing OSR leads to higher power consumption due to the increased speed requirement for the integrators and comparators in ΣΔ modulators. Due to the requirements of low supply voltage and low power dissipation in the mobile communications, the low order ΣΔ modulators of lower SNR are not suitable for wide bandwidth applications. Therefore, the high order multi-bit ΣΔ modulator circuit is design to increase the SNR.

While most of current commercial ΣΔ ADCs for wireless applications were implemented by using switched capacitor (SC) techniques which are also known as discrete-time (DT) ΣΔ ADCs [6-8], mainly due to mature design methodologies and robustness, more and more continuous-time (CT) ΣΔ ADCs were reported and showed impressive performance. Compared with DT counterparts, the CT ΣΔ ADCs have two main advantages. First, the inherent anti-aliasing characteristics of the CT ΣΔ ADCs reduce the performance requirement of the anti-aliasing filter further and hence reduce the power consumption of the transceiver. Second, the bandwidth requirement of the operational amplifiers (op amps) in CT ΣΔ ADCs is much lower than that of the op amps in DT ones for a given sampling rate, so the CT ΣΔ ADCs are more suitable for broadband applications. Hence we propose a low-voltage, lower power consumption and high resolution CT ΣΔ modulator. Our target is to design a 10 MHz input signal bandwidth and 160MHz sample-rate ΣΔ modulator implemented in TSMC 0.18 μm CMOS process.

This paper begins with a brief summary of the innovative CT ΣΔ circuit design. Section 2 introduces the system architecture of the wideband CT ΣΔ modulator. Section 3 describes the design of building blocks of the modulator, while Section 4 presents the measured results of the prototype. Section 5 summarizes the paper.

2. System Circuit Architecture

As high sampling frequency will restrict our design techniques, low OSR is more suitable for the bandwidth of 10 MHz structure. In order to achieve better resolution and reduce quantization noise, at least a third-order noise-transfer function is indispensable. **Figure 1** shows the proposed CT ΔΣ modulator architecture which consists of a 4-bit internal quantizer, operating at 160 MHz with an OSR of 8, and a third-order single-loop filter. In order to decrease power consumption and maintain a good alias filter characteristic, a combination of feedforward and feedback stabilized loop filters [9] is adopted. The 4-bit quantizer, including the NRZ feedback DAC is connected to the output of the loop filter. The quantizer delay is set to half of the sampling period. This large delay is compensated exactly by an additional feedback path K_{3fb}.

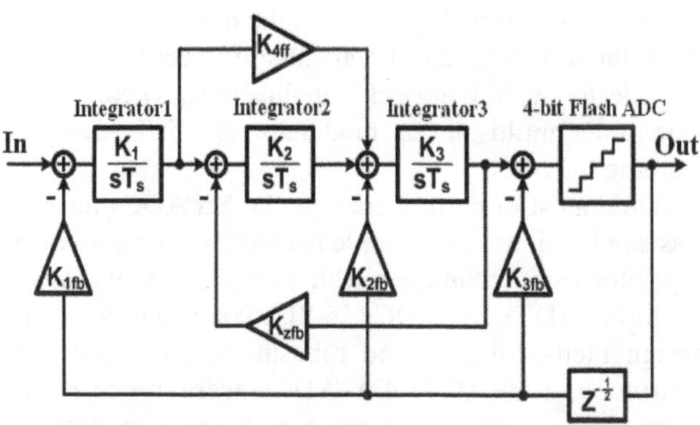

Figure 1. Continuous-time ΣΔ modulator architecture.

A possible design technique for CT modulators is described [10,11]. Specifying a DT modulator and trying to find the equivalent CT modulator between s-plane and z-plane can use the impulse-invariance transform expressed as:

$$Z^{-1}\{H(z)\} = L^{-1}\{R_D(s)H(s)\}\big|_{t=n\cdot T_s} \quad (1)$$

where $R_D(s)$ is the Laplace transform of impulse response of the DAC and $H(z)$ is the DT loop filter. Equation (1) is adopted to compensate the impairments of the circuit such that the resulting CT domain modulator still matches with the specified DT modulator. The followings outline the procedure used to determine the direct feedback coefficients such that quantizer delay is canceled exactly. First, a noise-transfer function (NTF) in the z-domain is chosen, then the loop transfer function $H_{loopz}(z)$ is derived as follows:

$$H_{Loopz}(z) = \frac{1-NTF(z)}{NTF(z)}. \quad (2)$$

Using the discrete-to-discrete (d2d) function in the MATLAB control system toolbox can easily transform z into $z^{1/2}$ shown in (3):

$$H'_{LoopZ}\left(z^{\frac{1}{2}}\right) = \frac{b'_{n-1}z^{\frac{n-1}{2}} + \cdots + b'_1 z^{\frac{1}{2}} + b'_0}{z^{\frac{n}{2}} + a'_{n-1}z^{\frac{n-1}{2}} + \cdots + a'_1 z^{\frac{1}{2}} + a'_0}. \quad (3)$$

After multiplying $z^{1/2}$ in the formula, a constant term b'_{n-1} can be easily separated from the transfer function $L_{filterD}\left(z^{1/2}\right)$ of the loop filter as follows:

$$L_{filterD}\left(z^{\frac{1}{2}}\right) = \frac{b'_{n-1}z^{\frac{n-1}{2}} + \cdots + b'_1 z^{\frac{1}{2}} + b'_0}{z^{\frac{n}{2}} + a'_{n-1}z^{\frac{n-1}{2}} + \cdots + a'_1 z^{\frac{1}{2}} + a'_0} \cdot z^{\frac{1}{2}} \quad (4)$$

Using the discrete-to-continuous (d2c) function in the MATLAB tool box converts this transfer function $L_{filterD}\left(z^{1/2}\right)$ to continuous time. A possible loop filter is then defined in the CT domain is RC loop filter.

3. Continus-Time ΣΔ Modulator Implementation

3.1. Continuous-Time ΣΔ Modulator Circuit

The 4-bit CT ΣΔ modulator circuit including the excess loop delay compensation is shown in **Figure 2** [12]. The modulator consists of a 4-bit internal quantizer, operating at 160 MHz with an OSR of 8, and a third-order single-loop filter. The loop filter is realized as an active RC filter. Due to the low supply voltage and the high-linearity requirement two-stage op amps with CT common mode feedback (CMFB) are used. The 4-bit quantizer is connected to the DWA circuit followed by the feedback

DAC. When multi-bit quantizer is used for better quantization resolution, in-band tones are often observed due to the element mismatch in the feedback DAC. To solve the mismatch problem, dynamic element matching is used in the circuit design. The RC time constant in the circuit dominating the entire NTF pole function, will keep stable and therefore the circuit phase margin will also be stable. Due to the process variation, the capacitor tuning circuit is used in this modulator. The DAC1 and DAC2 circuits provide the first and second feedback paths K_{1fb} and K_{2fb}, respectively. The third K_{3fb} is the feedback path around the 4-bit quantizer and its output is connected to the DAC2 output. In order to reduce the loop filter capacitive loading effects, all the comparators inside flash ADC input transistors must be the minimum-size.

General "zero-order" feedback path requires additional summing amplifier and return-to-zero (RZ) DAC contains additional logic control circuits. However, this will cause additional loop delay, increase power consumption and complicate the circuit. Therefore, to improve these drawbacks, in this work, a feedback path is directly connected to the last integrator input, and then the additional summing amplifier is eliminated. Obviously this way reduces power consumption and excess loop delay.

3.2. Loop Filter

There are three types of commonly used CT integrators: active-RC integrators, Gm-C integrators and MOSFET-C integrators. In this design, an active-RC integrator is chosen for the three stages of the third-order loop filter because it has high linearity and easy interface with DACs compared to Gm-C integrators. If active-RC integrators were used, resistive loading increases the power requirements due to the need for buffer stages. A higher frequency range is additionally demanded in connection with a high linearity, the active-RC filters are the preferred structure. The third-order noise shaping loop filter is realized by an active-RC op amp circuit as shown in **Figure 2**. The advantages of this implementation are high linearity and high output signal swing, and it also provides a good virtual ground for the modulator feedback DACs. This eases design, especially with low supply voltages. **Figure 3** show the architectures of the 1.2-V fully differential op amp [13] and the corresponding CMFB circuit is shown in **Figure 4**. The op amp shown in **Figure 3** is a two-stage that consists of a folded cascode input stage, a common source output stage and a CT CMFB which is similar to a transimpedence amplifier.

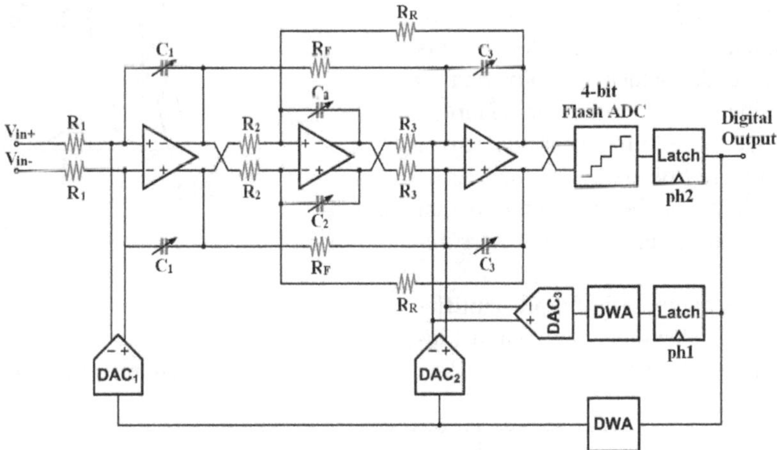

Figure 2. Four-bit CT ΣΔ modulator architecture.

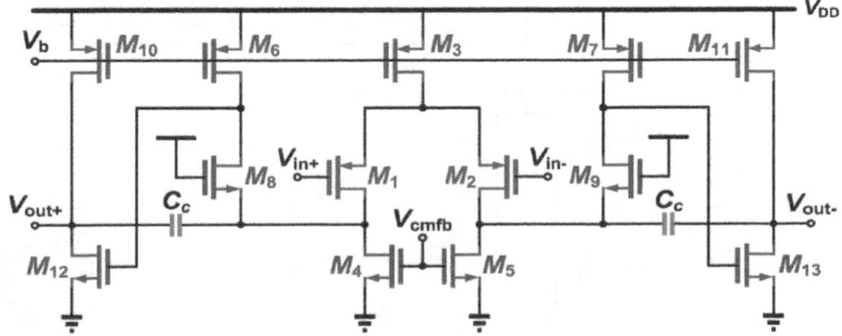

Figure 3. Fully differential 1.2-V op amp circuit.

As shown in **Figure 4**, two resistors with values equal to $2R_1$ are used to sense the output common mode voltage and produce a current I_1. This current is compared with I_2, which is set by the desired common-mode voltage ($V_{DD}/2$) and the resistor R_1. The difference between I_1 and I_2 is then converted into a control voltage labeled as V_{cmfb} by transistors M_3, M_6 and M_9. The control voltage will then be used to adjust the $V_{GS's}$ of M_4 and M_5, such that the output common-mode voltage is stabilized to about $V_{DD}/2$. The CMFB circuit has advantages of allowing rail-to-rail output swing. Furthermore, it does not need any level shift or attenuation on the common mode signal, unlike other CT CMFB circuits that use differential pairs.

3.3. Four-Bit Flash ADC

In ΣΔ modulators, the main specifications for the quantizer are offset, speed, area and power consumption requirements. Moreover the quantizer has to operate at the speed required by the oversampling process. Therefore it must be implemented as a flash ADC [14]. The block diagram of the 4-bit flash ADC used in the quantizer is shown in **Figure 5**. It consists of 15 differential comparators, a resistor ladder, and a thermal to binary encoder. These comparators compare the input signal with reference voltages by a resistor ladder biased by the full scale reference. Consequently, the comparator outputs constitute a thermometer code, which is converted to binary by the encoder. Since flash architectures employ comparators, they are susceptible to metastability errors. In order to lower the probability of metastable states, the thermometer-binary decoding can be pipelined so that potentially indeterminate outputs are allowed more regeneration time [15].

The clocked comparator is composed of a preamplifier and a regenerative latch. The schematic is shown in **Figure 6**. The comparator utilizes the advantages of the low kickback noise in static comparators and the high regeneration speed in dynamic comparators. On one hand, keeping the preamplifier continuously biased throughout the conversion period significantly reduces the kickback disturbance; on the other hand, the dynamic flip-flop in the latch circuit will shorten the regeneration and reset time [16].

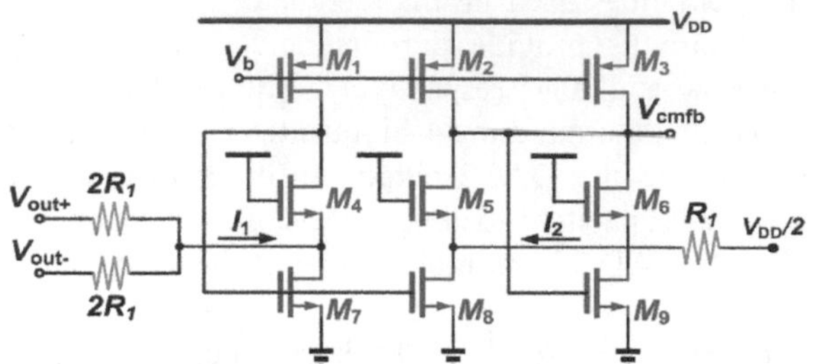

Figure 4. Continuous-time CMFB circuit.

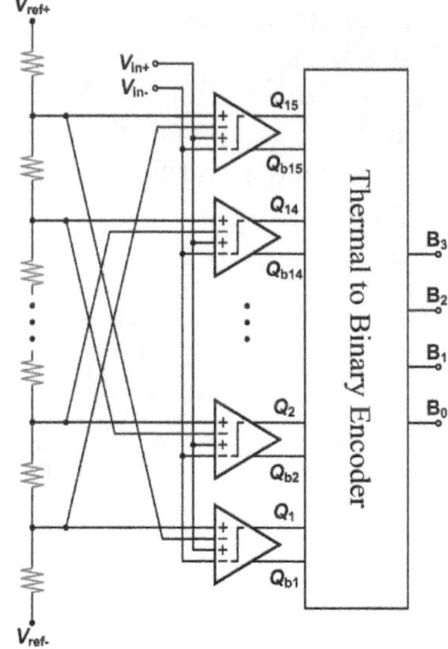

Figure 5. Four-bit quantizer and encoder structure.

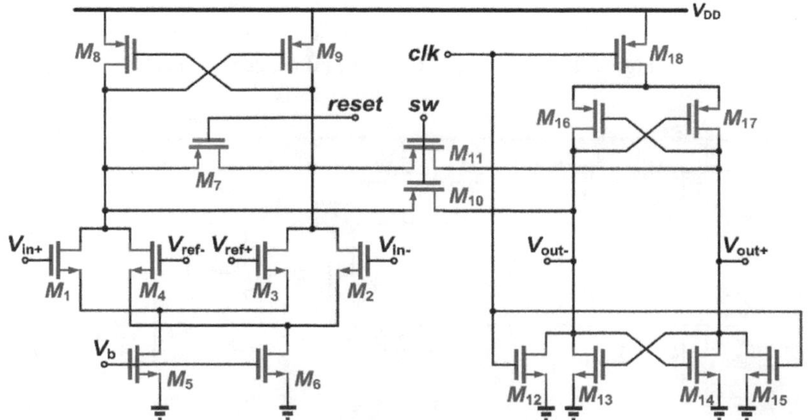

Figure 6. Schematic of the comparator circuit.

3.4. Feedback DACs

As shown in **Figure** 7, a multi-bit current-steering DAC, feeds current to the virtual grounds of the active-RC integrators, therefore good DAC linearity can be achieved. The improved DAC linearity is another advantage of active-RC integrators when compared to Gm-C integrators [17].

The CMFB circuit for the DAC along with the differential pairs connects to the op amp input. This DAC feedback circuit requires a 0.6-V voltage as a reference voltage, and this may operate in the virtual ground voltage. The reference voltage is connected by an external power supply. Two current sources inject common-mode currents to prevent a common-mode offset from appearing at the amplifier virtual grounds. The dynamic performance of current-steering DAC's is limited by the feedthrough of the control signals to the output lines. The coupling of the switching control signals to the output lines through the parasitic gate-drain capacitance of the switching transistors is also a source of glitches. The lower part of **Figure 7** is the simplified representation of the current-steering DAC. In this work, to minimize the feedthrough to the output lines, the drain of the switching transistors is isolated from the output lines by adding two cascaded transistors [18].

3.5. DWA Circuit

Combining ΣΔ modulators with multi-bit quantization is an effective means to achieve a high dynamic range and a wide bandwidth. The major obstacle in designing multi-bit ΣΔ modulators is that good component matching is required for internal DAC linearity. Good attenuation of DAC noise due to component mismatches can be provided by the DWA algorithm, which ideally can achieve a first-order DAC noise shaping. For DWA to be more useful in multi-bit SDM's, the DAC baseband tones must be removed. Conventionally, the problem is circumvented by adding dither. However, adding dither contributes additional noise to the base-band, degrades SNR and possibly destabilizes the modulator. A low- complexity high-speed circuit is proposed for the implementation of a DWA technique without adding dither, used for reducing DAC noise due to component mismatches [19].

The block diagram of the DWA logic is shown in **Figure 8**. The input of the DWA logic is connected to the four-bit quantizer output. The DWA logic converts the quantizer output code to the control signals, S_i, $i = 0, 1, \cdots, 15$, for the element selection of 4-bit DAC. A 4-bit adder and a 4-bit register produce two indexes which are converted to two sets of 16-bit thermometer codes by two binary to thermometer decoders. When the carry signal of the adder is low, the output control signals are the mutual XOR of the two 16-bit thermometer codes. When the carry signal is high, the control signals are the mutual XNOR of the two 16-bit codes. The DWA algorithm selects DAC components cyclically one by one. No unit is reselected before all the others are selected.

3.6. Time Constant Tuning Circuit

CMOS technologies usually do not have tight control over absolute values of R and C, so an automatic RC time constant tuning circuit is needed to ensure the ΣΔ modulator stability and SNR performance over large RC time constant variations. Therefore, a discrete capacitor tuning scheme is employed to calibrate the time constant of the active-RC integrators. The adjustable capacitor array is shown in **Figure 9**.

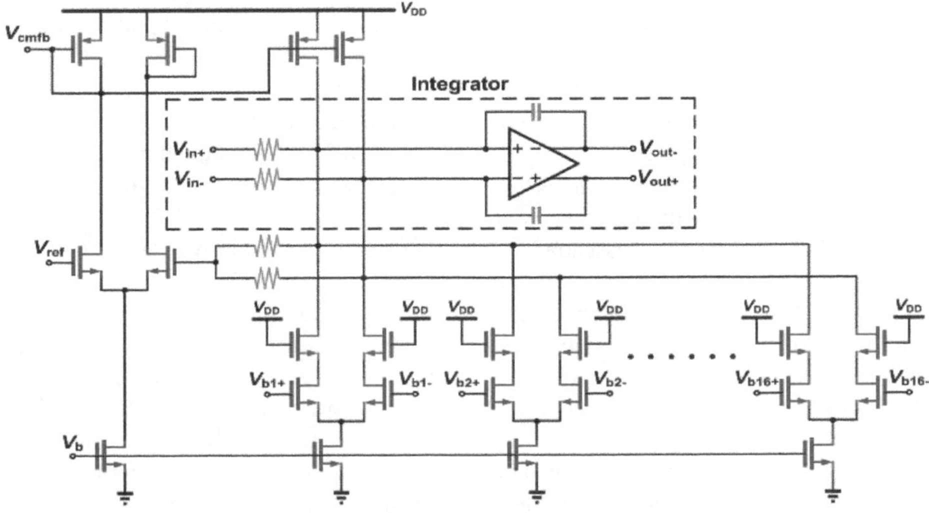

Figure 7. A multi-bit current-steering DAC schematic.

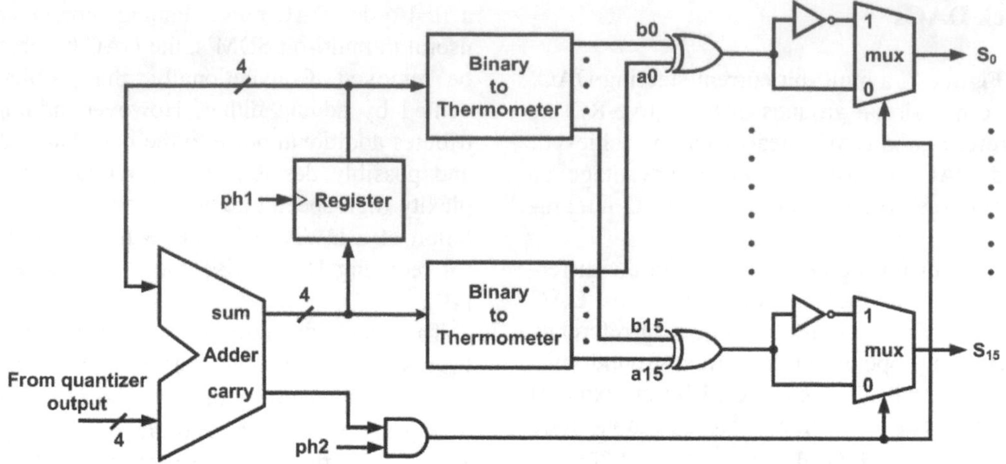

Figure 8. The block diagram for the DWA realization.

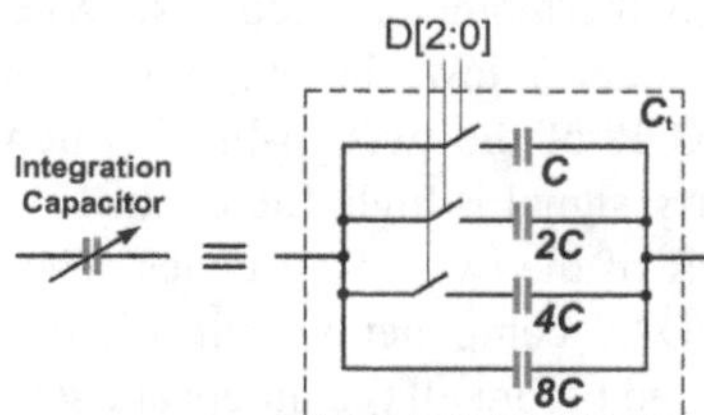

Figure 9. Tunable capacitor array.

The capacitors in the arrays are binary-weighted except the "always-in-use" capacitor which is equal to the most significant bit (MSB) capacitor, 8C. This sizing method provides constant tuning steps with the least number of capacitors. The 3-bit digital control codes are fed externally to choose which capacitors to use.

4. Measurement Results

The proposed third-order multi-bit CT ΣΔ modulator in this paper is implemented in TSMC 0.18-μm CMOS process. Post-processing was performed using MATLAB before tapout. The modulator samples signals at 160 MHz with 10 MHz signal bandwidth and oversampling ratio of 8 and operates with a 1.2 V supply voltage. The total power consumption is 19.8 mW. **Figure 10** shows the modulator die microphotograph including the wire bounding pads. The CT ΣΔ modulator is essentially a mixed-signal system which includes integrator, quantizer, and digital circuits. To achieve high resolution and linearity, caution should be taken in the layout design to reduce the effects of mismatch, parasitic and digital noise coupling to analog blocks. The total chip area including bonding pads is 0.9×1.284 mm^2.

The DWA circuit is located on the left of the chip. The noisy clock generator is placed in the bottom right-hand side to prevent interference with the weakly sensitive

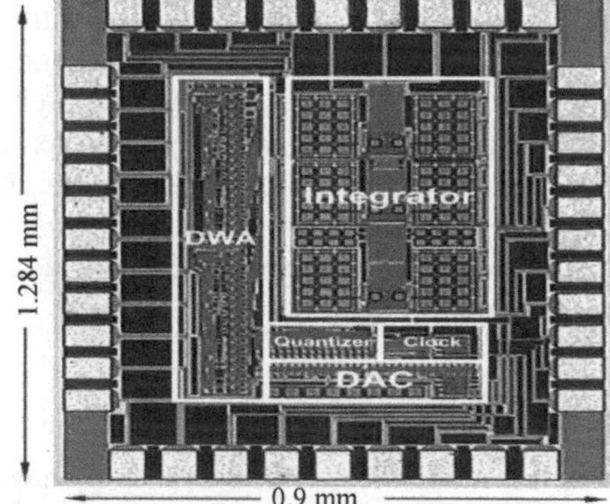

Figure 10. Microphotograph of the CT ΣΔ modulator.

analog blocks. A single-to-differential circuit converts the single-ended input signal to a balanced differential signal input to the ADC. The output data stream of the modulator was captured using a logic analyzer. **Figure 11** shows the digital outputs of the CT ΣΔ modulator measured by the logic analyzer for an input sinusoid at 3 MHz. The output spectrum density of the CT ΣΔ modulator analyzed by logic analyzer for an input sinusoidal signal of 3 MHz is shown in **Figure 12**. A peak SNDR of 48 dB which corresponds to a 7.7-bit within a bandwidth of 10 MHz is measured. The measured SNR and SNDR versus input signal level of the CT ΣΔ modulator for an input sinusoid at 3 MHz are plotted in **Figure 13**. The measured input peak dynamic range is 54 dB. **Figure 14** summarizes the measured SNR and SNDR for varying input frequencies. The SNR and SNDR fall to 46 dB and 43 dB respectively for a 9 MHz input signal. Because the integrator is basically a low pass filter, the modulator acts as low-pass filtering characteristic. When input frequency is increased, the SNR/SNDR values will be decreased.

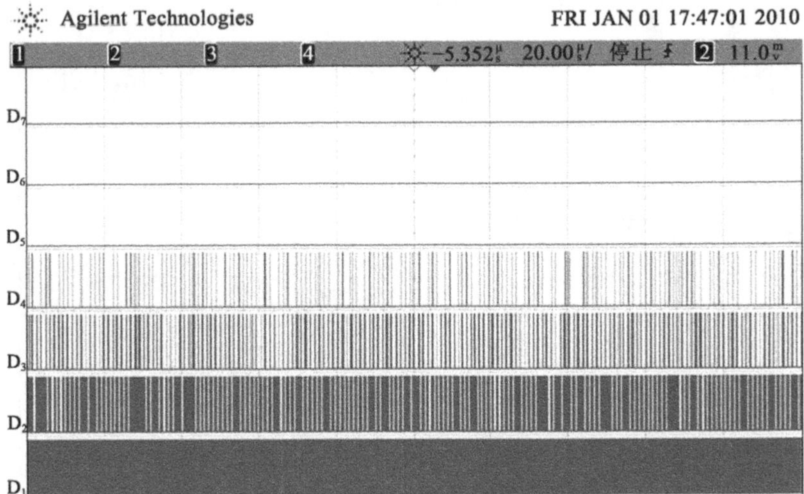

Figure 11. Measured digital output of the CT ΣΔ modulator at f = 3 MHz.

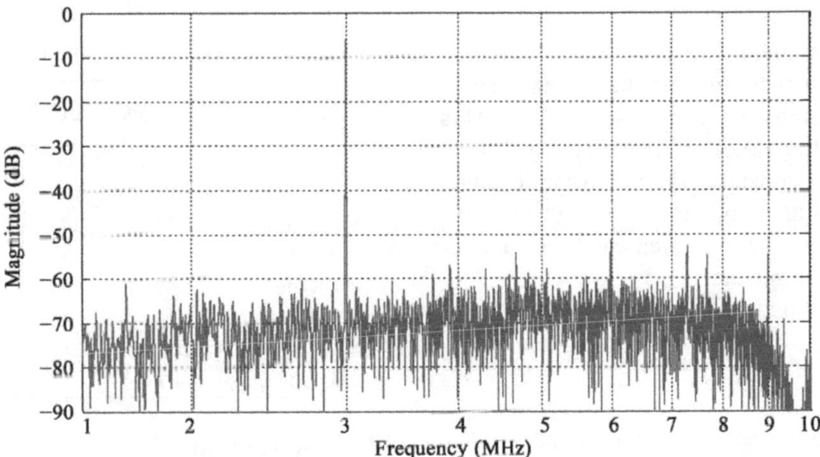

Figure 12. Measured output spectrum density.

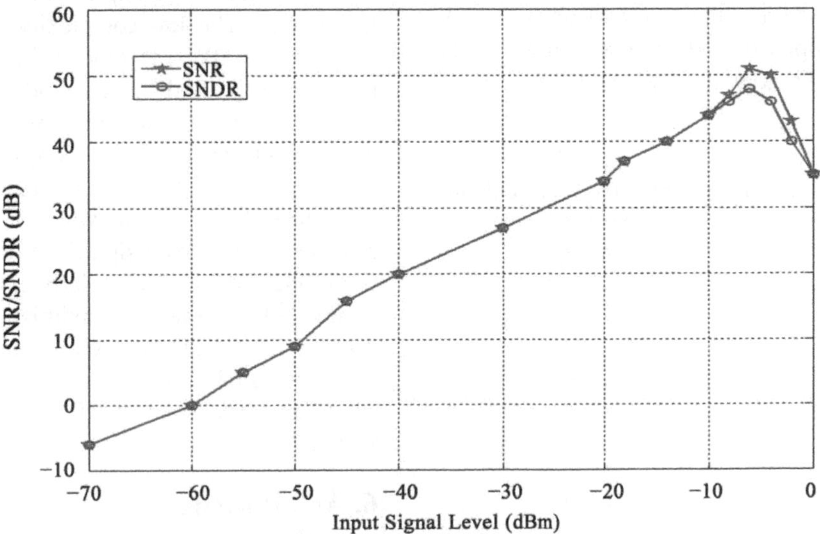

Figure 13. Measured SNR and SNDR vs. input signal level.

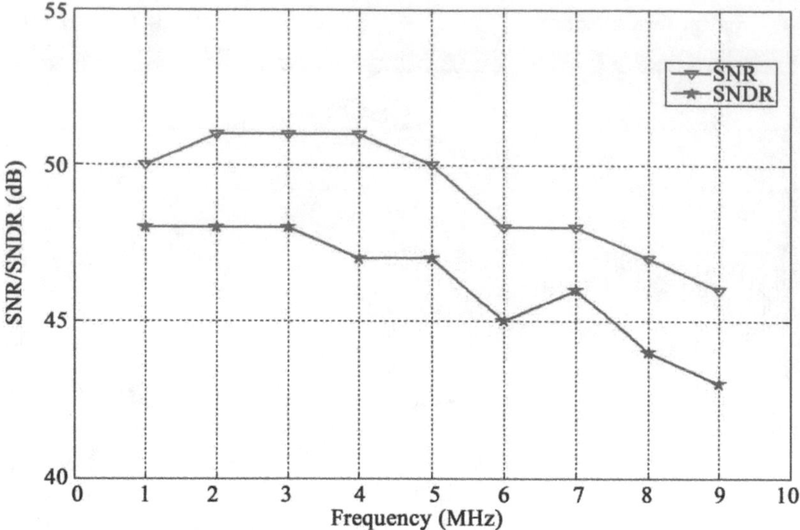

Figure 14. Measured SNR and SNDR vs. input frequency.

The performance parameters of this chip are summarized in **Table 1**. In this work, we use the design strategy for low-power CT ΣΔ modulator proposed by [20]. This concept is based on the figure of merit (FOM) which takes the overall power consumption, the dynamic range, and the signal bandwidth into account to find the most power-efficient ΣΔ modulator implementation with respect to these design parameters.

The FOM used is defined as

$$FOM = \frac{P}{2^B \cdot 2f_B}, \quad (5)$$

where P(mW) represents the power consumption, B is number of bits and f_B(MHz) is the bandwidth. The performance comparisons with other literatures are shown in **Table 2**. The smaller the FOM value is, the better the overall performance is. From this comparison table, it is confirmed that the proposed modulator with low voltage operations can achieve a wide bandwidth and lower power consumption.

Table 1. The performance summary of the CT ΣΔ modulator.

Parameters	Measured results
Sampling Frequency	160 MHz
Signal Bandwidth	10 MHz
SNR	51 dB
SNDR	48 dB
ENOB	7.7 bits
Dynamic Range	54 dB
Power Supply	1.2 V
Power Dissipation	19.8 mW
Chip Area	1.156 mm^2
Process	TSMC 0.18 um CMOS

Table 2. Performance comparisons with other literatures.

Parameter	This work	[21]	[22]	[23]	[24]
Technology	0.18 um	0.18 um	0.18 um	90 um	0.13 um
Voltage (V)	1.2	1.8	1.2	1.2	2.5
BW (MHz)	10	10	7.5	1.92	100
SNR (dB)	51	63	71	66.4	58.9
SNDR (dB)	48	56	67	62.4	53.1
ENOB (Bits)	7.7	9	10.8	10.1	8.5
Power (mW)	19.8	122.4	89	12.5	350
FOM (pJ/Conv.)	4.76	11.95	3.33	2.97	4.83

5. Conclusions

A low-voltage, low-power and wide bandwidth CT ΣΔ modulator has been implemented in a TSMC 0.18-um technology. The low-complexity high-speed implementation of the DWA technique for the reduction of baseband tones is used in this modulator. The excess loop delay set to half the sampling period of the quantizer has been used to avoid degradation of modulator stability in this architecture. All integration capacitors are tunable to overcome time constant variation. In addition, CT ΣΔ modulator provides a significant amount of inherent anti-aliasing, which is especially important when OSR is minimized in order to maximize the input bandwidth. The CT ΣΔ modulator itself occupies just 1.16 mm^2 and consumes 19.8 mW. The modulator achieves a SNR of 51 dB and SNDR of 48 dB over 10 MHz signal bandwidth.

6. Acknowledgements

The authors would like to thank the staff of the CIC for

the chip fabrication and technical supports with the number of T18-98D-158.

7. References

[1] J. Yu and B. Zhao, "Continuous-Time Sigma-Delta Modulator Design for Low Power Communication Applications," *Proceedings of IEEE ASICON*, October 2007, pp. 715-720.

[2] R. H. M. van Veldhoven, B. J. Minnis, H. A. Hegt and A. H. M. van Roermund, "A 3.3-mW ΣΔ Modulator for UMTS in 0.18-um CMOS with 70-dB Dynamic Range in 2-MHz Bandwidth," *IEEE Journal of Solid-State Circuits*, Vol. 37, No. 12, 2002, pp. 1645-1652.

[3] L. Dorrer, F. Kuttner, P. Greco, P. Torta and T. Hartig, "A 3-mW 74-dB SNR 2-MHz Continuous-Time Delta-sigma ADC with a Tracking ADC Quantizer in 0.13-um CMOS," *IEEE Journal of Solid-State Circuits*, Vol. 40, No. 12, 2005, pp. 2416-2427.

[4] S. R. Norsworthy, R. Schreier and G. C. Temes, "Delta-Sigma Data Converters: Theory, Design and Simulation," IEEE Press, New York, 1996.

[5] B. J. Farahani and M. Ismail, "Adaptive Sigma Delta ADC for WiMAX Fixed Point Wireless Applications," *IEEE Midwest Symposium on Circuits and Systems*, Vol. 1, Covington, 7-10 August 2005, pp. 692-695.

[6] T. L. Brooks, D. H. Robertson, D. F. Kelly, A. D. Muro and S. W. Harston, "A Cascaded Sigma-Delta Pipeline A/D Converter with 1.25 MHz Signal Bandwidth and 89 dB SNR," *IEEE Journal of Solid-State Circuits*, Vol. 32, No. 12, 1997, pp. 1896-1906.

[7] R. Jiang and T. Fiez, "A 14-bit Delta-Sigma ADC with 8X OSR and 4-MHz Conversion Bandwidth in A 0.18 um CMOS Process," *IEEE Journal of Solid-State Circuits*, Vol. 39, No. 1, 2004, pp. 63-74.

[8] A. Bosi, A. Panigada, G. Cesura and R. Castello, "An 80 MHz 4x Oversampled Cascaded ΔΣ-Pipelined ADC with 75 dB DR and 87 dB SFDR," *IEEE International Solid-State Circuits Conference*, 2005, pp. 174-175.

[9] F. Munoz, K. Philips and A. Torralba, "A 4.7 mW 89.5 dB DR CT Complex DS ADC with Built-In LPF," *IEEE International Solid-State Circuits Conference*, February 2005, pp. 500-501.

[10] J. A. Cherry and W. M. Snelgrove, "Continuous-Time Delta-Sigma Modulators for High-Speed A/D Conversion," Kluwer, Boston, 2000.

[11] S. Paton, A. D. Giandomenico, L. Hernandez, A. Wiesbauer, T. Potscher and M. Clara, "A 70-mW 300-MHz CMOS Continuous-Time ΣΔ ADC with 15-MHz Bandwidth and 11 Bits of Resolution," *IEEE Journal of Solid-State Circuits*, Vol. 39, No. 7, July 2004, pp. 1056-1063.

[12] G. Mitteregger, C. Ebner. S. Mechnig, T. Blon, C. Holuigue and E. Romani, "A 20-mW 640-MHz CMOS Continuous-Time ΣΔ ADC with 20-MHz Signal Band- width, 80-dB Dynamic Range and 12-Bit ENOB," *IEEE Journal of Solid-State Circuits*, Vol. 41, No. 12, 2006, pp. 2641-2649.

[13] S. Karthikeyan, S. Mortezapour, A. Tammineedi and E. Lee, "Low-Voltage Analog Circuit Design Based on Biased Inverting Opamp Configuration," *IEEE Transactions on Circuits and Systems II: Analog and Digital Signal Processing*, Vol. 47, No. 3, 2000, pp. 176-184.

[14] L. Lamarre, M. Louerat and A. Kaiser, "A Simple 3.8 mW, 300 MHz, 4-Bit Flash Analog-to-Digital Converter," *Proceedings of the SPIE*, Vol. 5837, No. 51, 2005, pp. 825-832.

[15] B. Razavi, "Principles of Data Conversion System Design," IEEE Press, New York, 1995.

[16] J. Chen, S. Kurachi, S. Shen, H. Liu, T. Yoshimasu and Y. Suh, "A Low-Kickback-Noise Latched Comparator for High-Speed Flash Analog-to-Digital Converters," *International Symposium on Communications and Information Technologies*, Beijing, 12-14 October 2005, pp. 250-253.

[17] Z. Li and T. S. Fiez, "A 14-Bit Continuous-Time Delta-sigma A/D Modulator with 2.5 MHz Signal Bandwidth," *IEEE Journal of Solid-State Circuits*, Vol. 42, No. 9, 2007, pp. 1873-1883.

[18] J. Bastos, A. M. Marques, M. S. J. Steyaert and W. Sansen, "A 12-Bit Intrinsic Accuracy High-Speed CMOS DAC," *IEEE Journal of Solid-State Circuits*, Vol. 33, No. 12, 1998, pp. 1959-1969.

[19] T. H. Kuo, K. D. Chen and H. R. Yeng, "A Wideband CMOS Sigma-Delta Modulator with Incremental Data Weighted Averaging," *IEEE Journal of Solid-State Circuits*, Vol. 37, No. 1, 2002, pp. 11-17.

[20] F. Gerfers, M. Ortmanns and Y. Manoli, "A 1.5-V 12-Bit Power-Efficient Continuous-Time Third-Order ΣΔ Modulator," *IEEE Journal of Solid-State Circuits*, Vol. 38, No. 8, 2003, pp. 1343-1352.

[21] L. J. Breems, R. Rutten and G. Wetzker, "A Cascaded Continuous-Time ΣΔ Modulator with 67-dB Dynamic Range in 10-MHz Bandwidth," *IEEE Journal of Solid-State Circuits*, Vol. 39, No. 12, 2004, pp. 2152-2160.

[22] S. D. Kulchycki, R. Trofin, K. Vleugels and B. A. Wooley, "A 77-dB Dynamic Range, 7.5-MHz Hybrid Continuous-Time/Discrete-Time Cascaded ΣΔ Modulator," *IEEE Journal of Solid-State Circuits*, Vol. 43, No. 4, 2008, pp. 796-804.

[23] M. Anderson and L. Sundstrom, "Design and Measurement of a CT ΔΣ ADC with Switched-Capacitor Switched-Resistor Feedback," *IEEE Journal of Solid-State Circuits*, Vol. 44, No. 2, 2009, pp. 473-483.

[24] A. Hart and S. P. Voinigescu, "A 1 GHz Bandwidth Low-Pass ΔΣ ADC with 20-50 GHz Adjustable Sampling Rate," *IEEE Journal of Solid- State Circuits*, Vol. 44, No. 5, 2009, pp. 1401-1414.

28

An Improved Chirplet Transform and Its Application for Harmonics Detection

Guo-Sheng Hu[1], Feng-Feng Zhu[2]

[1]*School of Computer, Shanghai Technical Institute of Electronics and Information, Shanghai, China*
[2]*School of Mathematics Science, South China University of Technology, Guangzhou, China*

Abstract

The chirplet transform is the generalization form of fast Fourier Transform, short-time Fourier transform, and wavelet transform. It has the most flexible time frequency window and successfully used in practices. However, the chirplet transform has not inherent inverse transform, and can not overcome the signal reconstructing problem. In this paper, we proposed the improved chirplet transform (ICT) and constructed the inverse ICT. Finally, by simulating the harmonic voltages, the power of the improved chirplet transform are illustrated for harmonic detection. The contours clearly showed the harmonic occurrence time and harmonic duration.

Keywords: Harmonics, Improved Chirplet Transform (ICT), *S*-Transform, Time-Frequency Representation (TFR)

1. Introduction

In many power quality analysis and disciplines, the concept of a stationary time series is a mathematical idealization that is never realized and is not particularly useful in the detection of power quality disturbances in power systems. Although the Fourier transform of the entire time series does contain information about the spectral components in a time series, for a large class of practical applications such as voltage signals in power systems, this information is inadequate. So in the year of 1996, Stockwell, Mansinha and Lowe presented a new S transform that provides a joint time-frequency representation (TFR) with frequency-dependent resolution [1] while, at the same time, maintaining the direct relationship, through time-averaging, with the Fourier spectrum. Several have been proposed in the past; among them are the Gabor transform [2], the related short-time Fourier transforms [3], the continuous wavelet transform (CWT) [4], and the bilinear class of time-frequency distributions known as Cohen's class [5], of which the Wigner distribution [6] is a member. The S transform was defined as following [1].

$$S(\tau,f)=\int_{-\infty}^{+\infty} h(t)\frac{|f|}{\sqrt{2\pi}}\mathrm{e}^{-\frac{(\tau-t)^2 f^2}{2}}\mathrm{e}^{-j2\pi ft}\mathrm{d}t. \tag{1}$$

It is easy to prove that

$$\int_{-\infty}^{+\infty} S(\tau,f)\mathrm{d}\tau = H(f). \tag{2}$$

where $H(f)$ is the Fourier transform of $h(t)$. It follows that $h(t)$ is exactly recoverable from $S(\tau,f)$. Thus

$$h(t)=\int_{-\infty}^{+\infty}\left\{\int_{-\infty}^{+\infty} S(\tau,f)\mathrm{d}\tau\right\}\mathrm{e}^{j2\pi ft}\mathrm{d}f. \tag{3}$$

The *S*-transforms have successfully been used in power system disturbance detection and identification [7]. Another time-frequency representation, Chirplet transform (CT), was defined by Mann Steven in 1992 [8].

$$C(b,\omega)=\frac{1}{\sqrt{2\pi}\sigma}\int_{-\infty}^{+\infty} h(t)\mathrm{e}^{-\frac{(t-b)^2}{2\sigma^2}}\mathrm{e}^{-i\left(\omega t+qt^2\right)}\mathrm{d}t. \tag{4}$$

From (4), it is easy to show that Chirplet transform is an extension of Gabor transform, short-time Fourier transform and continuous wavelet transform, furthermore, the time-frequency window of CT is more flexible than that of CWT. CT has been used successfully to classify power quality disturbance (including voltage sag, voltage swell, voltage interruption, and linear time-varying harmonics and nonlinear time-varying harmonics) [9], denoise the motor fault signals [10], and detect slight fault of electrical machines [11].

However, CT does not satisfy basic characters (2) and (3) and inconvenience in practical applications. So, in this paper, we present an improved Chirplet transform satisfying (2) and (3), moreover, the novel Chirplet transform is an extension of the *S*-transform.

This paper is organized as follows. The improved Chirplet transform is presented in Section 2, and the numerical algorithm is introduced in Section 3; Several simulated power quality harmonic waveforms are detected and identified using the proposed method in Section 4; Finally, The conclusions and references are given.

2. The Improved Chirplet Transform

Chirplet transform is considered as the "phase correction" of the CWT. The CWT $W(b,a)$ of a function $h(t)$ is defined by [4]

$$W(b,a)=\int_{-\infty}^{+\infty}h(t)w(t-b,a)\mathrm{d}t. \tag{5}$$

where $w(\bullet)$ is a scaled replica of the fundamental mother wavelet. The dilation *a* determines the "width" of the wavelet $w(\bullet)$ and thus controls the resolution. Along with (5), there exists an admissibility condition on the mother wavelet $w(\bullet)$ [4] that $w(\bullet)$ must have zero mean.

The improved chirplet transform of a function $h(t)$ is defined as a CWT with a specific mother wavelet defined as

$$w(t,f)=\frac{\sqrt{f^2+iq}}{\sqrt{2\pi}}\mathrm{e}^{-\frac{t^2(f^2-iq)}{2}}\mathrm{e}^{-i(2\pi ft+qt^2)}. \tag{6}$$

note that the frequency *f* and constant *q*.

The improved chirplet wavelet in (6) does not satisfy the condition of zero mean for an admissible wavelet; therefore, it is not strictly a CWT, Written out explicitly, the improved chirplet transform is

$$IC(b,f)=\frac{\sqrt{f^2+iq}}{\sqrt{2\pi}}\cdot\int_{-\infty}^{+\infty}h(t)\mathrm{e}^{-\frac{(t-b)^2(f^2-iq)}{2}}\mathrm{e}^{-i(2\pi f+q(t-b)^2)}\mathrm{d}t. \tag{7}$$

It is obvious that Equation (7) degenerates to be an *S*-transform as $q=0$ [1].

If the improved chirplet transform is indeed a representation of the local spectrum, one would expect a simple operation of averaging the local spectra over time to give the Fourier spectrum. It is shown as follows

$$\int_{-\infty}^{+\infty}IC(b,f)\mathrm{d}b=H(f). \tag{8}$$

where $H(f)$ is the Fourier transform of $h(t)$. It follows that $h(t)$ is exactly recoverable from $IC(b,f)$. Thus

$$h(t)=\int_{-\infty}^{+\infty}\left\{\int_{-\infty}^{+\infty}IC(b,f)\mathrm{d}b\right\}\mathrm{e}^{i2\pi ft}\mathrm{d}f. \tag{9}$$

Proof: from

$$\int_{-\infty}^{+\infty}\mathrm{e}^{-\frac{(t-b)^2(f^2-iq)}{2}}\mathrm{e}^{-iq(t-b)^2}\mathrm{d}b=\int_{-\infty}^{+\infty}\mathrm{e}^{-\frac{(t-b)^2(f^2+iq)}{2}}\mathrm{d}b$$
$$=\frac{1}{\sqrt{f^2+iq}}\int_{-\infty}^{+\infty}\mathrm{e}^{-\frac{u^2}{2}}\mathrm{d}u\left(set\quad u=\sqrt{f^2+iq}(b-t)\right)$$
$$=\frac{\sqrt{2\pi}}{\sqrt{f^2+iq}}\left(\because\int_{-\infty}^{+\infty}\mathrm{e}^{-\frac{u^2}{2}}\mathrm{d}u=\sqrt{2\pi}\right).$$

we can get

$$\int_{-\infty}^{+\infty}IC(b,f)\mathrm{d}b$$
$$=\int_{-\infty}^{+\infty}\frac{\sqrt{f^2+iq}}{\sqrt{2\pi}}\cdot\int_{-\infty}^{+\infty}h(t)\mathrm{e}^{-\frac{(t-b)^2(f^2-iq)}{2}}\mathrm{e}^{-i(2\pi ft+q(t-b)^2)}\mathrm{d}t\mathrm{d}b$$
$$=\frac{\sqrt{f^2+iq}}{\sqrt{2\pi}}\cdot\int_{-\infty}^{+\infty}h(t)\mathrm{e}^{-i2\pi ft}\mathrm{d}t\int_{-\infty}^{+\infty}\mathrm{e}^{-\frac{(t-b)^2(f^2-iq)}{2}}\mathrm{e}^{-i(q(t-b)^2)}\mathrm{d}b.$$
$$=\int_{-\infty}^{+\infty}h(t)\mathrm{e}^{-i2\pi ft}\mathrm{d}t=H(f).$$

Then (9) is the inverse of the above equation.

Alike FFT, STFT, WT, and CT, the improved chirplet transform has the linear property. This is an advantage over the bilinear class of time-frequency representations (TFR's). The presence of the cross terms makes it difficult to reliably estimate the signal. The improved chirplet transform can be written as operations on the Fourier spectrum $H(f)$ of $h(t)$

$$IC(b,f)=\int_{-\infty}^{+\infty}H(\alpha+f)\mathrm{e}^{-\frac{2\pi^2\alpha^2}{f^2+iq}}\mathrm{e}^{i2\pi\alpha b}\mathrm{d}\alpha \tag{11}$$

Proof:

$$\int_{-\infty}^{+\infty}H(\alpha+f)\mathrm{e}^{-\frac{2\pi^2\alpha^2}{f^2+iq}}\mathrm{e}^{i2\pi\alpha b}\mathrm{d}\alpha$$
$$=\int_{-\infty}^{+\infty}\int_{-\infty}^{+\infty}h(t)\mathrm{e}^{-i2\pi(\alpha+f)t}\mathrm{e}^{-\frac{2\pi^2\alpha^2}{f^2+iq}}\mathrm{e}^{i2\pi\alpha b}\mathrm{d}t\mathrm{d}\alpha$$
$$=\int_{-\infty}^{+\infty}h(t)\mathrm{e}^{-i2\pi ft}\mathrm{e}^{-\left(-\frac{f^2+iq}{2}(t-b)^2\right)}\mathrm{d}t\int_{-\infty}^{+\infty}\mathrm{e}^{-\left(\frac{\sqrt{2}\pi\alpha}{\sqrt{f^2+iq}}\right)^2}\mathrm{d}\alpha$$
$$=\frac{\sqrt{f^2+iq}}{\sqrt{2\pi}}\cdot\int_{-\infty}^{+\infty}h(t)\cdot\mathrm{e}^{-\left(\frac{(t-b)^2(f^2+iq)}{2}\right)}\mathrm{e}^{-i(2\pi ft+q(t-b)^2)}\mathrm{d}t$$
$$=IC(b,f).$$

The discrete analog of (11) is used to compute the discrete improved chirplet transform by taking advantage of the efficiency of the Fast Fourier transform (FFT) and the convolution theorem.

3. The Discrete Improved Chirplet Transform

Let $h[kT]$, $k=0,1,2,\cdots,N-1$ denote a discrete time series corresponding to signal $h(t)$ with a time sampling interval of T. The discrete Fourier transform is given by

$$H\left[\frac{n}{NT}\right]=\frac{1}{N}\sum_{k=0}^{N-1}h[kT]\mathrm{e}^{-\frac{i2\pi nk}{N}}. \quad (12)$$

where $n=0,1,2,\cdots,N-1$. In the discrete case, the improved chirplet transform is the projection of the vector defined by the time series $h[kT]$ onto a spanning set of vectors. The spanning vectors are not orthogonal, and the elements of the improved chirplet transform are not independent. Each basis vector (of the Fourier transform) is divided into N localized vectors by an element-by-element product with the N shifted Gaussians such that the sum of these N localized vectors is the original basis vector.

Using (11), the improved chirplet transform of a discrete time series $h[kT]$ is given by (letting $f\to n/NT$ and $\tau\to jT$)

$$IC\left[jT,\frac{n}{NT}\right]=\sum_{m=0}^{N-1}H\left[\frac{m+n}{NT}\right]\mathrm{e}^{-\frac{2\pi^2m^2}{n^2+i\tilde{q}}}\mathrm{e}^{\frac{i2\pi mj}{N}}. \quad (13)$$

where $n\neq 0$, $\tilde{q}=q(NT)^2$. For the $n=0$, it is equal to the constant defined as

$$IC[jT,0]=\frac{1}{N}\sum_{m=0}^{N-1}h\left(\frac{m}{NT}\right). \quad (14)$$

with j,m, and $n=0,1,2,\cdots,N-1$. The discrete improved chirplet transform suffers the familiar problems from sampling and finite length, giving rise to implicit periodicity in the time and frequency domains. The discrete inverse of the improved chirplet transforms (13) and (14) is

$$h[kT]=\sum_{k=0}^{N-1}\left\{\frac{1}{N}\sum_{j=0}^{N-1}IC\left[jT,\frac{n}{NT}\right]\right\}\mathrm{e}^{\frac{j2\pi nk}{N}}. \quad (15)$$

4. Examples

4.1. The Signal TFR Figure Using the Improved Chirplet Transform

Equations (7) and (9) are the improved chirplet transform (ICT) for the time-frequency representation (TFR) and its inverse ICT for the signal reconstruction. In the follow figures, **Figure 1(a)** is the A-phase current signal of the inductor motor with single phase grounding. **Figure 2(b)** shows the TFR of the A-phase current signal of the motor using (7). The reconstruction signal using (9) is illustrate in **Figure 2(c)**. From **Figure 1**, we know (7) and (9) are very effective for representing a time frequency feature of a signal and reconstructing from TFR.

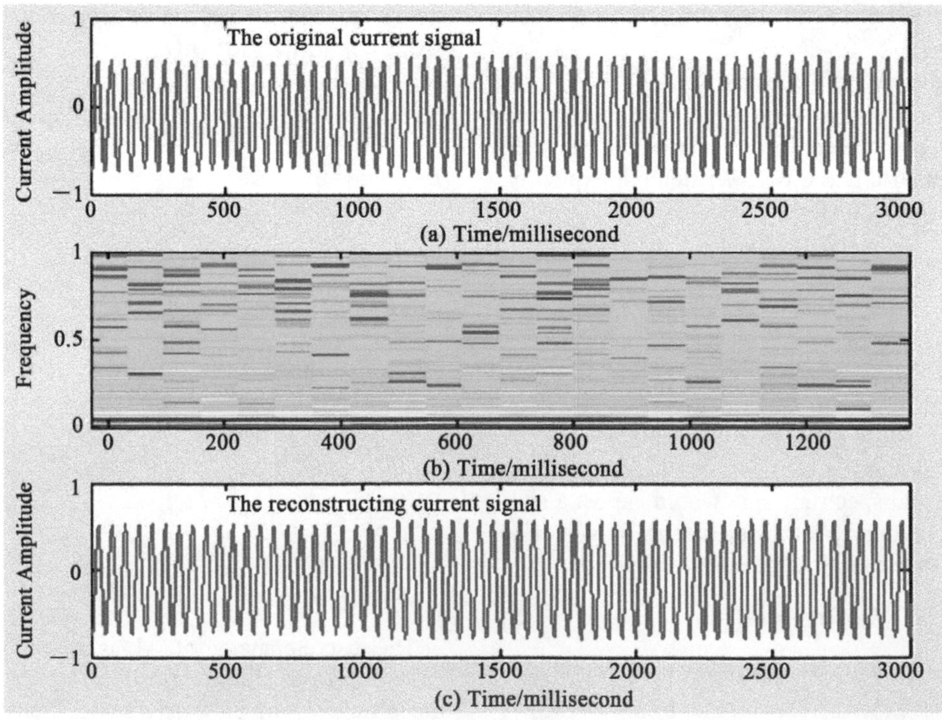

Figure 1. The motor A-phase current signal (a), its TFR (b), and the reconstructing signal.

4.2. The harmonics Detection

Figures 2 and **3** demonstrate the class of time series for which the improved chirplet transform would be useful; they highlight the advantages of such an approach as compared with other techniques.

Considering a simulating segment harmonic voltage with zero initial phase as follows.

$$f(t)=\begin{cases}\sin(2*pi*50*t) & (0\le t\le 0.3)\\ \sin(2*pi*50*t)+\sin(2*pi*150*t) & (0.3<t\le 0.6)\\ \sin(2*pi*(50+0.2*t)*t) & (0.6<t\le 1.4)\\ \sin(2*pi*50*t)+\sin(2*pi*350*t) & (1.4<t\le 1.7)\\ \sin(2*pi*50*t) & (1.7\le t\le 2)\end{cases} \tag{16}$$

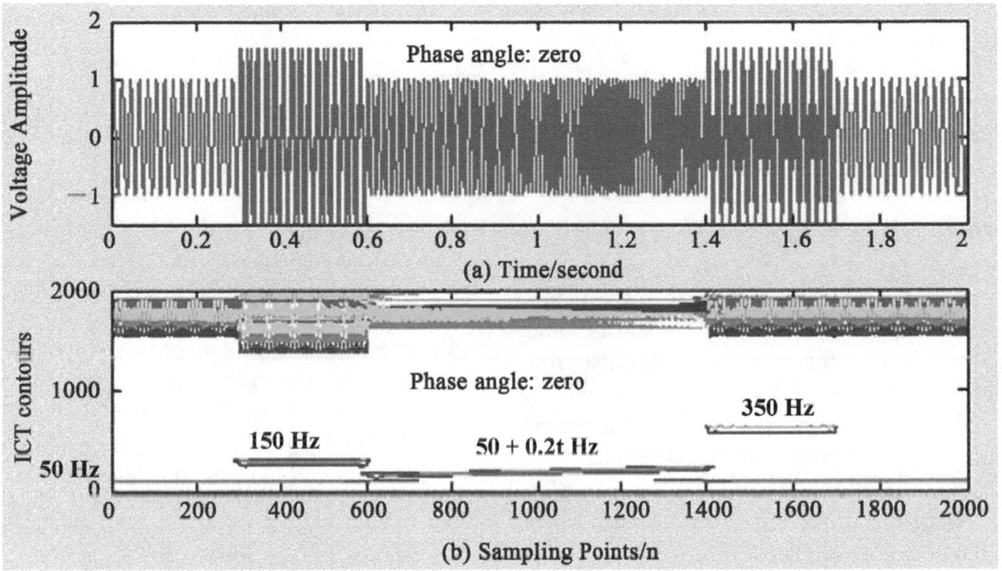

Figure 2. The simulating voltage with zero initial phase (a), and its ICT contour (b).

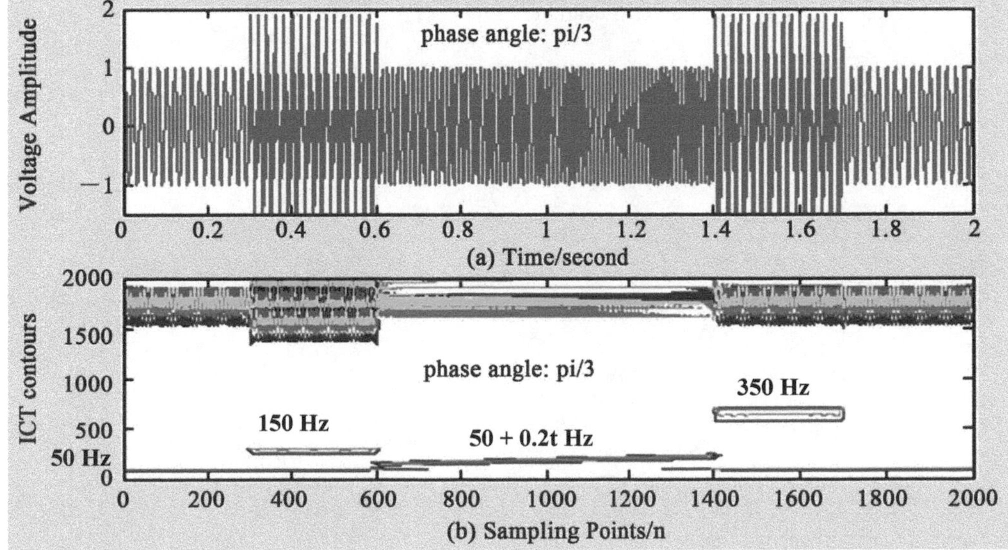

Figure 3. The simulating voltage with pi/3 initial phase (a), and its ICT contour (b).

The voltage signal divided into 5 time segments. In the first time interval, the voltage constrains only a frequency: 50 Hz. At time 0.3, the voltage constrains another harmonic: 150 Hz. In the time interval $0.6 < t \le 1.4$, the voltage constrains a linear time changing harmonic. Then at 1.4 s, the harmonic, 350 Hz, added to the signal. Finally, the voltage retain normally at 1.7 s.

The sampling frequency is 1000 Hz. **Figure 2 (a)** is the improved chirplet transform plot of (16). **Figure 2(b)** is the contour plot of the signal (a) using (13) and (14). Form **Figure 2(b)**, we find the ICT contour illustrates the work frequency 50 Hz, two harmonic frequency 150 Hz and 350 Hz, and the linear time changing frequency 50 + 0.2 t Hz.

Moreover, the contour in **Figure 2(b)** clearly shows the harmonic occurrence times and durations.

In order to investigate the influence of initial phase, we modulating the above simulating voltage signal with pi/3 phase. From **Figure 3**, we find that the initial phase does not influence the harmonic detection.

5. Conclusions

The chirplet transform is the generalization form of fast Fourier transform, short-time Fourier transform, and wavelet transform. It has the most flexible time frequency window and successfully used in practices. However, the chirplet transform has not inherent reconstructing formulae. So we proposed the improved chirplet transform (ICT) and constructed the inverse ICT. Finally, the power of the improved chirplet transform is apparent from the above examples.

6. References

[1] R. G. Stockwell, L. Mansinha and R. P. Lowe, "Location of the Complex Spectrum: The *S*-Transform," *IEEE Transactions on Signal Processing*, Vol. 44, No. 4, 1996, pp. 998-1001.

[2] D. Gabor, "Theory of Communication," *Journal of Institution of Electrical Engineers*, Vol. 93, No. 3, 1946, pp. 429-457.

[3] R. N. Bracewell, "The Fourier Transform and Its Applications," McGraw-Hill, New York, 1978.

[4] S. Mallat, "A Wavelet Tour of Signal Processing," 2nd Edition, Academic Press, Waltham, 2001.

[5] L. Cohen, "Time-Frequency Distributions—A Review," *Proceedings of the IEEE*, Vol. 77, No. 7, 1989, pp. 941-981.

[6] F. Hlawatsch and G. F. Boudreuax-Bartels, "Linear and Quadratic Time-Frequency Signal Representations," *Proceedings of Signal Processing Magazine*, Vol. 9, No. 2, 1992, pp. 21-67.

[7] M. V. Chilukur and P. K. Dash, "Multiresolution *S*-Transform-Based Fuzzy Recognition System for Power Quality Events," *IEEE Transactions on Power Delivery*, Vol. 19, No. 1, 2004, pp. 323-330.

[8] S. Mann and S. Haykin, "The Chirplet Transform: Physical Considerations," *IEEE Transactions on Signal Processing*, 1995, Vol. 43, No. 11, pp. 2745-2761.

[9] G.-S. Hu, F.-F. Zhu and Y.-J. Tu, "Power Quality Disturbance Detection and Classification Using Chirplet Transform," *Lecture Notes in Computer Science*, Vol. 4247, 2006, pp. 34-41.

[10] Z. Ren, G. S. Hu, W. Y. Huang and F. F. Zhu, "Motor Fault Signals Denosing Based on Chirplet Transform," *Transactions of China Electrotechnical Society*, Vol. 17, No. 3, 2002, pp. 59-62.

[11] G. S. Hu and F. F. Zhu, "Location of slight Fault in Electric Machine Using Trigonometric Spline Chirplet Transforms," *Power System Technology*, Vol. 27, No. 2, 2003, pp. 28-31.

Permissions

The contributors of this book come from diverse backgrounds, making this book a truly international effort. This book will bring forth new frontiers with its revolutionizing research information and detailed analysis of the nascent developments around the world.

We would like to thank all the contributing authors for lending their expertise to make the book truly unique. They have played a crucial role in the development of this book. Without their invaluable contributions this book wouldn't have been possible. They have made vital efforts to compile up to date information on the varied aspects of this subject to make this book a valuable addition to the collection of many professionals and students.

This book was conceptualized with the vision of imparting up-to-date information and advanced data in this field. To ensure the same, a matchless editorial board was set up. Every individual on the board went through rigorous rounds of assessment to prove their worth. After which they invested a large part of their time researching and compiling the most relevant data for our readers. Conferences and sessions were held from time to time between the editorial board and the contributing authors to present the data in the most comprehensible form. The editorial team has worked tirelessly to provide valuable and valid information to help people across the globe.

Every chapter published in this book has been scrutinized by our experts. Their significance has been extensively debated. The topics covered herein carry significant findings which will fuel the growth of the discipline. They may even be implemented as practical applications or may be referred to as a beginning point for another development.

The editorial board has been involved in producing this book since its inception. They have spent rigorous hours researching and exploring the diverse topics which have resulted in the successful publishing of this book. They have passed on their knowledge of decades through this book. To expedite this challenging task, the publisher supported the team at every step. A small team of assistant editors was also appointed to further simplify the editing procedure and attain best results for the readers.

Our editorial team has been hand-picked from every corner of the world. Their multi-ethnicity adds dynamic inputs to the discussions which result in innovative outcomes. These outcomes are then further discussed with the researchers and contributors who give their valuable feedback and opinion regarding the same. The feedback is then collaborated with the researches and they are edited in a comprehensive manner to aid the understanding of the subject.

Apart from the editorial board, the designing team has also invested a significant amount of their time in understanding the subject and creating the most relevant covers. They scrutinized every image to scout for the most suitable representation of the subject and create an appropriate cover for the book.

The publishing team has been involved in this book since its early stages. They were actively engaged in every process, be it collecting the data, connecting with the contributors or procuring relevant information. The team has been an ardent support to the editorial, designing and production team. Their endless efforts to recruit the best for this project, has resulted in the accomplishment of this book. They are a veteran in the field of academics and their pool of knowledge is as vast as their experience in printing. Their expertise and guidance has proved useful at every step. Their uncompromising quality standards have made this book an exceptional effort. Their encouragement from time to time has been an inspiration for everyone.

The publisher and the editorial board hope that this book will prove to be a valuable piece of knowledge for researchers, students, practitioners and scholars across the globe.

List of Contributors

Mitsuru Kawamoto and Koichi Kurumatani
Information Technology Research Institute, National Institute of Advanced Science and Technology, Tsukuba, Japan

Kiyotaka Kohno
Department of Electronic Control Engineering, Yonago National College of Technology, Yonago-city, Japan

Yujiro Inouye
Department of Electronic and Control Systems Engineering, Shimane University, Matsue, Japan

Hung-Yu Wang, Tzu-Yi Yang and Po-Yang Tsai
Department of Electronic Engineering, National Kaohsiung University of Applied Sciences, Kaohsiung, Taiwan, China

Sheng-Hsiung Chang
Department of Optoelectronic Engineering, Far East University, Hsin-Shih, Taiwan, China

Stefano Perticaroli and Fabrizio Palma
Department of Information Engineering, Electronics and Telecommunications, Sapienza Università di Roma, Rome, Italy

Adriano Carbone
Rhea System S. A., Louvain-La-Neuve, Belgium

Ibrahim Al-Bahadly and Joel White
School of Engineering and Advanced Technology Massey University, Palmerston North, New Zealand

Jiun-Wei Horng, Zhao-Ren Wang and Chih-Cheng Liu
Department of Electronic Engineering, Chung Yuan Christian University, Chung-Li, Taiwan, China

Yang Liu, Ashok Srivastava and Yao Xu
Department of Electrical and Computer Engineering Louisiana State University, Baton Rouge, U.S.A

Ling-ling Xie, Ren-xi Gong and Hao-ze Zhuo
College of Electrical Engineering, Guangxi University, Nanning, China

Kuang Wang
Airline Mechanical Company Ltd., Shenzhen, China

Sajai Vir Singh
Department of Electronics and Communications, Jaypee University of Information Technology, Waknaghat, India

Sudhanshu Maheshwari
Department of Electronics Engineering, Zakir Hussain College of Engineering and Technology, Aligarh Muslim University, Aligarh, India

Durg Singh Chauhan
Department of Electrical Engineering, Institute of Technology, Banaras Hindu University, Varanasi, India

Jiun-Wei Horng, Chun-Li Hou, Wei-Shyang Huang and Dun-Yih Yang
Department of Electronic Engineering, Chung Yuan Christian University, Chung-Li, Taiwan, China

Data Ram Bhaskar and Kasim Karam Abdalla
Department of Electronics and Communication Engineering, Faculty of Engineering and Technology, Jamia Millia Islmia, New Delhi, India

Raj Senani
Division of Electronics and Communication Engineering, Netaji Subhas Institute of Technology, Delhi, India

Peiman Aliparast
Young Research Club, Islamic AZAD University of Sofian, Sofian, Iran
Faculty of Electrical and Computer Engineering, University of Tabriz, Tabriz, Iran

Hossein B. Bahar, Ziaadin D. Koozehkanani, Jafar Sobhi and Gader Karimian
Faculty of Electrical and Computer Engineering, University of Tabriz, Tabriz, Iran

Ashish ranjan and Sajal K. Paul
Department of Electronics Engineering, Indian School of Mines, Dhanbad, India

Jun Liu
Key Laboratory of RF Circuits and Systems, Ministry of Education, Hangzhou Dianzi University, Hangzhou, China
School of Electronic Engineering, Dublin City University, Dublin, Ireland

Marissa Condon
School of Electronic Engineering, Dublin City University, Dublin, Ireland

Qais H. Alsafasfeh
Electrical Engineering Department, Tafila Technical University, Tafila, Jordan

Mohammad S. Al-Arni
Electrical Engineering Department, Tafila Technical University, Tafila, Jordan

Mohd Yusuf Yasin and Bal Gopal
Department of Electronics and Communication Engineering, Integral University, Lucknow, India

Jose-Ignacio Izpura and Javier Malo
Group of Microsystems and Electronic Materials, Universidad Politécnica de Madrid, Madrid, Spain

Nasreddine Benahmed, Fethi Tarik Bendimerad and Boumedienne Benyoucef
University Abou Bekr Belkaid-Tlemcen, Tlemcen, Algeria

Nadia Benabdallah
Preparatory School of Sciences and Technology (EPST-Tlemcen), Tlemcen, Algeria

Salima Seghier
University of Saida, Saida, Algeria

Rajiv Soundararajan and Ashok Srivastava
Department of Electrical and Computer Engineering, Louisiana State University, Baton Rouge, USA

Siva Sankar Yellampalli
Centre for Advanced Studies (VTU Extension Centre), UTL Technologies Ltd., Bangalore, India

Qassim Nasir
Department of Electrical and Computer Engineering, University of Sharjah, Sharjah, UAE

Saleh Al-Araji
Communication Engineering Department, Khalifa University of Science, Technology and Research, Sharjah, UAE

Wagah Farman Mohammad
Communications & Electronics Department, Faculty of Engineering, Philadelphia University, Amman, Jordan

Andrey Malkov, Dmitry Vasiounin and Oleg Semenov
Freescale Semiconductor, Moscow, Russia

Jin Young Choi and Choongkoo Park
Electronic & Electrical Engineering Department, Hongik University, Chungnam, South Korea

Sudeep Kanav and Satish Chand
Division of Computer Engineering, Netaji Subhas Institute of Technology, New Delhi, India

Arash Ahmadpour
Department of Electronic Engineering, Lahijan Branch, Islamic Azad University, Lahijan, Iran

Manoj Kumar and Sandeep Kumar Arya
Department of Electronics & Communication Engineering Guru Jambheshwar, University of Science & Technology, Hisar, India

Sujata Pandey
Department of Electronics & Communication Engineering, Amity University, Noida, India

Hüseyin Koçak and Ahmet Yıldırım
Department of Mathematics, Ege University, Bornova–İzmir, Turkey

Dahong Zhang
Department of Physics, South China University, Guangzhou, China

Karem Boubaker
École Supérieure des Sciences et Techniques de Tunis, University of Tunis, Tunis, Tunisia

Syed Tauseef Mohyud-Din
Department of Basic Sciences, HITEC University, Taxila Cantt., Pakistan

Jhin-Fang Huang, Yan-Cheng Lai, Wen-Cheng Lai and Ron-Yi Liu
Department of Electronic Engineering, National Taiwan University of Science and Technology, Chinese Taipei

Guo-Sheng Hu
School of Computer, Shanghai Technical Institute of Electronics and Information, Shanghai, China

Feng-Feng Zhu
School of Mathematics Science, South China University of Technology, Guangzhou, China